W9-ABI-843

HUNGER AND PUBLIC ACTION

WIDER

Studies in Development Economics embody the output of the
research programmes of the World Institute for
Development Economics Research (WIDER), which was
established by the United Nations University as its first
research and training centre in 1984 and started work in
Helsinki in 1985. The principal purpose of the Institute is
to help identify and meet the need for policy-oriented
socio-economic research on pressing global and
development problems, as well as common domestic
problems and their inter-relationships.

HUNGER AND PUBLIC ACTION

JEAN DRÈZE
and
AMARTYA SEN

CLARENDON PRESS · OXFORD
1989

Oxford University Press, Walton Street, Oxford OX2 6DP
Oxford New York Toronto
Delhi Bombay Calcutta Madras Karachi
Petaling Jaya Singapore Hong Kong Tokyo
Nairobi Dar es Salaam Cape Town
Melbourne Auckland
and associated companies in
Berlin Ibadan

Oxford is a trade mark of Oxford University Press

Published in the United States
by Oxford University Press, New York

© Jean Drèze and Amartya Sen 1989

All rights reserved. No part of this publication may be reproduced,
stored in a retrieval system, or transmitted, in any form or by any means,
electronic, mechanical, photocopying, recording, or otherwise, without
the prior permission of Oxford University Press

British Library Cataloguing in Publication Data
Drèze, Jean
Hunger and public action—(WIDER studies in development
economics).
1. Famines. Prevention
I. Title II. Sen, Amartya III. Series
363.8
ISBN 0-19-828634-1
ISBN 0-19-828365-2 (pbk)

Library of Congress Cataloging-in-Publication Data
Drèze, Jean.
Hunger and public action/Jean Drèze and Amartya Sen.
Includes bibliographical references.
1. Food supply—Government policy—Developing countries.
2. Famines—Prevention—Government policy—Developing countries.
3. Developing countries—Social policy. 4. Poor—Government policy—
Developing countries. 5. Nutrition policy—Developing countries.
I. Sen, Amartya Kumar. II. Title.
HD9018.D44D74   1990   363.8'56'091724—dc20   89-25504
ISBN 0-19-828634-1
ISBN 0-19-828365-2 (pbk)

Typeset by Rowland Phototypesetting Ltd
Bury St Edmunds, Suffolk
Printed by Clays Ltd, St Ives plc

FOREWORD

No social or economic problem facing the world today is more urgent than that of hunger. While this distressing state of affairs is not new, its persistence in spite of the remarkable technological and productive advances of the twentieth century is nothing short of scandalous.

The subject of world hunger therefore has the highest priority in WIDER's research programme. Since its creation in 1985, WIDER has consistently sought to promote research on contemporary development problems with a practical orientation. The focus of this book by Jean Drèze and Amartya Sen, one of the first fruits of this effort, is on action—action to banish both the threat of famine and the reality of chronic hunger affecting many parts of the world.

There is no instant remedy to the scourge of persistent world hunger. The impulse to rush ahead and do something practical to relieve suffering is laudable and necessary. But good motives do not by themselves guarantee effective action. While the task of eradicating hunger in the world is too serious to be left entirely to politicians and too immediate to be left entirely to academics, it is also too complex to be left entirely to the compassionate instincts of humankind. Action has to be based on clear thinking as well as on firm dedication.

This book, I believe, represents an important step towards a better understanding of the issues involved. There is, for instance, much to learn from its appraisal of the possible roles that can be respectively played by government intervention, market mechanisms and the activism of the public at large in encountering the problem of world hunger. As the authors show, the importance of these influences is well illustrated in a number of recent experiences of famine prevention. The response of the market to the demands generated by income support programmes, the involvement of the state in food distribution to prevent collusive practices on the part of private traders, and the impact of public pressure on the timing and nature of government action, can all be crucial ingredients of an effective programme of famine prevention. Similarly, in their analysis of strategies to deal with chronic hunger and deprivation, the authors stress the interlinked contributions which participative economic growth and direct public support can make to the improvement of living conditions in poor countries.

Besides clearer thinking, it is my hope that Drèze and Sen's work will lead to greater awareness and motivation, particularly by bringing out the social and political ramifications of the problem of world hunger. As the authors argue, to confront this problem involves not only being alive to opportunities for cooperative action but also addressing the multiple conflicts (e.g. of class and gender) that pervade social living.

The subject of hunger and poverty continues to occupy a major place in WIDER's research programme. This book will be followed shortly by three volumes of papers, written by international experts (and edited by Drèze and Sen), on 'the political economy of hunger'.

As the Director of WIDER, I am happy to be able to present this book as one of the first results of our programme of 'research for action'.

Lal Jayawardena
Director, WIDER
31 July 1989

PREFACE

This is a book about hunger. Not just about the extent of it, or about the havoc it causes—debilitating and killing people, enfeebling and devastating societies. While there are important issues of assessment and evaluation in this grisly field (and we do address many of these questions in this study), nevertheless the primary focus of the book is on action, rather than on measurement.

By public action we mean not merely the activities of the state, but also social actions taken by members of the public—both 'collaborative' (through civic cooperation) and 'adversarial' (through social criticism and political opposition). The state does, of course, have a major role to play in eradicating famines and in eliminating persistent deprivation, and the various aspects of this role we have tried to discuss fairly extensively in the light of general reasoning and empirical evidence. But the reach of public action goes well beyond the doings of the state, and involves what is done *by* the public—not merely *for* the public. We also argue that the nature and effectiveness of the activities of the state can deteriorate very easily in the absence of public vigilance and activism.

In the first four chapters, constituting Part I of the book, we have presented some general analyses of the economic, social, political and medical background to the problems of starvation and undernutrition in the contemporary world. Chapters 5 to 8, constituting Part II of the book, are concerned with analysing the major strategic and tactical issues in famine prevention. The diverse problems of persistent undernutrition and endemic deprivation are examined in Part III (Chapters 9 to 12).

In the fourth and final part, consisting only of one chapter (Chapter 13), the diverse roles of public action in removing hunger are considered together, with specific comments on some of the more debatable issues. It is not meant as a 'summary' of the main points of the book, but there is an attempt to provide an overall view of the general approach we have adopted and used. We have particularly highlighted the features of our approach that may appear to be controversial. We have tried to take full note of other points of view. But a practical treatise on the role of public action has to be, ultimately, rather assertive, and it is fair to say that we have not been afflicted by excessive shyness regarding what we recommend and why.

On stylistic issues, we should make two brief comments. First, we have tried to make the discussion as non-technical and accessible as possible. On occasion we have had to settle for formulations that are somewhat less rigorous than would have been possible had we chosen a different—more formal—style.

Second, the issue of gender is of special significance in our study, and it is perhaps particularly important for us to avoid the implicit 'sexism' of the standard language (e.g., referring to women as well as men generally as 'he'). On the other hand, the practice of 'inverting' the usage (e.g., by referring to all as 'she') is somewhat open to the same charge of sexism—in reverse—aside from looking rather self-consciously contrary. Also, the compound expression 'he or she', while fine in many cases, is a bit of a mouthful if used everywhere. The appropriate non-sexist practice may be to de-escalate the issue, and in particular to use 'he', 'she' and 'he or she' entirely interchangeably. That, at any rate, is what we have done.

This study is an outgrowth of our work for the project on 'Hunger and Poverty' of the World Institute for Development Economics Research (WIDER). At every stage of our research and the writing of this book, we have received good advice, encouragement and help from Lal Jayawardena, the Director of WIDER. Others too, at WIDER, have given us all the help we could have asked for. We are most grateful for that.

A part of WIDER's research in the area of 'Hunger and Poverty' is currently in the press in the form of a three-volume book, edited by us, entitled *The Political Economy of Hunger*, to be published by Clarendon Press, Oxford. The first versions of most of these papers were written during 1985–6 and were presented at a conference on 'food strategies' in July 1986. The papers have been extensively revised since, and some new papers have been added. Aside from us, the contributors to these volumes are: Sudhir Anand, Kaushik Basu, Partha Dasgupta, Meghnad Desai, Christopher Harris, Barbara Harriss, Judith Heyer, Francis Idachaba, Ravi Kanbur, Gopu Kumar, Siddiq Osmani, Kirit Parikh, Jean-Philippe Platteau, N. Ram, Martin Ravallion, Debraj Ray, Carl Riskin, Ignacy Sachs, Rehman Sobhan, Peter Svedberg, Samuel Wangwe, and Ann Whitehead. We have greatly benefited from their collaboration.

While undertaking the research, we had the efficient assistance of Robin Burgess, Peter Lanjouw, Shailendra Mehta, Shantanu Mitra, Sanjay Reddy, Sangeeta Sethi and Madhura Swaminathan, and we are most grateful to them. We are greatly in debt to Jacky Jennings who has looked after the secretarial and administrative side of the entire project with outstanding skill. We have also been very fortunate in having the superb assistance of Anna-Marie Svedrofsky.

We have benefited much from communications and discussions with several voluntary organizations, including OXFAM, Save the Children Fund, and Shramjivi Samaj, among others. In the course of our analysis we have had to be, at times, somewhat critical of particular aspects of the work of voluntary agencies, but we have in general nothing but admiration for their contributions, within their chosen spheres of action. As a small token of appreciation, the royalties from this book will go to these agencies.

We have profited greatly from suggestions and criticisms made by those who have taken an interest in this study. For detailed and enormously helpful comments on earlier drafts and notes, we are extremely grateful to Sudhir Anand, Philippe Autier, Robin Burgess, Lincoln Chen, Marty Chen, Stephen Coate, Monica Das Gupta, Mrinal Datta Chaudhuri, Meghnad Desai, Carl Eicher, Susan George, Keith Griffin, Judith Heyer, Allan Hill, Roger Hay, Athar Hussain, Nurul Islam, Jong-il You, Robert Kates, Jocelyn Kynch, Michael Lipton, John Mellor, Siddiq Osmani, Dwight Perkins, V. K. Ramachandran, Martin Ravallion, Shlomo Reutlinger, Carl Riskin, Frances Stewart, John Shaw, Paul Streeten, Per Pinstrup-Andersen, and Joachim von Braun.

We have also received very useful counsel and suggestions on general analyses and on case-studies from Brian Abel-Smith, Frédérique Apffel-Marglin, Harold Alderman, Alice Amsden, José Pablo Arellano, Surjit Bhalla, Bela Bhatia, Lars-Erik Birgegard, John Borton, L. Burgess, Diana Callear, David Campbell, Monique Chastanet, Robert Chambers, Robert Collins, Jane Corbett, George Cumper, Partha Dasgupta, Rob Davies, Angus Deaton, Stephen Devereux, Thomas Downing, Tim Dyson, Ricardo Ffrench-Davis, John Field, Alvaro Garcia, Catherine Gibb, Nancy Godfrey, Hugh Goyder, Jim Gordon, T. F. Grannell, Peter Greaves, S. Guhan, Charles Harvey, Akiko Hashimoto, Cynthia Hewitt de Alcántara, Abraham Horwitz, Solomon Inquai, Richard Jolly, Nanak Kakwani, David Keen, Qaisar Khan, Byung Whan Kim, Arthur Kleinman, Jane Knight, Gopu Kumar, Keon Lee, Francois-Regis Mahieu, Stephen Marglin, Robert McAdam, Wendy McLean, Carmelo Mesa-Lago, S. T. Mhiribidi, Siddharta Mitter, Richard Morgan, Jon Moris, Christopher Murray, Philip Payne, Pauline Peters, Jean-Philippe Platteau, Samuel Preston, Dagmar Raczynski, Sanjay Reddy, Norman Reynolds, Lenin Saenz, David Sanders, Chris Scott, John Seaman, Sunil Sengupta, Hans Singer, K. Subbarao, Luc Spyckerelle, Nicholas Stern, Jeremy Swift, J. Tagwireyi, William Torry, R. van der Hoeven, Megan Vaughan, Tony Vaux, Isabel Vial, Peter Walker, Daniel Weiner, Helen Young, and Richard Zeckhauser.

It may seem somewhat incredible that two people can have reasons to be grateful to such a large number of commentators ('never', to alter Churchill, 'has so much been owed by so few to so many'). But this has been an exacting work and we have tried to consider and take note of as much criticism as we could manage to secure. If the work is still very imperfect, it is not for the lack of good advice.

Helsinki   J.D.
25 July 1989   -   A.S.

CONTENTS

Part I
Hunger in the Modern World

Part II
Famines

LIST OF FIGURES

LIST OF TABLES

PART I

Hunger in the Modern World

1

Introduction

1.1 Past and Present

Hunger is not a new affliction. Recurrent famines as well as endemic under-nourishment have been persistent features of history. Life has been short and hard in much of the world, most of the time. Deprivation of food and other necessities of living has consistently been among the causal antecedents of the brutishness and brevity of human life.

Megasthenes, the envoy of Seleukos Nikator to the court of the Indian emperor Chandragupta Maurya in the fourth century BC, wrote—perhaps to impress his gullible Greek readers—that famine was completely unknown in Maurya India.[1] But Kautilya, the Indian political economist, who was an official adviser to Chandragupta, wrote extensively on how to deal with famines (on which more presently).[2] Ancient chronicles not only in India, but also in Egypt, Western Asia, China, Greece, Rome, North-east Africa, and elsewhere tell us about famines that ravaged ancient civilizations in different parts of the world.[3] Even when literary accounts are scarce or do not exist, archaeological data and other historical evidence tell stories of sudden depopulation and frantic migration, in addition to providing information concerning nutritional debilitation and significant stunting.[4] Hunger is not a modern malady.

Hunger is, however, intolerable in the modern world in a way it could not have been in the past. This is not so much because it is more intense, but because widespread hunger is so unnecessary and unwarranted in the modern world. The enormous expansion of productive power that has taken place over the last few centuries has made it, perhaps for the first time, possible to guarantee adequate food for all, and it is in this context that the persistence of

[1] See the translation by McCrindle (1877: 32). See also Dutt (1900, 1904).

[2] See Kautilya's *Arthaśāstra*, especially the 4th Book, particularly the section on 'Remedies against National Calamities'. There are various translations, e.g. Shama Sastry (1967).

[3] For interesting accounts of the history of famines in different parts of the world, see Walford (1878), Wright (1882), Dutt (1900, 1901), Loveday (1914), Mallory (1926), Ghosh (1944), Swann (1950), Cépède and Lengellé (1953), Pankhurst (1961), Masefield (1963), Bhatia (1967), Aykroyd (1974), Hussein (1976), Iliffe (1987), Alamgir (1980), Dando (1980), Will (1980), Cahill (1982), McAlpin (1983a), Rotberg and Rabb (1983), Bose (1987), Vaughan (1987), D'Souza (1988), Garnsey (1988), Newman et al. (forthcoming), among others. See also the bibliographies provided by Currey, Ali and Kohman (1981) and Golkin (1987).

[4] Old burial remains often provide tell-tale evidence of chronic stunting. The size of clothing, equipment, etc. also provides indirect data. It is not only that, say, the Roman soldiers and heroes, judging by such evidence, were astonishingly short (especially compared with Charlton Heston), but also that cases of clinically recognizable stunting are quite frequent. There is, of course, an interpretational issue as to whether stunting typically implies any significant impairment of human ability to function. This question and related nutritional disputes are taken up in Chapter 3.

chronic hunger and the recurrence of virulent famines must be seen as being morally outrageous and politically unacceptable. If politics is 'the art of the possible', then conquering world hunger has become a political issue in a way it could not have been in the past.

Aside from this political and ethical issue distinguishing modern hunger from past hunger, there are also a number of other important contrasts.

First, for a substantial part of humanity, the health problems connected with food consumption have ceased being the result of having too little and stem instead from having too much. While one part of humanity desperately searches for more food to eat, another part counts the calories and looks for new ways of slimming. Inequalities in the distribution of food are not a new phenomenon by any means, but while in the past affluence may have been confined to a small section of society, in the modern world the bulk of the population in many countries is now in the affluent category as far as food is concerned.

It is, of course, true that substantial pockets of hunger do survive in Europe and North America, and certainly call for serious attention in public policy.[5] We shall have some things to say on that problem of resilient undernourishment. But the fact that the *typical* person in Europe or North America tries to reduce—rather than increase—calorie intake makes the persistence of widespread nutritional deficiency and hunger in the rest of the world a particularly contrary phenomenon. This adds to the force of seeing world hunger as an international political issue in a way it has never been in the past.

Second, the persistence of hunger in many countries in the contemporary world is related not merely to a general lack of affluence, but also to substantial —often extreme—inequalities within the society. The issue of inequality in the genesis of hunger and famines is not in itself new. In his famous treatise on politics, diplomacy, and political economy called *Arthaśāstra* (roughly translated as 'instructions on material prosperity'), Kautilya, the ancient Indian political theorist and economist to whom we have already referred, included among his famine relief policies the possibility of raiding the provisions of the rich. In fact, he wrote with some eloquence on 'the policy of thinning the rich by exacting excess revenue [*karśanam*], or causing them to vomit their accumulated wealth [*vamanam*]'.[6]

The general issue of inequality has always been important in famine analysis. But with the development of modern economic relations and of extensive interdependences even between distant parts of the economy, there are many new ways in which different sections of the population can see their economic position and their command over food shift violently and suddenly. For example, aside from the more traditional 'slump famines', in which starvation develops along with a general economic decline (e.g. a crop failure leading to

<hr/>

[5] See e.g. the reports on hunger in the United States produced by the Harvard School of Public Health (1985, 1987).

[6] *Arthaśāstra*, 4th Book. In the translation by Shama Sastry (1967), see pp. 237–8.

impoverishment), famines can and have taken place in recent years even in boom situations. In a 'boom famine', many occupation groups may improve their economic position substantially, thereby commanding a bigger share of the available food, which can lead to a decline—even an absolute decline—of food command on the part of those less favourably placed in the uneven expansion of money incomes. For instance, the Bengal famine of 1943 (in which, it is estimated, 3 million people died) had many characteristics of being such a 'boom famine'.[7]

Third, the dependence of one group's ability to command food on its relative position and comparative economic power *vis-à-vis* other groups can be especially important in a market economy. The institution of markets is, of course, an old one, but the reach and role of market transactions has substantially expanded in recent times. On the one hand, this has added new economic opportunities and new ways of achieving prosperity through specialization and exchange, and the development of extensive markets has been a major force behind the enhancement of the wealth of nations, as Adam Smith rightly foresaw.[8] But, on the other hand, the expansion of markets has also added a new source of vulnerability for some groups. For example, pastoralist nomads can be reduced to starvation if the relative price of animal products falls in relation to that of staple food, since their subsistence depends on their ability to sell animals and animal products (including meat) to buy enough calories from *cheaper* food materials such as grain. Similarly, fishermen may go hungry if the price of fish fails to keep up with that of, say, rice.[9]

Fourth, the importance of the institution of wage labour is a particular aspect of this general problem. People who possess no means of production excepting their own labour power, which they try to sell for a wage in order to earn an adequate income to buy enough food, are particularly vulnerable to changes in labour market conditions. A decline in wages *vis-à-vis* food prices, or an increase in unemployment, can spell disaster for this class. While hiring labour has existed for a long time, its relative importance—especially in the form of wage labour—has dramatically increased with the spread of capitalism, even in developing countries. The class of landless wage labourers has indeed recurrently produced famine victims in modern times. For example, in

---

[7] On this see Sen (1977a, 1981a). See also Alamgir (1980) and Greenough (1982). Ravallion (1987a) provides an extensive and far-reaching analysis of the general economic relationships between markets and famines.

[8] Smith (1776). Smith was, however, fully aware—in a way some of his followers evidently were not—that the market may also help to spread deprivation and famines, e.g. through employment loss in a general economic crisis. Smith's analysis of famines is discussed in Sen (1986a).

[9] Of course, meat and fish are both food themselves, but the poor pastoralist or fisherman often survives by selling these 'luxury' foods and buying cheaper calories; the meat and the fish themselves may not provide enough calories to the population dependent on herding animals or catching fish for the market. On this see Sen (1981a: chapters 6–8), and Desai (1988a). See also Hay (1975), Rivers *et al.* (1976), and Seaman, Holt and Rivers (1978) on the relative costs of animal calories and grain calories and the conditions of exchange faced by Ethiopian pastoralists. On the equilibrium of pastoral survival, including exchange, see Swift (1982), McCann (1987) and Horowitz and Little (1987), among others.

the Indian subcontinent, the majority of famine victims in this century and the last has come from this group.[10]

The acute vulnerability of wage labourers in a market economy is a problem which applies, in fact, also to the richer countries (including those of Western Europe and North America), since even there wage labourers have little ability to survive on their own when unemployment develops as dramatically as it did, say, in the early 1980s. People in this predicament have been spared the necessity of starvation because of the supplementation of the market mechanism by institutionalized social security, and in particular by unemployment insurance, in the absence of which there would have been, it is easy to see, acute and widespread hunger in many of these countries.

The importance of the vulnerability of wage labourers to famines can be particularly acute in that *intermediate* phase in which the class of wage labourers has become large (unlike in precapitalist formations), but a system of social security has not yet developed (unlike in the more advanced economies). This is not to say that traditional means of social security in pre-wage economies are typically adequate. Indeed, as we shall see later, they are often altogether insufficient and meagre. But the wage system has added a particular source of vulnerability which has to be specifically addressed.

Fifth, recent times have witnessed not only a rapid expansion of market exchange, but also significant developments in the conditions of 'exchange with nature', i.e. production. On the one hand, advances in agricultural technology have increased the potential for improving living conditions in rural areas. On the other hand, in many countries environmental degradation (in the form of deforestation, desertification, etc.) poses a grave threat to the livelihood of the rural population. While these processes are, once again, not new, their pace and reach are often greater than ever. So is the scope for public action to influence and reshape them.

Sixth, the state has an important role to play in combating world hunger, and in this book we shall, in fact, go into many of the policy issues that are involved in playing this role effectively. At the same time, it would be a mistake to overlook the fact that many famines in the world have actually arisen from and been sustained by inflexible government policies undermining the power of particular sections of the population to command food. The Soviet famines of the 1930s and the Kampuchean famines of the late 1970s are obvious examples of systematic undermining of the economic power of a large part of the population through state policy. It is easy to cite other terrible cases in which political dogma and the use of authoritarian political power have led to disastrous government policies, making it impossible for millions of people to earn a living.

In a sense this feature is not really new, since kings and rulers in the past have also often imposed extraordinary sacrifices on sections of the population, not

---

[10] See Drèze (1988a).

least due to invasions and wars. But with the growth of modern politics, the importance of ideology has grown dramatically. That can, of course, be a creative force in providing political commitment for combating world hunger, and we shall have quite a bit to say on the positive role of determined state policy. But ideological state action can also include dogmatic pursuit of policies that force large sections of the population into penury and deprivation. Strongly ideological politics has become—both positively and negatively—an inescapable part of the economics of food and starvation, and this too is a feature that has to be kept in view in analysing the challenge of hunger in the modern world.

There are many other, subtler differences between hunger in the past and that in the modern world. Hunger is a common predicament, but this does not indicate the existence of one shared cause. People can fail in their ability to command food and other necessities in many different ways, and the genesis of these failures can vary greatly with the nature of the economy and the society. In this book we must pay particular attention to the special features of hunger in the modern world, in addition to investigating more traditional aspects of poverty and starvation.

1.2 Famine and Chronic Undernourishment

There are many different ways of seeing hunger. The dictionary meaning of the term, e.g. 'discomfort or painful sensation caused by want of food', takes us in a particular and extremely narrow direction. In the demand for 'ending hunger' the concern is not merely with making it possible to avoid that discomfort or pain (even though the suffering involved is often underestimated by people who have never really experienced this pain), but also to conquer food deprivation in general—seen in terms of its manifold consequences. These consequences include undernourishment, debilitation, fatigue, morbidity, and possibly mortality, with obvious effects on human well-being and productivity.

In trying to come to grips with the problem of hunger in the modern world, it is necessary to get a clear understanding of the different issues that constitute it. The distinction between the problem of chronic hunger (involving sustained nutritional deprivation on a persistent basis) and that of famine (involving acute starvation and a sharp increase of mortality) is particularly important. In this book we shall encounter several important contrasts in the strategic choices that arise in facing these respective problems. To take one example, in the context of famine prevention the crucial need for speedy intervention and the scarcity of resources often call for a calculated reliance on existing distributional mechanisms (e.g. the operation of private trade stimulated by cash support to famine victims) to supplement the logistic capability of relief agencies. In the context of combating chronic hunger, on the other hand, there is much greater scope for slower but none the less powerful avenues of action such as institution building, legal reforms, asset redistribution, or provisioning in kind.

The importance of the contrast between chronic hunger and acute starvation is also reflected in the experiences of different countries. There are countries in which famines in the form of acute starvation leading to large-scale mortality have not taken place in recent years, but where chronic hunger is quite widespread. An example is India since its independence in 1947. The last major famine in India took place before independence, viz. the Bengal famine of 1943, in which about 3 million people died. Since then there have been a number of threats of severe famine (e.g. in Bihar in 1967, in Maharashtra in 1973, in West Bengal in 1979, in Gujarat in 1987), but they did not materialize, largely due to public intervention. There is, however, a great deal of regular hunger and endemic undernourishment in India, especially in rural areas. The frequency of undernutrition-related diseases also remains distressingly high.[11]

On the other hand, it is possible for a country to deal effectively with chronic hunger as an endemic feature, and at the same time to fall prey to substantial famine as a transient phenomenon. That seems to have been the experience of China, in which the problem of regular hunger has been tackled with much success—considerably more effectively than in India—but where a famine on a gigantic scale took place during 1958–61, with an excess mortality that has to be counted in terms of tens of millions.[12] The contrast between India and China is really rather striking, especially since India's success in famine prevention seems to have done little to help it combat chronic hunger, and China's remarkable achievement in improving the nutritional well-being of its people in normal times (and in expanding the longevity of the Chinese to the high sixties) has not been accompanied by an absence of famine in the post-revolutionary period. The complex economic and political causation of this contrasting pattern—and other important features of the experience of these two giant countries—will be examined later on in this volume (Chapter 11). But, for the moment, we shall leave this issue here, using it only to illustrate the importance of the distinction between chronic hunger, on the one hand, and acute starvation involved in a famine, on the other.

As a matter of fact, famine is a much more confined phenomenon in the modern world than endemic undernutrition and persistent deprivation. Most famines in recent decades have occurred in sub-Saharan Africa, with a few exceptions such as the Bangladesh famine of 1974 and the Kampuchean famine of 1979–80. In sub-Saharan Africa famines have afflicted a great many countries, and we shall be paying particular attention to that region in Part II of

---

[11] See Banerji (1982), Rao (1982), Gopalan (1987b), Nutrition Foundation of India (1988), Srinivasan and Bardhan (1988), and Subbarao (1989). On the role of public intervention in preventing famines in India since independence, see Drèze (1988a).

[12] On the basis of the recently available Chinese demographic statistics, Ashton et al. (1984) estimate the number of excess deaths in that famine to be 29.5 million, while Peng's (1987) estimate is 23 million. On China's success in addressing the challenge of chronic hunger, see Riskin (1986), and also Chapter 11 below.

this volume (Chapters 5–8), concerned with analysing the causation and prevention of famines.

While famines have been rare outside Africa in recent decades, the problem of endemic hunger is serious—indeed often colossal—in many other parts of the world as well, particularly South Asia. Even in Latin America, which is very much richer in terms of GNP per head than Africa or South Asia, particular sections of the population—related to class and location—are significantly affected by the persistence of hunger (see Kanbur 1986b).

Furthermore, as we shall argue presently (Chapter 3), the problem of chronic undernutrition is closely related not only to deficiency of food intake, but also to deprivations of other kinds, particularly those of education, health care, basic facilities, and social environment (including water supply, sanitary provisions, etc.). The effects of these deficiencies can be seen in such elementary failures as low longevity and high morbidity, in addition to clinical undernutrition. While life expectancy at birth is more than 75 years in many of the prosperous countries of the world, the corresponding figure is estimated to be below 60 years in most poor countries, below 50 for a great many, and even below 40 years for some. When we address problems of endemic undernutrition and deprivation in Part III of this book (Chapters 9–12), we shall have to take a broad view of poverty and indigence, and also take note of the wide geographical coverage of rudimentary deprivation.

1.3 Some Elementary Concepts

In the analysis to be presented in this book a number of elementary concepts will be frequently used, and it may be convenient to say a few words on the underlying ideas in this introductory chapter. There is nothing particularly complex, nor anything alarmingly novel, about these concepts. But the presentation of the arguments may be helped by some initial clarification.

Entitlements

What we can eat depends on what food we are able to acquire. The mere presence of food in the economy, or in the market, does not entitle a person to consume it. In each social structure, given the prevailing legal, political, and economic arrangements, a person can establish command over some alternative commodity bundles (any one bundle of which he or she can choose to consume). These bundles could be extensive, or very limited, and what a person can consume will be directly dependent on what these bundles are. The set of alternative bundles of commodities over which a person can establish such command will be referred to as this person's 'entitlements'.[13]

---

[13] Entitlement is being defined here in terms of ownership rights. There are other types of rights of *use* that do not involve ownership as such, but which have the effect of guaranteeing use nevertheless. For a more comprehensive characterization of entitlements, see Sen (1981a). Some of these additional features will also be discussed later on in this book.

To illustrate, a peasant who grows his own food is entitled to what he has grown, adjusted for any obligations he may have (e.g. to money-lenders). He can sell, if he wants, a part of the product for cash to buy other goods and services, and all the alternative commodity bundles he can acquire through these means lie within his entitlement set. Similarly, a wage labourer's entitlement is given by what he can buy with his wages, if he does in fact manage to find employment.[14]

Endowment and Exchange

A person's entitlements depend both on what she owns initially, and what she can acquire through exchange. For example, a wage labourer owns her labour power, and by exchanging that for a wage (the exchange takes the form of employment), she acquires some money, which she can then exchange for some commodity bundle or other. Similarly, a landlord who owns some land and leases out that land for rent can use the proceeds to purchase different commodity bundles. The 'endowment' of a person is given by the initial ownership (e.g. the labourer's labour power, the landlord's holding of land), and these endowments can be used to establish entitlements in the form of holdings of alternative commodity bundles through trade (e.g. a labourer taking up employment and purchasing commodities with the wage, a landlord renting out land and purchasing commodities with the rent).

The exchange can also be with 'nature', and this is one way of seeing production, as opposed to trade. For example, a peasant farmer can exchange the use of his land and his labour power (along with a few other inputs such as seeds) for a crop. This exchange with nature in the form of production may, of course, be followed by trade in the form of selling a part (or indeed the whole) of the output and buying other commodities with the proceeds. The alternative bundles of commodities a person can acquire through exchange (i.e. production and trade) for each particular endowment are the person's 'exchange entitlement' for that level of endowment.

Extended Entitlements

While the concept of entitlement focuses on a person's *legal* rights of ownership, there are some social relations that take the broader form of accepted *legitimacy* rather than legal rights enforceable in a court. For example, if, by a well-established convention, the male head of a household receives more favourable treatment in the division of the family's total consumption (e.g. having the first claim on, say, the meat or the fish in the family's diet, or receiving greater medical attention in case of illness), that person can be seen as having a claim the legitimacy of which is accepted and is thus effective, even though it is not a claim that can be upheld in a court or enforced by the power of the state.

---

[14] The 'budget set' of elementary consumer theory is a simple example of an entitlement set.

Despite their legally weaker form, such socially sanctioned rights may be extremely important in determining the amount of food or health care or other commodities that different members of a family get, and this too will play a part in our analysis of hunger. 'Extended entitlements' is the concept of entitlements extended to include the results of more informal types of rights sanctioned by accepted notions of legitimacy. This notion is particularly relevant in analysing intrafamily divisions, but it has other uses in social analysis as well.

Cooperative Conflicts

In the social relations that *inter alia* determine the entitlements enjoyed by different people, there tends to be a coexistence of conflict *and* congruence of interests. There are, in most situations, clear advantages to be gained by different people through cooperation with each other, and yet there are also elements of conflict reflecting the partly divergent interests of the same people. 'Cooperative conflicts' refer to this coexistence of congruence and conflict of interests, providing grounds for cooperation as well as for disputes and battles.

Cooperative conflicts may be illustrated from many different fields of social relations. Consider the relation between workers and industrialists in a particular industry. If production is disrupted, both the industrialists and the workers may lose, so that it is in the interest of both to cooperate with each other in the process of production. But the division of benefits obtained from production may also involve an extensive tussle between the industrialists and the workers. It may be in the interest of the capitalists to get a larger share of the output produced, and in the interest of the workers to obtain higher wages and better working conditions and resist 'exploitation'. In the context of productive activities of other kinds, the relations between, say, a share-cropper and a landlord, or between the members of a production team, or between the different parties in a cartel, also involve obvious situations of cooperative conflict.

To take another example, it is typically in the interest of all the members of a family to cooperate in living together. But at the same time there is also the issue of *intra*family division, and it may be in the interest of, say, the husband to secure a higher share of benefits and a lower share of household chores *vis-à-vis* his wife. The conflicts involved in gender division may, thus, arise against a background of generally cooperative behaviour. Indeed, given the importance of cooperation in family living, the elements of conflict may be kept very well hidden, so that a serious awareness of the elements of conflict may be suppressed by the use of conventional norms. The questioning of these norms may even appear to be aberrant and deviant behaviour. The issue of perception can, thus, be a very important aspect of the problem of gender-based inequality.[15]

[15] The role of cooperative conflicts in gender relations and in intrafamily divisions, and the part played in all this by perception problems, are discussed in Sen (1985c, 1987c).

Analysing cooperative conflicts is particularly important for a better understanding of the causes and remedies of hunger. In addition to the problems involved in production relations and in intrafamily divisions, even at the more aggregative level there tends to be coexistence of a good deal of congruence and conflict of interests. For example, there may be great gains for everyone in cooperation for the preservation of the environment, for the prevention of droughts, for improving agricultural technology and infrastructure, for reducing industrial wastage, or for eliminating epidemics. And yet there may also be extensive battles between different groups for, say, a bigger share of the total food available in the economy. Sometimes even a famine may be principally associated with one group losing out in a 'food battle' of this kind.

Capability and Living Standards

In any economic analysis it is important to distinguish between the ends and the means. At the very beginning of his *Nicomachean Ethics*, Aristotle had noted, while discussing the role of economics, the need to be aware that 'wealth is evidently not the good we are seeking; for it is merely useful and for the sake of something else'.[16] Aristotle saw 'the good of human beings' in terms of the richness of 'life in the sense of activity', and thus argued for taking human functionings as the objects of value.[17]

In a similar line of reasoning, with more specific concentration on the quality of life, the object of public action can be seen to be the enhancement of the capability of people to undertake valuable and valued 'doings and beings'.[18] This can extend from such elementary capabilities as the ability to avoid undernourishment and related morbidity and mortality, to more sophisticated social capabilities such as taking part in the life of the community and achieving self-respect.

Capability is a broad concept, and it incorporates the concerns that are associated with what is often called the 'standard of living', but goes beyond it. Living standards relate specifically to the richness of the person's own life, whereas a person may value his or her capability also to be socially useful and influential (going well beyond the pursuit of his or her own living standards). The distinction between the broader notion of capability and the narrower concept of living standard can be relevant in many contexts.[19] Concern with

[16] Aristotle, *The Nicomachean Ethics*, Book I, section 5; in the translation by Ross (1980: 7).

[17] Book I, section 7; Ross (1980: 12–15). Marx followed this line of reasoning and argued for a reorientation of economic preoccupations: 'It will be seen how in place of the wealth and poverty of political economy come the rich human being and rich human need. The rich human being is simultaneously in need of a totality of human life-activities' (Marx, 1844).

[18] There are interesting and important problems in the characterization and analysis of capabilities, on which see Sen (1985a, 1985b). Formally, a person's capability is a set of functioning bundles, representing the various alternative 'beings and doings' that a person can achieve with his or her economic, social, and personal characteristics.

[19] For an analysis of this and related distinctions, see Sen (1977b, 1987a, 1987b). On related matters see Hart (1987), Hawthorn (1987), Kanbur (1987), Muellbauer (1987), B. Williams (1987), Griffin and Knight (1988, 1989).

the lives of others is clearly a crucial ingredient of public action. Without acknowledging this basic human motivation, it would be impossible to understand the part that political parties, social leaders, journalists, relief agencies and grass-roots activists can play in encountering famines and chronic deprivation. However, in the context of defining the *objectives* to be pursued in the battle against hunger, the finer distinction between capability and living standard may not be of central importance. The important thing at this stage (and in much of this book) is to note the general concern with 'doings' and 'beings' and the corresponding capabilities, rather than just with incomes or wealth or utilities.

The focus on capability helps to clarify the purpose of public action in different fields, including that of combating hunger. The object, in this view, is not so much to provide a particular amount of food for each. Indeed, the relationship between food intake and nutritional achievement can vary greatly depending not only on features such as age, sex, pregnancy, metabolic rates, climatic conditions, and activities, but also on access to complementary inputs such as health care, drinking water and so on. A more reasoned goal would be to make it possible for all to have the capability to avoid undernourishment and escape deprivations associated with hunger. The focus here is on human life as it can be led, rather than on commodities as such, which are means to human life, and are contingently related to need fulfilment rather than being valued for themselves.[20] The focus on entitlements, which is concerned with the command over *commodities*, has to be seen as only instrumentally important, and the concentration has to be, ultimately, on basic human capabilities.[21]

The implications of focusing on capabilities in the analysis of public action in combating hunger will become clearer as we go along. One particular consequence relates to the need to broaden our attention from the command over food to other influences, including the command over other commodities that have a substantial impact on nutrition and health. A person's capability to avoid undernourishment may depend not merely on his or her intake of food, but also on the person's access to health care, medical facilities, elementary education, drinking water, and sanitary facilities. Similarly, the prevalence of epidemics and disease in a particular region may also be a factor influencing the extent of undernutrition. In so far as we concentrate on entitlements, the case

[20] Marx (1887) discussed the problems associated with what he called 'commodity fetishism' (ch. 1). There is a good case for defining 'basic needs' in terms of capabilities as such rather than in terms of commodities, as they are usually defined. On this, see Sen (1984a), Streeten (1984), and F. Stewart (1988). See also Streeten *et al.* (1981).

[21] While the *entitlement* of a person is a set of alternative *commodity* bundles, the *capability* of a person is a set of alternative *functioning* bundles. Larger entitlements contribute to wider capabilities, but the relationship is not the same for different persons. For example, a pregnant woman has greater nutritional requirements and also special needs for medical attention, and hence having the same command over food and health care as another—non-pregnant—person may not give her the same capability to be well nourished and healthy. Public action has to be based on an adequately discriminating analysis, and this calls for causal investigations of capabilities and of variations in the relation between entitlements and capabilities.

for broadening the coverage from food as such to all the commodities relevant to nutritional capabilities and good health is strong. This has a direct and far-reaching bearing on the nature of public action for combating hunger and deprivation.

Undernourishment and Undernutrition

A capability is 'nutrition-related' if and only if it can be enhanced by greater or better food intake. Two clarifications are due. First, while many capabilities are 'nutrition-related' in this sense, some (e.g. the ability to survive) are clearly more important than others (e.g. fitness to hop, skip and jump). Our primary concern is with those nutrition-related capabilities that are crucial to human well-being. Second, while the boundaries of the concept of 'nutrition-related capability' are defined with reference to the relevance or otherwise of improved food intake, most capabilities of this kind also depend on many other factors. The importance of epidemiological protection, health care, basic education, sanitation, etc., for nutritional well-being will be one of the recurrent themes of this book.

A distinction is sometimes made—typically implicitly—between 'undernutrition' and 'undernourishment'. The former is usually seen in terms of *a shortage of food intake*, while the latter is taken to be an *unsatisfactory state of being*. In this contrast, undernutrition is connected with *commodities* (specifically food—someone having less food, or less variety of food, than some specified nutritional standard would demand), while undernourishment is connected with the state of *human beings* (specifically, a person being somehow inadequate in energy or strength or some other feature associated with nutritional sufficiency).

While there is a distinction here, it is arguable that it is not perhaps as much of a dividing line as might first appear. This is the case *if* 'undernutrition' is defined taking full note of personal characteristics. That is, undernutrition has to be seen in terms of a person not getting as much as he or she would need for reaching some specified nutritional standards. What those standards should be is, of course, a subject of considerable interest as well as great controversy (as we shall see in Chapter 3), but at this stage all that is immediately relevant is that the standards in question are related to the nutritional states of *people*, rather than being defined in terms of *given* amounts of food or nutrients, specified *irrespective* of personal characteristics (such as body size, metabolic rate, sex, pregnancy, age, etc.). A sensible identification of 'undernutrition' already brings in the *state of the person's being*—specifically the person being in some sense 'undernourished'. Given that connection between 'undernutrition' and 'undernourishment', the two must be seen as tied concepts.

Deprivation and Poverty

There are different ways of seeing the deprivations in human life with which public action has to be concerned. From what has been said already it should be clear that deprivation may be fruitfully seen in terms of the failure of certain human capabilities that are important to a person's well-being. If a person does not have the capability of avoiding preventable mortality, unnecessary morbidity, or escapable undernourishment, then it would almost certainly be agreed that the person is deprived in a significant way. There may be other—more subtle—types of deprivation on which too there could be general agreement, such as the inability to appear in public without shame because of one's evident penury.[22]

It is, in fact, possible to see 'poverty' itself as a severe failure of basic capabilities. That approach has much to commend, since it relates poverty to the failure of the ability to achieve precisely those things that are ultimately important.[23] On the other hand, the more common definition of poverty is in terms of inadequacy of incomes (e.g. a person's income level falling below the 'poverty line'). It is perhaps fruitless to spend much time arguing about which definition of poverty is superior. Undoubtedly, the failure of basic capabilities must ultimately be the central concern in the context of this analysis. Also, we have to take note of the fact that capabilities are influenced not merely by personal incomes but also by social facilities (such as public health). Whether poverty is seen as the failure of basic capabilities itself (e.g. 'a person is poor if she has to lead a very deprived life'), or as a causal antecedent of that failure (e.g. 'a person is poor if she has too low an income'), may not really make much difference *provided* we gear our analysis, ultimately, to matters of intrinsic concern and examine all causal influences on those matters. It is the need to avoid deprivation of basic capabilities on which we have to concentrate in the analysis of public action. This priority holds no matter whether 'poverty' is identified with that deprivation itself, or defined as the lack of economic means to escape that deprivation.

Social Security

Hunger is a many-headed monster. The undernutrition that haunts a large part of humanity relates to a wide range of deprivations. The connections between different types of deprivation are not only biological (e.g. between illness and undernutrition) but also economic and social (e.g. between unemployment and illness).

The idea of 'social security' is that of using social means to prevent deprivation and vulnerability. Social means can be of various types. Perhaps the most immediate is to provide direct support to the ability of the vulnerable to acquire the means to basic capabilities. Providing free food or cash to potential famine victims is an obvious example of this. On a more regular basis,

---

[22] The last is, in fact, a capability failure on which Adam Smith had a good deal to say; see Smith (1776), vol. I, Book V, Section II, in the edition by Campbell and Skinner (1976: 869–72).

[23] For a discussion of the rationale underlying this view of poverty, see Sen (1980, 1983*b*). See also Townsend (1985), Sen (1985*d*) and Seidl (1988).

providing unemployment insurance, free health services and basic education, etc., are other examples of such direct support.

The social means could also be indirect. For example, creating the social conditions of economic growth may make a substantial—and lasting— contribution to eliminating deprivation, if growth involves widespread parti- cipation of the population in the process of economic expansion. Later on in this book we shall study the different social means that may be used to reduce or eliminate failures of basic capabilities. We shall also have to study the interconnections between alternative approaches to social security.

We should stress that 'social security' as we see it here is a much broader and far-reaching notion than the technical sense in which the term is sometimes used in the professional literature on social administration in the richer countries. Debates on social security issues in the more prosperous countries have tended, perhaps for good logistic reasons, to focus on a number of specific forms of intervention such as unemployment benefits, medical insurance or old age pensions. Often the very definition of 'social security' is associated with these specific programmes (see e.g. the publications of the International Social Security Association). There is some debate as to the part that these program- mes can play in removing deprivation in developing countries.[24] But no matter what position we take on this issue, there is some obvious advantage in considering all the relevant forms of intervention in a common framework. We see 'social security' essentially as an *objective* pursued through *public means* rather than as a narrowly defined set of particular strategies, and it is important to take a broad view of the public means that are relevant to the attainment of this objective.[25]

It is useful to distinguish between two different aspects of social security, viz *protection* and *promotion*. The former is concerned with the task of preventing a decline in living standards as might occur in, say, an economic recession, or—more drastically—in a famine. The latter refers to the enhancement of general living standards and to the expansion of basic capabilities of the population, and will have to be seen primarily as a long-run challenge. In this book we shall be concerned with both aspects of social security.

It must be emphasized that while the terms 'promotion' and 'protection' both have a somewhat paternalistic ring, these terms refer to the objectives of the exercise rather than to the agency that may pursue these objectives. As we shall argue in the next section, public action for social security is neither just a matter of state activity, nor an issue of charity, nor even one of kindly

---

[24] On this see Mouton (1975), Gilbert (1976, 1981), Mesa-Lago (1978, 1983a, 1985c, 1986), Cockburn (1980), Mallet (1980), Guhan (1981, 1988), International Social Security Association (1982), Midgley (1984a, 1984b), Abel-Smith (1986), Atkinson and Hills (1988), and various contributions in Ahmad, Drèze, Hills and Sen (forthcoming).

[25] The social security measures that have been historically associated with the pursuit of social security objectives in the richer countries, and which are now formalized in the conventional usage of the term (e.g. in ILO publications), are best seen as contingently relevant for social security in the broader sense.

redistribution. The activism of the public, the unity and solidarity of the concerned population, and the participation of all those who are involved are important features of public action for social security.

1.4   Public Action for Social Security

It would be hard to deny that there is a straightforward public-interest issue involved in the elimination of starvation and of nutritional deprivation. The challenge of confronting in an effective manner the scourge that chastises and haunts a substantial part of humanity inescapably calls for diverse forms of public action. The provision of social security cannot exclusively rely either on the operation of market forces, or on some paternalistic initiative on the part of the state, or on some other social institution such as the family.

The *need* for public action does not, however, in itself point to the *nature* of the action to be undertaken. There are different areas of action, different strategies to pursue, different agents for undertaking action. The decision problems implicit in the choices involved are both complex and momentous. The issues include political and social phenomena as well as economic ones. The strategy of public action can be as difficult as it is urgent.

The various facets of the challenge of public action for the elimination of famines and endemic hunger will receive close attention in different parts of this book, but a few elementary considerations deserve immediate mention. First, the orientation of public action must clearly depend on the feasibilities of different courses of action. These feasibilities relate not merely to the causal factors that lead to deprivation and hunger, but also to the nature and power of the agencies involved. In particular, the character of the state, and the nature of the government undertaking state actions, can be crucial. The questions raised include not merely the administrative capabilities of governments, but also the political commitments and loyalties as well as the power bases of the holders of political power.

The countries with which we shall be concerned in this book have enormously divergent political systems and social balances of power, and the forms that public action can take will undoubtedly depend on these political and social parameters. For example, whether the Chinese success in subduing chronic hunger can be repeated, say, in India, or whether Indian achievements in the elimination of famines can be emulated in sub-Saharan Africa, or whether the sub-Saharan African record of lower gender inequalities in nutritional well-being can be duplicated in India or China or the Middle East, are all important and complex questions that call for careful scrutiny of the backgrounds against which these experiences have taken place.

Second, the public is not a homogeneous entity, and there are divisions related to class, ownership, occupation, and also gender, community and culture. While public action for social security is in some sense beneficial for all groups, the division of the benefits involved cannot escape differential pulls coming from divergent interest groups. The art of public action has to take note of these cooperative conflicts. To think of public action as action for the benefit of a homogeneous public is to miss a crucial aspect of the challenge.

Third, state action for the elimination of hunger can take enormously divergent forms. It need not involve only food production or food distribution. It can take the form of income or employment creation on a regular basis to combat endemic undernourishment. It can also involve famine relief operations in the form of employment for wages in cash or in kind to regenerate the purchasing power of hard-hit occupation groups. It can include the provision of health care and epidemic control, which may be important not merely as basic ingredients of the general well-being of the population, but also in preventing undernourishment, which is often associated with parasitic ailments and other forms of morbidity. State action can also take the form of enhancing economic development, in general, and the growth of incomes and other means of subsistence, in particular, through the expansion of productive activities. The discipline of public action may be widely different in these various fields, and the strategy of public action for social security has to be alive to the respective issues involved. The complementarities and tradeoffs between different avenues of action also have to be firmly faced in developing an overall effective public programme for eliminating hunger in all its forms.

Fourth, some public institutions, in particular the market, have often been seen as being an alternative to state action. To some extent this is right, since market mechanisms determine certain allocations and distributions, and state actions can alter or even take over many of these functions. While the conflicts between the reliance on markets and that on state action have to be fully acknowledged, it is also important not to see these two avenues as being in constant combat with each other. A purist philosophy can be awfully short of logistic means.[26]

The need to consider a plurality of levers and a heterogeneity of mechanisms is hard to escape in the strategy of public action for social security. The internal diversities involved in an effective public action programme can be quite extensive. For example, several countries have achieved some success in preventing famines by combining cash transfers to vulnerable groups in the form of wages for public employment with reliance on the private sector for moving food to affected regions, along with public participation in food distribution to prevent the emergence of collusive manipulations by private traders. These combined strategies illustrate the fruitfulness of taking an integrated and pluralist view of public action.

Fifth, public action should not be confused with state action only. Various

[26] The either-this-or-that 'exclusive' view often attributed to leaders of classical political economy was by no means universally endorsed. The effectiveness of the market mechanism in achieving certain types of efficiency was clearly seen by that great critic of capitalism, Karl Marx, and the fact that 'want, famine and mortality' can arise from unemployment in a market economy was explicitly noted by that great defender of the efficiency of markets, Adam Smith.

social and political organizations have typically played a part in actions that go beyond atomistic individual initiatives, and the domain of public action does include many non-state activities. Indeed, in many traditional societies, individual security has tended to depend greatly on support from groups such as the extended family or the community.[27] The active role of the state in the modern world should not be seen as replacement of what these non-governmental groups and institutions can achieve.

Finally, even as far as state action is concerned, there is a close relationship between public understanding and awareness, on the one hand, and the nature, forms and vigour of state action in pursuit of public goals, on the other. Political pressure plays a major part in determining actions undertaken by governments, and even fairly authoritarian political leaders have, to a great extent, to accept the discipline of public criticism and social opposition. Public enlightenment may, thus, have the role both of drawing attention to problems that may otherwise be neglected, and of precipitating remedial action on the part of governments faced with critical pressure. For example, the role of newspapers and public discussions, which can be extremely crucial in identifying famine threats (an energetic press may be the best 'early warning system' for famine that a country can devise), can also help to keep the government on its toes so that famine relief and preventive measures take place rapidly and effectively.

The question of public enlightenment and awareness involves both institutional features and the nature of social and political movements in the country. Since these are not immutable factors, the role of public action must be examined not merely in terms of consolidation of past achievements, but also with a view to possible departures in new directions. It is important to see the public as an agent and not merely as a passive patient.

---

[27] The profound concern of traditional societies for social security, and the variety of institutions they have evolved in pursuit of that objective, have been explored by Jean-Philippe Platteau (1988b). See also Chapter 5.

2

Entitlement and Deprivation[1]

2.1 Deprivation and the Law

When millions of people die in a famine, it is hard to avoid the thought that something terribly criminal is going on. The law, which defines and protects our rights as citizens, must somehow be compromised by these dreadful events. Unfortunately, the gap between law and ethics can be a big one. The economic system that yields a famine may be foul and the political system that tolerates it perfectly revolting, but nevertheless there may be no violation of our lawfully recognized rights in the failure of large sections of the population to acquire enough food to survive.

The point is not so much that there is no law against dying of hunger. That is, of course, true and obvious. It is more that the legally guaranteed rights of ownership, exchange and transaction delineate economic systems that can go hand in hand with some people failing to acquire enough food for survival. In a private ownership economy, command over food can be established by either growing food oneself and having property rights over what is grown, or selling other commodities and buying food with the proceeds. There is no guarantee that either process would yield enough for the survival of any particular person or a family in a particular social and economic situation. The third alternative, other than relying on private charity, is to receive free food or supplementary income from the state. These transfers rarely have the status of legal rights, and furthermore they are also, as things stand now, rather rare and limited.

For a large part of humanity, about the only substantial asset that a person owns is his or her ability to work, i.e. labour power. If a person fails to secure employment, then that means of acquiring food (e.g. by getting a job, earning a wage, and buying food with this income) fails. If, in addition to that, the laws of the land do not provide any social security arrangements, e.g. unemployment insurance, the person will, under these circumstances, fail to secure the means of subsistence.[2] And that can result in serious deprivation—possibly even starvation death. In seeking a remedy to this problem of terrible vulnerability, it is natural to turn towards a reform of the legal system, so that rights of social security can be made to stand as guarantees of minimal protection and survival.

---

[1] This chapter draws substantially on *Poverty and Famines* (Sen 1981*a*), and those familiar with the arguments presented there may wish to shun it.

[2] It is, of course, still possible for the person to survive on the basis of charity, but this is not a matter of right. If those who own more than they need are not willing to help this person adequately, the person will have to starve and perish.

We shall indeed explore this line of reasoning in this book, but at this stage we are primarily concerned with diagnostics rather than with cure.

It should also be added that even a person who is engaged in growing food and who succeeds in growing more (even, much more) than enough food for survival may not necessarily survive on this basis, and may not even have the legal right to do so. As we discussed in the last chapter, in many famines the majority of the victims come from the class of agricultural labourers. They are often primarily engaged in growing food. However, the legal nature of their contract, which is often informal, basically involves a wage payment in exchange for employment. The contract typically includes no right to the output grown by the person's own labour—no entitlement to the food output which could be the basis of survival for that person and his or her dependents.

Even if a person is lucky enough to find employment and is paid a certain sum of money for it as a wage, he or she has to convert that into food by purchase in the market. How much that wage commands would, of course, depend on the price of food. If food prices rise very rapidly, without money wages rising correspondingly, the labourers who have grown the food them-selves may fail to acquire the food they need to survive.[3] The food grown belongs to the employer (typically the owner of the land), and the wage payment is the end of the grower's right to the produce, even if that wage does not yield enough to survive.

Similarly, a person who acquires food by producing some other commodity and selling it in the market has to depend on the actual ability to sell that product and also on the relative price of that product *vis-à-vis* food. If either the sale fails to materialize, or the relative price of that product falls sharply *vis-à-vis* food, the person may again have no option but to starve.

It is also important to realize that uncertainty and vulnerability can be features of subsistence production (involving 'exchange with nature') as well as of market exchange. This precariousness is particularly visible in African famines, where a substantial proportion of the victims often come from the ranks of small farmers who are hit *inter alia* by a collapse of their 'direct entitlement' to the food they normally grow. It would be a misleading simplification to regard self-provisioning as synonymous with security. The peasant farmer, like the landless labourer, has no guaranteed entitlement to the necessities of life.

It is, of course, also the case that laws may be disrupted during a famine. But there is no necessity for that to happen in order for a famine to occur. Indeed, as it happens, quite a few famines have taken place without much violation of law and order. Even in the disastrous Irish famines of the 1840s (in which about an

---

[3] The exchange rate between labour and food (i.e. the ratio of money wage and food prices) may dramatically fall as a result of economic changes brought about by factors beyond the control of the labourer. On some examples of dramatic changes in labour–food exchange rates in the Bengal famine of 1943 and the Bangladesh famine of 1974, see Alamgir (1980), Sen (1981a), and Ravallion (1987a).

eighth of the population died, and which led to the emigration of a comparable number to North America), the law and order situation was, in many respects, apparently 'excellent'. In fact, even as the higher purchasing power of the English consumers attracted food away, through the market mechanism, from famine-stricken Ireland to rich England, with ship after ship sailing down the river Shannon laden with various types of food, there were few violent attempts to interfere with that contrary—and grisly—process. In many famines people starve and die in front of food shops, without attempting to seize law and order by the collar. It would be, particularly, a mistake to relate the *causation* of famines to violations of legality.

There have, of course, been well-known cases of protest and rebellion associated with food crises, and 'the food riot as a form of political conflict' has considerable historical significance.[4] Despite this important causal link, the exact period of a severe famine is often not one of effective rebellion. Indeed, the debilitation and general helplessness brought about by a famine situation is not typically conducive to immediate revolt and rebellion. This is not to deny that looting, raiding and other forms of unorganized crime can be quite frequent in famine situations. But the millions that die in a famine typically die in an astonishingly 'legal' and 'orderly' way.

2.2   Entitlement Failures and Economic Analysis

If a group of people fail to establish their entitlement over an adequate amount of food, they have to go hungry. If that deprivation is large enough, the resulting starvation can lead to death. There is nothing particularly novel in the recognition that starvation is best seen as a result of 'entitlement failure'. Since the aggregate food supply is not divided among the population through some distributive formula (such as equal division), each family has to establish command over its own food. Even though this fact is elementary enough, it is remarkable that food analysis is often conducted just in terms of production and total availability rather than taking note of the processes through which people establish their entitlements to food.[5]

The notion of entitlement in this context must not be confused with

---

[4] See Louise Tilly (1971, 1983) and Charles Tilly (1975, 1978). See also Walter and Wrightson (1976), Dirks (1980), Li (1982a) and Kynch (1988). The subject also relates to Sorokin's (1942, 1975) influential historical analysis, and to Hobsbawm's (1954) pioneering work on 'primitive rebellion'.

[5] The view of famines as entitlement failures (on which see Sen, 1976a, 1977a, 1981a) attempts to combine in one common framework various interrelated ideas that have been used to analyse specific cases of hunger and starvation for many centuries. Even though the lessons of these ideas have often been overlooked, it is possible to profit greatly from studying analyses of food command in the writings of various classical authors including Adam Smith (1776), Thomas Malthus (1800), David Ricardo (1822: 234–5), and Karl Marx (1857–8, 1887); on these links see Sen (1981a: Chapter 1 and Appendix B; 1986a).

normative ideas as to who might be 'morally entitled' to what. The reference instead is to what the law guarantees and supports.

The legal system that precedes and survives through the famine may not, in itself, be a particularly cruel one. The standardly accepted rights of ownership and exchange are not the authoritarian extravaganzas of a heartless Nero or some brutal Genghis Khan. They are, rather, parts of the standard legal rules of ownership and exchange that govern people's lives in much of the world. But when they are not supplemented by other rights (e.g. social security, unemployment insurance, public health provisions), these standard rights may operate in a way that offers no chance of survival to potential famine victims. On the contrary, these legal rights, backed by the state power that upholds them, may ensure that the 'have-nots' do not grab food from the 'haves', and the law can stand solidly between needs and fulfilment.

As was discussed in Chapter 1, the 'entitlement' of a person stands for the set of alternative commodity bundles that can be acquired through the use of the various legal channels of acquirement open to that person. In a private ownership market economy, the entitlement set of a person is determined by his original ownership bundle (what is called 'endowment') and the various alternative bundles that the person can acquire, starting with each initial endowment, through the use of trade and production (what is called his 'exchange entitlement').[6] A person has to starve if his entitlement set does not include any commodity bundle with an adequate amount of food.

A person can be reduced to starvation if some economic change makes it no longer possible for her to acquire any commodity bundle with enough food to survive. This 'entitlement failure' can happen either because of a fall in her endowment (e.g. alienation of land, or loss of labour power due to ill health), or because of an unfavourable shift in her exchange entitlement (e.g. loss of employment, fall in wages, rise in food prices, drop in the price of goods or services she sells, decline in self-employed production). Entitlement analysis has been used in recent years to study various famines, e.g. the Bengal famine of 1943, the Sahel famines of the 1970s, the Bangladesh famine of 1974, the Ethiopian famines of 1973–85, the Malawi (in fact, Nyasaland, as it was then

[6] Exchange entitlement is, mathematically, a 'mapping', specifying for each endowment bundle a set of alternative commodity bundles any one of which a person can choose to acquire. The formal structure of entitlement analysis (including definitions of endowments, exchange entitlement mappings, etc.) and the empirical relevance of this analysis are discussed in Sen (1981a). An interpretational error to guard against, which seems to have occurred in a number of contributions examining this approach, is to see the analysis exclusively in terms of exchange entitlements rather than in the more general terms of entitlements as such—influenced by endowments *as well as* exchange entitlements. While some famines have clearly resulted specifically from shifts in 'exchange entitlements' (e.g. the Bengal famine of 1943, analysed in Sen 1977a, 1981a), in general the 'entitlement approach' demands that attention be paid to both endowments and exchange entitlements.

called) famine of 1949–50, and also a number of historical and recent cases of widespread starvation.[7]

Entitlements need not, of course, consist only of rights of full ownership. The legal system of a country may—and typically does—include provisions for the right to *use* some commodities without owning them outright. This is often the case with durable goods for shared use such as public parks and roads. Free distribution of state-owned food for the purpose of public consumption might be construed as falling in the category of use without ownership. But given the single-use nature of food, it is perhaps more helpful to see a change of ownership as and when the public distribution takes place. These processes too are, in fact, matters of shifting entitlements (in this case, through public policy). However, the exact formal characterization of all this is far less important than the powerful empirical fact that such free-distribution arrangements—no matter how characterized—are rare even in socialist economies.

Just as there have been major famines in private ownership economies without state guarantee of basic subsistence rights, there have also been famines in socialist countries with their own systems of legality (e.g. in Ukraine in the early 1930s, in China during 1958–61, in Kampuchea in the late 1970s). The entitlements guaranteed by the law have, on those occasions, failed to provide the means of survival and subsistence to a great many people. In some cases, e.g. in the Ukrainian famines, state policy was in fact positively geared to undermining the entitlements of a large section of the population.[8]

In analysing the causation of famines and in seeking social changes that eliminate them, the nature of entitlement systems and their workings have to be understood and assessed. The same applies to the problem of regular hunger and endemic undernourishment. If people go hungry on a regular basis all the time, or seasonally, the explanations of that have to be sought in the way the entitlement system in operation fails to give the persons involved adequate means of securing enough food. Seeing hunger as entitlement failure points to possible remedies as well as helping us to understand the forces that generate hunger and sustain it. In particular, this approach compels us to take a broad view of the ways in which access to food can be protected or promoted, including reforms of the legal framework within which economic relations take place.

Since food problems have often been discussed in terms of the availability of food without going into the question of entitlement (there is a substantial tradition of concentrating only on food output per head, going back at least to Malthus's famous *Essay on Population* of 1798), it is particularly important to

---

[7] See Sen (1976a, 1977a, 1981a), Ghose (1982), Oughton (1982), Tilly (1983), Khan (1985), Snowdon (1985), Ratnavale (1986), Bose (1987), Griffin (1987), Ravallion (1987a), Vaughan (1987), Devereux and Hay (1988), Desai (1988b) D'Souza (1988), Garnsey (1988), Osmani (1988b), and various contributions to Drèze and Sen (forthcoming), among others.

[8] On the Soviet famines of the early 1930s, and their relation to Stalin's ruthless policies, see Dalrymple (1964), Hadzewycz *et al.* (1983), Bernstein (1984), Conquest (1986), Serbyn and Krawchenko (1986).

understand the relevance of seeing hunger as entitlement failures. Such failures can occur even when food availability is not reduced, and even when the ratio of food to population (on which Malthus concentrated) goes up rather than down.[9] Indeed, the relentless persistence of famines and the enormous reach of world hunger, despite the steady and substantial increase in food availability per head, makes it particularly imperative for us to reorientate our approach away from food availability to entitlements.

This can be done without losing sight of the elementary fact that food availability must be *among* the factors that determine the entitlements of different groups of people, and that food production is one of the important determinants of entitlements. But that is only part of the story (though an important part), and must not be seen as all of it. We examine this question further in the next section, since there has been considerable misunderstanding regarding what entitlement analysis does or does not assert.

2.3 Availability, Command and Occupations

The dissonance between the causal analysis of famines in terms of availability and that in terms of entitlement does not lie in the fact that availability and entitlements are unrelated to each other. In fact, the relations involved can be very important indeed. The links are worth pointing out, particularly to avoid the temptation—to which it seems easy to succumb—to replace the old error of concentrating *only* on food output and availability by a new error of ignoring altogether the influence of output and availability on the entitlements of different sections of the population.[10]

[9] In another contribution entitled *An Investigation of the Cause of the Present High Price of Provisions* (Malthus, 1800), published two years after the *Essay on Population*, Malthus did discuss illuminatingly the process of acquirement of food and the part that the market mechanism plays in it. In terms of *economic* analysis, that contribution contrasts sharply with the *Essay on Population*, even though Malthus himself tended to see the later analysis as a supplement to it (and the *motivational* links are indeed clear). On the two types of contributions by Malthus, see Sen (1981a: Appendix B).

[10] In the presentation of the so-called entitlement approach in Sen (1981a), care was taken to note the obvious fact that output and availability are *among* the several influences that determine entitlements, and that even though hunger is ultimately caused by entitlement failure, nevertheless changes in food output and availability can play significant parts in the⋅causal processes yielding or sustaining hunger (see pp. 7–8, 157–9, 179–81). In some of the later contributions in which this work has been cited (in support or in dissent), the thesis of the *inadequacy* of the availability perspective seems to have been somewhat confused with an imagined thesis of the *irrelevance* of food availability for famine analysis. It is also important to avoid the simplistic idea of seeing entitlement and availability as 'two sides' of the food story, with entitlement representing the demand side and availability the supply side and a 'synthesis' being worked out between the two. In fact, entitlement is influenced by both demand and supply factors, and food availability is one of the influences on it. These and several related issues have figured in a number of critiques of the entitlement approach to famines; see Muqtada (1981), D. R. Basu (1984, 1986), Rangasami (1985), Bowbrick (1986, 1987), Baulch (1987), Devereux (1988), Eicher (1988a), Kula (1988, 1989), Swift (1989). While some of the points raised have been based on misinterpreting the content of the entitlement approach, a number of interesting supplementary issues have *inter alia* emerged from these contributions. For further discussion of some of the underlying questions, see Sen (1981a, 1986a, 1986b, 1987d, 1987e).

The links between food availability and entitlements are indeed numerous and often important. First, for some people, the output of food grown by themselves is also their basic entitlement to food. For example, for peasants engaged mainly in growing food crops, the output, availability, and entitlement of food for the family can be much the same. This is a matter of what may be called 'direct entitlement'.[11] Second, one of the major influences on the ability of anyone to purchase food is clearly the price of food, and that price is, of course, influenced by the production and availability of food in the economy. Third, food production can also be a major source of employment, and a reduction in food production (due to, say, a drought or a flood) would reduce employment and wage income through the same process that leads to a decline in the output and availability of food. Fourth, if and when a famine develops, having a stock of food available in the public distribution system is clearly a major instrument in the hands of the authorities to combat starvation. This can be done either by distributing food directly (in cooked or uncooked form), or by adding to the supply of food in the market, thereby exerting a downward pressure or a moderating influence on possibly rocketing prices.

For these and other reasons, food entitlements have close links with food availability and output. It would be amazing if such links were absent, since the physical presence of food cannot but be an influence on the possibility of acquiring food through direct ownership or exchange. The dissonance does not arise from a denial of these obvious and important links. When questions of economic policy and political action are taken up in the later chapters of this volume, these links will be further investigated.

The conflict between the availability view and the entitlement view of food deprivation has to be seized along with making sure that the basic links have been recognized. The dissonance arises from the fact that the links do not establish a tight connection between availability and entitlement in such a way that the food commands of different sections of the population move up and down together, in the same way as the total availability of food in the economy. If food were to be distributed over the population on some egalitarian principles operated by some central authority, that assumption might have been sensible. However, as was discussed earlier, the actual command over food that different sections of the population can exercise depends on a set of legal and economic factors, including those governing ownership, production, and exchange. The overall availability of food is thus a very poor guide to the fortunes of different socio-economic groups.

The inadequacy of the availability view is particularly important to note in the context of the making of economic policy. Indeed, an undue reliance —often implicit—on the availability view has frequently contributed to the development or continuation of a famine, by making the relevant authorities

---

[11] On the distinction between 'direct' and 'trade-based' entitlement, see Sen (1981a: 50–1). The policy implications of failure of entitlements of distinct kinds can be quite different.

Table 2.1 The Bangladesh famine 1974: overall availability of food grains

Year	Per head availability (oz./day)	Index
1967	15.0	100
1968	15.7	105
1969	16.6	111
1970	17.1	114
1971	14.9	99
1972	15.3	102
1973	15.3	102
1974	15.9	106 (Famine!)
1975	14.9	99
1976	14.8	99

Source: Alamgir (1980), Table 6.23; see also Sen (1981*a*), Table 9.5.

smug about the food situation.[12] For instance, there have been famines, e.g. in Bengal in 1943 and in Ethiopia in 1973, when the absence of a substantial food availability decline has contributed to official smugness.[13]

The possibly contrary nature of the availability view and the entitlement view can be illustrated by considering the food availability picture during the Bangladesh famine of 1974. In Table 2.1, the availability of food per head (including food production and net imports) for the Bangladesh population as a whole is given for ten years during 1967–76. Treating the availability in 1967 as the base of the index (100), the availability in 1974—the year of the famine

[12] The 'role of theory in policy failures' (particularly in the making of policy relying heavily on an availability theory of famines) was discussed in the context of the 1943 Bengal famine in Sen (1981*a*), chapter 6. Just as the famine in Bengal was beginning to develop, the Viceroy of India could write to the Secretary of State for India in London that he had told the Premier of Bengal (in charge of the provincial government) that 'he simply must produce some more rice out of Bengal for Ceylon even if Bengal itself went short', and the Viceroy could report the cheerful possibility that he 'may in the result screw a little out of them' (Mansergh 1971: 544). Despite the possibility of viceregal callousness and low cunning, this apparently cruel remark can be understood only by recognizing the actual assessment of the food situation on the part of the Viceroy's advisers that the shortage in Bengal could not really be very great, given the fact that the food output and availability there were fairly normal. Indeed, as the famine was gathering momentum in late March, the Secretary of State for India received 'the comforting message' from the Viceroy that 'the food situation in India generally is at present much improved', that 'the situation in Bengal at present is disquieting', but that nevertheless the problem could be 'treated with guarded optimism, with special reference to the recent improvement of the situation in India generally and the excellent prospects of the rabi harvest' (Mansergh 1971: 825–6). Even in October 1943, when the famine had already peaked, the Governor of Bengal was still presenting calculations of 'the real shortage' based on comparing estimates of food availability with requirements of food per person, as if the distribution of food was determined by some kind of a rationing device, even though no such rationing existed in Bengal, except in Calcutta (see Sen 1981*a*: 82).

[13] See Sen (1981*a*), chapters 6–10. See also Cutler (1984*a*, 1985*b*), Snowdon (1985) and Kumar (1986) on recent Ethiopian famines.

Table 2.2 The Bangladesh famine 1974: famine districts *vis-à-vis* other districts

District	Rank of famine intensity among 19 districts[a]	Rank of per-head food availability among 19 districts[b]	Rank of per cent change in food availability per head *vis-à-vis* previous year among 19 districts[c]
Rangpur	1 (17%)	5 (126)	6 (*up* 10%)
Mymensingh	2 (12%)	2 (143)	5 (*up* 11%)
Dinajpur	3 (9%)	1 (158)	1 (*up* 23%)
Sylhet	4 (8%)	3 (139)	12 (*up* 3%)

  [a] Based on the share of the total population in the district seeking relief (shares given in brackets).
  [b] Index values *vis-à-vis* Bangladesh average in brackets.
  [c] Proportionate change in brackets.
Source: Sen (1981*a*), Tables 9.2 and 9.7; see also Alamgir (1980), from which the data are obtained, and which explains the primary sources.

—was 106. In fact, the availability of food that year was higher than in any other year during 1971–6. And yet the famine hit Bangladesh exactly in that year of peak food availability! The families of rural labourers and other occupation groups who died because of their inability to command food were affected by a variety of influences (including loss of employment, the rise in food prices, etc.), and this occurred despite the fact that the actual availability of food in the economy of Bangladesh was at a peak.

The failure of the availability view of famine can be further brought out by comparing different districts of Bangladesh in terms of their food availability in 1974 *vis-à-vis* their experience of famine. In Table 2.2 the so-called 'famine districts', which were most affected by the famine, are compared with other districts in terms of food availability.

It turns out that among the nineteen districts of Bangladesh, one of the famine districts (Dinajpur) had the *highest* availability of food in the entire country, and indeed all four of the famine districts were among the top five in terms of food availability per head. Even in terms of change in food availability per head over the preceding year, *all* the famine districts without exception had a substantial increase, and three of the four were among the top six in terms of food availability increase among all the nineteen districts.

The entitlement failure of the famine victims in Bangladesh related to a variety of factors, over and above output and availability of food.[14] The floods that afflicted Bangladesh (particularly the famine districts) caused some havoc during June to August of 1974. The availability of food in the economy, however, remained high since the primary crop of Bangladesh (the *aman* crop, which tended to contribute substantially more than half of the total food output

  [14] These factors have been studied by Alamgir (1980), Sen (1981*a*), Montgomery (1985), Osmani (1986), and Ravallion (1987*a*), among others.

of the country) is harvested during November to January, and this had been high in the *preceding* year (i.e. harvested in November 1973 to January 1974). The floods that hit Bangladesh did, of course, reduce the harvest in late 1974, including the primary *aman* crop. The famine, however, developed and peaked much before those reduced harvests arrived, and indeed by the time the primary crop (*aman*) was harvested, the famine was over and gone. During the famine months, the physical availability of food per head in Bangladesh thus remained high. And this was especially so for the famine districts, since they happened to have had rather good crops earlier, boosting the 1974 availability, even though the floods would eventually affect the availability of food in these districts in the *following* year (1975).

Among the influences that led to the collapse of entitlements of a large section of the population of Bangladesh in 1974 was the loss of employment as a result of the floods, which affected the planting and particularly the transplanting of rice, traditionally carried out in the period following the one in which the floods occurred. This would reduce the food output later, but its impact on employment was immediate and vicious.

The disruption of the economy of Bangladesh as a result of the floods was not, however, confined only to the decline of employment. The effect of the floods on the future output and availability of food and therefore on the expectation of food prices also played a major part. Indeed, as Ravallion's (1987*a*) careful analysis of the rice market of Bangladesh during the 1974 famine indicates, the expectation of high food prices in Bangladesh went far ahead of what would actually emerge in the future (i.e. the later *realized* future prices). The poor and chaotic functioning of rice markets, fed by alarmist anticipations, led to price explosions following the floods, resulting in a collapse of food entitlements for those who found the already low purchasing power of their earnings further undermined.

The failure of the government to institute a suitable stabilizing response also contributed to the unstable behaviour of the rice market.[15] Rural labourers found a sharply diminished ratio of food command per unit of employment, and on top of that many had, in fact, lost employment as a result of floods, especially in the famine districts.

There is, therefore, no paradox in the fact that the Bangladesh famine of 1974 occurred at a time when the physical availability of food in the economy was at a local peak. It is the failure of large sections of the population, particularly of the labouring families, to command food in the market that has to be examined in order to understand the causation of that major catastrophe.

The terrible story of the Bangladesh famine of 1974 brings out the folly of concentrating only on the physical availability of food in the economy, and points to the necessity of investigating the movements of food entitlements of the vulnerable occupation groups and the causal influences (including market

---

[15] On this see Alamgir (1980), Osmani (1986), and Ravallion (1987*a*).

operations) that affect these movements. Similar lessons can be drawn from other famines as well.

One of the central differences between the availability approach and the entitlement approach is the necessarily disaggregative nature of the latter, in contrast with the inherently aggregative perspective presented by the former. While it is possible to calculate how much food a country can command, and while such aggregative calculations of 'total food entitlement' for the economy as a whole may have some analytical value as one of the constituent elements in understanding the food situation affecting a particular economy,[16] the idea of entitlements applies ultimately to particular individuals and families.

When many individuals and families are in a similar situation (e.g. as a result of belonging to the same occupation group and having similar economic circumstances), it is possible and useful to study the entitlement relations of that group as a whole, to get some idea as to how typical members of the group may be faring. It is obvious that a totally disaggregative analysis would be quite impossible to pursue for a sizeable economy, since there may be many millions of people involved. But at the same time, the 'total food availability' for the economy as a whole is unduly aggregative as a concept, and for reasons that we have already discussed, an appropriate economic disaggregation would certainly be necessary.

The logic of the entitlement approach indicates that the analysis must *inter alia* concentrate on occupation groups. This is, of course, a tradition that goes back to classical political economy, and especially to the analyses presented by Adam Smith, David Ricardo, and Karl Marx. Marx in particular perhaps did more than any other author to emphasize the importance of analysing economic movements through disaggregation according to classes. The contrast between the economic positions of the proletariat, peasants, traders, capitalists, etc. formed the backbone of his analysis, which was fleshed out with details that fitted into that overall structure. That general perspective is of central importance in understanding the nature of entitlements, and the genesis of famines and starvation.

However, the extent of the aggregation that has to be sought depends on the nature of the exercise, and in analysing famines and hunger, it is often important to take a more disaggregative view of the economy than one might get from standard class analyses.[17] Sometimes, the entitlements of different families belonging broadly to the same class may move in divergent directions, depending on the particular economic influences that respectively operate on them. These influences can vary between different occupation groups. They can also lead to divergent experiences for different members of the *same* occupation group. For example, if there is a particular disease affecting one

----

[16] See e.g. Kanbur (1968a)

[17] There is, in fact, more to learn in this particular respect from Marx's highly disaggregated analysis presented in *The Eighteenth Brumaire of Louis Bonaparte* (1852) than from the broad political platform presented in the 'Communist Manifesto' (1848).

type of animal rather than another, a section of the pastoralists may be hit, but not another. Similarly, the collapse of regional fishing rights may affect one group of fishermen, leaving another group unaffected. Distinctions based on output structure, regional location, etc. have to be brought in to supplement the occupational picture.

Since the particular reference of entitlement analysis is to families and persons, any aggregation in analysing movements of entitlements has to be based on identifying similarities of circumstances that make such aggregation viable and useful. The usefulness involved in such aggregation may, of course, be very great indeed, since different people in the same occupation group in the same region are often affected by very similar economic and political forces. The skill of entitlement analysis would lie in being able to make use of these advantages of aggregation in understanding in a tractable way the influences affecting the fortunes of persons and families, without losing sight of the fact that it is the families and their members to whom entitlement analysis must ultimately relate.

2.4 The 'Food Crisis' in Sub-Saharan Africa

Alarm has often been expressed at the possibility of a decline in the amount of food available per person in the modern world. Indeed, there is a good deal of discussion centering on prospects of disaster, based on modern variants of Malthusian fears. As a matter of fact, however, there has not been any declining trend in food availability per head for the world as a whole in recent decades (nor, of course, any such trend since Malthus's own days).

On the other hand, there has been quite a flood of models—mostly fairly theoretical—predicting the onset of Malthusian decline in the 'near future'.[18] But the shrill announcements of impending disaster and doom have not, in fact, been based on a great deal of rigorous economic reasoning. The assumptions underlying the pessimistic models are rather arbitrary and often extreme. Since the results happen to be quite sensitive to the precise assumptions chosen, it is not obvious what faith can be put in these alarming predictions. Indeed, the more recent studies have not tended to confirm this pessimism. The underlying methodology has varied from model to model, but these studies have typically found less reason for general gloom, and also much more room for policy response.[19] Obviously, any such future gazing is hard to do,

[18] See e.g. Forrester (1971), Meadows et al. (1972), Mesarovic and Pestel (1974), among others. Various intellectual institutions of great standing and influence, such as the Club of Rome, seem to have been able to lend their support to these—at best tentative—studies.

[19] See particularly the 'United Nations World Model' (Leontief et al. 1977), the so-called 'Latin American World Model' (Herrera et al. 1976), the extensive study presented by 'Interfutures' under the leadership of Jacques Lesourne (Interfutures 1979), the IIASA study of world food systems (Parikh and Rabar 1981), the 'Global 2000 Report' commissioned by President Carter (Council on Environmental Quality and the Department of State 1982), and even the later study done for the Club of Rome—an original sponsor of the doom view—called the *Model of International Relations in Agriculture* (Linnemann 1981). See also Berry and Kates (1980) and Mellor and Johnston (1984).

Table 2.3 World trends in food output per head

Region	The last half decade: 1986–8 average over 1981–3 average	The last decade: 1986–8 average over 1976–8 average
All developed economies	up 2%	up 3%
All developing economies	up 5%	up 11%
Europe	up 5%	up 13%
USA	down 7%	up 7%
Africa	down 2%	down 8%
South America	unchanged	up 2%
Asia	up 8%	up 17%

Source: Calculated from data obtained from *FAO Production Yearbook 1988*, Table 4, and *FAO Quarterly Bulletin of Statistics*, vol. i, pt. 4, 1988.

but it seems unlikely that the real dangers in the near future can lie in the prospect of food output falling short of the growth of population.

Table 2.3 presents the trends in food output per head over the last half decade and the last decade (i.e. from 1981–3 to 1986–8, and from 1976–8 to 1986–8) for some of the major regions in the world. It would appear that for all *developed* economies taken together, food output per head went up by 2 per cent during the last half decade and by 3 per cent over the last decade. The corresponding increases for the *developing* economies taken together are, in fact, considerably higher, viz. 5 per cent and 11 per cent respectively.[20]

The fact that the trend of food output per head is so sharply upward for developing economies in particular is, naturally, a source of comfort. But it could be false comfort. In fact, different developing economies have done very differently over the last few decades. Specifically, in the last decade, when food output per head for all developing economies taken together went up by 11 per cent, that for Asia went up by 17 per cent and for South America by 2 per cent, while that for Africa came *down* by 8 per cent. Indeed, Africa has been plagued by production problems—in addition to other problems—over nearly two decades now. The aggregate picture for the developing economies put together is, thus, quite misleading.

Africa also has had—and continues to have—the fastest growth rate of population among the major regions of the world. However, it is easy to see that the contrasting trends of food output per head in Africa and other regions reflect differences in output performance at least as strongly as differences in

[20] There are certain weighting problems in these average figures. In fact, the same sources of information from which Table 2.3 has been derived give figures of increases of aggregate world food availability per head that are hard to tally with the separate figures for developed and developing countries. This contrariness arises from weighting problems, but also indicates that any such statistics must be taken with a pinch of salt, given the arbitrariness involved in such weighting exercises.

population growth rates (even with the assumption that the output growth rate in Africa is independent of the growth rate of population and labour supply).

This having been said, we must, however, resist the oversimplified suggestion that Africa's recent problems of hunger arise simply from declines in food output and supply. While food production and availability are undoubtedly among the more important influences in the determination of food entitlements, the connections are complex and there are also other matters involved (such as the performance of industries and non-food agriculture, and the general role of employment and economic participation).

It must be borne in mind that food production is not only a source of food supply, it is also a major source of income and livelihood for vast sections of the African population. As a result, any reduction in food output per head in Africa also tends to be associated with a reduction in overall income for many occupation groups. However, the observed decline in food output per head in Africa need not have resulted in a collapse of food entitlements, if that decline had been compensated by an expansion of alternative incomes usable to acquire food from other sources, e.g. through imports from abroad. The point can be illustrated by comparing the experiences of many of the sub-Saharan economies which have experienced declines in food output per head and have

Table 2.4 Declines in food production per head: intercountry comparisons

	1984–6 *vis-à-vis* 1979–81	1984–6 *vis-à-vis* 1974–6
Sub-Saharan Africa		
Sudan	down 4%	down 3%
Ethiopia	down 14%	down 10%
Somalia	down 10%	down 21%
Zimbabwe	down 7%	down 23%
Zambia	down 6%	down 24%
Mozambique	down 15%	down 30%
Senegal	down 1%	down 33%
Kenya	down 10%	down 33%
Botswana	down 20%	down 44%
Elsewhere		
Israel	up 2%	down 12%
Venezuela	down 11%	down 14%
Portugal	unchanged	down 15%
Costa Rica	down 11%	down 17%
Singapore	down 3%	down 19%
Hong Kong	up 15%	down 36%
Trinidad & Tobago	down 13%	down 40%

Source: Calculated from data presented in *FAO Production Yearbook 1986*, Table 4, and *FAO Monthly Bulletin of Statistics*, November 1987, Table 1.

also experienced food problems, with those of economies elsewhere which have also experienced declines in food output per head, but *without* experiencing famines or widespread undernourishment.

Table 2.4 compares the experiences over the decade 1974–6 to 1984–6 of nine sub-Saharan African economies with seven economies from elsewhere (Israel, Venezuela, Portugal, Costa Rica, Singapore, Hong Kong, and Trinidad and Tobago). Some of the sub-Saharan economies have indeed experienced famine in the middle eighties, and they did also have considerable declines in food output per head, e.g., Sudan (3 per cent), Ethiopia (10 per cent), Somalia (21 per cent), and Mozambique (30 per cent). On the other hand, several economies elsewhere have experienced comparable or even greater declines in food output per head (in some cases as large as 30 or 40 per cent), without having any problems of the kind which have afflicted these African countries.[21] This is so both because food production is a less important source of income and entitlement in these other economies, and also because they have achieved a more than compensating expansion of *non-food* production (with favourable effects on incomes and entitlements). What may superficially appear to be a problem of food production and supply in Africa has to be seen in the more general terms of entitlement determination.[22]

One important implication of this perspective is that even though current problems of hunger and famines in sub-Saharan Africa are undoubtedly connected *inter alia* with the decline of food production, remedial action need not necessarily take the form of attempting to reverse that historical trend. Other avenues of action, such as the diversification of economic activities and the expansion of public support, deserve attention as well. This general point will be further scrutinized in Chapter 9. We shall also have occasion, in Chapters 5–8, to discuss how a number of countries—including several African ones—have already achieved impressive success in preventing major (short-term or long-term) declines in food production or availability from causing famines or widespread deterioration in nutritional well-being.

---

[21] Table 2.4 also presents the figures of production change in the half-decade preceding 1984–6 (i.e. during 1979–81 to 1984–6), to confirm that the emerging picture of food output declines is not just a matter of the choice of base period.

[22] Among the adverse circumstances to consider here is the crippling burden of international debt on many economies of sub-Saharan Africa.

3

Nutrition and Capability

3.1 World Hunger: How Much?

The question is often asked, and we might as well face it. How many hungry people are there in the world? It is not easy to answer this question. This is not so much because we lack the data to do the estimation (though data limitations certainly exist), but primarily because there are great conceptual difficulties underlying the measurement exercise. While it is obviously not hard to recognize starving or acutely deprived people, it is much harder to find an agreed criterion in case of less severe food deprivation.

There is not much difficulty in agreeing that some estimates of the number of the hungry are obviously wrong, in terms of any reasonable criterion. For example, Lord John Boyd-Orr's well-known statement that 'a lifetime of malnutrition and actual hunger is the lot of at least two-thirds of mankind' would be hard to defend literally.[1] While not many estimators have reached the proportion specified by Boyd-Orr, it is by no means uncommon to encounter casual estimates of unbelievably many people suffering from crippling undernourishment.[2]

Moving away from casual figures to systematic and detailed estimation, a recent World Bank Policy Study, entitled *Poverty and Hunger*, calculates that the number of people suffering from nutritional deprivation (in the sense of not having an adequate calorie intake to prevent stunted growth and serious health risks) was 340 million in 1980, representing about 16 per cent of the population of the developing countries as a whole (about 23 per cent of the population in the 'low income countries'). The same study suggests that 730 million people in the developing world suffer from undernourishment in terms of having 'not enough calories for an active working life'. This amounts to 34 per cent of the population of developing countries as a whole (51 per cent in 'low income countries').[3]

These calculations are based on two particular methodological elements. One is to relate hunger to the low incomes of particular groups of people, rather

---

[1] Boyd-Orr (1950: 11). It should be mentioned that despite such exaggerated pronouncements, Lord Boyd-Orr did in fact play a very important and productive part in putting world hunger on the international agenda, and also in preparing the ground for scientific and systematic work in this difficult area. Whether the tendency to dramatize the extent of deprivation involved contributed to or detracted from the task that Boyd-Orr undertook is an interesting issue which we shall not address here.

[2] Poleman (1981) cites and critically discusses various examples of such high estimates.

[3] World Bank (1986: 17). For a succinct summary of some of the main findings and recommendations, see Reutlinger (1985).

than to food availability as such. In this respect the study involves the use of a more causal insight into the antecedence of hunger than would have been provided by the more traditional food-centred calculations.[4] The other element involves the use of particular 'calorie requirement' norms, and takes the form of relating income deficiency to alleged dietary deficiency, based on specified calorie norms.[5] The use of such norms has come under rather severe attack in recent years from critics who have stressed the importance of interpersonal variations as well as adaptive adjustments influencing the relation between food intakes and achieved nutritional levels. It has been suggested that many of those identified as falling below the calorie norms may, in fact, not be nutritionally deprived in any significant sense.[6]

It should be mentioned in this context that the report does not take the commonly used FAO–WHO 'requirement' figure, but only 80 per cent of that, to specify the calorie intake needed 'to prevent stunted growth and serious health risks', and 90 per cent of the FAO–WHO figure for identifying what amounts to 'not enough calories for an active working life'. Thus, a downward correction is introduced in the estimates of the number of the undernourished compared with what would have been obtained on the basis of the FAO–WHO norms. But the general methodological doubts still remain.

Other studies based on related methodologies have indicated figures of deprivation no less alarming than those derived in *Poverty and Hunger*, the World Bank study. For example, one estimate suggests that 'more than 500 million women, children and men are reported to suffer from chronic malnutrition or famine', and 'each year some 40 million people die from hunger and hunger-related diseases'.[7] To drive home the dimension of the problem, the same report presents the picture graphically by pointing out that this figure is 'equivalent to more than 300 jumbo jet crashes per day with no survivors, almost half of the passengers being children'.

---

[4] One of the major authors of the report *Poverty and Hunger*, viz. Shlomo Reutlinger, has been among the pioneers in shifting attention from food-supply-based analysis of hunger to an income-centred view. See particularly Reutlinger and Selowsky (1976), Reutlinger and Alderman (1980) and Reutlinger (1984). See also the contributions of Aziz (1975), Taylor (1975), Haq (1976), Griffin and Khan (1977) and Alamgir (1978).

[5] In fact, calorie is only one of the nutrients, and deprivation can also arise from the deficiency of proteins and other nutrients. There was a major controversy some years ago on the independent role that protein deficiency can play, and Sukhatme (1961, 1969, 1973, 1977) and Sukhatme and Margen (1978) have been enormously influential in showing the rather limited frequency of purely protein deficiency in the absence of calorie shortfall. As a matter of fact, for certain dietary patterns, meeting the calorie requirements automatically fulfils the protein norms given the proportions of these nutrients in these diets (see Osmani 1982). However, it must be noted that the problem of protein deficiency for children can be serious even when it is not so for the average adult. There are also interregional variations of dietary patterns. In concentrating only on calorie deficiency and in taking no note of protein deficiency in the absence of calorie shortfall, the report *Poverty and Hunger* introduces, if anything, a downward bias (in this particular respect) in the estimation of the number of the nutritionally deprived.

[6] See Sukhatme (1977, 1982a), Srinivasan (1981), Lipton (1983), and Payne (1987a).

[7] Nordic Conference on Environment and Development (1987: 1).

As was already mentioned, these estimates of the size of the population suffering from undernourishment are limited not only by the uncertainties of the data used but also by deep conceptual problems. Pertinent questions have been raised about the reliability of such estimates of undernourishment and hunger, based on fixed requirement norms, given the observed fact of (1) interpersonal variations of nutritional requirements, (2) the possibility of intertemporal variations of intake for a given person, and (3) the possibility of adjustment and perhaps even 'adaptation' to a long-run decline of nutritional intake.[8] The nature and force of these criticisms and the underlying methodological problems will be considered in the next section. But before we turn to that, it is worth asking whether this is an important issue at all. What difference can these figures make?

In one sense not a lot depends on the exactness of the figures. For example, even if the number of deaths from hunger and hunger-related diseases happened to be equivalent not to 300 jumbo jet crashes a day with no survivors, but only to 100 such crashes per day, the extraordinary nature of nutritional deprivation across the world would still be hard to dispute. The alarm that we ought to feel at these findings and the determination to work for a change may not be particularly sensitive to variations over a wide range of disastrous possibilities.

There is, however, an important policy aspect implicit in these measurement issues. A limited commitment of resources often forces certain choices as to whether economic or nutritional intervention should be aimed at a relatively small group of severely deprived people, or spread more broadly over a larger category of generally deprived population. To face these choices, the nutritional implications of deprivation have to be better understood. If a person falls a little below the nutritional norms, particularly the calorie requirement figures, what harm will come to such a person?

If the category of general deprivation is exaggerated, then there might possibly be a costly deflection of resources to tackle that problem, with comparative neglect of the less numerous but more urgent cases of extreme deprivation. Exaggeration can be, thus, counterproductive even for the cause of anti-hunger policy. On the other hand, underestimating the size of the affected population can lead to a neglect of the problem and underallocation of resources to anti-hunger programmes and policies altogether. There are hard choices to make, and the advantages of accurate evaluation cannot be summarily dismissed.

3.2   Food Deprivation and Undernourishment

How does the traditional nutritional analysis exactly work? Nutritional deprivation, in that approach, is judged by comparing a person's actual food intake

[8] Variations in nutritional needs can also lead to corresponding adjustments in food intakes. It can be hard to disentangle whether low nutritional intake in a particular case reflects deprivation *or* signifies an unusually low requirement level. See Osmani (1987a).

with some specific levels of 'requirements' for particular nutrients. Since different food items share common nutritional characteristics, the approach works through specifying the requirements not of particular foods, but of the nutritional characteristics themselves, e.g. calories or proteins. In practice, it is calorie norms which have been most widely used to identify the undernourished. If a person's actual intake of nutrients, in particular calories, falls short of the 'requirement', the person is taken to be 'undernourished'.

This approach to the nutritional problem has come under rather severe fire in recent years.[9] It has been pointed out that there are, first of all, significant *inter*individual variations in the conversion of nutrients into nutritional achievements, so that 'requirement' figures cannot be specified in an individual-independent way. Basal metabolic rates vary from person to person, and there can be substantial differences in the nutritional needs of different people. This makes it particularly problematic to identify undernourished individuals, though it need not rule out probabilistic arguments being used to estimate likely proportions of undernourished population, based on information on statistical patterns of interindividual variations of metabolic rates and other relevant factors.

Second, it has been argued that there can also be enormous '*intra*individual' variations over time and that a person can maintain a balanced equilibrium by compensating the lower intakes in some periods by higher intakes in others. Thus, a person who is observed to consume fewer calories than his or her own average 'requirements' are estimated to be (when such estimates are possible) may not, in fact, be in nutritional distress at all, but only in a low phase of his or her intake pattern. For this reason, the identification of all those falling below a calorie norm as being undernourished could quite possibly exaggerate the number of people with real nutritional deficiency, especially since intake data tend to be based on short-period samples.

Third, there may exist multiple equilibria, with the same person possibly achieving different states of balance at different average levels of nutritional intake. The scope for adjustment is widely accepted. The real issue concerns its forms, implications, and effects. Ultimately, the question is whether there is scope for much harmless adjustment—without detrimental effects on the person's well-being and productivity. The fact that a person being placed in a different nutritional regime would tend to adjust accordingly is plausible enough, and there is clear empirical evidence to suggest such responses. The question is whether the modification will be such that different levels of nutritional intake would produce essentially the same nutritional achievements judged in terms of the person's well-being and productive ability. Would the modification related to lower intakes be, in the relevant sense, curative?

[9] See particularly Sukhatme (1977, 1982a, 1982b), Srinivasan (1981), Seckler (1982, 1984), Sukhatme and Margen (1982), Lipton (1983), Blaxter and Waterlow (1985), Kakwani (1986), Payne (1985, 1987a), Payne and Lipton (1988).

Two types of curative adjustment have been suggested. The first works through body size, with 'small but healthy' people living on relatively low nutritional intakes without experiencing, in any real sense, a diminished quality of life or functioning ability.[10] The other is 'adaptation' of nutritional requirements to variations in nutritional intakes for a given body size and permitting unchanged levels of activity.[11] Both adjustments work in the direction of compensating nutritional deprivation, and if they are effective, low levels of food intake—in terms of nutrients consumed per person—may not amount to undernutrition in any consequential sense. The obvious questions are: how effective are these adjustments? In what way and to what extent do they affect the important functionings of a person? In terms of the nature of the life that a person can lead, how restrictive are the adjusted states? In short, what are the feasibilities and costs of adjustment?

The 'small but healthy' hypothesis has been strongly disputed from several distinct perspectives.[12] It is, of course, true that not every kind of activity requires a large body size. Indeed, for many functionings, such as making intellectual contributions, body size may be irrelevant. Further, it is not hard to think of some occupations in which smallness might indeed be an advantage (for a jockey, or a 'cat burglar'). On the other hand, there are clearly many other activities for which the largeness of body size *is* important, e.g., various types of physical activities requiring carrying capacity or strengths of particular types. Even if being small is no bar to being healthy, a small stature can indeed be a limitation to productivity and earning power, in particular economic or social circumstances.

As far as the basic issue of smallness and health is concerned, many complex medical and social questions arise in examining the implications of small body size, in general, and stunting, in particular. But considerable evidence does exist linking, for given communities, height to morbidity and mortality. On these grounds height has in fact, been plausibly used—within certain limits —as an indicator of general physical well-being.[13] The precise relationship between nutritional intake, height, weight, productivity, morbidity, and the quality of life certainly calls for much more extensive scrutiny. But as knowledge stands at the moment, to dismiss smallness as entirely costless would seem to be a dubious and premature position to take in the context of nutritional deprivation across the world. Indeed, given (1) the medical information on the observed relation between height, weight, morbidity, and learning (especially among children, and particularly for cases of severe stunting), (2) the economic information on the relevance of height for employment

[10] See Seckler (1982, 1984) and Sukhatme (1982a).

[11] See Sukhatme (1977, 1982a, 1982b), Srinivasan (1981), Lipton (1983), and Payne (1985).

[12] See particularly Gopalan (1983a, 1987a, 1987b). See also Beaton (1987a) and Osmani (1987a, 1987b).

[13] See the historical studies based on anthropometric measures of Floud and Wachter (1982), Fogel, Engerman and Trussell (1982), Fogel *et al.* (1983), Floud (1987), and Fogel (1987). See also Vaidyanathan (1985).

in some occupations and strength in others, (3) the social information on the relevance of height in moving up or down in the social ladder, and (4) the cultural information on people's own view of their height, weight, and strength, it would be difficult to view smallness of body size as being, in general, inconsequential and unproblematic.

The alternative avenue of costless adjustment would lie in the claimed possibility of nutritional adaptation for the same physical features and work abilities. That adaptations of this kind do take place has been forcefully argued by Sukhatme and others.[14] In this case the adjustment will not take the form of any change of stature or external appearance, nor of any variation in the actual ability to work—only a change in the efficiency with which the body converts nutritional intakes into results.[15]

The empirical support for extensive nutritional adaptation in a costless way is not very clear. It has been pointed out that the available clinical evidence cannot sustain the thesis of the presence of extensive and widespread costless adaptation mechanisms, or even the existence of such mechanisms in any significant sense.[16] Even if adaptation does take place in some cases, neither the ubiquity nor the quantitative reach of adaptation has been established in any way that can be taken to be scientifically definitive. In fact, from the point of view of nutritional planning and public health it may well be dangerous to proceed as if nutritional shortfall were typically costless over a wide range.

Scepticism about relying on curative adjustment mechanisms (whether the 'costless adaptation' version or the 'small but healthy' version) must not, however, be confused with defending the use of a set of fixed nutritional requirements to determine the number of the undernourished. The way in which calorie norms have been used in some of the policy literature does indeed leave room for considerable doubt. The motivation for specifying recommended energy intakes underlying the various studies produced by WHO, FAO, UNU and others was actually not so much to treat these as yardsticks for identifying *individuals* as being nutritionally deprived, but primarily to use them in aggregative contexts for rough estimations of the food needs of *communities*. If these norms are used for classifying individuals as being nutritionally deprived or otherwise, significant errors will be made both because of *inter*personal variations in basal metabolic rates and other factors, and because of *intra*personal variations of food intakes over time within normal intake profiles. These errors will be present even if no curative adjustment mechanism were to exist at all, since the prevalence of interindividual variations and intertemporal unevenness is hard to deny. It is, thus, important to

[14] See also Srinivasan (1981, 1987), Lipton (1983), and Payne (1985, 1987a).

[15] Biological adaptation relates to the reduction of nutritional requirements even for the same levels of activities. In addition, adaptation can be 'behavioural', and nutritional requirements may be reduced by varying the pattern of activities. See Payne and Lipton (1988).

[16] See particularly Dasgupta and Ray (1986a) and the clinical literature analysed there. See also Gopalan (1983b, 1987b), Blaxter and Waterlow (1985), Osmani (1987a, 1987b), Scrimshaw (1987), and Hossain (1989).

recognize that the inappropriateness of the mechanical use of calorie norms in individual nutritional monitoring (as opposed to group monitoring) transcends the heated controversies surrounding the specific theses on 'costless adaptation' or being 'small but healthy'.

The question remains, however, as to whether the calorie norms can be used to provide some kind of statistical guidance regarding the extent of undernourishment and nutritional deprivation in particular communities. Indeed, a probabilistic argument can be easily constructed. While it is possible for a person to fall frequently below the calorie norm and still remain well nourished (maintaining 'homeostasis' of nutritional balance), nevertheless the probability of being undernourished in the sense of being nutritionally deprived in some clinical way can be related to levels of calorie intakes *vis-à-vis* the standard norms. There is, thus, a stochastic argument in favour of using these norms to construct a probabilistic picture of nutritional deprivation based on intake figures.[17]

There is, however, no reason whatsoever why nutritional monitoring should be confined to intake figures excluding other indicators. For one thing, calorie information can be usefully supplemented by other data regarding incomes, employment, assets, etc., so that the shortfall of nutritional intakes compared with norms can be interpreted in a way which helps to discriminate between involuntary deficiencies of calories and other nutrients, on the one hand, and variations in intake patterns maintaining overall nutritional balance, on the other. Furthermore, even when nutritional shortfalls are clearly caused by factors beyond one's control, such as the seasonality of earnings, the clinical question as to whether this would have disastrous consequences can be interpreted only by probing more deeply into the economic and social circumstances leading to these shortfalls and their frequency and duration. In general, nutritional assessment will require a great deal more than food intake information.[18]

Within the field of nutritional statistics itself, it is not clear at all why information should be confined to intake figures alone. There are other ways of judging nutritional successes or failures (e.g. from anthropometric measures, or morbidity information), and these data—directly related to nutritional status—can be systematically used, rather than confining attention to food intakes. It is only when they are supplemented by these other nutritional data as well as economic and social statistics that analyses of nutrient intakes can be best used as one important basis for nutritional judgement.

The complexity of the relationship between nutrient intakes and nutritional

---

[17] Such analysis must take into account the possibility, discussed earlier, that the observed intake figures may include *inter alia* the adjustment of food consumption to variations in nutritional requirements. The probabilistic analysis has to be based on the *joint* distribution of intakes and requirements. See Anand and Harris (1987).

[18] For interesting models and their applications, see Lipton (1983, 1988a), Anand and Harris (1986, 1987).

achievement should not, however, make us lose sight of the fact that the magnitude of uncontroversial deprivation is enormously large in this hungry world. The subtler issues of nutritional intervention and support cannot, of course, be settled without expanding the information base and they do ultimately have policy relevance, but nevertheless there are many urgent and uncontroversially important matters that can—indeed must—receive attention without waiting for the informational base and the diagnostics to be fully refined. While this may be somewhat of a consolation from a 'scientific' point of view, it does, of course, only reflect the terrible state of the world in which we live. In order to show how terrible it is and how much needs to be urgently done, we do not have to construct precise estimates of the total number of nutritionally deprived people in the world.

3.3   Poverty and Basic Capabilities

Aside from the biological and related controversies discussed in the previous section, the assessment of nutritional deprivation has to address some broader conceptual problems arising in the evaluation of human deprivation in general. Some of the issues involved have been extensively examined in the literature on 'poverty'.[19] Perhaps the most elementary issue relates to the nature of the variables of ultimate interest when dealing with human deprivation, for example, whether a 'poverty line' should be drawn in terms of an income level (below which people count as poor), or in terms of some failure of basic functionings including nutritional performance.

In the first chapter of this book we argued that deprivation is best seen in terms of the failure of certain basic 'functionings' (such as being physically fit), rather than in terms of variables such as income or calorie intake which should be seen as means and not as ends in themselves. We have also suggested that once this substantive issue is resolved, the terminological question as to whether the expression 'poverty' should be used to refer to deprivation in this general sense, or to the low level of income or commodity command contributing to that deprivation, is of secondary importance.

Functioning failures can themselves be assessed either in terms of *achievement* or in terms of the *freedom to achieve*. The notion of 'capability' was introduced in Chapter 1 to refer to the extent of the freedom that people have in pursuing valuable activities or funtionings.[20] The distinction between achieved functionings and the capability to function is of particular importance in the context of those functionings in which individual choices and behaviour

[19] See the surveys and critiques of Atkinson (1983, 1987a), Foster (1984), Seidl (1988). See also Wedderburn (1974), Sen (1976b, 1985d), and Townsend (1979a).
[20] Freedom to achieve has obvious instrumental importance in achievement, but in addition it can be seen as having intrinsic value. The intrinsic importance of freedom has figured prominently in many ethical frameworks, including those of Marx (1844) and Mill (1859). These issues are discussed in Sen (1985b, 1988a).

patterns vary greatly (especially 'social' ones, such as 'taking part in the life of the community'). The occurrence of voluntary fasting brings out the fact that even in the context of food and eating there is a potentially important basis of distinction here.

In general the dichotomy between the ability to avoid hunger and the actual choice of that option may be relatively unimportant, given that the alternative of avoiding undernourishment is usually chosen when it is available.[21] But the distinction between capability and achieved functioning can be important even in the field of nutrition, for example, due to the influence of food habits, which can have a major influence on the choice of diet and thus on the *use* actually made of the capability to meet nutritional needs. Even if taste constraints are not entirely inflexible, with completely binding effects within particular cultures, they are not removable at will. Nor can we ignore the valuable and valued aspects of non-nutritional uses of food in social living.[22]

The use of the 'capability approach' can focus either on functionings or on the capability to function, or both.[23] While that is a fairly general approach to the assessment of well-being and advantage, its relevance for nutritional concerns as such is not negligible.

First, given the interpersonal and intrapersonal variations in the relation between nutritional intakes and human functionings (discussed earlier in this chapter), the distinction between income and commodities, on the one hand, and functionings and capabilities, on the other, can be very substantial indeed. In matters of nutrition and health, the need for being clear about the nature of the ultimate value-objects is especially strong. In particular, as we have already discussed, the removal of nutritional deprivation cannot be seen merely in terms of achieving certain specific levels of income or calorie intake. The distinction between opulence and income level, on the one hand, and the capability of being well nourished and healthy on the other, will be seen to be of pervasive importance in analysing endemic deprivation and in characterizing the needed remedial policies (see Chapters 9 to 12).

Second, the distinction between commodity command and functioning ability can be particularly important when dealing with groups that have systematic disadvantages for biological or social reasons. For example, the old

[21] Some recent empirical studies indicate that calorie consumption may not increase much with income, even when the calorie intake is low; see Behrman and Deolalikar (1987, 1988b). The generality of these findings, however, remains to be fully investigated. There are also important interpretational questions, including the particular role of calories in nutritional well-being. On these and related issues, see Chen (1986b), Bhargava (1988), Bouis and Haddad (1988), Ravallion (1988), Schiff and Valdés (1988), and Alderman (forthcoming).

[22] On the non-nutritional uses of food and in general the need to consider the social role of goods, see particularly Douglas and Isherwood (1979), Vatuk (1979), Douglas (1984), Khare and Rao (1986), and Marglin (1986).

[23] There are several empirical studies related to each perspective. See particularly Sen (1982b, 1984b, and 1985a), Kynch and Sen (1983), Kynch (1985), Brannen and Wilson (1987), Kumar (1987), Ringen (1987), A. Williams (1987), Wilson (1987a, 1987b), Griffin and Knight (1988), I. Hossain (1988), and Koohi-Kamali (1988).

and the infirm are not only handicapped in *earning* an income, they also have greater difficulty in *converting* incomes into functionings in the form of disease-free living, enjoying adequate mobility, and so on.

Women too have, in most societies, special disadvantages in achieving particular functionings. The roots of these problems can be social as well as physical, and the remedies sought have to take note of the nature of the constraints involved and the extent to which they can be removed. For example, the enhanced deprivation associated with pregnancy may arise partly from social factors (e.g. difficulty in maintaining employment) and partly from physical ones (e.g. greater need for food). While the physical factors cannot be altered in the same way as the social roots of deprivation can be, the depriving effects of the physical factors can be eradicated through public policy aimed at maintaining capability (e.g. through dietary supplementation, health care, and the creation of economic and social opportunities).

Third, the capability approach draws attention to the general need to consider inputs other than food as determinants of nutritional functioning and capability. Nutritional achievements may be strongly influenced by the provision of and command over certain crucial non-food inputs such as health care, basic education, clean drinking water, or sanitary facilities. It would, therefore, be a mistake to relate nutritional status to food inputs only. Undernourishment is often precipitated or enhanced by debilitating diseases and parasitic infections, and recent experiences of nutritional intervention, such as those of the UNICEF, have seized the importance of marshalling the delivery of vital non-food inputs in addition to monitoring food consumption.[24]

Even in famines the vast majority of people who die are killed by various diseases, and not directly by starvation as such.[25] This process takes the form

---

[24] On some of the medical issues involved in dealing with diseases that interfere with nutrition and survival, see UNICEF (1987a, 1988, 1989). On the interaction between undernourishment and infection, see Scrimshaw, Taylor and Gopalan (1968), Pacey and Payne (1985), Dasgupta and Ray (1986a), Leslie (1987), Osmani (1987a).

[25] This emerges clearly from a large number of empirical studies of famine mortality, including those of Foege (1971), Stein *et al.* (1975), Chen and Chowdhury (1977), Sen (1981a), Lardinois (1982), Maksudov (1986), de Waal (1988a, 1989a), Dyson (1988), and O'Grada (1988a), among others. On related matters, see also Sorokin (1942), Rotberg and Rabb (1983) and Hugo (1984). In spite of the role of epidemics in famines, the impact of excess mortality is usually far from neutral between different occupation groups (see e.g. Klein 1973, Sen 1981a, and Drèze 1988a on the 'class' nature of famine mortality patterns in a number of past Indian famines). Mortality patterns do not, however, always follow simple class lines. In a major study of famine mortality in Sudan in 1985, Alex de Waal (1989a) observes that mortality differentials between socio-economic groups within particular localities are far less striking than differentials between localities, the latter being related mainly to factors such as population displacements and water contamination. The author concludes that 'mortality can be explained simply by a changed disease environment during the famine', and that this change is completely unrelated to economic destitution or 'entitlements' (p. 24). But population displacements and water contamination are not just 'natural' events. There is a close link between destitution and displacement, which has been observed in numerous famines, in Africa as well as elsewhere. The roots of water contamination also include social elements, influenced by economic destitution, distress migration, and upheavals in living conditions.

of food deprivation, debilitation, enhanced morbidity, and increased mortality, and this sequence is supplemented by the encouragement that famines give to other influences in spreading disease (e.g. population movements and the spread of vectors of infection). The consumption and use of food fit into a complex process with biological and social links. The analysis of the relation between food deprivation, on the one hand, and undernourishment, morbidity, mortality, productivity and well-being, on the other, has to take note of the influence of the social environment, in addition to the variations of personal features emphasized in the literature on nutritional biology.

The widespread failure of basic capabilities relates to a diverse set of entitlement inadequacies. Even if we concentrate specifically on the capability failures related to nourishment, the parameters of policy have to be concerned with a much wider field of action than command over food. The domain of entitlement analysis has to be correspondingly broad.

4

Society, Class and Gender

4.1 Are Famines Natural Phenomena?

A distinction is sometimes drawn between 'man-made' famines and famines caused by nature. The purpose is, perhaps, to distinguish between those famines in which some kind of a natural event (e.g. a flood or a drought) causes the disaster, as opposed to a famine in which people die despite there being no such act of nature. Certainly, a distinction can indeed be made between famines in which the proximate initiator is some physical phenomenon and those in which social changes of one kind or other act as the prime mover. For example, the Bengal famine of 1943, which has often been described as being 'man-made',[1] had more to do with the uneven nature of the war boom and the oddities of public policy than with any great natural disaster,[2] whereas the 1972–3 drought in the Wollo province of Ethiopia had an important initiating role in the Wollo famine of 1973.

However, recognizing the varying role of physical nature in the development of a famine is not quite the same thing as classifying famines into 'man-made' and 'nature-made' types. That classification can, in fact, be deeply misleading. Famine is, by its very nature, a social phenomenon (it involves the inability of large groups of people to establish command over food in the society in which they live), but the forces influencing such occurrences may well include, *inter alia*, developments in physical nature (such as climate and weather) in addition to social processes. The idea that the causation of famines can be neatly split into 'natural' and 'man-made' ones would seem to be a bit of a non-starter.

No less importantly, it has to be recognized that even when the prime mover in a famine is a natural occurrence such as a flood or a drought, what its impact will be on the population would depend on how society is organized.[3] For example, a country with an extensive irrigation network is much less influenced by a drought than one without it (a distinction that has *some* bearing on the differential experience of India and sub-Saharan Africa, even though the

---

[1] See Ghosh (1944) and Uppal (1984).

[2] There was, in fact, a cyclone in a few parts of Bengal in October 1942 preceding the 1943 famine, but its impact on output and employment was fairly moderate, and its effect was mainly to supplement in a relatively minor way the forces of the famine that had their origin in the redistribution of purchasing power in the war economy of Bengal (see Sen 1977a, 1981a; see also Alamgir 1980, Chattopadhyay 1981). The view that the role of the cyclone was in fact crucial, argued by Peter Bowbrick (1986, 1987), is contradicted by output information, and also by the time pattern of price increases (see Sen 1986b, 1987d).

[3] The crucial role that social arrangements can play in the development of famines has been illuminatingly discussed in historical terms by Louise Tilly (1983).

main contrasts, as we shall argue in Part II, lie elsewhere).[4] Also, even when agricultural output goes down, or normal sources of incomes are hit, as a result of a drought or a flood, whether or not this would lead to a famine would depend on what arrangements society makes for protecting vulnerable groups from these adverse shocks, e.g. through public provision of employment or the public distribution of food.

Furthermore, even the occurrence of droughts, floods, and so on is not independent of social and economic policies. Many deserts have been created by reckless human action, and the distinction between natural and social causation is substantially blurred by the impact that society can have on the physical environment. For example, the problems of hunger and famine in sub-Saharan Africa are often seen, not entirely without reason, as being related to changes in climatic factors, particularly persistent drought conditions. But to see in those changes *the* causal explanation of African hunger makes the double error of (1) treating climatic change as independent of society, and (2) overlooking the role of economic, social, and political factors in determining the impact of a drought (or any other climatic change) on what people can produce or consume.

Blaming nature can, of course, be very consoling and comforting. It can be of great use especially to those in positions of power and responsibility. Comfortable inaction is, however, typically purchased at a very heavy price—a price that is paid by others, often with their lives. If the subject had not been such a terribly practical one, it would have been fine to discuss in leisurely peace whether in some intellectually defensible sense a class of famines can be seen as primarily caused by nature while others may not be so describable. Undoubtedly the direct or indirect role of nature may be quite a bit greater in some cases than in others. But these may not be the most useful distinctions on which to concentrate in planning urgent public action.

The points of overriding importance are: that there is no real evidence to doubt that all famines in the modern world are preventable by human action; that many countries—even some very poor ones—manage consistently to prevent them; that when people die of starvation there is almost invariably some massive social failure (whether or not a natural phenomenon had an initiating role in the causal process); and that the responsibilities for that failure deserve explicit attention and analysis, not evasion. There is, of course, much more to be said, but we have to say the first things first.

4.2 Society and Cooperative Conflicts

Given the crucial role of social conditions in the genesis of hunger and deprivation, it is important to have some understanding of certain basic

[4] Economic and social arrangements that make countries less prone to natural disasters can be an important part of development planning. On this see Berry and Kates (1980) and Glantz (1987a). See also Cannon (1978).

features of social relations in this field. One general characteristic that is, in some sense, quite obvious and that tends, nevertheless, to be neglected often enough is the coexistence of conflicts as well as congruence of interests in most forms of human interaction. There *are* many advantages to be gained by different people from cooperation and collaboration, and yet there are also elements of clash and divergence of interests. Such coexistence of cooperation and conflict is endemic in social relations (this general issue was discussed in Chapter 1).

The cooperative elements are often strongly emphasized in the context of describing the social challenge involved in confronting hunger and famines. That can be exactly right, and there are indeed great gains to be made for most people, possibly even all, through such matters as protecting the environment, preventing droughts, or eliminating epidemics. But at the same time, serious mistakes can be made in the analysis of deprivation in general, and of hunger in particular, if we do not pay attention to the pervasive elements of conflict that are among the constitutive features of any society.

Conflicts of class interests have received, rightly, a good deal of attention, partly in connection with Marxian analysis. These conflicts are relevant in an obvious and elementary way in matters of hunger and famine, and the broad categorization of classes can be fruitfully extended by seeking further divisions related to occupation groups.[5] Famines are always divisive phenomena. The victims typically come from the bottom layers of society—landless agricultural labourers, poor peasants and share-croppers, pastoralist nomads, urban destitutes, and so on. Contrary to statements that are sometimes made, there does not seem to have been a famine in which victims came from all classes of the society.[6]

Sometimes there is extensive competition and combat between different classes or occupation groups in trying to secure a larger share of a given supply of food that is fixed in the short run. For example, in the Bengal famine of 1943, the rural agricultural labourers who had to buy food with their wages were hit by the rise in food prices related, at least partly, to the increase in the purchasing power of the urban population in the war economy of Bengal. When there is a limited amount of food, with the market dividing it among the

---

[5] See Chapter 2. The diverse positions of different occupation groups have been discussed in the context of specific famines in various empirical studies, e.g. Sen (1981a), Oughton (1982), Snowdon (1985), Kumar (1986), Osmani (1986), Ratnavale (1986), Sobhan (1986), Mahieu and Nour (1987), Ravallion (1987a, 1987b), Drèze (1988a), Desai (1988a, 1986b), D'Souza (1988).

[6] There are folklores about 'kings going begging' in some famines, but little hard evidence in that direction. One allegedly true example of this, according to the prestigious *Encyclopaedia Britannica*, was the Indian famine of 1344–5, in which it is claimed that even 'the Moghul emperor was unable to obtain the necessaries for his household' (*Encyclopaedia Britannica*, 11th ed., vol. x, London 1910–11: 167). However, that engrossing story cannot be exactly accurate, not just because the Moghul empire was not established in India until 1526, but also because the Tughlak king in power in 1344–5 had in fact managed to organize one of the most ambitious programmes of famine relief, including distributing food and cash, and remitting taxes (on this see Loveday 1914, Chapters 1 and 4; also Sen 1981a: 43).

population according to their respective purchasing powers and market pulls, a worsening of the relative position of some groups in the scale of money incomes can lead to an absolute decline in their ability to command food. In 'food battles', the Devil takes the hindmost.

There are conflicts of interests of various kinds that operate in the economy, and the importance of cooperative elements in social relations should not make us lose sight of the extensive and vital role that interest conflicts can play in worsening the predicament of some groups as it improves the position of others. Indeed, 'cooperative conflict' (i.e. the presence of strong elements of conflict embedded in a situation in which there are mutual gains to be made by cooperation) is a pervasive feature of social living, and to take note of this 'mixed' structure is as important in the analysis of hunger and famines as it is in any other substantive social investigation.

The outcomes of cooperative conflicts depend on a variety of factors and can be analysed in different ways.[7] Generally, it seems reasonable to predict that one of the important factors is the 'breakdown position' in case cooperation fails.[8] The more a party has to fear from such a breakdown, the less able it will be to secure a favourable outcome in the choice over alternative cooperative solutions. The workers with no ownership of means of production are, of course, particularly vulnerable to the breakdown of employment arrangements, and this contributes to the bad terms of employment that workers tend to get—an issue that has been extensively discussed by Marx, among others. In the context of hunger analysis, it is important to note both (1) the vulnerable 'breakdown position' of those owning few productive assets other than their labour power (they are often the first to starve when the normal operation of the economy is disrupted), and (2) the influence of this vulnerability on the deals that such people tend to get, for instance in exploitative rural employment.

The other side of the same coin can be seen in the enhanced bargaining power of labour in private employment when alternative earning opportunities improve. For example, there is some evidence that the security provided by the Employment Guarantee Scheme in the state of Maharashtra in India has had a significant impact on the terms of employment in the rural economy, and

[7] What J. F. Nash (1950) called 'the bargaining problem' is a particular type of 'cooperative conflict', with certain specific features, e.g. the interests of each are representable by the respective cardinal utilities, perception problems about interest and contributions are not directly involved in the characterization of the game, ideas of acceptable distribution have to depend only on utility information, the solution must satisfy certain specific characteristics of symmetry and consistency (see Sen, 1970). Formal models of bargaining for intrafamily divisions have been presented by Clemhout and Wan (1977), Manser and Brown (1980), McElroy and Horney (1981), among others. See also Brown and Chuang (1980), Rochford (1981), Pollak (1983), Folbre (1986).

[8] This was one of the important insights provided by the original Nash (1950) model of bargaining, which made the predicted solution sensitive to the outcome that would emerge in the absence of cooperation (sometimes called, perhaps a little misleadingly, the 'status quo position'). This feature has been retained in some form in most of the later models of bargaining; see Schelling (1960), Kalai and Smordinsky (1975), Harsanyi (1976), Kaneko and Nakamura (1979), Roth (1985), Binmore (1987), Binmore and Dasgupta (1987).

generally on the economic and social positions of agricultural labourers.[9] The benefits received from the Employment Guarantee Scheme by vulnerable groups in Maharashtra may thus go well beyond the additional earnings from public employment. In assessing various forms of public intervention (e.g. land reforms, literacy campaigns, or employment programmes), importance has to be *inter alia* attached to their impact on the breakdown position of vulnerable groups and through that on the deal that these people receive in the economy and the society.

There are other determinants of outcomes of 'cooperative conflicts' than the breakdown position of the various parties involved, e.g. perceptions of contributions to joint prosperity, threats that the parties can respectively employ. The relevance of different influences will depend crucially on the nature of the congruent interests and the understanding of conflicts faced by the different parties. Here too, public action, e.g. in the form of education and politics, can have a far-reaching impact on the deal that vulnerable groups receive in the society.

Cooperative conflict takes a particularly important but complex form in matters of gender relations, such as the distribution of joint benefits between men and women in the family.[10] In that context, as we shall argue presently, the nature of the perception of each person's contribution to the joint benefits can play a particularly important part (for example, whether women are seen as 'contributing' much to the family's economic prosperity can become a crucial variable even in the division of food and health care).[11] But the need to take note of the nature of cooperative conflicts in the analysis of hunger and deprivation is a more general requirement that has pervasive relevance because of the extensive coexistence of congruent and conflicting interests in the social relations that govern people's ability to establish entitlement over food and related necessities.

4.3 Female Deprivation and Gender Bias

One of the difficult fields of 'food battle' is that of intrafamily divisions. While economic models are often constructed on the assumption that the distribution of commodities among different members of the family is done on the basis of

---

[9] On this see Deshpande (1982, 1984), Dandekar (1983), Walker *et al.* (1986), Acharya and Panwalkar (1988*a*, 1988*b*), Mencher (1988).

[10] This is analysed in Sen (1985*c*, 1987*c*) in terms of the notion of 'extended entitlement' discussed in Chapter 1 of this book, which broadens the focus of entitlement analysis from legal rights to a framework in which accepted social notions of 'legitimacy' can be influential. See also Kynch and Sen (1983), Bryceson (1985), Jain and Banerjee (1985), Whitehead (1985), Agarwal (1986, 1988), Boserup (1986), Tilly (1986), Vaughan (1987), Wilson (1987*a*, 1987*b*).

[11] The issue of perception has some relevance also in the analysis of class relations. Indeed, it was in that context that the Marxian analysis of 'false consciousness' was first used, and it can make a difference as to how people view and understand the nature of society and how it produces as well as distributes the jointly generated goods.

equalizing well-being or need-fulfilment, there is considerable evidence that intrafamily divisions often involve very unequal treatments. The systematic deprivation of women *vis-à-vis* men in many societies (particularly that of girls *vis-à-vis* boys) has attracted a good deal of attention recently, and there is a fair amount of evidence in that direction from many parts of the world, including South Asia, West Asia, North Africa, and China.

It is not, of course, easy to observe directly who is eating how much from a shared kitchen.[12] Claims regarding unequal treatment in the division of food are typically based on indirect information.[13] A natural direction in which to go is that of examining direct evidence of various nutritional and related functionings, such as clinical signs of undernourishment, morbidity rates, or comparative mortality patterns.[14] This also has the merit of establishing comparisons in terms of those things that ultimately matter (what kind of life a person can lead), rather than trying to observe just commodity intakes, which are means to achievements rather than being important in themselves. Our ultimate concern, as was argued in the last chapter, is not with the size of nutritional intakes, but with the extent of nutritional well-being and with the capability to achieve that well-being.

Since there can be substantial interpersonal and intrapersonal variations in the relation between nutritional intakes and health achievements or functioning ability (as was discussed in the last chapter), comparisons of inputs can be a defective basis for the assessment of relative treatments. If, on the other hand, it is found that women are more frequently undernourished than men, or that the ratio of female to male mortality rates is higher than what can be expected when there is no serious sex bias in the division of food or health care, there would indeed be a good ground for questioning the thesis of equal treatment.

Such evidence of inequality does exist in many developing economies. Even the elementary statistics of the ratio of female to male population bring out a picture of remarkable variations. To illustrate, Table 4.1 presents values of female–male ratio—FMR for short—for different regions of the world. For the more developed economies in Europe or North America the FMR tends to average around 1.05, mainly reflecting certain survival advantages that women seem to have over men in the absence of serious anti-female bias in the division

---

[12] For some interesting attempts in this direction and discussion of the problems involved, see Chen, Huq and D'Souza (1981), Chimwaza (1982) and Chaudhury (1987, 1988). See also Wheeler (1984), Harriss (1986), and Wheeler and Abdullah (1988).

[13] The usual techniques of 'equivalent scales' for the analysis of household consumption and welfare (see Deaton and Muellbauer 1980) are not easy to apply for intrahousehold divisions, since the purchase data do not discriminate between different users. But some deductions can be made on the basis of different regularities of consumption patterns among households with different demographic and social characteristics. On this see Muellbauer (1987) and Deaton (1987, 1988); on related matters see also Deaton and Case (1987) and Blackorby and Donaldson (1988).

[14] See Bardhan (1974, 1984, 1987), Mitra (1980), Chen, Huq and D'Souza (1981), Miller (1981), Kynch and Sen (1983), Sen (1984b, 1985a), Kynch (1985), Harriss (1986, 1988a), Harriss and Watson (1987), Lipton (1987b), Momsen and Townsend (1987), among many other contributions.

Table 4.1 Female–male ratio (FMR) and 'missing women', 1986

Region	FMR	Missing women in relation to sub-Saharan African FMR	
		Number (millions)	Proportion (%)
Europe	1.050		
Northern America	1.047		
Sub-Saharan Africa	1.022		
South-east Asia	1.010	2.4	1.2
Latin America	1.000	4.4	2.2
North Africa	0.984	2.4	3.9
West Asia	0.948	4.3	7.8
Iran	0.942	1.4	8.5
China	0.941	44.0	8.6
Bangladesh	0.940	3.7	8.7
India	0.933	36.9	9.5
Pakistan	0.905	5.2	12.9

Notes: (i) The *number* of 'missing women' for a particular country is calculated as the difference between (1) the number of women the country would have if its FMR was the same as that of sub-Saharan Africa (i.e. 1.022), given its actual male population, and (2) the number of women it actually has. The *proportion* of 'missing women' is the ratio of missing women to the actual number of women in a particular country. (ii) 'Sub-Saharan Africa' here includes all of Africa except North Africa and South Africa.

Source: Calculated from data on male and female populations provided in *UN Demographic Yearbook 1986*, Tables 2 and 3. This publication does not give separate male and female population figures for India. The Indian figures are therefore based on the female–male ratio of the 1981 census and the 1986 population total, respectively provided in *ILO Yearbook of Labour Statistics 1988*, Table 1, and *World Development Report 1988*, Table 27.

of such things as food and health care. In contrast, the FMR in South Asia, China, West Asia, and North Africa averages only around 0.93 or 0.94.[15] In India, not only is the mortality differential remarkably sharp among children (that is, mortality rates are much higher for girls than for boys), the higher mortality rate of females *vis-à-vis* males applies to all age groups until the late thirties.

However, not all poor regions of the world have very low female–male ratios. In fact, both South-east Asia and sub-Saharan Africa have female–male ratios higher than unity (though not as high as Europe or North America). We shall have to address the question as to why these differences are observed (on this

[15] For some comparative information on this, see Kynch and Sen (1983), Sen (1984a, 1985a, 1988c), Kynch (1985), Harriss and Watson (1987), Dyson (1988). The sex ratios observed in developed countries are not, of course, in any sense 'natural'. They reflect a complex interaction of biological, environmental and social differences affecting the lives of men and women. However, the fact that, on balance, biological factors work in the direction of general survival advantages for females relative to males (especially in infancy) is not in doubt. These and related issues are insightfully discussed by several contributors in Lopez and Ruzicka (1983), especially Lopez (1983), Ruzicka and Lopez (1983) and Waldron (1983).

see section 4.5). It is also interesting to probe these differences to throw light on the magnitude of the problem of shortfall of women in the total population—primarily reflecting excess female mortality at present and in the recent past of the concerned region.[16] It may, for example, be asked how many more women there would be in India or China (given the number of men in each) if they had the female–male ratio that obtains in sub-Saharan Africa. The number of 'missing women', calculated in this way, works out as 37 million in India and 44 million in China. Table 4.1 presents the estimates for a number of regions.

The number of 'missing women' reflects an aspect of a complex and terrible problem. The shortfall of women arises from a higher sex differential in mortality rates in India and China than obtains in the sub-Saharan African economies, and reveals in quiet statistics a gruesome story of anti-female bias in social divisions. It is also interesting to note that while sub-Saharan Africa is taken to be, in some respects, the 'problem region' of the world, when it comes to sex bias, the more problematic countries are elsewhere.

The number of 'missing women' as we have calculated it is highest in China, but proportionate to the population it is even higher in Southern Asia. Pakistan has, in fact, the highest proportion of 'missing women'—as high as 13 per cent. There are significant numbers of 'missing women' also elsewhere, including in West Asia, North Africa, and even Latin America. The numbers would have been larger if we had used, for comparison, not the sub-Saharan African female-male ratio, but that of, say, Europe or North America.

It should be mentioned that the differential mortality rates need not be wholly or even primarily connected with unequal treatments in the division of *food* as such, and the divergence can arise from other inequalities, such as those of access to health care.[17] As was argued earlier (in Chapter 3), it is a mistake to concentrate exclusively on the delivery of food and to ignore the tremendous interdependence and complementarity that obtain between the use of food and other resources (such as health care). Here as elsewhere, entitlement comparisons have to go beyond the limited focus of food entitlements to the more comprehensive concern for entitlements to the different goods and services which influence our nutritional opportunities and achievements.

[16] The female–male ratio is also, of course, affected by the relative numbers of female and male births. It is easily shown that the *differences* in the interregional birth ratios, in so far as they exist, are much too tiny to explain any significant part of the FMR differences *between the regions*. It has sometimes been suggested that the low FMR in India is due to a particularly high ratio of males in Indian births. That hypothesis can be rejected on the basis of demographic analysis; on this see Visaria (1961).

[17] There is indeed some direct evidence of the disadvantaged access of women to medical care, and also of enhanced morbidity rates. See Chen, Huq and D'Souza (1981), Miller (1981), Bhatia (1983), Kynch and Sen (1983), Sen (1984a, 1985a), Leela Visaria (1985), Basu (1987, 1988), Chaudhury (1987, 1988), Das Gupta (1987, 1989a, 1989b), Ramalingaswami (1987), Harriss (1988a). See also Wyon and Gordon (1971), Levinson (1972), Dyson and Moore (1983), Kielman et al. (1983). In an extensive review of the literature on the intrafamily allocation of food in South Asia, Barbara Harriss (1986) finds no conclusive evidence that women are discriminated against in the division of food as such. However, there is strong evidence of discrimination in health care and in parental attention.

The sharp contrast between South Asia and sub-Saharan Africa which emerges from the evidence on female–male ratios is of considerable significance, and has several interesting features. First, many studies of food intake, nutritional status and survival chances confirm the pattern of gender differentials indicated by a demographic examination of female–male ratios. Anti-female discrimination in health and nutrition is endemic in South Asia, but much less noticeable (perhaps even absent) in the case of sub-Saharan Africa.[18]

Second, there are many possible reasons for this interregional contrast. A full explanation would have to take into account the profound cultural, economic and social differences between South Asia and sub-Saharan Africa. It is worth noting, however, that the lower incidence of anti-female bias in the latter region fits well with the view that the vulnerability of the respective parties is one important influence on the outcome of cooperative conflicts (including those involved in gender divisions). There is indeed a good deal of anthropological and statistical evidence on the greater autonomy of African women (in terms of land rights, access to gainful employment, control over property, freedom of movement, etc.) in comparison with the general position of South Asian women.[19] This point is further discussed in section 4.5, particularly in relation to the role of 'gainful' employment.

Third, the extent of sex discrimination in health and nutrition is not an immutable feature of any society, and important changes have taken place over time in both regions. It has been argued that sex differentials in mortality are slowly narrowing in South Asia, while they seem to be widening in at least some countries of sub-Saharan Africa.[20] The latter phenomenon, if confirmed, may relate in part to the decline of agriculture in these countries, and the greater reliance on non-agricultural activities to which men have a privileged access.

Finally, the relative absence of sex discrimination in health and nutrition in sub-Saharan Africa does not imply, by any means, that sex discrimination *in general* is of little importance in African societies. Indeed, even in the rich countries of West Europe and North America, where nutrition and survival are no longer areas of intense discrimination between the sexes, women remain disadvantaged in numerous ways. Similarly, there is considerable evidence that the general status of women in African societies involves significant and pervasive inequities.[21]

[18] For references to studies on South Asia, see the preceding footnote. On the absence of systematic anti-female bias in health and nutrition in sub-Saharan Africa, see e.g. the demographic studies of Ohadike (1983), Caldwell and Caldwell (1987a), and Gbenyon and Locoh (1987), the nutrition surveys of Nash (1986), Brett (1987), and von Braun (1988), and the review of the evidence by Svedberg (1986, 1988).

[19] On these issues, see Boserup (1970), Hill (1975), Buvinic (1976), Whitehead (1986), Caldwell and Caldwell (1987b), and the literature cited in these studies. Kandiyoti (1988) contrasts the bargains faced by women in the very different 'patriarchal systems' of South Asia and sub-Saharan Africa. The interlinkages between cultural and economic relations involved in these interregional contrasts are discussed in Basu (1988) and Sen (1989a).

[20] See e.g. Dyson (1987) on South Asia, and Gbenyon and Locoh (1987) on sub-Saharan Africa.

[21] See Whitehead (1986) and the literature cited there. See also Boserup (1970), Rogers (1980) and Stichter and Parpart (1988).

4.4 Famine Mortality and Gender Divisions

There is considerable dispute as to whether the intensity of female deprivation increases in famine situations. It is, in fact, possible that two divergent tendencies come into play in this context. First, as was discussed earlier, women appear to have certain biological advantages over men in survival, and there is some evidence that these general advantages enhance the relative ability of women to cope with temporary distress situations *vis-à-vis* men.[22] Second, the factors that govern the distribution of food, health care and general attention among men and women may undergo changes in famine situations. This influence can act in the opposite direction to the previous one, if it takes the form of greater discrimination against women.

These divergent tendencies can result in a rather complex pattern of sex differentials in the experience of famine. On the one hand, there is considerable evidence that the proportionate increase of mortality is typically *lower* for women than for men in famine situations. This was, in fact, the observed pattern in most of the famines for which relevant demographic data are available.[23]

On the other hand, a number of studies also bring out the fact that, in many societies, the priorities of the family are often pro-male in distress situations.[24] In so far as *greater* physical distress coexists with a *smaller* increase in mortality for females *vis-à-vis* males, the explanation may have to be sought, at least partly, in terms of greater female ability to survive nutritional stress.

The empirical evidence on this entire subject remains to be fully investigated. The two—possibly opposite—tendencies noted earlier can lead to different patterns of sex differentials in food intake, anthropometric status, mortality rates and socio-economic indicators of stress. There can also be important interregional differences in the connections (1) between economic distress and patterns of sex-and-age specific deprivation of food and other commodities, (2) between the distribution of deprivation in intake and that of undernourishment, and (3) between the distribution of undernourishment and that of mortality.

The overriding fact that is altogether difficult to escape is the remarkable relative deprivation of women in many parts of the world in normal (non-famine) situations; the nature of sex bias in famine situations has to be assessed

[22] See Shettles (1958), Widdowson (1976), Rivers (1982), Payne and Lipton (1988).

[23] See e.g. Boyle and O'Grada (1986), O'Grada (1988a) and Voglaire (1988) on the Irish famines of the 1840s, Lardinois (1982) and Kynch (1987b) on 19th-century famines in India, Maksudov (1986) on the Ukrainian famines of 1927–38, Valaoras (1946) on the Greek famine of 1941–2, Greenough (1982) on the Bengal famine of 1943, Hill (1988) on the Chinese famines of 1958–61, and de Waal (1987) on the Sudan famine of 1985. It is, however, sometimes the case that in particular age groups the increase of female mortality is more pronounced than that of male mortality, even when the overall increase of mortality may affect men more; see e.g. Greenough (1982) and Agarwal (1988).

[24] See Chen *et al.* (1981), Greenough (1982), Rivers (1982), Kynch and Sen (1983), Sen (1984a), Fernandes and Menon (1987), Vaughan (1985, 1987), Agarwal (1988), Arnold (1988), Kabeer (1989).

in that light. The observation of widespread female disadvantage in nutritional conditions is of direct interest in the analysis of hunger and deprivation in a substantial part of the world, and cannot but be a matter of great concern in the making of economic and social policy in such regions as South Asia, West Asia, North Africa, and China. The issue of comparative position of women during famines is perhaps of less general interest if only because famines, with a few exceptions, have been confined in recent decades to sub-Saharan Africa, which is, on the whole, a part of the world in which there is little evidence of systematic anti-female bias in nutrition and survival.[25]

This is not to say that issues of sex discrimination in famine situations are altogether inconsequential in sub-Saharan Africa. Indeed, even for that region, a number of surveys have brought out the sharp social and economic disadvantages that women can face in coping with a subsistence crisis.[26] These problems deserve serious attention. However, as far as the question of famine mortality and nutritional damage is concerned, it appears that sex discrimination at worst only supplements in a relatively small way the enormous destructive forces that come into play in African famines.

4.5 Gender and Cooperative Conflicts

The part that the coexistence of congruent and conflicting interests plays in social relations was discussed earlier, and its bearing on the problem of hunger and related deprivations was explored. The presence of substantial anti-female bias in well-being and survival in many parts of the world can be seen to have clear connections with the way problems of cooperative conflicts in gender relations are tackled.[27]

It can be argued that the 'deal' that women get in the division of joint benefits in the family is unfavourably affected by the more precarious position of the female in the event of 'breakdown' (e.g. the separation of spouses or their cohabitation in a state of permanent strife). The greater vulnerability of women may be only partly due to biological differences (connected with reproduction, differences in physical strength, etc.), and is, in fact, often socially generated. Nevertheless this greater precariousness is typically influential in determining the relative shares on which women and men can respectively lay claims in the division of family resources.

[25] See section 4.3. Comparisons of nutritional status based on either calorie intake or anthropometric evidence for children do not reveal any general bias against girls *vis-à-vis* boys in sub-Saharan Africa, even in distress situations (see Nash 1986, Brett 1987, Deaton 1988, von Braun 1988, Svedberg 1988, Wheeler and Abdullah 1988; Médecins Sans Frontières Belgium, personal communication).

[26] See Campbell and Trechter (1982), Rivers (1982), Vaughan (1985, 1987), Matiza *et al.* (1988). Examples of anti-female discrimination observed in some African famines are the greater frequency of fasting for women and the abandonment of women by their husbands.

[27] The analysis that follows is more extensively developed in Sen (1985c, 1987c).

The greater vulnerability of women is closely connected with lesser opportunities for getting outside work and paid employment. The extent of so-called 'gainful activities' can also be a factor of influence on its own (in addition to acting through its impact on the 'breakdown' situations). In determining how the family benefits should be divided, importance seems to be attached, as many studies bring out, to who is 'contributing' how much to the joint prosperity of the family.[28] Even though the ability to do outside work on the part of some members of the family may depend crucially on the willingness of the other members to do housework, nevertheless in the accounting of respective 'contributions', paid employment and outside 'gainful' activities seem to loom particularly large. In so far as 'perceived contributions' are an influence of importance in determining who 'ought' to get how much in intrafamily divisions, the traditional structure of work division inside and outside the home may particularly disfavour women *vis-à-vis* men. In general, various perception problems enter into this complex issue of cooperative conflict, and many of these perceptions have close links with the traditions of work division between males and females.[29]

While considerations of cooperative conflicts (including the relevance of breakdown positions, perception biases, etc.) take us in one direction of analysis, those of economic calculations by household heads take us along another track. In recent years there have been a number of interesting attempts to relate the neglect of female children in South Asia to the greater 'investment value' of the survival of boys in comparison with girls.[30] This line of argument too brings in the greater earning power of men, related to the way society is organized in most parts of the world. However, it sees this information not as a determinant of cooperative conflict affecting the status and deal that women get, but as a part of the investment accounting of the household head. While the cooperative conflict approach concentrates on women and men, and sees the position of girls *vis-à-vis* boys as being related to the same basic influences that colour the way women's contributions and deserts are viewed, the investment approach sees the child-rearing problem in terms of relative returns to investment and does not directly address the issue of relative deprivation of adult women.

It is not easy to assess precisely what part hard-headed investment calculations play in the treatment of children, and there has been a certain amount of understandable questioning as to whether this is getting the social anthropology of child rearing right. Also, whether there is any wilful neglect of female children—compared with the attention that boys get—has also itself been

[28] See Sen (1985c) and the empirical studies reviewed there.

[29] See Boserup (1970, 1986), Chen and Ghuznavi (1976), Loutfi (1980), Kynch and Sen (1983), P. Bardhan (1984, 1987), K. Bardhan (1985), Sen (1985c, 1987c), M. Chen (1986a, 1986b), Das Gupta (1987), Joekes (1987), Papanek (1987, 1989), Wilson (1987a, 1987b), Agarwal (1988), Aslanbeigui and Summerfield (1989).

[30] See particularly Rosenzweig and Schultz (1982), Behrman and Deolalikar (1987), Behrman (1988a, 1988b).

questioned, especially in India.[31] There is scope for argument on this, but the evidence of preference for having male children is well documented in South Asia,[32] and it is hard to rule out the possibility that for poor families such hard-headed calculations may play some part in determining intrafamily divisions. However, it is also difficult to ignore the influence of the *perception* of greater male 'contribution'—related to the traditional patterns of work division—in determining views of relative deserts of the different family members. The general picture of anti-female bias in intrafamily divisions would seem to call for something more than just the accounting of relative values of 'returns to investment in child survival'. The whole issue may involve a much greater mixing of economic, social, and cultural influences than the narrow economic models may admit.

Be that as it may, there is considerable evidence that greater involvement with outside work and paid employment does tend to go with less anti-female bias in intrafamily distribution.[33] This has important policy implications no matter whether the influence is due to the impact of female 'economic activity' on the breakdown position of women, *or* to its influence on the perception of 'contributions' made by women, *or* to its effect on the accounting of returns to investment, *or* to some other chain of social or economic causation.

Table 4.2 Activity-rate ratios and life expectancy ratios, 1980

Regions	Activity-rate ratios (female–male)		Life expectancy ratios (female–male)	
	Values	Ranks	Values	Ranks
Non-Northern Africa	0.645	1	1.071	1
Eastern & South Eastern Asia	0.610	2	1.066	2
Western Asia	0.373	3	1.052	3
Southern Asia	0.336	4	0.989	5
Northern Africa	0.158	5	1.050	4

Source: Sen (1987c, 1988c), calculated from country data given in ILO (1986) and the United Nations tapes on 'Estimates and Projections of Population' (1985). The activity rate ratios represent the proportions of total population of each sex engaged in so-called 'economic' (or 'gainful') activities.

[31] See e.g. Alaka Basu (1987, 1988).
[32] See Miller (1981). The preference for male children appears to be especially strong after the birth of one or more daughters; see Das Gupta (1987, 1989a, 1989b) and Amin (1988).
[33] Various micro-economic studies have also brought out the importance of outside work for women's status and for their power within the family. On this see Boserup (1970, 1986), Standing and Sheehan (1978), Auerbach (1979), Cain *et al.* (1979), Croll (1978), Lloyd and Niemi (1979), Amsden (1980), Bhatty (1980), Loutfi (1980), Banerjee (1982, 1985), Beneria (1982), Deere and de Leal (1982), Dixon (1982, 1983), ILO (1982a, 1982b), Mies (1982), Phongpaichit (1982), Dandekar (1983), Sen (1984a), Jain and Banerjee (1985), Mahmud and Mahmud (1985), Agarwal (1986, 1988), Adnan (1988), Basu (1988), Blumberg (1988). See also an examination of the empirical literature in Sen (1985c).

It may be useful to examine whether the differential involvement of women in outside work in different regions of Asia and Africa provides any clues as to the possible causation of greater anti-female bias in Asia than in Africa, in North Africa than in sub-Saharan Africa, and so on. Given the broad cultural contrasts involved, the focus of comparison has to be correspondingly wide (rather than being based on political boundaries of state and province). We present and compare in Table 4.2 the ratios of 'economic activity rates' (roughly pertaining to outside work, including paid employment) of women *vis-à-vis* men, and the ratios of female life expectancy to male life expectancy.[34]

It turns out that the ranking of the different regions in terms of life expectancy ratios is almost the same as that in terms of activity-rate ratios.[35] In particular, the higher female participation in 'gainful' activities in sub-Saharan Africa dominates all the other regions, just as its female–male life expectancy ratio does. That dominance includes not merely an Asia–Africa divergence, but also a sharp dichotomy within Africa, between North Africa and sub-Saharan Africa.[36]

A simple finding of this kind does not, of course, establish any firm connections, but it is interesting that the relations that are expected on the basis of general economic and social analyses are on the whole confirmed rather than contradicted by these data.[37] When we come to policy, it would be hard to leave out the possible importance of female participation in 'gainful' economic activities as a material factor in combating the special deprivation of women in many parts of the world.

[34] On some conceptual and empirical issues related to this analysis, see Sen (1987c). Life expectancy figures tell us more about *current* mortality rates, whereas the female–male ratios reflect the effects of past mortality rates as well. Since the *activity-rate ratios* are current figures, it makes more sense to relate them to the *life expectancy ratios*.

[35] There is only one variation, with the relative position of Southern Asia and Northern Africa being reversed as we move from one ranking to the other—the fourth becomes fifth and vice versa. Note also that China has not been included in this table. The Chinese case has a number of special features, including problems of accounting as well as some particular policy variations such as the rule of 'one-child family' (on this see Chapter 11), but it is on the whole an exception to the picture revealed by the table, since China has a high activity-rate ratio but a relatively lower-ranked life expectancy ratio.

[36] There is a similar contrast within India between the North and the South, with the Southern states having both higher female participation and less gender bias in female survival. See Boserup (1970), Miller (1981), Bardhan (1987), Harriss (1988a). See also Caldwell and Caldwell (1987a).

[37] Krishnaji (1987) notes that the female–male ratio is higher in families of labourers and small peasants than in those of bigger farmers in rural India. This is also in line with the same relations, since the extent of female participation in economic activities is much higher in households of labourers and small peasants than in those of larger farmers (on this and related issues, see Gulati 1975, Jain 1980, ILO 1981, Mukhopadhyay 1981, Chatterji 1984, Reddy 1985, Chakravarty 1986, Nayyar 1987, Nagaraj 1989). But there can be other influences as well, as Krishnaji notes. He also comments, not without reason, on the tendency to calculate 'the economic value of women', by 'economists who do not distinguish human beings from commodities' (p. 897). In this respect, the 'cooperative conflict' model is quite different from the 'investment return' model, since the former sees the influence of outside earning on the status and clout of women (and views the treatment of girls in that light), rather than seeing it just as an influence on the relative 'returns' of investment 'in' girls and boys. The economic factors merge with social and cultural issues in this broader approach.

4.6   *Protection, Promotion and Social Security*

This book is concerned primarily with action. Even though we have been spending a good bit of time sorting out the diagnostics (this is necessary to analyse the strategies needed for action), our primary concern is with the role of public action in the provision of social security on a wide basis. The elimination of famines and endemic undernourishment fits into that general approach.

We have distinguished earlier (in Chapter 1) between two different—though not unrelated—aspects of social security, viz. *protection* and *promotion*. The former is concerned with preventing a decline in living conditions in general and with averting starvation in particular. The problem of protection is paramount in the context of famine prevention, which is the subject matter of Part II (Chapters 5–8) of this book. The other objective of social security is enhancing normal living conditions, including the elimination of persistent deprivation and endemic undernutrition. Part III (Chapters 9–12) is primarily concerned with this issue.

It is perhaps useful to make a few clarificatory remarks about the dual objectives of protection and promotion. First, while the objectives of protection and promotion are distinct, they are not independent of each other. Success with the promotional objective may make protection easier. For example, if the normal level of prosperity is socially enhanced across the board, the task of protection becomes less intensely crucial for survival, since there is then more of a margin to fall back on, and also since the family's own insurance arrangements may become more feasible in those circumstances.

Similarly, successful protection from famines and other crises can help to preserve the family's capital stock and make promotional objectives that much easier to pursue. Indeed, one of the side effects of famines typically is the demolition of the poor rural family's assets, and preventing that from happening helps to maintain and enhance the normal—'non-crisis'—capabilities and levels of living.

Second, the contrast between protection and promotion will arise in the specification of means as well as ends. While we have outlined the distinction here as a categorization of objectives, a similar differentiation can be made in the category of means as well. For example, it is often useful to distinguish between the instrumental role of protection of incomes (preventing sharp declines) and that of promotion of incomes (raising persistently low incomes). There is also an important difference between entitlement protection and entitlement promotion. The protection–promotion distinction has to be integrated with other contrasts used in policy analysis.

Third, while both the terms 'protection' and 'promotion' might be thought to have a somewhat 'statist' presumption, their use in this context is to clarify the distinction between different types of social objectives rather than to see the state as a great promoter and a heroic protector. As we argue throughout this book, public action is neither just a matter of state activity, nor an issue of acting from some 'privileged ground'.

Public action includes not just what is done *for* the public by the state, but also what is done *by* the public for itself. The latter includes not merely the directly beneficial contributions of social institutions, but also the actions of pressure groups and political activists. Indeed, even in the determination of what the government itself will do, the role of public pressure may be an important one. There is, for example, considerable evidence that timely governmental action in preventing famines has often been precipitated by powerful newspaper reports on early cases of starvation and by the pressure of political and social organizations demanding action.[38] Similarly, the combating of gender inequality relates, as was discussed earlier in this chapter, to the economic and social roles of women (e.g. female involvement in so-called 'gainful' activities), and also to the political awareness of existing economic, social and legal inequities and of the possibilities of radical change.[39]

Public action against hunger and deprivation involves the agency of the public as well as its role as the beneficiary. While the activities of the state fit into this general picture and can play an important—even crucial—role, it would be a mistake to see it as the only, or even the primary, part of that picture. Ultimately, public action will be determined by what the public is ready to do, what sacrifices it is ready to make, what things it is determined to demand, and what it refuses to tolerate. The vehicles of public action are immensely varied. We must not impoverish the richness of the set of possibilities by choosing—explicitly or by implication—a narrow conception of public action. The terrible problems of resilient hunger in the modern world call for a more adequate challenge.

[38] See Sen (1981*a*, 1983*a*), Ram (1986), Drèze (1988*a*, 1989), Reddy (1988). See also Chapters 5, 8 and 11.

[39] On the latter, and its connections with general political movements in the Third World, see Sobhan (1978), Omvedt (1980), Mazumdar (1985), Jayawardena (1986), Afshar (1987), Papanek (1989) and Tinker (forthcoming), among other contributions.

PART II
Famines

5

Famines and Social Response

5.1 Famine Prevention and Entitlement Protection

Faith in the ability of public intervention to avert famines is a relatively new phenomenon. Even as confident a utilitarian as James Mill felt compelled to use the most fatalistic language to tell his friend David Ricardo about the likely effects of a spell of adverse weather in England:

Does not this weather frighten you? . . . There must now be of necessity a very deficient crop, and very high prices—and these with an unexampled scarcity of work will produce a degree of misery, the thought of which makes the flesh creep on one's bones—one third of the people must die—it would be a blessing to take them into the streets and high ways, and cut their throats as we do with pigs.[1]

Ricardo had full sympathy for Mill's feelings, and assured him that he was 'sorry to see a disposition to inflame the minds of the lower orders by persuading them that legislation can afford them any relief'.[2]

Echoes of Mill's and Ricardo's pessimism can be found in abundance even today.[3] But an enormous amount of evidence now bears testimony to the potential effectiveness of public action for famine prevention. This part of the book examines the role of public intervention in the elimination of famines.

We discussed in Chapter 2 how famines develop from entitlement failures suffered by a large section of the population. Those who cannot establish command over an adequate amount of food have to perish from starvation. Famine prevention is essentially concerned, therefore, with the *protection of entitlements*. That much might be obvious enough, but a few interpretational issues should be addressed straightaway to avoid misunderstanding the content of that superficially simple message.

First, while famines involve—and are typically initiated by—starvation, many of the people who die from a famine die in fact not from starvation as such, but from various epidemic diseases unleashed by the famine. This happens primarily through the spread of infectious diseases helped by debilitation, attempts to eat whatever looks eatable, breakdown of sanitary arrangements, and massive population movements in search of food.[4] Famine

[1] Letter of Mill to Ricardo, August 14, 1816. Quoted in Jacquemin (1985), 'Annexe historique', p. 18.

[2] See Jacquemin (1985), 'Annexe historique', p. 18.

[3] The cult of the 'lifeboat ethics' (as well as the 'case against helping the poor' and the 'toughlove solution' advocated by Garrett Hardin 1974, 1981), discussing who to 'sacrifice' to let others survive, builds on a peculiarly heightened version of that pessimism.

[4] See Chapter 3, section 3.3, where the relation of these findings to the entitlement approach is also discussed.

prevention is, in fact, intimately connected with the avoidance of epidemics, even though the first and basic culprit may be the failure of food entitlements.

Thus, when acute deprivation has been allowed to develop, the task of containing famine mortality may require substantial attention to health care and epidemiological control. This consideration links with the general importance, discussed in Chapter 3, of seeing hunger and deprivation in terms of entitlement failures in a broader perspective than that of food entitlements only. At the same time, it is important to bear in mind that in the case of famines the collapse of food entitlements is the initiating failure in which epidemics themselves originate, and that the protection of food entitlements at an early stage is often a more effective form of action than medical intervention at a later stage.[5]

Second, while the entitlement approach asserts the inadequacy of aggregate food availability as a focus for the analysis of famines, it does not assert its irrelevance. Aggregate food availability remains important, but its influence has to be seen only as an element of a more complex entitlement process. This general point was discussed in Chapter 2 in the context of analysing the causation of famines, but it also has to be borne in mind when the attention is turned to the prevention of famines. In particular it is important to see that (1) the improvement of food availability can play a helpful or even crucial role in preventing the development of a famine, whether or not the threat of famine is accompanied by a decline in food availability, and (2) at the same time, many other influences are at work, and a broad view should be taken of possible options for action—including that of protecting the food entitlements of vulnerable groups even when it is not possible to bring aggregate food availability to a particular level.

Third, the protection of entitlements in the short run has to be contrasted with the general promotion of entitlements in the long run. In the short run, famine prevention is essentially a question of encountering an immediate threat of entitlement failure for vulnerable groups. In the long term, of course, much more is involved, and a durable elimination of vulnerability requires promotional policies, such as the expansion of general prosperity, the reduction of insecurity through economic diversification, and the creation of secure earning arrangements.

However, even within a long-term perspective, the task of building up reliable entitlement protection systems remains quite crucial. Indeed, in most cases it would be rather naïve to expect that efforts at eliminating vulnerability could be so successful as to allow a country to dispense with distinct and

---

[5] Many past experiences of famine prevention show the dramatic effectiveness that simple intervention measures can have on famine mortality. These measures have primarily taken the form of early protection of food entitlements, supplemented if possible with the provision of drinking water and basic health care (especially vaccination). For some examples (historical as well as contemporary), see Valaoras (1946), Ramalingaswami *et al.* (1971), Berg (1973), Krishnamachari *et al.* (1974), Binns (1976), Smout (1978), Will (1980), Kiljunen (1984), Otten (1986), de Waal (1987), and Drèze (1988a, 1989), among others.

specialized entitlement protection mechanisms. While famine prevention is not exclusively concerned with the protection of entitlements, much of the discussion in this part of the book will concentrate on this elementary and urgent aspect of the problem.

Fourth, the task of entitlement protection also has to be distinguished from the popular notion of 'famine relief' which conjures up the picture of a battle already half lost and focuses the attention on emergency operations narrowly aimed at containing large-scale mortality. Devising planned, coherent, effective and durable entitlement protection mechanisms is a much broader task. Entitlement crises have many repercussions on the rural economy and on the well-being of affected populations, and a comprehensive strategy for dealing with the scourge of famine must seek to ensure that human beings have both secure lives and secure livelihoods.

This is not just a question of immediate well-being, but also one of development prospects. Consider, for instance, the so-called 'food crisis in Africa'.[6] The current débâcle of agricultural production in much of sub-Saharan Africa has, not without reason, been held partly responsible for this region's continued vulnerability to famine. But it is legitimate to wonder how farmers who are condemned every so often to use up their productive capital in a desperate struggle for survival can possibly be expected to save, innovate, and prosper. There is indeed considerable evidence of the lasting adverse effects of famine on productive potential as well as on the distribution of assets.[7] It is reasonable to think that improved entitlement protection systems in Africa would not only save lives, but also contribute to preserving and rejuvenating the rural economy. The alleged dilemma between 'relief' and 'development' is a much exaggerated one, and greater attention has to be paid to the positive links between famine prevention and development prospects.

Finally, seeing famine prevention as an entitlement protection problem draws our attention to the plurality of strategies available for dealing with it. Just as entitlements can be threatened in a number of different ways, there are also typically a number of feasible routes for restoring them. Importing food and handing it over to the destitutes is one of the more obvious options. The overwhelming preoccupation of the journalistic and institutional literature on African famine relief has been with the logistics of food aid and distribution, reflecting the resilient popularity of this approach. But there is a good case for

[6] For valuable analyses of the problems involved, see Lofchie and Commins (1982), Berry (1984), Labonne (1984a, 1984b), IDS Bulletin (1985), Rose (1985), Society for International Development (1985), Eicher (1986a, 1988a), FAO (1986), Idachaba (1986), Lawrence (1986), Lofchie (1987), Mellor, Delgado and Blackie (1987), Platteau (1988a), Rukuni and Eicher (1987). See also Chapters 2 and 9.

[7] See e.g. Swanberg and Hogan (1981), Chastanet (1983), de Waal (1987), Glantz (1987b), McCann (1987), and Hay (1988). Numerous reports on the 1983–5 famines in sub-Saharan Africa also emphasize the acute problems caused (inter alia) by shortages of seeds, oxen, or human labour during the recovery period, often resulting in a shrinkage in sown area and other forms of production losses.

taking a broader view of the possible forms of intervention, and this part of our book will be much concerned with exploring other—often more effective —alternatives.

5.2   African Challenge and International Perception

It seems to be widely believed that most African countries lack the political framework (perhaps even the commitment) for successful pursuit of comprehensive strategies of entitlement protection. There may be truth in this in some cases. The inaction and confusion of some governments in the face of crises have been striking. The role of war in exacerbating food crises in Africa also needs persistent emphasis. Nevertheless, an excessive concentration on failure stories has given a vastly exaggerated and undiscriminating impression of the apathy, incompetence, and corruption of African governments in the context of famine prevention. In fact, contrary to popular belief, there is some evidence that the willingness and ability of many African countries to respond to crises have been improving over time, in some cases to a very considerable extent.[8]

Furthermore, as we shall argue later, state action is not immune to the influence of political ideology, public pressure, and popular protest, and there is nothing immutable in the nature of contemporary African politics. It is, of course, true that the development of a workable system of famine prevention calls for political as well as economic restructuring, but political changes—no less than economic transformations—are responsive to determined action and popular movements.

While examining experiences of success and failure in famine prevention, it has to be recognized that international perceptions of these past experiences are often seriously distorted. In particular, for reasons of journalistic motivation (which has its positive side as well, on which more presently), the media tend to overconcentrate on stories of failure and disaster. To the extent that successes do get reported, the balance of credit is heavily tilted in favour of international relief agencies, who enjoy—and need—the sympathy of a large section of the public.

This phenomenon is well illustrated by an episode of successful famine prevention in the state of Maharashtra in India in 1972–3. The impressive success achieved at the time by the government of Maharashtra in preventing a severe drought from developing into a famine by organizing massive public works programmes (at one point providing employment to as many as 5 million men and women) is described in Chapter 8. This event, however, caused very

[8] See e.g. Borton and Clay (1986), CILSS (1986), Caldwell and Caldwell (1987c), Hill (1987), Wood, Baron and Brown (1986), and World Food Programme (1986a). The last, for instance, reported on the basis of field missions in Burkina Faso, Chad, Mali and Niger after the crisis of 1983–5 that 'in all the countries visited, governments had made tremendous efforts to organise relief activities effectively' (p. 3). As we shall see, very impressive capabilities to respond are now clearly visible in such diverse countries as Botswana, Cape Verde, Kenya and Zimbabwe (see Chapter 8).

few ripples in the Western press, and received extraordinarily little attention from social scientists outside India.[9]

While the government of Maharashtra was employing millions of people on relief works, various international agencies were involved in feeding programmes on a relatively tiny scale—often importing modest amounts of wheat, biscuits, and milk powder from the other side of the globe. However, the role of the latter appeared to be oddly exaggerated. One of the relief organizations —indeed one that has altogether distinguished itself for many years by its far-sighted initiatives and actions—had no hesitation in reporting in its bulletin how a poor peasant sighed that the drought 'may be too big a problem for God; but perhaps OXFAM can do something'. There are other self-congratulatory snippets in the same vein about OXFAM's heroic deeds in Maharashtra and other drought-affected parts of India at that time:

'I suddenly realised that, driving 20 miles out of Ajmer on the road to Udaipur, all the scattered green patches I saw in the brown desert were in some way or another due to OXFAM.'

'In spite of the feeding programme the children have not gained weight. Stina at first thought her scale was wrong, but she discovered that the children now get almost nothing to eat at home. One shudders to think what would have happened to them without the feeding scheme. What's happening in other villages, where we aren't feeding?'[10]

The donor's exaggerated perception of its achievements is coupled with a comparatively patchy account of what the government was doing on an enormously larger scale. As late as December 1972, by which time the government-led relief programme was in full swing, the same bulletin reports: 'we have no information as yet of the extent of the Indian Government's programme'. The fact that an organization with as remarkable a record of helpful action and leadership as OXFAM could fall into this trap of making mountains out of molehills and molehills out of mountains shows the difficulties of objective perception and reporting on the part of an institution directly involved in the act of relief and dependent on the preservation of a heroic public image.

The highly selective focus of public discussions on famine is also evident in the case of Africa. For instance, until recently Botswana's remarkable record of famine prevention had received very little recognition, to the point that a

---

[9] The first in-depth analysis of the Maharashtra drought published in an international professional journal outside India is that of Oughton (1982). On the role of public policy in averting a possible famine and the lessons to be drawn from this experience, see McAlpin (1987) and Drèze (1988a). See also Chapter 8.

[10] These citations are from OXFAM (1972, 1973) and Hall (1973). It must be emphasized that it is not the intention here to blame OXFAM in particular for sharing in a form of disaster reporting that seems to be, in fact, common to the publications of many relief agencies when these are addressed to the wider public. The point is simply to illustrate certain biases which an institution of this kind seems to find hard to resist.

FAMINES

Table 5.1 Food and agricultural production in sub-Saharan Africa, 1983–1984

Country	Per capita food production 1983–4		Per capita agricultural production 1983–4	Growth rate of agricultural production per capita 1970–84
	(1979–81 = 100) (1)	(1976–78 = 100) (2)	(1979–81 = 100) (3)	(% per year) (4)
Cape Verde	62	n/a	n/a	n/a
Zimbabwe	73	68	82	−1.4
Niger	83	78	83	0.7
Botswana	83	n/a	84	−3.8
Kenya	87	82	93	−1.3
Senegal	88	70	89	−2.1
Mozambique	88	75	87	−4.3
Ethiopia	88	94	88	−0.6
Sudan	89	72	93	−0.5
Togo	90	93	90	−1.1
Zambia	92	89	93	−1.1
Angola	93	81	91	−5.6
Guinea	93	92	94	−1.0
Malawi	93	100	96	0.1
Tanzania	95	91	93	−0.6
Burundi	95	87	95	0.5
Côte d'Ivoire	95	111	90	0.5
Cameroon	96	83	95	−0.8
Burkina Faso	98	90	99	−0.2
Uganda	98	96	100	−1.7
Ghana	98	80	98	−3.9
Nigeria	98	88	98	−1.0
Zaire	101	97	102	−0.6
Liberia	102	100	99	−1.4
Benin	103	85	104	−0.3
Sierra Leone	104	84	101	−0.5
Mali	106	90	105	0.8
Guinea-Bissau	114	92	114	−0.9

Note: The countries included in this table are all those for which data are available from each of the three sources; Cape Verde has been added using van Binsbergen (1986), Table 3. Figures for 1983–4 have been calculated as an unweighted average of 1983 and 1984.

Sources: (1) and (3): Calculated from FAO, *Monthly Bulletin of Statistics*, Nov. 1987. (2): Figures given by the United States Department of Agriculture, reproduced in J. Downing *et al.* (1987), Table 1.1. (4): Food and Agriculture Organization (1986), Annex I, Table 1.2.

leading expert on Africa described it as 'Africa's best kept secret'.[11] Examples of worthwhile but underreported successes in famine prevention in Africa, most of them involving large-scale government intervention, can also be found *inter alia* in countries as varied as Burkina Faso, Cape Verde, Kenya, Lesotho, Mali, Mauritania, Niger, Tanzania, Uganda, Zimbabwe, and even to some extent Chad and Ethiopia.[12]

It is arguable that popular interpretations of the 'African famine' of 1983–5 have themselves involved important misperceptions. Though drought threatened a large number of African countries at that time, only some of them—notably war-torn ones—actually experienced large-scale famine. There was no uniform disaster of the kind that has often been suggested. In fact, a probing interpretation of the mounting evidence on this tragedy could well uncover many more reasons for hope than for despair.[13]

It is, moreover, far from clear that those countries in which large-scale famine did occur were the ones most affected by drought. Such an impression is certainly *not* borne out by available food and agricultural production indices (see Table 5.1).[14] We shall argue, in fact, that the sharp contrasts which can be observed in the relationship between drought and famine in different countries have a lot to do with the contrasting quality of public action in various parts of Africa. In particular, a number of countries where drought was extremely severe in 1983–4 (indeed often more severe than in the much-discussed cases of Ethiopia or Sudan, in terms of declines in food and agricultural production indices) met with notable success in averting large-scale famine. Powerful illustrations are found in the experiences of Botswana, Cape Verde, Kenya and Zimbabwe (see Table 5.2, and also Chapter 8). There is as much to learn from these 'quiet successes' as from the attention-catching failures that can also be observed in Africa.

5.3 Informal Security Systems and Concerted Action

Rural communities faced with a precarious environment often develop sophisticated institutions and strategies to reduce or cope with the insecurity of their lives. A few examples of this phenomenon are the diversification of crops and herds, the exploitation of geographical complementarities in the ecosystem, the pursuit of 'symbiotic exchanges' between different communities,

---

[11] Eicher (1986b: 5). The experience of this country will be further discussed in Chapter 8.

[12] See e.g. Kelly (1987) on Burkina Faso; Freeman *et al.* (1978) and van Binsbergen (1986) on Cape Verde; Borton and Clay (1986), Cohen and Lewis (1987) and Downing *et al.* (forthcoming) on Kenya; Bryson (1986) on Lesotho; Steele (1985) on Mali; UNDRO (1986) on Mauritania; de Ville de Goyet (1978), CILSS (1986) and World Food Programme (1986e) on Niger; Mwaluko (1962) on Tanzania; Brennan *et al.* (1984) and Dodge and Alnwick (1986) on Uganda; Bratton (1986) on Zimbabwe; Holt (1983), Nelson (1983), Firebrace and Holland (1984), Peberdy (1985), Grannell (1986) and World Food Programme (1986a) on Ethiopia (including Tigray and Eritrea); and Autier and d'Altilia (1985), Brown *et al.* (1986) and World Food Programme (1986b) on Chad.

[13] A large number of the references cited in the preceding footnote deal with the 1983–5 crisis.

[14] Nor is this impression confirmed by meteorological evidence (see J. Downing *et al.* 1987).

Table 5.2 Drought and famine in Africa, 1983–1984: contrasting experiences

Country	Percentage decline of production since 1979–81		Growth rate of per capita total gross agricultural production (1970–1984)	Outcome
	Food	Agriculture		
Cape Verde	38.5	n/a	n/a	Mortality *decline*. Nutritional *improvement*.
Zimbabwe	37.5	18.5	−1.4	Mortality *decline*. No sustained nutritional deterioration.
Botswana	17.0	16.5	−3.8	Normal nutritional situation. No starvation deaths.
Kenya	13.5	7.5	−1.3	No starvation deaths reported. Possibility of nutritional deterioration.
Ethiopia	12.5	12.5	−0.6	Large-scale famine.
Sudan	11.0	7.0	−0.5	Large-scale famine.

Sources: The figures on food and agricultural production performance are from the same sources as Table 5.1. On the assessment of 'outcome' in Botswana, Cape Verde, Kenya, and Zimbabwe, see Chapter 8. For estimates of excess mortality in Sudan and Ethiopia during the 1983–5 famines, see e.g. Otten (1986), de Waal (1987), Jansson *et al.* (1987) and Seaman (1987).

the development of patronage or reciprocal gift-giving, the recourse to complex dietary adjustments, and the storage of food or body fat.

It has been pointed out that informal security systems of this type have, *inter alia*, the great merit of not leaving the rural community at the mercy of undependable sources of external assistance. Appreciaton for these and other virtues of traditional responses to the threat of famine has, in fact, not infrequently resulted in an expression of considerable alarm at the prospect that traditional abilities to cope with the threat of famine might be dangerously weakened or even undermined by the interference of externally provided forms of entitlement protection.[15] This claim has to be taken seriously, and its

[15] For some variations around this theme, see Morris (1974, 1975), Colson (1979), Torry (1979), Wohlt *et al.* (1982), Cuny (1983), Turton and Turton (1984), Campbell (1986, 1987), Downing (1986), Zinyama *et al.* (1988), Devereux and Hay (1988), and Eldredge and Rydjeski (1988).

assessment must be based on a careful appreciation of how informal security systems function in practice.

Some of the coping strategies that have been referred to in the literature on informal security systems essentially consist of dealing with the risk of entitlement failure through some form of *individual precaution* at the household level. An important example is that of food storage, e.g. storing foodgrains, keeping animals, developing body fat. It is easy to see, however, that taking extensive precautions individually, without any pooling of risks, can be a difficult and costly business, and it can entail large losses of *average* entitlements compared to a situation where more efficient forms of insurance opportunities are available. For instance, storage has a high opportunity cost in the form of foregone investment in productive activities. Given their costs, therefore, it is hardly surprising that the scope for using precautionary measures can be rather limited for poor households. This way of tackling vulnerability may be nowhere near adequate.

Further opportunities for pursuing security arise from *mutual insurance*, and the attempt to obtain a better distribution of risks *across* households, rather than coping with them individually. A simple example may help to bring out the potentialities and limitations of mutual insurance. Consider a fishing community consisting of fishermen and their families, where fishermen go out every day to fish but their daily individual fortunes are not related to each other. If, every day, 'lucky' fishermen feel a social obligation to give some fish to the less fortunate ones, a measure of insurance against poor catches will exist.[16] In fact, if a well-developed system of mutual credit or reciprocal gift-giving operates, individual fluctuations in catches will not 'matter' at all: for each family the daily consumption of fish need bear no relation to the individual daily catch of the family. In this example, fishermen can costlessly insure against the entitlement risks arising from individual variations and fluctuations in catches, in the sense that—if the system works well—they have the opportunity to even out the consumption stream without lowering its average level.[17]

There are good reasons why, in practice, opportunities for costless insurance are often difficult to exploit. In fact, sometimes such opportunities can be altogether absent. In the last example, the possibility of costless insurance depended crucially on the fact that the fortunes of different individuals were

[16] The phenomenon of 'reciprocal gift-giving' has sometimes been interpreted by anthropologists as a mechanism of mutual insurance. For discussions of the anthropological literature on informal security systems, see Torry (1979, 1987), Posner (1980), Cashdan (1985), Dirks (1980), and Platteau (1988b). The last author investigates an instructive example of the operation of reciprocal gift-giving as a mutual insurance mechanism in an Indian fishing community. For economic analyses of gift exchange, see Lundahl (1983), Akerlof (1984), Platteau (1988b).

[17] The partners in a contract of mutual insurance need not, in general, make symmetric contributions to the reduction of risk as in this example. On the subtler distinctions between risk-sharing, risk-pooling, risk-shifting, etc., see Newbery and Stiglitz (1981) and Newbery (1987a).

not related to each other. Clearly, a system of reciprocal giving would be useless in dealing with collective risks. For instance, in the event of an adverse fluctuation in the total catch of the community (with the catches of individual fishermen going down together) there will be little scope for the 'unlucky' families to rely on the 'lucky' ones. Similarly, if fishermen rely on the exchange of fish for rice to survive, and if the price of fish in terms of rice collapses, the scope for evening out misfortunes within the fishing community will clearly be very limited. This is no small spanner in the wheel, since collective risks applying to large sections of a population are often precisely what we are most concerned with in the context of famine vulnerability.

Informal arrangements for mutual insurance are, therefore, deeply problematic when it comes to dealing with collective risks. Their failure in circumstances of widespread calamity is in fact well documented: in times of famine, the ordinary rules of patronage, credit, charity, reciprocity, and even family support tend to undergo severe strain and can hardly be relied upon to ensure the survival of vulnerable groups.[18] Nor is this failure a new phenomenon: during the famines of ancient Egypt several thousand years ago it was already found that 'each man has become a thief to his neighbour', and the story of biblical famines is similarly replete with tales of introversion, conflict, and even cannibalism on the part of famine victims.[19]

Quite aside from the problem of collective risks, there are many reasons why, in practice, the design and enforcement of insurance contracts tend to involve considerable difficulties.[20] The difficulties present (particularly those related to the revelation of information) are, in some respects, less acute in small face-to-face communities, but the fact remains that generally insurance opportunities are neither 'costless' nor even particularly attractive for poor households. The miserable employment conditions which permanent farm servants are often willing to accept in exchange for some security of employment are a telling example of the sacrifices that may be involved in insuring against the worst eventuality.[21]

[18] The so-called 'breakdown of the moral economy' in times of severe collective crisis, in the past as well as in the present, is one of the best documented aspects of social responses to food crises. Dirks (1980) provides a good discussion of this phenomenon, and a survey of the literature. For some relevant empirical studies, see Colson (1979), Greenough (1982), Jodha and Mascarenhas (1985), de Waal (1987), Vaughan (1987), Chen (1988), and Rahmato (1988), among others. It should be mentioned that the breakdown of social ties is a common feature of the *advanced* stages of famines, and that in the early stages *greater* sociality may well be observed.

[19] The citation is from an ancient inscription, mentioned in Aykroyd (1974: 25). On biblical famines, see Dando (1983). See also Garnsey (1988).

[20] These difficulties include the 'incentive' problems arising from the need for some parties to elicit information which other parties may have little interest in revealing (see Newbery 1987*a*, for an excellent discussion). These problems are particularly acute in large and anonymous societies, but some of them are also important even in small, face-to-face communities. See Cashdan (1985), Torry (1987), Rosenzweig *et al.* (1988), and Platteau (1988*b*).

[21] An extreme example is that of 'bonded labour'. There are, of course, many other aspects to the causation of this phenomenon than the quest for security on the part of dispossessed labourers. But this part of the story is, in some cases, clearly an important one. See Breman (1974), Deshpande (1982), and Ramachandran (1986), among other contributions.

These limitations of informal security systems have to be borne in mind—no less than the potentialities mentioned earlier—when assessing their place in a programme of public action for famine prevention. It has been argued by many that, in order to be effective, famine prevention strategies should strengthen rather than undermine traditional security systems. There is no doubt an element of wisdom in this, and there are several important examples of such strengthening. At the same time, it has to be recognized that there may be nothing embarrassing in famine prevention policies having a partial 'displacement' effect on informal security systems, as long as this displacement effect reflects the greater effectiveness of public intervention. While careful account always needs to be taken of the possible adverse effects of public intervention on informal security systems, it would be a poor principle of action to attempt to preserve the latter at all cost.

Consider, for instance, the case of private storage at the household level mentioned earlier. It is to be expected that, if they feel more secure (possibly as a result of successful public intervention), individual households will store less and devote their resources to other—perhaps more productive—purposes.[22] If this is really why the reduction of storage takes place, such a development may be welcome. An instinctive conservationism regarding traditional institutions may easily take the form of nostalgic hopes rather than contributing to a pragmatic integration of formal and informal security systems.

The revival or strengthening of informal security systems, important as it often is, cannot be an adequate response to the challenge of famine. The effective protection of vulnerable groups requires redistributive mechanisms going well beyond what individual precaution or traditional systems of mutual insurance can deliver. The need to devise famine prevention systems that do not leave the rural community to its own fragile devices is inescapable.

5.4 Aspects of Traditional Response

An effective programme of public action for famine prevention must be responsive to the empirical features of informal security systems. As a prelude to further discussion of the forms which concerted action for famine prevention might take, this section briefly recalls some relevant findings from the literature on traditional responses to the threat of famine.[23] The discussion will

[22] This is indeed a plausible interpretation of the considerable decline of on-farm storage in India since the last century (Drèze 1988a). The decline of private storage against a background of *decreasing* famine vulnerability in Kenya is also noted in Downing (1986).

[23] The empirical studies on which this section draws include Firth (1959), Morris (1974, 1975), Jodha (1975, 1978, 1981), Lallemand (1975), Jackson (1976), Bernus (1977a, 1977b, 1986), Faulkingham (1977), Gallais et al. (1977), Scott (1976), Colson (1979), Popkin (1979), Prindle (1979), Berlin (1980), O'Leary (1980), Campbell and Trechter (1982), Greenough (1982), Schware (1982), Chastanet (1983, 1988), Watts (1983, 1984), Campbell (1984, 1986, 1987), Cutler (1984a, 1985b, 1986), Turton and Turton (1984), Cashdan (1985), Jodha and Mascarenhas (1985), Negus (1985), Pankhurst (1985, 1986), Lombard (1985), Swift (1985), Tobert (1985), Caldwell et al. (1986), Downing (1986), Fleuret (1986), de Waal (1987), Akong'a and Downing (1987),

footnote continued overleaf

focus mainly on sub-Saharan Africa, and our remarks will concentrate on a few strategic elements of informal security systems, viz. (1) diversification and exchange, (2) dietary adjustments, (3) migration and employment, and (4) intrahousehold redistribution.

Diversification and Exchange

One of the earliest and most robust findings of anthropological studies in uncertain environments is that diversification is among the chief strategies adopted by vulnerable communities to reduce the precariousness of their lives. People learn not to put all their eggs in the same unreliable basket. The diversification motive is a pervasive aspect of economic decisions in uncertain environments, including those on cropping patterns, livestock management, occupational choices, and migration routes.

Opportunities for diversification can, of course, be greatly helped by the institution of exchange. While complete autarky may often be an admired achievement, it tends to be, in fact, a poor basis for security. Numerous historical and anthropological studies confirm that over the world vulnerable communities have consistently seen exchange as an opportunity for enhancing the security of their existence.[24]

Exchange itself can assume a multiplicity of forms, and the cash economy accommodates only one of them. Nevertheless, the acquirement of cash (especially through wage employment, but also through the sale of livestock, charcoal, craft work, assets, and even 'superior' foods) has now become one of the foremost responses to the threat of entitlement failure in sub-Saharan Africa.[25] The development of market exchange offers both new opportunities

---

footnote continued.

McCorkle (1987), Mamadou (1987a, 1987b), Sperling (1987a, 1987b), Vaughan (1987), Zinyama et al. (1988), M. Chen (1988, 1989), Dupré and Guillaud (1988), Matiza et al. (1988), Platteau (1988b), Pottier (1988), Rahmato (1988), Wheeler and Abdullah (1988), Brown (forthcoming), Kamau et al. (forthcoming), von Braun (forthcoming). Valuable discussions of informal security systems in more general terms can also be found in Torry (1979, 1986a, 1986b, 1987), Dirks (1980), Wynne (1980), den Hartog (1981), van Appeldoorn (1981), Lundahl (1983), Toulmin (1983), Scott (1984), Jiggins (1986), Longhurst (1986), Agarwal (1988), Corbett (1988), de Garine and Harrison (1988), Platteau (1988b), Chambers (1989).

[24] See Pankhurst (1985, 1986) for an illuminating discussion of this issue. The author insists, *inter alia*, on the importance of 'extensive pre-capitalist regional systems of exchange' in both East Africa and the Sahel, and on the role of market exchange as a 'safeguard against the vulnerability of subsistence economies to environmental risk' in pre-colonial African societies (Pankhurst, 1985: 42–3). The historical role of exchange in enhancing security is confirmed by examples of famines occurring as a result of the *disruption* of traditional exchange channels in some parts of Africa during colonial times. For some interesting examples, see Lugan (1976) and Herlehy (1984), among others. On the historical importance of market exchange in Africa, see also Gray and Birmingham (1970a, 1970b), Jones (1980), Eicher and Baker (1982), Hill (1986), and the literature cited in these studies.

[25] This observation is reflected in numerous recent studies of famine responses, including those of Faulkingham (1977), Bertlin (1980), O'Leary (1980), Campbell and Trechter (1982), Chastanet (1983), Watts (1983), Cutler (1985b), Swift (1985), Downing (1986), Fleuret (1986), Hale (1986), Pankhurst (1986), Akong'a and Downing (1987), de Waal (1987), Holland (1987), Bush (1988), Matiza et al. (1988), Pottier (1988).

and new threats. It is natural to expect that potential famine victims would attempt to use the market to overcome their problems, whether or not the problems themselves have been partly generated by a greater exposure to market fluctuations. When we turn to strategic issues of famine prevention in the next three chapters, we shall have to investigate the part that market operations can play both in undermining and in helping to protect the entitlements of vulnerable groups.

Dietary Adjustments

An important characteristic of dietary habits in vulnerable communities is their flexibility.[26] There is, of course, nothing particularly encouraging in the observation that, in times of crisis, affected groups resort to many ingenious forms of dietary adjustments. Indeed some of these strategies (such as programmed fasting or the gathering of wild foods) can be extremely painstaking and even dangerous. Of greater interest, however, are the general findings that (1) the reduction of food consumption tends to be an *early* response to the threat of entitlement failure, apparently motivated, at least partly, by the preservation of productive assets, and (2) substantial adjustments of consumption patterns are observed in times of economic adversity even in the behaviour of richer people who are not immediately at great risk of starvation.[27]

As we shall see in the next chapter, these findings are of far-reaching relevance for entitlement protection strategies. For example, they suggest that, in the event of a moderate but unpreventable decline in the availability of food, there is some scope for inducing a reduction of food consumption on the part of the relatively richer and not-so-vulnerable households. This adjustment can help to support the consumption of the most affected population. For instance, income support measures for the destitute population can, by putting an upward pressure on food prices, bring down the consumption levels of the more privileged groups, thus releasing food to meet the newly generated demands of the income-supported destitutes. The tightening of belts can be shared more easily given the priority that seems to be attached by rural households to preserving assets through adjusting consumption.

Migration and Employment

Two general points of crucial importance for public policy seem to have emerged from studies of migration patterns during subsistence crises in

[26] On this see Bernus (1977b), Fleuret and Fleuret (1980), den Hartog (1981), Campbell and Trechter (1982), Watts (1983), Fleuret (1986), Longhurst (1986), Downing (1988a, 1988b), and Drèze (1988a), among others. See also Chapter 8 below.

[27] The evidence from India, reviewed in Drèze (1988a) and recently supplemented by Pinstrup-Andersen and Jaramillo (1986) and M. Chen (1989), is fairly conclusive on this point. Few quantitative studies are available for Africa, but qualitative studies suggest a strikingly similar pattern—see Colson (1979), Watts (1983), de Waal (1987), Corbett (1988), Rahmato (1988), and Kamau et al. (forthcoming). See also the literature on survival during the period of 'soudure' in different parts of Africa, including Campbell and Trechter (1982), Dupré and Guillaud (1984), Lombard (1985), and the earlier studies reviewed in Mondot-Bernard (1982).

sub-Saharan Africa. First, among sedentary communities the migration of entire families is generally a last resort option.[28] The reasons for this are not difficult to understand. On the one hand, for a family used to a sedentary life, leaving a home can mean a severe social and psychological stress, extreme hardship for those too weak to travel, and selling off one's possessions or exposing them to theft.[29] On the other hand, when everything else has failed, migration does provide a hope, however faint, of access to new opportunities: the hospitality of relatives, the charity of city dwellers, or the presence of public relief camps.

Second, the migration of single adults in search of work appears, by contrast, to be an early response to the threat of entitlement failures in sub-Saharan Africa.[30] These movements mainly involve adult males, moving either to cities or to more prosperous rural areas. It is not immediately clear, of course, how this particular strategy can be expected to affect different household members. In principle, the departure of adult males can reflect the pursuit of three distinct objectives: (1) the *supplementation* of household resources through remittances (typically earned as wages); (2) the *release* of the migrant's share of joint household resources for the benefit of those who stay behind; and (3) the *abandonment* of other family members by the migrant.

Empirical examples can be found illustrating the operation of each of these three motives. But there is much evidence that the first motive is often the dominant one, and that remittances from absent adult males during periods of stress now represent a crucial form of entitlement support for vulnerable households in most African countries.[31] Particularly interesting in this respect are several recent studies showing a clearly positive association between food security and the migration of adult members in different households.[32]

There can, of course, be a problem of intrahousehold inequality in a process

[28] See Corbett (1988) for a review of the evidence on this point. The same observation has often been made in South Asia, where one turn-of-the-century commentator went so far as to assert that 'the dislike of the people to leave their homes was so strong that they would rather starve in their village' (Government of India 1898: 77, citing the Famine Commissioner of Madras). On the phenomenon of distress migration in South Asia, see Chakravarty (1986), Agarwal (1988), and the literature cited in these works.

[29] See Negus (1985: 15), Schware (1982: 215), and Hale (1986) for some examples of these anxieties.

[30] See e.g. Mwaluko (1962), Lallemand (1975), Caldwell (1977), Smale (1980), Watts (1983), Autier and d'Altilia (1985), Cutler (1985b), Swift (1985), Downing (1986), Hay (1986), McLean (1986), Akong'a and Downing (1987), de Waal (1987), Holland (1987), Government of Mali (1987), Dupré and Guillaud (1988), Brown (forthcoming).

[31] On the supportive role of cash remittances in the context of subsistence crises, and their close connections with wage labour, see Faulkingham and Thorbahn (1975) for Niger, Leys (1986) and Bratton (1987a) for Zimbabwe, Bush (1988) for Sudan, Akong'a and Downing (1987), Downing *et al.* (forthcoming) for Kenya, Dupré and Guillaud (1984) for Burkina Faso, Government of Mali (1987) for Mali, Hay (1988) for Botswana, Lombard (1985) and Chastanet (1988) for Senegal, Smale (1980) for Mauritania, van Binsbergen (1986) and Freeman *et al.* (1978) for Cape Verde.

[32] On this question, see particularly Lombard (1985: 38–40). Similar findings are reported for diverse sub-Saharan countries in the empirical studies of Dupré and Guillaud (1984: 31), Leys (1986), Akong'a and Downing (1987), and Vaughan (1987: 47), among others. See also Chapter 8.

which leaves the survival of women and children thoroughly dependent on the earnings and remittances of male migrants.[33] This intrahousehold consideration has to be kept in view when assessing the contribution of labour migration to the survival of different household members.

Intrahousehold Redistribution

The issue of intrahousehold divisions during famines has an important bearing on the strategy of public action for famine prevention. For instance, whether entitlement protection should be aimed at households or at individuals would depend quite importantly on the pattern and intensity of intrahousehold inequalities. We have already commented, in the previous chapter, on the question of gender discrimination during famines. A complementary aspect of the problem of intrahousehold divisions is that of the fate of children *vis-à-vis* adults.[34]

The history of famines over the world is full of gruesome stories of neglect, abandonment, sale, or even murder of children.[35] It is not really surprising that family ties can be significantly undermined by severe famines and crises. Whether the family also provides inadequate protection to children in subsistence crises of moderate intensity is a more open question. In fact, on this point empirical findings are much less clear-cut. If anything, the limited evidence available suggests the strong possibility that in early stages of a famine young children are *protected* at the expense of other family members.

There are three types of findings in that direction. First, a number of anthropological studies have found that, when food is short at the household level, young children tend to get priority in feeding. In their study of hunger and poverty in the state of Orissa in India, for instance, Fernandes and Menon report that 'during scarcity, children get first priority, then come men and then only women'.[36] Very similar observations regarding the preferential treatment of children in food allocation during crises have been reported in different parts of sub-Saharan Africa.[37]

---

[33] On the question of gender conflicts in African famines and particularly in the context of male migration, see Vaughan (1987). Vaughan's insightful analysis underlines the conflicts involved in the phenomenon of male migration during the famine of 1949 in Malawi (including the possible abandonment of women by their husbands). But it also brings out the positive overall contribution which male migration made to the survival chances of both men and women. Husbands who were reluctant to migrate in search of work or food appeared to be cursed by their wives in sarcastic songs (p. 32).

[34] Another problem of great social importance concerns the fate of the elderly. There is considerable evidence from anthropological studies that the old fare particularly badly during famines (see Dirks 1980, Greenough 1982, Vaughan 1987, de Waal 1988a, Rahmato 1988). This remains, however, an understudied problem, and its implications for public policy in particular need to be pursued much more extensively.

[35] For a detailed review, see Dirks (1980). The secret murder of starving children by their desperate mothers during the 1949 famine in Malawi is discussed by Vaughan (1987: 36).

[36] Fernandes and Menon (1987: 109).

[37] See e.g. Hale (1986), Rahmato (1988) and Wheeler and Abdullah (1988). See also Jelliffe and Jelliffe (1971).

Second, several quantitative studies of anthropometric status and nutritional intake during famines confirm that the burden of nutritional
adjustment often falls disproportionately on adults. For instance, the very
careful nutrition surveys carried out by Médecins Sans Frontières during the
1983–5 crisis in the Sahel found a pro-children bias in intrafamily distribution
compared to ordinary times.[38]

The third type of evidence, which is harder to interpret, relates to age
patterns of mortality during famines. Given the greater biological vulnerability
of young children to nutritional stress, one might expect that in spite of
special protection they would often suffer disproportionately from excess
mortality during crises. In fact, the evidence does not seem to support this
generalization.

Of course, the *absolute* mortality rates are almost invariably highest among
young children during famines. But this is true in ordinary times as well, and
there is no evidence that the *increase* in mortality is usually most pronounced
for the lower age groups. In fact, among the few studies presenting reasonably
accurate estimates of mortality by age groups both before and during a
subsistence crisis, a surprisingly large proportion indicate a lower (or at least no
higher) percentage increase in mortality for young children compared to other
age groups.[39]

The fact that intrahousehold divisions in famine situations appear to operate
often in favour of rather than against young children does not imply, of course,
that this group requires no special attention. Given the high fragility of their
lives, young children almost invariably account for a major share of famine
mortality even when the percentage increase in mortality is no higher for them
than for other age groups. The fact that systematic intrahousehold discrimination does not seem to be the clue to high infant and child mortality during
famines has important implications, however, for the choice of remedial
action. In particular, the case for striving to influence the intrahousehold
distribution of food in favour of young children during crises (e.g. through
direct feeding) would seem to lose some force to the extent that a bias in that

[38] See Autier and d'Altilia (1985) and Autier (1988). See also Binns (1976) on dietary change
among the Yana of Papua New Guinea during the 1972–3 food crisis, Biellik and Henderson
(1981) on the Karamoja famine of 1980, and Wheeler and Abdullah (1988) and Chaudhury (1988)
on the intrafamily distribution of nutritional stress during the lean seasons in Bangladesh and
Malawi.

[39] See e.g. Valaoras (1946) on the Greek famine of 1941–2, Sen (1981a: 210–4) and Greenough
(1982: 238) on the Bengal famine of 1943, O'Grada (1988a: 9) on the Irish famines of the 1840s,
Chen and Chowdhury (1977: Table 2) on the famines of 1971 and 1974 in Bangladesh, Maksudov
(1986) on the Ukrainian famines of 1927–38, Hill (1988) on the Chinese famines of 1958–61,
Meegama (1985: 324) on the food crisis of 974 in Sri Lanka, and the work of Dyson (1989) on the
demography of South Asian famines. In the case of *infants*, these findings have often been
attributed to the protective value of breast-feeding; but the studies mentioned here found
relatively low proportionate increases in mortality for non-infant young children as well. There
are, of course, exceptions to this pattern; see e.g. de Waal (1988a, 1989a) on the 1985 famine in
Darfur (Sudan).

direction often exists already within the family in such situations. We shall
return to this issue in Chapter 7.

From the analysis and evidence presented in this chapter and in Chapter 4,
some typical patterns do seem to emerge. It appears that, during the early
stages of subsistence crises: (1) the elderly are frequently neglected; (2) adult
women often bear a disproportionate share of the burden of adjustment in
comparison with adult men, but do not typically experience higher increases in
mortality; (3) young children seem to be comparatively protected, at least
initially, *vis-à-vis* other age groups; (4) in sub-Saharan Africa, there is no
evidence of widespread discrimination against girls in comparison with boys,
in the field of nutrition.

5.5 Early Warning and Early Action

Historical as well as contemporary documents on the subject of famine
prevention repeatedly stress the advantages of *early intervention*—in pre-
empting the disruption of population displacements, in containing the out-
break of epidemics, in preserving family solidarity, and in preventing the
emergence of famine expectations. These considerations are all the more
important if one accepts the view of famine prevention as being concerned not
just with containing mortality but also with preserving a certain normality of
life and preventing the loss of productive assets.

Arguing in favour of early intervention may sound like pushing against an
open door, since nobody, presumably, is in favour of 'belated intervention'.[40]
The sluggishness of action in the event of subsistence crises has indeed a lot
more to do with the politics of famine situations than with doubts about the
advantages of early intervention. But what bears emphasis is that the objective
of early intervention sometimes has distinct implications for the choice of
intervention method, and also that its attainment may require making con-
cessions on other fronts. For instance, while feeding centres and relief camps
may have a role to play in emergency operations, they clearly have little place in
early intervention strategies since (as we have seen) most people are not eager to
join relief camps until they have reached an advanced stage of destitution. And,
generally, the ambition of remedying intrafamily inequalities in famine
situations by *individual* intervention may have to be moderated in favour of
coarser but swifter intervention mechanisms operating at the level of *household*
entitlements.

This being said, the really important issues raised by the need for early
intervention are concerned not so much with detailed strategic considerations
as with the tougher problem of ensuring that resolute and early action will, in

[40] However, in some instances early intervention strategies *have* been criticized for involving
the risk of 'overreacting' in the form of intervening in a situation where in fact people are quite
capable of 'coping' (by which is usually meant surviving) on their own. See e.g. Morris (1974,
1975) and Waddell (1974), and the responses by Jodha (1975) and Binns (1976) respectively.

fact, be forthcoming in the event of a crisis. This is the context within which the related questions of preparedness, warning and response have to be seen.

The blame for delayed action is often put on inadequate information about the existence, or the exact character, of a crisis. There has, indeed, recently been a phenomenal surge of interest and involvement in so-called 'early warning systems'.[41] However, as we shall discuss in Chapter 8, it would be hard to see formal early warning techniques as having played a central role in recent experiences of successfully averted famine, whether in Botswana, Cape Verde, Kenya, Zimbabwe, or indeed India.

One frequently cited reason for the apparent redundancy of formal warning systems is their technical deficiency. There is certainly scope for refining existing approaches by moving away from mechanical analyses of the causation of entitlement failures. It is intriguing to note, for instance, that the Food and Agriculture Organization's Global Information and Early Warning System (this was, during the famine threats of 1983–5, the main source of regular information on potential food crises available to the member governments of the FAO) persists in concentrating on 'food balances' at the national level as the main variable of interest:

The Global Information and Early Warning System of the Food and Agriculture Organization (FAO) has three main functions. First, it monitors the *global food supply* position . . . Second, it monitors the food supply position at the national level and alerts governments to emerging *food supply problems* . . . Third, assistance is provided to strengthen national early warning capacities in developing countries . . . These national and regional projects aim at providing a low-cost system of monitoring which brings together all the indicators on the *food supply* position and prospects which are available in the country.[42]

This focus is perhaps not unnatural for an agency whose main concern is to assist various countries with food supply management. But it can clearly not form the basis of a reliable anticipation of threatening famines.[43]

---

[41] One study finds the current situation of duplication, heterogeneity and even inconsistency of independent efforts to be quite 'surrealistic' (CILSS 1986: 67). That study, which is not meant to be exhaustive, identifies no fewer than 39 different early warning systems in the Sahel alone, of which 14 are engaged in primary data collection and 25 'recycle' information collected by 'more or less competing agencies' (p. 69).

[42] Newhouse (1987: 6), italics added (on the GIEWS, see also FAO 1987*a*). Admittedly, the same document emphasizes that national early warning systems include the analysis of various 'socio-economic variables' of greater interest, such as 'cereal prices, cereal stocks, market arrivals, population movements, cattle prices and slaughter rates, length of queues at food shops, nutritional indicators, etc.' (p. 22). However, the role of these variables is seen as one of providing 'direct clues to emerging food supply problems', and the exercise therefore seems to remain instrumental to the ultimate purpose of gauging food supplies. It should be mentioned that many of the current problems of early warning systems are better understood when due recognition is given to the fact that, in practice, the purpose of these techniques is often more to *establish a credible claim for food aid* than to galvanize the domestic government into action.

[43] For a telling critique of the shortcomings of the 'food balances approach' with reference to the African crisis of 1983–5, see Torry (1988*a*). In the case of many African countries, the problem of misleading focus is compounded by that of atrocious production statistics, as a number of

Nor is the solution simply to shift the focus from food supply to another single variable (e.g. crop failures, changes in food prices, etc.), leaving out the rest of the system. The 'crop failures' approach, for instance, has been found quite useful in countries where the growing of crops (food *or* non-food) is, directly or indirectly, a major source of livelihood for vulnerable groups. But it can by no means be relied upon mechanically, and its predictive power has in some cases failed quite miserably.

A similar remark applies to early warning techniques based on food prices. Close association has been found between famine vulnerability and the level of food prices in a number of recent studies.[44] Indeed it is hard to think of a variable which exerts a comparable influence on the entitlements of large numbers of people. But it is also easy to see how starvation can hit particular occupational groups without being accompanied by a sharp increase in food prices. Again, historical experiences clearly point to the need for a more discerning assessment of the entitlement process.[45]

It is sometimes thought that a handy shortcut through this problem is to monitor nutritional status directly. This 'nutrition surveillance' approach has its uses, but for purposes of early warning it is now widely thought to be of limited value. The main reason is that, given the time needed for visible signs of increasing deprivation to develop, nutrition surveillance gives practically no advance indication of an impending crisis.[46]

There is no escape, then, from giving a solid place to economic and social analysis in attempts to predict future crises. Food balances, crop estimates, cereal prices, wage levels, population movements, and indeed many other variables are all useful clues, but the real challenge is to put them together to arrive at a coherent picture of the entitlement process. A number of recent

---

authors have emphasized; see e.g. Berry (1984), Lele and Candler (1984), Eicher and Mangwiro (1986), CILSS (1986), Hill (1986) and Lipton (1986). Some authors have gone so far as to question whether the alleged decline in food production in Africa during recent decades has been adequately ascertained; see e.g. Berry (1984), Hay (1986) and Hill (1986).

[44] See particularly the works of Peter Cutler on Ethiopia (Cutler 1985*b*) and Martin Ravallion on Bangladesh (Ravallion 1987*a*), as well as the historical studies of Meuvret (1946) and Lardinois (1982, 1985). See also Seaman and Holt (1980) and von Braun (forthcoming).

[45] In India, the Famine Commission of 1880 ended its pronouncement on the existence of a fairly systematic association between food price increases and famine with a strong word of caution: 'It is a well-ascertained fact that prices which would be regarded as indicating famine in one part of the country are quite compatible with undisturbed prosperity in another' (Government of India 1880, para. 78). The Ganjam famine of 1888–9 later revealed that 'food prices were no criteria of severity in a famine' (Srivastava 1968), and the Famine Commission of 1898 expressed an even more sceptical view on this general question (see e.g. Government of India 1898: 18, 44, 158). For similar observations in contemporary Ethiopia and Sudan, see Sen (1981*a*: Chapter 7) and de Waal (1988*a*).

[46] See e.g. Rivers *et al.* (1976), Mason *et al.* (1984), Autier and d'Altilia (1985), Borton and York (1987). Nutrition surveillance can, of course, have functions other than just early warning. It has, for instance, been used with good effect to monitor health conditions in non-crisis as well as crisis situations (see e.g., Morgan 1985 on its use in Botswana).

contributions to the development of early warning techniques have considerably advanced in that direction, and this progress deserves to be welcomed.[47]

It would, however, be a mistake to regard early warning only as a question of generating information for governmental policy making. As we have already discussed, the informational exercise has to be seen in the wider context of the need to trigger early action. In this process, the diffusion of information, and its use as a basis for public pressure, are no less important than the task of data gathering and analysis.

In that task, the media can play a crucial role, both as conveyors of information and as organs of public criticism and advocacy. Other important influences are the activities of political parties, of voluntary agencies, and indeed of the wider public. In Chapters 8 and 11 of this book, we shall encounter several instructive examples of the importance of adversarial politics in forcing an early response from governments in power in the event of a crisis. It will also be apparent how the interest that a political opposition typically has to find out, disseminate and use information about an impending food crisis can make a crucial difference, if the opposition is allowed to function.

Official tolerance of political pluralism and public pressure in many African countries is, at the moment, quite limited. The opposition is often muzzled. Newspapers are rarely independent or free. The armed forces frequently suppress popular protest. Further, to claim that there are clear signs of change in the direction of participatory politics and open journalism in Africa as a whole would be undoubtedly premature. However, there is now perhaps a greater awareness of the problem and of the need for change. The long-term value of creative dissatisfaction should not be underestimated.[48]

---

[47] See, for instance, the pioneering work of Médecins Sans Frontières in Chad (Autier 1988), the bulletins of the Système d'Alerte Précoce in Mali, the work of Jeremy Swift on Turkana in Kenya (Swift, forthcoming), and the econometric modelling by Meghnad Desai (1986). For a survey of the literature on early warning, see Walker (1988).

[48] A distinguishing feature of many of the African countries which have been relatively successful in responding adequately to the threat of famine in recent years is the greater accountability of their governments. This question is further discussed in Chapter 8 below. On the role of the press in the context of African famines, and the emerging signs of positive change in some countries, see Hoffer (1980), Yao and Kone (1986), Mitter (1988), Reddy (1988). On the general role of 'enfranchisement' in influencing entitlements of different groups, see Appadurai (1984).

6

Famines, Markets and Intervention

6.1   The Strategy of Direct Delivery

Famine prevention is primarily concerned with the protection of food entitlements where they are in danger of collapsing. The way of doing this that taxes the imagination least is to transport food into the affected area (possibly from abroad) and to feed the vulnerable population (distributing cooked food or food to be cooked). This is indeed how famine relief is very often instinctively conceived. As a USAID report on famine relief in Ethiopia put it, 'the number one priority was supplying food and getting to the people who needed it'.[1]

This particular strategy, which may be called the strategy of 'direct delivery', remains the most popular one today, and accordingly the key to the future prevention of famines is often seen primarily in terms of increased food aid, more trucks, better roads, more precise 'targeting' of food distribution, and the like. But the strategy of direct delivery is not always the most effective approach to the protection of entitlements. In fact, as we shall see in Chapter 8, it has played at best a secondary role in some of the most effective famine prevention systems in the world, not only in India but also in other regions including Africa. And the historical experience of famine prevention in different parts of the world actually includes a rather impressive variety of unevenly successful approaches to the protection of food entitlements: feeding, food distribution, public works, cash doles, price control, tax relief, crop insurance, the support of livestock prices, and many others.

The case for scrutinizing alternative entitlement protection strategies is all the more important because, apart from not being particularly ingenious, the strategy of direct delivery is intrinsically vulnerable to severe administrative and logistic failures. The requirement of transport makes the provision of relief dangerously contingent upon the successful and timely movement of food, sometimes all the way from the other end of the world to the very mouths of the starving, and often in painfully adverse conditions. The disruption of relief efforts as a result of the failed or delayed arrival of food is one of the most widely observed (and predictable) defects of the strategy of direct delivery, even in countries such as India and Botswana where management and logistic capabilities are comparatively good.

The difficulties arising in the process of distribution are no less important. If food is distributed through centralized feeding or distribution centres, intervention is inevitably confined to an advanced stage of distress (with all the

---

[1] Office of Foreign Disasters Assistance (1985: 27).

attendant disadvantages mentioned earlier). Indeed, the attendance at feeding centres requires the displacement of families, and, as we discussed in the previous chapter, sedentary populations typically resist—with good reason —the decision of abandoning their homes until they are completely hopeless and their hardship has become very acute indeed.[2]

The distribution of food need not, of course, take place in large feeding or distribution centres, and many countries have a growing experience with decentralized distribution systems. But here the scope for concentrating public support on the most vulnerable is usually much more limited, because the close monitoring of food distribution at the local level requires administrative resources far exceeding those of most famine-prone countries. One is, therefore, constrained to rely on rather indiscriminate allocation mechanisms, such as public distribution with universal eligibility, or distribution mediated by local institutions. Given the limited resources that are typically obtainable for famine prevention efforts, a serious consequence of indiscriminate distribution is that it may become impossible to provide enough support to the most vulnerable people to protect them from starvation.

The defects of the strategy of direct delivery are visible in the experience of relief operations during the crisis of 1983–5 in Africa. In spite of commendable experiments with innovative approaches to famine relief in a number of places, direct delivery was the main plank of entitlement protection in this event. A number of adverse but predictable consequences of this strategic priority are discernible in the evaluation reports dealing with this experience. First, logistic failures have been the most persistent drag on the progress of relief operations.[3] Second, while Africa benefited from a massive amount of food aid (about 5 million tonnes in 1984, enough to feed more than 25 million people throughout the year), much of it was given away in indiscriminate, inequitable or simply unascertained ways, with the consequence that in many places the most vulnerable groups did not get enough support to survive through the crisis.[4] Third, while the delivery of food through feeding centres, where it applied, obviously was not entirely indiscriminate, it did little to prevent

---

[2] Nomadic populations are, naturally, more mobile. But many of them have been found to be strongly reluctant to join the regimented life of relief camps except under the most extreme hardship.

[3] On this, see the various periodical publications of the World Food Programme, the Office for Emergency Operations in Africa, the Office of the United Nations Disaster Relief Coordinator, the United Nations High Commissioner for Refugees, and the numerous evaluations of these emergency operations, including especially World Food Programme (1986a, 1986b).

[4] See e.g. Ray (1984), Tobert (1985), Hale (1986), Holthe (1986), Pearson (1986), World Food Programme (1986a, 1986b, 1986c), Keen (1988), and also *The Economist*, 20 July 1985 and 30 Nov. 1985. The World Food Programme, under whose auspices the bulk of emergency relief was provided, recognized in a refreshingly frank evaluation that 'the well known difficulties that relief authorities face in selecting the beneficiaries of emergency assistance . . . led [them] to effect general distributions to entire populations of drought-stricken areas' (World Food Programme 1986a: 3), and that 'in most cases, neither WFP nor bilateral food could be properly traced to the beneficiaries' (World Food Programme 1986b: 13). For an even more critical account, see Torry (1988a).

population displacements, with which the development of famine situations was chiefly associated.[5] Fourth, in several countries a large part of the food aid intended for famine relief in 1984 in fact arrived after the bumper harvest of 1985, aggravating the glut of local markets.[6]

The real question, of course, is whether more effective alternatives really exist to a strategy of direct delivery. One way of seeing the unnecessarily restrictive nature of this strategy is to recognize that the protection of entitlements through direct delivery essentially conflates two distinct forms of intervention in the single act of food distribution: first, an injection of food in the system; and second, selective generation of income, i.e. of the means to acquire food. Greater effectiveness in the provision of relief can often be achieved by 'separating' the two—for instance, by selling food in the market and separately providing some form of income support to the needy.

The case for concentrating on direct delivery relies implicitly on the combination of two assumptions: (1) that no effective entitlement protection is possible without a commensurate and simultaneous increase in food availability, and (2) that no reliable channel for increasing food availability exists other than the famine relief system itself.[7] Much of our concern in this chapter will be to reconsider these assumptions carefully.

6.2 Availability, Prices and Entitlements

As we have stressed in the first part of this book, it would be a gross mistake to conclude from the entitlement approach that food availability is unimportant or unhelpful in protecting food entitlements. A greater abundance of food, if nothing else, usually means cheaper food, and lower food prices improve the entitlements of those who are on the demand side of the market—the side to which vulnerable groups typically belong. The advantages of a greater abundance of food will tend to apply irrespective of the process through which the entitlements of these groups are threatened in the first place, and in particular irrespective of whether or not the threat of famine is accompanied by any decline in the availability of food.

An improvement in food availability in regions threatened by famine can, of course, be achieved in a number of different ways. Food aid is an obvious possibility, which tends to capture a lot of attention. An alternative comes from

[5] See World Food Programme (1986b).

[6] See CILSS (1986), Pearson (1986) World Food Programme (1986a, Annex IV), and McLean (1987, 1988). Great care is, however, needed in assessing the precise impact of plummeting post-harvest grain prices on different occupation groups. For a helpful analysis of this problem in the case of Sudan, see de Waal (1987).

[7] Strictly speaking, while direct delivery of food by the state or a relief agency tends to add to the supply of food in the area, the net increase may be quite different from the gross amount directly delivered since there can be a 'displacement effect' on the normal—usually private—operations in the food market. Usually the displacement effect would be negative (since the price reduction consequent on direct delivery will reduce the incentive of private traders to bring in food), though in situations of manipulative speculation direct delivery may also have the effect of countering strategic hoarding.

commercial imports on government account, and during the 1983–5 food crisis in Africa many countries did indeed make use of this opportunity.[8] The depletion of public stocks, when these exist, is another option. Food can also be moved into the affected region through the channel of private trade, which again has played a prominent role not only in India but also, quite often, in Africa as well. Finally, in some instances the availability of food can be substantially improved by greater local production, including foraging, gathering wild foods, growing root crops, and slaughtering livestock. In planning public policy, it is important to recognize both the instrumental role that improved food availability can play in protecting entitlements, and the plurality of mechanisms that can be brought to bear on the supply of food.

Closely related to the question of food availability is that of food prices. The level of food prices is, in fact, one of the crucial variables mediating the relationship between aggregate food availability and individual entitlements.[9] As was noted in the previous chapter, sharp increases in food prices are a common, though not universal, feature of famines. It is also easy to see that the successful containment of increases in food prices would generally be helpful in protecting the entitlements of vulnerable groups.

One natural thought in dealing with high prices of provisions is that of imposing direct control on food prices. This has obvious attractions.[10] There are, however, serious difficulties in making good use of this strategy in a largely market-based economy without rationing. For one thing, effective enforcement is very hard, and the cases of successful reduction of prices through direct control have been quite rare. There is the further problem that even if prices are successfully kept low through control, this in itself does not guarantee that the available food will be equitably distributed. If prices are lowered below the level at which total demand is met by supply, the people failing to make a purchase might quite possibly be among those who were most vulnerable and deprived in the first place. An additional requirement will then be that of providing a minimal amount of food for all, or at least for the more deprived, through some form of direct rationing.

With adequate preparation, rationing can certainly make a big difference to the distribution of scarce food.[11] But the administrative and logistic requirements involved in successful controls on food prices along with extensive rationing can be extremely exacting. Moreover, the operation of rationing need not be conditional on directly controlling free market prices *as well*, and there can be dual markets with the coexistence of a limited 'ration' of food for all and,

[8] See Borton and Clay (1986).

[9] This is one of the major themes of Martin Ravallion's important and far-reaching study of *Markets and Famines* (1987a).

[10] See e.g. Jean Mayer (1975), who argues that 'price control is an essential measure in any famine situation', and that 'it has to be vigorously enforced' (p. 81).

[11] For example, in Britain, war-time rationing in the 1940s certainly played a major part in maintaining—indeed in some ways improving—nutritional levels despite the strain on food supplies. On this see Chapter 10, and also Titmuss (1950) and Hammond (1951).

along with that, ordinary market operations. There are good examples of effective entitlement protection through food rationing without resorting simultaneously to comprehensive price control.[12]

There are also other ways of influencing food prices than the imposition of direct controls, for example through the importation of food, the participation of the public sector in food distribution, or various forms of regulation of the activities of private traders. The merits of some of these forms of intervention in different contexts will be discussed in later sections of this chapter.

It would be a mistake, however, to see the moderation of food prices as the overriding objective of famine relief policies. Indeed, in some cases an increase in food prices can emerge as an acceptable side effect of entitlement protection policies themselves. For instance, it is often sensible to protect entitlements by generating cash incomes for vulnerable groups, and some increase in food prices may then result from their greater purchasing power. Price increases will, in this case, play a positive part in shifting food in the direction of the poor. This will take place partly through the reduction of consumption on the part of other—less vulnerable—groups, and partly through increased flows of food from other regions, greater depletion of stocks, and perhaps some increase in the production of food even in the reasonably short run.

Price increases of this kind obviously have an altogether different significance from the price increases that would result, say, from the manipulative activities of colluding traders. Conversely, it is easy to think of examples where the moderation of prices would be achieved at the expense of a deterioration in the entitlements of vulnerable groups. When evaluating alternative forms of intervention, the focus has to be on the entitlement process as a whole, rather than simply on the level of prices as such.

6.3   Private Trade and Famine Vulnerability

The possible influence of private trade in alleviating or exacerbating distress during famines is a theme that is not always approached dispassionately. For some, the business of trafficking in food amidst raging starvation is a particularly objectionable form of anti-social profiteering. For others, faith in the positive contribution of private trade is part and parcel of reliance on the logic of the price system. Correspondingly, government policies towards private trade during famines have often varied between the dangerous extremes of indiscriminate liberalism and paralysing control. Famine victims have sometimes been sacrificed at the altar of economic ideology even when a willingness to rescue them apparently existed.

There is, in fact, abundant empirical evidence from various famines of both negative and positive influence of private trade. At times it has been responsible for manipulative operations on the part of professional speculators.

---

[12] Effective use of this means can be related, for instance, to the nutritional achievements of Kerala and Sri Lanka (see Chapters 11 and 12). The role of public distribution, both in protecting entitlements and in effectively promoting them, will receive further attention later on in this book.

Large-scale exports of food from famine-affected areas have also been commonly observed. But in other cases private trade has performed a more positive function, typically by moving food towards famine-affected areas and containing the increase of prices in those regions. And the disastrous consequences of deliberate paralysing of private trade by governments have been a notable feature of several modern famines. These empirical observations suggest the need for discrimination in appraising the role of private trade in entitlement protection.

Private traders tend to move food from low-price to high-price areas. This is indeed how they make profits.[13] Such food movements normally lead to a moderation of food prices in high-price importing areas and an increase in low-price exporting areas. As a result, price disparities between different regions should tend to get reduced.[14]

This process will typically alleviate the intensity of famine if two conditions are satisfied. First, in a given locality a moderation of food prices should improve the food entitlements of vulnerable groups. This is quite a plausible assumption, since vulnerable groups are rarely on the selling side of the food market. The second condition is that, across different localities, there should be a positive association between the intensity of distress and the level of prices. If, in contrast, the worst-affected areas are in fact low-price areas, the movement of food towards high-price areas will exacerbate—rather than reduce—the intensity of famine.

As we saw in the previous chapter, the fulfilment of this second condition is by no means universal. The history of famines in fact contains abundant examples of *export* of food through private trade *from* famine-affected regions to elsewhere. The Famine Commission of 1880 in India, for instance, recognized with embarrassment but also resolute apathy the persistence (and in fact expansion) of large-scale exports of grain from the country all the way through the preceding years of famine:

Unluckily for the Indian consumer, there have been several bad harvests in England, and this and the exchange have stimulated a great export of grain for the last few years. This gain of the producing class and its adjunct, the bunyah [trader], has been so far the loss of the consuming class. This seems inevitable.[15]

Other well-documented examples, such as that of the Irish famine of 1845–8, inescapably confirm the genuine possibility of food 'counter-movements' during famines.[16] This contrary phenomenon was not absent during the recent

---

[13] Private traders also make profits by speculating over time. This raises separate issues which will be considered in the next section.

[14] There are exceptions to this process, to be discussed later on in this section.

[15] Government of India (1880, Appendix I: 112).

[16] Substantial amounts of food were shipped from famine-affected Ireland in the 1840s to more prosperous England, where the ability to pay a high price for superior food was much greater than in Ireland. A moving account of the distressing experience of witnessing these counter-movements can be found in Woodham-Smith (1962). For analyses of food counter-movements, see Sen (1981a) and Chichilnisky (1983).

famines in Africa. There have, for instance, been consistent reports of large-scale food exports from famine-affected Chad towards countries such as Cameroon and Nigeria where food prices were more rewarding.[17]

While the possibility of such food counter-movements must be kept firmly in view, it would be a mistake to ignore the positive function that market-based transactions can play in relieving the distress of famines. As was discussed in the last chapter, within a country famine-affected areas are also quite often areas of relatively high food prices. In such cases the operation of private trade may reasonably be expected to have the effect of driving down food prices in hard-hit regions and thereby alleviating the intensity of the famine. It would, of course, be silly to insist on the generalization that the overall impact of private trade will invariably contribute to reducing aggregate mortality. But there is nevertheless some sense in seeing the sharing of distress over a wider area as essentially a good thing, when the configuration of prices is such that private trade does move food in the 'right' direction.[18]

An illustration, discussed in greater detail in Chapter 8 below, may help to explain the issue. This illustration relates to the behaviour of food prices in Botswana and Kenya during the droughts of 1982–7 and 1984 respectively.[19] In Botswana, food moves freely throughout the country, and the food market is fairly active and competitive (the government also participates in food trade and distribution). In this country, food prices have been found to remain strikingly close to each other in different regions during the drought. The increase in prices, aside from being quite uniform, was also fairly moderate (see Table 8.13 in Chapter 8). In Kenya, by contrast, food trade between different districts was severely controlled during the drought of 1984. While in some districts food prices were *falling* during the drought as a result of the inability of private traders to export surpluses to other parts of the country, in drought-affected areas food prices were rising very sharply in spite of government attempts to rush in food bought on the international market. The result was the emergence of extremely large price differentials between different regions, with food prices being, at one point, as much as ten times higher in some regions than in others. It would be hard to sustain the thesis that the sharp intensification of food price increases in drought-affected regions of Kenya in 1984, evidently associated with the restrictions imposed on interregional trade, was in any way helpful to vulnerable groups. It is easy to find

[17] See e.g. Hoeffel (1986) and Diesler (1986). There have been other recent cases of reported food counter-movements during famines, such as in the Wollo famine of 1973, the Bangladesh famine of 1974 and the famine of 1979–80 in parts of Kenya (see Hussein 1976, Holt and Seaman 1976, Belete *et al.* 1977, Alamgir 1980, Sen 1981a, Herlehy 1984).

[18] Ravallion (1987a) investigates the process through which a reduction of price differentials can lead to a moderation of overall famine mortality.

[19] See Chapter 8 for a more detailed account of the recent experiences of drought and famine prevention in these two countries, as well as of their respective marketing and distribution policies.

further illustrations from other countries pointing clearly in the same direction.[20]

There are, however, several important qualifications to the foregoing argument. First, the assumption of a positive association between the level of prices and the intensity of distress, while frequently justified, is not invariably so. If the famine region or country happens to be particularly deprived of purchasing power (because of low income and few assets), food prices can be lower there along with starvation. In these circumstances, free movement of food can worsen the situation by exporting food away from the most affected regions. On the other hand, an effective solution of this problem involves not only providing the distressed population with the ability to purchase food, but also making it possible for food supply to respond to the newly created purchasing power. This can be brought about by a combination of income support in the affected region along with permitting the movement of food in response to the demand generated by that income. On this more presently.

Second, private trade can take a direct role in reducing price differentials only as long as these differentials exceed transport costs. Where transport costs are high, as in many parts of Africa, the operation of private trade may allow quite alarming price differentials between regions to persist. This observation does not, of course, provide an argument for introducing *further* restrictions on private trade, but it is relevant for correctly gauging the extent of its influence on price differentials. A very similar remark applies to other limitations restricting the operation of private trade, such as credit constraints, poor information, or insufficient communications.

Finally, collusive behaviour by traders can interfere with the expected movement of food from low-price to high-price localities. The collective interest of traders is often to 'segment' markets and, in this instance, they may wish to prevent the moderation of prices in famine-affected areas by restricting their trade. This possibility must be taken seriously, and its empirical relevance has to be assessed in specific context. Cases of gross manipulation of the market by traders have certainly been noted, and public policy-making in this field should not fall into the trap of simply assuming this possibility away.[21] On the other hand, it must also be remembered that in most countries of Africa and Asia the 'traders' are not all portly merchants sitting on heaps of grain, but also include millions of poor buyers and sellers (many of them women) who are

---

[20] See e.g. the comparison between the drought of 1966–7 in the state of Bihar and the drought of 1970–3 in the state of Maharashtra (both in India) in Drèze (1988*a*), and the comparison between the droughts of 1910–15 and 1968–74 in the Sahel in Kates (1981). The emergence of enormous price differentials between adjacent regions of Ethiopia during droughts has also been attributed partly to the suppression of private trade in that country, inadequately compensated by positive state involvement in food distribution (see e.g. Cutler 1985*b*, Griffin and Hay 1985, and Griffin 1987).

[21] See e.g. Pearson (1986) and Bush (1988) on the Darfur famine of 1985 in Sudan.

willing to travel long distances, on foot if necessary, in order to transact food at more advantageous prices.[22]

In those cases in which the collusive and restrictive practices of traders may worsen the sufferings involved, there is also a serious issue in deciding on the best means of dealing with this threat. Legal restrictions on private food movements rarely prove helpful in counteracting collusive practices (sometimes quite the contrary), and the paralysis of private trade without a compensating state involvement in food trade can be a particularly dangerous policy. A more constructive way of preventing the emergence or persistence of such practices is often to ensure a measure of government participation in food trade—we shall return to this point in the next section. In this field, as in many others, the government's ability to help through positive action is both more promising and more ofen overlooked than the martial art of doing good through slapping down negative restrictions.

As far as traders are concerned, their contribution—positive and negative —is much too diverse to be summarizable in the form of some simple favourable or critical slogan. There is, of course, some wisdom in Bertolt Brecht's aphorism that 'famines do not occur, they are organised by the grain trade', but as a piece of causal explanation of famines it has some obvious shortcomings. The same qualification applies to Malthus's belief that famines are never exacerbated by trade, only ameliorated by it. That too is poetry rather than prose. The choice of public action in countering famines has to make use of the wisdom that prompted these remarks, without being blinded by their misleading claim to generality.

6.4   Speculation, Hoarding and Public Distribution

Many of the considerations applying to interregional trade are also relevant to the phenomenon of intertemporal transactions. To some extent, similar influences will be operating in determining the activities of private trade and their consequences on a famine-threatened economy. There are private gains to be made by successful intertemporal arbitrage, and one of the effects of this activity will often be to reduce the fluctuation of prices over time. Qualifications similar to those examined in the preceding section have to be considered in accepting the presumed outcomes of such arbitrage.

But the analogy between the temporal and the spatial is imperfect, and the evaluation of the role of intertemporal arbitrage cannot be based simply on mirroring the evaluation of interregional trade. There is a real asymmetry of

---

[22] Peter Cutler has noted that, during the early stages of the Ethiopian famine in 1984: 'There was grain available at normal prices some 60 km away from the drought zone. Indeed, peasants were walking this distance in order to purchase food and bring it home again—a very cumbersome load of some 50 kg being carried over a weary journey' (Cutler 1985*b*: 61). Similar findings have been reported from Mali (J. Downing *et al.* 1987: 234), Chad (Pol Barbier, personal communication), Malawi (Vaughan 1987: 123), and Zambia (Pottier 1988).

knowledge (in addition to that of operations) that applies between two time periods, and which does not have a clear counterpart in the case of two regions.[23] In particular, the role played by *expectations* about the unknown future in the process of speculation over time brings in a crucial complication.

Consider, for instance, a situation in which the general public is hoarding food at a ferocious rate in anticipation of a severe price rise, while the government happens to have reliable information about the arrival of a substantial amount of food from abroad in the near future. Even if the government publicizes the information it has, the public may still have good reasons (perhaps based on past experience) to be sceptical of the veracity of governmental statements. The immediate price rise caused by misguided speculation may lead to great hardship and even starvation on the part of the more vulnerable, and the government under these circumstances may well have good reasons to interfere severely with private markets to prevent that outcome. One can think of similar cases with a different scenario in which the government has a role in supplementing and supplanting private trade to deal with the adverse effects of misguided speculation. This type of problem of general failure of public knowledge about the future can be a serious reason for seeing a more crucial role for public action in the field of intertemporal transactions than in interregional trade.[24]

Professional speculators may, of course, be typically quite well informed, unlike the general public. The point has also been variously made, by Malthus, Mill, Friedman and others, that the unsuccessful speculators get eliminated by the market mechanism, and that the activities of surviving speculators can be expected to be stabilizing rather than the contrary. This argument is flawed for a variety of reasons, chiefly its inability to take an adequately detailed view of the different channels through which the actions of speculators affect the market.[25] Speculation *can* be destabilizing.

The real issue concerns what the government can do, faced with the possibly damaging effects of misguided or mischievous speculation. The administrative problems involved in imposing direct and effective controls on the holding of stocks by the public and by professional speculators can be enormous

---

[23] These asymmetries have different aspects. If food can be moved from region A to region B, it typically can also be moved from B to A. On the other hand, while passing on food from the present to the future can frequently be easily achieved (through stocking), there is no corresponding ease in moving food backwards in time. No less importantly, the future is unknown to people living now in a way that the present may not be unknown to the historians in future. There would tend to be, typically, more symmetry between regions in terms of their knowledge of prices and other information relating to the other regions.

[24] See Ravallion (1987a) for a study of the contribution of misguided private speculation (and inadequate public involvement) to the development of the Bangladesh famine of 1974.

[25] Even under favourable assumptions about the competitiveness of markets, the accuracy of traders' foresight, and risk-neutrality of individual behaviour, speculation can be 'destabilizing' (see Hart 1977, Hart and Kreps 1986, Newbery 1987b, and the discussion of this in relation to famines in Ravallion 1987d). *Additional* difficulties can arise from (1) the lack of competitiveness of markets, (2) inaccurate foresight, and (3) risk aversion on the part of speculators.

(especially when, as in much of sub-Saharan Africa, food stocks are mainly held by small farmers). Also, the atmosphere of emergency created by forced requisition may aggravate rather than appease the apprehensions of the public.

One of the alternatives to consider is the possibility of influencing expectations, and the behaviour of traders and speculators generally, by vigorous government *participation* in food trade and storage. The existence of public stocks, for instance, can go a long way towards reducing fears of future scarcity and also defeating the manipulative practices of private traders.

There is considerable empirical evidence of the potential effectiveness of this strategy. For instance, in his instructive analysis of the prevention of famine in Bangladesh in 1979, Siddiq Osmani persuasively argues that the public distribution system played a major role in inspiring public confidence in the stability of prices.[26] Similarly, in his account of the 1984–5 famine in Sudan, Roger Pearson describes how even marginal participation in food distribution and transport on the part of relief agencies could have dramatic effects on local prices: 'When it was heard that the first batch of food aid was to arrive in El Obeid in November 1984 the price of a 90 kg sack of sorghum declined from 135 to 75 Sudanese pounds'.[27] Strikingly similar observations have also been reported in a number of other countries.[28]

In food policy, there is no panacea. The dangers of leaving matters entirely to private trade are obvious enough. At the same time, it is hard to escape the recognition that in famine situations many African governments have missed the opportunity of supplementing their own logistic resources by a skilful use of what market trade can offer. Making room for private trade must not be confused with giving it an unrestrained and commanding influence on market operations, even when that influence has damaging effects on vulnerable people. It is possible to utilize the advantages—direct and indirect—of public distribution systems without taking on the Herculean task of managing all transactions through bureaucratic controls.

6.5 Cash Support

In section 6.1 we suggested that one of the important factors accounting for the frequently belated and insufficiently effective nature of famine prevention

[26] See Osmani (1986), and also Clay (1985b), Crow (1987) and Ravallion (1987a).

[27] Pearson (1986: 52). The author also argues that food aid had the immediate effect of breaking a traders' cartel in Sudan, which was 'perhaps the most important effect that the emergency operation has had on the lives of the majority of the poor in Sudan' (p. 87). On this question, see also Bush (1988).

[28] A report from the FAO in Chad, for instance, notes how the maintenance of a small public food stock provides 'psychological pressure on prices' and ensures that 'traders will not hold precautionary stocks' (FAO 1987b: 7). In Kampuchea, rice prices have been reported to fall by 80% within two weeks of the introduction of free public distribution (Mason and Brown 1983: 82).

efforts in Africa is the dependence of the chosen entitlement protection measures on the timely arrival of food aid, and generally on the complicated logistics associated with the direct delivery of food. The question, however, is whether and how this situation can be remedied. Greater use of cash support is an obvious option.

Cash relief is not a new idea. It is mentioned in the Bible, and has a rich history covering many parts of the world.[29] But the suggestion that it has a contribution to make to famine prevention strategies in Africa today is often met with resilient suspicion. This suspicion cannot reasonably arise from the belief that the conversion of cash into food might prove impossible in a famine situation. Indeed, as we discussed in Chapter 5, the earning of cash is now one of the most vital survival strategies of famine victims in African countries.

But there is a deeper problem. Even if it is accepted that having cash can almost always help an individual to acquire food and avoid starvation, it is less obvious that cash support can help a *community* taken together. After all, one person's ability to command food through cash support may adversely affect other people's entitlements, e.g. by exerting an upward pressure on prices. As we have seen in Chapter 4, 'food battles' can be intense, and the competition for market command is one of the forms which such conflicts can take. The merits of cash support therefore need to be scrutinized with considerable care.[30]

The debate about the merits and limitations of cash support has, in fact, involved two distinct issues which should not be confused. The first issue concerns the relative merits of food and cash as the *medium* of entitlement protection. Is it better (1) to provide people directly with food, or (2) to give them an equivalent transfer in cash with the corresponding amount of food sold in the local market? In considering this question in its pure form, the amount of resources (food *and* cash) used by the relief system is held constant by hypothesis. The second issue concerns the wisdom of giving cash income to the potential victims *without* adding a corresponding amount of food to the system. Here the comparison is between (1) taking direct action using cash, and (2) waiting for an improvement in food availability (e.g. through food aid) before extending support to vulnerable groups. This is really where the question of potential conflicts in access to food comes in. For convenience we shall refer to

---

[29] On the former, see Dando (1983), Sider (1980), and The Bible, Acts 11: 27–30. Cash relief has a long history both in India (Loveday 1914; Drèze 1988a) and in China (Mallory 1926; Will 1980; Li 1987), and has also been an important feature of famine prevention in a number of African countries more recently, including Botswana (Hay et al. 1986), Cape Verde (van Binsbergen 1986), colonial Tanganyika (Mwaluko 1962), colonial Zimbabwe (Holland 1987), and contemporary Ethiopia (Bjoerck 1984; Hilsum 1984; RRC/UNICEF 1984, 1985; Kumar 1985; Padmini 1985; von Kohl 1988).

[30] For a lucid examination of some of the important issues involved, following a line of analysis rather different from the one used here, see Coate (1986, 1989).

these two distinct issues as the 'cash medium issue' and the 'cash injection issue', respectively.[31]

Regarding the cash medium issue, it seems plausible that in the specific context of famine prevention, the choice of support medium (cash or kind) would be unlikely to have a major influence on the effectiveness of entitlement protection strategies. One reason why the medium of entitlement protection is not completely irrelevant is that households often treat income acquired in the form of cash differently from income acquired in the form of food. A number of recent studies strongly suggest that, in ordinary times at least, using food as a medium of support tends to influence the consumption of families in the direction of greater food intake.[32] But it is not unreasonable to expect that the contrast applies with much less force in the case of famine victims, for whom food intake becomes an overriding concern and absorbs the bulk of the resources they may succeed in acquiring.[33] The choice between providing food and providing cash may still matter to some extent, but it is hardly likely to have momentous implications for the survival chances of famine victims.

The more important part of the debate about cash relief relates to the cash injection issue. To come to grips with it, consider a scheme of cash-based entitlement support to vulnerable populations, such as a cash-for-work programme or a scheme of cash hand-outs. This policy will have the immediate effect of exerting an upward pressure on food prices, since the effective demand for food increases. But, as we have already noted, this inflationary pressure may be functional: in this instance the increase of prices has its origin in the greater purchasing power of the needy and is part of the process of improving (rather than undermining) their command over food. In order to assess the precise impact of an income generation strategy of this kind on the allocation of food in the economy, one must examine carefully the effects it is likely to have, via the price mechanism, on (1) the total availability of food in the affected region (through changes in production, storage, and trade), and

[31] In the formulation of the 'cash medium issue', we are assuming that, when cash rather than food is given to the victims, the corresponding amount of food is additionally supplied in the *local* market. A further question is whether it is, in fact, important that the relief system itself should deliver the food all the way to the local market. In terms of standard 'general equilibrium' theory, if cash payments to the victims include the relevant transport costs, the location of food sale would not matter. However, that analysis takes little note of some specific problems which may be important in practice, e.g. the relative speed and efficiency of public delivery *vis-à-vis* private trade, the possible importance of preventing the destruction of the normal infrastructure of trade and commerce, and so on. Some of these issues are investigated in Kumar (1985), Coate (1986, 1989), Sen (1986a) and Johnson and Zeckhauser (1989).

[32] On this question, see the empirical studies of George (1979), Kumar (1979), Harbert and Scandizzo (1982), Senauer and Young (1986), Edirisinghe (1987), and especially Garcia and Pinstrup-Andersen (1987).

[33] This conjecture is particularly plausible if the different treatment of cash and food income in ordinary times is due to a form of 'illusion' on the part of recipients (rather than, say, to different treatments of intrahousehold conflicts depending on whether outside help is received by the family in the form of food *or* cash).

(2) the distribution of the food available between different sections of the population.[34]

To start with, higher prices can have the effect of stimulating the *production* of food. It is tempting to think that in a famine situation the production of food is not responsive to price changes, but there are in fact good reasons to be sceptical of this belief. The literature on informal security systems discussed in the previous chapter abundantly shows that repeated sowing, growing alternative crops, reducing livestock feeding, and gathering wild foods are all very common responses to food crises, and all these activities are—up to a point—rendered more attractive by increases in food prices. It has been widely observed, for instance, that wild foods ordinarily eaten only by the poorest households become prized objects of consumption *and* market transactions during famines.[35] Interestingly, one of the observed effects of a cash-for-work programme implemented in Ethiopia in 1984 was that peasants in the area 'began . . . growing more' in response to an increased demand for food.[36]

The likely effects of price increases on *storage* decisions during famines in Africa are not easy to assess. The discussion of the previous section points to serious difficulties in forming prior judgements on this question, and the empirical evidence is also very limited. Some researchers have argued that, in famine situations, an initial perturbation in the level of prices could escalate and spread, as farmers and traders withdraw their supplies from the market.[37] But others have come to much less pessimistic conclusions. The timely depletion of stocks during the 1973 famine in the Sahel, for instance, is reported by Caldwell:

Even in 1973 some areas received close to their seasonal rainfall and grew adequate crops. The market encouraged the fortunate populations to tighten their belts and to sell food that they could spare either from the current harvest or from stored stocks. Indeed, it was the very high prices induced by the drought that led some farmers to sell stored stocks just at a time when the outsider might at first assume that he was storing most desperately.[38]

This judgement is not isolated, and further indications pointing in the same direction can be found elsewhere.[39] Great caution is of course required in

---

[34] There are other, potentially important price-sensitive aspects of food allocation which will not be investigated here, e.g. animal feeding, wastage and diet composition. For some relevant empirical findings in the context of subsistence crises, many of which strengthen the case for greater use of cash support in famine situations, see e.g. Faulkingham (1977), Tobert (1985), McLean (1986), Fleuret (1986), McCorkle (1987), and O'Grada (1988a).

[35] See Bernus (1977b), Dando (1982), Tobert (1985), Fleuret (1986), Longhurst (1986), McLean (1986), de Waal (1987) and M. Chen (1988).

[36] *Africa Emergency Report*, Apr./May 1986, p. 6.

[37] See particularly Seaman and Holt (1980).

[38] Caldwell (1981a: 8).

[39] The evaluation of the UNICEF cash relief project in Ethiopia in 1984 to which we have already referred, for instance, 'discovered that as demand for food grew within the area, peasants with small food surpluses began introducing them to local markets' (*Africa Emergency Report*, Apr./May 1986, p. 6). In his review of food security issues in the Sudano-Sahel, Brandt even comes

drawing conclusions from specific information of this kind, but there is certainly no strong evidence to support the view that the price increases that might accompany cash relief programmes would systematically encourage damaging speculative activities in sub-Saharan Africa (especially if public policy is intelligently used to counter manipulative practices).

Increases in food prices can also stimulate private *trade* and cause enlarged flows of food towards the famine affected area (or a reduction of food exports, if these are taking place). Reliance on this mechanism has indeed been one of the central planks of famine prevention in India for a long time.[40] India's circumstances are perhaps somewhat favourable to the smooth functioning of this mechanism, since crop failures in one part of the country are often compensated—at least partly—by good crops elsewhere, communications are well developed, and private trade is fairly alert. But the contrast between Indian and African conditions in these respects, while very real, is perhaps not as sharp as is often asserted.

In the common international perception, connected largely with the nature of media reports, African famines are often seen in terms of acute and more or less uniform 'shortages' of food everywhere in the affected country or countries. This is, however, little more than a myth, and in fact the scope for interregional food movements to alleviate the intensity of distress is often considerable. Large variations in food output between different regions are common in Africa, and a marketable surplus usually remains in or near the famine-affected territory.[41] This is most clearly the case when dealing with 'food crises' of a localized nature, as recurrently occur in different parts of Africa.[42] But even during the African famines of 1973 and 1984, both of which were rather extreme in terms of the extent and spread of the crop failures that accompanied them, a considerable potential for interregional food movements certainly existed in many places. John Caldwell, for instance, has argued that large regional variations existed in the severity of crop failures during the Sahel

---

to the conclusion that 'semi-commercial storage by farmers is already making a tremendous contribution towards the elimination of seasonal fluctuations of supply in the internal markets of the Sahel countries' (Brandt 1984: viii). A commentator on the famine situation in Africa in 1983–5 noted that 'in the Sahel, when the cereal crops (millet, osrghum) fail, other farmers who produce tubers (cassava, yam) rush to sell their surplus to the cereal farmers' (*The Economist*, 20 July 1985, p. 21).

[40] See Chapter 8 and also Drèze (1988a). The same strategy of trade stimulation through income generation played a crucial role in the famine relief system of 18th-century China under the Qing dynasty, on which see the major work of Étienne Will (1980). At one point the usual practice was to provide food relief and cash relief in identical proportions (Will 1980: Chapter 3).

[41] For examples of the sharp contrasts that are typically found in Africa in the extent of crop failures, not only between different regions, but also between different villages and even fields, see Caldwell (1975, 1977), Lallemand (1975), Rivers *et al.* (1976), Faulkingham (1977), Relief and Development Institute (1985), CILSS (1986), Fleuret (1986), Green (1986a, 1986b), Morgan (1986), Bratton (1987a), Vaughan (1987), Koponen (1988), von Braun (1988).

[42] The references cited in the preceding footnote provide many examples of localized entitlement crises in Africa. The persistence of famine in various parts of Africa in 1985, despite record harvests in most countries, has also been widely noted.

famine of 1973, and that sizeable movements of food were taking place within as well as towards famine-affected countries.[43] It would be a mistake to disregard the opportunity of reducing the forces of famine through encouraging food movements between different areas.

A further aspect of the problem, however, is whether private trade can be expected to provide adequate food movement when interregional movements of food *are* potentially helpful. The answer to this question cannot but be contingent on many specific considerations. In several parts of Africa (including much of the Sahel), there is a strong tradition of private food trade, sometimes over long distances. The dynamism of this tradition has been observed in several places during recent famines *in spite* of official discouragement.[44] Generally, there is considerable evidence that private trade in Africa is alive to economic opportunities when it is allowed to operate without bureaucratic restrictions.[45] Of course, sharp contrasts exist between different African countries, and it may well be that in some places a major reliance on the operation of private food trade to respond to the demands generated by cash support would be problematic. There are, however, no serious grounds for general pessimism in this respect.

Despite the possibly important effects of cash support on the total supply of food in the market through stimulating production, de-stocking, and trade, it is very likely that the increase in food availability will fall short of the increase in the consumption of those receiving cash support. Indeed, the same price rise which has an expanding effect on supply will also have a contracting effect on the demand for food of those who do not receive cash support but now face

[43] See Caldwell (1975, 1977). Similar observations have been made in the context of the 1983–5 crisis for different parts of Africa (World Food Programme 1986b: 14), and even for Ethiopia (see *Africa Emergency Report*, Apr./May 1985, p. 6, and Government of Ethiopia 1986). On the important contribution that interregional food movements seem to have made in alleviating a number of recent African famines, see also Caldwell (1977, 1984), Kates (1981), Hill (1987), Iliffe (1987).

[44] For instance, private trade (often clandestine) is reported to have flooded Burkina Faso in 1984 with Ghanaian maize and cereals imported from distant Abidjan and Lomé (Hesse 1985); imported 150,000 tonnes of cereals into drought-affected Mali in 1985 (Steele 1985); ensured 'a remarkable uniformity of grain prices throughout Nigerian Hausaland' during the 1973 famine (Iliffe 1987: 257); reached 'every day' a Sudanese town which was said by UN agencies to be hopelessly cut off by road mining (Garden and Musa 1986); and, less happily, *exported* large quantities of food from Chad in 1984–5 towards countries such as Cameroon and Nigeria (as noted earlier). The active role of private trade is also evident in many accounts of African famines during the colonial period. See e.g. Mwaluko (1962), Lugan (1976), O'Leary (1980), Herlehy (1984), Holland (1987), and de Waal (1989b).

[45] On the characteristics and functioning of food markets in Africa, see Bauer (1954), Club du Sahel (1977), Eicher and Baker (1982), Harriss (1982), and Berg (1986), among others. Of course, food markets in most African countries are far from completely 'integrated', but it is hard to separate out the extent to which this is due to bureaucratic regulation and control as opposed to the underdevelopment of trade.

higher prices. To that extent, a redistribution of consumption towards the protected groups will take place.[46]

The prospect of dealing with the threat of famine partly by inducing a redistribution process operating *within* affected areas strikes terror in the heart of many observers. They see this as a failure to respond to the 'real problem' of 'shortage' and as an attempt 'to transfer food from one victim to another'. It must be remembered, however, that large inequalities are a pervasive feature of most famine-prone societies. As was discussed in the previous chapter, the readiness of populations (poor and less poor) to alter their consumption patterns under the pressure of price and income changes in times of famine also seems to be much greater than is often imagined. The scope for redistribution from the relatively privileged to the most vulnerable may therefore be far from negligible. When direct delivery of food through the public relief system is hampered or slowed down by administrative and logistic difficulties, cash support may be a useful option, especially compared with leaving the problem unaddressed.

The feasibility of the redistributive mechanism is clearly illustrated by the experience of famine prevention in Maharashtra during the 1972–3 drought, to which we have already referred in the previous chapter. In this event, the government resorted to large-scale cash relief (in the form of cash-for-work programmes), and *separately* organized the supply of food through the public distribution system. The latter efforts, however, were hampered by logistic difficulties, and left a large gap between the availability of food in the state of Maharashtra as a whole and the normal level of aggregate consumption. To a considerable extent, this gap was reduced by the operation of private trade, which moved large amounts of food into Maharashtra (where public employment programmes generated a considerable expansion of purchasing power).[47] In spite of these additional food movements, a substantial decline in food availability occurred in the state during the drought, but the effect of targeted income generation measures was precisely to ensure that the reduction of average consumption was remarkably evenly distributed between different socio-economic groups, rather than the burden of reduction being entirely borne by the most vulnerable.

The success of the redistributive strategy, however, depends to a great extent on the ability of the relief system to provide preferential support to the entire vulnerable population. If substantial numbers of vulnerable people are excluded from entitlement protection measures but have to take the conse-

---

[46] It is conceivable that, in some rather special circumstances, cash transfers could lead (through 'general equilibrium' effects) to a *deterioration* of food entitlements for the recipient groups. But the empirical relevance of this 'transfer paradox' is rather limited in the context of cash support for famine victims.

[47] Interestingly enough, the drought occurred at a time when there were severe official restrictions on private interstate movements of foodgrains, so that the helpful movements of food were, in fact, 'illegal', even though the authorities evidently turned a blind eye on such movements.

quences of price increases, the overall vulnerability of the population could conceivably be exacerbated rather than diminished by the relief system.[48] An important question therefore concerns the need to cover all the major vulnerable groups, while continuing to exclude the more privileged in order to preserve the redistributive bias on which the success of the strategy of cash support depends. These and related questions are further discussed in the next chapter.

6.6   An Adequate Plurality

This chapter has explored the part that markets can play in precipitating or relieving a famine. We have also examined the possibility of making deliberate use of the market mechanism in public policy for famine prevention, in particular by providing large-scale cash support to famine victims. This investigation has focused on the substantial scope for effective use of cash support in famine situations.

We should, however, also warn against a possible misinterpretation of this conclusion. To recommend greater use of cash support is not to suggest that importing food into famine affected countries or areas is undesirable or unnecessary. Cash support and food supply management are not, by any means, mutually exclusive activities. Often, in addition to a strong case for the use of cash support, there is also a good argument for increasing the availability of food (e.g. by accepting food aid). Our contention is not that cash support should *replace* efforts to improve food availability, but only that in many circumstances there is no need to make entitlement protection conditional on the direct delivery of food.[49]

A related observation of some importance is that taking full advantage of the scope for cash support may require a careful integration of income generation programmes with other aspects of famine prevention policies. For instance, the case for imposing bureaucratic controls on food movements seems much weaker when the incomes of the poor are protected through public policy. In fact, an adequate market response to the demands newly generated by a strategy of cash support will often call for a relaxation of such controls. In turn, the threat of manipulative activities on the part of private traders may be much reduced by a substantial measure of public involvement in food distribution.

---

[48] It should, however, be mentioned that some of the excluded groups could gain from *derived benefits* obtained from the income support provided to other groups. For instance, a reduction of distress livestock sales on the part of those who receive support could substantially benefit vulnerable livestock owners outside the relief system by arresting an impending collapse of livestock prices. As was discussed in Chapter 2, the deterioration of livestock–grain exchange rates is indeed a causal antecedent of many famines. Another example of potentially important 'derived effects' is the 'multiplier effect' of the increase in the purchasing power of those who do receive support, i.e. their additional purchases will add to the incomes of the sellers, and so on.

[49] From the point of view of the affected country, the financial implications of combining cash support with food imports and the sale of food in the market need not be more taxing than those of a strategy of 'direct delivery'.

In so far as cash support emerges as an effective form of intervention in famine situations, it appeals to a combination of public action and private participation that may be worth emphasizing. Cash support, such as public works with cash wages, is quintessentially a 'public' activity, but its success is dependent on an adequate response from the market in the form of meeting the demands generated. In this sense, the success of a strategy of this kind is neither a question of pure governmental action, nor one of leaving matters to private initiative.

The tradition of thinking of famine relief in pure and rather extreme terms can be very misleading. To think only in terms of either direct delivery and feeding by the state, or in terms of leaving matters to the mercy of the market mechanism, cannot begin to be an appropriate approach to the threat of famine in the modern world. There is need to go beyond the bounds of that tradition, and to consider major departures in the relief practices of some of the most famine prone countries in the world. The penalty of purism can be high.

7

Strategies of Entitlement Protection

7.1 Non-exclusion, Targeting and Selection

The minimal ambition of a sound famine prevention system should be to protect (directly or indirectly) the entitlements of *all* those who are vulnerable to starvation. This typically requires the adoption of a suitable range of support strategies which, taken together, reach all the vulnerable individuals. We shall refer to this as the *non-exclusion* objective.

The safest and most obvious way of guaranteeing the universal protection of entitlements is to provide direct and unconditional support to everyone without distinction. The method of *universal support* is obviously a rather coarse one, but it does have the advantage of altogether bypassing the various difficulties which any form of selectivity in the provision of relief is bound to entail. There is something simple, practical and ethically appealing in the notion that everyone should be regarded as having an inalienable and uncon-ditional right to the provision of a subsistence food ration—a notion that is actually widely supported when it comes to different types of basic necessities, such as education or health care. Universal support can be a simple expression of the much discussed 'right to food', and there was a time when, in European countries, the proposal of free bread for all was indeed considered seriously. More recently, universal suport has formed the basis of several highly impress-ive entitlement support schemes of a permanent nature, such as the early versions of the food subsidy systems of Sri Lanka (introduced in 1942) and Egypt.[1]

When it comes to famine prevention, however, the strategy of universal support would have several obvious disadvantages. To start with, it involves an administrative and logistic burden which can turn out to be quite exacting. More importantly, if it is to provide effective protection to those who depend entirely on public relief for their survival, universal support may require a commitment of resources that can be hard to obtain. We have to accept the fact that when limited resources are spread uniformly and indiscriminately over the whole population in a famine situation, lives are bound to be lost. Even in the event where adequate resources are available, one may still wish to impart a redistributive element to the entitlement protection process by restricting or 'targeting' support to selected groups. We shall refer to these redistributive considerations as the *targeting* objective.[2]

---

[1] The Sri Lankan experience is further examined in Chapter 12 of this book. For an excellent analysis of food subsidies in Egypt, see Alderman and von Braun (1984).

[2] While the principle underlying the notion of 'targeting' is simple enough, the operational notion of targeting-based protection is far from uncomplicated. Indeed, given the interdepend-

There can, in principle, be two different kinds of motivations underlying the targeting objective. One of them is to ensure the greatest *economy of resources* by *withholding* public support from less vulnerable groups. The other one is to make use of available resources to the greatest advantage of the most deprived groups, or in other words to promote the *redistribution of resources* by *concentrating* public support exclusively on these groups. In practice, it can of course be difficult to tell how the possibilities for improved targeting will be used —whether for reducing the resources devoted to entitlement protection, or for increasing the support given to vulnerable groups. The latter opportunity can be an important allocation issue for famine prevention, but it must be firmly distinguished from the fiscal temptations of the former.

There are, it must be said, good arguments for questioning the case for elaborate targeting even on distributional grounds. The ability of the poor to have access to public services, and the political support that the provision of these services can command, may depend crucially on the participation of a large part of the population in the benefits of public provisioning. For instance, the rapid expansion of public services in Britain during the Second World War, particularly impressive in contrast with the shocking apathy of the state in the 1930s, seems to have had much to do with factors of this kind:

That all were engaged in war whereas only some were affected with poverty and disease . . . had much to do with the less constraining, less discriminating scope and quality of the war-time social services . . . It was the universal character of these welfare policies which ensured their acceptance and success. They were free of social discrimination and the indignities of the poor law.[3]

We shall have more to say on this when we come to public action to deal with endemic deprivation, but there are good reasons to believe that in the context of famine prevention the case for targeting is fairly strong. Famines are typically situations where time is short and resources are limited, and the penalties of failing to come to the rescue of the most vulnerable by priority can be enormously high.

The potential importance of targeting for famine prevention can be illustrated by considering the experience of famine relief in Sudan in 1985.[4] As we saw in Chapter 5, there is little indication that the crisis of food and agricultural production which preceded famine in Sudan in that year was at all exceptional by the standards of what was happening elsewhere in Africa at the same time.

---

ences between different parts of the economy (including the so-called 'general equilibrium effects'), it must be recognized that in addition to direct beneficiaries any project will tend to influence—positively or negatively—the lives of many others.

[3] Titmuss (1950: 506, 514). The expansion of public services during and immediately after the Second World War in Britain, and the apparently dramatic impact of this expansion on the well-being of the population, are further discussed in Chapter 10.

[4] The following account draws on Chambers *et al.* (1986), Hale (1986), Pearson (1986), de Waal (1987, 1988a), Walker (1987), Bush (1988), Keen (1988), Maxwell (1988), Torry (1988b), and Borton and Shoham (1989b), as well as on personal communications from David Keen, Jeremy Swift, William Torry, Joachim von Braun and Peter Walker.

In fact, it has been argued that the extent of this crisis had initially been deliberately exaggerated for various political and tactical reasons.[5] Be that as it may, the country received massive amounts of food aid in 1984–5, and had the famine relief system succeeded in concentrating support on the most deprived, a famine could almost certainly have been averted.

Unfortunately it seems that the allocation of the bulk of food aid was far from redistributive. A careful study of this problem has put the situation thus:

> In general, it appears that wealthier people, and more politically influential groups, got more food aid than poorer and less influential groups. Broadly, the bigger towns got more than the smaller towns, townspeople got more than villagers, residents got more than migrants, and settled people got more than nomads . . . Areas designated as 'worst affected' received only a very small proportion of the grain distributed before the harvest . . . Within villages . . . richer households got more than poorer households.[6]

Sometimes the recipients of food aid were found to spend as much as 50 per cent of it on non-food items—a consumption pattern hardly compatible with extreme destitution. Even in feeding camps, it has been alleged that as few as 10 or 20 per cent of selected children were actually undernourished. The disquieting aspect of the story is not that too many people were helped, but rather that many were starving while relatively better-off groups were fattened by public support. In areas such as Darfur, the overall death rate in 1985 was estimated at three times the normal level.[7]

The simultaneous, and to some extent conflicting, objectives of 'non-exclusion' and 'targeting' can be pursued with varying emphasis, depending on the *selection* procedure adopted to determine the eligibility of different groups of people to public support. Common examples of alternative selection procedures are the reliance on village communities to allocate relief, the use of anthropometric measures of nutritional status as a criterion of eligibility for feeding, and the provision of support in exchange for work (leading to self-selection). Each of these approaches has many diverse implications aside from its ability to further the non-exclusion and targeting objectives, and it would be wrong to consider them solely from the point of view of selection issues. On the other hand, given the difficulty and importance of success-fully implementing satisfactory selection mechanisms, it is natural to pay special attention to these issues in an examination of alternative strategies of entitlement protection.[8]

---

[5] On this question, see particularly Pearson (1986).

[6] Keen (1988: 3–4). This study relates to the region of Darfur. For similar findings elsewhere in Sudan, see Alfred (1986) and Hale (1986). According to a personal communication from David Keen, 'targeting began to improve in late 1985–6 as agency control over food increased'.

[7] De Waal (1988a: 83). The same author estimates famine mortality in Darfur in 1985 as 85,000 excess deaths.

[8] The evaluation reports of relief agencies are replete with indications of the anxieties arising from the dilemmas involved in choosing between alternative selection procedures. For various discussions of these problems, see e.g. Seaman and Holt (1980), Gooch and MacDonald (1981a),

7.2 Alternative Selection Mechanisms

The extent of economic distress experienced by different individuals is, to a great extent, a matter of common knowledge within a given rural community. An apparent solution to the selection problem would take the form of making the selection process rely on local institutions to allocate public support according to individual needs.

Would this method work in practice? The leaders of a village community undoubtedly have a lot of information relevant for appropriate selection. But in addition to the informational issue, there is also the question as to whether the community leaders have strong enough motivation—or incentives—to give adequately preferential treatment to vulnerable groups. Much will undoubtedly depend on the nature and functioning of political institutions at the local level, and in particular on the power that the poor and the deprived have in the rural community.[9] Where the poor are also powerless—as is frequently the case—the reliance on local institutions to allocate relief is problematic, and can end up being at best indiscriminate and at worst blatantly inequitous, as numerous observers have noted in diverse countries.[10]

In Africa, the intermediation of local communities in the distribution of food has been observed in a large number of cases to result simply in uniform household rations or, at best, rations related to household size. For instance, a careful study of food distribution in the Red Sea Province of Sudan in 1985 noted that the local leaders (or 'responsible men') in charge of food distribution did have a very clear and accurate perception of the needs of different families, but that the allocation process made no discriminating use of this informational advantage: 'Every family had to have a share. No responsible man felt able to

---

Mason and Brown (1983), Tabor (1983), Autier and d'Altilia (1985), Hay et al. (1986), Pearson (1986), Wood et al. (1986), McLean (1987), and Borton and Shoham (1989a) among many others. The distinction between the non-exclusion and targeting objectives is an old one (already prominent in discussions of famine policy in 18th-century China and 19th-century India), and has been recently considered by different authors under various labels such as 'vertical targeting efficiency and horizontal targeting efficiency' (Weisbrod 1969), 'E-mistakes and F-mistakes' (Cornia et al. 1987, Kumar and Stewart 1987), or 'specificity and sensitivity' (Alderman 1988a).

[9] For example, the change in the balance of power in the rural society of West Bengal in favour of the poorer sections of the population, largely as a result of left-wing activisit movements, has certainly resulted in a much greater participation of the poor in poverty alleviation programmes. The contrast is particularly sharp with other states in Northern India such as Uttar Pradesh (see Drèze 1988b). The crucial difference that local institutions and the balance of power within a rural community can make to the success of public support measures is also clearly illustrated by the positive role attributed to participative village institutions in the context of recent famine prevention efforts in Tigray and Eritrea (Nelson 1983, English et al. 1984, Firebrace and Holland 1984, CAFOD 1986a, 1986b), and in independent Zimbabwe (see Chapter 8). In Ethiopia, the Peasant Associations are also widely reported to have greatly facilitated the equitable distribution of food and employment at the local level (McKerrow 1979, Holt 1983, Relief and Development Institute 1985, World Food Programme 1986d).

[10] For a few examples among many, see e.g. Bernus (1977a, 1977b), Gooch and MacDonald (1981a), van Appeldoorn (1981), Hartmann and Boyce (1983), Mason and Brown (1983), Watts (1983), Tobert (1985), York (1985), Bryson (1986), Hale (1986), Pearson (1986), and Bratton (1987a).

exclude any family on grounds of wealth. On the contrary, sheikhs, who usually had the largest herds, often got extra food.'[11] These findings are more or less echoed in a number of recent studies of famine prevention in sub-Saharan Africa.[12]

However, in sub-Saharan Africa it is sometimes the case that during a famine all sections of a particular village community experience acute deprivation and suffer from nutritional inadequacy. When intravillage inequalities are particularly less perspicuous than intervillage differences, *and* an effective procedure can be devised to identify the more vulnerable villages or areas, the rule of uniform distribution *within* the village community can be a commendable expedient.[13] While it may not be able to achieve the fine tuning that a full response to the non-extreme inequalities within the village would ideally call for, the non-divisive and participatory involvement of the entire village community in the exercise of public support can be seen to have distinct advantages. The reality and extent of these advantages in different social and cultural environments calls for cautious assessment.

Three ranges of alternative selection mechanisms suggest themselves: (1) using administrative criteria based on observable indicators of deprivation or need, such as anthropometric status, asset ownership, demographic characteristics, or geographical location; (2) intervening impersonally at the level of the market (e.g. by subsidizing food prices or supporting livestock prices), and letting the share of different groups in public support be determined by their market situation; and (3) relying on 'self-acting tests', such as the requirement of work in exchange for relief, in order to discourage privileged groups. We shall refer to these three ranges of options as *administrative selection*, *market selection* and *self-selection* respectively.

While these conceptual distinctions are helpful, it must be realized that most forms of intervention involve some explicit or implicit combination of these three elements. For instance, administrative selection methods almost invariably imply an element of self-selection as well, since the recipients usually have to present themselves and take some unpleasant or stigmatizing initiative to get

[11] Hale (1986: 36).

[12] See e.g. Ray (1984), Tobert (1985), Alfred (1986), World Food Programme (1986*d*), Keen (1988), Borton and Shoham (1989*a*, 1989*b*). See also Chapter 8. Another very common (and disquieting) observation is that the intermediation of local communites in food distribution tends to discriminate against displaced people, towards whom the administration or leadership of host communities often feel little responsibility (see Kelemen 1985, Relief and Development Institute 1985, Tobert 1985, Pearson 1986, McLean 1987, Keen 1988, Borton and Shoham 1989*b*).

[13] Daniel *et al.* (1984), for instance, argue that 'there are relatively few cases in SSA [sub-Saharan Africa] where inequality (and landlessness) within a low-income area makes it impossible to consider the people of the area as the target group, in the sense that households share similar levels of nutrition and income . . .' (p. 9). The apparent contrast in intrarural inequality between South Asia and sub-Saharan Africa is not surprising: economic inequality in South Asia is to a great extent derived from inequality in land ownership, which is typically less acute in sub-Saharan Africa, given the relative abundance of land. This contrast, while fairly uncontroversial, should not be exaggerated, and a number of authors have emphasized the existence of large inequalities in various African societies—see e.g. Watts (1983) and Hill (1986).

help based on the use of these indicators. Similarly, self-acting tests usually apply only to population groups possessing certain characteristics, such as being able-bodied enough for manual work in the case of the labour test. And most forms of intervention have important repercussions through the market, e.g. by influencing wages or food prices. Market selection mechanisms themselves are also usually of a mixed nature. For instance, the incidence of commodity subsidies depends on the regional focus of the subsidy (possibly involving administrative selection based on specific indicators), as well as on the individual behaviour patterns (e.g. dietary choices) of potential recipients.

Market responses are of pervasive relevance for famine prevention policies. It is always important to take them into account when evaluating alternative forms of intervention.[14] On the other hand, in most situations an exclusive reliance on market selection mechanisms to protect the entitlements of vulnerable groups would be a very doubtful approach. It is not only that market selection tends to be a blunt and inadequately discriminating mechanism for reaching the most vulnerable. In fact, market selection often has the effect of ending up discriminating against, rather than in favour of, the poor.

A good example of the perversely discriminating effects that market selection can have is provided by public policies of livestock price support. There are now several examples of famine relief schemes based on the idea that supporting livestock prices through public purchases would help pastoralists to survive droughts.[15] It is certainly the case that schemes of this kind do enhance the purchasing power of pastoralists *vis-à-vis* other occupation groups. On the other hand, it must be recognized that livestock price support helps pastoralists proportionately to the size of their herds, with large owners gaining much more than smaller ones.[16] Generally, what we have called 'market selection' is an undependable answer to the possibly crucial need of providing preferential support to the most vulnerable groups in famine situations.

7.3 Feeding and Family

When a food crisis has reached an advanced stage and extensive signs of enhanced deprivation or undernourishment have developed, it becomes possible even for outsiders to observe deprivation directly. The allocation of relief on the basis of observed nutritional status is one of the most widely used selection mechanisms, and the attractiveness of this method is easy to understand. Conflicting claims have been made, however, as to the real merits of this approach.

---

[14] For a careful analysis of market responses in relation to public policy for the prevention of famines and chronic hunger, see Ravallion (1987b).

[15] For examples of such schemes, see e.g. T. Downing et al. (forthcoming).

[16] Of course, it is possible to restrict public livestock purchases to particular sections of the pastoralist population. This would amount to supplementing the 'market selection' mechanism with some form of administrative selection or self-selection.

To start with, two important limitations of selection by nutritional status must be clearly recognized. First, contrary to popular belief the assessment of nutritional status is a skilled and complex task.[17] It is unfortunately often the case that nutritional assessment in famine situations is left—sometimes inevitably—to inexperienced and overworked staff. The risk of poor identification of vulnerable individuals and their nutritional problems as a result of this practice have been graphically brought out in several studies relating to recent African famines.[18] The requirements of competent nutritional assessment should therefore not be underestimated.

Second, there could conceivably be very important *incentive* problems associated with using individual nutritional status as a criterion of selection for support. One of the most common targeting techniques consists of providing support to households (e.g. in the form of take-home food rations) conditionally on the presence, in the recipient household, of at least one undernourished child.[19] It does not take a great deal of reflection to see the potential dangers of such a system in the form of disincentives against child care. Particularly in a famine situation it must be all too tempting for a household to 'ensure' that at least one child remains undernourished in order to retain eligibility for support. The operation of these adverse incentives can, of course, be extremely hard to observe, but there is a certain amount of anecdotal evidence confirming one's worst fears. It is worrying, for instance, to hear of the following response to feeding schemes in Ethiopia during the recent famine:

Undoubtedly, to some mothers, a malnourished child was seen as a 'meal ticket' for her and the family . . . Who would blame a mother who kept a child sufficiently undernourished to remain on the intensive feeding programme?[20]

---

[17] Some of the problems involved relate to the complexities of nutritional assessment discussed in Chapter 3.

[18] See e.g. W. Taylor (1983), Teuscher (1985), Chambers *et al*. (1986), Gibb (1986), Pearson (1986), and Soeters (1986). The last author describes how two independent survey teams from Médecins Sans Frontières and the League of Red Cross and Red Crescent Societies assessed the nutritional status of the same group of children on the same day using the same methods, and arrived at sharply different results (e.g. they respectively concluded that 24 per cent and 48 per cent of the children were below 80 per cent of a *common* weight-for-height standard). See also Borton and Shoham (1989*a*) on some disenchantment among relief agencies regarding the use of anthropometric measures of nutritional status for targeting purposes.

[19] This method is astonishingly widespread—it was, for instance, used in most of the feeding schemes run by OXFAM during the 1985–6 famine in Ethiopia (Helen Young, personal communication; see also Young 1987). Further examples can be found in many guidelines and evaluation studies of food distribution programmes. See, for instance, Gooch and MacDonald (1981*a*), Morgan (1986), Pearson (1986), OXFAM/UNICEF (1986), Garcia and Pinstrup-Andersen (1987), Brown and Mason (1988), Pinstrup-Andersen and Alderman (1988), Borton and Shoham (1989*b*) and Neumann *et al*. (forthcoming).

[20] Nash (1986). Other evaluations of recent supplementary feeding programmes in famine-stricken Ethiopia have also noted the problem of 'deliberate starving of children to obtain programme access' (Borton and Shoham 1989*b*, Case Study 12, p. 3). Personal communications from several relief agencies confirm that terrible events of this kind are unfortunately not isolated, though understandably enough they are not the object of much publicity.

Incentive problems of this specific kind do not arise when nutritional status is used as a criterion for helping undernourished *individuals*, rather than the households to which they belong. But there is an incentive problem in this case too. If a child is being looked after by a feeding scheme, that is so much less pressure on household resources. Thus, individual feeding still operates partly like an improvement in household entitlements and there remains an incentive for the household to do whatever is necessary to get one or more of its children selected for feeding. The temptation of neglect will, moreover, be no less if parents have genuine concern for the child's well-being. Indeed, the child's own interest may well be to undergo temporary undernourishment so as to become eligible for feeding. The widespread practices of 'discharging' children when their nutritional status improves, or of relating the amount of food provided to the extent of observed undernutrition, can create further disincentives against family care.

These important limitations being noted, it must be asked whether using nutritional status as a basis for selection has compensating advantages. Perhaps the greatest advantage of nutritional criteria is that, when carefully applied, they allow the identification of vulnerable individuals rather than households. An attempt can, thus, be made to help individuals directly, and to influence the distribution of food within households. This is how direct feeding schemes, especially, are thought to operate.

The desirability and importance of influencing intrahousehold distribution in this particular way raises many complex issues. For one thing, as was discussed in Chapters 4 and 5, the empirical evidence on the extent and typical patterns of intrahousehold discrimination during famines is not entirely clear. There is in particular a distinct possibility that, during the early stages of food crises at least, intrahousehold discrimination operates in favour, rather than against, young children (the main targets of feeding schemes). For another, there remains in any case a difficult ethical and practical question as to whether a relief worker is really better placed than a mother or a father to decide who should get food within a family.

But the feasibility of influencing intrahousehold allocation in the desired direction should also not be taken for granted. Indeed, it is not obvious why a household should treat the feeding of one of its members very differently from an improvement in household entitlements, if that member's share of the family food can be adjusted accordingly. There is considerable evidence from supplementary feeding programmes operating in ordinary times that this so-called 'leakage' problem is very real, although usually a certain degree of influence on intrahousehold allocation is in fact retained.[21] When food is badly short at the household level, as in a famine situation, the temptation to

[21] See particularly Beaton and Ghasseimi (1982), who discuss the leakage problem at length and conclude, after reviewing a large number of supplementary feeding schemes: 'Overall, the net increase in intake by the target recipient was 45 to 70% of the food collected' (p. 909). The more recent reviews of Kennedy and Knudsen (1985), Godfrey (1986a, 1986b) and Norgan (1988) arrive at broadly similar conclusions.

reduce the share of household food going to members who benefit from supplementary feeding could be particularly strong.

Many evaluations of feeding programmes have indeed insisted on the ineffectiveness of providing selective 'supplementary' feeding when 'basic rations' are themselves badly inadequate at the household level.[22] In the worst cases, supplementary feeding of this kind has been found to be not only ineffective but even counter-productive. This can happen, for instance, if the individual recipients of cooked food are no longer fed at home on the erroneous assumption that they have already been adequately fed.[23] While there is no reason to believe that disasters of this kind are a pervasive feature of feeding programmes, the general dangers of households overestimating the amount of nourishment received by the beneficiaries of feeding cannot be overlooked.

These problems can be avoided if a child is fed more than he or she would receive in the household in the absence of a feeding scheme. In this case, the child may well stop being fed at home, but there can be no 'leakage' beyond that, and in the end the child *is* better nourished. However, when the responsibility for the nutritional well-being of a child is entirely 'taken over' by a relief agency in this way, some of the incentive problems discussed earlier (e.g. the temptation of keeping a child famished for it to qualify for assistance) survive in a strong form. Moreover, it is well known that the resources required (in terms of personnel, logistics and administration) to spoon-feed every child individually and on a continuous basis make this type of intervention unsuitable for large-scale relief operations.

It seems, then, that providing direct support to vulnerable individuals when household entitlements are inadequate is a rather flawed procedure in many circumstances. The priority has to be to ensure adequate 'basic rations' to households, and direct feeding of individuals is best regarded as a possible supplementary measure.[24] Further, as we have stressed, it would generally be

[22] See e.g. Capone (1980), Autier and d'Altilia (1985), Lowgren (1985), Dick (1986), Godfrey (1986a, 1986b), Chambers et al. (1986), League of Red Cross and Red Crescent Societies (1986) and Borton and Shoham (1989a).

[23] In this event, the beneficiaries of selective feeding sometimes literally *lose* weight. For examples of such cases, and of other hazards associated with poorly designed or executed feeding schemes in famine situations, see Hall (1973), Barnabas et al. (1982), Kielman et al. (1982), Teuscher (1985), Wallstam (1985), Gibb (1986), Hay et al. (1986), Morris-Peel (1986) and Pearson (1986).

[24] This general conclusion is, in fact, in line with a number of recent evaluations of supplementary feeding programmes in famine situations. See e.g. Lowgren (1985), Dick (1986), Gibb (1986), Godfrey (1986a, 1986b), League of Red Cross and Red Crescent Societies (1986), Appleton (1987) and Borton and Shoham (1989a). There are, of course, important exceptions to the rule that household entitlements should be regarded as the priority. One of them arises when food *quality* strongly matters, as can be the case when undernutrition has reached an advanced stage. When an important objective of feeding is to influence the composition of the diet of vulnerable individuals (e.g. to give them a particular vitamin), the simplest procedure is to provide direct supplementation to these individuals (i.e. to give them the vitamins). Selective feeding can therefore be of special value when there is a concern for *both* quality and intrahousehold distribution. 'Therapeutic' feeding, addressed to severely malnourished children, is an example. The appropriateness of this type of intervention has to be assessed in the light of the qualifications discussed earlier.

very dangerous to use the nutritional status of children as a criterion of eligibility for support at the household level. A different selection procedure is needed.

The fact that nutritional status does not appear to perform very promisingly as a basic selection criterion does not mean that feeding schemes themselves have no role to play in famine prevention, since they can (1) operate on the basis of different selection criteria such as age, sex, or location; (2) complement rather than replace a strategy of household entitlement support. A successful use of individual feeding, however, would seem to depend on the existence of a reliable system of entitlement protection aimed at vulnerable households.

7.4   Employment and Entitlement

The provision of employment as a device for generating compensating income has been an important part of the entitlement protection systems of a number of countries in the past. One of the great advantages of this strategy is to make it possible to carry out large transfers to vulnerable households, while at the same time imparting a strong redistributive bias to the entitlement protection process. The employment mechanism involves a comparatively exacting selection procedure, but once the recipients are selected, they obtain what are, relatively speaking, fairly substantial payments in food or in cash. There is rarely a possibility of making transfers of a similar magnitude per head on a non-selective basis, since the total resources needed would be very much larger.

The strategy of employment provision has another important advantage which deserves special mention. Employment provision can go with either payments in kind or wages in cash. When the latter mode of payment is used, the employment approach to the protection of entitlements becomes a particular way of providing cash support. The advantages of cash support, as was discussed in the previous chapter, can be quite substantial in many contexts. Those advantages hold *inter alia* for cash-based employment programmes. In fact, the only effective and politically acceptable method of providing large-scale cash support is often that of employment provision with cash wages.

In addition to these two basic advantages, the strategy of employment provision has a number of further features (most of these will apply irrespective of whether the wages are paid in cash or in kind), the merits of which should be clear from the discussion in the two preceding chapters. These include: (1) being compatible with intervention at an early stage of a subsistence crisis (when affected people are looking hard for alternative sources of income but do not yet suffer from severe nutritional deprivation); (2) obviating the necessity of movements of entire families to feeding camps; (3) at the same time, obviating the necessity of taking food to every village (as in a system of decentralized distribution), to the extent that the work-seeking adult population is mobile; (4) preserving family ties, particularly when employment can be offered near homes (without families having to be huddled together with thousands of others into relief camps); (5) inducing positive market responses in the form of an upward pressure on local wages; (6) allowing reliance on 'self-selection'.

The last in particular is important in so far as it reduces the dependence on administrative selection. Apart from their high organizational burden, most forms of administrative selection involve greater risks of errors in coverage than a system where the initiative of joining the relief system rests with the affected people themselves.[25]

Employment provision has been extensively used as a tool of entitlement protection in India for many centuries (see Chapter 8). Even in the recent drought of 1987, which could have led to a very substantial famine given the disruption of the livelihood of hundreds of millions of people, employment provision in the form of large-scale public works programmes played a major part in averting that threat. In suggesting a greater use of this approach in Africa, we have to encounter the possible criticism (one which has been aired in response to some earlier presentations) that this is based on a hasty imitation of the 'Indian model'. This would be an undeserved accusation.

First, India is by no means the only country to have made extensive and effective use of employment provision for the prevention of famines.[26] In Africa itself, employment provision has already been a positive part of famine prevention efforts in a number of countries, including especially Botswana and Cape Verde.[27]

Second, as we have seen in Chapter 5, searching for employment has become one of the cornerstones of informal security systems in many African countries. Public provision of employment would seem to be a natural way of helping this effort. The common prescription, discussed at some length in section 5.3, that entitlement protection measures should seek to strengthen rather than undermine traditional security systems, would seem to point to employment provision as a commendable form of intervention.

Third, it is arguable that in some important respects the strategy of employment provision would in fact be *easier* to adopt in many parts of Africa than it has proved to be in India. Several of the problems which have limited the strategy of employment provision in India in the recent past would indeed

[25] For evidence of the high involvement of vulnerable groups in public works programmes, see e.g. Desai *et al.* (1979), Dandekar (1983), Chowdhury (1983), Osmani and Chowdhury (1983), and Drèze (1988*a*).

[26] Public works were, for instance, a major plank of famine prevention in China during the 1920s. On this see Edwards (1932), Nathan (1965), Li (1987), and various contributions to the *Chinese Recorder*, vol. 23 (1932).

[27] On these two countries, see Chapter 8. Positive experiences with the use of public works for famine prevention in Africa in recent years have also been reported in countries as diverse as Ethiopia (Holt 1983, Admassie and Gebre 1985, Grannell 1986, World Food Programme 1986*d*), Burkina Faso (Kelly 1987), Lesotho (Bryson 1986), Chad (Autier and d'Altilia 1985), and Uganda (Dodge and Alnwick 1986). On the contemporary African experience with public works in non-famine situations, see Thomas (1986).

seem to apply with less force in sub-Saharan Africa. For instance, public works programmes in India have been restrained by the scarcity of publicly owned land, and the attendant problems of property rights involved in finding suitable worksites. In this important respect, many African countries, with their relative abundance of land, would appear to be at considerable advantage compared to India in making good use of the employment strategy.

This being said, a number of difficulties associated with the employment strategy must also be considered.[28] Most of these difficulties are in no way specific to Africa, but their relevance for Africa deserves special attention.

One of the shortcomings of the employment approach is that it has the contrary feature of *increasing* calorie requirements precisely at a time when there is a strong case for reducing activity levels. This can no doubt be a serious problem, and it must be remembered in particular that the strategy of employment provision has been found quite impractical, indeed sometimes damaging, in situations of advanced distress when people are too enfeebled to provide the required effort. The strategy of employment provision must be seen, intrinsically, as a strategy of *early* intervention. It is primarily preventive rather than curative as an anti-famine strategy.

The criticism of enhanced calorie requirements, however, overlooks the crucial fact that, while raising the calorie requirements of the labourers, public works often more than commensurately increase their entitlements by preventing relatively privileged groups from taking advantage of the public support system. In fact, it can be shown that the resources needed to cover the 'requirements' of vulnerable groups would typically be much smaller when relief is provided in the form of employment (even after taking note of the additional calorie requirements of work) rather than in the form of indiscriminate distribution.

The question of increased calorie requirements is closely related to another objection that has often been raised against the provision of employment in situations of famine vulnerability, and which is concerned with the excessively 'punitive' nature of this approach. The fact that a person has to *work* to receive support may be thought to be a denial of what is owed to him or her by the society. However, the vulnerable population can gain greatly from the discrimination that can be achieved through the insistence on work requirement which would prevent the available resources from being squandered on the privileged. Also, it must be remembered that potential famine victims tend to look positively for employment in order to deal with their deprivation, and providing that employment can scarcely be described as being 'punitive'. In fact, famine victims often prefer the status of being employed rather than being mere receivers of charity. Perhaps most importantly, while public works are often accused of creating 'dependency' and doing little to improve the situation

---

[28] For a critique of employment provision as a strategy of famine prevention, see Mayer (1975). Arguments in different directions are also discussed in Maxwell (1978a), Shukla (1979), Jackson and Eade (1982), Klein (1984), Reynolds (1984), Clay (1986) and Hay (1986), among others.

and prospects of the poor in the rural economy and society, in some instances they have been found, on the contrary, to be instrumental in enhancing the economic and social position of vulnerable groups (e.g. by boosting local wages, strengthening the bargaining power of the poor, and providing them with an opportunity to organize around common interests).[29]

Another possible criticism of the strategy of employment provision is that it can only succeed in protecting entitlements at the *household* level, and obviously provides very little scope for directly redressing intrahousehold inequalities where these are large. It is quite possible that in some situations this shortcoming would be an important one, and might militate against this approach (and in favour of a strategy of individual support, e.g. direct feeding). As was discussed earlier, however, in the case of sub-Saharan Africa there is little evidence of sharp intrafamily discrimination against the most vulnerable family members (e.g. young children) in the early stages of food crises.

As far as discrimination against adult women is concerned, not only is there little evidence of systematic anti-female bias in nutrition and survival in sub-Saharan Africa, the strategy of employment provision could be seen as being particularly beneficial to women in so far as they often form a large part of the labour force on public works programmes.[30] Even when this is not the case as things stand, female participation can be promoted as a policy decision when women are ready to work for a wage. Indeed in some cases the promotion of female employment has been an important and effective part of entitlement protection policies.[31] The issue of intrafamily inequality always deserves careful attention, but there is no general presumption that this would necessarily undermine the case for a strategy of employment provision.

[29] See Drèze (1988b) for further discussion of this point with reference to India; also Mencher (1988). The positive contribution of employment provision to the enfranchisement of the rural poor is, for instance, quite clear from the experience of the Employment Guarantee Scheme (EGS) in Maharashtra. As a pamphlet issued by a social action group in rural Maharashtra explains, 'the Employment Guarantee Scheme is an important instrument for those who have been involved in organizing the poor, oppressed, and exploited classes in rural areas over the years' (Deshpande 1984: 5; our translation). On this and other aspects of the Employment Guarantee Scheme, see also Government of India (1980), Desphande (1982, 1984), Dandekar (1983), D'Silva (1983), Herring and Edwards (1983), Lieberman (1984, 1985), Ezekiel (1986), and Acharya and Panwalkar (1988a, 1988b).

[30] In most countries, female participation rates tend to be quite high in public works. The proportion of women among labourers employed on public works has been estimated at 80% in Botswana (Tabor 1983), about 50% in Cape Verde (Spyckerelle 1987), 52% in Chile (Cheyre and Ogrodnick 1982), between 27 and 65% in Ethiopia (Admassie and Gebre 1985), 64% in Jamaica (Girling and Keith 1977), 95% in Lesotho (Reynolds 1984), and more than half in Maharashtra (Dandekar 1983). Involvement in public works not only increases women's earning power, it also enhances their 'bargaining position' within the household (see Chapter 4). As a poor woman in drought-stricken Mauritania put it, 'if a woman earns her salary, the man can no longer command the woman' (cited in Abeille 1979). On the general importance of the 'breakdown position' of women in famine situations, see Agarwal (1988).

[31] This has been the case in Bangladesh (Marty Chen, personal communication). On the far-reaching impact which the expansion of female employment seems to have had on the status of women in Bangladesh in recent years, see Adnan (1988).

Another objection that has been raised is based on questioning the productive value of public works programmes. This can scarcely be a serious route of attack on the strategy of employment provision, if the alternatives take the form of giving something away for nothing (as in feeding or food distribution schemes). Considerations of productivity are, in any case, clearly of secondary importance in the short run in a situation of famine vulnerability.[32]

A more solid objection related to productivity considerations is that public works are liable to divert labour from other activities, including the growing of food. Again, this is a consideration which may well be important in particular cases, but as a general argument against the strategy of employment provision it is hardly persuasive. In many cases, vulnerable groups will have very little access to alternative employment, and in fact alternative opportunities may even be *enhanced* by greater security. When the diversion of labour from productive activities is important, the positive influences of this displacement (e.g. an upward pressure on local wages) must be evaluated along with the negative ones (e.g. a loss of agricultural output).

Finally, it is often asserted that the administrative and logistic requirements of organizing public works programmes must be much more demanding than those of direct distribution or feeding schemes. In some ways, there may be an element of truth in this assertion, especially if public works programmes suddenly have to be improvised from nowhere by bureaucrats unused to such a system. A sound strategy of entitlement protection through employment provision cannot dispense with the need for careful contingency planning —any more than other reliable systems of famine prevention.[33]

There is very little evidence, however, that with appropriate contingency planning, the administrative and logistic requirements of large-scale employment provision are more demanding than those of direct food distribution. A rigorous comparison would in fact not be easy to make, and in particular it must be remembered that a proper comparison should take into account not only the numbers of people helped with a given amount of resources under each alternative, but also the extent of relief provided per recipient, as well as the composition of the protected population. This qualification is important since, as we have seen, employment provision typically provides a unique

[32] It is worth noting, however, that little empirical evidence supports the view that public works programmes are *generally* 'unproductive'. Some evaluations have come to quite different conclusions. See e.g. Frances Stewart's review of evaluation studies (Stewart 1987), and also Thomas *et al.* (1976), Grannell (1986), Hay *et al.* (1986), van Binsbergen (1986), World Food Programme (1986*d*), and Gaude *et al.* (1987).

[33] It should be mentioned that the administrative and logistic burden involved in organizing public works on a large scale can depend significantly on the importance that is attached to providing work at short distances from the homes of affected people. Given that labour migration is a common—and early—household response to the threat of famine in many countries of sub-Saharan Africa (see section 5.4), even somewhat centralized public works schemes would often provide very substantial protection to vulnerable populations in times of crisis. This option is important to bear in mind when organizational capabilities are severely limited.

opportunity for implementing large, redistributive transfers to the most affected groups.

Furthermore, it must be noted that the strategy of employment provision with *cash* wages provides an excellent—indeed perhaps unique—opportunity to take advantage of the administrative economies of using the market mechanism in the movement and distribution of food. That the advantages can be quite considerable was discussed in the last chapter. In a situation where the bureaucratic structure of governmental operations is already overstrained, the merits of sharing the logistic tasks with private trade cannot be neglected. When doubts are raised about the administrative capability of particular governments to protect the entitlements of potential famine victims through employment schemes, it is often overlooked that a particular form of the employment strategy (viz. that of cash-for-work) permits a reduction in the tasks to be performed by the government. In comparison with what the government has to do if the entire charge of taking the food from one place to another and distributing it to the recipients were to fall on its slender shoulders, the task of the government with cash-for-work programmes is much more limited.

7.5 A Concluding Remark

Effective famine prevention calls for much more than simply rushing food to the victims when they have started dying of starvation. It involves a network of decisions relating to diverse policy areas such as the generation of incomes, the delivery of health care, the stabilization of food prices, the provision of drinking water, and the rehabilitation of the rural economy. The general problem of 'entitlement protection' has many different facets.

Further, as should be clear from the preceding chapters, the occupational characteristics of the affected population, the pattern of intrafamily divisions, the structure of markets, the nature of cooperative village institutions, the mobility of vulnerable groups, are only some examples of the numerous considerations that are relevant to the choice of a strategy of entitlement protection when a famine threatens. There are significant heterogeneities within Africa in all these respects, and any serious programme of public intervention to prevent famines must come to grips with these diversities.

We have chosen to discuss the pros and cons of entitlement protection through employment provision in some detail because of the potential importance of much greater use of this method in preventing famines in the future, especially in Africa. We have seen that this strategy has some notable advantages, which can in many circumstances be consolidated by combining the provision of employment with the payment of cash wages. The use of this technique in sub-Saharan Africa has been, so far, rather limited, but there are good economic and social grounds for going much further in this direction.

The employment strategy can be especially effective if it is adopted at an early stage of a famine threat, and its success will be that much easier if it is incorporated in a general system of relief that is in a state of preparedness to be invoked without undue delay. Sometimes, the value of having such a system seems to be overlooked. An illustration comes from the experience of Ethiopia during the famine of 1984.

Until that year, the government of Ethiopia had been relatively successful in using food aid to run extensive public works programmes, and these played an important part in averting large-scale famine in 1982 and 1983.[34] However, when fears of a big famine developed in 1984, the famine relief agencies (including international organizations) decided that the priority was no longer 'development' but 'relief', and that food aid should be diverted from public works to emergency programmes of food distribution and feeding. As a result, hundreds of thousands of people either lost employment or, even worse, continued working while arrears in wage payments were mounting. The improvisation of feeding programmes, on the other hand, rapidly ran into considerable logistic difficulties.[35] One has to wonder whether the crisis could not have been much more effectively dealt with by expanding existing employment programmes on a larger scale rather than winding up one system of entitlement protection to be replaced by a hastily built—and by no means flawless—alternative device.

In highlighting the advantages of employment provision, we are not suggesting that exclusive reliance could in any way be placed on this one method of entitlement protection. Provision must clearly be made for supporting those who are unable to work themselves and who do not have able-bodied relatives on whom they can rely for support. The proportion of such people may or may not be large (depending *inter alia* on the demographic characteristics of affected groups and the nature of family ties), but a comprehensive system of entitlement protection must pay adequate attention to their needs. This is especially

[34] See e.g. Holt (1983) and Relief and Development Institute (1985). Food-for-work programmes in Ethiopia are also discussed in Admassie and Gebre (1985), Grannell (1986), World Food Programme (1986*d*), and Government of Ethiopia (1987). During the two years preceding mid-1984, more than 130,000 tonnes of wheat were distributed through WFP-assisted employment programmes, mainly in the most vulnerable areas (World Food Programme 1986*d*, Annex II). This corresponds to something like 200 million person-days of nourishment.

[35] These events are briefly described and discussed in Admassie and Gebre (1985), Gill (1986), Grannell (1986), Jansson *et al*. (1987), Goyder and Goyder (1988), and particularly World Food Programme (1986*d*). We are grateful to Hugh Goyder (Oxfam), John Shaw (World Food Programme), and Thomas Grannell (World Food Programme) for very helpful personal communications on this issue. The disruption of supplies to Food-For-Work programmes in Ethiopia in 1984 seems to have been the combined result of (1) deliberate restraint in shipments as a result of an overestimation of the stocks available in Ethiopia at the end of 1983; (2) unsettled quarrels between international agencies and the Government of Ethiopia concerning the modalities of food aid; and (3) massive diversion of supplies for 'emergency' programmes (see World Food Programme 1986*d*, and Grannell 1986). Ironically, as a result of the disruption of public works programmes many wage earners lost their employment and had to become recipients of 'emergency assistance' (World Food Programme 1986*b*, 1986*d*).

Table 7.1 'Gratuitous relief' in three villages of Bhiloda Taluka (Gujarat), 1987

Name	Sex	Age	Marital status	Relatives living in the same household	Number of grown-up sons	Ability to work	Land owned	Other productive assets	Remarks
Chanchiben	F	old	Widow	None	None	n/a	None	None	
Valiben	F	old	Widow	None	None	No	None	None	
Manabhai	M	old	Widower	Daughter	None	No	None	None	Daughter on relief works
Koshiben	F	≈50	Widow	None	None	No	None	None	Begging
Danabhai	M	n/a	Widower	Young son	One	n/a	None	None	Blind
Dhuliben	F	≈50	Widow	None	None	No	None	None	
Paliben	F	old	Widow	None	None	No	None	None	
Ratanben	F	old	Widow	None	None	No	None	None	
Phoolaben	F	old	Widow	None	None	n/a	None	None	Stopped attending relief works
Ramabhai	M	≈50	Married	Wife	None	No	None	n/a	Some self-employment (craft)
Jamnaben	F	≈50	Married	Husband	None	No	None	n/a	Wife of Ramabhai (above)
Uniashankar	M	≈50	Unmarried	None	None	No	None	n/a	Mental illness
Shankarbhai	M	≈50	Married	Wife	None	No	None	None	Husband of Buriben (below)
Buriben	F	≈50	Married	Husband	None	No	None	None	Wife of Shankarbhai (above)
Manjiben	F	≈70	Widow	None	None	No	None	None	
Natiben	F	n/a	Widow	Santokben	None	n/a	None	None	
Santokben	F	n/a	Widow	Natiben	None	n/a	None	None	
Hiraben	F	old	Widow	None	None	No	None	None	Begging
Divaben	F	≈60	Widow	None	None	n/a	None	n/a	
Vekandas	M	old	Married	Wife	None	No	None	None	Husband of Urmilaben (below)
Urmilaben	F	old	Married	Husband	None	No	None	None	Wife of Vekandas (above)
Galbabhai	M	≈70	Widower	None	None	No	None	None	
Kalabhai	M	≈50	Unmarried	None	None	No	None	None	Disabled
Manguben	F	≈60	Widow	None	None	No	None	None	
Shantaben	F	≈60	Widow	None	None	No	None	None	
Hansaba	F	≈30	Widow	Father and brothers	n/a	Yes	n/a	n/a	Father seems quite affluent

Source: Drèze (1988b), Table 21.

important in view of the extremely high vulnerability of the elderly in famine situations which we noted earlier.

However, the inability to work is a relatively easily *observable* condition, and quite often this criterion can form a realistic basis for unconditional relief using what was called earlier 'administrative selection'.[36] To illustrate this point, Table 7.1 presents the characteristics of all the households who benefited from 'gratuitous relief' in three villages of Gujarat (India) during the 1987 drought.

It is remarkable that only one case out of the twenty-six (the last one in the table) can possibly be described as fraudulent in any sense. All the other recipients clearly belong to the intended target group of assetless households without able-bodied members. This success in identifying the most vulnerable is all the more impressive given that, in the same area, large-scale fraud can be observed in a number of other schemes of 'poverty alleviation' based on administrative selection with less easily observable criteria of eligibility such as 'having a low income'.[37]

Entitlement protection will almost always call for mixed systems, involving the use of different instruments to provide direct or indirect support to all vulnerable groups. The provision of employment—perhaps with cash wages —combined with unconditional relief for the 'unemployable' is likely to be one of the more effective options in many circumstances.

[36] This is especially the case when the able-bodied are already covered by employment provision. The able-bodied are not tempted to compete with the 'unemployable' in seeking unconditional relief, since the rewards from employment tend to be substantially higher (for obvious reasons).

[37] See Drèze (1988b) for details. This illustration of the feasibility of effecting direct transfers to the unemployable should not be taken to imply that the Indian system provides adequate support to households without fit adult members. In the area where the data presented in Table 7.1 were collected, only about half of all villages were actually covered by unconditional relief.

8

Experiences and Lessons

8.1   The Indian Experience

How has India avoided major famines since independence in 1947? It is tempting to attribute her success in this area to a steady improvement in food production. A close look at the facts, however, quickly reveals the inadequacy of this explanation. Indeed, the period during which the frequency of famines started to decline in India (the first half of this century) was actually one of steadily *declining* food production per head. Since independence, total food output has grown at a substantial rate, but per-head food production levels have not increased dramatically. They seem to remain, in fact, lower than late nineteenth-century levels, and also lower than per-capita food output levels in many countries affected by famines today. Moreover, the increase in per-capita production has resulted partly in the reduction of imports (and also to some extent the accumulation of large stocks), so that the net aggregate *consumption* of food per head has remained remarkably constant for the last forty years. Finally, almost every year large and heavily populated parts of India suffer from devastating droughts or floods which, through the disruption of rural livelihoods, remain quite capable of causing large-scale starvation.[1]

Nor is it possible to attribute India's success in preventing famines to a significant improvement in the general prosperity of the rural population. The removal of poverty in rural India since independence has, in fact, been shamefully slow.[2]

The prevention of famines in India cannot be understood without reference to the extensive entitlement protection efforts that have come into play on numerous occasions to sustain the rural population through a crisis. At the risk of oversimplification, it may be said that entitlement protection in India relies on the operation of two complementary forces, viz. (1) an administrative system that is intelligently aimed at recreating lost entitlements (caused by droughts, floods, economic slumps, or whatever), and (2) a political system that acts as the prime mover in getting the administrative system to work as and when required. We shall concentrate first on the administrative aspects, but we

---

[1] For an examination of the evidence supporting this assessment of post-independence trends in India, see Drèze (1988*a*).

[2] This question is further discussed in Chapter 11. On recent trends in the incidence of poverty in rural India, see e.g. Dandekar and Rath (1971), Bhatty (1974), Minhas (1974), Srinivasan and Bardhan (1974, 1988), Ahluwalia (1978), Dutta (1978), Gaiha and Kazmi (1981), Sundaram and Tendulkar (1981), Bardhan (1984), Gaiha (1987, 1988), Minhas *et al*. (1987), Sagar (1988), Sanyal (1988), and Subbarao (1989).

shall argue later that the administrative structure can be non-operational and ineffective in the absence of a political triggering mechanism.

The administrative aspects of the system can be traced to ideas championed —and to a limited extent used—in Indian history.[3] Kautilya, in the fourth century BC, spoke of employment creation and redistribution to the poor as parts of a sound administrative system to defeat famines. Various Indian rulers (such as Mohammad bin Tughlak in the fourteenth century) made extensive use of work projects and income creation for rebuilding lost entitlements.

As far as systematic exploration and exposition are concerned, the administrative analysis goes back, in many respects, to the detailed recommendations of the Famine Commission of 1880. The policy of governmental inaction that dominated British imperial administration in the early and middle nineteenth century gradually gave way to selective intervention concentrating mainly on the regeneration of cash incomes.

Among the more important of these recommendations of the Famine Commission of 1880 were (1) the framing of region-specific 'Famine Codes' embodying 'authoritative guidelines' to the local administration on the measures needed to anticipate and deal with the threat of famine, and (2) a strategy of entitlement protection based on the combination of guaranteed employment at a subsistence wage and unconditional relief (so-called 'gratuitous relief') for the unemployable. The reasoning behind this strategy is explained with great clarity in the Famine Commission Report, which is worth quoting at some length:

. . . we have to consider the manner in which the proper recipients of the public charity can be most effectually ascertained. The problem to be solved is how to avoid the risk of indiscriminate and demoralising profusion on the one hand, and of insufficient and niggardly assistance on the other—how to relieve all who really need relief, and to waste as little public money as possible in the process . . . where limited numbers have to be dealt with, and there is a numerous and efficient staff of officials, it may be possible to ascertain by personal inquiry the circumstances of every applicant for relief sufficiently for the purpose of admitting or rejecting his claim. But in an Indian famine the Government has to deal not with limited numbers, but with millions of people, and the official machinery at its command, however strengthened for the occasion, will inevitably be inadequate to the task of accurately testing the individual necessities of so great a multitude. Nor again is it possible to entrust the administration of public charity to a subordinate agency without providing sufficient checks against dishonesty and neglect on the part of its members. Some safeguards then are essential in the interests of the destitute people no less than of the public treasury, and they are best found in laying down certain broad self-acting tests by which necessity may be proved, and which may, irrespective of any other rule of selection, entitle to relief the person who submits to them . . . The chief of these tests, and the only one which in our opinion it is ordinarily

[3] On the history of famines and famine prevention in India, see Dutt (1900, 1901), Loveday (1914), Bhatia (1967), Srivastava (1968), Ambirajan (1978), Jaiswal (1978), McAlpin (1983a, 1983b), Brennan (1984), Klein (1984), and Drèze (1988a), among others.

desirable to enforce, is the demand of labour commensurate in each case with the labourer's powers, in return for a wage sufficient for the purposes of maintenance but not more. This system is applicable of course only to those from whom labour can reasonably be required . . . The great bulk of the applicants for relief being thus provided for, we believe that it will be possible for an efficient staff of officers to control with success the grant of relief, on the basis of personal inquiry and knowledge of the individual circumstances of each applicant, among the comparatively small numbers of destitute persons to whom the test of labour cannot be applied.[4]

Employment in public works was typically remunerated with cash wages. The expectation was that the demands generated by these wage payments would be met by the operation of private trade.

These broad principles are still relevant to the conception of India's entitlement protection system today. In particular the continued power of the strategy of employment generation supplemented by 'gratuitous relief' for the unemployable has been apparent in a number of experiences of successful famine prevention since independence.[5] At the same time, it would be a mistake to regard this system as a mere legacy of the British Administration. In fact, important advances have been made in famine prevention strategies since independence, even if we confine our attention to the administrative part of the story. One of the most important post-independence changes relates to the public distribution system.

The British Indian administration considered governmental involvement in food trade or distribution as sacrilegious. This position was grounded on a particular understanding of the teachings of classical economists (especially Adam Smith, John Stuart Mill, and Thomas Malthus), which were sometimes referred to as the 'Infallible Laws of the Great Masters of Economic Science'.[6] Suspicion of government interference with private trade extended also to any kind of public *participation* in food distribution.

While the government of independent India has, by and large, refrained from directly interfering with the activities of private traders, its own involvement in food trade and distribution has been extensive and important. In order

---

[4] Government of India (1880 36). In practice the British Administration did not, in fact, resist the temptation of providing 'niggardly assistance'. For instance, the failure of the relief system to prevent dramatic increases in mortality during the two famines which occurred in India at the very end of the 19th century has been partly attributed by several authors to the inadequate nature of relief measures (Bhatia 1967; Klein 1984; Guz 1987; Drèze 1988a). The stinginess of public provisions declined markedly after independence, though one may question how far the government of independent India has really departed from the earlier colonial view that 'while the duty of Government is to save life, it is not bound to maintain the labouring community at its normal level of comfort' (circular of the Government of India No. 44F, 9th June 1883), however low that 'level of comfort' is in the first place.

[5] See Singh (1975), Subramaniam (1975), Desai *et al.* (1979), McAlpin (1987), Drèze (1988a), and Chen (1989) for some case studies. It must be emphasized that the nature and effectiveness of the famine prevention system vary considerably between different regions of India. Some of these interregional contrasts are studied in Rangasami (1974) and Drèze (1988a).

[6] Etheridge (1868: 3). On the influence exercised by the teachings of classical economists on many prominent administrators in British India, see Ambirajan (1971, 1978) and Rashid (1980).

to assess correctly the contribution of India's public distribution system to famine prevention, we need to distinguish between its functions of *price stabilization* and *income generation*.

The stability of food prices in India today is quite remarkable (especially in comparison with the pre-independence period). For instance, during the most recent drought (that of 1987–8), which led to a considerable decline in food production, foodgrain prices increased by less than 10 per cent.[7] This was largely due to large-scale sales of food through the public distribution system, which held very large stocks at the beginning of the drought.[8] Clearly, the contribution of price stabilization measures to the protection of entitlements during crises in India today is a major one.

On the other hand, the income generation aspect of the public distribution of food has often been exaggerated. In per-capita terms, the subsidies involved in food sales to the rural population in so-called 'fair price shops' are very small indeed, even at times of drought.[9] In fact, in most states of India subsidized sales of food have a very limited coverage in rural areas. The really important vehicle of income generation in India during crises is that of large-scale public works, most frequently for cash wages. The irreplaceable role played by public works in sustaining the purchasing power of the rural poor is illustrated by the case-study of the Maharashtra drought of 1970–3 in the next section.

The distinction between the price stabilization role and the income generation role of the public distribution system has some bearing on the relevance of the Indian experience for other countries. The possible relevance of this experience for African countries, in particular, has often been dismissed on the grounds that (1) subsidized food sales to the rural population are the corner-stone of entitlement protection in India, and (2) most African countries lack a comparable infrastructure. This assessment is quite misleading. The generation of income through public works is not dependent on subsidized food sales. Adding to the incomes of the victims helps to prevent destitution, even without distributing cheap food. Furthermore, the price stabilization objective of the public distribution system can be pursued with substantial effect through *wholesale* food operations, and need not be dependent on the public network of 'fair price shops'.

---

[7] On this see Kumar (1988). According to the author, the prices of wheat, rice and 'all cereals' increased respectively by 7.3 per cent, 7.4 per cent and 7 per cent between 1986–7 and 1987–8 (p. 26). The decline in per-capita production of foodgrains during the 1987–8 agricultural year was of the order of 13 per cent compared to the 1984–6 average (calculated from Government of India 1989, Table 1.16). A little more than one century earlier, the Famine Commission of 1880 had boldly pronounced that 'in time of very great scarcity, prices of food grain rise to three times their ordinary amount (Government of India 1880: 27).

[8] Public food stocks amounted to 23.6 million tonnes in January 1987, and declined to 10 million tonnes during the drought period (Kumar 1988: 13).

[9] Also, in spite of the considerable expertise which India has acquired in the field of food logistics and distribution, the public distribution system routinely falls way below target in its supply of food to the rural population during droughts. See e.g. Bhatia (1988), Drèze (1988a), and Harriss (1988b).

While developments in the administrative aspects of entitlement protection policies since independence have been important, the really crucial changes have taken place in the domain of politics. The *existence* of the Famine Codes did not, after all, ensure their *application*, let alone their early and energetic application. The Famine Codes did include very specific instructions on how to recognize and 'declare' a famine, and the duty they imposed on the administrative structure made it harder to ignore a threatening crisis. However, this 'early warning system' existed *within* the Famine Codes, and could not guarantee their use in practice. Indeed, the problem of triggering remained an important one, since the Famine Codes did not impose any legal obligation to 'declare' a famine. During the Bengal famine of 1943, for instance, the Famine Codes were never invoked and were deliberately ignored, and this fact may well have been responsible for a large part of the extraordinary excess mortality associated with that famine.[10]

After independence, the political incentives to recognize emergencies, and to take action against the threat of famine, had to assume a new form. The vigour of political opposition has now made it impossible for the government to remain passive without major political risks, and the fear of losing elections reinforces the general sensitivity to political embarrassment in the state assembly and in the central parliament. In the process of making the facts known and forcing the hands of the respective state and central governments, the press too plays a leading role. The affected populations themselves have a much greater ability than in the past to make their demands felt and to galvanize the authorities into action (especially in view of the importance of winning the rural vote). This is one of the positive aspects of Indian democracy. We shall return to this question for fuller assessment in Chapter 11, when we reconsider the respective achievements of India and China in recent decades in combating hunger and famines.[11]

8.2   A Case-Study: The Maharashtra Drought of 1970–1973[12]

The state of Maharashtra in Western India, which in the early 1970s had a population of a little over 50 million, is one of the more 'developed' among Indian states by a number of conventional *aggregate* indicators (including

[10] See Sen (1981a), Greenough (1982) and Brennan (1988) for further discussion of the non-declaration of famine in that event.

[11] For further discussion of the role of public pressure in famine prevention in India, see also Sen (1982b, 1982c, 1983a), Ram (1986) and Drèze (1988a).

[12] This section is largely based on Drèze (1988a). The interested reader is referred to that paper for further discussion, as well as for a more detailed examination of the empirical evidence presented here. On the Maharashtra drought of 1970–3, see also Ladejinski (1973), Government of Maharashtra (1973), Krishnamachari *et al*. (1974), Kulkarni (1974), Mundle (1974), Borkar and Nadkarni (1975), Jodha (1975), Mathur and Bhattacharya (1975), Subramaniam (1975), Oughton (1982), Brahme (1983), and various contributions to the *Economic and Political Weekly* from 1971 to 1974.

literacy, urbanization, life expectancy, and average income). However, the divide between urban and rural areas in Maharashtra is very sharp, and the proportion of the rural population below the 'poverty line' in this state is among the highest in India.[13] Even within the rural sector, there are enormous

Table 8.1 District-wise cereal production in Maharashtra, 1967–1973

District	Index of Cereal Production (1967–8 = 100)				Cereal production per capita, 1972–3 (kg./year)
	1969–70	1970–1	1971–2	1972–3	
Greater Bombay	77	81	54	31	
Thana	88	110	97	42	46
Kolaba	78	101	81	67	131
Ratnagiri	99	117	103	86	85
Nasik	81	107	55	26	32
Dhulia	106	119	74	49	54
Jalgaon	89	74	59	70	72
Ahmednagar	109	80	59	33	47
Poona	90	70	73	43	38
Satara	98	103	91	41	45
Sangli	90	86	90	18	20
Sholapur	92	51	63	18	27
Kolhapur	93	110	115	65	53
Aurangabad	89	74	48	20	31
Parbhani	76	54	42	41	66
Bhir	120	97	54	17	27
Nanded	77	36	48	29	51
Osmanabad	108	54	58	45	61
Buldhana	122	68	82	63	86
Akola	132	55	89	61	64
Amravati	103	61	68	79	62
Yeotmal	131	65	104	85	86
Wardha	97	59	73	68	80
Nagpur	96	71	76	67	49
Bhandara	121	139	114	58	92
Chandrapur	129	109	105	71	118
MAHARASHTRA	99	83	74	47	51

Source: Calculated from the *Annual Season and Crop Reports* (Government of Maharashtra) of the corresponding years. Per-capita production figures for 1972–3 (last column) are based on district-wise population estimates (for 1973) obtained by assuming identical 1973/1971 population ratios for each District; the all-Maharashtra 1973/1971 population ratio is taken from the *Bulletin on Food Statistics*, 1982–4. District-wise population estimates for 1971 are from the Census (as given in Brahme 1983: 13–14.)

[13] See e.g. Vaidyanathan (1987).

regional inequalities in living standards, and in the semi-arid parts of the state the precariousness of life is particularly acute.

At the time of the onset of the terrible drought of 1970–3, rural Maharashtra was facing an alarming problem of environmental degradation, agricultural decline and threatened rural livelihoods, in many ways similar to the crisis faced by a number of African countries today. The sustained downward trend in per-capita agricultural and food production, which went back at least to the early 1960s, turned into a disastrous crash in the early 1970s, when the larger part of the state was affected by a drought of exceptional intensity for three years in succession. The statistics of food production for that period show a decline which, in terms of rapidity and magnitude, finds few equivalents in the recent history of droughts and famines elsewhere (see Table 8.1, Figure 8.1, and also Table 5.1 in Chapter 5 for an instructive comparison). During the peak year of the drought in 1972–3, the per-capita production of cereals in the state was as low as 51 kg.—less than one-third of the average level (itself very low) of per-capita consumption for India as a whole.

This acute crisis of food and agricultural production, and of the rural economy in general (with a virtual collapse of private employment and incomes for large sections of the population for a prolonged period), represented a considerable threat of large-scale entitlement failures. In spite of this, there are good indications that the sufferings caused by the drought, while far from negligible, were remarkably confined. There is, indeed, very little evidence that any of the usual signs of famine developed to a significant extent in this

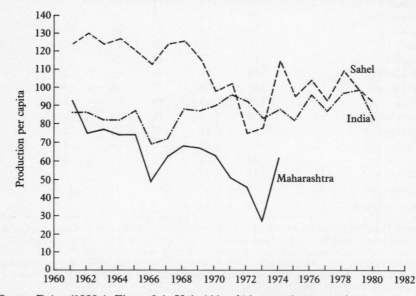

Source: Drèze (1988*a*), Figure 2.1. *Unit*: 100 = ½ kg. per day per capita.

Fig. 8.1   Production of cereals per capita, 1961–80: India, Maharashtra and Sahel

Table 8.2 Earnings from relief works and total income in seventy drought-affected villages, Maharashtra, 1972–1973

Percentage contribution of earnings on relief works to total income	Number of villages
0.0–20.0	7
20.1–40.0	8
40.1–50.0	9
50.1–60.0	10
60.1–70.0	14
70.1–80.0	15
80.1–90.0	6
90.1–100.0	1
TOTAL	70

Source: Brahme (1983: 59). The villages were located in the districts of Poona, Ahmednagar, Sholapur, Aurangabad, Bhir, and Osmanabad (all severely drought-affected).

event—whether 'starvation deaths', increases in mortality rates, nutritional deterioration, land sales, or migration to other states.[14]

How was famine averted? While it would be difficult to give a complete answer to this question, a major part of the story undoubtedly relates to public policies of entitlement protection. The cornerstone of these policies was the generation of employment for cash wages on a large scale, supplemented by 'gratuitous relief' for those unable to work and without able-bodied relatives. At the peak of the crisis, nearly 5 million labourers were employed on public works throughout the state. During the twelve months preceding July 1973 (the peak year of drought), relief works generated nearly one *billion* person-days of employment.[15] In the more severely drought-affected districts, the contribution of wage income from employment on public works to total income was well above 50 per cent for most villages (see Table 8.2).

One of the effects of this massive programme of income generation in drought-affected areas was to attract food from other parts of the country into Maharashtra through the channel of private trade. In theory, the drought period was one when severe restrictions were imposed on inter-state movements of food within India. But large amounts of foodgrains were imported into Maharashtra from neighbouring states in spite of these restrictions. This was an essential part of the mechanism of famine prevention, since the efforts made directly by the government to restore normal levels of food availability in

[14] See Drèze (1988a) for further discussion. The evidence on mortality rates is discussed in greater detail in the final version of that paper (to appear in Drèze and Sen, forthcoming), without major changes in the conclusions.

[15] Calculated from official figures given by Subramaniam (1975), Table II.3 (viii), based on attendance on the last day of each month.

Maharashtra (through public sales) fell far short of expectations.[16] In fact, had the trade restrictions been effectively enforced with an unchanged amount of food imported through the public distribution system, the aggregate consumption of foodgrains in the state would have been reduced by as much as 40 per cent. It would have been difficult to prevent a decline in *average* consumption

Table 8.3 Cereal consumption in Maharashtra: 1972–1973 compared to 'normal' years

Household class	Cereal consumption per capita (kg./month)	Percentage distribution of households by monthly per capita consumption class (kg./month)			
		<12	12–15	>15	Total
Large cultivators					
1967–8	15.6	25.5	28.7	45.8	100.0
1972–3	12.8	44.7	30.0	25.3	100.0
1973–4	15.3	n/a	n/a	n/a	100.0
Small cultivators					
1967–8	13.4	53.0	19.0	28.0	100.0
1972–3	11.1	61.2	25.2	13.6	100.0
1973–4	12.9	n/a	n/a	n/a	100.0
Farm labourers					
1967–8	14.5	41.4	19.9	38.6	100.0
1972–3	11.5	60.9	25.3	13.8	100.0
1973–4	13.7	n/a	n/a	n/a	100.0
Industrial workers					
1967–8	13.2	42.8	21.7	35.5	100.0
1972–3	12.0	65.3	27.1	7.6	100.0
1973–4	13.3	n/a	n/a	n/a	100.0
Others					
1967–8	12.4	n/a	n/a	n/a	100.0
1972–3	10.8	n/a	n/a	n/a	100.0
1973–4	12.1	n/a	n/a	n/a	100.0
All households					
1967–8	14.0	38.5	22.5	39.0	100.0
1972–3	11.7	59.9	25.2	15.9	100.0
1973–4	13.9	37.2	26.7	36.1	100.0

Source: Drèze (1988a), Tables 3.7 and 3.8. 1967–8 and 1973–4 were years of fairly normal harvest, and were the nearest (to 1972–3) 'normal' years for which data are available. The data cover the rural areas of ten drought-affected districts.

[16] The fact that the purchasing power generated by employment programmes had a dramatic impact on private food movements, and stimulated them in the right direction, does not imply that the public distribution itself played no important role in this episode of averted famine (or that it played a role that could have been easily supplanted by private trade). This should be clear from our earlier discussion of the interaction between private trade and public distribution (Chapter 6).

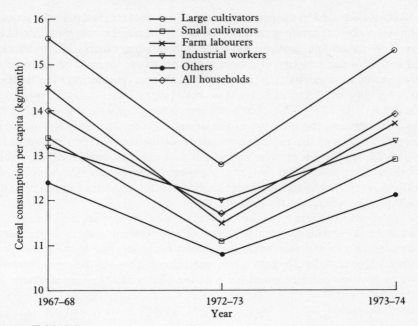

Source: Table 8.3.

Fig. 8.2 Cereal consumption in Maharashtra: drought year (1972–3) compared with normal years, by household class

of this magnitude (for a population as large as that of Maharashtra) from developing into a famine of major proportions.

In spite of large imports of food on both public and private accounts, a noticeable decline in average food consumption took place in Maharashtra in 1972–3. A striking feature of consumption patterns during that year, however, is that the reduction of aggregate consumption compared to ordinary years was distributed remarkably evenly among different socio-economic groups (see Table 8.3 and Figure 8.2). This phenomenon reflects the sustained purchasing power of vulnerable groups resulting from large-scale employment provision, and their ability to battle for their normal share of the available food in spite of the general penury. Correspondingly, the reduction of consumption on the part of relatively privileged groups resulted from the reduction of private money incomes, the increase of food prices, the desire of many asset owners to preserve their productive capital, and their reluctance to join relief works.[17]

---

[17] A decline in average consumption, along with a strikingly even reduction of intake for different socio-economic groups, is also observed by Marty Chen in her study of the impact of the 1987–8 drought on a village of Gujarat (Chen 1989). In fact, in that study the occupational group which experienced by far the *smallest* percentage decline in food consumption during the drought is found to be that of 'labourers' (Table 39). A completely different pattern has been found in the case of less well handled crises, such as the Bihar 'near-famine' of 1967, when the brunt of hardship was overwhelmingly borne by landless labourers (see Drèze 1988*a*).

As was discussed in the previous chapter, a crucial condition for the success of a redistributive strategy of this type is that preferential support should be given to vulnerable groups. An indication (among others) of the success achieved by the strategy of employment provision in reaching vulnerable groups and areas in this event can be obtained from considering the allocation of relief between different districts within Maharashtra. As can be seen from Figure 8.3, in 1972–3 a striking positive association was observable across districts between the intensity of the drought (as measured by the extent of crop failures) and the extensiveness of entitlement protection measures (as indicated by the proportion of the rural population employed on public works). This association is quite impressive considering the well-known difficulties that entitlement protection efforts often encounter in reaching the right people in famine situations.[18]

The success of a strategy based on large-scale cash support also depends, as discussed in Chapter 6, on the ability of the relief system to avoid the danger of large sections of the vulnerable population being left out of the purview of public support and at the same time remaining exposed to the price increases caused by the enhanced purchasing power of the others. This is where the

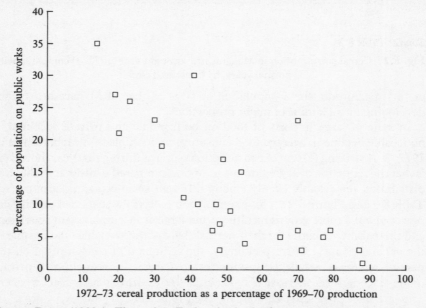

Source: Drèze (1988*a*), Figure 3.1. Each point in the figure represents one district of Maharashtra.

Fig. 8.3 Drought intensity and public relief in rural Maharashtra (1972–3), by district

[18] The difficulties and dilemmas involved in the 'selection problem' and the advantages of 'self-selection' were discussed in Chapter 7.

principle of *guaranteed* employment—imperfectly but usefully applied—played a crucial role.

The political factors involved in the response of the government, discussed in general terms in the previous section, are well illustrated by this particular event. The drought situation was the subject of 696 questions in the Maharashtra Legislative Assembly and Council in 1973 alone, and of numerous (often sharply critical) newspaper reports.[19] Much of the credit for galvanizing the government into action also belongs to the affected populations themselves, which pressed their demands in numerous ways—including marches, pickets and rallies. As one labourer aptly put it, 'they would let us die if they thought we would not make a noise about it'.[20]

8.3 Some African Successes[21]

In Chapter 5 of this book, we argued that African successes in famine prevention have failed to receive the attention they deserve. Of course, ultimately our concern has to be also with identifying mistakes and failures rather than taking idle comfort in past successes. However, there *is* a great deal to learn from the way in which various countries have successfully coped with the threat of entitlement failures. While the Indian experience is rich in general lessons, a number of recent successes with famine prevention in Africa are themselves of great interest. This section is devoted to a brief description and analysis of some of these successes. Their implications and lessons will be further discussed in the concluding section to this chapter.

Cape Verde

In his distinguished history of the Cape Verde Islands, Antonio Carreira wrote that 'everything in these islands combines to impose on man a hard, difficult and wretched way of life'.[22] A prominent aspect of the harshness of life in Cape Verde is the recurrence of devastating droughts, which have regularly affected the islands ever since their 'discovery' in 1460 by the Portuguese. Many of these droughts were associated with large-scale famine.[23]

[19] A useful guide to some of the newspaper reports on the drought can be found in Luthra and Srinivas (1976).

[20] Cited in Mody (1972: 2483). Many vivid accounts of popular protests during the drought can be found in the columns of *Economic and Political Weekly* (see e.g. Mody 1972, Anon. 1973, and Patil 1973). The demands involved often went beyond the mere provision of employment. For instance, in May 1973, a strike by 1.5 million labourers working on relief sites forced the government to grant them an increase in wages.

[21] We are extremely grateful to John Borton, Diana Callear, Jane Corbett, Rob Davies, Thomas Downing, Carl Eicher, Charles Harvey, Roger Hay, Judith Heyer, Francis Idachaba, Renée Loewenson, Siddhartha Mitter, S. T. W. Mhiribidi, Richard Morgan, Christopher Murray, David Sanders, Luc Spyckerelle, Samuel Wangwe, and Daniel Weiner for helpful comments, suggestions, and personal communications relating to the case-studies appearing in this section.

[22] Carreira (1982: 15). According to several analysts the climate of Cape Verde is even harsher and the droughts visiting it more frequent and severe than those of other Sahelian countries. See e.g. Meintel (1984: 56).

[23] For a chronology of droughts and famines in Cape Verde, see Freeman *et al.* (1978). For further discussion of famines in the history of Cape Verde, see Cabral (1980), Carreira (1982), Moran (1982), Meintel (1983, 1984), and Legal (1984).

Table 8.4 History of famine mortality in Cape
Verde, 1750–1950

	Mortality attributed to famine (percentage of total population)
1773–6	44
1830–3	42
1863–6	40
1900–3	15
1920–2	16
1940–3	15
1946–8	18

Source: Moran (1982), Table 1. The famines indicated
here are only those for which an estimate of famine
mortality is provided in that table. For the same period,
the author mentions 22 further large-scale famines for
which no mortality estimates are available.

In fact, it is hard to think of many famines in history that have taken a toll in
human life proportionately as high as those which have periodically decimated
Cape Verde in the last few centuries. Some of these famines are believed to have
killed nearly half of the population (see Table 8.4). Even after assuming some
exaggeration in these figures, there are very few parallels of such wholesale
mortality in the long and terrible history of famines in the world.

These historical famines went almost entirely unrelieved. When one of the
very few exceptions to this pattern occurred in 1825, the governor of the islands
was sacked for using Crown taxes to feed the people.[24] Left to its own devices,
the population had little other refuge than the attempt to emigrate—often
encouraged by the colonial authorities. Cape Verde's history of persistent
migration is indeed intimately connected with the succession of famines on the
islands. However, for most people this option remained a severely limited one,
and as recently as the 1940s large-scale mortality was a predictable feature of
prolonged drought.

In recent years, Cape Verde may well have been the worst drought-affected
of all African countries. Indeed, uninterrupted drought crippled the country's
economy for almost twenty years between 1968 and 1986—leading to a virtual
extinction of domestic food supplies and a near standstill of rural activity.[25]

[24] Freeman *et al*. (1978: 18). A strikingly similar incident occurred during the famine of the
early 1940s (Cabral 1980: 150–1). A significant attempt at providing relief was however made
during the famine of 1862–5, when employment was provided (with cash wage payments) on
road-building works (see Meintel 1984).

[25] In 1970, 70% of agricultural products consumed in Cape Verde were produced in the country
(CILSS 1976: 8). This ratio had fallen to 1.5% by 1973 (CILSS 1976:8), and only rose marginally
thereafter (van Binsbergen 1986). According to one study, 'during the drought over 70% of the
agricultural labour force has been unemployed' (Economist Intelligence Unit 1984: 38). It is not
clear, however, how this calculation treats labour employed on public works programmes (on
which more below).

Half-way through this prolonged drought in the middle 1970s, the event was already described as 'the longest and most severe [drought] on record' for the country.[26] In this case, however, not only was famine averted but, even more strikingly, significant *improvements* in living conditions took place during the drought period. The causation of these improvements is the centre of our interest here.

Famine prevention measures greatly gained in motivation and execution after the independence of Cape Verde in 1975. But even in the first period of the drought preceding independence (1968–75), the Portuguese rulers did make considerable efforts to provide famine relief (in contrast with the experiences earlier on in the colonial period).[27] Relief was provided almost exclusively in the form of employment for cash wages in makeshift work (the adequacy of food supplies being ensured separately by food imports). According to one study, as much as 84 per cent of total employment was provided by drought relief programmes in 1970 (this, however, still left 55.5 per cent of the labour force unemployed).[28]

These preventive measures succeeded to a great extent in averting a severe famine. There were no reports of large-scale starvation deaths, and the overall increase in mortality seems to have been moderate. The estimated infant mortality rate, for instance, which had shot up to more than 500 per thousand during the famine of 1947–8, was only a little above the 1962–7 average of 93.5 per thousand in the period 1968–75 (Table 8.5). On the other hand, a significant intensification of undernutrition during the same period has been reported in several studies.[29]

Since independence in 1975, Cape Verde has been ruled by a single party with a socialist orientation, viz. the Partido Africano da Independencia da Cabo Verde (PAICV).[30] This party, described by the current Prime Minister as 'reformist, progressist and nationalist',[31] is flanked by the Popular National Assembly, which is elected every five years by popular ballot (within a single party system). The government of independent Cape Verde has been consistently credited with progressive social reforms and development programmes. Notable areas of improvement have been those of education and health. Drought relief has been among the top political priorities.

Cape Verde's entitlement protection system since independence has

[26] Freeman *et al.* (1978: 98).
[27] Several commentators have argued that, in this case, action was motivated by the concern of the Portuguese government for its international image. See e.g. Meintel (1984: 68), CILSS (1976: 4), Davidson (1977: 394), and Cabral (1980: 134).
[28] Calculated from CILSS (1976: 3–4). This was the policy of *Apoio* or 'support', which was later criticized by the government of independent Cape Verde for the unproductive nature of the works undertaken (see CILSS 1976, Legal 1984, and Meintel 1983, 1984).
[29] See e.g. Meintel (1984: 68–9), CILSS (1976: 14), and Freeman *et al.* (1978: 149, 203).
[30] In fact, until 1981, Guinea-Bissau and Cape Verde were jointly ruled by the binational Partido Africano da Independencia da Guine e Cabo Verde, which had earlier led the independence struggle against the Portuguese rulers.
[31] *Courier* (1988: 27).

Table 8.5 Infant mortality in Cape Verde, 1912–1986

Year	Estimated infant mortality rate (deaths per 1000)	
	(1)	(2)
1912	220.6	
1913	174.2	
1915	117.9	
1920	155.0	
1927	217.6	
1931	206.7	
1937	223.4	
1943	317.9	
1946	268.7	
1947[a]	542.9	
1948[a]	428.6	
1949	203.9	
1950	130.7	
1962	106.1	
1963	109.7	
1964	85.3	
1965	76.7	
1966	83.6	
1967	99.9	
1968	91.7	
1969	123.1	
1970	95.0	
1971	130.9	
1972	90.9	
1973	110.6	
1974	78.9	
1975	103.9	104.9
1980–5		77.0
1985		70.0
1986		65.0

[a] Famine years.

Source: For the period 1912–75 (column 1), Freeman *et al.* (1978), Table V.26 (very close estimates are also reported for the 1969–74 period in CILSS 1976, Table VI). For 1975–86 (column 2), *World Health Statistics Annual 1985* and UNICEF (1987a, 1988).

consisted of three integrated components.[32] First, a competent and planned use of food aid has ensured an adequate and predictable food supply in spite of the nearly total collapse of domestic production. Food aid is legally bound to be *sold* wholesale in the open market, and the proceeds accrue to the National Development Fund.[33]

Second, the resources of the National Development Fund are used for labour-intensive public works programmes with a 'development' orientation. In 1983, 29.2 per cent of the labour force was employed in such programmes.[34] The works undertaken include afforestation, soil conservation, irrigation, and road building, and according to a recent evaluation 'the results of these projects are positive, even on the basis of high standards'.[35]

Third, unconditional relief is provided to selected and particularly vulnerable groups such as pregnant women, undernourished children, the elderly, and the invalid. This part of the entitlement protection system includes both nutritional intervention (such as school feeding) and cash transfers, and is integrated with related aspects of formal social security measures. In 1983, direct food assistance covered 14 per cent of the population (see van Binsbergen 1986: 10).

The effectiveness of this fairly comprehensive and well-integrated entitlement protection system is visible from the impact of the drought after 1975.[36] Indeed, the adverse effects of the drought on the living conditions of human beings seem to have been remarkably small.[37] In addition to the successful prevention of famine, there are indications that the post-1975 part of the drought period has witnessed: (1) a rapid *decline* in the infant mortality rate (see Table 8.5); (2) a significant *increase* in per-head food intake;[38] and (3) a significant *improvement* in the nutritional status of children (see Table 8.6).[39] By any criterion, the success achieved by the government of independent Cape

[32] For further details, see CILSS (1976), Davidson (1977), Freeman *et al.* (1978), USAID (1982), Meintel (1983), Legal (1984), Lesourd (1986), and particularly van Binsbergen (1986).

[33] This rule does not apply when the sale of food aid violates the conditions of delivery, e.g. in the case of the comparatively small quantities of food donated to Cape Verde under the World Food Programme. These are used for supplementary feeding.

[34] Economist Intelligence Unit (1984: 38).

[35] See van Binsbergen (1986: 9). See also *Courier* (1988).

[36] Both in the pre-independence and the post-independence periods, remittances from abroad also played an important role in mitigating the effects of the drought.

[37] There is a revealing contrast between this observation and the fact of huge livestock losses, which provide another measure of the intensity of the drought and of the threat of famine. The decline in livestock between 1968 and 1980 has been estimated at 12% for goats, 30% for pigs, 50% for sheep, and 72% for cows (calculated from Economist Intelligence Unit 1983: 43).

[38] On this, see Legal (1984: 12–16), who notes large increases in the consumption of maize, wheat, and rice in the post-independence period compared to the pre-drought period. The average consumption of calories, which 'for the vast majority of the population did not exceed 1500 calories per day' at the time of independence (CILSS 1976: 8; our translation), is now believed to have 'moved closer to the required level of 2800 calories per day' (van Binsbergen 1986: 3).

[39] A USAID study dated 1982 also mentions, without explicitly providing supporting figures, that 'by providing employment, the Government of Cape Verde's rural work program has had an acknowledged major effect on improving nutritional status' (USAID 1982: 15).

Table 8.6 Child undernutrition in Cape Verde, 1977 and 1984

District	Percentage of school children suffering from undernutrition (moderate to serious)	
	1977[a]	1984[b]
Boa Vista	41.8	7.8
Porto Novo	49.2	9.2
Ribeira Grande	54.3	5.8
São Vicente	38.1	10.7
Tarrafal	n/a	7.8
TOTAL	46.4	8.8

[a] Children aged 7–15 years.
[b] Children aged 6–18 years.

Source: van Binsbergen (1986), Table 2. According to the author, the two studies on which this table is based are 'reasonably comparable', and 'although the methodologies used by the different studies were not identical, it is safe to conclude that the nutritional status of school age children has significantly improved since 1977' (van Binsbergen 1986: 3–4). An independent study carried out in 1973 estimated that 38% of children aged 7–14 suffered from 'moderate protein-calorie malnutrition' (Freeman *et al*. 1978, Table V.24).

Verde in protecting the population from the adverse effects of a drought of unprecedented magnitude must be seen as exemplary.

Kenya

The history of Kenya, like that of Cape Verde, has been repeatedly marked by grim episodes of drought and famine.[40] As recently as 1980–1, famine struck substantial parts of the population in the wake of a drought of moderate intensity. The government of Kenya has been widely praised, however, for preventing a much more widespread and intense drought from developing into a famine in 1984. This event has been extensively studied elsewhere.[41] We shall only recall here the main features of this successful response, and comment briefly on some of its neglected aspects.

Like Cape Verde, Kenya has a single party system and an elected parliament. Since independence in 1963, the country has enjoyed a degree of political stability which compares favourably with many other parts of Africa. The freedom of the national media is limited, but nevertheless more extensive than in most African countries. The country also has a high degree of visibility in the international press.

More than 80 per cent of Kenya's population (around 19 million in 1984) is

[40] See e.g. Wisner (1977), O'Leary (1980), Herlehy (1984) and Ambler (1988).
[41] For in-depth analyses of the 1984 drought and the government's response, see Ray (1984), Deloitte *et al*. (1986), Cohen and Lewis (1987), Corbett (1987), J. Downing *et al*. (1987), and T. Downing *et al*. (forthcoming). A particularly useful and well documented account of this event can be found in Borton (1988, forthcoming).

rural, and derives its livelihood largely from agriculture and livestock. Compared to most other parts of Africa, the rural economy is quite diversified, and has experienced relatively rapid growth since the early 1960s. Despite these favourable factors, large parts of the country remain vulnerable to climatic and economic instability, particularly in the largely semi-arid areas of the Eastern and North-eastern Provinces.

The strategies adopted by rural households in Kenya to cope with drought or the threat of famine appear to be increasingly geared to the acquisition of food in the market and the diversification of economic activities (partly through wage employment).[42] The importance of off-farm activities in the rural household economy can be seen from the fact that, according to a survey carried out in six districts of the Central and Eastern Provinces in 1985, more than half of smallholder households had at least one member in long-term wage employment (see Table 8.7 below).

The 1984 crisis followed a massive failure of the 'long rains' in March and April 1984. According to Cohen and Lewis:

It was the worst shortage of rains in the last 100 years. Production of maize, the nation's principal food crop, was approximately 50% below that normally expected for the main rains of March–May. Wheat, the second most important grain, was nearly 70% below normal. Potato production was down by more than 70%. Pastoralists reported losing up to 70% of their stock. The situation had the potential for a famine of major proportions.[43]

Regional disparities compound the problems reflected in these aggregate statistics. In the Central and Eastern Provinces, maize production for the agricultural year 1984–5 was estimated by the FAO at 14 per cent and 26 per cent (respectively) of the average for the previous six years. In districts such as Kitui and Machakos, maize production was virtually nil both in 1983 and in 1984.[44]

While in specific areas the drought of 1984 meant the second or even third consecutive crop failure, for most areas the crisis was one of limited duration. The 'short rains' of October to December 1984 were above average. However, in terms of intensity and geographical coverage the drought of 1984 was certainly an exceptional one, and distress continued until the harvest of mid-1985.

The use of formal early warning techniques apparently played little role in precipitating action. The need for action seems to have been detected partly from the visible failure of rains in early 1984 (followed by evident crop failures), and partly from the unusual increase in food purchases from the

[42] On coping strategies in Kenya, see Wisner (1977), Bertlin (1980), Campbell (1984), Swift (1985), Downing (1988b), Akong'a and Downing (1987), Sperling (1987a, 1987b), Anyango et al. (forthcoming) and Kamau et al. (forthcoming).

[43] Cohen and Lewis (1987: 274). The existence of a serious threat of large-scale famine in this event is also argued in detail in Corbett (1987). For statistical information on rainfall patterns and crop production during the drought, see Downing et al. (forthcoming).

[44] See Borton (1988), Table 3, and Maganda (forthcoming), Table 9.4.

National Cereals and Produce Board later in the year.[45] While Cohen and Lewis stress the role of 'political commitment' in ensuring an early and adequate response, others comment that 'the government felt the need to forestall political instability that would result in the event of a widespread famine'.[46] The threat of political unrest seems to have been exacerbated by the fact that, somewhat unusually, the drought of 1984 strongly affected a number of politically important and influential areas of the Central and Eastern Provinces, as well as Nairobi.

Active public response to the crisis began in April 1984.[47] The first step taken by the government to deal with the threat of famine was to import large amounts of food on a commercial basis. The initial availability of substantial food stocks ensured that the lags involved in the importation of food did not have disastrous consequences. Food aid pledges were also obtained, but with a few minor exceptions their fulfilment occurred only in 1985, several months after the arrival of commercial food imports. The ability of the government to buy large amounts of food on the international market was greatly helped by the availability of foreign exchange reserves and the peak in export earnings resulting largely from high world prices for tea and coffee.

Entitlement protection measures took two different forms. First, the government used food imports to ensure the continued availability of food at reasonable prices through normal commercial channels. In ordinary times, interdistrict food movements are exclusively organized by the National Cereals and Produce Board, which subcontracts the transport and distribution of food to licensed private traders. This arrangement was preserved and intensified during the drought, and most of the imported food was sold through the intermediation of private traders at 'gazetted' prices fixed by the government.

Second, direct support was provided to vulnerable households in affected areas. Initially, the government intended to provide such support mainly in the form of employment for cash wages.[48] In practice, however, the generation of employment fell far short of target, due to a lack of preparedness and supervisory capacity. On the other hand, the provision of unconditional relief in the form of free food rations (mainly from food aid) assumed considerable importance. In August 1984, nearly 1.4 million people, or 7 per cent of the total

[45] Cohen and Lewis describe the symptoms of an impending crisis as follows: 'By April 1984, the situation was obvious. The sun was shining beautifully, when it should have been raining; no early warning system was required' (Cohen and Lewis 1987: 276). Other authors, however, have also stressed the role of rapidly increasing purchases from the National Cereals and Produce Board in arousing concern for the possibility of a crisis (see e.g. Corbett 1987, and Borton forthcoming).

[46] J. Downing et al. (1987: 266). It appears that the drought enjoyed only limited coverage in the local media, but attracted considerable international attention and concern (Downing 1988a).

[47] For detailed and documented accounts of the famine prevention measures, see Cohen and Lewis (1987), J. Downing et al. (1987), Borton (1988, forthcoming) and T. Downing et al. (forthcoming). This case study concentrates mainly on the government response, which represents the greater part of these measures, though the involvement of non-government agencies was not insignificant.

[48] The two slogans propounded by the government early on during the crisis were 'planning, not panic' and 'food imports and employment generation' (Ray 1984).

population, were estimated to be in receipt of free food distribution, and in January 1985 a very similar estimate was reported.[49] In drought-affected areas, the proportion of the population receiving food rations was much larger, and the survey of smallholders in Central and Eastern Kenya mentioned earlier found that over the same period the proportion of households receiving food assistance in the surveyed districts was as high as 45 per cent (see Table 8.7). The size of the rations distributed, however, appears to have been very small prior to the large-scale arrival of food aid in 1985.[50]

The allocation of relief to the needy was the responsibility of the provincial administration, which itself relied on local famine relief committees and 'chiefs' to identify those in need of support. The precise way in which this system actually worked is far from clear. According to some, the local chiefs 'knew the needs of their people, and by most reports did an effective, equitable job of distributing the government-supplied grain'.[51] Another account, however, states that 'moving in the path of least resistance, the GOK [Government of Kenya] would seem to rather divide the available food equally among recipients at the distributions thus defusing potentially uncomfortable situations'.[52]

It is not implausible that the allocation of food within specific communities was largely indiscriminate, and that 'targeting' operated mainly between different villages or regions (the impact of the drought varied greatly between different areas). On the other hand, an important factor facilitating the fair allocation of free food was the fact that most of it consisted of *yellow* maize, which is generally considered as an 'inferior' commodity in Kenya. The element of 'self-selection' involved in distributing yellow maize has been said by a number of commentators to have contributed to an allocation more geared to the most desperate.

Table 8.7 presents some indicators of the impact of the drought on the rural population in different ecological zones of Central and Eastern Kenya, arranged in increasing order of drought-proneness. The table brings out, *inter alia*, (1) the role played by wage employment and remittances in sustaining affected households, (2) the responsiveness of consumption patterns to price and income changes (the composition of food consumption changed for most households even in the less affected areas), and (3) the extensive nature of the

[49] Deloitte *et al.* (1986: 12). In 1985, the numbers in receipt of unconditional relief gradually decreased, though the amount of food distributed increased with the enlarged flow of food aid.

[50] The same survey reveals that, between July and December 1984, the median food ration per recipient household varied between 197 and 633 calories per day in different regions (Downing 1988a, Table 5.16; see also Downing 1988b, Table 4.19). For the same period, Anyango *et al.* (1987) estimate that 'the food relief averaged 5–10 per cent of individual requirements' for the recipients (see also Kamau *et al.* forthcoming). In 1985, the size of food rations was much larger, and did not in fact differ very much on average from the 'target' of 10 kg. of maize per person per month (Borton 1988, forthcoming).

[51] Cohen and Lewis (1987: 281).

[52] Ray (1984: 2). Communications from two persons who were involved in the 1984 relief efforts confirm that food distribution centres typically did not discriminate between different groups of people, and provided identical rations to all recipients.

Table 8.7 The 1984 drought and smallholder households in Central and Eastern Kenya

Characteristic	Percentage of households with the specified characteristic, by ecological zone					
	1	2	3	4	5	All zones
Household member moved during 1984	23	7	21	26	38	25
Has a member in permanent employment	58	47	61	54	54	56
Received cash remittances from relatives or friends during drought	34	28	40	57	46	43
Major food changed during 1984	84	78	76	67	67	73
Received famine relief (from govt or NGOs)	14	35	25	67	77	45
Slaughtered, sold, lost or consumed cattle[a]	41 (26)	45 (35)	33 (29)	44 (46)	32 (51)	38 (58)

[a] In brackets, the percentage decrease in cattle holding, averaged over all households surveyed in the respective zone.

Source: Anyango *et al.* (forthcoming), Tables 13.6 and 13.9. Based on survey data collected in January 1985 by the Central Bureau of Statistics on behalf of the National Environment Secretariat. In Kenya, a smallholder is 'typically defined as a rural landowner with less than 22 hectares' (Akong'a and Downing 1987: 92). Ecological zones appear in increasing order of drought-proneness, based on rainfall data.

coverage of food distribution in these districts at that time.[53] The large cattle losses also confirm the exceptional severity of the drought.[54]

The overall effect of the drought on the well-being of the affected populations has not been fully ascertained. Most commentators consider that 'famine was averted'. The apparent absence of confirmed reports of 'starvation deaths', as well as of distress migration on the part of entire families, lends some support to this view. On the other hand, there is clear evidence of widespread hunger as well as rising undernutrition in 1984.[55]

[53] The general significance for famine prevention policies of the phenomena related to the first two observations was discussed in Chapters 5 and 7.

[54] For further details of livestock losses, see Borton (1988), Downing *et al.* (forthcoming), Chapter 1, Kamau *et al.* (forthcoming), Anyango *et al.* (forthcoming) and Mwendwa (forthcoming). The picture presented in other surveys is, if anything, grimmer than that offered by Table 8.7. According to Borton (1988), the drought of 1984 may have depleted the *national* cattle herd by as much as 50 per cent (p. vii).

[55] See the surveys of Anyango *et al.* (forthcoming), Neumann *et al.* (forthcoming) and Kamau *et al.* (forthcoming). The relative absence of distress migration is discussed in Anyango *et al.* (forthcoming). Unfortunately, the available data do not permit us to estimate the extent of excess mortality during the drought.

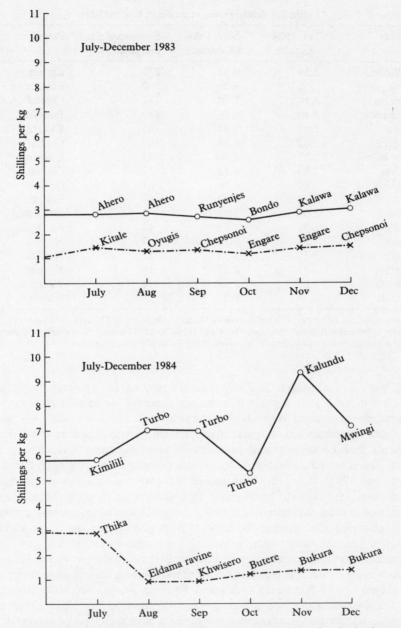

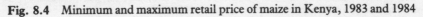

Source: As in Table 8.8. The upper line indicates the retail price of maize in the market where it was the highest in the corresponding month. The lower line indicates the retail price where it was the lowest.

Fig. 8.4   Minimum and maximum retail price of maize in Kenya, 1983 and 1984

Table 8.8 Retail prices of maize in Kenya, 1984

Market	Jan. 1984 (Kshs/kg.)	Nov. 1984 (Kshs/kg.)	Percentage increase	Province
Kalundu	2.50	9.31	272	Eastern
Mwingi	2.50	9.00	260	Eastern
Kiambu	2.14	5.30	148	Central
Machakos	2.40	5.76	140	Eastern
Iciara	2.53	5.94	135	Eastern
Limuru	2.02	4.19	107	Central
Runyenjes	2.57	4.70	83	Eastern
Thika	2.86	4.91	72	Central
Kandara	2.84	4.76	68	Central
Embu Town	2.92	4.89	67	Eastern
Eldoret	2.00	2.92	46	Rift Valley
Kitale	1.51	2.11	40	Rift Valley
Bondo	2.50	3.33	33	Nyanza
Ahero	2.51	3.19	27	Nyanza
Sondu	2.31	2.73	18	Nyanza
Mumias	2.35	2.69	14	Western
Luanda	2.71	2.57	−5	Western

Source: Republic of Kenya, Central Bureau of Statistics, Ministry of Finance and Planning, *Market Information Bulletin* (Jan.–June 1984 and July–Dec. 1984 issues). The markets in the table are all those for which data are provided in the Bulletin for both months.

While the credit which the Kenyan government has been given for averting a severe famine in 1984 appears to be largely deserved, an important query can nevertheless be raised as to whether the strategy it adopted made good use of available opportunities. A particularly relevant issue concerns the balance between income support and price stabilization measures. Considering the small size of food distribution to vulnerable households in per-capita terms (at least until 1985), it appears that famine prevention measures were geared to work mainly through the level of food *prices* rather than through the generation of compensating incomes.[56] In turn, the stability of prices was pursued through a policy of commercial imports from abroad into the worst affected districts. At the same time, however, government regulations prevented private traders from moving food from surplus to deficit areas within Kenya.

As was mentioned earlier, interdistrict food movements in Kenya are tightly regulated by the National Cereals and Produce Board, which subcontracts food transport to licensed private traders. Several studies have shown that these restrictions on interregional movements have the effect of exacerbating the intensity of local shortages and the disparity of retail food prices between

---

[56] According to Borton (1988), free distribution of food accounted for only 15 per cent of the cereals imported between September 1984 and June 1985 (p. 19).

regions.[57] This phenomenon was clearly visible during the drought year itself: while food prices were sharply rising in drought-affected districts, they were only sluggishly increasing or even *falling* in many others (see Figure 8.4 and Table 8.8). Maize prices in different markets varied, at one point, by a factor of nearly *ten*.[58] Even between adjacent districts, price disparities seem to have been exceptionally large (see Table 8.9).

The detrimental effects of this policy of trade restrictions on the entitlements of vulnerable groups in drought-affected areas are not difficult to guess. For instance, after stressing the role of food shortages and high prices in undermining the entitlements of poor households in the Samburu District of Northern Kenya, Louise Sperling comments:

[The] problem of local distribution was sufficiently severe to result in the convening of a district-level meeting as early as 14th June 1984. The District Commissioner called together the eleven or twelve wholesalers to discuss 'the erratic supply of commodities'. Maize prices are strictly controlled by the state, and the local traders claimed they were losing money on maize sales. The allowed mark-up could not cover the costs of transport and loading to these more remote areas. Even considerable government pressure to encourage traders to keep their shelves full did not result in an increase in the local availability of maize . . . Again, the poor disproportionately suffered from these shortages. They could not afford to buy grain in bulk when it did arrive. Equally, they did not have the means to purchase alternative, more costly foodstuffs.[59]

Table 8.9 Maize prices in Central and Eastern Kenya, 1984

Zone	Price of white maize (Kshs/kg.)		Percentage Increase (Jan.–Dec.)
	Jan.–Mar.	Oct.–Dec.	
1	3.98	5.94	49
2	3.25	5.50	69
3	2.80	6.20	121
4	2.94	7.22	146
5	3.49	10.24	193

Note: The ecological zones are the same as in Table 8.7.

Source: Anyango *et al*. (forthcoming), Table 13.10.

[57] On this, see particularly Olsen (1984). See also Akong'a and Downing (1987) and Sperling (1987a). Note that the volatility of *retail* prices is compatible with the control of 'gazetted prices' mentioned earlier.

[58] For details of food price patterns during the drought, see the Government of Kenya's *Market Information Bulletin*, and also Maganda (forthcoming). Careful econometric analysis of time-series data on food prices in Kenya confirms that the interregional disparity of prices sharply increased in 1984 (Jane Corbett, Food Studies Group, QEH, Oxford, personal communication).

[59] Sperling (1987a: 269).

To conclude, while the efforts made by the Government of Kenya in 1984 to import food into drought-affected areas well ahead of large-scale famine were no doubt remarkable, it may be that certain aspects of the relief programme are yet to receive adequately critical scrutiny. To some extent, the acute need to rush food from abroad into the worst affected regions was a result of the parallel efforts that were made, partly for political reasons, to prevent food exports from surplus areas, or to direct such exports towards Nairobi. It appears that, in some respects, government intervention during the drought was undoing with one hand the harm it had done with the other.

Zimbabwe

The so-called 'Zimbabwean miracle' in food production has received wide attention recently. By contrast, the impressive and largely successful programmes of direct entitlement protection pursued by the Zimbabwean government to prevent the prolonged drought of 1982–4 from precipitating a major famine seem to have been relatively neglected.[60] While it is tempting to think that a country with growing food supplies cannot possibly know the threat of famine, the experience of famines all over the world shows how misleading and dangerous this assumption can be. In the case of Zimbabwe too, a closer examination of the facts reveals that the prevention of a famine in 1982–4 must be attributed as much to far-reaching measures of public support in favour of affected populations as to the growth of food supplies.

The political system in Zimbabwe is that of a limited multi-party democracy. Since independence in 1980, the country has been ruled by the elected and re-elected ZANU (Zimbabwe African National Union) party led by Robert Mugabe. A notable feature of ZANU is its very wide and largely rural support base, inherited from the independence struggle. Political debate is intense in Zimbabwe. The press is relatively unconstrained and one of the most active in Africa. The press played, in fact, a conspicuous role in keeping the government on its toes throughout the drought period.[61]

In spite of the socialist aims of the government, the economy has retained private ownership and market incentives. On the other hand, the government of independent Zimbabwe has carried out a major revolution in the area of

[60] To the best of our knowledge an in-depth analysis of these events has not been published to this day. However, see Government of Zimbabwe (1986a, 1986b), Gaidzanwa (1986), Leys (1986), Bratton (1987a), Davies and Sanders (1987a, 1987b), Loewenson (1986), Loewenson and Sanders (1988), Mitter (1988), Tagwireyi (1988), and Weiner (1988), for many valuable insights.

[61] On the extensive coverage of the drought in the Zimbabwean press, see the accounts of Leys (1986), Bratton (1987a), and Mitter (1988). Some of the more widely circulated newspapers, such as the *Herald*, did not always take a sharply adversarial stance given their generally supportive attitude *vis-à-vis* the ZANU government. However, even they played a role in maintaining a strong sense of urgency by constantly reporting on the prevalence of undernutrition and hardship in the countryside, echoing parliamentary debates on the subject of drought, calling for action against profiteering, and exposing the 'scandal' of rural women driven to prostitution by hunger (on this see *Herald* 1983).

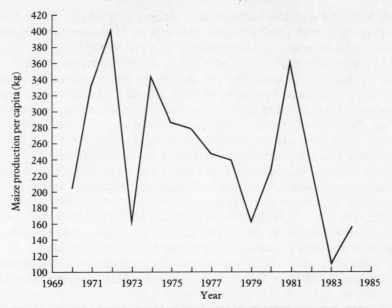

Source: Calculated from production figures provided in Rohrbach (1988), Figure 1, and from population data given in UNICEF (1988), Tables 1 and 5.

Fig. 8.5 Maize production per capita in Zimbabwe, 1970–84

social services. The great strides made since 1980 in the areas of health and nutrition have, in particular, received wide recognition.[62]

In comparison with most other African countries, Zimbabwe's economy (including the agricultural sector) is relatively prosperous and diversified. However, the heritage of the colonial period also includes massive economic and social inequalities. The agricultural sector is highly dualistic, the larger part of the more fertile land being cultivated by a small number of commercial farms while peasant production remains the dominant feature of 'communal areas'. Even within the communal areas, sharp regional contrasts exist both in productive potential and in access to infrastructural support.[63] Further divisions exist between racial and class groups as well as between rural and urban areas. As a result, large sections of the population live in acute poverty in

[62] See e.g. Donelan (1983), Government of Zimbabwe (1984), Waterson and Sanders (1984), Mandaza (1986), Davies and Sanders (1987a, 1987b), Loewenson and Sanders (1988), and Tagwireyi (1988). To mention only two important areas of rapid advance, the percentage of children fully immunized in Zimbabwe increased from 27 per cent in 1982 to 85 per cent in 1988 (Tagwireyi 1988: 8), and school enrolment increased at an annual rate of 20 per cent between 1979 and 1985 (Davies and Sanders 1987b: 297).

[63] This point is stressed in Weiner (1987) and Weiner and Moyo (1988). For further discussion of production relations in Zimbabwe's rural economy and their implications for living standards and famine vulnerability, see Bratton (1987a, 1987b), Rukini and Eicher (1987), Rukuni (1988) and Weiner (1988).

spite of the relative prosperity of the economy as a whole. At the time of independence, health and nutrition problems in Zimbabwe were extremely serious, even in comparison with other African countries.[64]

The 'production miracle' in Zimbabwe is of relatively recent origin. In fact, from the early 1970s until after the drought period, there was—to say the least—little evidence of any upward trend in food production per capita (see Figure 8.5). On the other hand, it must be remembered that, over the same period, Zimbabwe remained a net *exporter* of food in most years. The plentiful harvest which immediately preceded the drought ensured that large stocks of maize were available when the country faced the threat of famine.[65]

The drought lasted three years, and was of highest intensity in agro-climatic terms during the second year (i.e. 1983). In the drier parts of the country, the maize crop (Zimbabwe's principal staple crop) was 'a total failure throughout the drought years'.[66] Maize sales to the Grain Marketing Board fell by more than two-thirds between 1980–1 and 1982–3. Livestock losses between 1978 and 1983 have been estimated at 36 per cent of the communal herd.[67]

For many rural dwellers, remittances from relatives involved in regular employment or migrant labour were a crucial source of support during the drought. As in the Sahel and in Kenya (discussed earlier), it was found in Zimbabwe that 'the households most engaged in selling labour to the wider economy . . . are the least susceptible to drought'.[68] Many households, however, did not have access to this broader source of sustenance, and for them government relief was often the main or even the only source of food.

The drought relief programme of the government was an ambitious and far-reaching one. Famine prevention measures were taken early in 1982, and given a high political and financial priority throughout the drought. The main entitlement protection measures were large-scale food distribution to the adult

[64] See e.g. Sanders (1982), World Bank (1983b), Loewenson (1984), and Government of Zimbabwe (1984). These studies give a clear picture of the connections between this poor record and the massive inequalities in economic opportunities and access to public services of the colonial period. In the early 1970s, for instance, the life expectancy of a European female was more than *twenty* years longer than that of an African female (Agere 1986: 359).

[65] It is worth noting that while the Zimbabwean 'miracle' has often been attributed to the astonishing power of price incentives (see e.g. *The Economist* 1985, and Park and Jackson 1985), the expansion of the rural economy since independence has in fact involved a great deal more than a simple 'price fix'. On the extensive and fruitful involvement of the government of independent Zimbabwe in infrastructural support, agricultural extension, credit provision, support of cooperatives, etc., see Bratton (1986, 1987a), Eicher and Staatz (1986), Eicher (1988a), Rohrbach (1988) and Weiner (1988).

[66] Bratton (1987a: 224). This statement refers, in fact, to the two least fertile among Zimbabwe's five agro-ecological regions. These two regions account for 64% of Zimbabwe's land, 74% of the 'communal lands', and about two-thirds of the communal area population.

[67] Bratton (1987a: 223–5). Weiner (1988) reports declines in draught stock during the drought period of 47% and 21% respectively in the two agro-ecological regions mentioned in the last footnote.

[68] Leys (1986: 262). On the importance of wage labour and remittances for the rural economy in general, and for mitigating the impact of the drought on the rural population in particular, see also Bratton (1987a), Weiner (1987) and Weiner and Moyo (1988).

Table 8.10 Drought and drought relief in Chibi district, Zimbabwe, 1983–1984

Village	Number of households	Percentage of cattle which died in previous twelve months	Percentage of population receiving food rations[a]
A	52	28	62
B	36	34	64
C	44	32	68
D	39	47	54

[a] Per capita rations of 20 kg. per month.

Source: Constructed from Leys (1986). According to the author, Chibi District was one of the worst affected districts.

population, and supplementary feeding for children under five. Commenting on the importance of free food distribution for the survival of the poor, one study of drought relief in Southern Zimbabwe comments that 'for those without access to cash and other entitlements it was their only food intake'.[69]

It is not easy to assess how large a part of the population benefited from free food distribution. Estimates of 2 to 3 million people being fed in rural areas at the peak of the programme, as against a total rural population of 5.7 million in 1982, have been cited in various studies.[70] A survey of 464 households carried out in four communal areas selected for their environmental diversity found that more than 50 per cent of the surveyed households were receiving free maize in 1982–3 and 1983–4.[71] Another study, focusing on four villages in one of the most affected districts, reveals a proportion of population in receipt of free food rations ranging from 54 to 68 per cent (see Table 8.10). Very similar findings are reported in a number of further household surveys.[72] While the precise extent of food distribution is difficult to ascertain, its scale was undoubtedly impressive. The size of individual food rations—officially 20 kg. of maize per head per month—was also astonishingly large.

Of course, the task of organizing food distribution on such a gigantic scale was by no means an easy one. While the implementation of relief measures,

[69] Leys (1986: 270). Similarly, Weiner (1988) states that 'during the 1982–4 period the government drought relief programme became the primary means of survival for about 2.5 million people' (p. 71). While the present discussion focuses largely on the food distribution component of the drought relief programme, it is worth noting that (1) policy developments during the drought included an increasingly marked preference for public works programmes (supplemented by unconditional relief for the destitute) as opposed to large-scale distribution of free food, and (2) the drought relief programme had a number of other important components, such as water supply schemes, cattle protection measures, and inputs provision. On both points, see Government of Zimbabwe (1986a).

[70] See e.g. Government of Zimbabwe (1983: 21), Bratton (1987a: 237), Mitter (1988: 4). The official version seems to be that 'at the height of the drought about 2.1 million people had to be fed every month' (Government of Zimbabwe 1986a).

[71] Bratton (1987a), Table 10.8(b).

[72] See especially Weiner (1988), Table 6.4, and Matiza et al. (1988).

much helped by the popular mobilization and political stability associated with the post-independence reconstruction efforts, has attracted favourable comments from many observers, frequent complaints on the part of recipients about the delays, uncertainties, and frauds involved in food distribution have also been reported.[73] In relieving logistic constraints, the subcontracting of food delivery to the private sector played a major role. In fact, disruptions in food deliveries seem to have intensified after the attempt was made (in September 1983) to substitute government transport for private transport.[74]

The free distribution of food raised its own problems. The population eligible for food rations seems to have been confined in practice to households without a member in regular employment.[75] How fairly this criterion was applied in practice is not easy to ascertain, and conflicting views have been expressed on this question. For instance, one author reports on the basis of extensive field work in Southern Zimbabwe that 'as far as I could assess, these criteria were applied fairly and, at the sub-district level, were felt to be fair', and the evidence presented from four village studies in one of the worst-affected districts broadly supports this assessment.[76] But another author suggests the possibility that 'in practice, the distribution pattern was indiscriminate; those who were ineligible received relief food, while those who were truly needy may have gone short'.[77]

The politicization of food distribution during the drought was also apparent in a number of ways—with both negative and positive implications. First, party cadres have played a major role in many places in implementing the distribution of food, and this seems to have led to some favouritism along party lines.[78] Second, the coverage of the drought relief programme in Matabeleland, the stronghold of political dissidents, has been described as 'exceedingly patchy'.[79] Third, food distribution was restricted to rural areas—a highly interesting feature of the relief programme given the frequent bias of public distribution systems in favour of urban classes. It is tempting to interpret this

[73] See e.g. USAID (1983), Leys (1986), Bratton (1987a), Davies and Sanders (1987b), and Mitter (1988).

[74] Leys (1986: 270).

[75] Bratton (1987a) describes the eligible population as 'the "needy" . . . , defined as those with insufficient grain in the home granary and without a close family member working for a wage' (p. 238). Leys (1986), on the other hand, states that free food distribution was intended for 'the members of households in which the head of the household earned an income under the statutory minimum wage' (p. 269), but later adds that this involved 'distinguishing between those households where the head of household held a formal sector job' and others (p. 270). In practice it is likely that the two sets of criteria described by these authors did not diverge substantially.

[76] Leys (1986: 270). Another author gives credit to the ZANU government for 'the smooth running of the relief committees' (Mitter 1988: 5).

[77] Bratton (1987a: 238). The viewpoint expressed by Bratton is based on a personal communication from a colleague at the University of Zimbabwe and could have been less robustly founded than that of Leys.

[78] Daniel Weiner (University of Toledo), personal communication. See also Leys (1986).

[79] Leys (1986: 271). The government put the blame on dissidents for disrupting relief efforts, and even at one stage held them 'responsible for the drought' (see Mitter 1988, for further discussion).

Table 8.11 Nutritional status of children in Zimbabwe, 1981–2 and 1983

Area	Percentage of children (aged 0 to 5) suffering from second or third degree malnutrition			
	Weight for age		Weight for height	
	1981–2	1983	1981–2	1983
Commercial farming area	42	14, 20[a]	16	8, 7[a]
Communal area[b]	20	11	13	3
Mine area	22	9	6	4
Urban area	6	4	6	2

[a] These figures refer respectively to (1) farms benefiting from a health project initiated in 1981–2, and (2) farms excluded from the health project.
[b] Resurvey area adjacent to that of baseline survey.

Source: Loewenson (1986), Table 3. Based on a sample survey of nearly 2,000 children in Mashonaland Central. For further details and discussion, see also Loewenson (1984).

'rural bias' as a reflection of the politics of ZANU and the predominantly rural character of its support base.

In spite of these reservations, the overall effectiveness of entitlement protection measures during the drought is beyond question. It is not only that 'starvation deaths' have been largely and perhaps even entirely prevented.[80] The striking effect of the government's far-reaching relief programme, in combination with the general expansion of health and education facilities since independence, has been a noticeable *improvement* in the health status of the population of rural Zimbabwe in spite of the severe drought. The most striking aspect of this improvement has been the apparent *decline* in infant mortality throughout the drought period.[81] A significant decline in child morbidity, at least in relation to immunizable diseases, has also been reported, and related to the government's vigorous immunization campaigns.[82]

The evidence on the nutritional status of the population during the drought is mixed. Concern about sharply rising levels of undernutrition in the *early* phases of the drought has been expressed in many informal reports.[83] There is, however, some evidence of declining undernutrition after the relief programme expanded on a large scale in 1983 (see Table 8.11).[84] Taking the drought period as a whole, the available evidence suggests the absence of

[80] According to Bratton, 'it is safe to say that no person in Zimbabwe died as a direct result of starvation' (Bratton 1987a: 225). According to Leys, 'one consequence of the drought for some of the rural African population was hunger, and on occasion and specific places, deaths from starvation' (Leys 1986: 258).
[81] For detailed discussions of mortality decline in Zimbabwe since independence, see Davies and Sanders (1987a, 1987b), Loewenson and Sanders (1988) and Sanders and Davies (1988). It has been claimed that the extent of mortality reduction in Zimbabwe between 1980 and 1985 has been as large as 50% (*The Times* 1985; Bratton 1987a: 238).
[82] See Loewenson and Sanders (1988).
[83] See e.g. Bratton (1987a: 224), Mitter (1988: 3–4), Moto (1983).
[84] See Loewenson (1984, 1986) for further discussion of these findings.

marked change in the nutritional status of the Zimbabwean population.[85] This
is remarkable enough, given the severity of the initial threat.

Botswana

As a land-locked, sparsely populated, and drought-prone country experiencing rapid population growth, massive ecological deterioration, and shrinking
food production, Botswana possesses many of the features that are thought to
make the Sahelian countries highly vulnerable to famine. There are, of course,
also important contrasts between the two regions. One of them arises from the
highly democratic nature of Botswana's political regime, and—relatedly
perhaps—the comparative efficiency of its administration. Also, while many
Sahelian countries have suffered from declining or stagnating per-capita
incomes in recent decades, Botswana has enjoyed a growth rate which is
estimated as one of the highest in the world.

Economic growth in Botswana has, however, followed a highly uneven
pattern. In fact, much of this rapid growth has to do with the recent expansion
of diamond mining, a productive sector of little direct relevance to the rural
poor. Against a background of booming earnings in industry, there is some
evidence of increasing rural unemployment and falling rural incomes since the
early 1970s. One study goes as far as suggesting that rural incomes in Botswana
(inclusive of transfers and remittances) *declined* in real terms at the rate of 5 per
cent per year during the period 1974–81.[86] The year 1981–2 marked the
beginning of a prolonged and severe drought which lasted until 1986–7, and
would certainly have been accompanied by an even sharper deterioration of
income and employment opportunities in the absence of vigorous public
support measures. Fast overall economic growth is no guarantee of protection
against famine.

The rural economy, mostly based on livestock, crop production, and
derived activities, suffered a predictable recession during the drought. The
output of food crops fell to negligible levels (Table 8.12). Cattle mortality
increased substantially, and the decline of employment opportunities further
aggravated the deterioration of rural livelihoods.[87] In a socio-economic survey

[85] See Davies and Sanders (1987*a*, 1987*b*), Loewenson and Sanders (1988) and Sanders and
Davies (1988) for detailed reviews of the evidence. See also the results of regular surveys (carried
out by the government of Zimbabwe) presented in Tagwireyi (1988).

[86] See the study of Hay *et al.* (1986), especially Table 2. A published summary of the main
results of this major study of drought relief in Botswana can be found in Hay (1988). On the rural
economy of Botswana, see Chernichovsky *et al.* (1985).

[87] For details, see Hay *et al.* (1986) and Quinn *et al.* (1987). It should be mentioned that while
livestock losses during the drought were perhaps not dramatic in *aggregate* terms (according to
Morgan 1986, the size of the national cattle herd declined by 22 per cent between 1982 and 1986), it
has been frequently noted that these losses disproportionately hit small herds. Cattle deaths for
small herds have been estimated at 'more than 40 per cent for several years' (Diana Callear,
National Food Strategy Coordinator, personal communication). Also, poor households in rural
Botswana derive a greater than average part of their total incomes from crops (even harder hit by
the drought than livestock). The threat which the drought represented to the entitlements of
vulnerable groups was therefore much more serious than aggregate figures about livestock
mortality, and about the importance of livestock in the rural economy, would tend to suggest.

Table 8.12 Food crop performance in Botswana,
1968–1984

Year	Area planted (000 hectares)	Yield (kg./hect.)	Output (000 tonnes)
1968	200	180	36
1969	240	258	62
1970	202	69	14
1971	246	293	72
1972	251	343	86
1973	139	101	14
1974	255	290	74
1975	250	284	71
1976	261	295	77
1977	255	290	74
1978	260	192	50
1979	160	62	10
1980	268	172	46
1981	274	201	55
1982	193	89	17
1983	226	63	14
1984	197	36	7

Source: Hay *et al*. (1986), Tables 5 and 6.

of 284 rural households carried out in 1984, more than half of the respondents reported 'having no cash income' (other than relief income).[88]

By 1981–2, however, Botswana had set up an entitlement protection system exemplary in its scope and integration. This system was, in fact, the outcome of a long process of experimentation, evaluation and learning. Moderately successful but instructive experiments with famine relief in the 1960s and early 1970s were later followed by a series of evaluations and debates which provided the crucial foundation of Botswana's remarkable relief system.[89] The drought of 1979–80 played a particularly important role in this respect.

Famine relief during the 1979–80 drought was essentially an experiment in what we have called the 'strategy of direct delivery'.[90] The operation was considerably hampered by logistic difficulties connected with the transportation and distribution of food, though a noticeable improvement occurred after

[88] Hay *et al*. (1986: 85).

[89] The Sandford Report (Sandford 1977) provided a useful background investigation of drought in Botswana. The Symposium on Drought in Botswana (Botswana Society 1979) which was convened, quite remarkably, in spite of the then prosperity of agriculture and the economy, was an invaluable forum of discussion on numerous aspects of the problem. Gooch and MacDonald (1981a, 1981b) provided an illuminating evaluation of relief efforts during the 1979–80 drought and far-reaching recommendations for improvement. For an excellent analysis of the development of Botswana's entitlement protection system, see Borton (1984, 1986).

[90] The following details are based on Morgan (1985), Relief and Development Institute (1985), and especially Gooch and MacDonald (1981a, 1981b).

the adoption of extensive subcontracting to private truckers. Food deliveries in different parts of the country matched poorly with the extent of distress. The allocation of food within the rural population was largely indiscriminate, partly because the selective distribution of food was found to be 'socially divisive'.[91] While a large-scale famine was averted, the relief operations did not succeed in preventing increased malnutrition, excess mortality, or even starvation deaths.[92]

The lessons of this experiment were not lost, however. In fact, the detailed evaluation carried out by Gooch and MacDonald made a crucial contribution to the design of Botswana's entitlement protection system as it exists today. Their recommendations included (1) the issue of a Relief Manual providing clear and coherent advance guidelines to the administration about the provision of drought relief, and (2) the adoption of a famine prevention strategy based on the unlimited provision of employment (for a subsistence wage paid in cash) to the able-bodied supplemented by unconditional relief for vulnerable groups. These recommendations, while not literally implemented to this day, have provided the basis for a sustained improvement in famine prevention measures.

Careful planning (and buoyant government revenue) would not have gone far enough in the absence of a strong motivation on the part of the government to respond to the threat of famine. Drought relief, however, has consistently been a high political priority in Botswana, and an object of rival promises and actions on the part of competing parties. It is also interesting that, when drought struck the country again in 1981–2, early action was forthcoming in spite of the absence of a formal early warning system.[93] As in India, the politics of famine prevention in Botswana are intimately linked with the accountability of the ruling party to the electorate, the activism of opposition parties, the vigilance of the press, and—last but not least—the strong demands for public support on the part of the affected populations.[94]

The drought of 1982–7 provided a severe test of the country's growing ability to prevent famines. The entitlement protection measures invoked in this event involved three major areas of action: (1) the restoration of adequate food availability, (2) the large-scale provision of employment for cash wages, and (3) direct food distribution to selected groups.[95]

[91] Gooch and MacDonald (1981*b*: 11). In other cases, the distribution of food was vulnerable to frank abuses.

[92] On this, see Gooch and MacDonald (1981*b*: 12–13).

[93] Botswana does have a well developed 'nutrition surveillance' system, but this is used mainly for the purposes of monitoring and targeting rather than as a warning device. The decision to launch a major relief operation in 1982 was taken much *before* the system detected a significant increase in undernutrition (see Borton and York 1987). Nor do other components of Botswana's evolving early warning system seem to have played a major role in triggering the government's response (see e.g. Relief and Development Institute 1985).

[94] For a clear discussion of this issue, and of the 'political value of drought relief' in Botswana, see Holm and Morgan (1985) and Holm and Cohen (1988).

[95] It should be mentioned that the drought relief programme as a whole went much beyond

Table 8.13 Price of maize meal at selected centres, Botswana 1980–1983

Region	Price in August 1980 (Pula/bag)	Price in April 1983 (Pula/bag)	Percentage increase
Gaborone	3.39	4.51	33
Francistown	3.56	4.41	24
Lobatse	3.34	4.48	34
Selibe-Pikwe	3.33	4.71	41
Palapye	3.36	4.54	35
Mahalapye	3.48	4.86	40
Mochudi	3.41	4.55	33
Kanye	3.41	4.58	34
Serowe	3.56	4.80	35
Molepolole	3.70	4.81	30
Maun	4.22	5.38	27
Mmadinare	3.73	4.70	26
Tonota	3.59	4.68	30
Shoshong	3.38	4.82	43
Moshupa	3.38	5.02	49
Thamaga	3.35	4.97	48
Ramotswa	3.84	4.73	23
All regions, unweighted average	3.53	4.74	34

Source: Tabor (1983), Table 4.5.

Unlike in 1979–80, the restoration of food adequacy in 1982–7 relied on a more varied and discerning strategy than that of direct delivery. While Botswana did receive large amounts of food aid during the drought, the support of incomes through employment generation (financed out of general government revenue) was not tied to the receipt of food aid. Moreover, food aid was substantially complemented by private imports of food from abroad, and it is not implausible that had food aid been interrupted or delayed this alternative source of food supply would have enabled the relief system to operate with no major loss of effectiveness.[96]

Trade and distribution within the country has been largely ensured by

these measures of short-term entitlement protection. Public intervention was also very significant in areas such as the provision of water and the promotion of agricultural recovery. For comprehensive analyses of the drought relief programme, see Tabor (1983), Borton (1984, 1986), Holm and Morgan (1985), Relief and Development Institute (1985), Morgan (1985, 1986, 1988), Hay *et al.* (1986), Quinn *et al.* (1987), Hay (1988), Holm and Cohen (1988) and Moremi (1988). See also Government of Botswana (1980, 1985*a*, 1985*b*, 1987, 1988).

[96] Botswana belongs to the South African Customs Union (SACU), which *inter alia* allows the free movement of food between Botswana, South Africa, Lesotho and Swaziland. As a result, domestic variations in agricultural output have little effect on the availability and price of food in Botswana. For an econometric analysis of the effect of SACU membership on food prices and food security in Botswana, see Cathie and Herrmann (1988).

Botswana's 'widespread and highly competitive retail network operating in all but the remoter areas'.[97] The effectiveness of this system, and of the process of spatial arbitrage, is visible from the remarkable degree of uniformity in the level of food prices in different parts of the country during the drought (Table 8.13). The contrast with our earlier findings on Kenya is striking.

Another important contrast between drought relief in 1982–7 and in 1979–80 has been the much greater reliance, in the former case, on cash-based employment generation as a vehicle of income generation. The provision of employment has, in fact, fallen short of the vision of 'employment guarantee' contemplated by Gooch and MacDonald, and it has been repeatedly observed that the demand for employment has exceeded the number of jobs available.[98] Nevertheless, the extent of income support provided to vulnerable households by 'Labour-Based Relief Programmes' has been considerable. In 1985–6 they provided around 3 million person-days of employment to 74,000 labourers. It has also been estimated that Labour-Based Relief Programmes 'replaced' almost one-third of rural incomes lost from crop failures between 1983 and 1985.[99] Informal evaluations of the productive value of the works undertaken suggest that the contribution of these programmes to national investment has been far from negligible.[100]

Along with this strategy of employment generation, free food has been distributed on a large scale, mainly in the form of 'take-home' rations. The eligibility conditions for food distribution in various forms in rural areas are very broad, and include not only the destitutes but also other categories such as all pre-school children, all children in primary school, children aged 6–10 not attending school, and all pregnant or lactating women. As a result, the proportion of the total population in receipt of free food rations was as high as two-thirds in 1985.[101]

The experience of drought relief in Botswana in 1982–7 amply demonstrates the effectiveness of a famine prevention system based on the combination of adequate political incentives and insightful administrative guidelines. While the drought of 1982–7 was far more prolonged and severe than that of 1979–80, and led to a much greater disruption of the rural economy, the extent of human suffering was comparatively small. There is no significant evidence

[97] Morgan (1985: 49).

[98] See e.g. Hay et al. (1986) and Quinn et al. (1987). This finding must be interpreted bearing in mind that the level of wages paid is 'roughly equivalent to the salary earned by maids and security guards in urban areas and considerably more than cattle herders earned on cattle-posts' (Quinn et al. 1987: 18).

[99] Quinn et al. (1987: 18, 21). The population of Botswana was a little over one million at the time.

[100] See Hay et al. (1986) for a detailed discussion.

[101] Calculated from Hay et al. (1986), Tables 10 and 11. According to the same source the average size of rations amounted to nearly 60 kg. of food (mainly cereals) per recipient per year. For a helpful account of the various components of Botswana's food distribution programme, see Hay (1988).

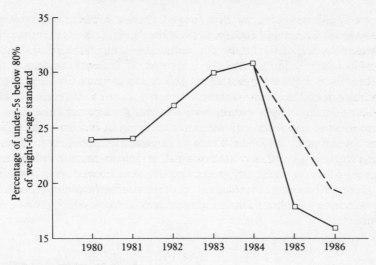

Source: Morgan (1988), Figure 5.

Note: The broken line shows the estimated incidence of undernutrition taking into account changes in the recording system in 1985. The figures are derived from Botswana's Nutrition Surveillance System, which covered about 60% of all under-fives in Botswana in 1984 (Morgan 1985: 45). The increase in observed undernutrition in the early years of the drought may partly reflect the large increase in the coverage of the surveillance system that took place during those years (Hay 1988: 1125).

Fig. 8.6 Incidence of child undernutrition in Botswana, 1980–6

of starvation deaths, or of distress migration on any significant scale.[102] The nutritional status of children only deteriorated marginally and temporarily (see Figure 8.6). One study also reports that 'those who have experienced previous droughts say that the decline in suffering among the disadvantaged is dramatic'.[103] Last but not least, drought relief measures in Botswana seem to have met with an impressive measure of success not only in preventing human suffering but also in preserving the productive potential of the rural economy.[104]

[102] According to Morgan (1988), 'starvation, even among extremely isolated communities, was entirely averted' (p. 33).

[103] Holm and Morgan (1985: 469). None of the studies cited in this section provide estimates of excess mortality during the drought. According to Borton, 'mortality estimates are poor in Botswana so it is not possible to estimate whether there has been a significant increase in the death rate' (Borton 1984: 92). Against the initial increase in undernutrition among children, it must be noted that (1) the incidence of *severe* undernutrition has been very small (Hay *et al.* 1986; Holm and Morgan 1985), and (2) seasonal fluctuations in nutritional status have virtually disappeared during the drought (Government of Botswana 1985: Table 5).

[104] On this, see Morgan (1986). The preservation of the productive potential of the rural economy is related partly to the entitlement protection measures discussed here, but also to a wide array of explicit rehabilitation and recovery programmes. Though they are not the focus of our attention in this chapter, the importance of these programmes must not be underestimated.

There is another aspect of Botswana's experience which deserves special mention here. A number of components of the drought relief programme, such as the distribution of food to certain vulnerable groups, the rehabilitation of undernourished children, and the provision of financial assistance to the destitute, have acquired a permanent status and are now an integral part of Botswana's social security system.[105] In the future, therefore, it can be expected that famine prevention measures will perhaps take the form of an *intensification* of social security measures applying in ordinary times. Such a policy development would be a natural extension of the current reliance on existing infrastructural and institutional arrangements for drought relief purposes. This approach to the protection of entitlements during crises has, in general, much to commend, in terms of administrative flexibility, likelihood of early response, simplification of logistics, and ability to elicit broad political support.

8.4   Lessons from African Successes

The African experiences analysed in the previous section illustrate the rich variety of political, social and economic problems involved in the protection of entitlements in a crisis situation. It would be stupid to attempt to derive from these case studies a mechanical blueprint for famine prevention in Africa. However, a number of commonalities involved in the recent experiences of famine prevention in Botswana, Cape Verde, Kenya and Zimbabwe provide, along with the general analyses of previous chapters, the basis of some useful lessons.

The Importance of Entitlement Protection Systems

There is a tendency, once the dust of an emergency has settled down, to seek the reduction of famine vulnerability primarily in enhanced economic growth, or the revival of the rural economy, or the diversification of economic activities. The potential contribution of greater prosperity, if it involves vulnerable groups, cannot be denied. At the same time, it is important to recognize that, no matter how fast they grow, countries where a large part of the population derive their livelihood from uncertain sources cannot hope to avert famines without specialized entitlement protection mechanisms involving direct public intervention. Rapid growth of the economy in Botswana, or of the agricultural sector in Kenya, or of food production in Zimbabwe, explain at best only a small part of their success in averting recurrent threats of famine. The real achievements of these countries (as well as of Cape Verde) lie in having provided direct public support to their populations in times of crisis.

---

[105] See Morgan (1986) and Holm and Cohen (1988) for further discussion of the interplay between drought relief and social security measures during the last few decades in Botswana.

Initiative and Agency

An important feature of recent famine prevention efforts in the four countries studied in the previous section is that, in each case, the initiative and responsibility of entitlement protection efforts rested squarely with the government of the affected country. This is not to say that international agencies played no positive part in such efforts. In fact, their contribution and partnership has, in each case, been helpful. But the essential tasks of coordination and leadership belonged primarily to the government and administration of the affected countries.

The general 'comparative advantage' that the governments of affected countries have in managing relief operations can indeed be important. This comparative advantage mainly takes the form of being able to draw at short notice on extensive networks of information, administration, communication, transport and storage. In a long term perspective, a sustainable and efficient system of famine prevention can hardly dispense with the close involvement and leadership of the governments of the concerned countries themselves. This makes it particularly important to see the current contribution of international agencies as cooperation with, rather than replacement of, the efforts of the respective governments.

Early Warning and Early Response

Formal 'early warning' techniques have played only a minor role in the famine prevention experiences studied in the preceding section. Early response has been much more a matter of political incentives and motivation than one of informational or predictive wizardry.

As was mentioned earlier, the political systems of the four countries concerned are, in comparison with most other African countries, relatively open and pluralist (e.g. they all have an elected parliament). All except possibly Cape Verde also have an active and largely uncensored press. The role of political opposition, parliamentary debate, public criticism and investigative journalism in galvanizing the national government into action has been central in Botswana as well as in Zimbabwe, and, to a lesser extent, in Kenya.

This does not mean that only countries with highly developed participatory institutions can consistently avert the threat of famine. Even fairly repressive governments are often wary of the prospects of popular discontent in the event of a famine. Political ideology—if it takes the form of a commitment to the more deprived sections of the population—can be another creative force in motivating response. In Cape Verde and Zimbabwe, this influence seems to have been important. As was pointed out in Chapter 5, the attitude of African governments to the threat of famine is not in general one of apathy and callousness.

Food Supply Management

In each of the four countries studied in the previous section, the government took necessary steps to ensure an adequate availability of food. But the exact nature of these steps varied a great deal, and appealed to different strategic elements such as government purchases on international markets, private trade, food aid and the depletion of public stocks.

This strategic diversity contrasts with the common belief that food aid is the only appropriate channel to enhance food availability in a famine-affected country. It is true that three of these four countries (namely, Botswana, Cape Verde and Kenya) have *made use* of substantial quantities of food aid in their efforts to avert famine, but in no case have their entitlement protection measures been significantly *contingent* on the timely arrival of food aid. In fact, entitlement protection policies have typically *preceded* the arrival of food aid pledged in response to the threat of famine. In this respect, entitlement protection measures in these countries have markedly departed from the strategy of 'direct delivery' discussed in Chapter 6.

A particularly significant departure from the strategy of direct delivery is the use of cash support to protect the entitlements of vulnerable groups. The general merits of this approach were discussed at some length in Chapter 6. It is worth noting that reliance on cash support, which is sometimes thought to be highly unsuitable in the context of African famines, has been used with excellent effect in two of the four countries concerned (Botswana and Cape Verde).

Private Trade and Public Distribution

Each of the four African countries discussed earlier have induced private trade to supplement the efforts of the public sector in moving food towards vulnerable areas. In Botswana and Cape Verde, this has taken the form of providing cash support to vulnerable groups on a large scale and leaving a substantial part of the task of food delivery to the market mechanism. In Kenya and Zimbabwe, it has taken the form of subcontracting to private traders the transport of food to specific destinations. In each case, private trade could be confidently expected to move food in the right direction, i.e. towards (rather than out of) affected areas.

At the same time, the direct involvement of the public sector in food supply management has also been substantial in each country. The benefits of this involvement were visible not only in terms of its direct effects on the flow of food, but also in the noticeable absence of collusive practices or panic hoarding in the private sector itself. The sharp contrast between the behaviour of food prices in Kenya and Botswana during recent droughts, discussed in sections 6.3 and 8.3, strongly suggests that the positive involvement of the public sector in food supply management is often a far more creative form of intervention than the imposition of negative restrictions on the operation of private trade.

Diversification and Employment

As a final observation, we should note the prominent role played by the diversification of economic activities (notably through wage employment), and the acquisition of food on the market, in the survival strategies of vulnerable groups in the countries studied in the previous section. As was discussed in Chapter 5, this observation is in line with a general assessment of survival strategies in Africa. Two of its implications are worth emphasizing.

First, while current problems of famine vulnerability in Africa clearly originate in part from the stagnation or decline of food production in that continent (leading to major losses of income and employment for the rural population), it does not follow that the remedy of this vulnerability must necessarily take the form of reversing that historical trend against all odds. Diversification and exchange have been an important part of the economic opportunities of rural populations in Africa for a long time, and open up alternative avenues of action that also need to be considered.

Second, there are strong reasons to think that the potential of employment provision as a tool of entitlement protection (e.g. in the form of public works programmes) is substantial in large parts of Africa. The general advantages of the strategy of employment provision (notably making possible the use of self-selection, and also the provision of cash support) were discussed in Chapter 7. The fact that affected populations positively look for work in crises situations, and do this long before reaching an advanced stage of destitution, strengthens the case for seeing this strategy as a natural avenue of entitlement protection. In many circumstances, the spade is a more powerful tool of famine prevention than the spoon.

PART III

Undernutrition and Deprivation

9

Production, Entitlements and Nutrition

9.1 Introduction

This part of the book is primarily concerned with public action to combat persistent undernutrition and endemic deprivation (as opposed to transient famines and crises). In this chapter, we shall deal with questions related to the role of food production in this context. Other aspects of the problem of 'social security' will receive scrutiny in subsequent chapters.

Let us begin by distinguishing four different questions about a country's achievements in relation to ensuring adequate nutrition for all. Each points to a particular focus of attention:

1. Is the country *self-sufficient* in food?
2. Does the country have an adequate *food availability*?
3. Do the people in the country have sufficient *food entitlement*?
4. Do the people have adequate *nutritional capability*?

Substantial parts of this chapter will be concerned with discussing the far-reaching implications of distinguishing between these different questions.

There are causal links between the respective points of attention in these questions. For example, achieving food *self-sufficiency* can be one way for a country to ensure *adequate food availability*. Having an adequate supply of food will generally help, to a varying extent, the guaranteeing of sufficient *food entitlements* for all. And securing an adequate entitlement to food must contribute to a person's *nutritional capability*. But there are also complexities —indeed gaps—in such causal relationships. Public action to combat hunger has to take note both of the causal links and of the gaps in those links.

Reasoned decision in this field is hampered not merely by the difficulty of causal analysis, but also by the fact that certain canons of wise policy have acquired such intellectual standing and such widespread acceptance that they are not subjected to adequately critical scrutiny. These canons do, of course, have their rationale, and some of them can serve the purpose of drawing our attention forcefully to the causal links in a simple form. While there is a clear gain in this, there is also the danger of taking too simple a view of these links. A half-truth can be a dangerous source of wisdom.

9.2 Food Self-Sufficiency?

Few objectives of economic policy seem to be as widely valued as that of national self-sufficiency in food. Both India and China, for instance, have placed enormous emphasis on this objective, and they get a great deal of credit and acclaim for that achievement, even though both countries have also met with some failures in their attempt to eliminate hunger and famines.[1] The objective of food self-sufficiency has been forcefully stressed for Africa in the famous Lagos Plan of Action, which set the year 2000 as the target date for its fulfilment. Most African governments seem to take the need for food self-sufficiency as axiomatic, and even proclaim the attainment of this objective as imminent. The endorsement of self-sufficiency as a major goal also surfaces regularly in the publications of influential international organizations such as the Food and Agriculture Organization, the Club du Sahel, and even the World Bank.[2]

It has been argued, with some justice, that the dependence of a country on importing food from abroad for the survival of its own population can be a major source of vulnerability for that country. This is particularly so in, say, war situations. At a very elementary level, the desire to be less dependent on outsiders for the most basic necessity of life is easy to sympathize with.[3]

This does not, however, imply that a country less dependent on importing food from abroad would necessarily be better off in terms of food consumption or nutritional levels than another which is more dependent in this respect. The issue of self-sufficiency is, obviously, quite a distinct one from that of the adequacy of food supply, and nothing is gained by confounding the two concepts. Countries like Japan, Switzerland, or the United Kingdom depend a great deal on importing food from abroad, but their populations do not, to say the least, suffer from food inadequacy, compared with, say, the people of self-sufficient Burma, Uganda, or—for that matter—India. And even within Africa, we have seen in Chapter 8 that some countries (such as Botswana and Cape Verde) have succeeded in considerably enhancing the nutritional security of their population in spite of a poor record in terms of food self-sufficiency. Given the possibility of relying on the international market to acquire food,

---

[1] The comparative experiences of India and China are discussed in Chapter 11. It will be seen that their successes as well as their failures are related to administrative, economic, and political strategies that go well beyond food self-sufficiency.

[2] See e.g. Ross (1983), Please and Amoako (1984), and Food and Agriculture Organization (1986).

[3] Arguments for food self-sufficiency have sometimes sought added strength from the historical observation that many dependent economies lost their food self-sufficiency in the age of imperialism. Lappé and Collins, for instance, have argued: 'Food dependency originated with imperialism . . . Food self-reliance is the cornerstone of genuine self-determination and it is possible for every country in the world' (Lappé and Collins 1980: 139, 145). This historical observation certainly does apply to many countries, and the *possibility* of universal food self-sufficiency given adequate concentration of resources also seems plausible. The question is whether this policy serves the interest of the deprived and hungry population best. Lappé and Collins suggest some reasons why this might be the case. There are arguments on the other side as well, and the decision has to depend on the relative force of these conflicting arguments as they apply to the contemporary world, no matter what the historical explanation for the loss of food self-sufficiency of the pre-imperial world might be.

the issue of self-sufficiency and that of adequacy can and must be firmly distinguished.

One factor that has been responsible for the confounding of the two different ideas of food self-sufficiency and food adequacy is the observed fact that many economies that have become increasingly dependent on food imports from abroad have also developed problems of food inadequacy and hunger within the economy. Sub-Saharan Africa is, of course, an area in which many countries fit this description. Indeed, as was mentioned in Chapter 2, Africa is the only major region in the world in which food output per head has gone down substantially during recent decades. In many African countries the problem of hunger is thought to have greatly intensified in the last decade or two, and food imports have also had to be quite dramatically increased.

This relationship is not, of course, surprising. Indeed, it is easy to see the causal links that operated in the process through which Africa became both more dependent on food supply from abroad, and more prone to persistent hunger as well as recurring famines. If the food production of a country fails to keep pace with domestic demand, its imports from abroad will tend to increase. If, in addition, the failure of food production to keep up with demand is caused by a production crisis, with less output and perhaps less employment, then it will be natural to expect that there will be economic hardship too. If, furthermore, in the country in question substantial sections of the population derive their incomes and entitlements primarily from the production of food, then the proportion of the population affected by this economic hardship would be large. And, if those who are thus affected happen to be normally quite poor, with relatively little economic reserve to fall back on, then the result of that large-scale hardship may well be quite a major increase in hunger and deprivation. Finally, if no social security system of any sort is in operation, then that hunger and deprivation may remain unrelieved.

As it happens, all these conditions are, unfortunately, met for many of the sub-Saharan African countries, and there is, therefore, nothing particularly surprising in the association over time that we observe in Africa between the intensification of the problem of hunger at home and the increased dependence on food imports from abroad. But that temporal relationship is not a reflection of causal inevitability. There are sources of incomes and entitlements other than food production, and an increase in food imports would have gone with no intensification of hunger had these countries been able to expand non-food production and provide the population with enough income to buy imported food. Indeed, this has happened in many countries elsewhere, as was discussed in Chapter 2.

In seeking a remedy for Africa's current problems we have to examine *all* the real prospects—and *only* those—that exist now, rather than trying just to undo the changes that have been associated with its past decline. The extensive debate about 'Africa's food crisis' has often fallen prey to the fallacy involved in the assertion that since Africa's ills are caused by a crisis in food production, the remedy of this situation must lie exactly in countering that historical change. It could, of course, emerge on the basis of an unbiassed assessment of current prospects that giving priority to food production—perhaps even seeking food self-sufficiency—is the right policy to pursue for many African countries. But if that proves to be so, the ground for that conclusion will not be provided just by the observation of the simple historical fact that in these countries food output has declined or food imports have increased. Policy decisions have to be based on assessing the present circumstances and anticipated future ones rather than taking the simplistic form of trying to recreate the past.

9.3   Food Production and Diversification

As we have stressed in Chapter 2, it is important to distinguish clearly between (1) food production as a source of income and entitlement, and (2) food production as a source of supply of the commodity food. While it is certainly true that in terms of observed changes over time there may well be noticeable associations between variations in incomes and entitlements and changes in food production and imports from abroad, a better understanding of the former variations can be found by looking directly at the sources of entitlements and at the changes in the factors that govern them. In that more comprehensive picture, food production and trade will undoubtedly have a role. But given the possibility of earning incomes from activities other than food production, and given the complex relationship between production and distribution, one could not by any means simplify the lesson of all this in the form of a general slogan in favour of giving total priority to food production, irrespective of economic and social circumstances.

In so far as the crisis of food production in Africa relates, at least partly, to climatic uncertainties and to environmental deterioration, that itself may be a good ground for considering other avenues of productive expansion. The ecological problems must, of course, themselves be encountered, and further the adverse impact of weather variations on economic activity must be reduced (through irrigation or other means). Perhaps there is a good chance that in the long run a much more favourable environment for agricultural expansion in general and increased food production in particular will materialize in Africa. But economic policies should not be determined on the basis of imagining that such a change has already taken place. If it turns out that given the actual climatic uncertainties and ecological problems, food production will remain very vulnerable to fluctuations in the near future, then it will be a mistake to rely too much on that uncertain source of income and entitlements, putting all one's eggs in the same fragile basket. This is an argument for making use of opportunities offered by other types of production, from which benefits may be derivable with greater certainty for the population in question.

Of course, an issue that has to be examined in considering the case for economic diversification is the nature of international markets. The level and variability of rewards associated with economic diversification away from food production will obviously depend *inter alia* on the stability and mode of operation of international markets for food as well as for the products to be exported by the country in question (the proceeds of which would provide the means to buy food from abroad). The experience of fluctuating commodity prices suggests caution, and points to the need to supplement the calculation of average returns by taking note of the variability in those returns.[4] However, the risks involved in self-provisioning (e.g. greater vulnerability to crop failures) have to be given due recognition as well. The important thing, in assessing the merits of alternative intersectoral balances, is to consider carefully the opportunities and uncertainties associated both with self-provisioning as well as with international trade.

The need for diversification has often not been adequately stressed in outlining possible solutions to the problem of hunger in Africa. As a matter of fact, diversification has been a part of the African tradition for a long time (see Chapter 5). In the anxiety to deal with the severe problems encountered in Africa in expanding and sustaining the production of food, we must not lose sight of the benefits that diversification has offered in the past and of the tremendous opportunities it can bring in the future.

As far as the current situation is concerned, it may be pointed out that the role already played by economic diversification in rural Africa tends to be severely underestimated. A considerable variety of economic activities can indeed be found in most African economies in the form of (1) diversification within the agricultural sector (e.g. between food crops and cash crops, or between crops and livestock), (2) combination of agricultural and non-agricultural activities (e.g. crafts and trade) within the rural sector, and (3) use of the extensive links between different rural regions as well as between rural and urban areas (especially through wage employment and remittances). As a study of the economy of rural Sudan notes:

So-called subsistence cultivators should not be seen as consuming only what they produce nor producing only for their own consumption. Even the most humble family participates and anticipates participating in the market place. Peasants expect to sell their labor, gather and sell firewood, make charcoal, migrate seasonally for work, produce cash crops, sell excess livestock and otherwise supplement their incomes.[5]

[4] These issues have received a good deal of attention in recent years. The imperfections and manipulations to which international food markets lend themselves have been emphasized by Susan George (1976, 1988) in particular; see also Lappé and Collins (1979, 1980). Others have stressed the potential gains of making use of the possibilities offered by international trade in food. See e.g. the discussions in Reutlinger and Bigman (1981), Valdés (1981), Donaldson (1984), Huddleston (1984), Bigman (1986), Mann and Huddleston (1986), World Bank (1986).

[5] Eldredge and Rydjeski (1988: 3). On the pervasive importance of economic activities other than food and agricultural production in rural Africa, see Heyer (1986), Hill (1986), Kilby and Liedholm (1988), Weber *et al.* (1988), von Braun (1988), and Liedholm and Kilby (1989), among other contributions.

As was discussed in Chapters 5–8, there is also considerable evidence that the rural population in Africa attaches enormous importance to these prospects for diversification. The picture of the typical African rural poor as a self-sufficient peasant exclusively engaged in food production is, for most African countries, little more than a misleading cliché.

These are elementary points, and they are worth mentioning only because the debates on this subject have often been so confusing. Specifically, so far as Africa is concerned, the case for giving an adequate place to the diversification of production in economic analysis and policy is undoubtedly strong, especially in view of the exposure of many parts of that continent to a variety of environmental uncertainties. Simple alleged solutions of the problem of African hunger based on putting all the resources in food or agricultural production, or on raising food prices to boost production incentives,[6] may deliver substantially less than they seem to promise. There is no substitute for a careful assessment of the gains and losses, including the respective uncertainties associated with alternative intersectoral balances.

9.4   Industrialization and the Long Run

The recognition that anti-hunger policies in Africa may profit greatly from diversification and from giving a very solid place to the expansion of non-food production raises the question as to whether industrial production may have an important role to play in that diversified strategy. There is a noticeable reluctance to consider the promise of industrialization in contemplating the future of Africa. Sometimes this reluctance arises from being unduly impressed by the favourable land–population ratio of most African countries compared with, say, Asia. But the choice between industry and agriculture has to be influenced by many considerations of advantages and costs, in addition to the availability of land.

On the positive side, the opportunity for economic growth that is provided by branching out into industries has been well demonstrated by the historical experience of many countries in different parts of the world, and Africa cannot ignore these long-run opportunities. An important consideration is the contribution that industrialization makes to skill formation and to the modernization of the economy and the society. The indirect influence of that technological transformation on agricultural productivity itself cannot, by any means, be ignored.

As it happens, most of the successful and highly productive agricultural economies in the world also happen to be industrialized, and this fact is not a

[6] Grand solutions of this kind, especially through price incentives for agricultural expansion, are a favourite theme of several recent World Bank reports. That case is well presented in the *World Development Report 1986*. Despite raising many interesting and diverse policy issues concerning African economic problems, it nevertheless comes down sharply in favour of solving Africa's food problems by 'getting prices right'. On this, see also the exchange between Michael Lipton (1987*a*, 1988*b*) and Anandarup Ray (1988*a*, 1988*b*).

mere accident. Skill is as important an input for agricultural production as land, and diversification of production helps the formation of skill. The favourable nature of the land–population ratio has, rightly, not been seen as a good ground for eschewing industrial production in Australia, Canada, or the United States. Dismissing that economic alternative for Africa on the grounds of its high land–population ratio would reflect, at the very least, some economic short-sightedness.

That is not to deny that industrialization is a long-run process, and that in the immediate future no great radical transformation can be brought about in Africa through the pursuit of industries. But the process of industrialization, if it is to be pursued, has to be started at some stage, for it to yield fruit in the future. Also, as the experience of many developing countries (e.g., the fast-growing economies of East Asia but also many others) have shown, rapid progress can be made by new entrants in some branches of industry, yielding benefits without much delay. The fact that some unassessed and badly planned efforts in the industrial direction have come to grief in Africa is not in itself an argument for closing the books in that field. The issue of industrialization has to be squarely faced sooner or later.[7]

To recognize the need for diversification is not, of course, to deny the importance of expanding food production. Expansion of agriculture in general and of food production in particular will undoubtedly be a major instrument in combating hunger in sub-Saharan Africa. Various strategic aspects of enhancing food production in sub-Saharan Africa have received expert attention and scrutiny in recent years, and there are many lessons to be learned from economic reasoning as well as from the empirical observation of actual experiences.[8] Given the number of people who derive their entitlements from food production in Africa, and given the limited speed at which this dependence can be reduced, enhancing food production in Africa has to be one of the principal strategies to combat hunger in that continent.

If we are attaching special importance to the case for considering production other than that of food, and emphasizing the need for diversification, the reason for that does not lie in any belief that African food production is unimportant in that diversified approach. Quite the contrary. It is rather that the needs of expanding food production in Africa are more easily—and more often—acknowledged than some of the other components of anti-hunger strategy. It is a question of trying to get the right balance of emphases and of making sure that less obvious but important issues are not ignored in an undue concentration on a partial picture.

[7] On the case for less pessimism on the prospects for industrialization in Africa and some relevant empirical studies, see Riddell *et al.* (1989) and the literature cited there.

[8] See e.g. Eicher (1986*b*, 1988*a*), Food and Agriculture Organisation (1986), and Mellor, Delgado and Blackie (1987). See also World Bank (1981, 1984*b*, 1986), Berry (1984), Eicher and Staatz (1984), Rose (1985), IDS Bulletin (1985), Commins, Lofchie and Payne (1986), Berg and Whitaker (1986), Idachaba (1986), Swaminathan (1986), Wangwe (1986), Lipton (1987*a*), Platteau (1988*a*) and the December 1984 issue of *African Studies Review*.

9.5 Cash Crops: Problems and Opportunities

There are many ways in which diversification can be achieved. Diversification within the rural economy, which itself can take many forms, is particularly important to consider. The part that can be played in this process by the so-called 'cash crops' deserves special examination if only because of the controversies that have surrounded this subject.[9]

Since cash crops are agricultural crops, they are, of course, exposed to climatic uncertainties similar to those affecting food crops. They also involve —as has often been stressed—additional vulnerability arising from greater dependence on markets. Cash crops have to be sold and the proceeds then used in buying food, and the food entitlements thus generated can be vulnerable to fluctuations in the markets for food as well as those for cash crops. But it is also true that cash crops are often highly remunerative in comparison with food crops, and if the income thus generated can be marshalled to support and secure the livelihood of the rural population, there need be no general reason to fear their expansion.

The promotion of cash crops in developing countries has, however, come under severe attack in recent years, and it has even been held responsible for a great deal of hunger in the modern world.[10] It is easy to see the need for caution regarding excessive reliance on cash crops. However, the evidence does not always support an unqualified censure of extensive use of cash crops. For instance, cash crop growers have often—though not invariably—been found to fare significantly better than subsistence farmers during famines.[11] And a number of countries have met with commendable success in using the economic opportunities provided by the cultivation of cash crops to enhance the nutritional status of the population.[12] A balanced assessment of the economic impact of cash crops has to account for these experiences as well as for the darker side of this complex picture.

[9] The notion of 'cash crops' is, in fact, rather complex, and can be confusing. This notion has been variously used to designate a number of distinct categories such as (1) crops which are exported instead of being consumed in the country where they are grown; (2) crops which are exchanged for cash by the people who grow them, instead of being consumed directly; (3) non-food crops as opposed to food crops. These alternative definitions overlap but do not coincide, and they would clearly lead to different crop classifications. Crops like potatoes or rice, for instance, are mainly subsistence crops in some countries, objects of local exchange in others, export crops in still others, and in many countries they are in fact a combination of all of these. We need not sort out these definitional problems here, but the potential difficulties of making precise sense of the notion of cash crops as an economic category is useful to bear in mind, especially in the context of blanket arguments for their condemnation or promotion.

[10] It is interesting that pastoralism, which from an economic point of view can be regarded as having much the same features as growing cash crops (including the use of land to produce something that is later exchanged for food), has not been viewed with nearly the same suspicion as 'cash crops'.

[11] For some examples of this in India and in Africa, see Oughton (1982), Derrick (1984), Herlehy (1984), Schmidt-Wulffen (1985), and de Waal (1987).

[12] Costa Rica, Cuba, Malaysia, Mauritius, and the state of Kerala in India are a few among many examples. The experiences of some of these economies will be discussed in later chapters.

A common argument implicitly or explicitly underlying the thesis that cash crops are responsible for exacerbating hunger in the modern world is that cash crops displace food crops and therefore lead to a reduction in the availability of food. This apparently appealing argument has in fact gained enormous popularity, and there is admittedly something contrary in the suggestion that a country in which masses of people are hungry could reasonably divert a large part of its productive agricultural resources away from growing food. However, as we have already seen, such simple availability-centred arguments can be misleading in analysing the problem of food entitlement. If cash crops provide greater means of acquiring food, then there is no reason why that avenue should be rejected in favour of sticking to growing only food crops even when the latter option provides comparatively meagre (or riskier) entitlements to food. To take for granted that increasing the production of cash crops could not bring in more food for the households is to beg the central question.

A more discerning case against cash crops would have to be based on the argument that their expansion undermines the entitlements of vulnerable groups, directly or indirectly.[13] But, we have to ask, why should people choose to produce cash crops rather than food crops if the expansion of cash crops makes them more vulnerable to hunger? Broadly speaking, the answer to this question can take four different forms: (1) Households are driven to adopt cash crops against their own interests, through coercion or delusion. (2) Economic and social changes, of which expansion of cash crops is an integral part, lead to impoverishment and vulnerability, even though in these reduced circumstances an individual household may gain from growing cash crops. (3) Some household members adopt cash crops to the detriment of *other members* of the household. (4) The adoption of cash crops by some households makes them rich at the cost of undermining the entitlements of *other households*. We examine each of these possibilities in turn.

It has been pointed out that peasants are often forced or persuaded to grow cash crops against their real interest, say by multinationals or predatory governments. In particular, agri-business interests have been accused of driving poor peasants off the land and reducing them to the status of wage labourers. Such things undoubtedly occur, but it is hard to explain the widespread adoption of cash crops primarily in these terms.[14] While the need to resist abuse and malpractice is by no means negligible (and not just in the context of cash crops), the reason for concern about cash crops goes much beyond these gross transgressions.

[13] For insightful analyses of various arguments along these lines, see Jalée (1965), Amin (1974, 1975), Meillassoux (1974), Raynaut (1977), Fleuret and Fleuret (1980), Franke and Chasin (1980), George (1984), Twose (1984), Bennett (1987), among others.

[14] On the variety of motivations and consequences linked to the expansion of cash crops in different parts of the world, see De Wilde (1984), Pinstrup-Andersen (1985a), von Braun and Kennedy (1986, 1987), Kennedy and Cogill (1987), Maxwell and Fernando (1987), Longhurst (1988), von Braun et al. (1989), and the special issue of *IDS Bulletin* on 'Cash Crops in Developing Countries' (Volume 19, Number 2, 1988).

In the second line of argument, the greater vulnerability of many sections of the rural African population in recent decades has been attributed—at least partly—to a shift in the pattern of economic production and activity towards greater 'commoditization', of which the expansion of cash crops is an integral part. This has involved, it has been argued, greater reliance on the sale of marketable commodities and the purchase of food on the market, with greater exposure to the uncertainties of exchange, sharper economic inequalities, and also important changes in the nature of social bonds within the rural community.[15]

These are important issues, and more can be said on each side. But the complex economic and social relationships involved in the economic changes with which the expansion of cash crops is associated must not be reduced to a simple question of shifts only in cropping patterns. The right variables to look at in this context are the relations of production and the nature of exchange, rather than the type of crop as such.

When commercialization of agriculture in the form of expanding cash crops goes hand in hand with more market-based uncertainty and exacerbates inequalities in the ownership of the means of production, the argument that cash crops are on the average and in total more remunerative than food crops can be seriously undermined. But the possible dangers of this process also have to be assessed against the sometimes enormous potential gains that can be made from a widening of economic opportunities through greater access to market exchange.

There is a certain amount of political interest in all this, since opposition to changes involving cash crops has sometimes come from Marxian analysts. It may be noted in this context that among the countries that have made good use of the opportunities provided by cash crop cultivation to promote the entitlements of vulnerable groups are several socialist ones, including Cuba and Nicaragua.[16]

Ultimately it is a matter of seeing the economic process as a whole, of which the growth of cash crops may be a part. If the development of cash crop production is associated with growing concentration of land, more unequal income distribution, uncertainty of wage employment, and insecurity of earnings, then that is indeed an unfavourable change, but it is not the fact of cash crop production as such that makes it so. The same cash crops can be

[15] See particularly Amin (1974, 1975), Comité Information Sahel (1974), Meillassoux (1974), Copans et al. (1975), Dalby et al. (1977), Raynaut (1977), Watts (1983, 1984), and Bryceson (1984).

[16] Marx, who was aware of the potentialities of market exchange (as well as of the related dangers), rightly saw economic exploitation as arising primarily from inequalities in ownership rather than from exchange per se, and cautioned against the mistake of focusing unduly on the latter: 'The relation of capitalist and wage labourer . . . has its foundation in the social character of production, not in the mode of exchange . . . It is, however, quite in keeping with the bourgeois horizon, everyone being engrossed in the transaction of shady business, not to see in the character of the mode of production the basis of the mode of exchange corresponding to it, but vice versa' (Marx 1893: 120). For an analysis of Lenin's views on these and related matters, see Desai (1976).

associated with a more favourable development of earnings and entitlements in a different overall economic situation without the dispossession and vulnerability associated with the first case. The role of cash crops has to be assessed in the fuller economic context.

The third problem in the list of four mentioned earlier relates to intrafamily divisions. Cash crops, it has been argued, are typically grown by men, and benefit men to the relative or even absolute detriment of women. Sometimes this view has taken the form of asserting that cash crops are 'male' crops whereas food crops are 'female' crops, but there is not much empirical evidence to support this overpowerful generalization.[17] On the other hand, it is plausible enough that the adoption or expansion of cash crops can in many circumstances intensify conflicts of interest within households. These could take the form of men having a privileged access to the new opportunities provided by cash crops (e.g. because of their greater mobility), or enjoying a greater control over household resources as a result of the enhanced role of cash in the household economy.

These considerations can be important, but it must be recognized that the complex changes in gender relations taking place along with a process of expansion in economic opportunities cannot be reduced to the simple format of a dilemma between food crops and cash crops. We have to look at the nature of labour markets, the access of women and men to employment opportunities, the gender features in land ownership, and the social traditions in the intrafamily division of consumption and work.

As Megan Vaughan emphasizes in her study of gender and famine in Malawi, 'the mere existence of a cash-cropping economy . . . does not define the economic role and status of women, and needs to be seen as acting together with a number of other variables, the most crucial being the availability of land and the degree of control over it exercised by women'.[18] Once again, policy decisions call for attention being paid to specific empirical features of the choices involved, and to the economic and social circumstances that condition the influence of cash crops on the entitlements of different groups.

The fourth issue mentioned earlier involves the potential conflict of interest between cash crop growers and non-growers. It is easy to see that the large-scale adoption of cash crops by some households can, in some circumstances, pose an important threat to the entitlements of other—possibly more

[17] It is easy to find examples of rural economies in Africa where the reverse pattern corresponds more closely to the truth, with women being more involved in cash crop cultivation than men. For some illustrations, involving countries as diverse as Senegal, Zambia, and Sierra Leone, see e.g. Chastanet (1983), World Health Organization (1986: 47), and Richards (1986: 105). For a general discussion of the ambiguities and pitfalls involved in discriminating between cash crops and food crops along gender lines, see Whitehead (1986).
[18] Vaughan (1987: 144). It is possible to find examples of socio-economic settings in which the expansion of cash crops appears to have *improved* rather than undermined the bargaining position of women. In her anthropological study of cocoa-farming in Ghana, for instance, Polly Hill argues that, for women, 'cocoa-farming ownership was a new and most welcome form of insurance against poverty arising from divorce' (Hill 1975: 131).

vulnerable—groups. For instance, in economies where many or most of the poor are landless labourers, an increase in food prices resulting from a switch towards cash crops on the part of farmers could clearly lead to a deterioration of the entitlements of the most vulnerable groups. Other possible forms of conflicts have been pointed out, such as conflicts arising from the damaging environmental effects of some cash crops,[19] or conflicts between pastoralists and cash crop growers who put under cultivation fallow land previously available for grazing animals.[20]

At the same time, it is important to recognize that the influence of cash crops on the entitlements of those who are not growing them can be positive as well as negative. Many cash crops, for instance, are enormously more labour-intensive than most food crops, and in an economy where many of the poor are wage labourers this factor could count heavily in favour of promoting cash crops.[21] Once again, there is no escape from analysing the entitlement process as a whole rather than relying on instant wisdom from simple slogans in favour of or against cash crops.

It is hardly surprising that there can be no invariant answer to the question as to whether cash crops help or hinder the battle against hunger. Indeed, in seeking straightforward and rigid links between the capabilities enjoyed by people (e.g. nutritional capabilities) and the production of particular commodities in the economy (specifically food crops), there is a danger of falling prey to a particular version of 'commodity fetishism' (discussed in the first part of this book).

In many contexts, the production of cash crops is likely to deserve an important place within a diversified strategy for the promotion of food entitlements in Africa. This recognition, which relates particularly to the distinction between food production and food entitlement and which connects up with the economic case for diversification, does not in any way overlook the possibility that, in some circumstances, the growing of cash crops can have an adverse effect on the ability of many people to establish entitlements over food.[22]

---

[19] In Western India, the rapid expansion of sugarcane cultivation by large farmers owning irrigated land, and encouraged by wealthy 'sugar barons', has been an object of considerable and often justified criticism (see e.g. Anon. 1985). The expansion of eucalyptus cultivation in India has also been repeatedly denounced as a clear case of anti-social private gains. On the damaging environmental effects of cash crops in the Sahel, see Franke and Chasin (1980).

[20] For examples of this type of conflict and their contribution to the vulnerability of pastoralists in Ethiopia and the Sudan, see Sen (1981a: Chapters 7 and 8), and the literature cited there.

[21] It has been estimated that in Kenya, where wage labour is a very important source of livelihood for the poor, a crop such as tea requires more than four times as much labour per hectare as maize, and more than eight times as much as wheat (Mwangi, 1986). A switch from cash crops (in this case jute) to less labour-intensive food crops as a result of price changes is alleged to have caused starvation among agricultural labourers in some parts of Assam in India in 1975 (Prabhakar 1975).

[22] To dispute that cash crops must be vigorously and systematically discouraged is not to deny that, in many countries, they may have been *excessively encouraged*, especially during the colonial period.

9.6   From Food Entitlements to Nutritional Capabilities

So far in this chapter we have discussed the related issues of self-sufficiency, food production and economic diversification in terms of the ability of alternative policy options to improve food entitlements. At this stage it is important to link up the question of entitlement guarantees with the importance of non-food items in ensuring the capability to be nourished, as well as other capabilities closely associated with nourishment, e.g. avoiding escapable morbidity and mortality. As we argued earlier (in Chapters 1 and 3), it is a mistake to view hunger in terms of food deprivation only. This is not merely because there are significant interindividual and intraindividual variations in food requirements for nutritional achievement. But also, the capability to be nourished depends crucially on other characteristics of a person that are influenced by such non-food factors as medical attention, health services, basic education, sanitary arrangements, provision of clean water, eradication of infectious epidemics, and so on. If we compare different countries, or different regions within a country, we may find considerable dissonance between the ranking of food intakes and the ranking of nutritional achievements.

The recognition of this point does not, of course, imply that we must not attach any importance to the deficiency of food intakes as such, and concentrate only on the achieved qualities of nourishment. Eating is a major aspect of living, and the physical and psychological aspects of hunger (related directly to food intake) must command our attention.[23] Avoiding hunger, in the most elementary sense of the term, is certainly one part of the bigger programme of combating hunger in the broader sense.

The importance of food is obviously crucial in the prevention of hunger in the narrow sense, but the fact remains that the prevention of hunger in the broader sense, including nutritional deprivation, depends substantially also on an adequate access to vital non-food items. For example, in seeking an explanation of the contrast between the Sri Lankan life expectancy figure of 70 years at birth and the South African average of 55 years, we would get little help from comparing the calorie consumption levels in Sri Lanka and South Africa, viz. 2,385 calories and 2,979 calories respectively (in 1985).[24] Even if the inequalities in the respective distributions of calories were taken into account, the contrast would remain. The difference lies to a great extent in the fact that the health services, education and other features of the social environment of

---

[23] See Chapter 3. We also do know that, in personal consumption behaviour, a strong emphasis is placed on the maintenance of food intake and expenditure, in spite of possible short-run fluctuations in total income or total expenditure. See particularly Anand and Harris (1986, 1987). By showing the relative stability of food expenditure (in comparison with income and total consumption expenditure), and by placing the analysis of consumer behaviour in that perspective, Anand and Harris have argued for the use of food expenditure, even in the short run, as a better guide to long-run opulence than the more traditional variables used for this purpose, such as current income or expenditure.

[24] *World Development Report 1987*, Tables 1 and 30.

Sri Lanka are far more broadly distributed and equitable than those of South Africa.[25]

It is in the uneven delivery of crucial non-food items that the causation of some of the sharpest contrasts in the qualities of life of different countries and communities lie. The divergence, for example, between Sri Lanka with 93 per cent of the population having access to health services and Bhutan with a corresponding figure of 19 per cent, can make an extraordinary difference to the nature of the life that people can lead. One aspect of that is reflected in the widely different levels of life expectation at birth in the two countries, viz. 70 years for Sri Lanka and 44 years for Bhutan (contrasting with calorie consumption figures of 2,385 and 2,572 respectively).[26]

This broadening of our concern from food entitlements to more general entitlements (including crucial non-food items as well as food) has many significant consequences. One of them, which is of central importance in policy-making, relates to the fact that while food is typically purchased in a market (even when influenced by subsidies, rationing, etc.), provisions for medical, educational, and related facilities are more often—for good reasons —made directly by public institutions. In such matters as the operation of general health services, the provision of clean water, the elimination of infectious epidemics, and so on, the role of the state is typically even more direct and immediate. Entitlement guarantees in the context of these non-food items have to be seen mainly in terms of public planning rather than just the enhancement of purchasing power in the market. These issues will be taken up further in the analysis to follow.

In this chapter we have argued for broadening our attention respectively (1) from food self-sufficiency to food adequacy, (2) from food adequacy to food entitlements, and (3) from food entitlements to nutritional and related capabilities (involving *inter alia* entitlements to crucial non-food items). There are important links between these variables, but the links depend significantly on other variables of which note has to be taken. When we study the strategy of public action against endemic undernourishment and deprivation, we shall have to come to grips with the plurality of influences affecting nutritional capabilities and achievements.

---

[25] On Sri Lanka's record in public health, educational expansion and related matters, see Chapter 12 below. On South Africa, see Wilson and Ramphele (1989).

[26] *World Development Report 1987*, Tables 1 and 30, and UNICEF (1987a), Table 3.

10

Economic Growth and Public Support

10.1 Incomes and Achievements

The mistake involved in analysing hunger just in terms of food output and availability has been discussed extensively in earlier chapters of this book. The main issue concerns the power of vulnerable groups to command food and other essentials, rather than just the physical availability of commodities. While focusing on entitlements rather than on what is available has many complex implications (we have tried to analyse some of them and to draw lessons for policy), the basic contrast between command and availability is fairly straightforward.

Sometimes the position that hunger is essentially due to a *command* failure not necessarily caused by an output failure is summarized in the form of the simple slogan 'hunger is caused by a lack of income, not of food supply'. Extending this line of straightforward analysis, it is often argued that the real problem lies in the shortage of purchasing power, rather than of anything else.

That conclusion has some obvious sense, but as a causal theory it is rather misleading. This is so not merely because income is itself a derived variable which depends on ownership and exchange and therefore provides a rather poor focal point for the analysis of entitlement failures. But no less importantly, it is also the case that many essential commodities are not bought and sold in the market in the usual way, and conventional estimates of real income may not give us a good idea of the command over a number of inputs which, as we have seen, can play a crucial role in the removal of hunger, such as educational services, health care, clean water, or protection from infectious epidemics. The importance of these non-food commodities and facilities for nutrition and health was discussed earlier (in Chapters 3 and 9). Since their use may have a major impact on the nutritional status and health of a population, and since they are often provided directly through public delivery, the lacuna involved in concentrating on purchasing power is quite limiting. Income is a rather dubious indicator of the opportunity of being well nourished and having nutrition-related capabilities.

This is one reason, among others, why the association between Gross National Product per capita, on the one hand, and health, nutrition, morbidity, and mortality, on the other, is far from simple. In Table 10.1, we present some relevant figures for five selected countries to illustrate the point. South Africa, with nearly six times the GNP per head of China and Sri Lanka, has a

Table 10.1 Average opulence and survival achievement: selected intercountry comparisons, 1985

Country	GNP per head (dollars)	Infant mortality rate (per 1,000)	Expectation of life at birth (years)
China	310	35	69
Sri Lanka	380	36	70
Brazil	1,640	67	65
South Africa	2,010	78	55
Oman	6,730	109	54

Source: *World Development Report 1987*, Tables 1 and 29.

life expectancy of only 55 years, compared with 69 and 70 years respectively for the two poorer countries.[1] Similarly Brazil, with many times the income per head of China and Sri Lanka, has nevertheless lower life expectancy than the latter. Oman, with about 20 times the GNP per head of China or Sri Lanka, offers a life expectancy of only 54 years at birth.

The contrast of infant mortality rates brings out the same dissonance between GNP per head and the capability to survive premature death. Brazil, Oman, and South Africa, despite their much greater opulence, have enormously higher infant mortality rates than China and Sri Lanka.

There are, in fact, two distinct—and in principle separable—causes underlying the dissonance between GNP and achievements of quality of life. First, the GNP gives a measure of the aggregate opulence of the economy, and the translation of this into the pattern of individual prosperity would depend also on the distribution of income over the population.[2] Second, as we have seen, the capabilities enjoyed by people depend on many factors other than the command over commodities which can be purchased in the market. Among such factors, public provisions made by the state for health, education, sanitation, etc., are especially important.

While we must recognize this dissonance, there is no reason to dismiss GNP altogether.[3] There are, in fact, good grounds for expecting a positive *general*

---

[1] The figure of 69 years for China appearing in the *World Development Reports* may be a bit of an overestimate. On this see Chapter 11. There have been abrupt and unexplained upward revisions of the reported life expectancy for South Africa in the later *World Development Reports*.

[2] It is worth noting that just as we may be concerned with the distribution of GNP in addition to its mean value per capita, similarly also in the case of such indicators as life expectancy, there is the need to distinguish between their mean values and their patterns of distribution over the population.

[3] Cf. Robert Kennedy's remark: GNP 'measures everything, in short, except that which makes life worthwhile.' (Statement made by Robert Kennedy at the University of Kansas during his presidential campaign in 1968; cited in Dowd 1987.)

association between GNP and nutrition-related capabilities. This is partly because the increased incomes associated with greater general affluence do indeed offer the opportunity to buy a number of commodities that are *inter alia* crucially important for nutrition-related capabilities, the most notable of which is, of course, food itself. But, in addition, a higher GNP per capita enlarges the material base for public support in areas such as health care and education, and generally facilitates the provision of social security to the more vulnerable sections of the community.

The governments of some of the oil-rich countries, for example, have been able to use their unusual and relatively recent opulence to make widespread public provisions for their citizens, and this is one of the reasons why life expectancy at birth and similar indicators have, in recent decades, moved to comparatively high figures in countries such as Kuwait and United Arab Emirates (e.g. life expectancies above 70 years). The examples of these countries are admittedly rather exceptional, but the general principle that an expanded basis for public support *can be* one of the fruits of economic growth applies to other countries too. There are also many cases where average opulence has reached a high level, but public support has been comprehensively neglected, with correspondingly low levels of nutritional and related achievements.

At the risk of oversimplifying the problem, it can be argued that a high level of GNP per head provides an *opportunity* for improving nutrition and other basic capabilities, but that opportunity may or may not be seized. In the process of transforming this opportunity into a tangible achievement, public support in various forms (and influencing both the distribution of income and the relationship between income and basic capabilities) often play a crucial role.

Improvements in the quality of life are sometimes seen simply as the result of increases in overall affluence *per se*, when in fact the expansion of public support may have been the crucial intermediator. Common perceptions of the historical experience of Western countries in enhancing life expectancy often involve this misleading belief in the power of simple opulence *per se* (e.g. high GNP per head). In fact, the idea that the rich countries have achieved high levels of basic capabilities simply because they are rich is, to say the least, an oversimplification. A good illustration of this point is provided by the history of longevity expansion in Britain during this century.

Table 10.2 presents the *increase* in life expectancy at birth in England and Wales in each of the first six decades of this century (starting with a life expectancy figure no higher than that of most developing countries today). Note that while the increase in life expectancy has been between one to four years in each decade, there were two decades in which the increase was remarkably greater (around seven years approximately). These were the decades of the two world wars, with dramatic increases in many forms of public support including public employment, food rationing and health care

Table 10.2 Longevity expansion in England
and Wales

Decade	Increase in life expectancy per decade (years)	
	Male	Female
1901–11	4.1	4.0
1911–21	6.6	6.5
1921–31	2.3	2.4
1931–40	1.2	1.5
1940–51	6.5	7.0
1951–60	2.4	3.2

Source: Based on data presented in Preston, Keyfitz,
and Schoen (1972: 240–71). See also Winter (1986)
and Sen (1987e).

provisions.[4] The decade of the 1940s, which recorded the highest increase in British life expectancy during the century, witnessed an enormous expansion of public employment, extensive and equitable food rationing, and the birth of the National Health Service (introduced just after the war).

The nature of these experiences illustrates both the importance of the distinction between commodity availability and functioning achievement (discussed earlier), and the role that social intervention and public support played in the expansion of a very basic capability in the history of the first industrial nation.[5]

---

[4] See Winter (1986) for an illuminating analysis of the effects of the First World War on public distribution and public involvement, and their impact on living conditions in Britain. The experience of the Second World War is discussed in great detail by Titmuss (1950: Chapter 25), who examines the evidence indicating a strong relationship between the surprisingly good health conditions of the British population during the war (including a rapid improvement of the health status of children) and the extensive reach of public support measures in that period. As Titmuss put it, 'by the end of the Second World War the Government had, through the agency of newly established or existing services, assumed and developed a measure of direct concern for the health and well-being of the population which, by contrast with the role of Government in the nineteen-thirties, was little short of remarkable' (p. 506). According to Titmuss, the most influential part of social policy during the war related to employment provision and food rationing. This conclusion is strongly corroborated by Hammond's detailed study of the 'revolution in the attitude of the British State towards the feeding of its citizens' which took place after 1941 (Hammond 1951). On these issues, see also Marrack (1947), McKeown and Lowe (1966: 131–4), McNeill (1976: 286–7), Szreter (1988).

[5] It is of some interest to note that in the case of Japan, too, the rate of expansion of longevity was substantially higher during the period covering the Second World War and immediately after (see the figures presented in Preston *et al.* 1972, as well as the further discussion in Drèze and Sen 1988). This was also a period of rapid expansion of public support, and it is plausible that, as in the case of Britain, this expansion was a crucial factor in the reduction of mortality rates especially after the war. We are grateful to Akiko Hashimoto for helpful discussions on the empirical evidence related to this observation. See also Taeuber (1958), Shigematsu and Yanagawa (1985) and Morio and Takahashi (1986).

10.2   Alternative Strategies: Growth-Mediated Security and Support-Led Security

Given the distinct, though interconnected, roles played by overall opulence and public activism in enhancing capabilities, it is possible in principle to distinguish two contrasting approaches to the removal of precarious living conditions. One approach is to promote economic growth and take the best possible advantage of the potentialities released by greater general affluence, including not only an expansion of private incomes but also an improved basis for public support. This may be called the strategy of 'growth-mediated security'. Another alternative is to resort *directly* to wide-ranging public support in domains such as employment provision, income redistribution, health care, education, and social assistance in order to remove destitution without waiting for a transformation in the level of general affluence. Here success may have to be based on a discriminating use of national resources, the efficiency of public services, a redistributive bias in their delivery. This may be called the strategy of 'support-led security'.

The possibility of success through either approach is credible enough in principle. The real question is whether in practice they can be utilized in the way we might expect in theory. There have been, in fact, serious detractors questioning the viability of each of these two strategies. Some have questioned the soundness of a strategy which gives precedence to public support over growth on grounds of the allegedly extravagant nature of generous public provisions for a poor economy. They have argued that deflecting resources to social services from investment reduces economic growth and adversely affects future opportunities.[6] State provisioning as such has also been regarded, at times, with considerable suspicion, and it has in fact become a target of relentless criticism in the contemporary intellectual atmosphere of great faith in 'the market'.

Others have questioned the soundness of a strategy of growth-mediated security on the grounds that high growth is often accompanied by increased inequality in the distribution of incomes, so that the people in greatest need of capability enhancement may end up benefiting least (if at all) from the general process of economic expansion. It has also been argued that the potential opportunity for expanded public provisioning may not be typically seized by a growth-oriented government, because of its preoccupation with the expansion of material opulence rather than with the basic quality of human life. It is the slowness or absence of the so-called 'trickle down' (in itself not an electrifying prospect) that makes growth an unreliable means of general advance of a community.

[6] This line of reasoning has also been influential in bringing about drastic reductions in social services as part of 'adjustment programmes' in developing countries faced with mounting debts and trade imbalances. On the adverse social impact of such cut-backs, see Jolly and Cornia (1984), Cornia *et al*. (1987) Bell and Reich (1988), and the WIDER studies by Nora Lustig and others in Jayawardena (forthcoming).

Table 10.3 Proportionate reduction in U5MR (1960–1985): the top ten countries[a]

Country	Percentage reduction in U5MR	Percentage growth rate of GNP/capita		GNP per head (US dollars)	Level of U5MR
	(1960–85)	(1960–82)[b]	(1965–85)	(1985)	(1985)
Hong Kong	83	7.0	6.1	6,230	11
Chile	82	0.6	−0.2	1,430	26
UAE	82	−0.7	n/a	19,270	43
Costa Rica	81	2.8	1.4	1,300	23
Kuwait	80	−0.1	−0.3	14,480	25
Cuba	78	n/a	n/a	n/a	19
Singapore	76	7.4	7.6	7,420	12
China	75	5.0	4.8	310	50
Jamaica	72	0.7	−0.7	940	25
South Korea	71	6.6	6.6	2,150	35

[a] Excluded from the comparison are the countries of Eastern and Western Europe, Japan, New Zealand, Australia, USA, USSR, and Canada.
[b] In this column, figures in italics are for a period not exactly corresponding to 1960–82, due to non-availability of data for the early 1960s (see *World Development Report 1984*, Table 1).
Source: UNICEF (1987a), Table 1; *World Development Report* (1984, 1987), Table 1.

What have the actual experiences been in different countries of the world? While intercountry comparisons of performance are often quite unreliable and misleading, they sometimes do provide at least a tentative basis for noting certain elementary relationships and possibilities. We shall examine here in some detail one particular set of intercountry comparisons of performance, based on the observed reduction in infant and child mortality between 1960 and 1985 in different parts of the world. Of course, infant and child mortality can by no means be interpreted as a summary index of the quality of life as a whole, or even of the nutritional status of the population, and the performance of various countries in areas related to nutrition will call for further investigation later on in this book. However, as a starting-point for our enquiry the incidence of mortality among infants and children in different countries is a useful indicator to examine.

An internationally comparable set of estimates of the 'under-5 mortality rate' (hereafter U5MR) has been constructed recently by UNICEF, and provides a useful basis for a comparative assessment of performance.[7] From the information provided about under-5 mortality rates in 1960 and 1985, it is possible to calculate the percentage reduction of the U5MR in different countries over these 25 years. The ten best performers according to this

[7] The nature of the U5MR index is explained in UNICEF (1987a: 126). The information on U5MR for 130 countries, on which our analysis is based, appears in Table 1 of the same publication. In the remainder of this chapter, the term 'developing countries' will be used to refer to the hundred countries left in that table after excluding the countries of Western and Eastern Europe, North America, Japan, New Zealand, Australia and the USSR.

criterion, among the developing countries, are the following (in decreasing order of performance): Hong Kong, Chile, United Arab Emirates, Costa Rica, Kuwait, Cuba, Singapore, China, Jamaica, and South Korea.[8] The actual figures are presented in Table 10.3.[9]

On the basis of the information contained in Table 10.3, and of what is known about the experiences of the countries involved, it is possible to divide these ten countries into two distinct groups. Growth-mediated security has clearly been an important part of the experiences of Hong Kong, Singapore, and South Korea. In fact, it is interesting to note that these three countries were among the five *fastest* growing economies in the world during the period under consideration, in terms of the growth rate of real GNP per capita.[10] The United Arab Emirates and Kuwait can also be put broadly in the same group, even though in this period their growth rates of GNP per capita, as it is standardly measured, are not high. The phenomenal increase in the incomes of these two countries that has in fact taken place as a result of changes in international prices (in this case involving oil) fails to be captured by the growth rate of the real *quantity-index* of GNP per capita.[11] The fact is that both these countries have become very rich over this period, and their remarkable

---

[8] In fact, North Korea was also in our preliminary list of countries selected for highest reduction in U5MR. However, it was removed from the list because it turns out that the figures of U5MR for North Korea published by UNICEF were not obtained independently but were simply *assumed* to be the same as those applying to South Korea. Note also that the recorded reduction in U5MR for the period 1960–85 in China would be completely misleading if the base-level mortality rate actually corresponded to 1960, when famine was raging and mortality had shot up sharply (see Chapter 11). However, the 1960 figure given in UNICEF (1987a) is clearly *not* one based on the famine years, and rather appears to be based on an extrapolation from pre-famine figures (see the infant mortality data in Piazza 1986, and Jamison and Piazza 1987).

[9] It could be argued that a given percentage reduction in U5MR between 1960 and 1985 provides different indications about a country's 'performance' in mortality reduction depending on the *initial* level of U5MR in 1960. However, when percentage reductions in U5MR over this period are examined after 'controlling' for these initial levels (this is done by looking at the residuals of a regression of the 1985 U5MR levels on the 1960 levels, both in logarithmic form), the identification of the best performers is not substantially affected. In fact, by this alternative criterion *all* the 'top ten' countries appearing in Table 10.3 still outperform *all* other developing countries except three (viz. Jordan, Saudi Arabia, and Syria).

[10] See *World Development Report 1987*, Table 1. This statement refers to the period 1965–85 (rather than 1960–85), the only one for which the figures are presented in that report. For the period 1960–82, however, these three countries are also among the five fastest growing economies in the world (see *World Development Report 1984*, Table 1).

[11] This problem is explicitly mentioned in the Technical Notes accompanying the *World Development Reports*, with special reference to oil-producing countries (see e.g. *World Development Report 1984*, p. 275). In the case of these countries, the use of, say, a Consumer Price Index to deflate nominal GDP figures (instead of the GDP deflator applied in the *World Development Report* figures) gives a much fairer idea of the massive increase in purchasing power experienced by their populations in recent decades. For instance, using the Consumer Price Index published in the *Annual Statistical Abstract of Kuwait* as a deflator, the annual growth rate of real GDP in Kuwait after 1973 (the starting year of this price index series) is of the order of 11% until the early 1980s (after which it decelerates due to a sharp reduction in oil prices). The annual growth rate of real consumption expenditure (public and private) over the 1973–81 period is even higher, of the order of 14% (all figures have been calculated from the 1970, 1982, and 1987 issues of the *Annual Statistical Abstract of Kuwait*).

success in reducing under-5 mortality rates has been much helped by their —relatively new—opulence. Thus, a half of the ten highest performers in terms of percentage reduction of under-5 mortality rate seem to have resorted to a strategy of growth-mediated security, of one sort or another.

On the other hand, the other five countries (viz. Chile, Costa Rica, Cuba, China, Jamaica) have had quite different experiences. Their growth rates have been comparatively low. Moreover, as we shall discuss later in this chapter, these countries stand out sharply in having achieved far lower mortality rates than most other countries at a comparable income level. The basis of their success does not seem to rest primarily in rapid income growth, and suggests the possibility of support-led security.[12]

Before we move on, two points must be stressed. First, the outstanding record of these five countries can by no means be dismissed as a statistical artefact. The demographic and health records of *each* of these countries have, in fact, attracted widespread attention on their own, and the statistical evidence establishing their record has been extensively scrutinized in each case.[13] As will be discussed later, there is also strong independent evidence (e.g. in the form of anthropometric data and morbidity indicators) of very rapid nutritional improvement in these five countries, in addition to the observed trends in infant and child mortality rates.

Second, the prominent role of public support in bringing about these successes is also well established. All the five countries under consideration have repeatedly attracted attention for their active public involvement in various forms of social support, including the direct provision of vital commodities and social services. We shall return to this at greater length in

[12] The Chinese growth rate appearing in Table 10.3 is quite impressive, and might be seen as suggesting that the basis of China's success may well lie as much in economic growth as in direct public support. This question is further discussed in the next chapter, where it is argued that (1) China's growth rate during the period of interest has been much exaggerated, and (2) economic growth has followed rather than preceded the wide-ranging measures of public support which must be seen as the main source of China's success.

[13] There tend to be many gaps in international statistics of life expectancy and related indicators (on this see Murray 1987). However, the reliability of such statistics is much greater for these five countries. The abundance and quality of demographic and health statistics in Costa Rica and Chile since the 1950s are rather exceptional, and the impressive records of these two countries in the areas of health and nutrition have attracted very wide attention—the experiences of these two countries are further discussed in Chapter 12. Cuban statistics have to be used with great care, but health and demographic statistics are among the more reliable ones (see the thorough discussions in Mesa-Lago 1969, 1979, Diaz-Briquets 1983, and Santana 1987: Appendix), and Cuba's achievements in the area of health and nutrition are well established—see Brundenius (1981, 1984), Handelman (1982), Diaz-Briquets (1983), Valdes-Brito and Henriquez (1983), Werner (1983), Muniz *et al.* (1984), Meegama (1985), Eckstein (1986), and Santana (1987). The literature on China's experience of rapid health and nutritional improvement (further discussed in the next chapter) is enormous. Some useful references, which also carefully discuss the statistical evidence, include Jamison and Trowbridge (1984), World Bank (1983a, 1984a, 1985), Jamison *et al.* (1984), Jamison (1985), Xu Su-en (1985), Piazza (1986), Riskin (1986), Banister (1987), Jamison and Piazza (1987), Hussain (1987), and Hussain and Feuchtwang (1988). On the Jamaican experience, which too will be commented on (Chapter 12), see Jameson (1981), Cumper (1983), Gunatilleke (1984), Boyd (1987), Samuels (1987), Moran *et al.* (1988), and Mesa-Lago (1988a).

Chapters 11 and 12, but at this point it must already be noted that the evidence in favour of the feasibility of support-led security is quite substantial.

10.3 Economic Growth and Public Support: Interconnections and Contrasts

The distinction made in the previous section between growth-mediated security and support-led security reflects an important strategic aspect of public action, but many interconnections are also involved, which have to be noted to avoid a false, total dichotomy. The precise nature of the contrast should become clearer as we re-examine the experiences of growth-mediated security in different countries later on in this chapter, but a few preliminary clarifications and general disclaimers might be helpful here.

First, the distinction involved is definitely not a question of activism versus disengagement on the part of the state. The governments of some of the countries which have pursued growth-mediated security have, in fact, often been active in widely disseminating the fruits of growth. In these distributive efforts, the constructive role of the state has not been confined only to the domain of public provisioning. This role has also been geared to facilitating wide participation of the population in the process of economic growth. This has been done particularly through widespread promotion of skills and education, and the maintenance of full employment. In addition, state policies have in many cases been crucial in promoting growth itself.

Second, the contrast we have pursued is also not a simple one of market versus state provisioning. The masses can gain a share in general opulence not only through the increase of private incomes, but also through wide-ranging public provisioning. A striking example is that of Kuwait, where enhanced opulence has provided the material basis for what is clearly one of the most comprehensive welfare states in the world.[14] But in fact all the countries which we have identified as pursuing the strategy of growth-mediated security have taken considerable advantage of the enhanced opportunities for public support provided by rapid economic growth. Other countries with high economic growth but little effort to combine it with social provisioning (e.g. Brazil or Oman) have done much worse in terms of the index of mortality decline, as we have already noted earlier in this chapter.

Third, the distinction made in the last section has little to do with the dilemma that has sometimes been construed between the pursuit of 'growth' and the satisfaction of 'basic needs'. A strategy of 'growth-mediated' *security* is not at all the same thing as the pursuit of economic growth *tout court* (an issue further pursued in the next section). The former need not conflict with the satisfaction of basic needs—indeed it is an *approach* to their satisfaction. Conversely, support-led security does not imply surrendering the goal of

---

[14] See section 10.5 below. It is important to note that welfare provisions in Kuwait, while generally extensive, also discriminate sharply in favour of Kuwaiti citizens as opposed to other residents.

economic growth. In fact, often improvements in the quality of human life (e.g. through better health and education) also substantially enhance the productivity of the labour force. And economic growth can be crucial to the sustainability of a strategy based on generous public support. The interconnections and contrasts between the two strategies are both more extensive and more complex than would be portrayed by a simplistic dichotomy between growth and basic needs.

The real source of the contrast lies in the fact that the countries which have been identified as having made substantial use of the strategy of support-led security have not *waited* to grow rich before providing large-scale public support to guarantee certain basic capabilities. The contrast is a real one, but it should not obscure the complementarities that exist between economic growth and public support—and in particular, the prominent role played by public support in the strategies of growth-mediated as well as support-led security.

Despite these complementarities, dilemmas can arise in seeking a balance between the two strategies. Both growth-oriented measures and support-oriented measures make substantial claims on public resources as well as on public administrative capabilities. There are choices to be made in public policy-making, and we have to face the conflicts involved.

The strategy of growth-mediated security and the strategy of support-led security are basically distinct, but they are not unconnected. It is just as important to recognize that much can be done to improve living standards even when growth has not yet led to a high level of GNP per head, as it is to see that economic growth can be used to provide the basis for raising the quality of life.

10.4   Growth-Mediated Security and Unaimed Opulence

The strategy of growth-mediated security is of somewhat deceptive simplicity, and it is important to realize how widely it actually differs from the indiscriminate pursuit of economic expansion or what might be called a strategy of 'unaimed opulence'. A particularly crude version of the latter approach, which is in fact not uncommon, consists of attempting to *maximize* economic growth without paying any direct attention to the transformation of greater opulence into better living conditions. Unaimed opulence, in general, is a roundabout, undependable, and wasteful way of improving the living standards of the poor. In countries like Brazil where the poorest quintile of the population have to get by with as little as 2 per cent of national income, exclusively relying on the enhancement of general opulence would amount to accepting the need for generating 50 units of income for *one* unit that would go to the poor.[15] In addition, opportunities for the conversion of private incomes into basic

---

[15] Even this is conditional on the assumption that the distribution of income remains unchanged; in fact, inequalities may well increase with the single-minded pursuit of economic growth. The income distribution figures are from *World Development Report 1987*, Table 26.

capabilities might be expected to be particularly poor in a country where public services are persistently sacrificed at the altar of economic growth.

There are remarkable heterogeneities in what has been achieved by different countries through economic expansion and enhanced opulence. At the simplest level, the effect of increased affluence on the quality of life can be expected to depend strongly on the *distribution* of income. The twenty-five developing countries for which income distribution data are available in the *World Development Report 1987* include Hong Kong and South Korea from the group of five growth-mediated successes; both have among the least inegalitarian distributions in the entire list of twenty-five countries. In contrast, Brazil emerges as the country where the share of the richest quintile is highest, and the share of the poorest quintile second lowest. It is hardly surprising, then, that rapidly increasing general opulence in Brazil seems to have yielded so little in terms of improvements in basic aspects of the quality of life.[16] It would not be difficult to find other examples to illustrate how a strategy of unaimed opulence can lead to a tremendous waste of the opportunities provided by rapid economic growth. For example, as was discussed earlier the living-standard records of countries such as South Africa and Oman (also highly inegalitarian, with the poor left mostly to their own devices) are quite dismal, despite their relative opulence.

In many cases, an important part of the difference between unaimed opulence and growth-mediated security relates to the expansion of employment opportunities. Each of the five countries with successful pursuit of growth-mediated security has in fact experienced extraordinarily low rates of unemployment by the standards of developing economies, and several of them have in fact been large importers of labour power.[17] The role of the state in promoting full employment in these countries has also been quite conspicuous.

Note that the actual means employed to promote or guarantee full employment have themselves displayed a great variety in different countries. In South Korea, for instance, employment promotion has been based on (1) the encouragement of labour-intensive export industries, (2) the maintenance of comparative advantage in labour-intensive manufacturing through the ruthless preservation of highly competitive labour markets, (3) an active policy of education, skills diffusion and training, and (4) supplementary public works

[16] In 1985, Brazil had exactly the same U5MR as Burma, even though the latter had just about one-tenth of Brazil's GNP per capita. In fact, Burma had started off with a 43% higher U5MR in 1960, and grew at about only a quarter of the rate of Brazil, and still caught up with Brazil in terms of U5MR by 1985. Among all developing countries, Brazil had the tenth fastest growing economy between 1960 and 1982 (with an estimated annual growth rate of GNP per capita of 4.8%), but only occupies the 56th position in terms of percentage reduction in U5MR (1960–85). See UNICEF (1987a), Table 1, and *World Development Report 1984*, Table 1. For an informative analysis of Brazil's experience, see Sachs (1986).

[17] For further evidence and discussion of the outstanding employment records of these five countries, see al-Sabah (1980), Ismael (1982), Koo (1984), Sherbiny (1984), Hajjar (1985), Nijim (1985), Government of Hong Kong (1986), Krause (1988), Richardson and Kim (1986), and Hahn (1989).

programmes.[18] In Kuwait, on the other hand, the munificence of the welfare state has extended to nothing short of guaranteeing a job in the public sector to every Kuwaiti not employed in the private sector.[19] Here too, one finds a plurality of strategic options for public action. But the instrumental role of the expansion of employment opportunities to share the benefits of affluence must generally be seen as a crucial one.

10.5   Opulence and Public Provisioning

We should recall that a strategy of growth-mediated security does not necessarily make private incomes an exclusive vehicle for spreading the fruits of growth. Direct provisioning by the state can, as we have emphasized, assume an important role even when security is mediated by general economic growth. This fact is clearly illustrated by the experience of several of the countries which we have identified as having pursued the strategy of growth-mediated security. One obvious case is that of Kuwait.[20]

The genesis of Kuwait's present affluence goes back to 1946, when the country started exporting oil. Since then, earnings in the oil sector have grown to remarkable heights, and in 1980 they accounted for two-thirds of Kuwait's Gross Domestic Product.[21] Until 1975, when the Kuwait Oil Company (KOC) was fully acquired by the Government of Kuwait, oil earnings accrued mainly in the form of taxes and royalties levied on the foreign-owned KOC. At the time of nationalization, oil and gas exploitation provided employment only to a tiny fraction of the labour force. The same pattern continued after 1975, though the KOC was from then run by the government, which therefore appropriated its entire profits.

The livelihood of the bulk of Kuwait's population depends directly or indirectly on the use of these huge oil earnings through government activities and transfers. The percolation of oil revenues from the KOC to the masses has of course not assumed a particularly egalitarian character. A sizeable chunk, for instance, goes straightaway to various members of the ruling family in the form of permanent salaries, which allow this privileged élite to live in the material abundance that has often made the headlines in the Western press. Nevertheless, the greater part of oil revenues has been allocated to a massive programme of development activities, public sector employment, social services provision, and direct transfers.

A very large proportion of domestic government expenditure is accounted

---

[18] See section 10.6 of this chapter.

[19] See e.g. Ismael (1982). We should stress that the guarantee of employment applies only to Kuwaiti *nationals*. With respect to non-Kuwaiti residents (a large part of the population), full employment seems to be ensured through the no-nonsense method of stipulating that 'a non-Kuwaiti must leave the country once unemployed' (Ismael 1982: 119).

[20] The factual basis of the following account is derived from al-Sabah (1980), Ismael (1982), Harrison (1985), Nijim (1985), Public Institution for Social Security (1985), Hammoud (1986, 1987), and Nagi (1986), aside from official statistical sources.

[21] *Annual Statistical Abstract of Kuwait 1987*, pp. 266–7. As noted earlier, the contribution of oil revenues to Kuwait's economy declined after 1980 due to the fall in oil prices.

Table 10.4 Kuwait, 1960–1985: selected indicators

	1960	1965	1970	1975	1980	1985
Population (000s)	322[a]	467	739	995	1,357	1,697
Government oil revenue (million KD)	159	216	289	2,440	5,187	2,295
Public health expenditure (million KD)	n/a	6	16	39	105	193
Public education expenditure (million KD)	n/a	15	32	81	172	275
Number of teachers in government schools	2,133	4,625	8,652	14,842	22,219	26,463
Number of students in government schools (000)	43	85	134	192	294	361
Number of physicians in government hospitals	n/a	451	540	932	1,921	2,528
Rate of illiteracy (percentage of population aged 10 and above)	n/a	46	39	36	29	16

[a] For the year 1961.

Source: Government of Kuwait, Ministry of Planning, Central Statistical Office, *Annual Statistical Abstract* (1970, 1974, 1978, 1980, 1982, 1984, 1987).

for by wages and salaries, and the magnitude of public sector employment has indeed assumed staggering proportions. As we have already noted, every Kuwaiti citizen not otherwise employed is guaranteed a job in the public sector. The army of government employees has primarily busied itself with implementing the multitudinous activities of the welfare state, and in 1975 as much as 69 per cent of the Kuwaiti labour force was employed in the 'social services' sector.[22] As Ismael (1982) puts it, Kuwait is a 'total service society with almost every human need from the cradle to the grave serviced by institutional arrangements'.[23]

The availability of public services in Kuwait has indeed expanded in record time from one typical of low-income countries to one typical of rich, industrialized economies; on this see Table 10.4. The stick of compulsory school attendance (first brandished in 1965), combined with the carrot of free education, free books, free meals, free transport, and even free clothes, has lured the younger generation to school in spite of some conservative resistance (particularly regarding girls). In 1977, government subsidies on education exceeded $600 per student.[24] The male secondary-school enrolment ratio of 86 per cent in Kuwait in 1982–4 is bettered only by South Korea and a handful of industrialized market economies (interestingly enough, the Kuwaiti ratio is

[22] *Annual Statistical Abstract of Kuwait 1987*, p. 136.
[23] Ismael (1982: 105).   [24] al-Sabah (1980: 58).

higher than those of France and the United Kingdom). The female secondary-school enrolment ratio of 79 per cent is a little lower but is still extremely impressive, especially by the standards of developing economies. This ratio of 79 per cent compares, for instance, with 19 per cent in Oman and 36 per cent in Brazil.[25]

Sophisticated medical services are provided free of charge to the entire population, Kuwaiti and non-Kuwaiti. Far-reaching public provisions are also made in areas such as housing, water supply (a precious commodity in Kuwait), electricity, transport and communications, and the subsidization of basic commodities. In addition, Kuwait has a system of large-scale direct transfers and financial help to low-income families which is by any standards one of the most generous in the world.[26] If socialism were reduced simply to state ownership of the means of production and generous provision of 'social wages', Kuwait would appear to be one of the most obviously socialist countries in the world!

The case of Kuwait is admittedly a special one in many respects, but the general notion that growth can facilitate public support applies more generally. In fact, it is rather striking how extensively the governments of the five 'growth-mediated security' countries have been driven (under the influence of a variety of political pressures and motivations) to use wide-ranging public provisioning in order to transform the material fruits of growth into secure minimal living standards for the greater part of the population. This applies even to governments which have a fierce reputation of non-interventionism in the private enterprise economy, of which Hong Kong is a classic example.

It is true that the government of Hong Kong, in sharp contrast with that of Kuwait, commands a relatively small proportion of the national income. However, within total government expenditure social services are the main item, with a share as large as 38 per cent in 1986.[27] This has permitted not only substantial improvements in the provision of educational facilities and health care but also the development of a sophisticated system of social assistance, including means-tested income support along similar lines to the Supplementary Benefits in the UK. It also includes huge housing subsidies which, in terms of generosity and coverage, count among the most substantial income support schemes in the world.[28] The results of economic growth as well as

[25] UNICEF (1987a), Table 4.

[26] According to al-Sabah, the percentage of Kuwaiti families benefiting from direct financial aid from the government is the highest in the world (about 25 per cent), and the government of Kuwait is strongly committed to the 'lower-income Kuwaitis', the latter being defined as those 'whose *monthly* income does not exceed $550' (al-Sabah 1980: 57, 158; emphasis added).

[27] Government of Hong Kong (1987), Appendix 8a.

[28] The strides that have been made in Hong Kong during the last few decades in the areas of health care, education, social assistance, and housing are discussed in Heppell (1973, 1974), Chow (1981), Drakakis-Smith (1981), King and Lee (1981), Lee (1983), Yeh (1984), and Government of Hong Kong (1987). The role played by welfare provisions in the development experience of the 'four little tigers' (Hong Kong, South Korea, Singapore, and Taiwan) is also investigated in Midgley (1986).

public support founded on it include a remarkably high life expectancy (viz. 76 years, which is comparable with the expectation of life in the most advanced industrial economies).

The opportunity for enlarged public provisioning provided by rapid growth has also been seized to various degrees by the other three of the five countries identified earlier as cases of 'growth-mediated security'. The experience of the United Arab Emirates bears some resemblance to that of Kuwait.[29] In Singapore, the government has an impressive record of extensive activism in both economic and social matters, which has been seen as a major factor behind the rapid improvement of living conditions in that country in the last few decades.[30] The experience of South Korea is discussed at greater length in the next section.

10.6   Growth-mediated Security: The Case of South Korea

A good illustration of the subtleties involved in a strategy of growth-mediated security, and of the role played at different levels by public action, is provided by South Korea. As we have seen, the growth rate of GNP per capita in that country over the last few decades has by any standards been a highly impressive one. Nor can it be denied that in this case rapid growth has provided the basis for very tangible improvements in basic components of the quality of life. We have already noted South Korea's outstanding reduction in infant and child mortality rates. There are many other, direct and indirect, indications of rapid advances in living standards. Indeed, there is solid evidence that during the period under consideration (viz. 1960 to 1985), the nutritional status of children has markedly improved; morbidity rates for communicable diseases have shrunk very fast; the incidence of absolute poverty (as standardly measured) has rapidly decreased, both in rural and in urban areas; the unemployment rate has stabilized at a remarkably low value (around 4 per cent); general educational standards have reached exceptionally high levels; and real wage rates have consistently increased, both in agriculture and in manufacturing. Some relevant indicators are presented in Table 10.5.[31]

The extent of government involvement in income redistribution and social welfare programmes has been, until recently, rather small by international standards. To take only one example, before 1976, South Korea had no public

[29] See e.g. Taryam (1987), especially Chapter 7.

[30] On this see the in-depth analysis of Ng Shui Meng (1986b). The pervasive influence of the government on economic and social life in Singapore (which ranges from housing 81% of the population in 1986 to 'discouraging long hair and corrupting music and dance') is also discussed in detail by Krause (1988).

[31] See also Suh (1984) on nutrition and morbidity; Richardson and Kim (1986) on employment; and McGinn et al. (1980) on education. According to UNICEF (1987a), Table 4, in 1985 South Korea had the fourth highest male literacy among all developing countries. Its secondary-school enrolment rate was the highest among developing countries for males (92%), and second highest for females (86%). In the latter respect South Korea surpassed a large number of developed, industrialized countries.

Table 10.5 South Korea, 1960–1985: selected indicators

| Year | Infant mortality rate (per 1,000) | Height of children aged 6 (cm.) | | Incidence of poverty (%) | Gini index of income inequality | Unemployment rate (%) | Index of real wages in industry (1970 = 100) | Secondary school enrolment (%) |
| | | Male | Female | | | | | |
	(1)	(2a)	(2b)	(3)	(4)	(5)	(6)	(7)
1960	85	111.1[a]	110.4[a]	n/a	0.448	n/a	n/a	n/a
1965	n/a	111.7	110.8	41	0.344	7.4	58	54
1970	53	112.7	111.7	23	0.332	4.5	100	66
1975	41	113.3	112.3	15[b]	0.391	4.1	127	77
1980	37	115.0	113.7	10	0.389	4.5	219	96
1985	27	116.5	115.4	7	0.363	4.0	286	99

[a] Figure relating to 1962.
[b] Figure relating to 1976.

Sources: (1) Suh (1984: 162) and UNICEF (1987a), Table 1. (2) Government of the Republic of Korea (1963, 1965, 1970, 1987). (3)–(5) Hahn (1989), Figures 5, 7, and 13b. (6) Calculated from Hasan and Rao (1979), Table D.38, and Hahn (1989), Figure 22. (7) Hahn (1989), Figure 28. We are extremely grateful to Byung Whan Kim (London School of Economics) for guidance to South Korean statistics.

health care system worth the name, and no form of broad-based medical assistance or medical insurance scheme. Health care was predominantly in the hands of private professionals, especially pharmacists.[32] Many other aspects of social welfare have also been rather neglected until recently, and the South Korean government has consistently rejected the option of developing into a 'welfare state'.[33] Nor has it expressed much direct concern about income redistribution.[34]

One could be led by all this to conclude that in South Korea private enterprise has been the driving force not only of economic growth in the narrow sense (as is widely recognized), but also of wider improvements in the quality of life. It is perhaps not without reason, then, that South Korea has been variously seen as an archetype of the fecundity of capitalism, a 'free enterprise model' for other developing countries, an illustration of the redundancy of planning, and, generally, a brilliant product of what some have called the 'market order'.[35]

There is clearly an element of truth in these characterizations. However, there are also serious qualifications to be made from several different perspectives.

First, it must be pointed out that the South Korean economy in the late 1940s offered a rather unusual base for equitable growth. A particularly important factor was the relatively equal distribution of assets (including skills, education and land), in the creation of which the government played a major role.[36] Equitable growth was reinforced by the labour-intensive orientation of industry (we have already noted South Korea's remarkable wage and employment figures), and this orientation took place within a structure of incentives and inducements carefully planned by the government. It is impossible to understand South Korea's experience without reference to the major role which the government has played in enabling the population at large to *participate* fruitfully in the process of economic growth.

Second, as has been widely noted, the hands which signalled South Korea's economic expansion have been much less 'invisible' than would appear at first sight. It is true that South Korean economic policy and planning has mainly taken the form of creating an environment conducive to private enterprise of

[32] South Korea's health care system is discussed in detail in Park and Yeon (1981) and Yeon (1982, 1986). See also Golladay and King (1979), Suh (1984), Yoon and Park (1985a), and Bahl *et al.* (1986). The year 1976 marked a turning-point in the development of health care policy in Korea, with the introduction of the medical assistance and medical insurance programmes. In recent years increasing efforts have also been made to develop the public health care system.

[33] See the references cited above, and also Republic of Korea (1979). It is worth noting that important changes have taken place in South Korea in the area of social welfare policy since the mid-1970s—see e.g. Suh (1984), Government of Korea (1986), Midgley (1986), and Suh and Williamson (1987).

[34] See e.g. Kim and Yun (1988).

[35] On these various characterizations and important analyses related to these perspectives, see Bauer (1972, 1981, 1984), Little (1982), Lal (1983) and Balassa (1988).

[36] See e.g. Suh (1984), Bahl *et al.* (1986), Michell (1988).

the favoured kind. However, the role of government policy in planning the nature of economic growth and in intervening to shape the direction of investment and expansion has been both pervasive and enormously effective.[37]

Government involvement in this field has taken a wide variety of forms, including extensive credit controls and incentives, import substitution measures, infrastructural investments, the dissemination of information, a sophisticated tax administration system, and the promotion of an active and competitive labour market.[38] As far as the alleged 'redundancy of planning' is concerned, South Korea has, in fact, had regular Five-Year Plans since 1962 and also the rare distinction of implementing them successfully.[39] The various instruments of state policy for shaping the South Korean economy are systematically put together in this exercise of integrated planning.

Third, a further question concerns the precise involvement of the South Korean government in measures of direct public support. The record in this respect has been highly uneven between different areas of intervention, and is therefore difficult to assess. For instance, while public provisions for health care were rather meagre until the late 1970s (as noted earlier), the state has been extremely active in the area of education for a long time.[40] And while it is true that the South Korean government has, at least until recently, eschewed the idea of large-scale welfare programmes, it has, on the other hand, had a long-standing and (in some ways) pioneering concern for the prevention of acute destitution.[41]

Moreover, there have been important policy developments within the period under consideration (viz. 1960 to 1985). Specifically, the commitment of the government to social policies has rapidly increased in the second half of this period. In the area of health care, for instance, ambitious programmes of medical assistance and medical insurance initiated in the late 1970s have marked a reorientation of earlier policies.[42] Government expenditure on health, education, housing, and social security has grown

[37] Numerous writers have stressed and documented this point. See, for instance, Datta Chaudhuri (1979), Hasan and Rao (1979), Sen (1981b), Wade (1983), Evans and Alizadeh (1984), Koo (1984), Bahl et al. (1986), Hamilton (1986), Midgley (1986), Richardson and Kim (1986), Bagchi (1987), Toye (1987), Amsden (1989), Kim and Yun (1988), Kuznets (1988), Michell (1988), Qi (1988), White (1988), and Alam (1989).

[38] On the last point, see e.g. Richardson and Kim (1986). It must be noted in particular that the South Korean government's anxiety to maintain competitive labour market conditions has had a counterpart in very energetic and effective policies aimed at upgrading skills through education and training.

[39] See Suh (1984) and Kuznets (1988).

[40] See McGinn et al. (1980) and Amsden (1989).

[41] This concern has been visible, for instance, in the promotion of a 'Work-conditioned Assistance Programme' (initiated in 1964) and in the provisions associated with the Livelihood Protection Act of 1961. For further discussion of these and related social security measures, see Yoon and Park (1985a, 1985b).

[42] On this, see e.g. Park and Yeon (1981) and Yeon (1986).

very fast since then—as fast as 33 per cent per year during the period 1978–82.[43]

The important role played by direct measures of public support in supplementing the normal operation of the economy in South Korea has been particularly clear during the recession of the early 1980s. It has been observed that, in this event, direct measures of public support (such as public works programmes and direct transfers to the needy) emerged as crucial policy instruments for the protection of vulnerable groups.[44]

The Korean experience is thus far from one of *laissez-faire*, and in fact richly illustrates the diverse roles that state planning and action can play in influencing—directly and indirectly—the expansion of basic capabilities within a strategy of growth-mediated security. The active nature of state policy in South Korea within the structure of promoting security through participatory growth would be hard to deny.

The positive involvement of the state in promoting participatory growth may seem surprising given the repressive nature of the Korean government over this period. The possible contribution of—open or latent—political opposition in influencing the state in the direction of promoting living standards should not, however, be underestimated. The government has had to cope with vocal political dissent (especially from the student community) and frequent outbursts of public protest, which have also been widely reported abroad.[45] The precise role of adversarial public action in affecting the direction of state policy is an aspect of the South Korean experience that merits further attention.

10.7 Support-Led Security and Equivalent Growth

In the preceding sections we have discussed the experiences of some of the countries that have successfully pursued what we have called 'growth-mediated security'. In Chapters 11 and 12, we will examine selected cases of 'support-led security'. In this last section of the present chapter, we discuss some general issues related to assessing the effectiveness of the strategy of support-led security.

To start with, it is of some interest to consider briefly how the levels of under-5 mortality in the countries which we have identified as having pursued a strategy of support-led security compare today with the levels observed in

[43] Suh (1984), Table XII.3. As Yeon observes: 'In recent years government policy in the Republic of Korea has recognised the fact that rapid economic growth is a necessary but not sufficient condition for improving the income and standard of living of the population' (Yeon 1986: 153). This concern is indeed evident in recent planning documents (e.g. Government of Korea 1986).

[44] For a detailed analysis of this issue, see Suh and Williamson (1987), as well as Cornia *et al.* (1987), vol. i.

[45] See Steinberg (1988) on adversarial politics in South Korea and their relation to economic policies. See also McGinn *et al.* (1980).

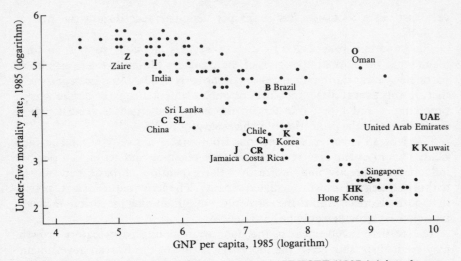

Source: Based on data for 120 countries provided in UNICEF (1987*a*) (nine observations represent two countries each due to 'superimposition'). Data on GNP are not available for Cuba.

Fig. 10.1   GNP per capita and under-5 mortality (1985): international comparison

other countries with a similar level of GNP per capita. This can be appreciated from a simple scatter diagram showing the levels of GNP per capita and U5MR (in 1985) for different countries—see Figure 10.1 and also Table 10.6.[46]

The interpretation of the position of different countries requires some caution. For instance, it would not make much sense to presume that any country with a low U5MR relative to other countries at a comparable income level must be particularly exemplary (as is sometimes assumed in analysing 'basic needs performance'). This is so not only because one simple way to reach that position is to do it, as it were, the Zaire way, to wit, by producing *negative* growth![47] As income goes down, the U5MR looks better in comparative terms. But more importantly, this way of identifying successful countries would hide the success of countries that have achieved a low U5MR *through* a growth-mediated strategy.

The goal of development is to improve the quality of life, not to improve the

[46] Note that Figure 10.1 is drawn on the basis of logarithmic scales. This means that, each time we move one unit up the vertical axis, U5MR is multiplied by a little less than *three* (and correspondingly for GNP per capita along the horizontal axis). Table 10.6 is based on a log-linear, ordinary-least-squares regression of U5MR (1985) on per-capita GNP (1985) for 120 countries. The over-all results reported in this section are quite robust to alternative specifications of the set of countries considered in the analysis (e.g. including or excluding developed economies, or oil-exporting countries).

[47] Zaire had a growth rate of −2.1% in 1965–85 (*World Development Report 1987*, Table 1). It has also experienced a steady deterioration of its living standards in recent years.

Tabel 10.6 Actual value of U5MR (1985) as percentage of
value predicted on the basis of GNP per capita

	Ratio (%)	Growth rate of GNP per head (1965–85)
Ten developing countries with lowest ratio		
China	32	4.8
Jamaica	33	−0.7
Sri Lanka	35	2.9
Guyana	36	−0.2
Costa Rica	37	1.4
Burma	42	2.4
Chile	45	−0.2
Mauritius	46	2.7
Hong Kong	50	6.1
Madagascar	52	−1.9
Other (selected) countries		
Singapore	61	7.6
Zaire	73	−2.1
South Korea	79	6.6
Brazil	172	4.3
Kuwait	216	−0.3
Oman	819	5.7

Note: Calculated from the same sources as Table 10.3. The 'predicted value' of U5MR is obtained from OLS regression of U5MR on GNP per capita (both in logarithmic form). The regression involves 120 countries for which data were available on both variables (for 10 countries, including Cuba, U5MR estimates existed but not GNP estimates).

quality of life *relative* to income. In pursuing the former goal, the growth of income can, as we have already seen, play an important role. The achievement of a low level of under-5 mortality relative to income (through, say, extensive public provisioning) would give little grounds for congratulation if the expenses involved had the effect of slowing down the growth of incomes to the extent that the *absolute* value of U5MR ended up being higher than it would have been with less public support and more growth.

In spite of these reservations, the information provided by Figure 10.1 and Table 10.6 is instructive in giving us a part—an important part—of the picture. It can, in fact, assist our understanding of the gains that can be obtained through public support for a given level of opulence. The figures indicate the extent to which the success of the five countries which we have identified as having made effective use of a support-led strategy (viz. Chile, China, Costa Rica, Cuba, Jamaica) has indeed relied on their ability to deviate from the 'standard' relationship between GNP and mortality. Their record in breaking the shackles of low income and poverty is indeed impressive, with (for instance) China achieving a level of under-5 mortality rate (U5MR) less than a *third* of that predicted on the basis of its income level alone. Similarly striking advantages are enjoyed by the other countries in this group.[48]

This exercise is also helpful in identifying other countries which have achieved great success in reducing mortality despite low incomes, but did not appear in our initial group of 'top ten' performers because the period of rapid improvement in their case failed to overlap substantially with the time period used in this classification (viz. 1960–85). On the basis of Figure 10.1 and Table 10.6, the most obvious candidate for this diagnosis is Sri Lanka. It can be seen that Sri Lanka, like China, has a level of U5MR about a third of what one would expect (on the basis of international comparisons) given its level of GNP per capita. But the period of spectacular advance in Sri Lanka did not lie primarily in the last two or three decades, and for the 1960–85 period specifically Sri Lanka has not been an outstanding performer. Accelerated breakthrough in mortality reduction occurred earlier, during the 1940s and 1950s. These were, in fact, also the decades of rapid growth of public support in the form of free or subsidized distribution of rice (introduced in 1942) and intensive expansion of public health services (beginning in the forties, partly related to a campaign to conquer malaria). Though it has a different time pattern from the other countries discussed in this chapter, Sri Lanka's pioneering experience is of great general interest, and will be further investigated in Chapter 12.[49]

A careful examination of the levels of per-capita GNP and under-5 mortality can also help us to assess the relative gains that different countries might expect to obtain from alternative strategies. We could, for instance, examine questions of the following sort. If a country like, say, China had resorted to a 'standard' amount of public support instead of an exceptional one, how much *faster* would it have had to grow over a specified period in order to reach the level of U5MR it is observed to have in 1985? Clearly, only rather speculative —and at best approximate—answers to this question can be arrived at. Simple examinations of the current relationship between U5MR and per capita GNP in different countries can, however, assist our intuition about the plausibility of different answers.

An elementary but nevertheless useful answer to the question posed can, for instance, be obtained in the following manner. First, we estimate the level of

[48] For Cuba, however, the relevant data (particularly GNP estimates) needed for inclusion in Table 10.6 are not available.

[49] The case of Mauritius (also appearing in Table 10.6) bears some resemblance to that of Sri Lanka. Indeed, the links between public policy and social achievements in Mauritius in the 1940s and 1950s have attracted considerable attention. On this and related aspects of Mauritius's development experience, see Meade *et al.* (1968), Titmuss and Abel-Smith (1968), Tabutin (1975), Mehta (1981), Minogue (1983), Tabutin and Sombo (1983), Selwyn (1983), Joynathsingh (1987).

per-capita GNP which an 'average' country appears to need in order to experience China's current level of infant and child mortality.[50] Second, we calculate the extra growth of income that China would have been required to achieve over a specified period to reach that level of GNP per capita.[51] The results of such a calculation, taking 1960–85 as the reference period, are presented in the first column of Table 10.7. They suggest that, to reach the observed level of U5MR in 1985 in the absence of outstanding public support measures, China would have had to raise its annual growth rate over the whole period by 7 to 10 per cent of the GNP per capita (e.g., if the actual growth rate experienced was 4 per cent, it would have had to raise it to somewhere between 11 and 14 per cent per year).

It may be argued that this calculation can be somewhat misleading in that it attributes the whole of China's deviation from the average relationship between GNP and U5MR to its outstanding measures of public support. What if China's outstanding record is due, say, to favourable ecological circumstances, or some other advantage applying to China as a country? There is no obvious reason to believe that such advantages—ecological or otherwise—are enjoyed by China. Nevertheless, Table 10.7 also presents (in the last three columns) alternative estimates assuming different levels of 'country advantage', where the latter is defined as the proportion of China's deviation from the average relationship between GNP and U5MR that can be attributed to favourable circumstances unrelated to public support.[52] For reasonable values of country advantage, *additional* growth requirements over the 1960–85 period in the absence of outstanding public support measures remain very high—5 per cent of GNP per capita each year under the set of assumptions most favourable to the growth scenario.[53]

Furthermore, there is an important source of *downward* bias in the figures of 'extra growth requirements' appearing in Table 10.7. In effect, it is assumed in this exercise that higher incomes have an immediate effect on infant and child

---

[50] This estimated level of income, say $y^\star$, is inferred from the regression relating U5MR (1985) to per-capita GNP (1985), mentioned earlier.

[51] It is easy to show that, if y is China's actual per-capita GNP in 1985, and t the length of the specified period, then this 'extra growth requirement', say g, is simply $(\ln y^\star - \ln y)/t$. Note that this formula does *not* require us to know China's *actual* growth rate at any time. This is fortunate since, as we shall see in the next chapter, China's past growth rates are extremely hard to ascertain.

[52] Formally, the 'country advantage' is the proportion of China's 'residual' in the earlier regression that is considered attributable to favourable circumstances rather than to public support. It can be shown that, if the assumed value of the country advantage is α, then the 'extra growth requirement' is simply $(1 - \alpha).g$, where g is calculated as before.

[53] The highest value of 'country advantage' for China used in Table 10.7 is 30 per cent. This upper bound is obtained by treating country advantage analogously to a 'fixed effect', and attributing *all* of China's favourable deviation from the international regression line around 1960 to its country advantage. Note that this is likely to be a substantial *overestimate* of China's 'country advantage' since by that time China already had an outstanding history of public support. Of course, whether there is *any* 'country advantage' at all for China is far from clear, and our use of this 'scaling down' of the achievements of support-led strategy is motivated by making as conservative an estimate as possible.

Table 10.7 Extra annual growth of per-capita GNP required
by China between 1960 and 1985 in order to reach its observed
level of U5MR in 1985 in the absence of outstanding public
support measures (%)

Additional growth requirement for alternative assumed values of 'country advantage' (CA)			
CA = 0	CA = 0.10	CA = 0.20	CA = 0.30
7.1	6.4	5.7	5.0
(9.9)	(8.9)	(7.9)	(6.9)

Source: See text. The numbers without brackets are based on a
regression involving all countries for which the relevant data are
available in UNICEF (1987*a*, 1988). The numbers within brackets are
based on a regression involving only developing countries.

mortality. In practice, however, there are likely to be lags involved, as the
recent experience of oil-exporting countries illustrates. Incorporating such
lags in the analysis would lead to considerably larger estimates of 'extra growth
requirements'.[54]

In spite of their illustrative nature, the calculations we have presented bring
out that the 'economic growth equivalent' of well-planned public support is
very large indeed.[55] That is, the results that countries such as China have
achieved through direct public support could only have been obtained through
extremely fast economic growth if they had followed a 'path' similar to that
typical of other developing countries.[56]

Whether immediate and extensive measures of public support in a poor
country *lead to* slower economic growth is, of course, an extremely complex
question, and we shall not pursue it here. As was mentioned earlier, the
interactions between public support and economic growth include not only
dilemmas and trade-offs (e.g. the allocation of resources between immediate
consumption and investment), but also many positive links (e.g. the effects of
improved health and nutrition on productivity). What is worth noting here is
that, given the very large 'growth equivalent' of public support, only the
existence of some remarkably powerful (and negative) trade-off between
public support and economic growth would seriously undermine the case for
extensive involvement in public support at an early stage of development.

[54] Indeed, when the 1960 value of U5MR is included as an 'explanatory variable' in the earlier
regression, the coefficient of 1985 per-capita GNP drops dramatically. Correspondingly, estimates
of 'extra growth requirements' sharply increase.

[55] An alternative approach to the analysis of the 'growth equivalent' of public support, leading
to a similar general conclusion, was presented in Sen (1981*b*). For a critical examination of the
possible interconnections, see Birdsall (1988, 1989).

[56] It must be emphasized that this 'standard' path as it exists today is *not* the same as what we
have called 'growth-mediated security'. In fact, it is interesting that *all* the countries identified
earlier as having followed that strategy have large negative residuals in regressions of U5MR (1985)
on GNP (1985) and U5MR (1960). This confirms that their experiences have involved a great deal
more than a vague reliance on economic growth, as with 'unaimed opulence'.

In the next two chapters, we shall discuss in some detail the experiences of selected countries in the pursuit of support-led security. Some of the general issues and dilemmas arising from a programme of public action for social security will be reconsidered in the concluding part of this book.

11

China and India

11.1 Is China Ahead?

When development planning began in China after the revolution (1949) and in India after its independence (1947), both countries were starting from a very low base of economic and social achievement. The gross national product per head in each country was among the lowest in the world, hunger was widespread, the level of illiteracy remarkably high, and life expectancy at birth not far from 40 years. There were many differences between them, but the similarities were quite striking. Since then things have happened in both countries, but the two have moved along quite different routes. A comparison between the achievements of China and India is not easy, but certain contrasts do stand out sharply.

Perhaps the most striking is the contrast in matters of life and death. Life expectancy at birth in China appears to be firmly in the middle to upper 60s (close to 70 years according to some estimates),[1] while that in India seems to be around the middle to upper 50s.[2] The under-5 mortality rate, according to UNICEF statistics, is 47 per thousand in China, and more than three times as much in India, viz. 154.[3] The percentage of infants with low birth weight in 1982–3 is reported to be about 6 in China, and five times as much in India.[4] Analyses of anthropometric data and morbidity patterns confirm that China has achieved a remarkable transition in health and nutrition.[5] No comparable transformation has occurred in India.

Things have diverged radically in the two countries also in the field of elementary education. The percentage of adult literacy is about 43 in India, and around 69 in China.[6] If China and India looked similar in these

[1] The *World Development Report 1988* puts the Chinese life expectancy at birth in 1986 at 69 years. The Chinese official statistics based on the 1982 census place it at 68 years in 1981. Judith Banister (1987) gives a lower estimate based on corrections for incomplete reporting, viz. 65 years, for the same year.

[2] The *World Development Report 1988* gives the figure of 57 years as life expectancy at birth in India in 1986. The last reliable estimate based on sample registration survey for 1976–80 puts the figure at 52.3 years, but later estimates also exist suggesting a life expectancy in the mid-50s.

[3] See UNICEF (1988), Table 1.

[4] UNICEF (1988), Table 2. Serious doubts have, however, been expressed about the reliability of these figures of birth weights, for purposes of international comparison, especially since there are some variations in the criteria used.

[5] See World Bank (1983a, 1984a, 1985), Piazza (1986), Hussain (1987), Jamison and Piazza (1987), and Hussain and Feuchtwang (1988).

[6] UNICEF (1988), Table 4. The male and female adult literacy rates given by UNICEF for each country are respectively 82 and 56 in China and 57 and 29 in India. The total population averages have been obtained from these data by weighting the female and male figures by the ratio of females to males in the two countries.

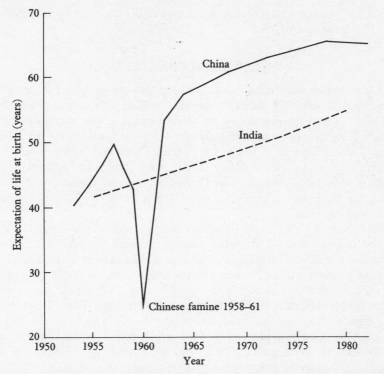

Sources: J. Banister, 'An Analysis of Recent Data on the Population of China', *Population and Development Review*, 10 (1984); S. Preston and P. N. Mari Bhat, 'New Evidence on Fertility and Mortality Trends in India', *Population and Development Review*, 10 (1984), for 1966–81 based on 'the low variant' procedure; *Statistical Pocket Book of India 1984* (New Delhi, 1985), for 1955 (as the 1951–61 decade average).

Fig. 11.1 Life expectancy at birth in China and India

matters at the middle of this century, they certainly do not do so now.[7]

The comparison is not, however, entirely one-sided. There are skeletons in China's cupboard—millions of them from the disastrous famine of 1958–61. India, in contrast, has not had any large-scale famine since independence in 1947. We shall take up the question of comparative famine experience later on (in section 11.3), and also a few other problems in China's success story (sections 11.4 and 11.5), but there is little doubt that as far as morbidity, mortality and longevity are concerned, China has a large and decisive lead over India.[8]

---

[7] The picture is more diverse if *intra*country differences are also considered. In particular, the public intervention programmes in the state of Kerala in India seem to have made the achievements of that state comparable to China's. The mixed nature of these contrasts also points towards some policy lessons. The issue is taken up in the last section of this chapter.

[8] China's lead in the field of literacy is also clear enough, though India has a much more extensive tertiary education sector with a much higher percentage of the relevant age-cohort going to the universities.

What has brought about that lead is a matter of very considerable interest, and to that issue we now turn.

11.2 What Put China Ahead?

In the last chapter we distinguished between 'growth-mediated security' and 'support-led security'. Is China's success based mainly on rapid economic growth, or is it primarily the result of developing a vast system of public support? It might not be immediately obvious what has been the main factor behind China's lead over India. Of course, China has had a much more extensive system of public delivery of food, health care, and education. But, according to widely quoted standard statistics, it is also credited with having had a much faster rate of economic growth than India. We have to scrutinize both sets of information.

Comparison of China's and India's rates of growth of per-capita GNP has attracted a good deal of attention among experts, and the difficulties of comparison are indeed formidable. The consensus has been in the direction of accepting a much higher growth rate in China than in India, though the difference appears to be somewhat smaller after corrections are made to account for the different bases of the respective estimates. There are also some non-comparabilities arising from differences in the way in which the two economies function (e.g. in the role of the service sector, which is much larger in India and has been growing fast), and the authors of these studies have warned us to be careful in interpreting the comparative estimates.[9]

World Development Report 1988 gives the growth rate of GNP per head during 1965–86 as 1.8 per cent in India and 5.1 per cent—nearly three times as large—in China. If the comparative growth picture is really something like that, it would be natural to assume that the Chinese achievement in matters of life and death must have been substantially 'growth-mediated'. Growing at 5.1 per cent per year over decades would, for one thing, make a country's per-capita income a great deal higher than what would result from hastening slowly at 1.8 per cent, and that—as the arguments of the last chapter indicated—could make a lot of resources potentially available for public support in addition to enhancing average personal affluence.

These comparative growth figures do not, however, bear any scrutiny. Indeed, the same *World Development Report 1988* gives the Chinese per-capita GNP in 1986 as $300 and that of India as $290. If the figures of GNP level and GNP growth are put together, it would appear that in 1965 India had about twice the per-capita GNP of China (about $200 for India and $106 for China at 1986 prices). That is, in order for the Chinese GNP per head to have grown at

[9] Wilfred Malenbaum (1956, 1959, 1982) has provided careful and illuminating comparisons of economic growth in the two countries over the decades. See also Swamy (1986*a*), and the previous literature cited there and in Malenbaum (1982). See also Perkins (1983, 1988) on methodological problems and substantive results in assessing China's growth performance.

5.1 per cent while India's grew at 1.8 per cent, and for the two to have ended up with their respective 1986 GNP figures, the Chinese per-capita GNP in the middle 1960s would have had to be only a little over a half that of India.[10]

That inference would be contrary to all available estimates of Chinese and Indian GNP for the 1960s. It would have also made China then a great deal poorer than the *poorest* country in the contemporary world.[11] In fact, Simon Kuznets's estimates indicated a similar GNP per head in 1958 for China and India, with 'product per head' about 20 per cent *higher* in China.[12] The story of the Chinese GNP per head growing about three times as fast as the Indian simply does not bear empirical scrutiny.

In fact, the World Bank's own *World Tables 1987* puts the GNP per head in the mid-1960s, specifically 1966, at $110 for China and $90 for India, i.e. 22 per cent *higher* in China. *World Tables 1987* also gives the 1986 GNP per head of China and India as $300 and $270 respectively. Putting their 1966 and 1986 figures together indicates implicit growth rates that are very similar for the two countries (5.1 per cent per year for China and 5.6 per cent in India). That is a very different picture from that of China's growth rate of 5.1 per cent per year being nearly three times as high as India's 1.8 per cent, as given by the more widely used publication of the same World Bank—the *World Development Report*. The picture is confused and confounded, to say the least.

One should not make heavy weather of these inconsistencies. We do know that international comparisons of GNP are plagued by the usual complications of exchange-rate variations and changes in relative prices.[13] But the complete lack of relation between GNP levels and growth rates in *World Development Report*'s account of China's and India's respective performance makes it hard to put much reliance on the respective growth statistics.[14] In particular, the

[10] These results are not particularly sensitive to the exact years chosen for the backward extrapolation based on World Bank data. Putting together the GNP figures for 1982 and the growth rates for 1960–82, as given in *World Development Report 1984*, yields 1960 per-head GNP figures of $106 for China and $196 for India, i.e. a Chinese GNP per head 46% *lower* than India's (on this see Sen 1985a: 78–80 and Table A.2).

[11] The poorest country covered in the *World Development Report 1988* is Ethiopia with a GNP per head of $120 in 1986 (see Table 1, p. 222). This figure is much higher than the attributed GNP per head in China of $106 in 1965 (at 1986 prices).   [12] Kuznets (1966: 36).

[13] *World Development Report 1988* itself shows the limitations of its estimates and draws attention to the assumptions on the basis of which the figures are arrived at (see pp. 290–1). The issue here is not one of accusing the World Bank of deception or perfidy, but to see the case for rejecting the comparative numbers that are presented in some of these widely used tables and which are in fact quoted again and again in discussions relating to China and India.

[14] On the rapid revisions of China's GNP figures made by the World Bank, see Malenbaum (1982): 'As noted, Bank data for China's GNP per capita were of the order of $400 for 1976 and 1977 (current US prices). Comparable figures for India were $150, some 37.5% of the Chinese levels. In 1980, the respective figures for 1978 were listed as $230 and $180 (1978 US prices); the ratio was 78.5%. The levels for 1979 are now shown as $260 and $190. A comparative development history that pictured China with a long-period growth advantage of about 150% per capita over India by the late 1970s now shows an advantage only one-quarter as large, some 30%–35%, over the same period. No structural explanation is offered for this radical revision' (pp. 81–2). To continue the story where Malenbaum left off, the World Bank made the figures converge for all practical purposes by 1986, with (as mentioned in the text) a GNP per head of $300 for China and

footnote continued overleaf

story of a growth rate in China very much higher than that of India (5.1 per cent against India's 1.8 per cent) is difficult to firm up. It is hard to see the Chinese attainment in health and nutrition as primarily a 'growth-mediated' success.

In fact, it seems fairly clear that the Chinese growth rate was not radically higher than that of India before the economic reforms of 1979, by which time the tremendous surge ahead in health and longevity had already taken place.[15] In the pre-reform period, agricultural expansion in particular was sluggish in China, as it was in India, and the dramatic reduction in hunger and undernourishment and expansion of life expectancy in China were not ushered in by any spectacular rise in rural incomes or of food availability per head. As Judith Banister notes: 'It also appears that the quantity of food produced per capita and the quality of the Chinese diet did not improve between 1957 and the late 1970's. . . . annual per capita grain production through 1977 was about the same as in the late 1950's: it averaged 301 kilograms in 1955–57 and 305 kilograms in 1975–77.'[16]

This is indeed the crucial point. The Chinese level of average opulence judged in terms of GNP per head, or total consumption per capita, or food consumption per person, did not radically increase during the period in which China managed to take a gigantic step forward in matters of life and death, moving from a life expectancy at birth in the low 40s (like the poorest countries today) to one in the high 60s (getting within hitting distance of Europe and North America).

Since the far-reaching economic and social reforms introduced in 1979 (with much greater use of market-based incentives), the Chinese growth rate has been fast—very much faster than earlier. But this has not been a period of further reduction in mortality. In fact, quite the contrary. The death rate in China reached, according to official statistics, its lowest level in 1978, just *before* the reforms, and went *up* in the period following the reforms, precisely when the growth of output and income accelerated impressively. On the lessons of the post-reform period in China, we shall have to say more (see section 11.4).

At the moment we only note the fact that the great increase in longevity and reduction in mortality took place in China before the reforms, during a period of fairly moderate economic growth, whereas the post-reform period of rapid growth has witnessed no further rise and possibly some deterioration in survival chances. China's remarkable achievements in matters of life and death

---

footnote continued
$290 for India. While the GNP figures for China were made to come down closer to India's GNP per head, the figures for GNP growth rates of China were kept sharply higher than those of India. What we are looking at here is not an account with just some little inconsistency somewhere, but one that is altogether contrary within its own internal structure.

[15] See Riskin (1986, 1987).

[16] See Banister (1987: 354). See also Carl Riskin's (1986) paper on the strategy of 'feeding China', and the empirical studies cited there.

cannot in any way be ascribed simply to a strategy of 'growth-mediated' security.

As far as support-led security is concerned, the Chinese efforts have been quite spectacular. The network of health services introduced in post-revolutionary China in a radical departure from the past—involving cooperative medical systems, commune clinics, barefoot doctors, and wide-spread public health measures—has been remarkably extensive.[17] The contrast with India in this respect is striking enough. It is not only that China has more than twice as many doctors and nearly three times as many nurses per unit of population as India has.[18] But also these and other medical resources are distributed more evenly across the country (even between urban and rural areas), with greater popular access to them than India has been able to organize.[19]

Similar contrasts hold in the distribution of food through public channels and rationing systems, which have had an extensive coverage in China (except in periods of economic and political chaos, as during the famine of 1958–61, on which more presently). In India public distribution of food to the people, when it exists, is confined to the urban sector (except in a few areas such as the state of Kerala where the rural population also benefits from it, on which, too, more presently). Food distribution is, in fact, a part of a far-reaching programme of social security that distinguishes China from India.[20] The impact of these programmes on protecting and promoting entitlements to food and basic necessities, including medical care, is reflected in the relatively low mortality and morbidity rates in China.

The contrast between China and India in public distribution systems and in social security programmes is certainly very striking, and it is plausible to see China's success story as one of support-led security. The growth-mediated interpretation would be much harder to defend, especially since there are so many uncertainties about what GNP growth rates China did, in fact, achieve. We shall come back to the growth question again in section 11.4 when we review the impact of the recent experience of high economic growth in China

[17] See World Bank (1983a, 1985), Jamison et al. (1984), Perkins and Yusuf (1984), L. C. Chen (1988), and Shao (1988), among many other contributions.

[18] World Development Report 1988, Table 29, p. 278. Population per physician is reported to be 3,700 in India and 1,730 for China in 1981. The corresponding figures for population per nursing person are 4,670 in India and 1,670 in China. It is often claimed, with some justice, that the medical training programmes in India are typically more exacting than the Chinese programmes have been (at least until recently). But the big difference in having some medical services available across the country (even in the remotest parts) makes the Chinese overall situation altogether distinct from that in India, and in this achievement the logistic advantages of having many more doctors and nurses per unit of population have been quite crucial.

[19] For some interesting comparisons between China and India in the domain of health, see A. Bhalla (1987); see also Chen (1987). The Chinese arrangements, especially for the rural areas, provide a major contrast with the lack of penetration of health services in rural India, especially among vulnerable groups (see Bose and Tyagi 1983, and Murthy et al. 1988).

[20] On the nature and reach of the social security system and public services in China, see Riskin (1986, 1987), Ahmad and Hussain (1988) and Hussain et al. (1989), and the literature cited there.

since the reforms. But before that we examine the big blot in China's past record, viz. the famine of 1958–61.

11.3   The Chinese Famine and the Indian Contrast

The Chinese famine of 1958–61 followed the débâcle of the so-called Great Leap Forward that was tried out from late 1957 onwards.[21] While the failure of the Great Leap Forward came to be widely recognized after the initial euphoria, the existence of the famine oddly escaped open scrutiny and even public recognition, until very recently.[22] This is particularly interesting given the monumental scale of the famine—arguably the largest in terms of total excess mortality in recorded history.

Comparing actual mortality with pre-famine mortality yields remarkably high figures of extra deaths in this famine. Estimates of extra mortality vary from 16.5 million to 29.5 million.[23] These figures are extraordinarily large. For example, the excess mortality in the last Indian famine, viz. the so-called Great Bengal famine of 1943 (occurring four years before independence), is estimated to be about 3 million.[24] In the scale of 'extra deaths' the Chinese famine was, thus, about five to ten times as large as the largest famine in India in this century.[25]

Many things are still uncertain about the causation of the famine, but it is clear that there was an enormous collapse of agricultural output and income. Food availability decline certainly played an important part in the genesis of hunger that gripped China for three years. Taking the average national grain output per capita of 308 kg. in 1956 and 1957 as the point of reference, the 1959 output was 17 per cent below this and by 1960 the per-capita grain output was as much as 30 per cent down. Even in 1961, the shortfall vis-à-vis the 1956–7

---

[21] Various regions of China also suffered from adverse weather conditions during 1959–61, involving drought and flooding in different parts of the country. These conditions certainly contributed to the production problems, but it is hard to escape the conclusion that the bulk of the problem was caused by the failure of the policy changes initiated by the Great Leap Forward. In fact, the adverse climatic conditions were particularly important in making it harder to identify precisely how fully the 'Leap' had failed.

[22] On this see Sen (1982c, 1983a), Bernstein (1983), Riskin (1986, 1987).

[23] See Coale (1981), Aird (1982), Ashton et al. (1984), Peng (1987). The largest estimate of 29.5 million (Ashton et al. 1984) attempts to take full note of unreported deaths. Peng's (1987) estimation based on provincial demographic data suggests a figure of 23 million.

[24] That figure was obtained also by using the same method of comparing actual mortality with pre-famine mortality, and making allowances for unreported deaths (Sen 1981a, Appendix D). The official estimate of excess mortality was 1.5 million, but that involved an undercounting due to incomplete temporal coverage.

[25] It must, however, be remembered that since the Chinese mortality rates had come down sharply already prior to the famine, the 'extra death' estimates based on pre-famine mortality rates are in comparison with a pre-famine death rate lower than that of most poor countries in the world. But even if considerably higher pre-famine mortality rates are used, the excess mortality in China still amounts to astonishingly high figures.

average was 28 per cent, and the pre-famine figure was not reattained until the latter half of the 1960s.[26]

Further, some regions suffered particularly serious declines and the sharp differences between food availability in the different regions continued through the period of distress.[27] For example, in 1960, while the provinces of Heilongjiang and Yunnan had respectively 229 and 209 kg. of grains per head for their rural population, the corresponding figures for Henan, Sichuan, and Hebei were respectively 143, 137, and 122 kg. The contrast between the rural and urban areas was also striking (for example, between 288 kg. in urban Hebei as against 122 in the rural areas of that province).[28]

Public distribution at the local level was comprehensively disrupted. The problem for the rural areas was made much worse by the sharp increase in state procurement of foodgrains, and the rural communes were in many cases desperately short of food. In addition to that, there were also remarkable inequalities in the distribution of whatever food was available. This applied not only between the regions and between urban and rural areas, but even within a given rural region. Some provinces evidently suffered from much sharper *intra*regional inequalities than others did, with correspondingly higher mortality. For instance, rural Sichuan and Henan suffered from much greater death rates than rural Hebei which did not have, on the average, any more food. Particularly, there was a great deal of wastage and excess consumption in particular 'commune mess halls'.[29]

The Chinese famine of 1958–61 was closely linked with policy failures —first in the débâcle of the Great Leap Forward, then in the delay in rectifying the harm done, and along with that in accentuating distributional inequalities through enhanced procurement and uneven sharing. The remarkable aspect of the famine is its continuation over a number of years without an adequate recognition of the nature of the crisis (and without leading to the necessary changes in public policy).

This is one respect in which India's record since independence must be seen to be very much superior. The fact that there has been no large-scale famine in India since independence is a positive contrast with the Chinese experience. The contrast is particularly interesting when account is taken of the fact that there have been several alarming dips in food output and availability in India over the same period (the latest being in the drought of 1987), and that on many occasions the entitlements of large parts of the population have been severely threatened both directly and indirectly (particularly through employment declines associated with droughts or floods).

[26] See Peng (1987: 653–5, esp. Table 3).
[27] See Riskin (1986, 1987) and Peng (1987).
[28] The data are taken from Peng (1987).
[29] On this see Peng (1987). 'Ironically,' notes Peng, 'almost all the provinces that were praised by a *People's Daily* article for their "good performance" in establishing rural mess halls experienced severe excess mortality' (p. 664).

The Indian system of famine prevention was discussed in Chapter 8 of this book. There are, as was argued, two different features involved in the system. One is a worked-out procedure for entitlement protection through employment creation (usually paying the wages in cash), supplemented by direct transfers to the 'unemployable'. The origins of this procedure go back to the 1880s and the Famine Codes of the late nineteenth century, though a number of important developments (including the use of the public distribution system to stabilize food prices) have taken place since independence. The other part is a political 'triggering mechanism' which brings the protection system into play and indeed which keeps the public support system in a state of preparedness. It was this triggering mechanism that was lacking in the famine prevention system of British India after the Famine Codes were set up. In the Bengal famine of 1943, not only were the Famine Codes not invoked, that was indeed a deliberate decision of the government.[30]

On the other hand, given the political system of post-independence India, it is extremely hard for any government in office—whether at the state level or at the centre—to get away with neglecting prompt and extensive anti-famine measures at the first signs of a famine. And these signs are themselves more easily transmitted given India's relatively free media and newspapers, and the active and investigative role that journalists as well as opposition politicians can and do play in this field. The adversarial participation of newspapers and opposition leaders is, as we have discussed earlier, an important part of the Indian famine prevention system. It yields a rapid triggering mechanism and encourages preparedness for entitlement protection.

The contrast with China is striking primarily in the second respect. Given its system of public distribution, China did not lack a delivery and redistribution mechanism to deal with food shortages as the famine threatened in 1958 and later. Despite the size of the decline of food output and the loss of entitlement of large sections of the population, China could have done a much better job of protecting the vulnerable by sharing the shortage in a bearable way.

What was lacking when the famine threatened China was a political system of adversarial journalism and opposition.[31] The Chinese famine raged on for three years without it being even admitted in public that such a thing was occurring, and without there being an adequate policy response to the threat. Not only was the world ignorant of the terrible state of affairs in China, even the population itself did not know about the extent of the national calamity and the extensive nature of the problems being faced in different parts of the country.

Indeed, the lack of adversarial journalism and politics hit even the govern-

---

[30] The Governor of Bengal, Sir T. Rutherford, wrote to the Viceroy of India explaining that a famine had not been declared to avoid the obligation to undertake the relief measures mandated by the Famine Codes. See Mansergh (1973, 363, Document No. 158).

[31] The reasons for this diagnosis and the empirical evidence for this view are discussed in Sen (1982c, 1983a).

ment, reinforcing the ignorance of local conditions because of politically motivated exaggeration of the crop size during the Great Leap Forward and the fear of local leaders about communicating their own problems. The pretence that everything was going all right in Chinese agriculture and rural economy to a great extent fooled the national leaders themselves. 'Leaders believed in 1959–60', as Bernstein puts it, 'that they had 100 MMT more grain than they actually did.'[32] This misconception was crucial in keeping down Chinese imports of foodgrains, which fell to virtually nothing in 1959 (about two thousand tons compared with 223 thousand tons in 1958), and stayed incredibly low in 1961 (66 thousand tons), before jumping to 5.8 million tons in 1961 as the fact of the famine and the agricultural débâcle became at long last clear. Chinese exports of foodgrains, similarly, peaked in 1959, and stayed high in 1960, before beginning to come down in 1961. The Chinese net exports of cereals rose from 1.9 million tons in 1957, to 2.7 in 1958, 4.2 in 1959, and 2.7 in 1960—as the famine devastated the lives of tens of millions of people across the country.[33]

The misinformation and misreading also led to a sharp *increase* in the extent of food procurement from the rural areas. The percentage net procurement out of total output went up from 15 to 17 per cent in 1956 and 1957 to 21 per cent in 1958 and 28 per cent in 1959.[34] The rural Chinese—hit by a production decline—were hit again by having to part with a larger proportion of the reduced output as procurement by the state.

The misinformation also contributed to the non-revision of production and distribution policies and to the absence of any emergency entitlement-protection programme.[35] Aside from the government's informational inadequacy, which made its own assessment of the situation disastrously wrong, the absence of an adversarial system of politics and journalism also meant that there was little political pressure on the government from any opposition group and from informed public opinion to take adequate anti-famine measures rapidly.

We end this section with three interpretative remarks. First, as was dis-

[32] Bernstein (1984: 13).

[33] The figures are from the *Statistical Yearbook of China 1981*. See also Riskin (1986, 1987) and Jowett (1988).

[34] Riskin (1987), Table 6.5. See also Bernstein (1984) and Peng (1987).

[35] In 1962, shortly after the famine, when the recent experiences were being reviewed, Mao Zedong noted the problem of informational failure for planning in the absence of local democracy: 'If there is no democracy and ideas are not coming from the masses, it is impossible to establish a good line, good general and specific policies and methods . . . Without democracy you have no understanding of what is happening down below; the situation will be unclear; you will be unable to collect sufficient opinions from all sides; there can be no communication between top and bottom; top-level organs of leadership will depend on one-sided and incorrect material to decide issues, thus you will find it difficult to avoid being subjectivist; it will be impossible to achieve unity of understanding and unity of action, and impossible to achieve true centralism' (Mao Zedong 1974: 164). On this pronouncement and its context and relevance, see Sen (1983*a*, 1984*a*).

cussed in Chapter 8, famine prevention is an important achievement of India, and there is something to learn from that experience in this famine-ridden world. The fact that even post-revolutionary China, with its outstanding record of entitlement promotion and enhancement of living conditions, could fall prey to a gigantic famine indicates that the lesson may be far from negligible. In fact, the precise feature of absence of adversarial politics and open journalism that may have contributed to the occurrence, magnitude and duration of the Chinese famines of 1958–61 are also present in most sub-Saharan African countries today. While the political systems are quite different, this feature of absence of political opposition and free journalism in African politics is a cause of famine vulnerability in Africa as it was in China at the time it had its own disaster. Also, greater tolerance of criticism and more open journalism in China would have a positive effect on helping to make China secure against the kind of political and economic crisis that ushered in the famines of 1958–61. But unfortunately political democratization in China has not really kept pace with the speed of economic liberalization (on which more presently).

Second, as India's experience shows, open journalism and adversarial politics provide much less protection against endemic undernutrition than they do against a dramatic famine. Starvation deaths and extreme deprivation are newsworthy in a way the quiet persistence of regular hunger and non-extreme deprivation are not. Endemic hunger may increase the morbidity rate and add to the mortality rate (in these respects India's performance continues to be quite awful), but that is primarily a statistical picture rather than being immediately palpable and—no less importantly—being 'big news'. To bring endemic deprivation into the fold of news reporting and to make it a major focus of political confrontation are inherently more difficult tasks, and seem to have been largely beyond the normal activities of journalists and politicians in India.[36] That situation could change (there are some signs of that already), and this is clearly a field in which there is scope for the public to play a very creative role in India. But as things stand, the Chinese political commitment—not unrelated to the ideological predispositions of the Chinese political system—seems to have served the country well for combating endemic deprivation, despite its failure as a defence against famines.

Finally, it is important to note that despite the gigantic size of excess mortality in the Chinese famine, the extra mortality in India from regular deprivation in normal times vastly overshadows the former. Comparing India's death rate of 12 per thousand with China's of 7 per thousand, and applying that difference to the Indian population of 781 million in 1986, we get an estimate of excess normal mortality in India of 3.9 million per year. This implies that every eight years or so more people die in India because of its higher regular death rate than died in China in the gigantic famine of

[36] On this see Sen (1982c, 1983a, 1984a) and Ram (1986).

Table 11.1 China since the 1979 reforms

	Gross value of output (index)		Death rate (index)		Female–male ratio (value)
	Industry	Agriculture'	National	Rural	
1979	100	100	100	100	94.3
1980	109	104	102	101	94.4
1981	113	111	102	102	94.2
1982	122	123	106	110	94.1
1983	135	135	114	120	93.9
1984	154	159	108	105	93.7
1985	181	181	106	104	93.5
1986	197	201	108	105	93.6

Source: People's Republic of China, *Statistical Yearbook of China 1986* (in English); *1987* (in Chinese).

1958–61.[37] India seems to manage to fill its cupboard with more skeletons every eight years than China put there in its years of shame.

11.4 Chinese Economic Reforms: Opulence and Support

The economic reforms introduced in China in 1979 have now gone through nearly a decade of practice, and it is possible to begin assessing some of their impacts. On the side of commodity production, there is little doubt that the Chinese economy has surged ahead in response to market incentives, and the agricultural sector has really had—at long last—a proper 'leap forward'. As Table 11.1 indicates, the gross value of agricultural output doubled between 1979 and 1986 (a growth rate of more than 10 per cent per year). Growth in the agricultural sector has also kept pace with industrial expansion, which is in fact quite remarkable in itself, particularly since industrial expansion has been very fast as well. There may be some questions about the exact figures (there might have been incentives to understate output prior to the reforms), and it is not easy to be certain of the exact growth rates achieved. There has also been a slow-down after the initial leap, as well as some worry that the production of food crops has not kept up with the expansion of other types of production. Nevertheless, taking everything into account, there can be little doubt that the economic reforms have been quite remarkable in expanding the supply of nutrients in China as well as agricultural outputs and incomes in general.[38]

The economic reforms can be and have been questioned from many points of view. The fact that the reforms have led to an inflationary situation with price

[37] This is so with the highest of the estimated mortality figures, viz. 29.5 million (due to Ashton *et al*. 1984). If instead we take, say, Peng's figure of 23 million, then every *six* years there is more extra mortality in India than in the Chinese famine of 1958–61.

[38] See Riskin (1986, 1987), Johnson (1988) and Perkins (1988). On the incentive problems of collective agriculture, see Putterman (1986), and also Nee (1986).

rises destabilizing the consumers' equilibrium has been widely acknowledged, and this has caused some rethinking on how far and how fast to go on the path of economic change. There have also been fears that the price mechanism, while successful in raising total outputs and incomes, may increase inequalities in the distribution of incomes. But, again, even after taking note of these qualifications, it is quite clear that the average opulence of the Chinese population, especially the rural population, has expanded greatly since the reforms.

Even in the reduction of poverty, calculated in terms of personal incomes, a great deal has been recently achieved. It appears that the number of rural Chinese below the poverty line of 200 yuan in 1986 prices has fallen from 200 million in 1979 to 70 million in 1986.[39] That is a striking decline of which there are few parallels. If 'growth-mediated security' were the chief means of promotion of longevity in China, this post-reform experience should have provided an excellent basis for further enhancement of life expectancy at a rapid rate.

In fact, however, this has not occurred, as we noted earlier. The death rate in China, rather than declining rapidly, seems to have gone *up* after the reforms, as Table 11.1 indicates. Indeed, in no year since 1979 has the death rate—as given in Chinese official statistics—been lower than that achieved by 1978 and 1979, viz. 6.2 per thousand. The death rate, as reported in the *Statistical Yearbook of China*, went up to 7.1 by 1983, and even after coming down, it has hovered around 6.6 and 6.7 in 1985 and 1986.

There is much room for doubt about the correctness of the official Chinese mortality data. It must be particularly noted that an increase in the coverage of mortality statistics may have the effect of raising the reported death rate. It is quite possible that at least some part of the apparent increase in mortality rates after 1979 is connected with better coverage of death data. Also, we have to take note of the changing age composition of the Chinese population when interpreting overall death rates.[40] But even after note has been taken of these factors, there is evidence of an increase in forces of mortality since the reforms compared with what had been achieved before them.[41] The downward trend in mortality which made China reach truly unusual levels of longevity (given its low per-capita income) has been at least halted, and possibly reversed.

The effect of the changing age composition can be eliminated by looking not at the crude death rate, which is in effect a simple average, but at the life expectancy figures. Life expectancy is estimated by using 'endogenous weights' (in the sense that the population in different age groups is estimated

---

[39] See Riskin (1988: 21).

[40] See Banister (1987) and Hussain and Stern (1988).

[41] Hussain and Stern (1988) argue that 'the year to year fluctuations [in death rates] are likely to be largely the result of changing data sources and methods', but confirm a broad pattern of 'a reduction [in the death rate] to the end of 1970s followed by an increase of around 7% in the death rate from 1979–86' (p. 18).

Table 11.2 Life and death in China, 1978–1984

Year	Crude death rate (per thousand): Banister's adjusted estimates	Life expectancy at birth (years): Banister's estimates	Infant mortality rate (per thousand)	
			Banister's adjusted estimates	Yang and Dowdle indirect estimates
1978	7.5	65.1	37.2	40
1979	7.6	65.0	39.4	41
1980	7.7	64.9	41.6	44
1981	7.7	64.8	43.7	53
1982	7.9	64.7	45.9	61
1983	8.0	64.6	48.0	—
1984	8.0	64.6	50.1	—

Source: Banister (1987) Table 4.18 and Yang and Dowdle (1985).

by using the mortality rates in the previous age groups), and does not depend on the actual age structure of the existing population. Thus, concentrating on life expectancy gives us a good idea of what we are looking for.

Judith Banister's estimates of life expectancy at birth are given in Table 11.2. These suggest a steady decline in life expectancy since 1978 (up to and including 1984, which is the last year in Banister's series). The fall is moderate, though firm and consistent, but it has to be judged particularly as a contrast with steadily declining mortality rates and expansion of life expectancy up to the late 1970s (with the exception, of course, of the period of the famine of 1958–61, discussed earlier). The real issue is the slowing down of social progress just when overall economic growth has quickened.

While the reduction of life expectancy is fairly moderate, the rise of infant mortality according to some estimates appears to be sharp (see Table 11.2). This is so according to both Banister's estimates and also the indirect estimates made by Yang and Dowdle (1985) on the basis of a fertility survey questionnaire. The extent to which this is connected with China's enforced population policy introduced also in 1979—especially the insistence on a one-child limit in many parts of the country and a two-child limit elsewhere—is not crystal clear, but there is strong circumstantial evidence in that direction.[42] One of the sinister signs is a decline in the reported birth ratio of females to males, and this can reflect infanticide, or at least death due to severe neglect, of female children, with their births as well as deaths remaining unregistered.[43] The recent

[42] See Banister (1987: Chapter 7). 'Many couples, determined to have a son, have killed their infant daughters, either outright or by severe neglect, so that they could try again for a son' (Banister 1987: 40).
[43] See Hull (1988) on this general question, and also on the results of a 1 per cent survey of the population carried out by the State Statistical Bureau in 1987.

Table 11.3 Gender differential in mortality in China, 1978–1984

Year	Life expectancy at birth (years)			Infant mortality per thousand		
	Females	Males	Female advantage	Females	Males	Female advantage
1978	66.0	64.1	1.9	37.7	36.8	−0.9
1979	65.7	64.3	1.4	42.7	36.3	−6.4
1980	65.3	64.4	0.9	47.7	35.8	−11.9
1981	65.0	64.5	0.5	52.6	35.3	−17.3
1982	64.7	64.7	0.0	57.5	34.9	−22.6
1983	64.4	64.8	−0.4	62.4	34.4	−28.0
1984	64.1	64.9	−0.8	67.2	33.9	−33.3

Source: Banister (1987), Table 4.12.

relaxation of the one-child limit when the first child is a girl may have been the result of recognizing the prevalence of this problem.

No matter what role the population policy may have played in this, there is considerable evidence that the mortality picture has possibly darkened for girls in comparison with boys in recent years. In fact, Banister's estimations suggest that in the post-reform period while male infant mortality has continued to fall (though only quite slowly), it is female infant mortality that has apparently had an *upward* jump (see Table 11.3). Similarly and correspondingly, male life expectancy at birth has continued to rise (again, very moderately since the reforms), but female life expectancy reached a peak in the pre-reform year of 1978 and has fallen apparently since then. These estimates are speculative and must not be taken too seriously, but altogether there is much evidence of (1) a slow down or a halt in the steadily improving survival chances of both men and women, and specifically children, and (2) on top of that, an evident increase in gender bias, specifically affecting female children.

The increase in gender bias, if confirmed, would no doubt relate (at least partly) to recent population policies. However, enforced limitation of population size, since it is in principle 'gender neutral', can have a devastating effect on female children *only* when there is already a strong parental preference for male children, and ultimately we have to be concerned also with the causal roots of that preference.

Such male-preference is not, of course, a new thing in China, but it is arguable that the responsibility system may itself have contributed a little to the undermining of the position of women. As was argued in Chapter 4, there is considerable evidence that the involvement of women in so-called 'gainful employment' tends to reduce gender bias against females. In this respect, the communal form of agriculture used in pre-reform China provided much easier scope for female 'gainful' involvement, and the proportion of women in such employment had risen quite radically in the 1960s and 1970s. However, with the new responsibility system, Chinese agricultural production has become more family-based, with the usual division of labour that tends to place women in activities of the typical 'household' kind.[44]

This can indeed be an influence towards worsening the position of women in 'cooperative conflicts', and through a general regression of women's economic position and social status, can also strengthen the anti-female bias in the caring of children. It is not obvious that this type of effect, which—if important—is most likely to be so only in the long run, could have had any role already in the Chinese rural society. But no matter what view is taken of that question (and more generally of any strengthening of anti-female bias in the Chinese society), the pre-existing level of anti-female bias would, in any case, tend to make any restrictive policy fall disproportionately on the female child.

The restrictive developments of the post-reform period include not merely the enforced control of family size, but also a considerable reduction in the general medical care and health services available in rural China. The 'support-led security' on the basis of which China had achieved so much prior to the reforms has been weakened rather than strengthened in some important ways by the reforms affecting the economy and the society.[45] In fact, despite the increase in outputs and incomes, the support system that the Chinese had built up with such success has been under severe strain. There is a clear weakening of commitment to public support measures, which may be partly ideological, related to the recent passion for economic liberalism.[46] But it is also connected with the undermining of the financial and institutional basis of public support measures at the local level in rural areas, as a result of the abandonment of previous communal arrangements and their replacement by the 'responsibility system', which we discussed earlier.[47]

The rural production brigades used to offer a widespread cooperative medical system of health insurance, but the proportion offering this support has declined from 90 per cent in 1977 to about 34 per cent by 1985.[48] It appears that the earlier cooperative health insurance survives only in 5 per cent of the villages, according to the Ministry of Public Health.[49] The number of village-level medical workers has fallen from 3.3 million in 1975 to 1.2 million by 1984. The number of 'barefoot doctors' working in Chinese villages and brigade

[44] On this see Aslanbeigui and Summerfield (1989). On the comparison with the pre-reform situation, see also Croll (1983), Hemmel and Sindbjerg (1984), Nee (1986), Wolf (1987) and Kelkar (1989).

[45] It is, in fact, also possible that the breakdown of social support provisions regarding old age security may have added to the existing 'pro-male-child' bias, given the association of male-preference with the motive of insuring support in old age. On related matters, see Hussain et al. (1989).

[46] Riskin (1988) notes that the style is a hybrid one involving 'a strange mixture of residual socialist rhetoric and Chicago School values'. But the socialist rhetoric has been distinctly in retreat in recent years.

[47] On this see Banister (1986, 1987), Nee (1986), Panikar (1986), Bhalla (1987), Ahmad and Hussain (1988), Johnson (1988), Shao (1988), and Hussain et al. (1989).

[48] See Banister (1986: 2–3).

[49] See Shao (1988).

clinics went down from 1.8 million in 1977 to 1.3 million by 1984, and is known to have fallen greatly since. The number of female barefoot doctors fell even more sharply. By now, that entire system of medically imperfect but socially useful service is in complete decline, and the number of barefoot doctors is no longer reported in the *Statistical Yearbook*.[50]

Further, the balance between urban and rural areas in terms of medical services—less unequal in China than in most developing countries—has also been disrupted by the changes accompanying the reforms. By 1983 the three-quarters of China's total population who happen to live in rural areas had to make do with the services of only half the practising doctors, i.e. a third of what the urban areas had in per capita terms.[51]

The impact of these declines in rural health services must have been significant in general and particularly detrimental to vulnerable groups, and its role in halting the rapidly declining trend of Chinese mortality would have been substantial. Also, the burden of decreased health services seems to have been unequally shared between boys and girls, and given the pre-existing anti-female bias (whether strengthened or not in the post-reform period), the gender inequalities can be expected to be most consequential in periods of general contraction.[52]

Despite these disruptions of communal health facilities, China does, of course, remain considerably ahead of India in terms of its widespread public health provisions and related social security facilities. The Chinese also remain firmly in the lead in the fields of longevity, nutrition and health. But the recent economic reforms, with their negative effects on public support (especially at the local level in the rural areas), have moved China a little bit in the direction of India, and that—in this context—is not a particularly helpful development. The weakening of the support-led system has not been outweighed by a growth-mediated new development.

It is too early to judge what kind of a new equilibrium China will achieve. At the moment it is clear that there is a pause and perhaps even some regress in the expansion of longevity and in the reduction of morbidity, despite the progress in incomes and opulence. The authoritarian nature of Chinese politics has permitted an abrupt reduction in the social security provisions that had contributed so much to China's earlier successes.

It is not our purpose to prognosticate what will happen in China in the long run. From the point of view of public action against hunger and deprivation, what is especially important is an understanding of the policy issues raised by China's varied experience. A particularly important one concerns the role of public support, especially the universality of the coverage of public support. The contribution that universal (or near-universal) support-led security can

[50] From 1986 the *Statistical Yearbooks* discontinued giving the numbers of barefoot doctors, and the last year of report is 1984. See also World Bank (1984a) and Banister (1986).

[51] See Banister (1986: 2).

[52] On the general issue of gender bias and intrahousehold distribution, see Chapter 4.

make to living conditions is exemplified both by (1) China's progress in expanding some of the most basic capabilities up to the late 1970s despite little increase in per-capita GNP and food consumption, and (2) her comparative regress in these vital fields in the post-reform period despite rapidly rising outputs and incomes.

11.5   China, India and Kerala

India offers within its own boundaries quite a variety of experiences. There are great interstate differences, and one state in particular, viz. Kerala, deserves special attention in terms of public action against hunger and deprivation. Kerala is one of the poorer Indian states.[53] Yet it has achieved a remarkably high level of life expectancy—by a long margin higher than any other Indian state, including the richest states of Punjab and Haryana.

The last rigorous estimate of life expectancy at birth in India available at the time of writing this monograph is for the period 1976–80. The figures for the next half-decade 1981–5 have not yet been published. The all-India average figure in 1976–80 was 52 years, but that for Kerala was as high as 66 years (68 for females and 64 for males), which is not materially different from China's achievement.[54] Early estimates indicate considerable increases in life expectancy in India as a whole, but Kerala's overwhelming lead has been maintained.

Doubts have been raised as to whether Kerala's outstanding longevity indicators are reflective of a comparable breakthrough in general health and nutritional well-being.[55] These doubts have arisen mainly from the additional evidence provided by (1) low calorie intakes, and (2) high self-reported morbidity rates. The significance of these indicators is, however, open to serious question. As was discussed at some length in Chapter 3, calorie intake offers a poor basis of assessment of nutritional status, and when it comes to more direct measures of nutritional well-being (especially the avoidance of severe undernourishment), it appears that Kerala remains firmly ahead of other Indian states.[56] As far as high morbidity rates are concerned, these are

[53] The standard comparative data can be found in Agrawal, Verma and Gupta (1987). For a probing analysis of the comparative real incomes of the different Indian states (taking note of distributional differences), see Bhattacharya, Chatterjee and Pal (1988). See also Sanyal (1988) on Kerala's comparative poverty in terms of landholding.

[54] This figure of 65.5 years is, in fact, a little higher than Judith Banister's estimate of life expectancy for China even before the reforms (65.1), and a fortiori so afterwards (64.6 in 1984 according to Banister's estimate). It must, of course, be mentioned that there is a lot of regional diversity within China (on this see Prescott and Jamison 1985), and the life expectancies in the more advanced regions are higher than that in Kerala.

[55] See e.g. Panikar and Soman (1984) and B. G. Kumar (1987).

[56] See e.g. the anthropometric evidence presented in B. G. Kumar (1987), Table 6.7, and Subbarao (1989), Table 6 (both based on survey data collected by the National Nutrition Monitoring Bureau). The very low incidence of 'severe undernutrition' in Kerala is particularly striking—a matter of particular importance for health, well-being and survival (on this see Lipton 1983, and also Chapter 3 above). The percentage of 'severe undernutrition' for children between 1 and 5 years of age in 1982 was 6.1 for India as a whole and only 1.5 for Kerala (Kumar 1987, Table 6.7).

Table 11.4 China, India and Kerala: selected comparisons

	Adult literacy rate (per cent)		Life expectancy at birth (years)		Female–male ratio
	Female	Male	Female	Male	
China[a]	56	82	64.1	64.9	0.935
India[b]	26	55	52.1	52.5	0.934
Kerala[b]	71	86	67.6	63.5	1.032

[a] 1985
[b] 1981

Notes and sources: Adult literacy rates for China for 1985 are taken from UNICEF, *The State of the World's Children 1988*, and for India and Kerala, they are calculated from the data presented in the *Census of India 1981*. Life expectancy figures for China are taken from Banister (1987), Table 4.18, and relate to 1984. The official *Statistical Yearbook of China 1986* gives figures of 69.3 years for females and 66.4 years for males for 1982. The life expectancy figures for India and Kerala relate to the period 1976–80, and are taken from *SRS Based Abridged Life-Tables 1976–80* (Occasional Paper No. 1, 1985), published by the Registrar General of India. The female–male ratio for China in 1985 is obtained from *Statistical Yearbook of China 1986*, and that for India and Kerala for 1981 from the *Census of India 1981*.

based on *self-reported* illnesses, and it is not easy to determine the extent to which they reflect a greater level of articulation of a population that is enormously more literate and health-conscious than people anywhere else in India. It has been argued, in fact, that self-reported morbidity indicators as they exist today are extremely misleading in the context of interpersonal comparisons of well-being.[57] While there is some scope for disputation as to the precise relationship between longevity and other aspects of nutrition or health in Kerala, the overall picture of success is hard to deny.

The role of public support in Kerala's achievement has attracted justified attention.[58] This has partly taken the form of extensive medical coverage of the population through public health services, helped by the determination of the population—much more educated than elsewhere in India—to seek medical attention.[59] Kerala is also the only Indian state in which the public distribution

[57] For the evidential basis of this claim, see Murray and Chen (1989). As shown by these authors, many contrary findings arise from assessments of well-being based on self-reported morbidity data. For instance, while self-reported morbidity rates in India are highest in Kerala (and lowest in Uttar Pradesh, where the expectation of life is about 25 years *shorter* than in Kerala), they are even higher in the United States, and within the United States they are highest in the higher income groups. Such findings do not imply, of course, that self-reported morbidity data are entirely useless. Self-perception of morbidity as well as articulate reporting are of obvious interest in the social analysis of *perception* and *communication*.

[58] See Centre for Development Studies (1975), S. K. Kumar (1979), Gwatkin (1979), Gwatkin *et al.* (1980), Jose (1984), Panikar and Soman (1984), Halstead *et al.* (1985), Krishnan (1985, 1989), Stewart (1985), Caldwell (1986), B. G. Kumar (1987), Osmani (1988*a*).

[59] It is arguable that the higher incidence of reported morbidity can be seen as a positively contributory factor in Kerala's success in dealing with diseases and in expanding longevity. Treatment can begin only when attention is paid to the disease from which one is suffering. A large proportion of the Indian rural population die from undiagnosed—often ignored—diseases.

of food goes well beyond the limits of urban areas and provides significant support to the rural population.

The high literacy level of Kerala is also a major asset, especially in making people more eager and more skilled in seeking modern remedies for treatable ailments. It may also have a role in facilitating public participation in social change and in generating public demand for social security.[60] The innovative programmes in the distribution of health care and food in Kerala have frequently followed articulated social and political demands.[61] The same is true of a range of institutional changes, notably wage legislation and land reforms.

In contrast with the all-India adult literacy rate of 41 per cent (age 15 or over) in 1981, Kerala's literacy rate is 78 per cent. That ratio is also substantially higher than China's 70 per cent for 1985. There is also a particularly important feature in Kerala's pattern of literacy. It shows relatively less gender bias. The percentage of adult literacy in Kerala in 1981 was 71 for women and 86 for men, compared with 26 and 55 respectively for India as a whole. The gender bias in literacy is also substantially less in Kerala than in China, as Table 11.4 indicates. The female literacy rate of 71 per cent in Kerala compares well with the corresponding rate of 56 per cent in China.

In fact, the history of literacy expansion through public action goes back a long time in Kerala. The state of Kerala was formed at the time of independence by amalgamating, on grounds of linguistic uniformity and cultural unity, two so-called 'native Indian states' (viz. Travancore and Cochin) with a part of the old Madras Presidency in British India (viz. Malabar). As it happens, public policy in both the native Indian states put much greater emphasis on general education and literacy than was the case in the rest of India, and the emphasis on female education was particularly exceptional. In fact, as early as 1817, the ruler of Travancore, Rani (Queen) Gouri Parvathi Bai, had issued a rescript commanding that 'the State should defray the entire cost of the education of its people in order that there might be no backwardness in the spread of enlightenment among them, that by diffusion of education they might become better subjects and public servants and that the reputation of the State might be advanced thereby'.[62] The Rani was probably right, and the wide educational base in Kerala seems to have had a major impact on other public policies in that state (including medical care and food policy), in addition to encouraging intelligent health practice at the family level.

Gender bias is a topic of some interest in the context of both China and India. As was noted in Chapter 4, both China and India have an exceptionally low female–male ratio (FMR) in the population, and the issue of female survival is

---

[60] See Halstead *et al.* (1985) and Caldwell (1986). See also Mencher (1980).

[61] The radicalism of Kerala's politics found some expression in 1957 in its being the first Indian state to elect a communist government. Since then different political coalitions have ruled the state, and the parties in office have been typically kept on a short leash.

[62] Quoted in *Census of India, 1931*, vol. xxviii (Trivandrum, 1932), 301.

an important one in both countries. Life expectancy at birth has been lower for females than for males in India until very recently and the cross-over—bringing India in line with much of the rest of the world—is supposed to have occurred only in this decade.[63] In China, the move in recent years has been in the opposite direction, and the female life expectancy, which used to be higher than the male, has now become lower (see Table 11.4 and the discussion in the last section). In both countries the female–male ratio remains dismally low —around 93 females per 100 males. It contrasts with the ratio of 1.05 or higher observed in those countries (e.g. in Europe or North America) in which there is little gender bias in health care and food distribution (though there may be much sexism in other areas), and it is much lower (as discussed in Chapter 4) than the sub-Saharan African ratio of 1.02.

In contrast with both China and the rest of India, the female–male ratio in Kerala was higher than 1.03 in the last census, and is taken to have risen further since then. This is a higher female–male ratio than that for every region of the developing world for which we examined aggregated data in Chapter 4 (including sub-Saharan Africa, which was the basis for our calculation of 'missing women').

To what extent the relative absence of gender bias in Kerala relates to its radical public policy (discussed earlier) is hard to say. It would be surprising if a greater level of female education—and less gender inequality in the sharing of education—had not contributed to better prospects of a plausible life for women, both through raising the status of women and through increasing female economic power and independence in 'cooperative conflicts' (discussed in Chapter 4).

But there are also other factors to be considered here, including the partially matrilineal system of inheritance in parts of Kerala and the relatively long history of its left-wing activist politics. It would be well beyond the scope of the present inquiry to go into this important but difficult question, and the sorting out of different but interrelated causal influences can be a particularly hard exercise. But it is worth noting, as a preliminary observation for closer scrutiny, that the one state in India that has made extensive use of support-led security has also been able to avoid some of the disastrous implications of gender bias that plagues so many parts of the world. The possibility of support-led systems making a contribution to gender equality is something that would deserve further investigation.[64]

[63] See Dyson (1987).

[64] It should be mentioned here that the female–male ratio being greater than unity has been a feature of Kerala since before this century. In the *Census of India* for 1881, it was remarked: 'In Travancore, as in other southern populations, the proportions of the sexes approach more nearly to European standards than is the case in the northern states and Provinces' (*Report on the Census of British India*, vol. i (London: HMSO 1883), 70). This fact should not be seen as automatically turning the table against the importance of support-led security for reducing gender bias, since the active promotion of primary education, especially female education, in Kerala (in particular in

The success of Kerala in achieving support-led security adds force to the plausibility of following this route even when the economy is very poor. The fact that Kerala has achieved such success through careful and wide-coverage public support shows how much can be achieved even at a low level of income, if public action is aimed at promoting people's basic entitlements and capabilities.

People's capability to conquer preventable illness and to escape premature mortality depends crucially on their command over basic necessities and their ability to use these with skill. Public support of education, health, employment, etc. can contribute both to that command and to the necessary abilities. The varying experiences of China and India, and the internal diversity of those experiences (both over time and over regions), bring out the importance of these roles in varying contexts.

Travancore and Cochin) goes back to early in the last century. *Both* the features of higher FMR and higher involvement in basic education (especially for girls) go back to the 19th century in the case of Kerala.

12

Experiences of Direct Support

12.1 Introduction

In this chapter, we examine the strategy of support-led security as it is reflected in the experiences of some selected countries, in particular Sri Lanka, Chile, and Costa Rica. The distinction between 'growth-mediated security' and 'support-led security' has already been discussed in some detail in the two preceding chapters. It was explained, in particular, that the distinction between the two does not lie in the use of public support in one case and not in the other. Even the cases of growth-mediated security (e.g. in South Korea and Kuwait) studied in Chapter 10 involved crucial use of public support provisions utilizing the resources generated by economic growth, and indeed in this respect the contrast between growth-mediated security and 'unaimed opulence' can be both striking and important.

The strategy of support-led security is distinguished by the use of public support without waiting for the country in question to get rich as a result of sustained economic growth. The rationale of this approach consists of using public support directly for raising the standard of living, rather than waiting for economic growth to do this (by increasing private incomes *and* providing resources for public support at a later stage). It is the direct use of public support in expanding the capabilities of people, not qualified by achieved growth, that characterizes the distinct nature of this strategy.

The countries that are studied in this chapter are all relatively poor in terms of GNP per head. Even for the two richer ones, viz. Costa Rica and Chile, the levels of GNP per capita (respectively $1,480 and $1,320 in 1986) are substantially lower than that of, say, South Korea ($2,370), in spite of superior achievements in some aspects of quality of life (e.g. expectations of life of 74 and 71 years respectively, as against 69 years for South Korea). The contrast is much sharper in the case of Sri Lanka, with its GNP per capita of only $400 and a life expectancy of 70 years.[1] In this respect, Sri Lanka's position is somewhat similar to that of China and Kerala, discussed in the last chapter.

Before we turn to the country experiences, one general point is perhaps worth mentioning. It may be wondered whether a poor country—especially one as poor as, say, Sri Lanka—can at all 'afford' to have programmes of public support in any way comparable with those of countries many times richer. That worry is a legitimate one, but in considering feasibilities one must not fall into the trap of assuming exactly similar real costs in different countries. In

---

[1] These figures are taken from *World Development Report 1988*, Table 1.

particular, in a poor country not only are the GNP and the public budget quite restricted, the labour costs involved in providing, say, education and health care are also low (because of tinier wages).[2] Indeed, even the cost of support of public employment is lower in these economies for the same reason. This does not make the resource problem disappear for the poorer economies (health services in particular tend to have substantial non-labour costs as well), but the apparent enormity of the gap between what the richer and the poorer countries can afford has to be scaled down considerably to take note of this fact. The ambitious public support programmes in the low income countries to be studied in this chapter would have been probably unaffordable had this not been the case.

12.2 Sri Lanka

The case of Sri Lanka was singled out earlier as one of remarkable achievement despite its low GNP. Judged in terms of life expectancy, child mortality, literacy rates, and similar criteria, Sri Lanka does indeed stand out among the poor countries in the world.[3]

Sri Lanka's experience is particularly worth studying not only for the exceptional nature of its achievement, but also for its timing. Large-scale expansion of basic public services began early in Sri Lanka. The active promotion of primary education goes back to the early decades of this century.[4] The sharp increase in public health measures took place later, but still as early as the middle 1940s. The radically innovative scheme of providing free or heavily subsidized rice to all was introduced in 1942. The fruits of this expansion were also reaped early, and by the end of the 1950s, Sri Lanka was altogether exceptional in having an astonishingly higher life expectancy at birth than any other country among the low-income developing countries.[5]

The issue of timing is of some importance in assessing Sri Lanka's experience. Given the much wider availability of internationally comparable data in later periods, such as 1960 onwards, it is tempting to compare the changes in Sri Lanka's achievement in the post-1960 world with those of other countries.

---

[2] This applies even in terms of market wages, but the contrast may be sharper in terms of social cost of labour, because of underemployment and surplus labour. On this issue, see Dobb (1960), Sen (1960, 1984a), Chakravarty (1969), Marglin (1976), and Drèze and Stern (1987).

[3] In view of the domestic problems that Sri Lanka has had in recent years, involving political violence and social strife, it is easy to think of Sri Lanka as a much troubled country. That it certainly is, even though it is also the country with the highest life expectancy among all the low income countries of the world. There are, *inter alia*, considerable disparities between the different communities, and the appreciation of Sri Lanka's achievements has to be qualified by an adequate recognition of these—and other—inequalities.

[4] There is a similarity in this respect with the expansion of literacy in the Indian state of Kerala. Kerala too, as was discussed in Chapter 11, reaped the rewards of early expansion in literacy.

[5] Nutrition indicators based on anthropometric measurements as well as on dietary intakes confirm that the post-war period in Sri Lanka was one of rapid improvements in living conditions. On this see Gray (1974) and the literature cited there.

Table 12.1 Sri Lanka: intervention and achievement

Year	Public distribution of food	Number of medical personnel	Death rate per thousand
1940	No (introduced 1942)	271	20.6
1950	Yes	357	12.6
1960	Yes	557	8.6
1970	Yes (reduced 1972, 1979)	693	7.5
1980	Yes	664	6.1

Source: Sen (1988*d*), Table 7.

This does not bring out the nature of Sri Lanka's achievement, since it managed a radical transformation in life expectancy *earlier* than 1960, and the absence of further radical expansion later on was partly due to the high level of longevity accomplished already. The right period for examining Sri Lanka's transformation is the one *preceding* 1960, rather than following it.

Indeed, judged in terms of further reduction of under-5 mortality rate during 1960–85, Sri Lanka is only a moderately good performer—not an exceptional one—even though in terms of absolute levels its current record remains better than that of any other low-income developing country. The same applies to life expectancy and other related indicators. The neglect of the timing of Sri Lanka's public intervention programme can lead to the spurious conclusion that its achievements are not exceptional, or that public intervention achieved little in that country. This is worth mentioning since that interpretational error has often been made, and since the alleged debunking of the role of public support in Sri Lanka has received wide attention.[6]

The temporal relation between the expansion of public support and the reduction of mortality rates in Sri Lanka is brought out by Table 12.1. Between 1940 and 1960 the death rate fell from 20.6 per thousand to 8.6 per thousand —a level not far from that of Europe and North America. This occurred along with the radical expansion of health services brought in with great vigour in the middle 1940s and with the bold introduction of free rice distribution in 1942.[7]

It should also be noted that the vigour of public intervention slackens a good

[6] On this see Bhalla and Glewwe (1986) and Bhalla (1988), and also Bhagwati (1987). On some technical problems in the Bhalla–Glewwe analysis, in addition to the issue of the misleading choice of time period, see Anand and Kanbur (1987), Glewwe and Bhalla (1987), Isenman (1987), Pyatt (1987), and Ravallion (1987*c*). See also Sen (1988*f*).

[7] The eradication of malaria was one of the first targets of public health care measures, and this campaign was remarkably successful. However, this success only accounts for a part of total mortality reduction during this period. For an excellent discussion of this question, and a review of earlier contributions, see Gray (1974). The author concludes on the basis of careful statistical analysis that the control of malaria altogether accounted for 23 per cent of the decline in average crude death rates in Sri Lanka in the post-war period. Somewhat higher estimates, with a 'preferred value' of 44 per cent, were obtained by Peter Newman (1970, 1977).

deal in the later decades, particularly in the 1970s, with a decrease (rather than an increase) in the number of medical personnel and a sharp reduction in the subsidized distribution of food. Given these disengagements, the slowing down of Sri Lanka's expansion of life expectancy in the later decades would not be any kind of 'proof' against the effectiveness of public support as a policy—quite the contrary.[8]

The temporal connection between the expansion of public support in Sri Lanka and the corresponding achievements is easy to see.[9] To move from time-relations to asserting causal connections is, of course, always problematic, and this can be done only with careful attention being paid to the evidence on the causal links that can explain the observed relations. The causal role of health services and public distribution of food has been the subject of a good deal of empirical analysis recently, and there is much evidence of the causal connections proceeding the way that time-relations suggest.[10]

Sri Lanka's experience in support-led security is particularly interesting not merely because it was one of the first developing countries to go that way (preceding even the spectacular case of China), but also because it was then—and still is—a good deal poorer than many other countries that have traversed the path of security through direct support (e.g. Costa Rica, Chile, or Jamaica). Sri Lanka's strategic experience as a pioneer in overcoming the major penalties of low income remains one of great significance for understanding the prospects for support-led security in poor countries.

12.3   Chile

Is there a natural affinity between the strategy of support-led security and particular political regimes? An association of this kind is not implausible, since the attempt to remove hunger through direct public support rather than through the intermediation of growth naturally involves a strong bias in favour of the more deprived sections of the population. Not unexpectedly, regimes where political power is particularly concentrated in the hands of the rich have a tendency to favour development models which give greater prominence to economic growth—whether as an element of a strategy of growth-mediated security, or in the form of unaimed opulence (or indeed in the form of opulence aimed at the privileged classes!).

An examination of the political systems of the six countries (China, Costa

[8] This is quite aside from the fact that by 1960 Sri Lanka's achievements in longevity and low mortality were already high. This made further improvements in absolute terms that much harder compared with countries having still a long distance to go.

[9] There is also some indication of a possible temporal relation between the reduction of public support from the late 1970s and the increase in morbidity and mortality of the affected groups. On this see Edirisinghe (1987), Jayawardena *et al.* (1987), Sahn (1987), UNICEF (1987b), Sahn and Edirisinghe (forthcoming). See also Anand and Kanbur (1987).

[10] See Newman (1970, 1977), Jayawardena (1974), Gwatkin (1979), Fields (1980), Isenman (1980), Alailima (1985), Basu (1986), Anand and Kanbur (1987), Samarasinghe (1988), among others.

Rica, Cuba, Chile, Jamaica, and Sri Lanka) identified earlier as illustrations of the strategy of support-led security reveals an interesting pattern. The only country in the list which can be described as being ruled by a right-wing dictatorship is Chile. The others have either communist governments (China and Cuba), or are multi-party democracies (Costa Rica, Sri Lanka and Jamaica).[11] Chile was democratic until 1973 when Allende was overthrown and replaced by General Pinochet.

There is something intriguing in the fact that continued improvements in basic aspects of the quality of life should have taken place in Chile during the grim period of its contemporary history following the coup of 1973—a period marked not only by enormous economic instability but also by the rapid deterioration of many social services, ruthless political repression, and systematic violation of basic human rights. And yet there is, as we shall see, fairly incontrovertible evidence that, in the area of nutrition and particularly child health, the very rapid progress that was already taking place in the 1960s has continued and consolidated throughout the 1970s.[12] Since General Pinochet does not have a reputation of being a soft-hearted do-gooder, the unusual record of the post-1973 period stands in need of some explanation.

Chile's experience must be seen in historical perspective. Particularly relevant here is the very long tradition of public action for the improvement of living standards, especially in the areas of health care, education, nutrition intervention, and social insurance. This tradition, which goes back to the social reforms of the 1920s, has been intimately linked with the trade union movement and other forms of political activism. Social provisions have been a sensitive political issue, and an area of intense competition among political parties—many pieces of social legislation were indeed enacted in the context of electoral tactics or promises.[13]

Initially, social services were importantly biased towards the more vocal constituencies of the various parties, and especially towards urban dwellers and the organized sections of the working classes. But the reach of public intervention spread systematically over the years, and by the 1960s Chile had not only the most comprehensive social insurance system in Latin America but also a unified National Health Service (with nearly universal coverage), large-scale nutrition intervention programmes, and virtually free education at

[11] The state of Kerala in India was also separated out as having a distinguished record of support-led security (see Chapter 11). Kerala has, of course, a multi-party system, as in the rest of India. It has also had substantial periods of communist government within that system.

[12] During the early 1980s, progress continued but apparently at a slower pace.

[13] This applies, right from the start, to the Social Security Act of 1924, which inscribed itself in a broad range of social and constitutional reforms, represented Chile's pioneering introduction of social insurance in the American continent and also marked the beginning of supplementary feeding in Chile (Mesa-Lago 1985b, Vial et al. 1987). On the history of social services in Chile, and its intimate connection with adversarial politics until 1973, see Arellano (1985a, 1985b). See also Hakim and Solimano (1978), who provide a particularly instructive account of the development and politics of milk distribution programmes.

all levels.[14] Since then, there have been further advances in primary health care (including birth attendance and vaccination), female education, family planning, nutrition intervention, sanitation, and related areas. Today, Chile is probably the only country in the world where public health services ensure not only the monitoring of nearly all young children in the country, but also the provision of food supplements, primary care, and, when identifiably necessary, direct nutritional rehabilitation.[15]

After the abandonment of Allende's socialist experiment in 1973 following a military coup intended to 'rescue the country from the clutches of Marxism–Leninism' (Pinochet 1976), the new government adopted orthodox monetarist policies which put heavy emphasis on 'liberalizing' the economy, drastically reducing the scope of government intervention in the economic sphere, and restoring macro-economic balance through fiscal restraint, greater competition, outward orientation, devaluation, and other tenets of the 'Chicago school'. This so-called 'monetarist experiment', which lasted until 1982 in its pure form, has been the object of much controversy, but few have claimed it to be a success.[16] The failure of the monetarist experiment to lead to a sustained and broad-based increase in economic prosperity is apparent from the macroeconomic indicators presented in Table 12.2 (see also Figure 12.1). The most conspicuous feature of the post-1973 period is that of considerable instability, with two sharp recessions (in 1975–6 and again in 1983–5) and no firm and consistent upward trend (to say the least) in the conventional indicators of economic prosperity.

The question of whether or not the disengagement of the state in the economic sphere during this period has also taken the form of a decline in the provision of social services has been a matter of some disputation. The government has claimed a sustained and in some ways even increased involvement in this area. This claim, however, has been forcefully challenged by a number of critics, who have emphasized the disengagement of the state and the deterioration of many social services since 1973.[17]

[14] On these and other aspects of social services in contemporary Chile, see e.g. Hakim and Solimano (1978), Foxley et al. (1979), Harbert and Scandizzo (1982), Gonzalez et al. (1983), Monckeberg (1983), Wallich (1983), Arellano (1985a, 1985b), Mesa-Lago (1985b, 1985d), Valiente et al. (1985), Ffrench-Davis and Raczynski (1988), and Vial et al. (1987). The redistributive effects of social services in Chile, and particularly of public health and nutrition programmes, have been clearly brought out in a number of studies—see e.g. Foxley et al. (1979), Grossi (1985), and Torche (1985).

[15] It is important to note that while the National Health Service (through which the most important nutrition and health programmes are implemented) does not quite provide universal coverage of infants and young children, there is no indication that the excluded population consists primarily of disadvantaged groups. In fact, the reverse may often be nearer the truth. On this see Torche (1985), Valiente et al. (1985), and Vial et al. (1987).

[16] For various evaluations of this experiment, see Harberger (1982), Ffrench-Davis (1983), Foxley (1983), Sigmund (1984), Corbo (1985), Edwards (1985), and Moran (1989), among others.

[17] See e.g. Ruiz (1980), Foxley and Raczynski (1984), Solimano and Haignere (1984), Scarpaci (1985), Raczynski (1987), Scheetz (1987), Arellano (1988), and Ffrench-Davis and Raczynski (1988), among others.

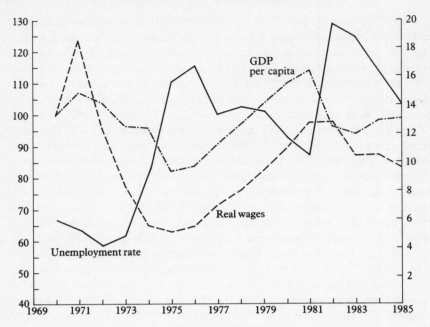

Source: Table 12.2. The right-hand vertical axis indicates the unemployment rate. The left-hand vertical axis provides the relevant scale for the indices of per-capita GDP and real wages (1970 = 100).

Fig. 12.1　Chile, 1970–85: selected economic indicators

Some relevant indicators (constructed from official statistics) appear in Table 12.3, and they do seem to confirm the latter view. At the same time, it is arguable that the observed reduction of social expenditure since 1973 has perhaps been surprisingly *smaller* in aggregate terms than one might have expected given the ideological predilections of the Pinochet regime. Though total social expenditure per capita was considerably reduced during the recession of the mid-70s, it was, on average, only 4% below the 1970 level during the 1981–5 period.[18]

More striking, however, is the noticeable shift in the *composition* of social expenditures since 1973. This point deserves some elaboration. Right through the monetarist experiment, the official policy of the government has been to 'target' social expenditures much more sharply than in the past towards the

---

[18] As shown in Cabezas (1988), alternative studies and sources lead to very similar conclusions regarding broad post-1973 trends in aggregate 'public social expenditure' (shown in the second column of Table 12.3). The concept of public social expenditure has to be distinguished from the narrower notion of 'fiscal social expenditure', which has been used as a basis of the official claim that social expenditures have risen in per-capita terms under the Pinochet regime (see Scheetz 1987, and Arellano 1988).

Table 12.2 Chile, 1960–1985: selected economic indicators

Year	GDP per capita (1970 = 100)	Private consumption per capita (1970 = 100)	Index of real wages and salaries (1970 = 100)	Index of wage earnings per capita[a] (1970 = 100)	Unemployment rate (percentage)
	(1)	(2)	(3)	(4)	(5)
1960–4	86.4	90.9			
1965–70	96.4	97.4	90.9[b]		
1970	100.0	100.0	100.0	100.0	5.9
1971	107.0	111.1	122.7	124.1	5.2
1972	103.8	117.6	96.1	96.5	4.1
1973	96.4	108.0	77.6[c]	75.2[c]	4.8
1974	95.8	86.8	65.0	61.9	9.1
1975	82.1	75.7	62.9	54.2	15.6
1976	83.7	74.7	64.7	54.8	16.7
1977	90.6	85.5	71.4	62.8	13.3
1978	96.7	90.6	76.0	69.7	13.8
1979	103.2	95.1	82.2	75.8	13.5
1980	109.5	100.0	89.3	83.8	11.7
1981	113.7	108.9	97.3	94.4	10.4
1982	96.0	94.1	97.6	81.8	19.6
1983	93.7	89.4	86.9	69.5	18.7
1984	98.0	89.0	87.1	76.3	16.3
1985	98.7	86.5	83.2	76.1	14.1

[a] Calculated as the ratio of total wage earnings (real wage index multiplied by employment) to population.
[b] This value refers specifically to 1969.
[c] This value is for the last trimester of the year.

Sources: (1)–(3) Arellano (1988), Tables 1 and 3. (4) Calculated from Arellano (1988), Table 3, and Ffrench-Davis and Raczynski (1988), Tables 7 and A27. (5) Ffrench-Davis and Raczynski (1988), Table 7.

poorest groups, and to put greater reliance on the private sector for general provisioning. This strategy is reiterated in a large number of official documents.[19] It has been accompanied by an important reorientation in the pattern of public support, including (1) the large-scale 'privatization' of social insurance, (2) the freezing or reduction of mass provisions in the areas of health, housing, and education (in particular a dramatic decline of *investment* in

[19] For statements of the official view of social policy in Chile since 1973, and of the general philosophy of the government in economic and social matters, see Government of Chile (1974), Pinochet (1976), Mendez (1979, 1980), Banco Central de Chile (1984), and particularly Government of Chile (1988). The last document describes the 'new objectives' of the 'social reforms in Chile since 1973' as (1) the eradication of extreme poverty, and (2) the promotion of true equality of opportunities (p. 6). The former objective is explicitly distinguished from, and contrasted with, a policy of income redistribution. The second objective alludes essentially to the virtues of privatization.

Table 12.3 Chile, 1970–1985: social policies

Year	Public social expenditure per capita (1970 = 100)						Public investment in social sectors (1970 = 100)		Percentage of labour force on emergency programmes	Quantity of milk distributed through PNAC (000 tons)
	Total	Education	Health	Social insurance and social assistance	Housing	Other	Total	Health		
	(1)	(2)	(3)	(4)	(5)	(6)	(7)	(8)	(9)	(10)
1970	100.0	100.0	100.0	100.0	100.0	100.0	100.0	100.0	0.0	17.1
1971	n/a	n/a	n/a	n/a	n/a	n/a	n/a	n/a	0.0	19.0
1972	n/a	n/a	n/a	n/a	n/a	n/a	n/a	n/a	0.0	19.3
1973	n/a	n/a	n/a	n/a	n/a	n/a	n/a	n/a	0.0	20.3
1974	75.9	79.9	86.6	59.6	129.8	127.3	148.7	124.9	0.0	20.8
1975	63.4	63.2	67.1	60.6	74.1	39.2	80.3	55.4	2.0	23.6
1976	61.9	67.6	62.7	59.9	54.8	101.7	55.0	37.4	5.2	24.5
1977	71.0	78.9	67.8	68.6	61.4	195.4	69.6	18.1	5.6	28.7
1978	79.3	83.0	75.0	82.0	57.4	171.6	46.1	23.1	4.2	29.8
1979	87.6	90.8	73.8	91.6	71.7	209.1	57.2	30.4	3.8	28.7
1980	90.1	88.7	82.4	95.3	71.2	211.4	55.3	20.6	5.3	29.2
1981	97.5	92.1	74.8	110.7	70.5	174.5	39.2	32.1	4.7	29.8
1982	104.4	93.0	78.4	127.6	49.4	135.4	28.3	30.6	6.5	30.3
1983	93.6	78.8	62.4	118.4	40.9	205.6	n/a	n/a	12.6	22.0
1984	93.7	76.2	65.9	117.9	47.8	180.1	n/a	n/a	8.4	27.8
1985	90.0	75.6	63.6	108.0	65.6	172.9	n/a	n/a	7.9	30.3

Note: PNAC stands for the National Programme of Supplementary Feeding. The contributions of different sectors to total public social expenditure in 1970 were as follows: education (25%), health (13%), social insurance and social assistance (51%), housing (10%), other (1%).

Source: (1)–(6): Calculated from Cabezas (1988), Table 11. (7)–(8): Calculated from Foxley and Raczynski (1984), Table V.5. (9): Calculated from Ffrench-Davis and Raczynski (1988), Table 7. (10): Vial *et al* (1987), Tables 1 and 2; Ffrench-Davis and Raczynski (1988), Table A. 19.

these sectors), (3) the maintenance, and in some cases an expansion, of nutrition programmes, along with a reorientation towards the most vulnerable groups, and (4) a very large expansion of emergency employment programmes in years of high unemployment (see Table 12.3).

Against this background, there is unambiguous evidence of rapid improvement in infant and child mortality as well as in anthropometric measures of the nutritional status of children during the post-1973 period. Health statistics in Chile have a long history and a reputation of high reliability, and from 1975 annual statistics on the nutritional status of children have been produced on the basis of very large samples. The indications provided by these statistics are striking: between 1973 and 1985, the infant mortality rate plunged from 66 to 19 per thousand live births, while between 1975 and 1985 the assessed percentage of undernourished children below 5 years of age declined from 15.5 to 8.7 (see Table 12.4). It is important to note that critics of government policies have mostly focused on the interpretation of these figures rather than on their validity.[20]

Conflicts of interpretation have taken place around the question of whether or not the advances we have just noted can be taken as reflective of broader improvements in living standards. Critics have argued that, on the contrary, the decline in infant and child mortality has taken place against a background of steady deterioration in living standards as a whole, and they have attributed this apparent paradox to the effects of specific intervention in the domains of child health and nutrition.[21]

The question of whether or not general living standards have indeed deteriorated since 1973 is, again, a controversial one. Some have claimed a sharp reduction in 'extreme poverty' as a result of government policies, and even an improvement in income distribution.[22] But many others have documented sharp declines in real wages and wage income, rapidly increasing inequality of incomes, rising incidence of certain diseases, deterioration of housing conditions, falling primary school enrolment ratios, and other indications of adverse changes in living standards.[23]

Given the turbulence of the period, and the opposite directions in which different variables may move, it is not easy to find one's way through these apparently conflicting indications and claims. Among the contrary evidential

---

[20] See in particular Ruiz (1980), Foxley and Raczynski (1984), Solimano and Haignere (1984), Ffrench-Davis and Raczynski (1988), Raczynski (1987), and Arellano (1988). Solimano and Haignere, for instance, acknowledge in spite of their severe criticisms of recent government policies that 'Chile, fortunately, has had a highly competent system for collecting health statistics since the early 1950s, and there is evidence that the reliability of mortality data has not deteriorated significantly' (p. 5), and note in connection with trends in the incidence of child malnutrition that 'there is no reason to believe that the overall decline is unreal' (p. 9).

[21] This view has been expressed by a large number of authors, including those cited in the preceding footnote.

[22] See e.g. Haindl and Weber (1986), Mujica and Rojas (1986), Rojas (1986), and Government of Chile (1988). For rejoinders see Arellano (1988) and Ffrench-Davis and Raczynski (1988).

[23] See the critiques of government policies cited earlier.

Table 12.4 Chile, 1960–1985: child health and nutrition

| Year | Infant mortality rate (per 1,000) (1) | Prevalence of undernourishment among children aged 0–5 (%) | | | | Percentage of low birthweights (6) | Percentage of under-5s under nutrition surveillance (7) |
		Total (2)	Mild (3)	Moderate (4)	Severe (5)		
1960	119.5						
1965	97.3						
1970	82.2						
1971	73.9						
1972	72.7						
1973	65.8						
1974	65.2						
1975	57.6	15.5	12.1	2.7	0.7	11.4	72
1976	56.6	15.9	12.1	3.0	0.8	11.4	74
1977	50.1	14.9	11.9	2.5	0.5	10.9	75
1978	40.1	13.0	10.8	1.8	0.3	9.1	72
1979	37.9	12.2	10.4	1.6	0.2	9.0	69
1980	33.0	11.5	10.0	1.4	0.1	8.6	70
1981	27.0	9.9	8.7	1.1	0.1	7.8	70
1982	23.6	8.8	7.8	0.9	0.1	6.9	75
1983	21.9	9.8	8.7	1.0	0.1	6.5	76
1984	19.6	8.4	7.5	0.8	0.1	6.5	77
1985	19.5	8.7	7.8	0.8	0.1	n/a	78

Source: (1) Banco Central de Chile, *Boletín Mensual*; no. 725 (1988), 2055. (2)–(7) República de Chile, Instituto Nacional de Estadísticas, *Anuario de Recursos y Atenciones*, various issues (1975 to 1985). The prevalence of undernourishment is based on weight-for-age measurements.

Table 12.5 Life expectancy in Chile

Year	Infant mortality rate (per 1,000)	Life expectancy at age 1 (years)	Life expectancy at birth (years)
1960	119.5	64.4	57.6
1965	97.3	66.0	60.5
1970	82.2	68.9	64.2
1971	73.9	68.6	64.5
1972	72.7	68.8	64.8
1973	65.8	68.6	65.1
1974	65.2	68.9	65.4
1975	57.6	68.7	65.6
1976	56.6	68.9	65.9
1977	50.1	68.7	66.2
1978	40.1	68.2	66.5
1979	37.9	68.4	66.7
1980	33.0	68.3	67.0
1981	27.0	68.1	67.3
1982	23.6	68.1	67.5
1983	21.9	68.3	67.8
1984	19.6	68.4	68.0
1985	19.5	68.6	68.3

Source: Banco Central de Chile, *Boletín Mensual*, no. 725 (1988), 2055 (original source: Instituto Nacional de Estadísticas).

directions is the combination of a stagnating life expectancy at age 1 with an increase in life expectancy at birth (reflecting a strong reduction in infant mortality). The relevant figures are given in Table 12.5, and would seem to provide some support for the view that favourable infant mortality trends in Chile since 1973 have not been reflective of a corresponding general improvement in living conditions.[24]

It also seems possible that a distinction would have to be made between the living standards of the poorer sections as a whole (particularly of the working class as a class), and the incidence of extreme poverty among particular groups.

---

[24] After pointing out that infant mortality and life expectancy in Chile are strongly correlated, and stating that 'life expectancy is a very general indicator of quality of life' (p. 9), Hojman (1988) ʾgues against the 'widely held preconception that infant mortality has been artificially reduced with purposes of propaganda, by means which have no relation whatsoever to wider quality of life indicators' (p. 19). Note, however, that *by construction* life expectancy at birth is very sensitively related to infant mortality. This does not apply to the expectation of life *at age one*, and when this indicator is compared with infant mortality, the strong (inverse) correlation on which Hojman's claim is based seems to disappear (see Table 12.5).

Given the explicit and consistent policy of concentrating public support on the poorest, the hypothesis of a decline in extreme poverty is not obviously incompatible with the picture of falling living standards for the poorer groups as a whole.[25]

These methodological issues are not without importance. They bring out, in particular, the limitations involved in concentrating exclusively on health and nutrition indicators for children and infants for the purpose of assessing changes in basic living conditions (even when the primary concern is confined to nutrition and related capabilities). It is certainly sometimes the case that movements in these indicators *can* be taken as reflective of general trends in health, nutrition and related capabilities. But this is not always true, and the case of Chile illustrates the possible difficulties arising from divergent trends coexisting with each other.

As far as the question of the effectiveness of public support is concerned, however, there is little disagreement as to what caused the observed improvements in the area of child health and nutrition. There have, as discussed earlier, been important debates regarding the relation of these improvements to general trends in the quality of life in Chile since 1973, and also regarding overall changes in the government's commitment to public support. But the role and effectiveness of public support in the specific domain of child health and nutrition is not in dispute.

There is, moreover, nothing really surprising in the fact that targeted intervention programmes (including income support) should have been responsible for a large part of the observed improvements.[26] In fact, it would be hard to attribute the impressively steady decline in infant mortality during the last three decades (despite several major economic recessions and political upheavals) to anything *else* than the maintenance of extensive public support measures, and in particular the remarkable consistency of child health and nutrition programmes. Moreover, the noticeable impact of nutrition and health programmes in Chile has been convincingly brought out in a large number of studies (including several econometric investigations), and it is natural to expect that this impact would continue and be consolidated as these programmes were more vigorously extended to disadvantaged groups.[27]

[25] The role of public works programmes in this context is particularly noteworthy. At their peak in 1983, emergency employment programmes employed as much as 13% of the labour force, and their importance for poor households is easily seen (e.g. Cheyre and Ogrodnik 1982, Raczynski and Serrano 1985, and Raczynski 1987).

[26] Of course, other factors have also played a role, notably the continued expansion of female education and the reduction in fertility (according to Valiente *et al.* 1985, the contribution of the latter to the decline of infant mortality has been estimated at about 20% by two different studies). These factors are themselves closely linked with various forms of public action, e.g. in the domains of education and family planning.

[27] For studies and discussions of the impact of health and nutrition intervention in Chile, both before and after 1973, see Hakim and Solimano (1978), Harbert and Scandizzo (1982), Medina and Kaempffer (1982), Castaneda (1984, 1985), Torche (1985), Valiente *et al.* (1985), and various contributions in Underwood (1983) as well as the review by Vial *et al.* (1987).

This account leaves open the intriguing question why a government which had no hesitation in resorting to the most brutal political repression in order to protect the privileges of the dominant classes was so interested in looking after child health and extreme poverty. As far as *non-withdrawal* is concerned, an obvious explanation lies in the political difficulties of withdrawing what different sections of the population had come to regard as their legitimate claim to state support in various forms.[28] This is perhaps most visible in the domain of health, and in the preservation of the National Health Service along with a dramatic reduction of investment in this sector.[29]

In some respects, however, there has been an *expansion* of public support, notably in the area of public works and nutrition programmes. It is tempting to interpret this as a strategy for checking popular discontent at a time of political repression, economic instability, and diminished general social provisions. It has been persuasively argued, for instance, that the expansion of emergency employment programmes was largely a response to the shifting political threats represented respectively by unionized and unemployed workers as a result of mounting unemployment and massive clampdown on trade unions.[30] The expansion of targeted nutrition and health programmes also has an obviously populist ring in a country where popular expectations of public provisioning are very high, and the Chilean government has indeed consistently endeavoured to build political capital from its achievements in the area of child nutrition.[31]

In recognizing Chile's achievements, we have to see the role of public intervention in selected aspects of the quality of life, but also we cannot but observe the part that political pressure and a search for a popular mandate may play even in a country with an authoritarian political atmosphere. Chile does, of course, have a long tradition of democratic and pluralist politics. But the general lesson about the power of adversarial politics even under authoritarian systems may have a wider relevance.

[28] An official document on social policy states that Chile's 'long history of State intervention in social matters' has 'both positive and negative aspects . . . On the negative side, it is difficult to modify already existing social programs and to adapt them to the ever changing reality of poverty' (Government of Chile 1988: 33).

[29] This 'concealed disengagement', and a number of other aspects of social policy under Pinochet (e.g. the emphasis on 'targeting' and 'privatisation'), bear interesting analogies with recent experiences of liberalization in a number of other countries, including Sri Lanka since 1977 (Sahn and Edirisinghe, forthcoming) and Britain in the 1980s (Atkinson *et al.* 1987 and Welfare State Programme, forthcoming).

[30] On this, see particularly Arellano *et al.* (1987, 1988). The authors claim, *inter alia*, that 'whereas in 1973 there were almost 10 times more unionized than unemployed workers or "pobladores", by 1983 the number of unemployed ("pobladores") was more than three times that of unionized workers' (Arellano *et al.* 1987: 16).

[31] Official documents and public speeches since 1973 are full of self-congratulatory references to the rapid progress achieved in the area of child health and nutrition, and to this day 'the pro-Pinochet press regularly runs stories noting that Chilean newborns are among the fattest in the hemisphere' (Contrera 1988: 24).

12.4 Costa Rica

If 'development' is to be recognized by the expansion of basic capabilities, there is little doubt that Costa Rica is one of the most outstanding success stories of the last few decades. In areas related to health and nutrition, the record of this country is particularly clear from the convergent indications of many direct and indirect pieces of evidence (see Tables 12.6 and 12.7). Infant mortality, which had already declined to the respectable level of 76 per thousand live births in 1960, further plunged to 19 over the next 20 years.[32] During the same period, life expectancy at birth leapt by an entire decade to reach 73 years, a figure comparable to those of most European countries. The percentage of women (aged 20–34) having completed primary education increased from 27 to 66. Severe undernourishment as a phenomenon virtually disappeared, and nutritional standards attained levels comparable to those of rich countries. The marital fertility rate (which had been rising steadily before 1960) declined from 7.3 to 3.7. The incidence of a wide range of parasitic and infectious diseases retreated dramatically, and morbidity patterns approached those typical of affluent countries. The extent of poverty as measured by conventional income criteria also declined.[33]

Table 12.6 Costa Rica, 1960–1980: selected well-being indicators

Year	GNP per capita (1960 = 100)	Infant mortality rate (per 1,000)	Life expectancy (years)	Percentage of women aged 20–34 with completed primary education	Total marital fertility rate	Percentage of newborns below 2.5 kg.
1960	100	76	62.6	27	7.3	12.5
1965	115	75	62.9	31	6.5	
1970	138	63	65.4	43	4.9	9.1
1975	164	38	69.6	55	3.8	
1980	185	19	72.6	66	3.7	7.0

Source: Mata (1985), Table 7; Mata and Rosero (1988), Tables 4.1, 2.25, and 2.26.

[32] As in the case of Chile, the pace of improvement in living conditions seems to have decelerated in the 1980s under the impact of world recession—see Peek and Raabe (1984), Mesa-Lago (1985a) and Mata and Rosero (1988). The general issues of world recession, adjustment policies and human well-being are discussed in Jolly and Cornia (1984), Cornia *et al.* (1987), Taylor (1988a), Jayawardena (forthcoming). It must be stressed that the economic difficulties of Costa Rica in the 1980s are overwhelmingly attributable to world-wide fluctuations in economic activity as well as commodity prices, and in this respect Costa Rica shares the common predicament of most Latin American countries.

[33] These trends have been established and discussed in a large number of studies, and the statistical evidence establishing them is robust enough. See e.g. Haines and Avery (1982), Saenz

Table 12.7 Costa Rica, 1960–1980: selected indicators of public support

Year	Percentage of the population covered by 'Social Insurance' and 'Social Assistance'	Per capita real public expenditure on education (1970 US $)	Percentage of births taking place in hospital	Percentage of rural population with water supply connection
1960	15.4	19.3	50	n/a
1965	30.6	23.8		34[a]
1970	38.2	35.4	71	39
1975	54.7	49.3		58[a]
1980	85.1	63.6	91	62

[a] These figures are in fact for the proximate years, respectively 1966 and 1974.

Source: Mesa-Lago (1985*a*), Table 2; Mata (1985), Tables 7 and 8; Mata and Rosero (1988), Table 4.1.

Two factors have accounted for these impressive trends. First, the fairly healthy growth of the economy during these two decades, led by a rapid expansion in the export of 'cash crops' (such as coffee), and resulting in this case in a broad-based improvement of private incomes. Second, the exceptionally rapid expansion of the 'welfare state', and in particular extensive public efforts in the domains of health, education, social insurance and income support.

The expansion of the welfare state in Costa Rica must in turn be understood against a unique political background. Located in the heart of a region where social and political repressions are rife, Costa Rica is widely regarded as a leading exception. In fact, since independence in 1821, Costa Rica has had a long history of active democracy, minimal violence and progressive social legislation.[34] Slavery was abolished as early as 1813, and capital punishment in 1882. The abolition of the army (*sic!*) itself took place in 1949. A high value has consistently been placed on education, and secondary schooling has been free and compulsory since 1869. Elections take place every four years under the supervision of the autonomous Supreme Electoral Tribunal, and Costa Rica

(1982, 1985), Jaramillo (1983), Mohs (1983*a*, 1983*b*), Rosero (1984, 1985*a*, 1985*b*), Peek and Raabe (1984), Halstead *et al.* (1985), Mata (1985), and the meticulous review by Mata and Rosero (1988). The last authors present, *inter alia*, clear evidence of nutritional improvement as indicated by anthropometric measurements.

[34] For an excellent account of the nature of Costa Rican democracy, see Ameringer (1982). For background details on the economy and society of Costa Rica we have also drawn on Rosemberg (1979, 1983), Seligson (1980), Castillo *et al.* (1983), Mesa-Lago and Diaz-Briquets (1988), Peek and Raabe (1984), Wesson (1984*a*), Gonzalez-Vega (1985), Mesa-Lago (1985*a*), Fields (1988), and Mata and Rosero (1988).

has been said to enjoy 'the freest and fairest electoral machinery of any country in the world'.[35] Turn-out at the polls is very high (about 80 per cent), and quite often the opposition wins. Most of the police force are replaced at the time of election.[36]

Costa Rica's achievements have sometimes been seen as a reflection of an egalitarian society and economy. This thesis, while not entirely dismissible, is somewhat misleading. Although inequalities were non-extreme in the early colonial days, the relatively egalitarian land tenure pattern did not survive the emergence of large coffee and banana estates in the nineteenth century.[37] Today the distribution of land in Costa Rica is highly unequal even in comparison with other Latin American countries, and approximately two-thirds of the agricultural labour force consists of landless wage earners.[38] It is true that the distribution of *income* is much less unequal, and that income inequality in Costa Rica is relatively small by Latin American standards. But these standards are hardly exacting, and it is very hard to see a great contrast between Costa Rica and other developing countries in terms of income distribution.[39] The fact is that Costa Rica's economic system is a fundamentally inegalitarian one, and falls far short of guaranteeing adequate entitlements to all—as widespread hunger during the depression of the 1930s had dramatically illustrated. However, cooperative social and political traditions have recently found a new expression in the welfare state, whose far-reaching activities have provided an increasingly important source of security for the poor.

The foundations of the modern welfare state in Costa Rica were firmly laid down by the social reforms of the 1940s. During the first forty years of this century, the Costa Rican state, dominated by a small and conservative oligarchy, had maintained essentially non-interventionist policies. However, changes occurred in the early 1940s under the presidency of Calderón Guardia, an enterprising pediatrician turned politician who, among other things, promoted innovative legislation in the area of social insurance, and proposed the introduction of wide-ranging 'social guarantees' to protect the interests of workers. The constitution of 1949 not only consolidated the advances made under Guardia, but also institutionalized the process of social reforms and

---

[35] Ameringer (1982: 33).

[36] It would be an exaggeration, of course, to describe Costa Ricans as 'non-violent', as has often been done. The homicide rate in Costa Rica, for instance, is much smaller than in neighbouring Latin American countries, but it is not negligible, and some concern has recently been expressed at the fact that homicides increasingly take more violent forms than 'the traditional straight killing', partly as a result of rising alcoholism (Mata and Rosero 1988). Another important social problem in Costa Rica is the disadvantaged position of ethnic minorities.

[37] See Seligson (1980), who discusses the importance of Costa Rica's colonial history, including the evolution of land tenure and the relatively homogeneous ethnic composition of the population.

[38] Peek and Raabe (1984: 12).

[39] See e.g. the tables on income distribution in recent issues of *World Development Report*. For a careful study of land and income distribution in Costa Rica, see Peek and Raabe (1984).

government intervention in economic and social matters by creating a large number of 'autonomous institutions' responsible for the pursuit of various forms of supportive government activity—including *inter alia* educational and health programmes, social insurance, assistance to the needy, land reforms, and public works. These legal foundations, and the pressures generated by the democratic process, have ensured the continued vitality of the welfare state.[40]

Two closely related and interconnected areas of active intervention deserve special attention here: 'fiscal social security measures' and the public health care system.[41] The system of fiscal social security measures, which includes contributory and non-contributory pensions, health insurance, various social welfare programmes and direct financial assistance to needy families, is of a markedly different nature from similar systems in other countries of Latin America. In most of these countries, the fiscal social security system has evolved into a regressive form of large-scale government support to the more influential groups, especially the urban élites.[42] In Costa Rica, this criticism does not seem to apply today. A constitutional amendment was passed in 1961 calling for 'universalization' of social security within a decade, and since then the drive in that direction has been very strong. According to Mesa-Lago, 'in 1980 practically all the population was covered, between two-thirds and three-fourths by social insurance and the rest through social assistance and public health programmes'.[43]

Fiscal social security measures cover a part of the system of public health[44] (e.g. in the form of health insurance). But the latter also includes community health and primary health care programmes implemented directly under the Ministry of Health. These programmes underwent a leap forward in the 1970s with the formulation of a National Health Plan in 1971, and the subsequent

[40] On the role of democratic politics in shaping social policy in Costa Rica, see e.g. Ameringer (1982), Rosemberg (1983), and Mesa-Lago (1985c).

[41] By 'fiscal social security measures' we understand social security in the narrower and more conventional sense than the broader idea of 'social security' used in this book (discussed in section 1.3). This conventional notion is perhaps best reflected by the legislative concerns of the ILO covering 'social insurance' and 'social assistance'. On fiscal social security measures in Costa Rica, see e.g. Green (1977), Rosemberg (1979, 1983), Briceño and Méndez (1982), Mesa-Lago (1985a, 1985c), and Rodriguez (1986).

[42] This verdict is extensively defended and documented in numerous writings by Carmelo Mesa-Lago—see e.g. Mesa-Lago (1978, 1985b, 1985c, 1986, 1988b). It is worth noting that the three countries which Mesa-Lago singles out as departing from this pattern happen to be Chile, Costa Rica, and Cuba (see Mesa-Lago 1985d). These three countries distinguish themselves by having unified fiscal social security systems with universal (or nearly universal) coverage.

[43] Mesa-Lago (1985b: 45; our translation).

[44] The literature on public health in Costa Rica is enormous. Some useful references include Mata (1978, 1985), Haines and Avery (1982), Jaramillo (1983), Mohs (1983a, 1983b), Tomic (1983), Asociación Demográfica Costarricense (1984), Mesa-Lago (1985a), Rosero (1985a, 1985b), Caldwell (1986), and various contributions in Halstead et al. (1985). For a particularly useful and up-to-date account, which also summarizes neatly the existing evidence on the relation between health intervention and health and nutritional improvement, see Mata and Rosero (1988).

implementation of vigorous health campaigns, including especially the Rural Health Programme (started in 1973) and the Community Health Programme (started in 1976). There is considerable evidence that these programmes have made a major contribution to rapid health and nutritional improvement in Costa Rica since their inception.[45]

The links between public support and the improvement of living conditions in Costa Rica are particularly well reflected in the decline of infant and child mortality. The decline of infant mortality over the period 1960–85 in Costa Rica has been overwhelmingly concentrated in the decade of the 1970s. Indeed, the 70 per cent decline in infant mortality over that single decade (from 63 to 19 per thousand live births) may well be an all-time record—all the more impressive because the base mortality level was itself already quite low. Not surprisingly, many factors seem to have accounted for this achievement. The moderate but broad-based growth of private incomes must have exercised its influence.[46] The expansion of female education, which is known to exercise a strong influence on infant mortality, almost certainly played a role as well. The decline of fertility (itself partly the result of declining infant and child mortality) made a further contribution, which has indeed been quantitatively estimated.[47]

Interestingly enough, one factor that does *not* seem to have played a significant role in mortality reduction is the quantitative increase of nutritional intakes. Indeed, nutritional intakes do not seem to have increased much (if at all) over the period under consideration (see Table 12.8). This confirms once again the need to relate nourishment and health not to food entitlements as such but to a broader notion of entitlements including command over crucial non-food items.[48]

The relative unimportance of quantitative increases in nutritional intake in Costa Rica's success contrasts with the crucial role that has been widely ascribed to the vigorous health programmes initiated in the 1970s. Careful statistical studies confirm that, in addition to the positive factors mentioned

[45] The evidence on this point is discussed in many of the contributions cited in the preceding footnote.

[46] The rate of decline of infant mortality in Costa Rica since 1911 seems to have been more rapid during periods of economic prosperity than through recessions. See Rosero (1985b) and Mata and Rosero (1988). Note, however, that the growth of income per capita in Costa Rica does not seem to have been more rapid in the 1970s than in the 1960s. According to the *World Development Report 1984*, the growth rate of GDP per capita in Costa Rica was 3.2% over the 1960–70 period, and only 2.0% between 1970 and 1982 (calculated from Tables 2 and 19).

[47] According to Rosero, the decline of fertility is estimated to have been responsible for 24% of the observed reduction in infant mortality in Costa Rica between 1960 and 1977 (Rosero 1985a: 131). Note that the decline of fertility is itself closely related to social policy, including education and family planning programmes—see Stycos (1982) for a detailed analysis. In 1981, two-thirds of those using contraception utilized state-provided services—the proportion rising to 90% among agricultural labourers (Rosero 1985a: 131).

[48] Of course, it must be remembered that Costa Rica is more prosperous than most countries of Africa or South Asia, and it is not clear that substantial improvements in nutritional status could be easily achieved in much poorer countries without *inter alia* an increase in calorie intake.

Table 12.8 Nutritional status and nutritional intake in Costa Rica, 1966–1982

Year	Percentage of stunted children	Percentage of wasted children	Average calorie intake (Kcal./cap.)		Average protein intake (g./cap.)	
			Rural	Urban	Rural	Urban
1966	16.9	13.5	1,894	2,330	53.6	67.3
1975	7.2	12.5				
1978	7.6	8.6	2,020	1,947	54.0	58.2
1982	n/a	4.1				

Source: Mata and Rosero (1988), Tables 2.10 and 2.13, summarizing a number of surveys conducted by the Ministry of Health.

earlier, these programmes have indeed had a strong independent effect on mortality decline. The evidence presented is of two kinds. First, it is observed that while until 1970 the infant mortality rate in Costa Rica could be reasonably accurately 'predicted' from its general social and economic indicators on the basis of the relationships (between these indicators and infant mortality) observed elsewhere in Latin America, during the 1970s infant mortality in Costa Rica deviated markedly downward from its predicted value. Second (and more importantly), by utilizing the rich data available at the canton level in Costa Rica, it has been possible to carry out statistical tests to ascertain whether mortality decline was more rapid in regions where the coverage of rural health programmes was more comprehensive, controlling for the effect of regional differences in incomes, education levels, fertility, sanitation, and so on. Detailed investigations of this type have tended to demonstrate that the influence of health care programmes in the 1970s was indeed extremely important.[49]

Table 12.9 gives a very elementary illustration of the results obtained. It is clear from this table that the rural health programmes of the 1970s were targeted to the cantons with higher initial infant mortality rates (this was indeed a conscious and declared policy). It can be seen that the annual declines of infant mortality, which were relatively slow in these cantons in the 1960s, sharply accelerated in the 1970s. Indeed the ranking of mortality reduction rates in different cantons got largely reversed as a result of these programmes. Basically the same conclusion is retained when the exercise is extended by 'controlling' for factors such as education, fertility and economic development.[50]

[49] On both types of evidence, see the detailed review of evidence in Mata and Rosero (1988). Rosero (1985*a*) estimates that 41% of the infant mortality decline between 1972 and 1980 is attributable to the expansion of primary health care, and another 32% to secondary health care (mainly out-patient consultations at hospitals). See also Haines and Avery (1982) on the importance of maternal and child health programmes during the period 1968–73.
the period 1968–73.
[50] See Mata and Rosero (1988) for details.

Table 12.9 Rural health programmes and mortality reduction in cantons in Costa Rica, 1968–1980

Ranges of coverage of population in community and rural health programmes in different cantons	Percentage of all births in Costa Rica taking place in the cantons within the respective ranges of coverage	Health indicators in the corresponding cantons			
		Infant Mortality Rate (per 1,000)		Annual Decline in IMR (%)	
		1968–9	1979–80	1965–72	1973–80
0–9	(15)	49	21	8	7
10–24	(25)	49	19	8	7
25–49	(13)	64	23	3	14
50–74	(37)	76	22	4	15
75–100	(10)	80	17	5	16
All cantons	(100)	64	21	5	12

Source: Mata and Rosero (1988), Table 4.10. All 79 cantons of Costa Rica are included in the Table.

There is, of course, nothing contrary in these results. Many of the studies mentioned earlier have noted that the decline of infant mortality in Costa Rica over the last few decades has been associated with an impressive retreat of infectious and parasitic diseases. It would be rather odd if carefully managed programmes of primary health care concentrating on enterprises such as immunization, deworming, environmental improvements, oral rehydration and prenatal care did not succeed in substantially accelerating this process and making a dent in the undernutrition-infection complex. Costa Rica went directly at the problem and has reaped as it sowed.

12.5 Concluding Remarks

In this chapter and the previous one, we have examined selected country experiences of direct support. We have paid special attention to China, Costa Rica, Chile, Sri Lanka and the Indian state of Kerala. All these experiences suggest a close connection between the expansion of public support measures and the improvement of living conditions. Public support can take various forms, such as public health services, educational facilities, food subsidies, employment programmes, land redistribution, income supplementation, and social assistance, and the country experiences that were examined have involved various combinations of these measures.

While there are significant contrasts in the relative importance of these different forms of public support in the different country experiences, the basic commonality of instruments is quite striking (especially in view of the great diversity of the political and economic regimes). Underlying all this is something of a shared approach, involving a public commitment to provide direct support to raise the quality of life, especially of the deprived sections of the respective populations.

The causal links between public efforts and social achievements in these as well as other countries have received a good deal of attention in the recent development literature. The investigations have taken different forms. One group of studies have been concerned with examining similarities in the nature of public support efforts in *different countries* (each with good records in mortality reduction and other achievements), and the commonalities involved in their respective efforts have been assessed, especially in contrast with the experience of other countries.[51] A second group of studies have been concerned with *interregional comparisons within single countries*, comparing the achievements of regions with greater or lesser involvement in public support.[52] A third set of studies have presented *intertemporal comparisons within single countries* of public efforts and social achievements.[53] A fourth set of studies have examined the direct impact of public support measures, such as health and nutrition programmes, at the *micro* level.[54] The causal links between public support provisions and social achievements have been clearly brought out in different ways in these diverse empirical investigations.

In this chapter and the preceding one, our focus has been concentrated on five specific 'case-studies'. Three of the five cases studied (viz. China, Chile and Costa Rica) were among the five countries identified in Chapter 10 as being the top performers in the 'support-led' category in reducing child mortality during the period 1960–85.[55] The other two countries in this identified list were Jamaica and Cuba. These countries are harder to study for a variety of reasons, including data limitation. Nevertheless, we may make a few brief remarks on particular aspects of the experiences of these two countries.

Regarding Jamaica, the data on infant and child mortality rates, already examined in Chapter 10, suggest a rapid improvement in basic living

[51] See e.g. Sen (1981b), Flegg (1982), Halstead et al. (1985), Stewart (1985), Caldwell (1986).

[52] See e.g. Patel (1980), Castaneda (1984, 1985), Jain (1985), Nag (1985), Prescott and Jamison (1985), Morrison and Waxler (1986), Kumar (1987), Mata and Rosero (1988).

[53] See e.g. Castaneda (1984, 1985) on Chile, Anand and Kanbur (1987) on Sri Lanka, and Mata and Rosero (1988) on Costa Rica.

[54] See e.g. Gwatkin et al. (1980), Harbert and Scandizzo (1982), Garcia and Pinstrup-Andersen (1987), Berg (1987a), Mata and Rosero (1988), and the studies of health and nutrition programmes cited earlier in this chapter in connection with specific country studies.

[55] The two other cases studied did not qualify in the 'top performer' list in Chapter 10 for rather special reasons. In the case of Sri Lanka the programme of support-led security began substantially earlier (and gathered particular momentum in the 1940s) and by 1960 Sri Lanka already had a very low level of child mortality, leaving less scope for exceptional performance in the period 1960–85 on which the international comparison in Chapter 10 concentrated (see section 12.2). In the case of Kerala as well, the interventionist history pre-dates 1960, but, more importantly, it did not even 'qualify' to be included in the international comparisons in Chapter 10 since Kerala is not a country but only a state within India.

conditions during the last few decades. This is indeed confirmed by other relevant indicators. By 1985, the expectation of life at birth in Jamaica was 74 years, a level as high as that of Britain or West Germany. Adult literacy was virtually universal for both men and women. And morbidity patterns had undergone a radical transformation, including a considerable retreat of infectious and parasitic diseases.[56]

As far as programmes of public support are concerned, Jamica has an impressively activist record. This includes 'a distinguished history of accomplishments in public health care since early in the twentieth century'.[57] The record of public involvement in the provision of basic education is equally strong, with the bulk of Jamaica's outstanding literacy record being attributable to public, rather than private, educational institutions. The supportive role of the state, kept alive by a highly assertive electorate, has extended to many other fields of action including those of housing, sanitation, public employment, food subsidies, nutritional intervention, social insurance and social assistance.[58]

It is plausible enough that, as with the other countries studied in this chapter, a strong link exists between public support and social achievements in this case. This view is all the more convincing given that, during the period under consideration (1960–85), the rate of economic growth in Jamaica has been dismally low—in fact *negative* (see Table 10.3 in Chapter 10).

There is a further and rather striking aspect of Jamaica's experience which deserves mention here. The negative growth rate of GNP per capita for the 1960–85 period is mainly due to the record of the economy between 1973 and 1980, when Jamaica had the unique distinction of a negative growth rate *every year*.[59] This was also a period of socialist government, when the People's National Party (PNP, elected in 1972 and re-elected in 1976) was in office. It is possible that the PNP's policy of retaining an essentially capitalistic economy, while simultaneously cracking down in many ways on private initiative, reinforced the negative external factors to produce the economic morass of this period. But the socialist programme of the PNP government also included many positive and ambitious initiatives in domains such as health care, education, housing, food subsidies and public employment. Under the circumstances, if it were to turn out that the 1970s were also a decade of particularly rapid improvements in health and nutrition, Jamaica's experience

---

[56] See UNICEF (1987a), Cumper (1983) and Moran *et al.* (1988).

[57] Moran *et al.* (1988: 13). For a detailed investigation of these accomplishments, and of their economic and political basis, see Cumper (1983).

[58] On various aspects of public support in Jamaica today, see G. Cumper (1972), Gobin (1977), Girling and Keith (1977, 1980), Jameson (1981), G. E. Cumper (1983), Gunatilleke (1984), Samuels (1987), Mesa-Lago (1988a, 1988c), and Moran *et al.* (1988). The prominent role of public assertiveness and participatory politics in Jamaica's experience of support-led security is evident from several of these contributions. On this see also Duncan (1984).

[59] See e.g. the data presented in Boyd (1987), Table 5.1. In the 1960s, the economy had enjoyed a period of positive and fairly substantial economic growth.

would provide strong confirmation of the powerful influence that public support measures can have in removing hunger and deprivation even in the face of highly adverse macroeconomic circumstances.[60]

The available demographic evidence supports this hypothesis, with, *inter alia*, a decline of infant mortality of the order of 50 per cent during the decade of the 1970s.[61] Nutrition surveys provide some further evidence in the same direction. For instance, the incidence of rural undernutrition among children aged 5 and below appears to have declined from 12.1 per cent to 8.3 per cent between 1970 and 1978.[62] There is, thus, a strong possibility that indicators of economic opulence and nutritional well-being were moving in sharply contrasting directions during the 1970s.

This interpretation of Jamaica's experience calls for fuller investigation. The potential adverse effects of rapidly declining incomes on living conditions, with a decline in average real incomes of as much as 25 per cent or so between 1973 and 1980, should not be taken lightly. The combined evidence from independent nutrition surveys must be handled with some caution. Even mortality data are much less reliable for Jamaica than for the other countries studied in this chapter.[63] A closer examination of the available evidence (from anthropometric data, morbidity surveys, demographics statistics, etc.) would be needed to confirm the apparent achievements of the 1970s. As things stand, however, the period of socialist government in Jamaica does appear to be one of substantial success in support-led security.

In the case of Cuba, there is—as with Jamaica—a clear temporal association between expansion of public support on the one hand and improvements in health and nutrition on the other. Indeed, the sharp decline in infant and child mortality since 1960 (observed in Chapter 10) coincides with the post-

[60] The People's National Party was beaten in the 1980 election by the rival Jamaica Labour Party, which immediately adopted extensive measures of economic liberalization and 'adjustment', including very severe cuts in social programmes and public support. In spite of some economic recovery, the 1980–5 period seems to have been one of stagnation and possibly even deterioration in living standards. On this, see Boyd (1987), Melville *et al.* (1988*a*, 1988*b*), Mesa-Lago (1988*c*) and Moran *et al.* (1988).

[61] See Government of Jamaica (1985), Annex 6, Table A3, Moran *et al.* (1988), Table A1, and FAO (1988), Table 2.6. The precise magnitude of the decline is hard to ascertain, and substantially different estimates are provided by different studies.

[62] Samuels (1987), Table 4.11, based on weight-for-age measurements (the incidence of stunting also decreased considerably). Striking improvements during the 1970s have also been observed in the studies of Alderman *et al.* (1978) and Marchione (1977, 1984), which cover specific 'Parishes'. The data presented by Marchione (1984) apparently indicate some setback between 1975 and 1978–80 in the parish studied, but the 1978–80 figures—as Marchione explains—are not comparable with the earlier ones. Comparable figures for 1973 and 1975 indicate a decline of about 40% in the incidence of undernutrition for children below age 3 (calculated from his Table 3 first column). For evaluations of recent nutrition surveys in Jamaica, see Omawale and McLeod (1984), Davis and Witter (1986), Landman and Walker (1987), and Melville *et al.* (1988*a*, 1988*b*).

[63] There is, in fact, a possibility that the UNICEF estimates used in Chapter 10 give a slightly exaggerated picture of Jamaica's recent achievements, due to some decline in the quality of death reporting (George Cumper, London School of Hygiene and Tropical Medicine, personal communication).

revolutionary period, which has witnessed not only a radical land reform and a great deal of income redistribution, but also ambitious initiatives in the domains of health care, fiscal social security measures, nutrition programmes, basic education and food rationing. To cite only a few relevant facts, between the years immediately preceding the revolution of 1959 and the mid-1970s, the share of the poorest 20 per cent of the population in national income appears to have roughly quadrupled, secondary school enrolment ratios increased more than eightfold, the rate of open unemployment dropped by around 75 per cent, and the number of nurses per inhabitant more than tripled.[64]

The successes of China and Cuba in removing endemic undernutrition and deprivation are of some relevance in assessing the development experience of post-revolutionary socialist countries. The economic performances of these countries have been the object of a good deal of criticism—both internal and external—in recent years. The reprimands have often been well deserved, and the inefficiencies of bureaucratic planning have emerged powerfully enough. But the criteria of appraisal have often been rather limited, e.g. focusing on the size of commodity production rather than on the achievements in nutrition, health, education, morbidity, longevity and other basic aspects of the quality of life. As was discussed earlier (Chapter 1) and illustrated with empirical experiences (Chapters 10 and 11), aggregate economic opulence can be a very misleading indicator of achievements in developing basic human capabilities. The growth of GNP is no more than one important *means* to deeper ends, and as the variations in the intertemporal experiences of China show, the growth of commodity production can have quite a contrary pattern to that of life expectancy and related indicators (see Chapter 11).

The impressive records of Cuba and pre-reform China in the fields of health, education, nutrition and life expectancy have to be incorporated in a fuller and fairer assessment of the performance of these socialist economies. Of course, in this broader assessment other aspects of the quality of life must also be brought in, including the political freedoms enjoyed or denied. Sometimes the lack of these freedoms may not only vitiate the quality of life directly, it could indirectly also affect adversely health and longevity themselves. We have discussed, for example, the role of political suppression in the genesis of the Chinese famines of 1959–62 (see Chapter 11). But these complex considerations contribute to (rather than detract from) the need to broaden the criteria of success from the narrow concentration—currently fashionable—on the growth of commodity production and GNP. In that broadened evaluation, the successes of the socialist economies of China and Cuba in nutrition and health

[64] The figures are based on Brundenius (1982), Tables 8.1, 8.4, 8.5, 8.6. On the transformation of living conditions in Cuba since 1959, and the role of public support in bringing about this transformation, see Brundenius (1981, 1982, 1984), Eckstein (1980, 1982, 1986), Aldereguia (1983), Diaz-Briquets (1983), Muniz *et al.* (1984), Halebsky and Kirk (1985), Santana (1987), Ghai *et al.* (1988), among others. For interesting comparisons of the experience of Cuba with those of Costa Rica, Jamaica, Sri Lanka, and Chile, see Jameson (1981), Monckeberg (1983), Meegama (1985), Mesa-Lago and Diaz-Briquets (1988).

must figure prominently, along with other relevant assessments (many of which would be much less favourable). A proper reassessment of the experiences of socialist countries cannot be carried out in the narrow format that has come to be used so widely.

Before concluding the empirical investigations of this part of the book, something should be said about the resource requirements (and affordability) of the kind of public support measures that we have found crucial to the strategy of support-led security. Scepticism regarding the feasibility of large-scale public provisioning in a poor country often arises precisely from the belief that these measures are inordinately 'expensive'. The experiences studied in this chapter and the previous one (particularly those that have succeeded in spite of a low GNP per capita, e.g. China, Sri Lanka and Kerala) suggest that this diagnosis is, at least to some extent, misleading.

Indeed, the costs of many of the social security programmes in the countries we have studied have been in general astonishingly small. This applies, in particular, to public provisioning of health care and education. It has been estimated, for instance, that in China the percentage of GDP allocated to public expenditures on health has been only around 2 per cent. Moreover, only about 5 per cent of total health expenditure has tended to go to preventive health care, which has been one of the major influences behind the fast retreat of infectious and parasitic diseases.[65] There are similarly striking figures for the other experiences of support-led success we have studied.[66]

As was discussed in the first section of this chapter, the relatively inexpensive nature of public provisions in the domains of health and education is not, in fact, so suprising given the low level of wages in many developing countries.[67] The distinction of China or Kerala or Sri Lanka does not lie in the size of financial allocations to particular public provisions. Their real success

[65] Baumgartner (1989). On this general question, see also World Bank (1984a) and Jamison (1985).

[66] The percentage of GDP allocated to public expenditures on health in Sri Lanka in 1981 was barely 1% (Perera 1985: Table 8). The corresponding figure for Cuba was around 2.7% (Muniz et al. 1984: Tables VI.1 and VI.6). In Kerala, per-capita government expenditure on health is not much greater than in the rest of India (Nag 1985: Table 16). In Costa Rica, overall government expenditure on health is relatively high, but the public health programmes described in the preceding section accounted for only 2% of the total (Saenz 1985: 143). For further evidence and discussion of the scope for low-cost public provisions in the domain of health, with special reference to China, Costa Rica, Kerala and Sri Lanka, see various contributions in Halstead et al. (1985), and also Caldwell (1986).

[67] There are also other considerations that would lead to a reduction of the real resource burden of public support in developing countries. First, financial costs are not always a good reflection of social costs, and in particular a good case can often be made for regarding the social cost of labour in labour-surplus economies as being lower than the market wage. Second, the opportunities for raising revenue are not independent of the existence of a social security system. For instance, the scope for resorting to exacting indirect taxation may be much larger when vulnerable groups are protected from possibly severe deprivation. Third, there is an element of investment in public provisioning (e.g. through the relation between health, nutrition, education and productivity). This reduces the diversion from investment opportunities that is apparently involved in a programme of public support.

seems to be based on creating the political, social and economic conditions under which ambitious programmes of public support are undertaken with determination and effectiveness, and can be oriented towards the deprived sections of the population.

We should close this part of the book with a few general remarks about the empirical experiences of 'support-led security' examined in this chapter and the preceding one. The connection between programmes of public support and achievements in the quality of life has obvious relevance for policy making, and that is why we have attempted to study various aspects of these experiences in some detail. But the existence of such a connection is not in itself particularly remarkable. It is, in fact, not enormously surprising that efforts in providing extensive public support are rewarded by sustained results, and that public sowing facilitates social reaping.[68]

Perhaps what is more remarkable is the fact that the connections studied here are so frequently overlooked in drawing up blueprints for economic development. The temptation to see the improvement of the quality of life simply as a consequence of the increase in GNP per head is evidently quite strong, and the influence of that point of view has been quite pervasive in policy making and policy advising in recent years. It is in the specific context of that simple growth-centred view that the empirical connections between public support measures and the quality of life deserve particular emphasis.

Indeed, the simple growth-centred view is misleading not only because of the importance of public support in the successful implementation of 'support-led security' (with which this chapter and the last one have been concerned), but also because of the role that public support clearly plays even in the successful experiences of what we have been calling 'growth-mediated security'. As was discussed earlier (in Chapter 10), the contrast between a strategy of 'growth-mediated security' and the tactics of 'unaimed opulence' can be very significant indeed, and there are plenty of examples of countries with high growth rates of GNP, real incomes, food output, etc., with extremely sluggish improvement of the quality of life. A shared feature of support-led security and growth-mediated security is that they *both* involve crucial use of public support. Neither strategy hands over the job of raising life expectancy, reducing undernutrition, morbidity, illiteracy, etc. to an unaimed process of GNP growth.

What the particular studies of support-led security—on which we have concentrated in this chapter and the last—bring out is the force with which public support programmes can work even when a country is quite poor in

[68] Hunger and deprivation are, to a large extent, social conditions that cannot be seen only in isolated individual terms. There are strong interdependences and so-called 'externalities' involved in health (e.g. through the spread of diseases), education (e.g. through influencing each other), and nutrition (e.g. through food habits being dependent on social customs). The importance of social intervention in ensuring adequate entitlements to 'public goods', and in dealing with externalities generally, has been well recognized for a long time in economics (see Samuelson 1955, and Arrow 1963).

terms of GNP per head. This makes it possible to do something immediately about conquering deprivation and raising the quality of life without having to wait quite some time before ploughing back the fruits of economic growth into improved health and longevity. That immediacy is an important aspect of the promise of support-led security, and it can substitute for a good deal of fast economic growth (on which see section 10.7 of Chapter 10). Given that most countries are in situations such that they cannot hope to grow as fast as Kuwait or South Korea or Hong Kong have done over the last few decades, immediacy is a distinct advantage of the strategy of support-led security over that of growth-mediated security.

This recognition should not, however, be seen as establishing any general superiority of 'support-led security' over 'growth-mediated security'. Indeed, it is arguable that the latter strategy has its own advantages too. In particular, it makes it possible to establish the material basis of *further* progress in the future—even in the fields of health and longevity—going well beyond the elementary task of eradication of undernutrition and acute deprivation on which we have concentrated in this book.

Moreover, an assessment of the respective advantages of each strategy ultimately has to go beyond the concerns that have been the focus of this book. High incomes and extensive public support are both important to many other basic capabilities than those of being well nourished and healthy. High incomes provide individual access to commodities (such as better housing and more elaborate forms of entertainment) which can be used to lead a more varied life. Public support, on the other hand, can be an effective route to enhancing capabilities in domains where social interdependences are particularly strong, e.g. higher education.

Both growth-mediated security and support-led security have much to offer. Their advantages are partly congruent and partly divergent. In this chapter and the preceding one, the empirical analyses have pointed *inter alia* to the merits of support-led security and the process through which these merits are realized. The possibility of immediacy in encountering hunger and acute deprivation is certainly a serious virtue in that context. But this and related virtues of support-led security have to be assessed in the light of more comprehensive considerations relevant to this evaluation, including those brought out by the empirical and evaluative analyses in the *earlier* chapters of this book.

PART IV

Hunger and Public Action

13

The Economy, the State and the Public

13.1 Against the Current?

This is a book about what public action can do to eradicate hunger in the modern world. A question that would occur to many people is this. Is this not a hopeless time to write in defence of public action? The world has, in recent years, moved decisively towards unhesitating admiration of private enterprise and towards eulogizing and advocating reliance on the market mechanism. Socialist economies—from China to the USSR and East Europe—are busy de-socializing. Capitalist economies with a tradition of 'welfare state' policies —from the UK and the USA to Australia—have been absorbed in 'rolling back the frontiers of the state', with a good bit of privatization of public enterprise. The 'heroes' at this moment are the private ownership economies with high growth rates—not only old successes such as Japan, but also the new 'trail blazers'—South Korea, Hong Kong, Singapore. What chance is there of getting much of a hearing at this time for an argument in favour of *more* public action? And, more importantly, how can we possibly *defend* such a case, given the empirical regularities that are taken to have emerged in the recent decades?

There is indeed some sense in seeing the developments in the modern world in these terms. But there is also a good deal of nonsense mixed with that sense. We have had the occasion, in earlier parts of this book, to discuss fairly extensively the enormously positive role of public action in the success stories in the modern world. This applies *inter alia* to the outstanding and decisive contribution made by constructive public action in eradicating famines (see Part II), as well as in eliminating endemic undernutrition and deprivation (see Part III).

In the field of famine prevention, the decisive role of public action is illustrated not only by the elimination of famines in India since independence, but also by the unsung and underappreciated achievements of many African countries (see Chapters 5 and 8). These experiences firmly demonstrate how easy it is to exterminate famines if public support (e.g., in the form of employment creation) is well planned on a regular basis to protect the entitlements of vulnerable groups. Ensuring that the concerned governments take early and effective steps to prevent a threatening famine is itself a matter of public action. It is also clear that the eradication of famines need not *await* a major breakthrough in raising the per-capita availability of food, or in radically reducing its variance (even though these goals are important in themelves and can be—and must be—promoted in the long run by well-organized public policy). Public action can decisively eliminate famines *now*, without waiting for some distant future.

Regarding the elimination of regular, persistent deprivation (as opposed to the eradication of intermittent famines), the analysis presented here has indicated the positive contribution that can be made by public provisioning (especially of education and health services) and more generally by public support (including such different policies as epidemiological control, employment generation and income support for the vulnerable). Expectations based on general reasoning are, in fact, confirmed by the empirical experiences of different countries.

Public support in these different forms has played a major part in combating endemic deprivation not only in economies that are commonly seen as 'interventionist' (e.g., China, Costa Rica, Jamaica, Sri Lanka), but also in the market-oriented economies with high growth (e.g., Hong Kong, Singapore, South Korea); on this see Chapters 10–12. Indeed, the contrast between what was called 'growth-mediated security' (as in, say, South Korea) and 'unaimed opulence' (as in, say, Brazil) relates closely to the extensive and well-planned use of public support in the former cases, in contrast with the latter (see Chapter 10). When it comes to enhancing basic human capabilities and, in particular, beating persistent hunger and deprivation, the role played by public support—including public delivery of health care and basic education —is hard to replace.

The crucial role of public support in diverse economic environments is well illustrated by the intertemporal variations in the experience of China. The radical transformation in the health and nutritional status of the Chinese population (visible *inter alia* in a sharp increase in life expectancy, a dramatic decline of infectious and parasitic diseases, and improved anthropometric indicators) took place *before* the reforms of 1979, at a time of relatively moderate growth of GNP but enormously effective public involvement in the promotion of living conditions. The post-reform period has seen an impressive acceleration in the growth of GNP and private incomes, but also a crisis of public provisioning (especially of health services), and an *increase* in mortality. Much more is involved in increasing human capabilities—and in preventing their decline—than the stimulation of economic growth through revamping private incentives and market profits.

We have also discussed how the crucial role of public support in removing endemic deprivation is visible not only in the achievements and failures of developing countries today, but also in the historical experiences of the rich and industrialized countries. This is well illustrated by the sharp increases in longevity in Britain during the decades of the world wars, which were periods of rapid expansion of public support in the form of public food distribution, employment generation and health care provisioning (not unconnected with the war efforts).[1] There is nothing particularly *ad hoc* in the findings regarding the contribution of public support to human lives in the developing countries today.

Public action is not, of course, just a question of public delivery and state initiative. It is also, in a very big way, a matter of participation by the public in the process of social change. As we have discussed, public participation can have powerful positive roles in both 'collaborative' and 'adversarial' ways *vis-à-vis* governmental policy. The collaboration of the public is an indispensable ingredient of public health campaigns, literacy drives, land reforms, famine relief operations, and other endeavours that call for cooperative efforts for their successful completion. On the other hand, for the initiation of these endeavours and for the government to act appropriately, adversarial pressures from the public *demanding* such action can be quite crucial. For this adversarial function, major contributions can be made by political activism, journalistic pressures and informed public criticism. Both types of public participation —collaborative and adversarial—are important for the conquest of famines and endemic deprivation.

To emphasize the vital role of public action in eliminating hunger in the modern world must not be taken as a general denial of the importance of incentives, nor indeed of the particular role played by the specific incentives provided by the market mechanism. Incentives are, in fact, central to the logic of public action. But the incentives that must be considered are not only those that offer profits in the market, but also those that motivate governments to implement well-planned public policies, induce families to reject intrahousehold discrimination, encourage political parties and the news media to make reasoned demands, and inspire the public at large to cooperate, criticize and coordinate.[2] This complex set of social incentives can hardly be reduced to the narrow—though often important—role of markets and profits.[3]

This *is* indeed a good time to keep in view the crucial role that public action—in various forms—can play in eradicating hunger in the modern world. The empirical experiences of different countries point to certain systematic connections, and it is important not to lose sight of them in the scramble to be more 'private'—more exclusively 'market-based'—than the next country. We have to recognize the functions of public action and the rewards they can bring. The cost of overlooking them can be very high—in terms of unnecessary misery, morbidity and mortality.

[1] On this and related experiences, see Chapter 10. Some contemporary developments point to similar lessons to these historical experiences. For instance, the resilient persistence of hunger and deprivation in some sections of the population even in the richest countries of the world (e.g., the USA) seems to have a clear connection with the neglect of public support (see Harvard School of Public Health 1985, 1987). This is an important issue for further exploration in analysing the survival of undernutrition and preventable morbidity (and the persistence of inequalities in health and longevity between different classes and regions) within the rich countries of North America and Europe (see, e.g., Townsend and Davidson 1982).

[2] See Chapters 4, 5–8, 10–12.

[3] We have also discussed the importance of combining and connecting state action and market response in strategies to combat hunger (see particularly Chapters 6 and 7).

13.2   Famines and Undernutrition

The two forms of calamity related to hunger with which this book is concerned are (1) famines, and (2) endemic undernutrition and deprivation. The distinction between the intermittent and explosive occurrence of famines and the quieter and persistent phenomenon of regular undernutrition is important both from the point of view of diagnosis (they have different features and often quite dissimilar causal antecedents) and that of action (they call for substantially distinctive policies and activities).

In the earlier chapters we have had the occasion to discuss the shared conceptual background and interconnected causal circumstances of the two phenomena (Part I: Chapters 1–4). We have also examined and assessed the specific demands on strategies and actions imposed respectively by famines (Part II: Chapters 5–8) and by endemic deprivation (Part III: Chapters 9–12). The distinction relates closely to the different demands of what we have respectively called 'entitlement *protection*' and 'entitlement *promotion*'.[4] The task of entitlement protection is largely a matter of making sure that vulnerable groups do not face a collapse of their ability to command food and related necessities. Possible threats can arise not only from production failures—of non-food commodities as well as food—but also from worsening opportunities of acquiring the basic necessities (e.g. through unemployment, collapse of real wages, worsening of terms of trade). The concentration here has to be on preventing sharp declines in the economic circumstances of those who live close to the borderline of starvation. In contrast with the largely conservative task of entitlement protection, the exercise of entitlement *promotion* is, in many respects, more radical. In this case the concentration has to be on expanding the general command that people—particularly the more deprived sections of the population—have over basic necessities.

Of the two phenomena, famine clearly is much more visible and easier to diagnose. It is also a good deal easier to eradicate than regular undernutrition. Indeed, it is remarkable that famines continue to occur in the modern world despite the relative ease with which they can be totally eliminated through public action. The possibility of such termination has been amply illustrated by the experiences of many countries that have successfully achieved the transition.[5]

To make the eradication of famines more universal, some of the common tactics of anti-famine policy would have to be replaced by strategies that take fuller account of the economic and social realities in the famine-prone coun-

---

[4] See Chapter 1 on the respective definitions and characterizations, including that of the notion of 'entitlements' itself. In this concluding chapter, as in the earlier ones, several specific concepts and categories are freely used without redefinition, since they have been explicitly discussed and explained in the first chapter of this book.

[5] As was mentioned earlier, this applies not only to the often-discussed case of India, but also to many success stories from sub-Saharan Africa, e.g., in Botswana, Cape Verde, Zimbabwe (on these and other experiences, see Chapter 8).

tries. We have tried to clarify the nature of these required strategies (Part II), and we shall make a few further remarks on them in the next section.

Endemic undernutrition is a less obvious—less 'loud'—phenomenon than famine. Though it kills many more people in the long run than famines do, it does not get the kind of dramatic media attention that famines generate. But even in terms of sheer mortality, many times more people are killed slowly by regular undernourishment and deprivation than by the rarer and more confined occurrence of famine. Endemic deprivation is also a more complex social condition, involving deep-rooted economic and social deficiencies. Eliminating it is a much more difficult task than preventing famines. But it has been achieved to varying extents by many different developing countries, and there are lessons in these experiences.

The objectives of public action against endemic hunger have to go well beyond the enhancement of food intake. Human well-being relates to the lives that people can live—their 'capabilities'—rather than only to the commodities they can command. In the context of hunger, we are concerned with the ability that people have to lead a life without undernourishment, and not with the quantities of their food intake as such (on this see Chapter 3).

Even as far as *entitlements* are concerned (i.e. the command over commodities that people have), the relevant characterization must take note of all the commodities that can significantly influence a person's ability to lead a life without undernourishment. This would typically include not only food, but also health care and medical attention, since parasitic and other diseases contribute substantially to undernourishment as well as ill health. The list of important commodities must also include such items as clean water, living space and sanitation.

In fact, capabilities depend not only on the commodities consumed, but also on their *utilization*, as was discussed in Chapter 1. Variations in utilization (i.e. in the conversion of commodities into capabilities) can arise from the biological and social characteristics of persons, e.g., a pregnant woman may need more nutrients to achieve the same level of nourishment as another person. These variations can be important for policy planning, and entitlement analysis —focused as it always is on commodities as opposed to capabilities—cannot be a fully adequate basis for assessment of public action. Even when the utilization rates are not much influencible by policy, the fact of varying utilization rates has to be taken into account, particularly for assessing distributions of commodity entitlements (e.g. between women and men).[6]

But quite often rates of utilization may well be influencible by public action and policy. For example, if lack of information and knowledge about nutrition and health, or blind acceptance of injurious practices and traditions, reduces the capabilities that a person can get from a given entitlement to food and health care, then an expansion of education can—quite possibly—much

[6] On this see Sen (1984a, 1985a, 1987c).

enhance the person's nutritional capabilities. In this case, the entitlement to—and the actual use of—educational opportunities must also be included among the relevant focal points for policy. Education is not only of direct importance to living (e.g., in broadening a person's horizon of perception and thought), it can also influence the conversion of other entitlements into human abilities (e.g., the conversion of incomes into nutritional capabilities).

In fact, the expansion of basic education in general, and of female education in particular, can have several distinct roles in reducing endemic undernourishment.[7] Some of the influences of educational expansion may operate *through* affecting the person's entitlement to food and health care, e.g., by making the person more employable (and thus raising her income), or by making her more influential in demanding public provisioning of these basic essentials (through informed criticism of public policy and more articulate demands). The influence of education may also work through increasing the person's ability to *use* the available opportunities and entitlements (including the public services offered, e.g., through more extensive and better informed utilization of health services).[8] Finally, educational expansion can also lead to a less prejudiced intrahousehold distribution of food and health care. For example, greater female literacy tends to increase the bargaining power of women within the household and can reduce anti-female bias in nutritional division.[9]

In assessing the policies and programmes that have been used in different countries to promote entitlements and to expand basic capabilities of the people, we identified some common elements in the effective strategies, but also noted some genuine plurality of possible approaches (see Part III). We shall comment briefly on the similarities and pluralities in section 13.4 of this chapter.

13.3   Famine Prevention

In Chapters 5 to 8 of this book we have examined various aspects of anti-famine strategies. While there is much to learn from the informal security systems that have existed for a long time in famine-prone countries, it is also clear that an adequate system of famine prevention has to go well beyond strengthening these traditional security systems. For example, sometimes informal insurance arrangements based on community-centred mutual support can be of great use

[7] The positive connection between female education and the elimination of undernutrition has been investigated in a number of recent studies; see, e.g., Caldwell (1979), Behrman and Wolfe (1984, 1987), Cornia (1984), Ware (1984), Jain (1985), Mosley (1985a), Cleland and van Ginneken (1987), Levine (1988), Senauer and Garcia (1988), Thomas et al. (1988a, 1988b).

[8] For example, there is considerable evidence that the high level of basic education, especially female literacy, in Kerala leads to a better search for and exploitation of available medical services compared with the rest of India (see Nag 1985, 1989, and Caldwell 1986). This reinforces Kerala's advantage in having more public health services on offer. On Kerala's experience, see Chapter 11.

[9] On this issue, see Chapter 4, and also Chapter 11.

(as has indeed been found on different occasions in the past), but in other cases such arrangements can help very little since the economic viability of the entire community may be simultaneously undermined leaving little room for mutual support. The entitlements of the vulnerable groups may be threatened in many different ways, and the preventive system has to cover all the likely sources.

In the recent literature on famine prevention, much attention has been paid to formal systems of 'early warning' of famine threats. The advantages of getting such warnings are clear enough, but nevertheless we have not found the refinement of formal 'early warning systems' to be a crucial requirement of an effective anti-famine strategy. Countries that have been remarkably successful in preventing famines through timely public action typically have not made much use of such formal systems. This applies to countries as diverse as India, Botswana, Cape Verde and Zimbabwe.

Indeed, most often the warnings of imminent dangers have tended to come from general reports of floods or droughts or economic dislocations and from newspaper coverage of early hardship and visible hunger. In countries with relatively pluralist political systems, open channels of protest have also helped to direct forcefully the attention of the authorities to the need for preventive action without delay. Varieties of administrative, journalistic and political communications have served the 'early warning' role in the absence of elaborate systems of famine prediction or of formal procedures of 'early warning'.

Of course, informal ways of anticipating famine threats can sometimes mislead. But so can formal systems of 'early warning', which are often based on some rather simple model (explicitly invoked or implicitly presumed), paying attention to a few variables and ignoring many others. There is undoubtedly scope for improving famine warning systems based on economic analysis.[10] But there is little chance that a formal model can be developed that would be practically usable (with all the necessary data inputs being marshallable with the required speed) and that would take adequate note of all the variables that may possibly be relevant in the wide variety of cases that can, in fact, arise. The supplementation of formal economic models by more informal systems of communication and analysis is, to a great extent, inescapable.

In fact, most cases of neglected famine threats reflect not so much a lack of knowledge that could have been remedied only with formal systems of prediction, but negligence or smugness or callousness on the part of the non-responding authorities. In this context it is important to note that such informal systems of warning as newspaper reports and public protests carry not only information that the authorities *can* use, but also elements of pressure that may make it politically compelling to respond to these danger signals and do something about them urgently. It is, we have argued, no accident that the

---

[10] On different lines of possible improvement, see e.g. Cutler (1985b), Desai (1986), Borton and York (1987), Autier (1988), Walker (1988), Autier et al. (1989), Swift (forthcoming).

countries that have been most successful in famine prevention in the recent past have typically had rather pluralistic politics with open channels of communication and criticism. A relatively free newspaper system may be the most effective 'early warning' system a famine-prone country can rely on.

The issue of early warning is closely linked to that of preparedness. There is great advantage in being able to rely on ongoing famine prevention systems that do not have to be devised as and when a particular threat arises. Contingency plans indicating what to do and when to do it can make the exercise of famine prevention a great deal more reliable. Aside from avoiding the confusions that are typical of suddenly devised *ad hoc* response, a general system of this kind also has the advantage of integrating different programmes of action in which many agents may be involved but which do call for coordination at the national level.

As far as policies for entitlement protection are concerned, in Chapters 6 to 8 we had the opportunity to assess various methods that have been tried. Since most of the particular findings were put together in the concluding sections of these chapters, we need not cover that specific ground again. However, it is perhaps worth mentioning that we have argued in favour of strategies of entitlement protection based on employment creation, particularly in the form of public works programmes. This strategy is an efficient counter-measure to the loss of entitlements resulting from one of many possible changes (such as loss of employment or income or output due to droughts or floods) which may induce starvation of the affected group of people. This policy is also in line with the fact that, in most sub-Saharan African countries, seeking wage labour has become, these days, one of the chief survival strategies for vulnerable populations in times of crisis. Further, public employment is also a particularly effective solution to the 'selection problem', i.e., identifying *whom* to assist (discussed in Chapter 7).

The other major advantage of a strategy of employment provision (discussed in Chapter 6) is that it offers the possibility of greater reliance on 'cash support' (as opposed to the direct provision of food, cooked or uncooked). Indeed the payment of cash wages in exchange for labour may be the only practicable form of large-scale cash support in famine situations. Given the urgency of relief in a situation of famine threat, the advantages of being able to avoid the delays involved in moving and distributing food through bureaucratic channels can be quite crucial. By combining (1) public intervention (through cash wage payments—rather than leaving potential famine victims unaided), and (2) selective use of markets (in allowing food to be moved by the normal channels of trade—in response to the newly generated demand), it is possible to avoid both the inefficiency of bureaucratic food distribution and the unreliability of depending only on market-generated entitlements. It is the combination of different institutional arrangements that seems to provide, in many cases, the most reliable means of preventing famines effectively.

The possibility of using the market mechanism to supplement public intervention should not, however, be interpreted to imply that there is, then, no need for a substantial public stock of food grains. Public holding of food stocks can be crucial, even when the main burden of entitlement protection is carried by income generation programmes, and even when food movements and trade are largely left in private hands.

As was discussed in Chapter 6, public food stocks can help famine prevention in a variety of ways. First, they may be important to prevent collusive actions by traders in response to the enhanced demand for food resulting from income generation programmes. The 'threat' of breaking artificially generated price increases through releasing public stocks of food in the market can be very effective in preventing traders' collusion. Second, public food stocks can also prevent price rises due to panic and overestimation of future increases in food prices. This can be important even if there is no collusion on the part of traders.[11] Third, while we have argued that entitlement protection measures need not necessarily *await* an improvement of food availability through the public distribution system, the process of famine prevention can, of course, be very substantially helped by the release of food in the market—exercising a downward pressure on rising prices. Public stocks of food can be particularly important for market stabilization given the delays that are typically involved in importing food.

Famine prevention strategies are often designed on the assumption that it is crucial to achieve a strong influence on the intra-family distribution of food (e.g., in favour of young or undernourished children). We have argued that, in practice, the information and control needed for such discrimination are typically hard to obtain. There may, in fact, be good grounds for seeking the cooperation of the family unit in situations of famine vulnerability, rather than threatening its cohesiveness through divisive distribution practices.[12] This view relates partly to the incentive problems associated with attempts to influence the distribution of food within the family (see Chapter 7), and partly

---

[11] See Ravallion (1987a) on the process through which a market can 'overshoot' in anticipating price increases even without much collusion by traders. See also his analysis of the overreaction of food markets in the Bangladesh famine of 1974. Those food markets undoubtedly suffered from the general knowledge that there was relatively little food in public stock held by the government in Bangladesh. The suspension of US food aid to Bangladesh in the crucial period also added to the helplessness of the government to break the price rise through its own stock. The US government resumed its food aid only after Bangladesh accepted its demand that it should stop exporting jute to Cuba—by which time the famine was nearly over (on this see Rothschild 1976, McHenry and Bird 1977, Sobhan 1979, 1986). The lessons of that experience certainly underline further the advantages of holding a sizeable public stock of food grains as a general precautionary strategy.

[12] This point refers specifically to famine situations, and is not meant to indicate any general scepticism regarding the merits of nutritional intervention through individual feeding. In fact, rather different issues are raised in assessing such intervention in the context of chronic hunger and endemic undernutrition. See Chapters 3 and 6, and also Berg (1973, 1981, 1987a, 1987b), Gwatkin et al. (1980), Austin and Zeitlin (1981), Beaton and Ghasseimi (1982), Underwood (1983), Sen and Sengupta (1983), Pinstrup-Andersen and Biswas (1985), Godfrey (1986a, 1986b), Field (1987), Kumar and Stewart (1987), Norgan (1988), among others.

to the evidence of preferential treatment of young children in the early stages of a famine in many societies (Chapter 5).

As far as gender discrimination is concerned, we have found ample evidence of the enormity of the problem of chronic female disadvantage in nutrition and health in many parts of the world (Chapter 4). This problem is, however, distinctly less acute in sub-Saharan Africa—where most famines tend to take place these days—than in, say, South Asia or China or West Asia. Also, there is little evidence that gender discrimination plays a major additional role in the causation of *famine mortality* in particular, despite its importance in the determination of mortality in general (see section 4.4). The need to counter gender inequality—important in general—would not, therefore, seem to undermine, in the specific context of famines, the case for greater reliance on prevention strategies which concentrate on the regeneration of *household* incomes (e.g., through employment provision) rather than on *individual* support (e.g., through feeding). In fact, given the very high rates of female participation in public works programmes observed in most parts of the developing world, and the importance of female employment for the reduction of intra-family inequalities, gender considerations would seem to add strength to the case for employment-based famine prevention strategies.

The provision of employment cannot, of course, be an answer to all the different aspects of the famine prevention problem. For one thing, the choice of selection mechanism requires enough versatility to take note of the diversity of potential famine victims. In particular, additional provision must always be made for those (usually in relatively small numbers) who can neither work nor rely on the support of able-bodied relatives. However, the inability to work is a relatively easily observable condition, which can form the basis of administrative selection for 'unconditional relief'. Direct distribution of cash or food on the basis of fairly unambiguous selection criteria has indeed been found eminently practicable in many countries (see the case studies of Chapter 8).

It must also be remembered that the strategy of employment provision operates mainly through private incomes. While a good case can be made for regarding income generation as the most urgent and basic task in a situation of famine vulnerability, the survival of vulnerable groups also depends substantially on adequate access to a number of crucial public goods and services, including especially clean water, health care and sanitation. A comprehensive strategy of entitlement protection requires paying adequate attention to these public provisions.

13.4   Eliminating Endemic Deprivation

As was mentioned earlier, the elimination of regular hunger and undernutrition is a much harder task than the eradication of famines. The phenomenon of endemic deprivation is more pervasive; it affects many times the number of people who are threatened by famines. It is also more resistant to change, since it requires widespread promotion—on a long-term basis—of entitlements beyond well-established levels, and not just protecting established entitlements from short-term declines (as in the case of famine prevention).

Nevertheless, it is not hard to see what is needed for the elimination of endemic undernutrition and deprivation. People earn their means of living through employment and production, and they use these means to achieve certain functionings which make up their living. Entitlements and the corresponding capabilities can be promoted by the expansion of private incomes on a widespread basis, including all the deprived sections of the population. They can also be promoted by extensive public provisioning of the basic essentials for good living such as health care, education and food. Indeed, participatory growth and public provisioning are among the chief architects of the elimination of endemic deprivation—illustrated amply by historical experiences across the world. The basic challenge of 'social security' (in the broad sense in which we have used this term) is to combine these instruments of action to guarantee adequate living standards to all.

The problem of undernutrition cannot be divorced from that of morbidity and ill health—both because undernourishment makes one prone to illness and also because a good deal of the observed undernourishment in the world is due to the effect of parasitic and other diseases which make the absorption and retention of nourishment that much more difficult. Thus—as was discussed earlier—the entitlements that have to be promoted for eliminating persistent undernutrition are not merely of food, but also of health care, medical attention and epidemiological environment (just as the entitlements to be promoted for eliminating preventable morbidity include food as well as medical care).

Further, as we discussed earlier, basic education too has a major role in the eradication of both undernourishment and preventable morbidity. This is not merely because education helps in the use of one's personal means to buy food and medicine in a more informed way, but also because widespread elementary education leads to greater utilization of public health services. It can also generate more effective political demand that such services be provided. Furthermore, an educated public can more easily participate in national economic growth—partly through the expansion of remunerative employment—making the fruits of growth more widely shared. All this is in addition to the part that education directly plays in making human lives more worthwhile through broadening one's horizon of thought and experience.

The essential entitlements to be promoted for eliminating endemic deprivation and undernutrition, thus, include basic health care and elementary education in addition to food as such. They also include other necessities such as clean water, living space and basic sanitation. Many countries have achieved great success over the last few decades in widespread promotion of these essential entitlements and the corresponding capabilities to function. In terms of a simple criterion of the promotion of elementary capabilities (specifically, the reduction of infant and child mortality), ten countries were identified in Chapter 10 as having produced the fastest transformation since 1960. All of them have impressive records of gearing public policy towards guaranteeing widespread access to these basic ingredients of living.

However, there are also interesting diversities in their experiences. We have distinguished between two broad strategies for promoting basic social security for all. One strategy—called 'growth-mediated security'—has taken the form of fast growth of real national income per head and the use of the fruits of this growth to enhance the living conditions on a wide basis. Countries in this category among the identified ten include both newly industrializing countries such as South Korea, Hong Kong and Singapore, and also countries that have benefited from the rise in oil prices, in particular Kuwait and United Arab Emirates. All these countries have not only achieved much higher real income per head, they have used the fruits of that growth to expand the basic entitlements to food, health care and elementary education for all (see Chapter 10). Indeed, despite the role of private enterprise in these economies, in all cases the state has played a major part in promoting social security by bringing the basic ingredients of living within the reach of all the citizens—either through direct provisioning or through ensuring a participatory form of economic growth.

The other strategy, which has been called 'support-led security', has taken the form of promoting—through direct public support—entitlements to education, health care and food, without waiting for the national income per head to rise to a high level through general economic growth. Countries in this category among the ten include not only China and Cuba, but also Costa Rica, Chile and Jamaica.[13] The experiences of these countries (on which see Chapters 11 and 12) bring out the possibility of avoiding a longish 'wait' in the elimination of hunger and acute deprivation by immediate use of extensive public support.

In seeing the range of possibilities that are open to different developing countries, it is important to examine both the common elements and the contrasting features of the experiences of successful countries. The strategies of support-led security and growth-mediated security have the common feature of marshalling public action to involve diverse sections of the population in the process of social and economic transformation. In particular, countries in both groups have made extensive use of public provisioning

---

[13] One country that has achieved no less than any of these five in terms of support-led security is Sri Lanka. But in its case the main expansion took place *prior to* 1960, and it is thus not included in the list of top performers in the 1960–85 comparison. On this and on the assessment of Sri Lanka's policies, see Chapter 12. Another interesting experience is that of the state of Kerala in India which has also achieved extraordinary success in support-led security. Kerala is not included in the list of top performing countries since it is not a country but only a state in a federal country (even though in population size it is much larger than several of the countries actually included in the list, such as Hong Kong, Singapore, Kuwait and United Arab Emirates). For an analysis of Kerala's experience, see Chapter 11.

(especially in health care, basic education and food distribution) to enhance living conditions.

The experience of each group here contrasts with that of countries which have grown fast—in terms of GNP or real income per head—without using the fruits of growth to bring the essential ingredients of living within the reach of most people. In this respect the contrast between, say, Kuwait or South Korea or Singapore, on the one hand, and Brazil or Oman, on the other, is very sharp indeed. While the latter countries too have experienced fast economic growth, they have failed to ensure widespread public participation in the process of expansion of private incomes, and have not used extensive public support programmes to guarantee basic entitlements to the vulnerable sections of the population. For example, the fruits of growth have been used for public provisioning of education and health care in Kuwait, South Korea and Singapore in a way that simply has not happened in, say, Brazil or Oman.

The experiences of what we called 'unaimed opulence', of which Brazil provides a good illustration, show that growth as such is not a dependable strategy for enhancing elementary well-being and capability. If it is to serve as a solid basis for promoting living conditions, growth must take a participatory form (e.g., with widespread creation of remunerative employment), *and* a substantial part of the resources made available by economic growth has to be devoted to the expansion of public provisioning. Since the participatory nature of the growth process, particularly in the form of widespread access to remunerative employment, is itself dependent on certain preconditions that can be influenced by public provisioning (e.g., of elementary education), the role of public provisioning in distinguishing between 'unaimed opulence' and 'growth-mediated security' is quite central.

The use of public support in general—and of public provisioning in particular—is, thus, a common element in the experiences of growth-mediated security and support-led security, and the main difference is one of timing and sequencing. In the case of China or Cuba or Sri Lanka or Costa Rica, the countries concerned have not waited to get rich before embarking on ambitious programmes of public support. In the case of Kuwait, opulence has come first, but the gains from wealth have been transformed into better living conditions mainly through generous public provisioning. In South Korea, the expansion of private incomes played a relatively larger part, but public support—especially in the promotion of education, skills and employment —was crucial in ensuring participatory growth.[14] There are clearly different

---

[14] Another major factor in this success story of private enterprise has been Korea's fairly comprehensive land reforms, which took place early and contributed greatly to the sharing of the fruits of economic growth. Further, the role of the state in that country's planned economic expansion based on guided private enterprise is also important to study (e.g., the part played by state planning in industrial expansion, in a way not altogether dissimilar to what had happened in Japan earlier). As was discussed in Chapter 10, the Korean 'miracle' must not be seen in terms of an imaginary policy of *laissez faire*, since that has not been a feature of that country's route to success.

time patterns of social and economic change in the two broad strategies identified here, but also a commonality of the use of state involvement and public action in particular fields that are directly relevant for enhancing the basic capabilities of the population.

In promoting the elementary capabilities of living without undernourishment, escapable morbidity and preventable mortality, major contributions are made by the entitlements that people enjoy to food, health services, medical attention, good epidemiological environment and basic education. In the promotion of guaranteed entitlements to these essentials, public provisioning can play an important part. In fact, in most countries in the world, public provisioning is—for good economic and social reasons—a standard part of the delivery system of many of these vital ingredients of basic living. This applies even to the richer—more industrialized—countries in the world, and, as was discussed in Chapter 10, the history of longevity expansion in these countries has commonly involved crucial contributions of direct public provisioning. What the experiences of the countries with 'support-led security' bring out is the possibility of making these vital ingredients of quality of life widely available even when the country is still quite poor.

We have discussed earlier (in Chapter 12) the apparently perplexing question as to how this type of public provisioning could possibly be affordable by poor countries. One simple point to note is that some of the epidemiological transformations in health care, e.g., the elimination of infectious vectors, are remarkably economic in terms of resource use, and a great deal can be achieved in reducing preventable morbidity and premature mortality through fairly simple and inexpensive public policy. The same applies to the promotion of literacy and basic education.

A more complex aspect of this issue is the relevance of relative prices in the determination of real costs. Both elementary education and health care are extremely labour-intensive in their provisioning, and one of the characteristics of a poor economy is the cheapness of labour—and of training labour for elementary education and basic medical services. Thus, the poorer economies not only have less money to spend on providing these services, they also *need* less money for making these provisions. The handicap of national poverty is, therefore, to some extent reduced through the cheapness of labour costs as far as these public services are concerned, provided the country orientates its public policy to generate enough training of the appropriate kind. The bite of the financial constraints can also be substantially reduced by giving priority to basic services and to the needs of the most deprived people.[15]

13.5 *Food Production, Distribution and Prices*

The recognition of the role of direct public support in enhancing capabilities does not, of course, deny the importance of aggregate production. Indeed,

[15] See Chapters 11 and 12.

public provisioning should not be seen simply as a distributive device, even though it may be aimed at bringing basic ingredients of living within the reach of all. When elementary education or basic health services are provided more widely, the total production of these commodities is also expanded, so that the process is one of enlargement of production as well as of equitable distribution. It is not so much that the same bundle of commodities is more equally distributed as a result of this process, but that larger aggregate outputs of education and health services are produced, and it is from this enhanced production that the new recipients get their own share.[16]

This is not to deny that there can be, in particular cases, a conflict between aggregative and distributive considerations in policy making. A number of such conflicts were discussed earlier on in this book in the context of specific policies. In the particular context of food policy as such a conflict that has received some attention recently is that between the productive influences of high food prices *vis-à-vis* their possibly regressive distributional effects.[17] That low food prices tend to depress production incentives is certainly correct, and it has been argued with some force that this has been one of the factors behind the food production crisis in sub-Saharan Africa. While there are clearly many other aspects of the African food production problem (as was discussed in Chapters 2 and 9), low food prices can be seen as being among the contributory factors.

There is not much difficulty in accepting fairly readily that higher food prices can lead to a larger volume of food output being produced, but it would be a mistake to assume that, whenever that is the case, good public policy would require a considerable raising of food prices. We have to be concerned not only with the total volume of food produced, but also—indeed primarily —with the food consumption of the different sections of the population. Higher food prices, even as they increase the total food output, may reduce drastically the ability of the poor to buy food, and thus a larger volume of aggregate food output might actually go with a reduced consumption of the most vulnerable people. There is a real issue of conflict involved between the positive production incentives and the reduced affordability associated with

---

[16] Indeed, even the greater *use* of available health services as a result of the expanded education of the population (discussed earlier) must be seen as an enhancement of actual *production* of these services, since more of these services are then produced and used. Unfortunately, the usual estimations of the 'output' of public health services often does not record this basic fact. One reason for this is the tendency to measure the output generated by public provisioning in some mechanical way, e.g., in terms of the volume of public expenditure itself, or in units of theoretically available capacities rather than the actual volume of services used by the public.

[17] It is a common belief that the problem of regressive distributional effects of high food prices does not apply in much of sub-Saharan Africa, where most of the poor are thought to be peasant farmers who would *benefit* from an increase in the ordinary level of food prices. Recent empirical studies, however, suggest that in many African countries the number of poor who depend on market purchases of food for their survival is in fact large (and rapidly growing). On this see, among other contributions, Iliffe (1987), von Braun (1988), Weber *et al.* (1988), Liedholm and Kilby (1989).

high food prices. Which way the balance of advantages would lie is not just a matter of being either a hard-nosed 'productionist' or a soft-hearted 'distributionist', but also of knowing precisely how the different groups of consumers would be affected by the new equilibrium with higher food prices.[18]

In this book we have not tried to argue in general for 'high' or 'low' food prices. These are instrumental issues and can be resolved only in terms of the relevant features of each case, taking into account the production effects as well as distributional impact.[19] That itself amounts to a denial of such often-advocated policies as total reliance on 'getting prices right'. This is not only because the 'rightness' of prices depends ultimately on our overall objectives (including the assessment of social welfare) and must not be seen simply as a matter of what the market mechanism would have determined, but also because there is so much more to a sound food strategy than just fiddling with food prices.[20] Other issues include policy matters (e.g., technology, environmental improvement) related to the production of food and also of crucial non-food commodities (e.g., other outputs that generate income, or the supply of commodities such as health and education). The solution of the food problem requires a great deal more than getting food prices 'right'.

We have also emphasized the links between the economic and the political aspects of the food problem. Even in the context of the general diagnosis that the food production crisis in, say, sub-Saharan Africa arises partly from having unduly low food prices, the question can be asked as to why this is the direction in which food prices tend to 'err' in so many different countries. It would be amazing if the answer had nothing to do with the relative political powers enjoyed by the different classes and groups, e.g., the contrasting interests of food-growing peasants and the food-buying urban élite. Whether we see this in terms of the hold of a handful of administrators with interests of their own, or in line with what has been called a general 'urban bias' in development policies, or in terms of some other political analysis, it would be naïve to concentrate on 'getting prices right' without also addressing the underlying political factors that lead to these price biases.[21]

---

[18] Dharm Narain (1988) in particular has clarified a number of issues involved in this conflict. On his contributions and their general bearing on economic policy, see also Mellor and Desai (1985). On different aspects of 'food price dilemmas' in developing countries, see Timmer (1984, 1986), Pinstrup-Andersen (1985b), Ghai and Smith (1986), Kanbur (1986a), Lipton (1987a), Streeten (1987), Besley and Kanbur (1988), Mellor and Ahmed (1988), Ray (1988a, 1988b), among others.

[19] These effects would, of course, depend inter alia on the particular way in which it is proposed to influence food prices (e.g. through devaluation, imports, indirect taxes, food price subsidies).

[20] For analyses of the relationship between general development problems and food strategies, see Valdés (1981), Basu (1984), Swaminathan (1986), Boyce (1987), Gittinger et al. (1987), Mellor et al. (1987), Pinstrup-Andersen (1987, 1988b), Rukini and Eicher (1987), Eicher (1988a), Lipton (1988a). Many of the underlying issues have been investigated by various authors in the papers included in Drèze and Sen (forthcoming).

[21] On various political aspects of these economic relations, see among others Bauer (1954), Lipton (1977), Mitra (1977), Byres (1979), Bates (1981, 1983, 1986), Sobhan (1986), Hopkins (1988), Streeten (1989).

Discussion of food problems in Africa and elsewhere has often suffered from a systematic narrowing of vision to a few variables, overlooking the reach and relevance of many other factors. This can be seriously misleading for public policy. We have discussed earlier on in this book how the nature of the problem of hunger—both famines and endemic deprivation—calls for a broader political economic analysis taking note of the variety of influences that have a bearing on the commodity commands and basic capabilities that people enjoy. The case for such a broader focus—rejecting a cramped analysis—should not be interpreted as being something equally simplistic, though on the 'opposite' side, e.g., being 'anti-price-policy' or 'anti-production'. Production and prices belong to the analysis, but do so along with other concerns.

13.6   International Cooperation and Conflict

The agents of change in conquering hunger can come from inside or outside the country in question. It may be thought that the focus of this book has been primarily on forces that operate from *inside*. This would be fair comment. We have indeed mainly concentrated on what can be done through public action *within* the country to eradicate hunger. This should not be taken to imply that we believe that international help cannot be of any great use in combating hunger. We do believe that both famine prevention and the eradication of endemic undernutrition call for leadership and coordination coming from inside rather than outside the country, but that does not imply that international help cannot supplement these efforts effectively.[22] Nor that international conflicts of interest do not hinder an adequate solution of the problem of hunger in the modern world.[23]

Some of the policies we have discussed will undoubtedly call for international reform and coordination. Environmental protection is an obvious example. This type of international effort will be increasingly important in the future. There is also a good case for making sure that the countries battered by famines or undernutrition do not have to face severely restricted world markets, e.g., markets in the rich countries from which their goods are systematically excluded. The need for confronting and eliminating collusion and manipulation in food markets can also be important. Further, there is need for international cooperation in dealing with the excessive burden of debt that is borne by some of the poorest countries, especially in sub-Saharan Africa.[24]

[22] We have discussed in the context of famine prevention the helpful part that international agencies can play in strengthening and supplementing national efforts. But we have also discussed the advantages of the leadership of famine prevention being in the hands of national governments, with public participation (see Chapters 6–8).

[23] Various aspects of the bearing of international interest conflicts on the problem of hunger have been investigated by George (1976, 1984, 1988), Lappé and Collins (1979, 1980), Byron (1982), Twose (1984), Parikh (1986), among others.

[24] On the scope for 'cooperative debt relief', with special reference to Africa, see Jacques Drèze *et al.* (1989).

These and many other areas of possible international cooperation are of obvious importance.

There has recently been a great deal of debate about the pros and cons of aid in general and of food aid in particular. This is not the occasion to attempt a general assessment of that complex and tangled problem.[25] There is indeed a need to 'de-escalate' the issue. It is not hard to find cases in which aid will help, e.g., by providing timely relief, by permitting a larger investment for the benefit of living standards. Nor is it difficult to find other cases in which much harm does follow from aid, e.g., through economic or political dependency, or through the spread of corruption. It is hard to believe that aid can emerge as being just generally good or generally bad. Like all other policies and institutions, aid too has to be assessed by balancing its positive and negative consequences in the respective contexts.

It may, however, be worth commenting briefly on a particular argument that has often been used to argue generally against food aid as such. It has been pointed out that food aid tends to depress food prices and thus reduces the incentive to produce more food. There is some truth in this way of looking at the problem, but it can scarcely be seen as a decisive rebuttal of the case for food aid. First, production is, as was discussed earlier, only one part of the overall picture of entitlement determination, and has to be supplemented by distributive considerations, which can be especially important when the use of food aid is geared to giving relief to the needy. Second, food production is only one part of total production, and the ability of people to command food will depend also on the effects on the production of *other* goods which generate employment and income; it is quite inadequate to look only at the incentive effects on food output. Third, what the impact of food aid will be on food prices is not a fact of nature but a matter of policy. It is not particularly complex to make sure, if it is so desired, that food aid does not lower the food prices that producers receive. Indeed, the element of income-gain involved in receiving food aid makes it also possible to have a consumer subsidy that makes the prices that producers receive exceed the prices the consumers have to pay. In general the effects of food aid on prices will depend on what is done with it. The tendency to believe that it must—of necessity—adversely affect incentives is far from correct.

While aid is often seen as the central 'international' aspect of the problem of world hunger, it is possible to argue that an international issue that is no less important is that of war and peace. The problem of hunger is made much worse by the war-torn nature of the world. Many of the great famines in the world have been associated with actual wars—varying from armed conflicts in Biafra and Eritrea to the 'killing fields' of Kampuchea. Wars increase a country's

---

[25] For a general analysis of the contribution of aid, see Cassen *et al.* (1986). For a strong defence of food aid, see Dawson (1985), Singer *et al.* (1987); see also Clay and Singer (1985). On the other side, see Jackson and Eade (1982), Bauer (1984), Griffin (1987).

vulnerability to famines in many different ways: (1) through the destruction of crops, (2) by destroying resources including land and the environment, (3) by deflecting resources from economic development and welfare programmes to military expenditure, (4) by disrupting trade, commerce and economic activity, (5) by making the provision of organized relief for the hungry much harder, (6) by causing population displacements and generating masses of destitute refugees, and (7) through the suppression of the freedom of the press and civil rights, and by making the country less tolerant of protest and pluralism.

Sub-Saharan Africa in particular has been especially torn by strife and warfare, with terrible consequences on hunger and deprivation. Angola, Chad, Ethiopia, Mozambique, Somalia, Sudan, and many other countries have been transformed to a greater or lesser extent into veritable battlefields. Quite a few of these wars have been directly or indirectly associated with global conflicts and the cold war, with the African governments falling in line with one international side or another. The big powers have also been remarkably tolerant of regimes on their respective sides despite persistent violations of the very principles of democracy and socialism on behalf of which the big powers allegedly wage their respective battles. It is a story in which there is little honour—either locally, or in the distant capitals from which many international conflicts have been pursued with such vigour and lethal arms pushed with such energetic cunning. It is arguable that one of the biggest contributions that the big powers can make to the solution of the problem of world hunger is to refrain from exacerbating armed conflicts in the 'third world'.

The disastrous effects of wars (and war preparations) on the problem of human well-being and hunger sharply contrast with the success that some of the poorer countries have achieved by giving low priority to military expenditure. Costa Rica which abolished its army in 1949 is the most obvious example. The saving of resources involved has certainly helped to channel economic efforts to the improvement of living standards.

The international aspects of world hunger are indeed extensive. In addition to the much-debated issues of aid, trade and debt, they include problems of international coordination involved in environmental protection and—less palpably but most surely—the problems of war and peace, which can have such a crucial influence on the successes and failures of different countries in eradicating famines and endemic hunger. Once again the need is to take an adequately broad view of the causal antecedents of starvation and undernutrition. That general theme has, of course, been a recurrent one in this book.

13.7   Public Action and the Public

The persistence of widespread hunger is one of the most appalling features of the modern world. The fact that so many people continue to die each year from famines, and that many millions more go on perishing from persistent deprivation on a regular basis, is a calamity to which the world has, somewhat incredibly, got coolly accustomed. It does not seem to engender the kind of shock and disquiet that might be reasonable to expect given the enormity of the tragedy. Indeed, the subject often generates either cynicism ('not a lot can be done about it'), or complacent irresponsibility ('don't blame me—it is not a problem for which I am answerable').

Perhaps this is what one should expect with a resilient and continuing calamity of this kind. But it is not at all easy to see why we do not owe each other even the minimal amounts of positive sympathy and solidarity that would make it hard for us to cultivate irresponsible complacency.[26] While we shall not wait for an answer to that ethical question, we must address the issue of cynical pessimism (i.e., the belief that 'not a lot can be done'). There is, in fact, little reason for presuming that the terrible problems of hunger and starvation in the world cannot be changed by human action. Much of this book has been concerned with exploring and clarifying what can be done and how.

As we have discussed, the eradication of famines is a fairly straightforward task, and there is not much difficulty in achieving it given systematic preparedness and the will to act quickly to protect or recreate threatened entitlements (Part II). Indeed, the successes achieved in different Asian and African countries in eliminating famines seem eminently repeatable in others. While the problem of endemic undernutrition and deprivation is harder to deal with, here too the possible lines of policy are clear enough and well illustrated by particular strategies that have already been used in one form or another (Part III). There is little room for cynical pessimism or for paralysing scepticism.

The types of public action needed in different contexts have been discussed earlier on in the book, and there is no need here—in this final section—to go once again into these questions. But it is worth emphasizing that throughout this book, we have seen public action as something involving a great deal more than activities of the state. This is partly because the public can do a great deal for itself even without governmental assistance, but also because the nature of government policy can depend very extensively on the nature of public activism, including articulated demands and criticisms. The connections are easy to identify in many contexts, e.g., the role of adversarial politics and of an active press in forcing the hands of the government to act rapidly enough to abort threatening famines (see Chapter 5). In other contexts, the precise part played by public activism may be harder to identify exactly, even though the influence may be understood to be generally quite strong. For example, the social impact of women's political movements and economic organizations —and more generally of informed discussion and criticism of women's relative deprivation—can be recognized to be quite substantial even when it is

---

[26] This book is not directly concerned with exploring ethical issues as such, and we shall resist going into the question as to what we owe each other as human beings. On the ethical issues raised by the hunger and suffering of people at a distance from us, see Onora O'Neill's (1987) powerful and far-reaching analysis. See also Sen (1982d, 1985a, 1988e).

hard to specify the exact details of the process of influence (see Chapters 4 and 11).

It is also worth noting, in general, that effective action is not only a matter of informed analysis, but also one of determination and will. The idea of the 'political will' has often been invoked in social analysis. That concept, however, is hard to make very precise, and the tendency to treat it as a 'black box' for 'completing' incomplete explanations has been viewed—rightly —with some suspicion. There are, in fact, many problems in trying to specify the exact process through which a 'political will' is supposed to operate, and there are certainly many connections here that are hard to observe. But, at the same time, it would be a mistake to leave no room whatever in our social analysis for the general influence of firm commitment, uncompromising resolve and dedicated action by the political leadership, and to take no account of the way in which an inspired leadership can generate effective social response.

Indeed, without bringing in the class of concepts that are associated with the general idea of political will and determination, it is difficult to provide an adequate analysis of the process through which, say, a country like China achieved a remarkably rapid improvement in longevity and general health even without a massive increase in GNP per head or in aggregate economic opulence. This success was based on a politically inspired and forcefully led transformation of the access to basic ingredients of living enjoyed by the Chinese population, and we have discussed some of the ways in which that transformation took a concrete shape (see Chapter 11). While there are technical issues here concerning institutional structure, financing arrangements and relative costs, underlying all this was the force provided by a politically committed leadership determined to achieve a radical transformation.

However, it must also be acknowledged that dogmatic commitment and inflexible resolve on the part of the leadership can sometimes be associated with a negative—rather than a constructive—role in combating hunger and deprivation. For example, the same China that achieved so much success through determined public action in transforming health conditions, also carried out—with misplaced confidence—a disastrous set of public policies leading to the largest famine in this century in 1958–61 in the wake of the so-called Great Leap Forward (see Chapter 11). Despite their destructive consequences, these wrong-headed policies could not be modified by the pressure of public criticism both because the leadership was uncompromising and overconfident and because the system did not encourage—or indeed allow—such criticism.[27]

[27] Similarly, the reduction of communal health services in rural China and the imposition of the 'one child' policy and related measures of compulsory birth control, which accompanied the reforms of 1979, were carried out with remarkably little public discussion and opportunity of social criticism, despite the dangers of serious adverse effects on mortality rates (especially on infant mortality).

Aside from this issue of political commitment, we have had several occasions to note the positive role that political *pluralism* can play in the eradication of hunger and deprivation. The contribution of political pluralism relates to the importance of adversarial politics and social criticism in influencing state action in the direction of greater sensitivity to the well-being of the population. The power of public pressure is not, of course, confined to pluralist political systems, and indeed we have discussed how even fairly authoritarian political regimes may have strong incentive to respond to popular demands (as in South Korea or Chile). But it is clear that the scope for effective public influence on the activities of the state tends to be greater in political systems that make room for opposition and criticism. We have discussed, for instance, how the accountability of the Indian government to the electorate (combined with a relatively free press) has made the prevention of famines a political compulsion, in a way that has not applied in China (or in sub-Saharan Africa). We have also noted the crucial role played by participatory politics in the development of public support systems in countries such as Costa Rica, Sri Lanka and Jamaica.

This is not to say that the political systems of these countries are in any way 'exemplary' as far as pluralism and participation are concerned. The demands of different classes typically do not receive equal attention because of the strong links between economic inequality and the distribution of political power. Ultimately, genuine political participation involves a great deal more than the elementary political rights that are recognised in these countries. Also, formal political rights may fall far short of providing a sound basis for political participation when large sections of the public are deprived of the means of effectively exercising these rights and of articulating their demands. We have noted, for instance, how the extraordinary persistence of mass illiteracy in India has contributed to the neglect of many social problems, and has tended to prevent chronic deprivation from becoming a politically sensitive issue in the way that famine has become.[28] But these qualifications, however real and important, do not detract from the general connection that can be observed between the scope for pluralist politics and the role of public activism.

The distinction between the 'collaborative' and 'adversarial' roles of the public has some relevance to this dichotomy between the advantages of political commitment *vis-à-vis* those of political pluralism. While a leadership committed to radical social change can often inspire more public collaboration, having a committed leadership is not adequate for—and may even be hostile to—the exercise of the adversarial role of the public. Since both the roles have value in combating deprivation, it is natural to look for the possibility of combining the advantages of committed leadership with those of pluralist tolerance. Whether such combinations are possible, especially in the circum-

[28] The Indian state of Kerala is an exception to this pattern, and we have discussed how the longstanding achievements of this state in the field of education have borne fruit in the form of a more effective and broad-based system of public support than exists in the rest of India.

stances that rule in most developing countries, remains a challenging question.[29] There is no reason, in principle, why a political system that allows, encourages and helps the public to be active (both adversarially as well as collaboratively) cannot also lead to governments that provide bold initiatives and inspiring leadership. But it is obvious that in practice the actual possibilities are much constrained by social, political and economic circumstances, and the 'ideal combinations' are hard to realize, as the history of the world has shown again and again.

In these concluding comments, we have taken the liberty of raising some very broad questions, drawing on—but going beyond—the analyses presented earlier in the book. Some of these questions are easier to raise than they are to answer. But it is nevertheless important to ask these bigger questions even when the answers are far from clear. While much of this book has been concerned with issues of diagnosis and policy that admit of relatively clear-cut answers (and these we have tried to present sharply enough), it would be misleading not to point to the broader—and 'grander'—questions that lie close to the fields of our inquiry and which can profoundly influence the nature of these fields.

It is important, in this concluding section, to re-emphasize our focus on public participation—collaborative and adversarial—in eradicating famines, undernutrition and deprivation. It is, as we have tried to argue and illustrate, essential to see the public not merely as 'the patient' whose well-being commands attention, but also as 'the agent' whose actions can transform society. Taking note of that dual role is central to understanding the challenge of public action against hunger.

---

[29] This is a question that has come even more to the forefront with the recent demands for democratic rights in China and Eastern Europe.

REFERENCES

ABEILLE, B. (1979), 'A Study of Female Life in Mauritania', mimeo, Office of Women in Development, US Agency for International Development, Washington, DC.

ABEL-SMITH, B. (1986), 'Funding Health for All: Is Insurance the Answer?', *World Health Forum*, 7.

ABELSON, P. H. (ed.) (1975), *Food, Politics, Economics, Nutrition and Research* (Washington, DC: American Association for the Advancement of Science).

ABRAHAM, A. (1980), 'Maharashtra's Employment Guarantee Scheme', *Economic and Political Weekly*, 15.

ACHARYA, S., and PANWALKAR, V. G. (1988*a*), 'The Maharashtra Employment Guarantee Scheme: Impacts on Male and Female Labour', Regional Research Paper (South and South East Asia), The Population Council, Bangkok.

—— —— (1988*b*), 'Labour Force Participation in Rural Maharashtra: A Temporal, Regional and Gender Analysis', Studies on Women Workers No. 2, Asian Employment Programme, International Labour Organization, New Delhi.

ADAMS, M. E. (1986), 'Merging Relief and Development: The Case of Turkana', *Development Policy Review*, 4.

ADMASSIE, Y., and GEBRE, S. (1985), *Food-for-Work in Ethiopia: A Socio-economic Survey* (Addis Ababa: Institute of Development Research, Addis-Ababa University).

ADNAN, S. (1988), 'Birds in a Cage: Institutional Change and Women's Position in Bangladesh', paper presented at a IUSSP Conference on Women's Position and Demographic Change held in Asker (Norway), June 1988.

AFSHAR, H. (ed.) (1987), *Women, State and Ideology: Studies from Africa and Asia* (London: Macmillan).

AGARWAL, B. (1986), 'Women, Poverty and Agricultural Growth in India', *Journal of Peasant Studies*, 13.

—— (1988), 'Social Security and the Family', paper presented at a Workshop on Social Security in Developing Countries held at the London School of Economics, 4–5 July 1988; to be published in Ahmad, S. E., *et al.* (eds.) (forthcoming), *Social Security in Developing Countries*.

—— (ed.) (1989), *Structures of Patriarchy* (London: Zed).

AGERE, S. T. (1986), 'Progress and Problems in the Health Care Delivery System', in Mandaza, I. (ed.) (1986), *Zimbabwe: The Political Economy of Transition 1980–1986*.

AGRAWAL, A. N., VERMA, H. O., and GUPTA, R. C. (1987), *Economic Information Yearbook 1987–88* (New Delhi: National Publishing House).

AHLUWALIA, M. S. (1978), 'Rural Poverty and Agricultural Performance in India', *Journal of Development Studies*, 14.

AHMAD, Q. K. (1985), 'Food Shortages and Food Entitlements in Bangladesh: An Indepth Enquiry in Respect of Selected Years', mimeo, Food and Agriculture Organization, Rome.

AHMAD, S. E., and HUSSAIN, A. (1988), 'Social Security in China: A Historical Perspective', paper presented at a Workshop on Social Security in Developing Countries held at the London School of Economics, 4–5 July 1988; to be published in Ahmad, S. E., *et al.* (eds.) (forthcoming), *Social Security in Developing Countries*.

—— DRÈZE, J. P., HILLS, J., and SEN, A. K. (eds.) (forthcoming), *Social Security in Developing Countries* (Oxford: Oxford University Press).

AIRD, J. (1982), 'Population Studies and Population Policy in China', *Population and Development Review*, 8.

AKERLOF, G. A. (1984), *An Economist's Book of Tales* (Cambridge: Cambridge University Press).

AKONG'A, J. (1982), *Famine, Famine Relief and Public Policy in Kitui District* (Nairobi: Institute for Development Studies).

—— and DOWNING, T. (1987), 'Smallholder Vulnerability and Response to Drought', in Akong'a, J., *et al.* (1987), 'The Effects of Climatic Variations on Agriculture in Central and Eastern Kenya'.

—— —— KONIJN, N. T., MUNGAI, D. N., MUTURI, H. R., and POTTER, H. L. (1987), 'The Effects of Climatic Variations on Agriculture in Central and Eastern Kenya', mimeo, IIASA, Laxenburg; preprinted from Parry, M. L., *et al.* (eds.) (forthcoming), *The Impact of Climatic Variations on Agriculture* (Dordrecht: Reidel).

ALAILIMA, P. (1985), 'Evolution of Government Policies and Expenditure on Social Welfare in Sri Lanka During the 20th Century', mimeo, Colombo.

ALAM, M. S. (1989), 'The South Korean "Miracle": Examining the Mix of Government and Markets', *Journal of Developing Areas*, 23.

ALAMGIR, M. (1978), *Bangladesh: A Case of Below Poverty Level Equilibrium Trap* (Dhaka: Bangladesh Institute of Development Studies).

—— (1980), *Famine in South Asia* (Cambridge, MA: Oelgeschlager, Gunn and Hain).

ALDEREGUIA, J. (1983), 'The Health Status of the Cuban Population', *International Journal of Health Services*, 13.

ALDERMAN, H. (1986), *The Effects of Food Price and Income Changes on the Acquisition of Food by Low-Income Households* (Washington, DC: International Food Policy Research Institute).

—— (1987), 'Allocation of Goods Through Non-Price Mechanisms: Evidence on Distribution by Willingness to Wait', *Journal of Development Economics*, 23.

—— (1988*a*), 'Do Food Subsidies Reach the Poor?', mimeo, International Food Policy Research Institute, Washington, DC.

—— (1988*b*), 'Food Subsidies and State Policies in Egypt', in Richards, A. (ed.) (1988), *Food, States and Peasants: Analysis of the Agrarian Question in the Middle East* (Boulder: Westview Press).

—— (forthcoming), 'Poverty and Undernutrition: How Strongly Linked?', mimeo, International Food Policy Research Institute, Washington, DC.

—— and VON BRAUN, J. (1984), 'The Effects of the Egyptian Food Rationing and Subsidy System on Income Distribution and Consumption', Research Report No. 45, International Food Policy Research Institute, Washington, DC.

ALDERMAN, M. H., WISE, P. H., FERGUSON, R. P., LAVERDE, H. T., and D'SOUZA, A. J. (1978), 'Reduction of Young Child Malnutrition and Mortality in Rural Jamaica', *Journal of Tropical Pediatrics*, 24.

ALFRED, C. (1986), 'Famine and Food Aid Among the Beja', mimeo, OXFAM, Oxford.

ALLEN, G. (1986), 'Famines: The Bowbrick–Sen Dispute and Some Related Issues', *Food Policy*, 11.

ALLISON, C., and GREEN, R. (eds.) (1985), 'Sub-Saharan Africa: Getting the Facts Straight', special issue of *IDS Bulletin*.

AL-SABAH, Y. S. F. (1980), *The Oil Economy of Kuwait* (London: Kegan Paul).

AMBIRAJAN, S. (1971), 'Political Economy of Indian Famines', *South Asia*, 1.

—— (1978), *Classical Political Economy and British Policy in India* (Cambridge: Cambridge University Press).

AMBLER, C. H. (1988), *Kenyan Communities in the Age of Imperialism: The Central Region in the Late Nineteenth Century* (New Haven: Yale University Press).

AMERINGER, C. D. (1982), *Democracy in Costa Rica* (Stanford: Praeger).

AMIN, S. (1988), 'The Effect of Women's Status on Sex Differentials in Infant and Child Mortality in South Asia', mimeo, Office of Population Research, Princeton University.

AMIN, SAMIR (1974), *Neo-colonialism in West Africa* (New York: Monthly Review Press).

—— (ed.) (1975), *L'Agriculture africaine et le capitalisme* (Paris: Anthropo-Idep).

AMSDEN, A. H. (ed.) (1980), *The Economics of Women and Work* (Harmondsworth: Penguin).

—— (1989), *Asia's Next Giant: Late Industrialization in South Korea* (Oxford: Oxford University Press).

ANAND, S., and HARRIS, C. (1986), 'Food and Standard of Living: An Analysis Based on Sri Lankan Data', paper presented at a Conference on Food Strategies held at WIDER, Helsinki, 21–5 July 1986; to be published in Drèze, J. P., and Sen, A. K. (eds.) (forthcoming), *The Political Economy of Hunger*.

—— —— (1987), 'Issues in the Measurement of Undernutrition', paper presented at a Conference on Poverty, Undernutrition and Living Standards held at WIDER, 27–30 July 1987; to be published in Osmani, S. R. (ed.) (forthcoming), *Nutrition and Poverty*.

—— and KANBUR, S. M. R. (RAVI) (1987), 'Public Policy and Basic Needs Provision: Intervention and Achievements in Sri Lanka', mimeo, to be published in Drèze, J. P., and Sen, A. K. (eds.) (forthcoming), *The Political Economy of Hunger*.

ANDREU, J. (1984), 'Health Sector Development Issues', mimeo, World Bank, Washington, DC.

Anon. (1973), 'Food Riots: Hungry Stomachs Must Hunger On', *Economic and Political Weekly*, 28 Apr.

Anon. (1984), 'Cape Verde: Drought as a Way of Life', *West Africa*, 6 Feb.

Anon. (1985), 'Fighting Famine', *Economic and Political Weekly*, 2 Nov.

Anon. (1988), 'Cash for Food in Ethiopia', *UNICEF/INTERCOM*, 47.

ANYANGO, G. J., et al. (forthcoming), 'Drought Vulnerability in Central and Eastern Kenya', in Downing, T. E., et al. (eds.) (forthcoming), *Coping with Drought in Kenya: National and Local Strategies*.

APPADURAI, A. (1984), 'How Moral is South Asia's Economy? A Review Article', *Journal of Asian Studies*, 43.

APPLETON, J. (1987), *Drought Relief in Ethiopia: Planning and Management of Feeding Programmes* (London: Save the Children Fund).

—— (1988), 'Nutritional Status Monitoring in Wollo, Ethiopia, 1982–1984: An Early Warning System', mimeo, Save the Children Fund, UK.

ARELLANO, J. P. (1985a), 'Social Policies in Chile: An Historical Review', *Journal of Latin American Studies*, 17.

—— (1985b), *Políticas sociales y desarrollo, Chile 1924–1984* (Santiago: CIEPLAN).

—— (1988), 'La situación social en Chile', Notas técnicas No. 94, CIEPLAN, Santiago.

—— CORTÁZAR, R., and SOLIMANO, A. (1987), 'Chile', Country Study No. 10, Stabilization and Adjustment Policies and Programmes, WIDER, Helsinki.

—— —— —— (1988), 'Medium-Term Development: Some Issues Relevant for Chile', paper prepared for a Conference on Medium Term Development Strategy, WIDER, Aug. 1988.

ARNOLD, D. (1988), *Famine: Social Crisis and Historical Change* (Oxford: Blackwell).

ARROW, K. (1963), 'Uncertainty and the Welfare Economics of Health Care', *American Economic Review*, 53.

ASHTON, B., HILL, K., PIAZZA, A., and ZEITZ, R. (1984), 'Famine in China, 1958–61', *Population and Development Review*, 10.

ASLANBEIGUI, N., and SUMMERFIELD, G. (1989), 'Impact of the Responsibility System on Women in Rural China: An Application of Sen's Theory of Entitlements', *World Development*, 17.

Asociación Demográfica Costarricense (1984), *Mortalidad y fecundidad en Costa Rica* (San José: ADC).

ATKINSON, A. B. (1983), *Social Justice and Public Policy* (Brighton: Wheatsheaf and Cambridge, MA: MIT Press).

—— (1987a), 'On the Measurement of Poverty', *Econometrica*, 55.

—— (1987b) 'Income Maintenance and Social Insurance: A Survey', in Auerbach, A., and Feldstein, M. (eds.) (1987), *Handbook of Public Economics* (Amsterdam and New York: North-Holland).

—— and HILLS, J. (1988), 'Social Security in Developed Countries: Are There Lessons for Developing Countries?', paper presented at a Workshop on Social Security in Developing Countries held at the London School of Economics, 4–5 July 1988; to be published in Ahmad, S. E., *et al.* (eds.) (forthcoming), *Social Security in Developing Countries*.

—— —— and LEGRAND, J. (1987), 'The Welfare State', in Dornbusch, R., and Layard, R. (eds.) (1987), *The Performance of the British Economy* (Oxford: Oxford University Press).

AUDETTE, R. and GROLLEAUD, M. (1984), *Le Stockage non-étatique des grains dans les pays sahéliens: bibliographie générale, inventaire, analyse et recommandations* (Paris: Club du Sahel).

AUERBACH, L. S. (1979), 'Women's Jobs Means Women's Money: The Social Ramifications of the Increased Participation of Women in the Work Structure of a Tunisian Town', paper presented at the annual meeting of the American Anthropological Association.

AUSTIN, J. E., and ZEITLIN, M. F. (1981), *Nutrition Intervention in Developing Countries: An Overview* (Cambridge, MA: Oelgeschlager, Gunn and Hain).

AUTIER, P. (1988), 'Nutrition Assessment Through the Use of a Nutritional Scoring System', *Disasters*, 12.

—— and D'ALTILIA, J. P. (1985), 'Bilan de 6 mois d'activité des équipes mobiles médico-nutritionnelles de Médecins Sans Frontières', mimeo, Médecins Sans Frontières, Brussels.

—— —— DELAMALLE, J. P., and VERCRUYSSE, V. (1989), 'The Food and Nutrition

Surveillance System of Chad and Mali: The "SAP" after Two Years', mimeo, European Association for Health and Development, Brussels.

AYKROYD, W. (1974), *The Conquest of Famine* (London: Chatto and Windus).

AZBITE, M. (1981), 'A Famine Relief Operation at Qorem, Ethiopia in 1966', *Disasters*, 5.

AZIZ, S. (ed.) (1975), *Hunger, Politics and Markets* (New York: New York University Press).

BAGCHEE, S. (1984), 'Employment Guarantee Scheme in Maharashtra', *Economic and Political Weekly*, 19.

BAGCHI, A. (1987), *Public Intervention and Industrial Restructuring in China, India and Republic of Korea* (New Delhi: ILO).

BAHL, R., KIM, C. K., and PARK, C. K. (1986), *Public Finances During the Korean Modernization Process* (Cambridge, MA: Harvard University Press).

BALASSA, B. (1984), 'Política económica en Chile: 1973–83', Estudios Públicos, No. 14, Centro de Estudios Públicos, Santiago.

—— (1985), 'The National Economic Policies of Chile', in Altman, E., and Walker, I. (eds.) (1985), *Contemporary Studies in Economic and Financial Analysis*, No. 51, Graduate School of Business Administration, New York University, New York.

—— (1988), 'The Lessons of East Asian Development: An Overview', *Economic Development and Cultural Change*, 36.

BALL, N. (1981), *World Hunger: A Guide to the Economic and Political Dimensions* (Santa Barbara, California and Oxford: ABC-Clio Press).

Banco Central de Chile (1984), *Economic Report of Chile 1983* (Santiago: Central Bank of Chile).

BANERJEE, N. (1982), *Unorganised Women Workers: The Calcutta Experience* (Calcutta: Centre for Studies in Social Sciences).

—— (1985), 'Women's Work and Discrimination', in Jain, D., and Banerjee, N. (eds.) (1985), *Tyranny of the Household: Investigative Essays in Women's Work*.

BANERJI, D. (1982), *Poverty, Class and Health Culture in India* (New Delhi: Prachi Prakashan).

BANG, F. B. (1981), 'The Role of Disease in the Ecology of Famine', in Robson, J. R. K. (ed.) (1981), *Famine*.

BANISTER, J. (1984a), 'An Analysis of Recent Data on the Population of China', *Population and Development Review*, 10.

—— (1984b), 'Population Policy and Trends in China 1978–83', *China Quarterly*, 100.

—— (1986), 'China: Recent Trends in Health and Mortality', Paper No. 23, Center for International Research, Washington, DC.

—— (1987), *China's Changing Population* (Stanford: Stanford University Press).

BARDHAN, K. (1985), 'Women's Work, Welfare and Status', *Economic and Political Weekly*, 20.

BARDHAN, P. K. (1974), 'On Life and Death Questions', *Economic and Political Weekly*, 9, Special Number.

—— (1984), *Land, Labor and Rural Poverty* (New York: Columbia University Press).

—— (1987), 'On the Economic Geography of Sex Disparity in Child Survival in India: A Note', paper presented at the BAMANEH/SSRC Workshop on Differential Female Mortality and Health Care in South Asia, Dhaka.

BARNABAS, G., LOVEL, H. J., and MORLEY, D. C. (1982), 'Supplementary Food for the Few in a Refugee Camp', *Lancet*, July 3.

BASTA, S. S. (1977), 'Nutrition and Health in Low Income Urban Areas in the Third World', *Ecology of Food and Nutrition*, 6.

BASU, A. (1987), 'Is Discrimination in Food Really Necessary for Explaining Sex Differentials in Childhood Mortality?', mimeo, National Council of Applied Economic Research, New Delhi.

—— (1988), *Culture, Status of Women and Demographic Behaviour* (New Delhi: National Council of Applied Economic Research).

BASU, D. R. (1984), 'Food Policy and the Analysis of Famines', *Indian Journal of Economics*, 64.

—— (1986), 'Discussion: Sen's Analysis of Famine: A Critique', *Journal of Development Studies*, 22.

BASU, K. (1981), 'Food for Work Programmes: Beyond Roads that Get Washed Away', *Economic and Political Weekly*, 16.

—— (1984), *The Less Developed Economy* (Oxford: Basil Blackwell).

—— (1986), 'The Elimination of Endemic Hunger in South Asia: Some Policy Options', paper presented at a Conference on Food Strategies held at WIDER, Helsinki, 21–5 July 1986; to be published in Drèze, J. P., and Sen, A. K. (eds.) (forthcoming), *The Political Economy of Hunger*.

BATES, R. H. (1981), *Markets and States in Tropical Africa: The Political Basis of Agricultural Policies* (Berkeley: University of California Press).

—— (1983), *Essays on the Political Economy of Rural Africa* (Berkeley: University of California Press).

—— (1986), 'The Political Framework for Price Policy Decisions' in Mann, C. K., and Huddleston, B. (eds.) (1986), *Food Policy: Frameworks for Analysis and Action*.

—— and LOFCHIE, M. F. (eds.) (1980), *Agricultural Development in Africa: Issues of Public Policy* (New York: Praeger).

BAUER, P. T. (1954), *West African Trade: A Study of Competition, Oligopoly and Monopoly in a Changing Economy* (London: Cambridge University Press).

—— (1972), *Dissent on Development* (London: Weidenfeld).

—— (1981), *Equality, the Third World and Economic Delusion* (London: Weidenfeld).

—— (1984), *Reality and Rhetoric: Studies in the Economics of Development* (London: Weidenfeld and Nicholson).

BAULCH, B. (1987), 'Entitlements and the Wollo Famine 1982–1985', *Disasters*, 11.

BAUMGARTNER, R. (1989), 'China: Long-Term Issues in Options for the Health Sector', mimeo, World Bank, Washington, DC.

BEATON, G. (1983), 'Adaptation to an Accommodation of Long-Term Low Energy Intake', in Pollitt, E., and Amante, P. (eds.) (1983), *Current Topics in Nutrition and Disease: Energy Intake and Activity* (New York: Alan R. Liss/UNU).

—— (1987a), '"Small but Healthy?": Are We Asking the Right Question?', paper presented at the 86th Annual Meeting of the American Anthropological Association, Chicago, Nov. 1987.

—— (1987b), 'Energy in Human Nutrition: A Reconsideration of the Relationship between Intake and Functional Consequences', in Gittinger, J. P., *et al.* (eds.) (1987), *Food Policy*.

—— and GHASSEIMI, G. (1982), 'Supplementary Feeding Programs for Young Children in Developing Countries', *American Journal of Clinical Nutrition*, 34 (Suppl.).

BEHM, H. (1982), 'Determinantes socioeconómicos de la mortalidad en América Latina', *Boletín de población de las Naciones Unidas*, 13.

BEHRMAN, J. R. (1987), 'Intrahousehold Allocation of Nutrients and Gender Effects', paper presented at a Conference on Poverty, Undernutrition and Living Standards held at WIDER, 27–30 July 1987; to be published in Osmani, S. R. (ed.) (forthcoming), *Nutrition and Poverty*.

—— (1988a), 'Nutrition, Health, Birth Order and Seasonality: Intrahousehold Allocation in Rural India', *Journal of Development Economics*, 28.

—— (1988b), 'The Impact of Economic Adjustment Programs', in Bell, D. E., and Reich, M. R. (eds.) (1988), *Health, Nutrition and Economic Crises*.

—— and DEOLALIKAR, A. B. (1987), 'Will Developing Country Nutrition Improve with Incomes? A Case Study for Rural South India', *Journal of Political Economy*, 95.

—— —— (1988a), 'How Do Food Prices and Income Affect Individual Nutritional and Health Status? A Latent Variable Fixed-Effects Analysis', mimeo, University of Pennsylvania.

—— —— (1988b), 'Health and Nutrition', in Chenery, H., and Srinivasan, T. N. (eds.) (1988), *Handbook of Development Economics*.

—— —— (1988c), 'The Intrahousehold Demand for Nutrients in Rural South India: Individual Estimates, Fixed Effects and Permanent Income', mimeo, University of Pennsylvania.

—— and Wolfe, B. L. (1984), 'More Evidence on Nutrition Demand: Income Seems Overrated and Women's Schooling Underemphasized', *Journal of Development Economics*, 14.

—— —— (1987), 'How Does Mother's Schooling Affect Family Health, Nutrition, Medical Care Usage, and Household Sanitation?', *Journal of Econometrics*, 36.

BELETE, S., GEBRE-MEDHIN, M., HAILEMARIAM, B., MAFFI, M., VAHLQUIST, B., and WOLDE-GABRIEL, Z. (1977), 'Study of Shelter Population in the Wollo Region', *Journal of Tropical Pediatrics and Environmental Child Health*, 23.

BELL, D. E., and REICH, M. R. (eds.) (1988), *Health, Nutrition and Economic Crises* (Dover, MA: Auburn House).

BENERIA, L. (ed.) (1982), *Women and Development: The Sexual Division of Labour in Rural Societies* (New York: Praeger).

BENNETT, J. (1983), 'The Tigray Drought', mimeo, Relief Society of Tigray, London.

—— (1987), *The Hunger Machine: The Politics of Food* (Cambridge, England: Polity Press).

BERG, A. (1973), *The Nutrition Factor* (Brookings Institution).

—— (1981), *Malnourished People: A Policy View* (Washington, DC: The World Bank).

—— (1987a), *Malnutrition: What Can be Done?* (Baltimore: Johns Hopkins).

—— (1987b), 'Rejoinder: Nutrition Planning is Alive and Well, Thank You', *Food Policy*, 12.

BERG, E. (1986), 'La Réforme de la politique céréalière dans le Sahel', SAHEL D(86) 294, Club du Sahel.

BERG, R. J., and WHITAKER, J. S. (eds.) (1986), *Strategies for African Development* (Berkeley: University of California Press).

BERNSTEIN, T. P. (1983), 'Starving to Death in China', *New York Review of Books*, 30.

—— (1984): 'Stalinism, Famine, and Chinese Peasants', *Theory and Society*, 13.

BERNUS, E. (1977a), 'Les Éleveurs face à la sécheresse en Afrique sahélienne: exemples nigériens', in Dalby, D., *et al.* (eds.) (1977), *Drought in Africa 2*.

—— (1977b), 'Famines et sécheresses chez les Touaregs sahéliens', in Dalby, D. *et al.* (eds.) (1977), *Drought in Africa 2*.

—— (1986), 'Mobilité et flexibilité pastorales face à la sécheresse', *Bulletin de Liaison*, No. 8, ORSTOM, Paris.

BERRY, L., and KATES, R. (1980), *Making the Most of the Least* (New York: Holmes and Meier).

BERRY, S. S. (1984), 'The Food Crisis and Agrarian Change in Africa: A Review Essay', *African Studies Review*, 27.

BERTLIN, J. (1980), 'Adaptation and Response to Drought: Traditional Systems and the Impact of Change', a special study submitted in part fulfilment of the requirements for the M.Sc. in Agricultural Economics, Wye College, University of London.

BESLEY, T. (1989), 'Ex Ante Evaluation of Health Status and the Provision for Ill-Health', *Economic Journal*, 99.

—— and KANBUR, S. M. R. (RAVI) (1988), 'Food Subsidies and Poverty Alleviation', *Economic Journal*, 98.

BHAGWATI, J. (1987), 'Poverty and Public Policy', *World Development*, 16.

BHALLA, A. (1987), 'Access to Health Services in China and India', mimeo, Geneva.

BHALLA, S. (1988), 'Is Sri Lanka an Exception? A Comparative Study in Living Standards', in Srinivasan, T. N., and Bardhan, P. K. (eds.) (1988), *Rural Poverty in South Asia*.

—— and BANDYOPADHYAY, S. (1988), 'The Politics and Economics of Drought in India', paper presented at a Conference on Development Economics and Policy held at the Delhi School of Economics, 18–21 Dec. 1988.

—— and GLEWWE, P. (1986), 'Growth and Equity in Developing Countries: A Reinterpretation of Sri Lankan Experience', *World Bank Economic Review*, 1.

BHARGAVA, A. (1988), 'Estimating Short and Long Run Income Elasticities of Food and Nutrients for Rural South India', mimeo, Department of Economics, University of Pennsylvania.

BHATIA, B. M. (1967), *Famines in India: A Study in Some Aspects of the Economic History of India 1860–1965* (Bombay: Asia Publishing House).

BHATIA, BELA (1988), 'Official Drought Relief Measures: A Case Study of Gujarat', *Social Action*, 38.

BHATIA, S. (1983), 'Traditional Practices Affecting Female Health and Survival', in Lopez, A. D., and Ruzicka, L. T. (eds.) (1983), *Sex Differentials in Mortality: Trends, Determinants and Consequences*.

BHATTACHARYA, N., CHATTERJEE, G. S., and PAL, P. (1988), 'Variations in Level of Living across Regions and Social Groups in Rural India, 1963/64 and 1973/74', in Srinivasan, T. N., and Bardhan, P. K. (eds.) (1988), *Rural Poverty in South Asia*.

BHATTY, I. (1974), 'Inequality and Poverty in Rural India', in Srinivasan, T. N., and Bardhan, P. K. (eds.) (1974), *Poverty and Income Distribution in India*.

BHATTY, Z. (1980), 'Economic Role and Status of Women: A Case Study of Women in the Beedi Industry in Allahabad', ILO Working Paper.

BIELLIK, R. J., and HENDERSON, P. L. (1981), 'Mortality, Nutritional Status, and Diet During the Famine in Karamoja, Uganda, 1980', *Lancet*, 12 Dec.

BIENEN, H., and GERSOVITZ, M. (1986), 'Consumer Subsidy Cuts, Violence and Political Stability', *Comparative Politics*, 19.

BIGMAN, D. (1986), *Food Policies and Food Security under Instability* (Lexington, MA.: Lexington Books).

—— and REUTLINGER, S. (1979), 'Food Price and Supply Stabilization: National Buffer Stocks and Trade Policies', *American Journal of Agricultural Economics*, Nov.

BINMORE, K. (1987), 'Nash Bargaining Theory', in Binmore, K., and Dasgupta, P. (eds.) (1987), *The Economics of Bargaining.*

—— and DASGUPTA, P. (eds.) (1987), *The Economics of Bargaining* (Oxford and New York: Basil Blackwell).

BINNS, C. W. (1976), 'Famine and the Diet of the Enga', *Papua New Guinea Medical Journal*, 19.

BINSWANGER, H. P., DOHERTY, V. S., BALARAMAIAH, T., BHENDE, M. J., KSHIRSAGAR, K. G., RAO, V. B., and RAJU, P. S. S. (1984), 'Common Features and Contrasts in Labor Relations in the Semiarid Tropics of India', in Binswanger, H. P., and Rosenzweig, M. R. (eds.) (1984), *Contractual Arrangements, Employment, and Wages in Rural Labor Markets in Asia* (New Haven: Yale University Press).

BIRDSALL, N. (1988), 'Thoughts on Good Health and Good Government', paper presented at a Colloquium on Development, Cambridge, MA, May 19–20.

—— (1989), 'Pragmatism, Robin Hood, and Other Themes: Good Government and Social Well-Being in Developing Countries', mimeo, World Bank, Washington, DC.

—— and GRIFFIN, C. C. (1988), 'Fertility and Poverty in Developing Countries', *Journal of Policy Modelling*, 10.

BJOERCK, W. A. (1984), 'An Overview of Local Purchase of Food Commodities (LPFC)', mimeo, UNICEF.

BLACKORBY, C., and DONALDSON, D. (1988), 'Adult Equivalence Scales and the Economic Implementation of Interpersonal Comparisons of Well-Being', mimeo, University of British Columbia.

BLAXTER, K. (1985), 'Energy Intake and Expenditure', in Blaxter, K., and Waterlow, J. C. (eds.) (1985), *Nutritional Adaptation in Man.*

—— and WATERLOW, J. C. (eds.) (1985), *Nutritional Adaptation in Man* (London: John Libbey).

BLIX, G., HOFVANDER, Y., and VAHLQUIST, B. (eds.) (1971), *Famine: Nutrition and Relief Operations in Times of Disaster* (Uppsala, Sweden: Swedish Nutrition Foundation).

BLUMBERG, R. L. (1988), 'Income under Female and Male Control: Hypotheses from a Theory of Gender Stratification and Data from the Third World', *Journal of Family Issues*, 9.

BONGAARTS, J., and CAIN, M. (1982), 'Demographic Responses to Famine', in Cahill, K. M. (ed.) (1982), *Famine.*

BORKAR, V. V., and NADKARNI, M. V. (1975), *Impact of Drought on Rural Life* (Bombay: Popular Prakashan).

BORTON, J. (1984), 'Disaster Preparedness in Botswana', report prepared for the Ford Foundation, Relief and Development Institute, London.

—— (1986), 'Botswana Food Aid Management', paper presented at the WFP/ADB Conference on Food Aid for Development, Abijan, Sept. 1986.

—— (1988), 'The 1984/85 Drought Relief Programme in Kenya: A Provisional Review', Discussion Paper No. 2, Relief and Development Institute, London.

—— (forthcoming), 'Overview of the 1984/85 National Drought Relief Program', in Downing, T., *et al.* (eds.) (forthcoming), *Coping with Drought in Kenya: National and Local Strategies.*

—— and Clay, E. (1986), 'The African Food Crisis of 1982–86', *Disasters*, 10.

—— and Shoham, J. (1989a), 'Experiences of Non-governmental Organisations in the

Targeting of Emergency Food Aid', report on a workshop held at the London School of Hygiene and Tropical Medicine, Jan. 1989.

—— —— (1989*b*), 'Emergency Food Aid Targeting: Case Studies', collection of background papers prepared for a workshop held at the London School of Hygiene and Tropical Medicine, Jan. 1989.

—— STEPHENSON, R. S., and MORRIS, C. (1988), 'ODA Emergency Aid to Africa 1983–86', Evaluation Report EV 425, Overseas Development Administration, UK.

—— and YORK, S. (1987), 'Experiences of the Collection and Use of Micro-level Data in Disaster Preparedness and Managing Emergency Operations', *Disasters*, 11.

BOSE, A., and TYAGI, R. P. (1983), 'Rural Health Services: Present Status', in Goyel, R. P., *et al.* (eds.) (1983), *Studies in Social Dynamics of Primary Health Care* (Delhi: Hindustan Publishing).

BOSE, S. (1987), 'Starvation Amidst Plenty: The Making of Famine in Bengal, Honan and Tonkin, 1942–45', paper presented at the India–China Seminar, Fairbank Center, Harvard University, Dec. 1987.

BOSERUP, E. (1970), *Women's Role in Economic Development* (London: Allen and Unwin).

—— (1980), 'The Position of Women in Economic Production and in the Household, with Special Reference to Africa', in Presvelan, C., and Spijkers-Zwart, S. (eds.) (1980), *The Household, Women and Agricultural Development*.

—— (1983), 'The Impact of Scarcity and Plenty on Development', in Rotberg, R. S., and Rabb, T. K. (eds.) (1983), *Hunger and History*.

—— (1986), 'Economic Change and the Role of Women', mimeo.

Botswana Society (1979), *Symposium on Drought in Botswana* (Gaborone: Botswana Society).

BOUIS, H. E., and HADDAD, L. J. (1988), 'Comparing Calorie–Income Elasticities Using Calories Derived from Reported Food Purchases and a Twenty-four Hour Recall of Food Intakes: An Application Using Philippine Data', Discussion Paper No. 88, Development Economics Research Centre, University of Warwick.

BOWBRICK, P. (1986), 'The Causes of Famine: A Refutation of Professor Sen's Theory', *Food Policy*, 11.

—— (1987), 'Rejoinder: An Untenable Hypothesis on the Cause of Famine', *Food Policy*, 12.

BOYCE, J. K. (1987), *Agrarian Impasse in Bengal* (New York: Oxford University Press).

BOYD, D. (1987), 'The Impact of Adjustment Policies on Vulnerable Groups: The Case of Jamaica, 1973–1985', in Cornia, G., *et al.* (eds.) (1987), *Adjustment With a Human Face*.

BOYD-ORR, J. (1950), 'The Food and People Dilemma', *Scientific American*, 183.

BOYLE, P. P., and O'GRADA, C. (1986), 'Fertility Trends, Excess Mortality, and the Great Irish Famine', *Demography*, 23.

BRAHME, S. (1983), *Drought in Maharashtra 1972*, Gokhale Institute Series No. 68, Pune, India.

BRANDT, H. (1984), *Food Security Programmes in the Sudano-Sahel* (Berlin: German Development Institute).

BRANNEN, J., and WILSON, G. (eds.) (1987), *Give and Take in Families* (London: Allen and Unwin).

BRASS, P. R. (1986), 'The Political Uses of Crisis: The Bihar Famine of 1966–1967', *Journal of Asian Studies*, 45.

BRATTON, M. (1986), 'Farmer Organizations and Food Production in Zimbabwe', *World Development*, 14.

—— (1987*a*), 'Drought, Food and the Social Organization of Small Farmers in Zimbabwe', in Glantz, M. (ed.) (1987*a*), *Drought and Hunger in Africa*.

—— (1987*b*), 'The Comrades and the Countryside: The Politics of Agricultural Policy in Zimbabwe', *World Politics*, 29.

BREMAN, J. (1974), *Patronage and Exploitation: Changing Agrarian Structure in South Gujarat, India* (Berkeley: University of California Press).

BRENNAN, L. (1984), 'The Development of the Indian Famine Codes: Personalities, Politics and Policies', in Currey, B., and Hugo, G. (eds.) (1984), *Famine as a Geographical Phenomenon*.

—— (1988), 'Government Famine Relief in Bengal, 1943', *Journal of Asian Studies*, 47.

—— HEATHCOTE, R. L., and LUCAS, A. E. (1984), 'The Role of the Individual Administrator in Famine Relief: Three Case Studies', *Disasters*, 8.

BRETT, A. (1987), 'Nutrition Survey, Basic Needs Assessment Survey Cycle 3, December 1986–January 1987, Dawi Rahmedo Wareda and Delanta Wareda', mimeo, OXFAM.

BRICEÑO, A., and MÉNDEZ, E. A. (1982), 'Salud pública y distribución del ingreso en Costa Rica', *Revista ciencias económicas*, 1.

BROWN, E. P. (forthcoming), 'Sex and Starvation', to be published in Downs, R. E., Kerner, D. O., and Reyna, S. P. (eds.) (forthcoming), *The Political Economy of African Hunger*.

BROWN, L. R. and ECKHOLM, E. P. (1974), *By Bread Alone* (Oxford: Pergamon).

—— (1987), 'Food Growth Slowdown: Danger Signal for the Future', in Gittinger, J. P., *et al.* (eds.) (1987), *Food Policy*.

BROWN, M., and CHUANG, C. F. (1980), 'Intrahousehold Power and Demand for Shared Goods', mimeo, SUNY, Buffalo, NY.

BROWN, R., and MASON, L. (1988), 'Fire Blown by Wind: Famine in the Sudan', mimeo.

BROWN, V. W., BROWN, E. P., ECKERSON, D., GILMORE, J., and SWARTZENDURBER, H. D. (1986), 'Evaluation of the African Emergency Food Assistance Program 1984–1985: Chad', report submitted to USAID, Washington, DC.

BRUNDENIUS, C. (1981), *Economic Growth, Basic Needs and Income Distribution in Revolutionary Cuba* (Lund, Sweden: Research Policy Institute, University of Lund).

—— (1982), 'Development Strategies and Basic Needs in Revolutionary Cuba', in Brundenius, C., and Lundhal, M. (eds.) (1982), *Development Strategies and Basic Needs in Latin America: Challenges for the 1980s*.

—— (1984), *Revolutionary Cuba: The Challenge of Economic Growth with Equity* (Boulder: Westview).

—— and LUNDAHL, M. (eds.) (1982), *Development Strategies and Basic Needs in Latin America: Challenges for the 1980s* (Boulder: Westview).

BRYCESON, D. (1981*a*), 'Colonial Famine Responses: The Bagamoyo District of Tanganyika, 1920–61', *Food Policy*, 6.

—— (1981*b*), 'Changes in Peasant Food Production and Food Supply in Relation to the Historical Development of Commodity Production in Pre-colonial and Colonial Tanganyika', *Journal of Peasant Studies*, 7.

—— (1984), 'Nutrition and the Commoditization of Food Systems in sub-Saharan Africa', paper presented at a Conference on Political Economy of Health and Disease in Africa and Latin America sponsored by the Social Science Research Council, UK.

—— (1985), *Women and Technology in Developing Countries* (Santo Domingo: United Nations).

BRYSON, J. C. (1986), 'Case Study: The Lesotho Food for Work Programme of Catholic Relief Services', paper presented at the WFP/ADB Conference on Food Aid for Development, Abijan, Sept. 1986.

BUCKLEY, R. (1988), 'Food Targeting in Darfur: Save the Children Fund's Programme in 1986', *Disasters*, 12.

BURGESS, R., STERN, N. H., (forthcoming), 'Social Security in Developing Countries: What, Why, Who and How?', in Ahmad *et al.* (forthcoming), *Social Security in Developing Countries*.

BUSH, R. (1987), 'Explaining Africa's Famine', *Social Studies Review*, 2.

—— (1988), 'Hunger in Sudan: The Case of Darfur', *African Affairs*, 87.

BUVINIC, M. (1976), *Women and World Development: An Annotated Bibliography* (Washington, DC: Overseas Development Council).

—— LYCETTE, M., and McGREEVEY, W. P. (eds.) (1983), *Women and Poverty in the Third World* (Baltimore: Johns Hopkins).

BYRES, T. J. (1979), 'Of Neo-populist Pipe Dreams: Daedalus in the Third World and the Myth of Urban Bias', *Journal of Peasant Studies*, 6.

BYRON, W. (ed.) (1982) *The Causes of World Hunger* (New York: Paulist Press).

CABEZAS, M. (1988), 'Revisión methodológica y estadística del gasto social en Chile: 1970–86', Notas Técnicas No. 114, CIEPLAN, Santiago, Chile.

CABRAL, N. E. (1980), *Le Moulin et le pilon: les Îles du Cap Vert* (Paris: L'Harmattan).

CAFOD (1986a), 'Emergency Relief Programmes in Eritrea 1985: A Report by CAFOD on Food, Medical and Transportation Programmes Implemented by the Eritrean Relief Association', mimeo, Catholic Fund for Overseas Development, London.

—— (1986b), 'Report on CAFOD Assistance to the Relief Society of Tigray (REST) in 1985', mimeo, Catholic Fund for Overseas Development, London.

CAHILL, K. M. (ed.) (1982), *Famine* (New York: Orbis Books).

CAIN, M. (1978), 'The Household Lifecycle and Economic Mobility in Bangladesh', Center for Policy Studies Working Paper, Population Council, New York.

CAIN, M., KHONAM, S. K., and NAHAR, S. (1979), 'Class, Patriarchy and the Structure of Women's Work in Rural Bangladesh', Center for Policy Studies Working Paper, Population Council, New York.

CALDWELL, J. C. (1975), 'The Sahelian Drought and Its Demographic Implications', Overseas Liaison Committee Paper No. 8, American Council of Education, Washington, DC.

—— (1977), 'Demographic Aspects of Drought: An Examination of the African Drought of 1970–74', in Dalby, D., *et al.* (eds.) (1977), *Drought in Africa 2*.

—— (1979), 'Education as a Factor in Mortality Decline: An Examination of Nigerian Data', *Population Studies*, 33.

—— (1981a), 'Food Production and Crisis in the West African Savannah', Occasional Paper No. 25, Development Studies Centre, Australian National University.

—— (1981b), 'Maternal Education as a Factor in Child Mortality', *World Health Forum*, 2.

—— (1984), 'Desertification: Demographic Evidence, 1973–1983', Occasional Paper No. 37, Development Studies Centre, Australian National University.

—— (1986), 'Routes to Low Mortality in Poor Countries', *Population and Development Review*, 12.

—— and CALDWELL, P. (1985), 'Education and Literacy as Factors in Health', in Halstead, S. B., *et al.* (eds.) (1985), *Good Health at Low Cost*.

—— REDDY, P. H., and CALDWELL, P. (1986), 'Periodic High Risk as a Cause of Fertility Decline in a Changing Rural Environment: Survival Strategies in the 1980–1983 South Indian Drought', *Economic Development and Cultural Change*, 34.

CALDWELL, P., and CALDWELL, J. C. (1987*a*), 'Where There is a Narrower Gap Between Female and Male Situations', mimeo, Australian National University.

—— —— (1987*b*), 'The Cultural Context of High Fertility in Sub-Saharan Africa', *Population and Development Review*, 13.

—— —— (1987*c*), 'Famine in Africa', paper presented at a IUSSP Seminar on Mortality and Society in sub-Saharan Africa, Iford, Yaoundé, Cameroon, Oct. 1987.

CAMPBELL, D. J. (1984), 'Response to Drought Among Farmers and Herders in Southern Kajiado District, Kenya', *Human Ecology*, 12.

—— (1986), 'Coping Strategies as Indicators of Food Shortage in African Villages', paper presented at the Annual Meeting of the American Anthropological Association, Philadelphia, Dec. 1986.

—— (1987), 'Strategies for Coping with Severe Food Deficits in Northeast Africa', *Northeast African Studies*, 9.

—— and TRECHTER, D. D. (1982), 'Strategies for Coping with Food Consumption Shortage in the Mandara Mountains Region of North Cameroon', *Social Science and Medicine*, 16.

CAMPBELL, R. H., and SKINNER, A. S. (eds.) (1976), *Adam Smith: An Inquiry into the Nature and Causes of the Wealth of Nations* (Oxford: Clarendon Press).

CANNON, T. G. (1978): 'The Role of Environmental Influence and "Natural" Disasters', mimeo, Thames Polytechnic.

CAPONE, C. (1980), 'A Review of an Experience with Food-Aided Nutrition Programs', *Nutrition Planning*, 3.

—— JACOB, F., and O'LAUGHLIN, A. (1978), 'Catholic Relief Services: Nutrition Intervention Programme for the Drought Areas of Kenya (1975–1976)', *Disasters*, 2.

CARLSON, D. G. (1982), 'Famine in History: With a Comparison of Two Modern Ethiopian Disasters', in Cahill, K. (ed.) (1982), *Famine*.

CARREIRA, A. (1982), *The People of the Cape Verde Islands: Exploitation and Emigration* (London: Hurst & Co).

CASHDAN, E. (1985), 'Coping with Risk: Reciprocity Among the Basarwa of Northern Botswana', *Man*, 20.

CASSEN, R., and associates (1986), *Does Aid Work?* (Oxford: Clarendon).

CASTANEDA, T. (1984), 'Contexto socioeconómico y causas del descenso de la mortalidad infantil en Chile', Documento de Trabajo No. 28, Centro de Estudios Públicos, Santiago, Chile.

—— (1985), 'Determinantes del descenso de la mortalidad infantil en Chile 1975–1983', *Cuadernos de economía*, 22.

—— and RACZYNSKI, D. (1984), 'Contexto socioeconómico del descenso de la mortalidad infantil en Chile', *Estudios públicos*, No. 16, Santiago.

CASTILLO, G., FIGUEROA, E., GUTIÉRREZ, J. M., *et al.* (1983), *Costa Rica: Disarmed Democracy* (San José: Imprenta Nacional).

CATHIE, J. and HERRMANN, R. (1988), 'The Southern African Customs Union, Cereal

Price Policy in South Africa, and Food Security in Botswana', *Journal of Development Studies*, 24.

Centre for Development Studies (1975), *Poverty, Unemployment and Development Policy: A Case Study of Selected Issues with Reference to Kerala* (New York: United Nations).

CÉPÈDE, M., and LENGELLÉ, M. (1953), *Economie alimentaire du globe* (Paris: Librairie de Médicis).

CESPEDES, V. H., and GONZALEZ-VEGA, C. (1985), *Growth and Equity: Changes in Income Distribution in Costa Rica, 1960–1980* (New York: DIESA, United Nations).

CHAKRAVARTY, L. (1986), 'Poverty Studies in the Context of Agricultural Growth and Demographic Pressure (Case of Post-Independence India)', mimeo, Indraprastha College, Delhi.

CHAKRAVARTY, S. (1969), *Capital and Development Planning* (Cambridge, MA.: MIT Press).

CHAMBERS, R. (1983), *Rural Development: Putting the Last First* (New York: Longman).

—— (ed.) (1989), *Vulnerability: How the Poor Cope*, special issue of *IDS Bulletin*.

—— LONGHURST, R., and PACEY, A. (eds.) (1981), *Seasonal Dimensions to Rural Poverty* (London: Frances Pinter).

—— *et al.* (1986), 'An Independent Review and Evaluation of the Africa Drought Relief Operations 1984–86 of the League of Red Cross and Red Crescent Societies', IDS, Report No. 1, mimeo.

CHASTANET, M. (1983), 'Les Crises de subsistances dans les villages Soninke du Cercle de Bakel de 1858 à 1945', *Cahiers d'études africaines*, 89–90/23.

—— (1988), 'Survival Strategies of a Sahelian Society: The Case of the Soninke in Senegal from the Middle of the XIXth Century to Nowadays', paper presented at a Conference on Afro-Asian Studies on Social Systems and Food Crises, New Delhi, Mar. 1988; to be published in Floud, J., and Rangasami, A. (eds.) (forthcoming), *Essays on Famine and Society* (New Delhi).

CHATTERJI, R. (1984), 'Marginalisation and the Induction of Women into Wage Labour: The Case of Indian Agriculture', WEP Working Paper No. 32, ILO.

CHATTOPADHYAY, B. (1981), 'Notes Towards an Understanding of the Bengal Famine of 1943', *CRESSIDA Transactions*, 1.

CHAUDHURY, R. H. (1987), 'Dietary Adequacy and Sex Bias', *Social Action*, 37.

—— (1988), 'Adequacy of Child Dietary Intake Relative to That of Other Family Members', *Food and Nutrition Bulletin*, 10.

CHAZAN, N., and SHAW, T. M. (eds.) (1988), *Coping with Africa's Food Crisis* (Boulder: Lynne Rienner).

CHEN, L. C. (1986*a*), 'Primary Health Care in Developing Countries: Overcoming Operational, Technical, and Social Barriers', *Lancet*, 29 Nov.

—— (1986*b*), 'Explorations of Food Consumption and Nutritional Status: Bangladesh', in Mann, C. K., and Huddleston, B. (eds.) (1986), *Food Policy: Frameworks for Analysis and Action*.

—— (1987), 'Coping with Economic Crisis: Policy Developments in China and India', *Health Policy and Planning*, 2.

—— (1988), 'Health Policy Responses: An Approach Derived from the China and India Experiences', in Bell, D. E., and Reich, M. R. (eds.) (1988), *Health, Nutrition and Economic Crises*.

—— and CHOWDHURY, A. K. M. (1977), 'The Dynamics of Contemporary Famine', paper presented at the International Population Conference of the International Union for the Scientific Study of Population, Mexico.

—— Huq, E., and D'Souza, S. (1981), 'Sex-Bias in the Family Allocation of Food and Health Care in Rural Bangladesh', *Population and Development Review*, 7.

—— *et al.* (1980), 'Anthropometric Assessment of Energy Protein Malnutrition and Subsequent Risk of Mortality Among Pre-school Age Children', *American Journal of Clinical Nutrition*, 33.

Chen, M. (1986*a*), *A Quiet Revolution: Women in Transition in Rural Bangladesh* (Dhaka: BRAC).

—— (1986*b*), 'Poverty, Gender, and Work in Bangladesh', *Economic and Political Weekly*, 21.

—— (1988), 'The Drought Situation in Devdholera Village', mimeo, Harvard Institute for International Development.

—— (1989), 'Coping with Seasonality and Drought: The Study of a Village in a Semi-arid Region of India', mimeo, Harvard Institute for International Development; to be published as a monograph.

—— and Ghuznavi, R. (1976), *Women in Food-for-Work: The Bangladesh Experience* (Rome: World Food Programme).

Chenery, H., *et al.* (eds.) (1974), *Redistribution with Growth* (London: Oxford University Press).

Chenery, H., and Srinivasan, T. N. (eds.) (1988), *Handbook of Development Economics* (Amsterdam: North-Holland).

Chernichovsky, D., Lucas, R. E. B., and Mueller, E. (1985), 'The Household Economy of Rural Botswana: An African Case', World Bank Staff Working Paper No. 715, World Bank, Washington, DC.

Cheyre, H., and Ogrodnick, E. (1982), 'El programa de empleo mínimo: análisis de una encuesta', *Revista de economía*, Nov.

Chichilnisky, G. (1983), 'North–South Trade with Export Enclaves: Food Consumption and Food Exports', mimeo, Columbia University.

Chimwaza, B. M. (1982), 'Food and Nutrition in Malawi', unpublished Ph.D. thesis, London University.

Chow, N. W. S. (1981), 'Social Security Provision in Singapore and Hong Kong', *Journal of Social Policy*, 10.

Chowdhury, A. K. M. (1988), 'Child Mortality in Bangladesh: Food versus Health Care', *Food and Nutrition Bulletin*, 10.

Chowdhury, O. H. (1983), 'Profile of Workers in the Food for Work Programme in Bangladesh', *Bangladesh Development Studies*, 11.

CILSS (1976), 'Aperçu sur la situation aux Îles du Cap Vert du fait de la continuation de la sécheresse', DPP/5-10-1976, Comité Permanent Intérétats de Lutte Contre la Sécheresse dans le Sahel, Paris.

—— (1986), *La Prévision des situations alimentaires critiques dans les pays du Sahel: systèmes et moyens d'alerte précoce* (Paris: OECD).

Clay, E. (1985*a*), 'Organizing Food Security: Lessons from South Asia', mimeo, Institute of Development Studies, University of Sussex.

—— (1985*b*), 'The 1974 and 1984 Floods in Bangladesh: From Famine to Food Crisis Management', *Food Policy*, 10.

—— (1986), 'Rural Public Works and Food-for-Work: A Survey', *World Development*, 14.

—— and HARRISS, B. (1988), 'Emergency Measures for Food Security: How Relevant to Africa is the South Asian Model?', in Curtis, D., *et al.* (eds.) (1988), *Preventing Famines*.

—— and SHAW, J. (eds.) (1987), *Poverty, Development and Food* (London: Macmillan).

—— and SINGER, H. W. (1985), 'Food Aid and Development: Issues and Evidence', Occasional Paper No. 3, World Food Programme, Rome.

CLELAND, J., and VAN GINNEKEN, J. (1987), 'The Effect of Maternal Schooling on Childhood Mortality: The Search for an Explanation', paper presented at a Conference on Health Intervention and Mortality Change in Developing Countries, University of Sheffield, Sept. 1987.

CLEMHOUT, S., and WAN, Jr., H. Y. (1977), 'Symmetric Marriage, Household Decision Making and Impact on Fertility', Working Paper No. 152, Department of Economics, Cornell University.

Club du Sahel (1977), *Marketing, Price Policy and Storage of Food Grains in the Sahel: A Survey* (University of Michigan: Center for Research on Economic Development).

COALE, A. (1981), 'Population Trends, Population Policy and Population Studies in China', *Population and Development Review*, 7.

—— (1984), *Rapid Population Change in China 1952–82* (Washington, DC: National Academy Press).

COATE, S. (1986), 'Should Food Aid Be Given Away or Sold During a Famine?', Discussion Paper No. 701, Center for Mathematical Studies in Economics and Management Science, Northwestern University, Evanston.

—— (1989), 'Cash Versus Direct Food Relief', forthcoming in *Journal of Development Economics*.

COCKBURN, C. (1980), 'The Role of Social Security in Development', *International Social Security Review*, 33.

COHEN, J., and LEWIS, D. (1987), 'Role of Government in Combatting Food Shortages: Lessons from Kenya 1984–85', in Glantz, M. (ed.) (1987a), *Drought and Hunger in Africa*.

COHEN, J. M., and ISAKSSON, N. I. (1988), 'Food Production Strategy Debates in Revolutionary Ethiopia', *World Development*, 16.

COHEN, M. M. (1977), *The Food Crisis in Prehistory: Overpopulation and the Origins of Famine* (New Haven: Yale University Press).

COLLINS, J., and LAPPÉ, F. M. (1980), 'Food Self-Reliance', in Galtung, J., *et al.* (eds.) (1980), *Self-Reliance: A Strategy for Development*.

COLSON, E. (1979), 'In Good Years and in Bad: Food Strategies of Self-Reliant Societies', *Journal of Anthropological Research*, 35.

Comité Information Sahel (1974), *Qui se nourrit de la famine en Afrique?* (Paris: Maspéro).

COMMINS, S., LOFCHIE, M., and PAYNE, R. (1986), *Africa's Agrarian Crisis* (Boulder: Lynne Rienner).

CONQUEST, R. (1986), *The Harvest of Sorrow: Soviet Collectivization and the Terror-Famine* (London: Hutchinson).

CONTRERA, J. (1988), 'Glow of Prosperity: Most of Chile is Riding High on an Economic Boom', *Newsweek*, 22 Aug.

COPANS, J., *et al.* (1975), *Sécheresses et famines du Sahel* (Paris: Maspéro).

CORBETT, J. (1987), 'Drought and the Threat of Famine in Kenya in 1984', mimeo, Food Studies Group, Oxford.

—— (1988), 'Famine and Household Coping Strategies', *World Development*, 16.

CORBO, V. (1985), 'Reforms and Macroeconomic Adjustments in Chile During 1974–84', *World Development*, 13.

CORNIA, G. (1984), 'A Survey of Cross-Sectional and Time-Series Literature on Factors Affecting Child Welfare', in Jolly, R., and Cornia, G. (eds.) (1984), *The Impact of World Recession on Children*.

—— (1987), 'Adjustment at the Household Level: Potentials and Limitations of Survival Strategies', in Cornia, G., *et al.* (eds.) (1987), *Adjustment with a Human Face*.

—— JOLLY, R., and STEWART, F. (1987), *Adjustment with a Human Face* (Oxford: Clarendon).

CORTAZAR, R. (1980), 'Distribución del ingreso, empleo y remuneraciones reales en Chile, 1970–78', Colección Estudios CEIPLAN, No. 3., Santiago, Chile.

Council on Environmental Quality and the Department of State (1982), *The Global 2000 Report to the President: Entering the Twenty First Century* (New York: Penguin).

Courier (1988), 'Country Report: Cape Verde', *Courier*, No. 107.

CROLL, E. (1978), *Feminism and Socialism in China* (London: Routledge and Kegan Paul).

—— (1983), *Chinese Women Since Mao* (New York: Zed).

CROW, B. (1987), 'US Policies in Bangladesh: The Making and the Breaking of Famine?', Development Policy and Practice Working Paper No. 4, The Open University, UK.

CULLEN, L. M., and SMOUT, T. C. (eds.) (1978), *Comparative Aspects of Scottish and Irish Economic and Social History, 1600–1900* (Edinburgh: Donald).

CUMPER, G. (1984), *Determinants of Health Levels in Developing Countries* (Letchworth, UK: Research Studies Press).

CUMPER, G. E. (1983), 'Jamaica: A Case Study in Health Development', *Social Science and Medicine*, 17.

CUMPER, GLORIA (1972), *Survey of Social Legislation in Jamaica* (Mona: University of West Indies Institute for Social and Economic Research).

CUNY, F. C. (1983), *Disasters and Development* (Oxford: Oxford University Press for Oxfam-America).

CURREY, B., ALI, M., and KOHMAN, N. (1981), *Famine: A First Bibliography* (Washington, DC: Agency for International Development).

—— and HUGO, G. (eds.) (1984), *Famine as a Geographical Phenomenon* (Dordrecht, Holland: Reidel).

CURTIS, D., HUBBARD, M., and SHEPHERD, A. (1988), *Preventing Famine: Policies and Prospects for Africa* (London and New York: Routledge).

CUTLER, P. (1984*a*), 'Famine Forecasting: Prices and Peasant Behaviour in Northern Ethiopia', *Disasters*, 8.

—— (1984*b*), 'Food Crisis Detection: Going Beyond the Balance Sheet', *Food Policy*, 9.

—— (1985*a*), 'Detecting Food Emergencies: Lessons from the 1979 Bangladesh Crisis', *Food Policy*, 10.

—— (1985*b*), 'The Use of Economic and Social Information in Famine Prediction and Response', report prepared for the Overseas Development Administration, London.

—— (1986), 'The Response to Drought of Beja Famine Refugees in Sudan', *Disasters*, 19.

DALBY, D., HARRISON CHURCH, R. J., and BEZZAZ, F. (eds.) (1977), *Drought in Africa 2* (London: International Africa Institute).

DALRYMPLE, D. (1964), 'The Soviet Famine of 1932–34', *Soviet Studies*, 15.

DANDEKAR, K. (1983), *Employment Guarantee Scheme: An Employment Opportunity for Women* (Pune: Orient Longman).

—— and SATHE, M. (1980), 'Employment Guarantee Scheme and Food for Work Programme', *Economic and Political Weekly*, 15.

DANDEKAR, V. M. and RATH, N. (1971), *Poverty in India* (Poona: Indian School of Political Economy).

DANDO, W. A. (1980), *The Geography of Famine* (London: Edward Arnold).

—— (1983), 'Biblical Famines, 1850 B.C.–A.D.46: Insights for Modern Mankind', *Ecology of Food and Nutrition*, 13.

DANIEL, P., GREEN, R., and LIPTON, M. (1984), 'Towards a Strategy for the Rural Poor in Sub-Saharan Africa', Discussion Paper No. 193, Institute of Development Studies, University of Sussex.

DAS, T. (1949), *The Bengal Famine (1943)* (Calcutta: University of Calcutta).

DAS, V., and NICHOLAS, R. (1981), 'Welfare and "Well-Being" in South Asian Societies', ACLS–SSRC Joint Committee on South Asia (New York: SSRC).

DAS GUPTA, M. (1987), 'Selective Discrimination Against Female Children in Rural Punjab', *Population and Development Review*, 13.

—— (1989a), 'Death Clustering, Maternal Education and the Determinants of Child Mortality in Rural Punjab, India', mimeo, Center for Population Studies, Harvard University.

—— (1989b), 'The Effects of Discrimination on Health and Mortality', mimeo, Center for Population Studies, Harvard University.

DASGUPTA, P., and RAY, D. (1986a), 'Adapting to Undernourishment: The Biological Evidence and Its Implications', paper presented at a Conference on Food Strategies held at WIDER, Helsinki, 21–5 July 1986; Economic Theory Discussion Paper No. 106, Department of Applied Economics, University of Cambridge, 1987; to be published in Drèze, J. P. and Sen, A. K. (eds.) (forthcoming), *The Political Economy of Hunger*.

—— —— (1986b), 'Inequality as a Determinant of Malnutrition and Unemployment: Theory', *Economic Journal*, 96.

—— —— (1987), 'Inequality as a Determinant of Malnutrition and Unemployment: Policy', *Economic Journal*, 97.

DATTA CHAUDHURI, M. K. (1979), 'Industrialization and Foreign Trade: An Analysis Based on the Development Experience of the Republic of Korea and the Philippines', Working Paper II-4, Asian Employment Programme, ARTEP, ILO, Bangkok.

DAVIDSON, B. (1977), 'Mass Mobilization for National Reconstruction in the Cape Verde Islands', *Economic Geography*, 53.

DAVIES, R., and SANDERS, D. (1987a), 'Stabilisation Policies and the Effects on Child Health in Zimbabwe', *Review of African Political Economy*, 38.

—— —— (1987b), 'Adjustment Policies and the Welfare of Children: Zimbabwe, 1980–1985', in Cornia, G., *et al.* (eds.) (1987), *Adjustment With a Human Face*.

DAVIS, O., and WITTER, M. (1986), *Issues in Food Security in Jamaica* (Kingston: Caribbean Food and Nutrition Institute).

DAWSON, A. (1985), 'In Defence of Food Aid: Some Answers to its Critics', *International Labour Bulletin*, 124.

DEACON, B. (1983), *Social Policy and Socialism: The Struggle for Socialist Relations of Welfare* (London: Pluto Press).

DEATON, A. (1987), 'The Allocation of Goods Within the Household: Adults, Children and Gender', mimeo, Princeton University.

—— (1988), 'Household Behavior in Developing Countries', Occasional Paper No. 1, The Economic Growth Center, Yale University.

—— and CASE, A. (1987), 'Analysis of Household Expenditure', Working Paper No. 28, Living Standards Measurement Study, World Bank, Washington, DC.

—— and MUELLBAUER, J. (1980), *Economics and Consumer Behaviour* (Cambridge and New York: Cambridge University Press).

DEERE, C. D., and DE LEAL, M. L. (1982), *Women in Andean Agriculture* (Geneva: ILO).

DE GARINE, I., and HARRISON, G. A. (eds.) (1988), *Coping with Uncertainty in Food Supply* (Oxford: Clarendon).

Deloitte, Haskins and Sells Management Co. (1986), 'Final Monitoring Report on the Drought Emergency Relief Program for USAID Mission to Kenya', report prepared for USAID.

DEMENY, P. (1986), 'Population and the Invisible Hand', Working Paper No. 123, Center for Policy Studies, Population Council, New York.

DEN HARTOG, A. (1981), 'Adjustment of Food Behaviour During Famine', in Robson, J. (ed.) (1981), *Famine: Its Causes, Effects, and Management*.

DERRICK, J. (1984), 'West Africa's Worst Year of Famine', *African Affairs*, 83.

DESAI, G. M., SINGH, G., and SAH, D. C. (1979), 'Impact of Scarcity on Farm Economy and Significance of Relief Operations', CMA Monograph No. 84, Indian Institute of Management, Ahmedabad.

DESAI, M. (1976), 'The Role of Exchange and Market Relationships in the Economics of the Transition Period: Lenin on the Tax in Kind', *Indian Economic Review*, 11.

—— (1986), 'Modelling an Early Warning System for Famines', paper presented at a Conference on Food Strategies held at WIDER, Helsinki, 21–5 July 1986; to be published in Drèze, J. P., and Sen, A. K. (eds.) (forthcoming), *The Political Economy of Hunger*.

—— (1988a), 'Rice and Fish', Discussion Paper No. 14, Development Economics Research Programme, London School of Economics.

—— (1988b), 'The Economics of Famine', in Harrison, G. A. (ed.) (1988), *Famines*.

—— (ed.) (1989), *Lenin's Economic Writings* (London: Lawrence and Wishart).

—— and SHAH, A. (1988), 'An Econometric Approach to the Measurement of Poverty', *Oxford Economic Papers*, 40.

DESHPANDE, V. D. (1982), *Employment Guarantee Scheme* (Pune: Tilak Maharashtra Vidyapeeth).

—— (1984), *Rojgar Hami* (Pune: Gramayan Prakashan).

DEVEREUX, S. (1988), 'Entitlements, Availability and Famine: A Revisionist View of Wollo, 1972–1974', *Food Policy*, 13.

—— and HAY, R. (1988), 'Origins of Famine: Theories and Management', mimeo, Food Studies Group, Oxford.

Devres, Inc. (1986), *Evaluation of the African Emergency Food Assistance Pro-*

gram 1984–1985: Synthesis Report (Washington DC: US Agency for International Development).

DE VILLE DE GOYET, C. (1978), 'Disaster Relief in the Sahel: Letter to the Editor', *Disasters*, 2.

—— SEAMAN, J., and GEIJER, U. (1978), *The Management of Nutritional Emergencies in Large Populations* (Geneva: WHO).

DE WAAL, A. (1987), 'Famine That Kills: Darfur 1984–85', mimeo, Save the Children Fund UK, London; to be published by Clarendon Press, Oxford.

—— (1988*a*), 'Famine Early Warning Systems and the Use of Socio-Economic Data', *Disasters*, 12.

—— (1988*b*), 'A Re-assessment of Entitlement Theory in the Light of Recent Famines in Africa', Ld'A-QEH Development Studies Working Paper No. 4, Queen Elizabeth House, Oxford.

—— (1989*a*), 'Famine Mortality: A Case Study of Darfur, Sudan 1984–5', *Population Studies*, 43.

—— (1989*b*), 'The Sudan Famine Code of 1920: Successes and Failures of the Indian Model of Famine Relief in Colonial Sudan', mimeo, Nuffield College, Oxford.

—— and EL AMIN, M. M. (1986), 'Survival in Northern Darfur 1985–1986: Report of the SCF Survey Team', mimeo, Save the Children Fund, London.

DE WILDE, J. (1984), *Agricultural Marketing and Pricing in Sub-Saharan Africa* (Los Angeles: University of California African Studies Centre and African Studies Association).

DHAGAMWAR, V. (1987), 'The Disadvantaged and the Law', paper presented at a Workshop on Poverty in India held at Queen Elizabeth House, Oxford, Oct. 1987.

DIAZ-AMADOR, C. (1982), 'Situación nutricional de la población Costarricense', in Saenz, L. (ed.) (1982), *Análisis de la situación alimentaria-nutricional en Costa Rica*.

DIAZ-BRIQUETS (1983), *The Health Revolution in Cuba* (Austin: University of Texas Press).

DICK, B. (1986), 'Supplementary Feeding for Refugees and Other Displaced Communites: Questioning Current Orthodoxy', *Disasters*, 10.

DIESLER, E. (1986), 'Rapport analytique sur les operations de la ligue au Tchad (1984–1986)', internal report, League of Red Cross and Red Crescent Societies, Geneva.

DIRKS, R. (1980), 'Social Responses During Severe Food Shortages and Famine', *Current Anthropology*, 21.

DIXON, J. (ed.) (1987), *Social Welfare in the Middle East* (London: Croom Helm).

DIXON, R. (1982), 'Mobilizing Women for Rural Employment in South Asia: Issues of Class, Caste, and Patronage', *Economic Development and Cultural Change*, 30.

—— (1983), 'Land, Labour and the Sex Composition of the Agricultural Labour Force: An International Comparison', *Development and Change*, 14.

DOBB, M. (1960), *An Essay on Economic Growth and Planning* (London: Routledge).

DODGE, C. P., and ALNWICK, D. (1986), 'Karamoja: A Catastrophe Contained', *Disasters*, 10.

DOMES, J. (1982), 'New Policies in the Communes: Notes on Rural Societal Structures in China, 1976–1981', *Journal of Asian Studies*, 41.

DONALDSON, G. (1984), 'Food Security and the Role of the Grain Trade', *American Journal of Agricultural Economics*, 66.

DONELAN, A. (1983), 'Zimbabwe: A Study of the New Nation's Attempts to Progress

Since Independence, with Particular Reference to Health and Nutrition', report submitted to the University of London in partial fulfilment of the requirements for the Diploma in Food Resources related to Community Development.

DOUGLAS, M. (1984), 'Fundamental Issues in Food Problems', *Current Anthropology*, 25.

—— and ISHERWOOD, B. (1979), *The World of Goods* (New York: Basic Books).

DOWD, M. (1987), 'Discreet Use of Flattery Hurts Biden', *Herald Tribune*, 17 Sept.

DOWNING, J., BERRY, L., DOWNING, L., DOWNING, T., and FORD, R. (1987), 'Drought and Famine in Africa, 1981–1986: The U.S. Response', report prepared for USAID, Settlement and Resources Systems Analysis, Clark University/Institute for Development Anthropology.

DOWNING, T. (1986), 'Smallholder Drought Coping Strategies in Central and Eastern Kenya', paper presented at the Annual Meeting of the Association of American Geographers, Minneapolis, 3–7 May 1986.

—— (1988a), 'Coping with Drought in Kenya: National and Household Strategies, 1984–1985', transcript of a presentation made at a Workshop on Famine and Famine Policy, Tufts University, 24 Sept. 1987.

—— (1988b), 'Climatic Variability and Food Security Among Smallholder Agriculturalists in Six Districts of Central and Eastern Kenya', unpublished Ph.D. dissertation, Clark University, Worcester, MA.

—— AKONG'A, J., MUNGAI, D. N., MUTURI, H. R., and POTTER, J. L. (1987), 'Introduction to the Kenya Case Study', in Akong'a *et al.* (1987), 'The Effects of Climatic Variations on Agriculture in Central and Eastern Kenya'.

—— GITU, K., and KAMAU, C. (eds.) (forthcoming), *Coping with Drought in Kenya: National and Local Strategies* (Boulder: Lynne Rienner).

DOWNS, R. R., KERNER, D. O., and REYNA, S. C. (eds.) (forthcoming), *The Political Economy of African Hunger: The Class and Gender Bias of Hunger* (New York: Gordon and Breach).

DRAKAKIS-SMITH, D. (1981), *Urbanization, Housing and the Development Process* (London: Croom Helm).

DRÈZE, J. H., KERVYN DE LETTENHOVE, A., PLATTEAU, J. P., and REDING, P. (1989), 'A Proposal for "Cooperative Relief of Debt in Africa" (CORDA)', Working Paper No. 60, WIDER, Helsinki.

DRÈZE, J. P. (1988a), 'Famine Prevention in India', Discussion Paper No. 3, Development Economics Research Programme, London School of Economics; to be published in Drèze, J. P., and Sen, A. K. (eds.) (forthcoming), *The Political Economy of Hunger*.

—— (1988b), 'Social Insecurity in India', paper presented at a Workshop on Social Security in Developing Countries held at the London School of Economics, 4–5 July 1988; Discussion Paper, Development Economics Research Programme, London School of Economics.

—— (1989), 'Famine Prevention in Africa', Discussion Paper No. 17, Development Economics Research Programme, London School of Economics; to be published in Drèze, J. P., and Sen, A. K. (eds.) (forthcoming), *The Political Economy of Hunger*.

—— and SEN, A. K. (1988), 'Public Action for Social Security', paper presented at a Workshop on Social Security in Developing Countries held at the London School of Economics, 4–5 July 1988; to be published in Ahmad, S. E., *et al.* (eds.) (forthcoming), *Social Security in Developing Countries*.

—— —— (eds.) (forthcoming), *The Political Economy of Hunger* (Oxford: Clarendon Press).

—— and STERN, N. H. (1987), 'The Theory of Cost-Benefit Analysis', in Auerbach, A., and Feldstein, M. (eds.) (1987), *Handbook of Public Economics* (Amsterdam and New York: North-Holland).

D'SILVA, E. (1983), 'The Effectiveness of Rural Works Programs in Labor-Surplus Economies: The Case of the Maharashtra Employment Guarantee Scheme', Cornell International Agriculture Mimeo No. 97, Cornell University, Ithaca, NY.

D'SOUZA, F. (1988), 'Famine: Social Security and an Analysis of Vulnerability', in Harrison, G. A. (ed.) (1988), *Famines*.

DUNCAN, W. R. (1984), 'Jamaica: Alternative Approaches', in Wesson, R. (ed.) (1984), *Politics, Policies and Economic Development in Latin America*.

DUPRÉ, G., and GUILLAUD, D. (1984), 'Rapport préliminaire sur la situation alimentaire dans le pays d'Aribinda', mimeo, ORSTOM, Ouagadougou.

—— —— (1988), 'L'Agriculture de l'Aribinda (Burkina Faso) de 1875 à 1983', *Cahiers sciences humaines*, 24.

DUTT, R. C. (1900), *Famines and Land Assessment in India* (London).

—— (1904), *The Economic History of India* (London: Kegan Paul Trench, Trubner; repr. 1969, New York: A. M. Kelley).

DUTTA, B. (1978), 'On the Measurement of Poverty in Rural India', *Indian Economic Review*, 15.

DYSON, T. (1987), 'Excess Female Mortality in India: Uncertain Evidence on a Narrowing Differential', to be published in Srinivasan, K., and Mukerji, S. (eds.) (forthcoming), *Dynamics of Population and Family Welfare* (Bombay: Himalaya).

—— (1988), 'The Population History of Berar Since 1881 and its Potential Wider Significance', mimeo, Department of Population Studies, London School of Economics.

—— (1989), 'On the Demography of South Asian Famines', mimeo, London School of Economics.

—— and CROOK, N. (eds.) (1984), *Indian Demography* (New Delhi: South Asia Publishers).

—— and MOORE, M. (1983), 'On Kinship Structure, Female Autonomy, and Demographic Behavior in India', *Population and Development Review*, 9.

EASTERLIN, R. A. (ed.) (1980), *Population and Economic Change in Developing Countries* (Chicago: University of Chicago Press).

ECKSTEIN, S. (1980), 'Income Distribution and Consumption in Post Revolutionary Cuba', *Cuban Studies*, 10.

—— (1982), 'The Impact of Revolution on Social Welfare in Latin America', *Theory and Society*, 11.

—— (1986), 'The Impact of the Cuban Revolution: A Comparative Perspective', *Comparative Studies in Society and History*, 28.

The Economist (1985), 'Where Africans Feed Themselves', *The Economist*, 12 Jan. 1985.

Economist Intelligence Unit (1983), 'Quarterly Economic Review of Angola, Guinea Bissau, Cape Verde, São Tomé, Príncipe: Annual Supplement 1983'.

—— (1984), 'Quarterly Economic Review of Angola, Guinea Bissau, Cape Verde, São Tomé, Príncipe: Annual Supplement 1984'.

EDIRISINGHE, N. (1987), 'The Food Stamp Scheme in Sri Lanka: Costs, Benefits, and

Options for Modification', Research Report No. 58, International Food Policy Research Institute, Washington, DC.

EDWARDS, D. W. (1932), 'The Missionary and Famine Relief', *Chinese Recorder*, 63.

EDWARDS, S. (1985), 'Stabilization with Liberalization: An Evaluation of Ten Years of Chile's Experiment with Free Market Policies: 1973–83', *Economic Development and Cultural Change*, 33.

EICHER, C. K. (1985), 'Famine Prevention in Africa: The Long View', in *Food for the Future: Proceedings of the Bicentennial Forum* (Philadelphia: Philadelphia Society for Promoting Agriculture).

—— (1986a), 'Transforming African Agriculture', The Hunger Project Papers, No. 4, The Hunger Project, San Francisco.

—— (1986b), 'Food Security Research Priorities in Sub-Saharan Africa', key-note address presented at the OAU/STRC/SAFGRAD International Drought Symposium held at the Kenyatta International Center, Nairobi, May 1986.

—— (1988a), 'Food Security Battles in Sub-Saharan Africa', paper presented at the 7th World Congress for Rural Sociology, Bologna, 25 June–2 July 1988.

—— (1988b), 'An Economic Perspective on the Sasakawa–Global 2000 Initiative to Increase Food Production in Sub-Saharan Africa', mimeo, Department of Agricultural Economics, Michigan State University, East Lansing.

—— and BAKER, D. C. (1982), 'Research on Agricultural Development in Sub-Saharan Africa: A Critical Survey', International Development Paper No. 1, Michigan State University, East Lansing.

—— and MANGWIRO, F. (1986), 'A Critical Assessment of the FAO Report on SADCC Agriculture and Agricultural Sector Studies', mimeo, Department of Agricultural Economics and Extension, University of Zimbabwe, Harare.

—— and STAATZ, J. M. (eds.) (1984), *Agricultural Development in the Third World* (Baltimore: Johns Hopkins).

—— —— (1986), 'Food Security Policy in Sub-Saharan Africa', in Maunder, A., and Renborg, U. (eds.) (1986), *Agriculture in a Turbulent World Economy* (London: Gower).

ELDREDGE, E., and RYDJESKI, D. (1988), 'Food Crises, Crises Response and Emergency Preparedness: The Sudan Case', *Disasters*, 12.

ENGLISH, J., BENNETT, J., and DICK, B. (1984), 'Tigray 1984: An Investigation', mimeo, OXFAM, Oxford.

ETHERIDGE, A. T. (1868), *Report on the Past Famines in the Bombay Presidency* (Bombay: Education Society's Press).

ETTEMA, WM., and MSUKVA L. (1985), *Food Production and Malnutrition in Malawi* (Zomba: Centre for Social Research, University of Malawi).

EVANS, D., and ALIZADEH, P. (1984), 'Trade, Industrialization and the Visible Hand', *Journal of Development Studies*, 21.

EZEKIEL, H. (1986), 'A Rural Employment Guarantee Scheme as an Early Warning System', mimeo, International Food Policy Research Institute.

FAI-MING WONG (1981), 'Effects of the Employment of Mothers on Marital Role and Power Differentiation in Hong Kong', in King, A. Y. C., and Lee, R. P. L. (eds.) (1981), *Social Life and Development in Hong Kong*.

FAULKINGHAM, R. H. (1977), 'Ecologic Constraints and Subsistence Strategies: The Impact of Drought in a Hausa Village, A Case Study from Niger', in Dalby, D. *et al.* (eds.) (1977), *Drought in Africa 2*.

—— and THORBAHN, P. F. (1975), 'Population Dynamics and Drought: A Village in Niger', *Population Studies*, 29.

FENELON, K. (1976), *The UAE: An Economic and Social Survey* (London: Longman).

FERNANDES, D. F. S. (1985), 'Health Statistics in Sri Lanka, 1921–80', in Halstead, S. B., *et al.* (eds.) (1985), *Good Health at Low Cost.*

FERNANDES, W., and MENON, G. (1987), *Tribal Women and Forest Economy: Deforestation, Exploitation and Status Change* (New Delhi: Indian Social Institute).

FEUCHTWANG, S., HUSSAIN, A., and PAIRAULT, T. (eds.) (1988), *Transforming China's Economy in the Eighties* (London: Zed).

FFRENCH-DAVIS, R. (1983), 'The Monetarist Experiment in Chile: A Critical Survey', *World Development*, 11.

—— and RACZYNSKI, D. (1988), 'The Impact of Global Recession on Living Standards: Chile, 1973–87', Notas Técnicas No. 97 (2nd edn., updated), CIEPLAN, Santiago.

FIELD, J. O. (1987), 'Multisectoral Nutrition Planning: A Post-Mortem', *Food Policy*, 12.

FIELDS, G. S. (1980), *Poverty, Inequality and Development* (Cambridge: Cambridge University Press).

—— (1988), 'Employment and Economic Growth in Costa Rica', *World Development*, 16.

FIREBRACE, J., and HOLLAND, S. (1984), *Never Kneel Down—Drought, Development and Liberation in Eritrea* (London: Spokesman).

FIRTH, R. (1959), *Social Change in Tikopia* (London: Allen and Unwin).

FLEGG, A. T. (1982), 'Inequality of Income, Illiteracy and Medical Care as Determinants of Infant Mortality in Underdeveloped Countries', *Population Studies*, 36.

FLEURET, A. (1986), 'Indigenous Responses to Drought in Sub-Saharan Africa', *Disasters*, 10.

FLEURET, P., and FLEURET, A. (1980), 'Nutrition, Consumption, and Agricultural Change', *Human Organization*, 39.

FLOUD, R. C. (1987), 'Anthropometric Measures of Nutritional Status in Industrial Societies: Europe and North America Since 1750', paper presented at a Conference on Poverty, Undernutrition and Living Standards held at WIDER, 27–30 July 1987; to be published in Osmani, S. R. (ed.) (forthcoming), *Nutrition and Poverty.*

—— and WACHTER, K. W. (1982), 'Poverty and Physical Stature: Evidence on the Standard of Living of London Boys 1770–1870', *Social Science History*, 6.

FOEGE, W. H. (1971), 'Famine, Infections and Epidemics', in Blix, G., *et al.* (eds.) (1971), *Famine: Nutrition and Relief Operations in Times of Disaster.*

FOGEL, R. W. (1987), 'Second Thoughts on the European Escape from Hunger: Crop Yields, Price Elasticities, Entitlements, and Mortality Rates', paper presented at a Conference on Poverty, Undernutrition and Living Standards held at WIDER, 27–30 July 1987; to be published in Osmani, S. R. (ed.) (forthcoming), *Nutrition and Poverty.*

—— ENGERMAN, S. L., and TRUSSELL, J. (1982), 'Exploring the Use of Data on Height: The Analysis of Long-Term Trends in Nutrition, Labour Welfare and Labour Productivity', *Social Science History*, 6.

—— *et al.* (1983), 'Secular Changes in American and British Stature and Nutrition', in Rotberg, R. I., and Rabb, T. K. (eds.) (1983), *Hunger and History.*

FOLBRE, N. (1986), 'Cleaning House: New Perspectives on Household and Economic Development', *Journal of Development Economics*, 22.

Food and Agriculture Organization (1984), *Assessment of the Agriculture, Food Supply and Livestock Situation: Kenya* (Rome: Office for Special Relief Operations, FAO).

—— (1985), 'Guidelines for Use by FAO Crop Assessment Missions to Africa', W/R6323, FAO Global Information and Early Warning System on Food and Agriculture, FAO, Rome.

—— (1986), *African Agriculture: The Next 25 Years* (Rome: FAO).

—— (1987a), 'Methodology for the Assessment of the Food Supply Situation and Requirements for Exceptional Assistance Arising from Crop Failure or Unusual Crop Surplus', FAO Global Information and Early Warning System on Food and Agriculture, FAO, Rome.

—— (1987b), 'Approche d'une politique céréalière: quelques idées forces tirées de l'expérience vécue sur le terrain', mimeo, Food and Agriculture Organization, N'Djaména, Chad.

—— (1988), *Potentials for Agricultural and Rural Development in Latin America and the Caribbean, Annex II: Rural Development* (Rome: FAO).

FORBES, J. D. (1985), *Jamaica: Managing Political and Economic Change* (Washington and London: American Enterprise Institute for Public Policy Research).

FORRESTER, J. W. (1971), *World Dynamics* (Cambridge, MA: Wright-Allen).

FORSTER, N., and HANDELMAN, H. (1985), 'Food Production and Distribution in Cuba: The Impact of the Revolution', in Super, J. C., and Wright, T. C. (eds.) (1985), *Food, Politics and Society in Latin America*.

FOSTER, J. (1984), 'On Economic Poverty: A Survey of Aggregate Measures', *Advances in Econometrics*, 3.

FOXLEY, A. (1983), *Latin American Experiments in Neo-conservative Economics* (Berkeley: University of California Press).

—— ANINAT, E., and ARELLANO, J. P. (1979), *Redistributive Effects of Government Programmes* (Oxford: Pergamon).

—— and RACZYNSKI, D. (1984), 'Vulnerable Groups in Recessionary Situations: The Case of Children and the Young in Chile', in Jolly, R., and Cornia, G. A. (eds.) (1984), *The Impact of World Recession on Children*.

FRANKE, R., and CHASIN, B. H. (1980), *Seeds of Famine: Ecological Destruction and the Development Dilemma in the West African Sahel* (Montclair: Allanheld and Osmun).

FREEMAN, P. H., GREEN, V. E., HICKOK, R. B., MORAN, E. F., and WHITAKER, M. D. (1978), 'Cape Verde: Assessment of the Agricultural Sector', Report CR-A-219A submitted to USAID, General Research Corporation, McLean, VA.

GAIDZANWA, R. (1986), 'Drought and the Food Crisis in Zimbabwe', in Lawrence, P. (ed.) (1986), *World Recession and the Food Crisis in Africa*.

GAIHA, R. (1987), 'Micro Data on Rural Poverty', paper presented at a Workshop on Poverty in India held at Queen Elizabeth House, Oxford, Oct. 1987.

—— (1988), 'On Measuring the Risk of Rural Poverty in India', in Srinivasan, T. N., and Bardhan, P. K. (eds.) (1988), *Rural Poverty in Asia*.

—— and KAZMI, N. P. (1981), 'Aspects of Rural Poverty in India', *Economics of Planning*, 17.

GALLAIS, J., et al. (1977), *Stratégies pastorales et agricoles des Sahéliens durant la sécheresse 1969–1974* (Bordeaux: Centre d'Études de Géographie Tropicale).

GALTUNG, J., O'BRIEN, P., and PREISWERK, R. (eds.) (1980), *Self-Reliance: A Strategy for Development* (London: Bogle-L'Ouverture Publications).

GANGRADE, K. D., and DHADDA, S. (1973), *Challenge and Response: A Study of Famines in India* (Delhi: Rachana Publications).

GARCIA, M., and PINSTRUP-ANDERSEN, P. (1987), 'The Pilot Food Price Subsidy Scheme in the Philippines: Its Impact on Income, Food Consumption, and Nutritional Status', Research Report No. 61, International Food Policy Research Institute, Washington, DC.

GARCIA, R. (ed.) (1985), *Chile: 1973–1984* (Stockholm: Institute of Latin American Studies).

GARCIA, R. V. (1981), *Drought and Man: The 1972 Case History*, i: *Nature Pleads not Guilty* (Oxford: Pergamon).

—— and ESCUDERO, J. C. (1982), *Drought and Man: The 1972 Case History*, ii: *Constant Catastrophe: Malnutrition, Famines and Drought* (Oxford: Pergamon).

—— and SPITZ, P. (1986), *Drought and Man: The 1972 Case History*, iii: *The Roots of Catastrophe* (Oxford: Pergamon).

GARDEN, B., and MUSA, K. (1986), 'Deterioration, Improvement Mark Crisis in Sudan', *Africa Emergency Report*, Apr./May 1986.

GARNSEY, P. (1988), *Famine and Food Supply in the Graeco-Roman World: Responses to Risk and Crises* (Cambridge: Cambridge University Press).

GAUDE, J., GUICHAOUA, A., MARTENS, B., and MILLER, S. (1987): 'Rural Development and Labour-Intensive Schemes: Impact Studies of Some Pilot Programmes', *International Labour Review*, 126.

GAVAN, J., and CHANDRASEKERA, I. (1979), 'The Impact of Public Foodgrain Distribution on Food Consumption and Welfare in Sri Lanka', Research Report No. 13, International Food Policy Research Institute, Washington, DC.

GBENYON, K., and LOCOH, T. (1987), 'Différences de mortalité selon le sexe dans l'enfance en Afrique au sud du Sahara', paper presented at the Séminaire sur Mortalité et Société en Afrique Sud du Sahara, Yaoundé, Cameroon, Oct. 1987.

GENDELL, M. (1985), 'Stalls in the Fertility Decline in Costa Rica, Korea and Sri Lanka', World Bank Staff Working Paper No. 693, World Bank, Washington, DC.

GEORGE, P. S. (1979), 'Public Distribution of Foodgrains in Kerala: Income Distribution Implications and Effectiveness', Research Report No. 7, International Food Policy Research Institute, Washington, DC.

GEORGE, S. (1976), *How the Other Half Dies* (Harmondsworth: Penguin).

—— (1984), *Ill Fares the Land* (Washington, DC: Institute for Policy Studies).

—— (1987), 'Food Strategies for Tomorrow', The Hunger Project Papers, No. 6, The Hunger Project, San Francisco.

—— (1988), *A Fate Worse Than Debt* (London: Penguin).

GHAI, D., KAY, C., and PEEK, P. (1988), *Labour and Development in Rural Cuba* (Basingstoke: Macmillan).

—— and SMITH, L. D. (1986), *Agricultural Prices, Policy, and Equity in Sub-Saharan Africa* (Boulder: Lynne Rienner).

GHOSE, A. K. (1982), 'Food Supply and Starvation: A Study of Famines with Reference to the Indian Subcontinent', *Oxford Economic Papers*, 34.

GHOSH, K. C. (1944), *Famines in Bengal, 1770–1945* (Calcutta: Indian Associated Publishing Co.).

GIBB, C. (1986), 'A Review of Feeding Programmes in Refugee Reception Centres in Eastern Sudan', *Disasters*, 10.

GILBERT, N. (1976), 'Alternative Forms of Social Protection for Developing Countries', *Social Services Review*, 50.

—— (1981), 'Social Security in Developing Countries', in Wallace, H. M., and Ebrahim, G. (eds.) (1981), *Maternal and Child Health Around the World*.

GILL, P. (1986), *A Year in the Death of Africa: Politics, Bureaucracy and the Famine* (London: Paladin).

GIRLING, R., and KEITH, S. (1977), 'Jamaica's Employment Crisis: A Political Economic Evaluation of the Jamaican Special Employment Program', World Employment Programme Research Working Paper 8, ILO, Geneva.

—— —— (1980), 'The Planning and Management of Jamaica's Special Employment Programme: Lessons and Limitations', *Social and Economic Studies*, 29.

GITTINGER, J. P., LESLIE, J., and HOISINGTON, C. (eds.) (1987), *Food Policy: Integrating Supply, Distribution and Consumption* (Baltimore: Johns Hopkins).

GLANTZ, M. (ed.) (1976), *The Politics of Natural Disaster: The Case of the Sahel Drought* (New York: Praeger).

—— (ed.) (1987a), *Drought and Hunger in Africa: Denying Famine a Future* (Cambridge: Cambridge University Press).

—— (1987b), 'Drought and Economic Development in Sub-Saharan Africa', in Glantz, M. (ed.) (1987), *Drought and Hunger in Africa*.

GLEWWE, P., and BHALLA, S. (1987), 'Response', *World Bank Economic Review*, 1.

GOBIN, M. (1977), 'The Role of Social Security in the Development of the Caribbean Territories', *International Social Security Review*, 30.

GODFREY, N. (1986a), 'Supplementary Feeding in Refugee Populations: Comprehensive or Selective Feeding Programmes', *Health Policy and Planning*, 1.

—— (1986b), 'Supplementary Feeding in Refugee Populations: A Review and Selected Annotated Bibliography', Evaluation and Planning Centre Paper No. 11, London School of Hygiene and Tropical Medicine.

GOLKIN, A. (1987), *Famine: A Heritage of Hunger* (Claremont, Calif.: Regina Books).

GOLLADAY, F., and KING, T. (1979), 'Social Development', in Hasan, P., and Rao, C. C. (eds.) (1979), *Korea: Policy Issues for Long-Term Development*.

GONZALEZ, N., INFANTE, A., SCHLESSINGER, C., and MONCKEBERG, F. (1983), 'Effectiveness of Supplementary Feeding Programs in Chile', in Underwood, B. (ed.) (1983), *Nutrition Intervention Strategies in National Development*.

GONZALEZ-VEGA, C. (1985), 'Health Improvements in Costa Rica: The Socioeconomic Background', in Halstead, S. B., *et al.* (eds.) (1985), *Good Health at Low Cost*.

GOOCH, T., and MACDONALD, J. (1981a), *Evaluation of 1979/80 Drought Relief Programme* (Republic of Botswana: Ministry of Finance and Development Planning).

—— (1981b), *Evaluation of 1979/80 Drought Relief Programme: Synopsis* (Republic of Botswana: Ministry of Finance and Development Planning).

GOODY, J. (1987), 'Futures of the Family in Rural Africa', paper presented at the Expert Consultation on Population and Agricultural and Rural Development, FAO, Rome, June–July 1987.

GOPALAN, C. (1983a), ' "Small is Healthy"? For the Poor not for the Rich!', *Bulletin of the Nutrition Foundation of India*, Oct.; also reprinted in *Future*, Autumn, 1983.

—— (1983*b*), 'Measurement of Undernutrition: Biological Considerations', *Economic and Political Weekly*, 18.

—— (1987*a*), 'Undernutrition: Concepts, Measurement and Implications', paper presented at a Conference on Poverty, Undernutrition and Living Standards held at WIDER, 27–30 July 1987; to be published in Osmani, S. R. (ed.) (forthcoming), *Nutrition and Poverty*.

—— (ed.) (1987*b*), *Combating Undernutrition* (New Delhi: Nutrition Foundation of India).

GORDON, A. M., Jun. (1983), 'The Nutriture of Cubans: Historical Perspective and Nutritional Analysis', *Cuban Studies*, 13.

Government of Botswana (1980), *A Human Drought Relief Programme for Botswana* (Gaborone: Ministry of Local Government and Lands).

—— (1985*a*), *The Drought Situation in Botswana* (Gaborone: Ministry of Finance and Development Planning).

—— (1985*b*), *Report on the National Food Strategy* (Gaborone: Ministry of Finance and Development Planning).

—— (1987), 'The Drought Situation in Botswana, March 1987, and Estimated Requirements for Relief and Recovery Measures', *aide-mémoire*, Ministry of Finance and Development Planning, Gaborone.

—— (1988), 'The Drought Recovery Situation in Botswana, March 1988, and Estimated Requirements for Relief and Recovery Measures', *aide-mémoire*, Ministry of Finance and Development Planning, Gaborone.

Government of Chad (1986), 'Système d'alerte précoce', various monthly bulletins (Ministère de la Sécurité Alimentaire et des Populations Sinistrées, N'Djaména).

Government of Chile (1974), 'Declaration of Principles of the Chilean Government', reprinted in Mendez, J. C. (ed.) (1979), *Chilean Economic Policy*.

—— (1988), *Social Reforms in Chile Since 1973 (An Experience in Infant Nutrition)* (Santiago: Secretaria de Desarrollo y Asistencia Social, Government of Chile).

Government of Ethiopia (1986), '1985 Meher (Main) Crop Season Synoptic and 1986 Food Supply Prospect—Final Report', Early Warning and Planning Services, Relief and Rehabilitation Commission, Addis Ababa.

—— (1987), *Workshop on Food-for-Work in Ethiopia, Proceedings of the Workshop Held in Addis-Ababa in July 1986* (Addis Ababa: Office of the National Committee for Central Planning).

Government of Hong Kong (1986), *Hong Kong Annual Digest of Statistics 1986* (Hong Kong: Census and Statistics Department).

—— (1987), *Hong Kong 1986* (Hong Kong: Government Information Services).

Government of India (1880), *Report of the Indian Famine Commission 1880* (London: HMSO).

—— (1898), *Report of the Indian Famine Commission 1898* (Simla).

—— (1901), *Report of the Indian Famine Commission 1901* (Calcutta).

—— (1945), *Famine Inquiry Commission, Report on Bengal* (New Delhi: Manager of Publications).

—— (1980), 'Joint Evaluation Report on Employment Guarantee Scheme of Maharashtra', Planning Commission and Directorate of Economics and Statistics, New Delhi.

—— (1989), *Economic Survey 1988–89* (New Delhi: Ministry of Finance).

Government of Jamaica (1985), Economic and Social Survey of Jamaica 1984 (Kingston: Planning Institute of Jamaica).

Government of Kenya (1985), 'CBS/NES Survey of Drought Responses: Preliminary Findings', mimeo, National Environment Secretariat, Nairobi.

Government of Maharashtra (1973), Report of the Fact Finding Committee for Survey of Scarcity Areas of Maharashtra State (Bombay).

Government of Mali (1987), 'Projet système d'alerte précoce', various bulletins (Bamako: Comité National d'Aide aux Victimes de la Sécheresse).

Government of the Republic of Korea (1963), Annual Survey of Education (Seoul: Ministry of Education).

—— (1965), Annual Survey of Education (Seoul: Ministry of Education).

—— (1970), Statistic Yearbook of Education (Seoul: Ministry of Education).

—— (1986), The Sixth Five-Year Economic and Social Development Plan (Seoul: Government of Korea).

—— (1987), Social Indicators in Korea (Seoul: Economic Planning Board).

Government of Sri Lanka (1984), Nutritional Status and Its Determinants and Intervention Programmes (Colombo: Ministry of Plan Implementation).

Government of Zimbabwe (1983), 'Development Policies and Programmes for Food and Nutrition in Zimbabwe', Ministry of Finance, Economic Planning and Development, Harare.

—— (1984), 'Planning for Equity in Health: A Sectoral Review and Policy Statement', Ministry of Health, Harare.

—— (1986a), 'Zimbabwe's Experience in Dealing with Drought 1982 to 1984', mimeo, Ministry of Labour, Manpower Planning and Social Welfare, Harare.

—— (1986b), 'Memorandum on Drought Relief 1986', mimeo, Ministry of Labour, Manpower Planning and Social Welfare, Harare.

GOYDER, C., and GOYDER, H. (1988), 'Famine in Ethiopia', in Curtis, D., Hubbard, M., and Shepherd, A. (eds.) (1988), Preventing Famine: Policies and Prospects for Africa.

GRANDIN, N. E., and LEMBUYE, P. (1987), 'The 1984 Drought: A Case Study from a Maasaai Group Ranch in South-Eastern Kajiado District', Pastoral Network Paper No. 23e, Overseas Development Institute, London.

GRANNELL, T. F. (1986), 'Ethiopia: Food-for-Work for the Rehabilitation of Forest, Grazing and Agricultural Lands in Ethiopia', paper presented at the WFP/ADB Conference on Food Aid for Development, Abijan, Sept. 1986.

GRANT, J. P. (1978), Disparity Reduction Rates in Social Indicators (Washington, DC: Overseas Development Council).

—— (1985), 'Famine Today—Hope for Tomorrow', Working Paper No. 1, The Alan Shawn Feinstein World Hunger Program, Brown University, Providence.

GRAY, R. H. (1974), 'The Decline of Mortality in Ceylon and the Demographic Effects of Malaria Control', Population Studies, 28.

GRAY, R., and BIRMINGHAM, D. (eds.) (1970a), Pre-colonial African Trade (Oxford: Oxford University Press).

—— (1970b), 'Some Economic and Political Consequences of Trade in Central and Eastern Africa in the Pre-colonial Period', in Gray, R. and Birmingham, D. (eds.) (1970a), Pre-colonial African Trade.

GREEN, D. W. (1977), 'Some Effects of Social Security Programs on the Distribution of Income in Costa Rica', unpublished Ph.D. dissertation, University of Pittsburgh.

GREEN, R. H. (1986*a*), 'Food Policy, Food Production and Hunger in Sub-Saharan Africa: Retrospect and Prospect', *International Journal*, 41.

—— (1986*b*), 'Hunger, Poverty and Food Aid in Sub-Saharan Africa: Retrospect and Potential', paper presented at the WFP/ADB Conference on Food Aid for Development, Abijan, Sept. 1986.

GREENOUGH, P. R. (1982), *Prosperity and Misery in Modern Bengal: The Famine of 1943–1944* (Oxford: Oxford University Press).

GRIFFIN, K. (1976), *Land Concentration and Rural Poverty* (London: Macmillan).

—— (1978), *International Inequality and National Poverty* (London: Macmillan).

—— (1987), *World Hunger and the World Economy* (London: Macmillan).

—— (1988), *Alternative Strategies for Economic Development* (London: Macmillan).

—— and HAY, R. (1985), 'Problems of Agricultural Development in Socialist Ethiopia: An Overview and a Suggested Survey', *Journal of Peasant Studies*, 13.

—— and JAMES, J. (1981), *The Transition to Egalitarian Development* (London: Macmillan).

—— and KHAN, A. R. (1977): *Poverty and Landlessness in Rural Asia* (Geneva: ILO).

—— and KNIGHT, J. (1988), 'Human Development in the 1980s and Beyond', report for the United Nations Committee for Development Planning.

—— —— (eds.) (1989), *Human Development in the 1980s and Beyond*, special issue of *Journal of Development Planning*, No. 19; to be published as a book.

GROSSI, J. R. (1985), 'El acceso a la salud, la eficacia hospitalaria y la distribución de los beneficios de la salud pública', *Cuadernos de economía*, 22.

Grupo de Investigaciones Agrarias (1984), 'Coyuntura agraria 1984: el costo de la reactivación', mimeo, GIA, Academia de Humanismo Cristiano, Santiago, Chile.

GUHA, S. (1981), 'Income Redistribution Through Labour-Intensive Rural Public Works: Some Policy Issues', *International Labour Review*, 120.

GUHAN, S. (1981), 'Social Security: Lessons and Possibilities from the Tamil Nadu Experience', *Madras Institute of Development Studies Bulletin*, 11.

—— (1988), 'Social Security and Insurance: Looking One Step Ahead', keynote address, Annual Conference, Insurance Institute of India, Madras.

GULATI, L. (1975), 'Female Work Participation: A Study of Inter-state Differences', *Economic and Political Weekly*, 10.

GUNATILLEKE, G. (ed.) (1984), *Intersectoral Linkages and Health Development*, Offset Publication No. 83, World Health Organization, Geneva.

—— (1985), 'Health and Development in Sri Lanka: An Overview', in Halstead, S. B., *et al.* (eds.) (1985), *Good Health at Low Cost*.

GUPTA, A. K. (1987), 'The Role of Women in Risk Adjustment in Drought Prone Regions', Working Paper No. 704, Indian Institute of Management, Ahmedabad.

GUZ, D. (1987), 'Population Dynamics of Famine in 19th Century Punjab, 1896–7 and 1899–1900', mimeo, London School of Economics.

GWATKIN, D. R. (1979), 'Food Policy, Nutrition Planning and Survival: The Case of Kerala and Sri Lanka', *Food Policy*, 4.

—— WILCOX, J. R., and WRAY, J. D. (1980), *Can Health and Nutrition Interventions Make a Difference?* (Washington, DC: Overseas Development Council).

HADZEWYCZ, R., ZARYCKY, C., and KOLOMAYETS, M. (eds.) (1983), *The Great Famine in Ukraine: The Unknown Holocaust* (Jersey City, NJ: The Ukrainian National Association for the National Committee to Commemorate Genocide Victims in Ukraine 1932–33).

HAHN, S. (1989), 'The Effects of an Export-Led Strategy of Growth on Income Distribution: South Korea, 1963–1985', unpublished undergraduate thesis, Harvard University.

HAIFENG, C., and CHAO, Z. (eds.) (1984), *Modern Chinese Medicine* (Lancaster: MTP Press).

HAIGNERE, C. S. (1983), 'The Application of the Free-Market Economic Model in Chile and the Effects on its Population's Health Status', *International Journal of Health Services*, 13.

HAINDL, E., and WEBER, C. (1986), 'Impacto redistributivo del gasto social', Series de Investigación, Departamento de Económica, Universidad de Chile.

HAINES, M., and AVERY, R. (1982), 'Differential Infant and Child Mortality in Costa Rica: 1968–1973', *Population Studies*, 36.

HAJJAR, S. G. (ed.) (1985), *The Middle East:From Transition to Development* (Leiden: E. J. Brill).

HAKIM, P., and SOLIMANO, G. (1978), *Development, Reform, and Malnutrition in Chile* (Cambridge, MA: MIT Press).

HALE, S. (1986), 'The OXFAM Food Targeting and Monitoring Programme in the Red Sea Province, Sudan', mimeo, OXFAM, Oxford.

HALEBSKY, S., and KIRK, J. M. (eds.) (1985), *Cuba: Twenty-Five Years of Revolution 1959 to 1984* (New York: Praeger).

HALL, E. (1973), 'One Shudders to Think What Would Have Happened to the Children Without the Feeding Scheme', *Oxfam News*, July.

HALSTEAD, S. B., WALSH, J. A., and WARREN, K. S. (1985), *Good Health at Low Cost* (New York: Rockefeller Foundation).

HAMILTON, C. (1986), *Capitalist Industrialization in Korea* (Boulder: Westview).

HAMILTON, S., POPKIN, B., and SPICER, D. (1984), *Women and Nutrition in Third World Countries* (South Hadley, MA: Bergin and Garvey Publishers).

HAMMOND, R. J. (1951), *History of the Second World War: Food* (London: HMSO).

HAMMOUD, H. R. (1986), 'The Impact of Technology on Social Welfare in Kuwait', *Social Service Review*, 60.

—— (1987), 'Kuwait', in Dixon, J. (ed.) (1987), *Social Welfare in the Middle East*.

HANCOCK, G. (1985), *Ethiopia: The Challenge of Hunger* (London: Gollancz).

HANDELMAN, H. (1982), 'Cuban Food Policy and Popular Nutritional Levels', *Cuban Studies*, 11 and 12.

HANSEN, A., and MCMILLAN, D. E. (eds.) (1986), *Food in Sub-Saharan Africa* (Boulder, CO: Lynne Rienner).

HAQ, M. (1976), *The Poverty Curtain* (New York: Columbia University Press).

HARBERGER, A. (1982), 'The Chilean Economy in the 1970s: Crisis, Stabilization, Liberalization, Reform', in Brunner, K., and Meltzer, A. (eds.) (1982), *Economic Policy in a World of Change*, Carnegie-Rochester Conference Series on Public Policy, Vol. 17.

HARBERT, L., and SCANDIZZO, P. (1982), 'Food Distribution and Nutrition Intervention: The Case of Chile', World Bank Staff Working Paper No. 512, World Bank, Washington, DC.

HARDEE-CLEAVELAND, K., and BANISTER, J. (1988), 'Fertility Policy and Implementation in China 1986–88', *Population and Development Review*, 14.

HARDIN, G. (1974), 'Lifeboat Ethics: The Case Against Helping the Poor', *Psychology Today*, 8.

—— (1981), 'The Toughlove Solution', *Newsweek*, 26 Oct.

HARREL-BOND, B. (1986), *Imposing Aid: Emergency Assistance to Refugees* (Oxford: Oxford University Press).

HARRIS, N. (1983), *Of Bread and Guns* (Harmondsworth: Penguin).

HARRISON. A. (1985), 'Les Services de santé du Koweit et leurs usagers', *Forum mondial de la santé*, 6.

HARRISON, G. A. (ed.) (1988), *Famines* (Oxford: Oxford University Press).

HARRISS, B. (1982), 'The Marketing of Foodgrains in the West African Sudano-Sahelian States', Progress Report 31, Economics Program, ICRISAT, Hyderabad.

—— (1983), 'Markets and Rural Undernutrition', mimeo, London School of Hygiene and Tropical Medicine, London.

—— (1986), 'The Intrafamily Distribution of Hunger in South Asia', paper presented at a Conference on Food Strategies held at WIDER, Helsinki, 21–5 July 1986; to be published in Drèze, J. P., and Sen, A. K. (eds.) (forthcoming), *The Political Economy of Hunger*.

—— (1988*a*), 'Differential Female Mortality and Health Care in South Asia', mimeo, Queen Elizabeth House, Oxford; forthcoming in *Journal of Social Studies*.

—— (1988*b*), 'Policy is What it Does: State Trading in Rural South India', *Public Administration and Development*, 8.

—— (1988*c*), 'Limitations of the "Lessons from India"', in Curtis, D., Hubbard, M., and Shepherd, A. (eds.) (1988), *Preventing Famine: Policies and Prospects for Africa*.

—— and WATSON, E. (1987), 'The Sex Ratio in South Asia', in Momsen, J. H., and Townsend, J. (eds.) (1987), *Geography of Gender in the Third World*.

HARSANYI, J. (1976), *Rational Behaviour and Bargaining Equilibrium in Games and Social Situations* (Cambridge: Cambridge University Press).

HART, K. (1987), 'Commoditisation and the Standard of Living', in Sen, A. K. (1987*a*), *The Standard of Living*.

HART, O. D. (1977), 'On the Profitability of Speculation', *Quarterly Journal of Economics*, 91.

—— and KREPS, D. M. (1986), 'Price Destabilizing Speculation', *Journal of Political Economy*, 94.

HARTMANN, B., and BOYCE, J. (1983), *A Quiet Violence: View from a Bangladesh Village* (London: Zed Press).

Harvard School of Public Health (1985), *Hunger in America: The Growing Epidemic* (Cambridge, MA: Harvard University).

—— (1987), *Hunger Reaches Blue Collar America* (Cambridge, MA: Harvard University).

HASAN, P., and RAO, C. C. (eds.) (1979), *Korea: Policy Issues for Long-Term Development* (Baltimore: Johns Hopkins).

HAWTHORN, G. (1987), 'Introduction', in Sen, A. K. (1987*a*), *The Standard of Living*.

HAY, R. W. (1975), 'Analysis of Data from Ogaden-Hararghe Province' (Addis Ababa: Consolidated Food and Nutrition Information System, Ethiopian Food and Nutrition Surveillance Programme).

—— (1986), 'Food Aid and Relief-Development Strategies', *Disasters*, 10.

—— (1988), 'Famine Incomes and Employment: Has Botswana Anything to Teach Africa?', *World Development*, 16.

—— BURKE, S., and DAKO, D. Y. (1986), 'A Socio-economic Assessment of Drought

Relief in Botswana', report prepared by UNICEF/UNDP/WHO for the Inter-ministerial Drought Committee, Government of Botswana, Gabrone.

—— and CLAY, E. J. (1986), 'Food Aid and the Development of Human Resources', paper presented at a WFP/ADB Conference on Food Aid for Development, Abijan, Sept. 1986.

—— and RUKUNI, M. (1988), 'SADCC Food Security Strategies: Evolution and Role', *World Development*, 16.

HEBERT, J. R. (1987), 'The Social Ecology of Famine in British India: Lessons for Africa in the 1980s?', *Ecology of Food and Nutrition*, 20.

HEMMEL, V., and Sindbjerg, P. (1984), *Women in Rural China: Policy Towards Women Before and After the Cultural Revolution* (Copenhagen: Humanities Press).

HENDERSON, P. L., and BIELLIK, R. J. (1983), 'Comparative Nutrition and Health Services for Victims of Drought and Hostilities in the Ogaden: Somalia and Ethiopia, 1980–1981' *International Journal of Health Services*, 13.

HEPPELL, T. S. (1973), 'Social Security and Social Welfare: A "New Look" from Hong Kong', *Journal of Social Policy*, 2.

—— (1974), 'Social Security and Social Welfare: A "New Look" from Hong Kong', *Journal of Social Policy*, 3.

Herald (1983), 'Hungry Buhera Women Search for Husbands', *Herald*, 16 Mar. 1983.

HERLEHY, T. J. (1984), 'Historical Dimensions of the Food Crisis in Africa: Surviving Famines along the Kenya Coast 1880–1980', Working Paper No. 87, African Studies Center, Boston University.

HERRERA, A. O., *et al.* (1976), *Catastrophe or New Society? A Latin American World Model* (Ottawa: IDRC).

HERRING, R. J. (1987), 'Openness and Democracy in the Rise and Decline of Economic Interventionism: Liberalization in Sri Lanka', paper presented at the Annual Meeting of the American Political Science Association, Sept. 1987.

—— and EDWARDS, R. M. (1983), 'Guaranteeing Employment to the Rural Poor: Social Functions and Class Interests in the Employment Guarantee Scheme in Western India', *World Development*, 11.

HESSE, C. (1985), 'An Evaluation of the 1984–1985 Food Situation in Burkina Faso', *Disasters*, 9.

—— (1988), 'Famine Early Warning Systems as a Famine Prevention Tool', mimeo, OXFAM, Oxford.

HEWITT, K. (ed.) (1983), *Interpretation of Calamity From the View Point of Human Ecology* (Winchester, MA: Allen and Unwin).

HEYER, J. (1986), 'Poverty and Food Deprivation in Kenya's Smallholder Agricultural Areas', paper presented at a Conference on Food Strategies held at WIDER, Helsinki, 21–5 July 1986; to be published in Drèze, J. P., and Sen, A. K. (eds.) (forthcoming), *The Political Economy of Hunger*.

HILL, A. (ed.) (1985), *Population, Health and Nutrition in the Sahel* (London: Routledge and Kegan Paul).

—— (1987), 'Demographic Responses to Food Shortages in the Sahel', paper presented at the Expert Consultation on Population and Agricultural and Rural Development, FAO, Rome, June–July 1987.

HILL, K. (1988), 'Demographic Trends in China from 1950 to 1982', Discussion Paper No. 22, World Bank, Washington, DC.

HILL, P. (1970), *Studies in Rural Capitalism in West Africa* (Cambridge: Cambridge University Press).

—— (1975), 'The West African Farming Household', in Goody, J. (ed.) (1975), *Changing Social Structure in Ghana* (London: International Africa Institute).

—— (1986), *Development Economics on Trial: The Anthropological Case for a Prosecution* (Cambridge: Cambridge University Press).

HILSUM, L. (1984), 'Ethiopia: Coping with Drought: Cash Instead of Food', *Ideas Forum*, 18 (UNICEF).

HOBSBAWM, E. J. (1954), *Primitive Rebels* (Manchester: Manchester University Press).

HOEFFEL, P. H. (1986), 'Famine, Harvests Co-exist in Sahel', *Africa Emergency Report*, Feb.–Mar.: 3.

HOFFER, W. (ed.) (1980), *Formation des journalistes en Afrique: l'esquisse d'une vue d'ensemble* (Bonn: Fondation Friedrich Naumann).

HOJMAN, D. E. (1988), 'Infant Mortality in Chile: Issues in Employment, Welfare, Nutrition and Care from Import Substitution to the Neo-liberal Period', mimeo, Department of Economics, University of Liverpool; to be published in Abel, C., and Lewis, C. M. (eds.) (forthcoming), *Welfare, Equity and Development in Latin America* (London: Macmillan).

—— (1989), 'Neoliberal Economic Policies and Infant and Child Mortality: Simulation Analysis of a Chilean Paradox', *World Development*, 17.

HOLLAND, P. (1987), 'Famine Responses in Colonial Zimbabwe: 1912–1947', mimeo, London School of Economics.

HOLM, J. D., and COHEN, M. S. (1988), 'Enhancing Equity in the Midst of Drought: The Botswana Approach', *Journal of Social Development in Africa*, 3.

—— and MORGAN, R. (1985), 'Coping with Drought in Botswana: An African Success', *Journal of Modern African Studies*, 23.

HOLT, J. (1983), 'Ethiopia: Food for Work or Food for Relief', *Food Policy*, 8.

—— and SEAMAN, J. (1976), 'The Scope of the Drought', in Hussein, A. M. (ed.) (1976), *Rehab: Drought and Famine in Ethiopia*.

HOLTHE, K. (1986), 'Final Report', internal report, League of Red Cross and Red Crescent Societies, Khartoum.

HOPKINS, R. (1988), 'Political Considerations in Subsidizing Food', in Pinstrup-Andersen, P. (ed.) (1988), *Consumer-Oriented Food Subsidies: Costs, Benefits, and Policy Options for Developing Countries*.

—— and PUCHALA, D. J. (1978), *The Global Political Economy of Food* (Madison: University of Wisconsin Press).

HOROWITZ, M. M., and LITTLE, P. O. (1987), 'African Pastoralism and Poverty: Some Implications for Drought and Famine', in Glantz, M. (ed.) (1987), *Drought and Hunger in Africa*.

HOSKEN, F. P. (1981), 'Female Genital Mutilation in the World Today: A Global Review', *International Journal of Health Services*, 11.

HOSSAIN, I. (1988), 'Poverty as Capability Failure', mimeo, WIDER, Helsinki.

—— (1989), 'Measuring Undernourishment: Some Empirical Difficulties', mimeo, University of Stockholm.

HUDDLESTON, B. (1984), *Closing the Cereals Gap with Trade and Food Aid*, Research Report No. 43, International Food Policy Research Institute, Washington, DC.

HUGO, G. J. (1984), 'The Demographic Impact of Famine: A Review', in Currey, B., and Hugo, G. (eds.) (1984), *Famine as a Geographical Phenomenon*.

HULL, T. H. (1988), 'Implications of Rising Sex Ratios in China', mimeo, Australian National University.

HUSSAIN, A. (1987), 'Nutrition and Nutritional Insurance in China 1949–84', mimeo, London School of Economics.

—— and FEUCHTWANG, S. (1988), 'The People's Livelihood and the Incidence of Poverty', in Feuchtwang, S., *et al.* (eds.) (1988), *Transforming China's Economy in the Eighties*.

—— LIU, H., and LIU, X. (1989), 'Compendium of Literature on the Chinese Social Security System', Discussion Paper, Development Economics Research Programme, London School of Economics.

—— and STERN, N. H. (1988), 'On the Recent Increase in Death Rates in China', mimeo, London School of Economics.

HUSSEIN, A. M. (ed.) (1976), *Rehab: Drought and Famine in Ethiopia* (London: International Africa Institute).

IDACHABA, F. S. (1986), 'Policy Options for African Agriculture', paper presented at a Conference on Food Strategies held at WIDER, Helsinki, 21–5 July 1986; to be published in Drèze, J. P., and Sen, A. K. (eds.) (forthcoming), *The Political Economy of Hunger*.

—— (1987), 'Sustainability Issues in Agricultural Development', invited symposium lecture presented at the Seventh Agriculture Symposium, Agriculture and Rural Development, World Bank, Washington, DC.

IDS Bulletin (1985), *Sub-Saharan Africa: Getting the Facts Straight*, Vol. 16, No. 3.

ILIFFE, J. (1987), *The African Poor: A History* (Cambridge: Cambridge University Press).

ILLANES, J. P. (1984), 'Desarrollo social e indicadores de salud', Documento de Trabajo No. 27, Centro de Estudios Públicos, Santiago, Chile.

ILO (1981), *Women in the Indian Labour Force* (Bangkok: ILO-ARTEP).

—— (1982*a*), *Rural Development and Women in Asia* (Geneva: ILO).

—— (1982*b*), *Rural Women Workers in Asia* (Geneva: ILO).

—— (1986), *Economically Active Population Estimates and Projections, 1950–2025* (Geneva: ILO).

Independent Commission on International Humanitarian Issues (1985), *Famine: A Man-Made Disaster?* (London: Pan).

Institute of Social Studies (1979), *Impact on Women Workers: Maharashtra Employment Guarantee Scheme—A Study* (New Delhi: Institute of Social Studies).

Interfutures (1979), *Facing the Future* (Paris: OECD).

International Institute for Environment and Development (1986), *Report on the African Emergency Relief Operation 1984–1986* (London: IIED).

International Social Security Association (1982), *Medical Care under Social Security in Developing Countries* (Geneva: ISSA).

ISENMAN, P. (1980), 'Basic Needs: The Case of Sri Lanka', *World Development*, 8.

—— (1987), 'A Comment on "Growth and Equity in Developing Countries: A Reinterpretation of the Sri Lankan Experience" by Bhalla and Glewwe', *World Bank Economic Review*, 1.

ISMAEL, J. S. (1982), *Kuwait: Social Change in Historical Perspective* (Syracuse, NY: Syracuse University Press).

JACKSON, A. J. K. (1976), 'The Family Entity and Famine Among the 19th Century

Akamba of Kenya: Social Responses to Environment Stress', *Journal of Family History*, 2.

JACKSON, T., and EADE, D. (1982), *Against the Grain: The Dilemma of Project Food Aid* (Oxford: OXFAM).

JACQUEMIN, J. C. (1985), 'Politiques de stabilisation par les investissements publics', unpublished Ph.D. thesis, Facultés des Sciences Economiques et Sociales, University of Namur, Belgium.

JAIN, A. K. (1985), 'Determinants of Regional Variations in Infant Mortality in Rural India', *Population Studies*, 39.

JAIN, D. (1980), *Women's Quest for Power* (Ghaziabad: Vikas).

—— and BANERJEE, N. (eds.) (1985), *Tyranny of the Household: Investigative Essays in Women's Work* (New Delhi: Vikas).

JAISWAL, N. K. (1978), *Droughts and Famines in India* (Hyderabad: National Institute of Rural Development).

JALÉE, P. (1965), *Le Pillage du Tiers-Monde* (Paris: Maspéro).

JAMESON, K. P. (1981), 'Socialist Cuba and the Intermediate Regimes of Jamaica and Guyana', *World Development*, 9.

—— and WILBER, C. K. (1981), 'Socialism and Development: Editors' Introduction', *World Development*, 9.

JAMISON, D. (1985), 'China's Health Care System: Policies, Organization, Inputs and Finance', in Halstead, S. B., *et al.* (eds.) (1985), *Good Health at Low Cost*.

—— and PIAZZA, A. (1987), 'China's Food and Nutrition Planning', in Gittinger, J. P., *et al.* (eds.) (1987), *Food Policy: Integrating Supply, Distribution and Consumption*.

—— and TROWBRIDGE, F. L. (1984), 'The Nutritional Status of Children in China: A Review of the Anthropometric Evidence', Population, Health and Nutrition Department Technical Note GEN 17, World Bank, Washington, DC.

—— EVANS, J., KING, T., PORTER, I., PRESCOTT, N., and PROST, A. (1984), *China: The Health Sector* (Washington, DC: World Bank).

JANSSON, K., HARRIS, M., and PENROSE, A. (1987), *The Ethiopian Famine* (London: Zed).

JARAMILLO, J. (1983), *Los problemas de la salud en Costa Rica* (San José, Costa Rica: Litografía Ambar).

JAYAWARDENA, K. (1986), *Feminism and Nationalism in the Third World* (London: Zed Press).

JAYAWARDENA, L. (1974), 'Sri Lanka', in Chenery, H., *et al.* (eds.) (1974), *Redistribution with Growth*.

—— (ed.) (forthcoming), *The Impact of the Global Recession on Living Standards*.

—— MAASLAND, A., and RADHAKRISHNAN, P. N. (1987), 'Sri Lanka', Country Study No. 15, WIDER Series on Stabilization and Adjustment Policies and Programmes, WIDER, Helsinki.

JAYNE, T. S., and WEBER, M. T. (1988), 'Market Reform and Food Security in Sub-Saharan Africa: A Review of Recent Experience', MSU International Development Working Paper, Department of Agricultural Economics, Michigan State University, East Lansing.

JELLIFFE, D. B., and JELLIFFE, E. F. P. (1971), 'The Effects of Starvation on the Function of the Family and of Society', in Blix, G., *et al.* (eds.) (1971), *Famine: Nutrition and Relief Operations in Times of Disaster*.

JIGGINS, J. (1986), 'Women and Seasonality: Coping with Crisis and Calamity', *IDS Bulletin*, 17.

JODHA, N. S. (1975), 'Famine and Famine Policies: Some Empirical Evidence', *Economic and Political Weekly*, 10.

—— (1978), 'Effectiveness of Farmers' Adjustment to Risk', *Economic and Political Weekly*, 13.

—— (1981), 'Role of Credit in Farmers' Adjustment Against Risk in Arid and Semi-arid Tropical Areas of India', *Economic and Political Weekly*, 16.

—— and MASCARENHAS, A. C. (1985), 'Adjustment in Self-Provisioning Societies', in Kates, R. W., Ausubel, J. H., and BERBERIAN, M. (eds.) (1985), *Climate Impact Assessment* (John Wiley and Sons).

JOEKES, S. (1987), *Women in the World Economy: An INSTRAW Study* (New York: Oxford University Press).

JOHNSON, D. G. (1988), 'Economic Reforms in the People's Republic of China', *Economic Development and Cultural Change*, 36.

JOHNSON, D. H., and ANDERSON, D. M. (eds.) (1988), *The Ecology of Survival: Case Studies from Northeast African History* (Boulder: Westview).

JOHNSON, S., and ZECKHAUSER, R. (1989), 'Robin Hooding Rents: A New Case for In-Kind Redistribution', mimeo, Kennedy School of Government, Harvard University.

JOLLY, R. (1985), *Adjustment with a Human Face*, Barbara Ward Lecture (New York: UNICEF).

—— and CORNIA, G. A. (eds.) (1984), *The Impact of World Recession on Children* (Oxford: Pergamon).

JONES, L. P., and SAKONG, I. (1980), *Government, Business and Entrepreneurship in Economic Development: The Korean Case* (Cambridge, MA: Harvard University Press).

JONES, W. O. (1988), 'Agricultural Trade within Tropical Africa: Historical Background', in Bates and Lofchie (1980), *Agricultural Development in Africa*.

JORGENSON, D. W., and SLESNICK, D. T. (1987), 'Redistributional Policy and the Measurement of Poverty', paper presented at a Conference on Poverty, Undernutrition and Living Standards held at WIDER, Helsinki, July 1987; to be published in Osmani, S. R. (ed.) (forthcoming), *Nutrition and Poverty*.

JOSE, A. V. (1984), 'Poverty and Inequality: The Case of Kerala', in Khan, A. R., and Lee, E. (eds.) (1984), *Poverty in Rural Asia*.

JOWETT, A. J. (1988), 'Famine in the People's Republic of China', Occasional Paper No. 21, Geography Department, Glasgow University.

JOYNATHSINGH, M. (1987), 'Mauritius', in Dixon, J. (ed.) (1987), *Social Welfare in Africa* (London: Croom Helm).

KABEER, N. (1989), 'Monitoring Poverty as if Gender Mattered: A Methodology for Rural Bangladesh', Discussion Paper No. 255, Institute of Development Studies, University of Sussex.

KADYAMPAKENI, J. (1988), 'Pricing Policies in Africa with Special Reference to Agricultural Development in Malawi', *World Development*, 16.

KAKWANI, N. (1985), *Income Inequality and Poverty* (New York: Oxford University Press).

—— (1986), 'On Measuring Undernutrition', Working Paper No. 8, WIDER, Helsinki.

—— (1988), 'Economic Crisis in the 1980s and Living Standards in Eighty Developing Countries', mimeo, WIDER, Helsinki.

KALAI, E., and SMORDINSKY, M. (1975), 'Other Solutions to Nash's Bargaining Problem', *Econometrica*, 43.

KAMAU, C. M., GITAU, M., WAINAINA, M., ANYANGO, G. J., and DOWNING, T. E. (forthcoming), 'Case Studies of Drought Impacts and Responses in Central and Eastern Kenya', to be published in Downing, T. E., *et al.* (eds.) (forthcoming), *Coping with Drought in Kenya: National and Local Strategies*.

KANBUR, S. M. R. (RAVI) (1986a), 'Global Food Balances and Individual Hunger: Three Themes in an Entitlements Based Approach', paper presented at a Conference on Food Strategies held at WIDER, Helsinki, 21–5 July 1986; to be published in Drèze, J. P., and Sen, A. K. (eds.) (forthcoming), *The Political economy of Hunger*.

—— (1986b), 'Malnutrition and Poverty in Latin America', mimeo, WIDER, Helsinki; to be published in Drèze, J. P., and Sen, A. K. (eds.) (forthcoming), *The Political Economy of Hunger*.

—— (1987), 'The Standard of Living: Uncertainty, Inequality and Opportunity', in Sen, A. K. (1987a), *The Standard of Living*.

KANDIYOTI, D. (1988), 'Bargaining With Patriarchy', *Gender and Society*, 1.

KANEKO, M., and NAKAMURA, K. (1979), 'The Nash Social Welfare Function', *Econometrica*, 47.

KAPLAN, R. (1988), *Surrender or Starve: The Wars Behind the Famine* (Boulder: Westview).

Kasongo Project Team (1983), 'Anthropometric Assessment of Young Children's Nutritional Status as an Indicator of the Subsequent Risk of Dying', *Journal of Tropical Pediatrics*, 29.

KATES, R. (1980), 'Disaster Reduction: Links Between Disaster and Development', in Berry, L., and Kates, R. (eds.) (1980), *Making the Most of the Least*.

—— (1981), 'Drought Impact in the Sahelian–Sudanic Zone of West Africa: A Comparative Analysis of 1910–1915 and 1968–1974', Environment and Development Background Paper No. 2, Center for Technology IDS, Clark University.

—— CHEN, R. S., DOWNING, T. E., KASPERSON, J. X., MESSER, E., and MILLMAN, S. R. (1988), 'The Hunger Report 1988', The Alan Shawn Feinstein World Hunger Program, Brown University, Providence.

KEEN, D. (1988), 'Some Problems with Targeting Emergency Grain in Western Sudan, 1985', paper presented at a Workshop on Food Security in the Sudan held at the Institute of Development Studies, University of Sussex, Oct. 1988 (revised version).

KELEMEN, P. (1985), 'The Politics of the Famine in Ethiopia and Eritrea', Occasional Paper No. 17, Department of Sociology, University of Manchester.

KELKAR, G. (1989), '. . . Two Steps Back? New Agricultural Policies in Rural China and the Woman Question', in Agarwal, B. (ed.) (1989), *Structures of Patriarchy*.

KELLMAN, M. H. (1987), *World Hunger: A Neo-Malthusian Perspective* (New York: Praeger).

KELLY, C. (1987), 'The Situation in Burkina Faso', *Disasters*, 11.

KENNEDY, E., and ALDERMAN, H. (1987), *Comparative Analysis of Nutritional Effectiveness of Food Subsidies and Other Food Related Interventions* (Washington, DC: IFPRI, and New York: UNICEF).

—— and COGILL, B. (1987), 'Income and Nutritional Effects of the Commercialization of Agriculture in South-Western Kenya', Research Report No. 63, International Food Policy Research Institute, Washington, DC.

—— and KNUDSEN, O. (1985), 'A Review of Supplementary Feeding Programmes and Recommendations on their Design', in Pinstrup-Andersen, P., and Biswas, M. (eds.) (1985), *Nutrition and Development*.

KHAN, A. R. (1977), 'Poverty and Inequality in Rural Bangladesh', in Griffin, K., and Khan, A. R. (1977), *Poverty and Landlessness in Rural Asia* (Geneva: ILO).

KHAN, Q. M. (1985), 'A Model of Endowment Constrained Demand for Food in Agricultural Economy with Empirical Applications to Bangladesh', *World Development*, 13.

KHARE, R. S. (1986), 'The Indian Meal: Aspects of Cultural Economy and Food Use', in Khare, R. S., and Rao, M. S. A. (eds.) (1986), *Food, Society and Culture*.

—— and RAO, M. S. A. (eds.) (1986), *Food, Society and Culture* (Durham, NC: Carolina Academic Press).

KIELMAN, A. A., AJELLO, C. A., and KIELMAN, N. S. (1982), 'Nutrition Intervention: An Evaluation of Six Studies', *Studies in Family Planning*, 13.

—— et al. (eds.) (1983), *Child and Maternal Health Services in Rural India: The Narangwal Experiment*, i (Baltimore: Johns Hopkins).

KILBY, P., and LIEDHOLM, C. (1988), 'The Role of Nonfarm Activities in the Rural Economy', in Rukuni, M., and Bernsten, R. H. (eds.) (1988), *Southern Africa: Food Security Policy Options*.

KILJUNEN, K. (ed.) (1984), *Kampuchea: Decade of the Genocide* (London: Zed).

KIM, W. S., and YUN, K. Y. (1988), 'Fiscal Policy and Development in Korea', *World Development*, 16.

KING, A. Y. C., and LEE, R. P. L. (eds.) (1981), *Social Life and Development in Hong Kong* (Hong Kong: The Chinese University Press).

KLEIN, I. (1973), 'Death in India, 1871–1921', *Journal of Asian Studies*, 32.

—— (1984), 'When the Rains Failed: Famine, Relief and Mortality in British India', *Indian Economic and Social History Review*, 21.

KOO, H. (1984), 'The Political Economy of Income Distribution in South Korea: The Impact of the State's Industrialization Policies', *World Development*, 12.

KOOHI-KAMALI, F. (1988), 'The Pattern of Female Mortality in Iran and Some of its Causes', Applied Economics Discussion Paper No. 62, Institute of Economics and Statistics, Oxford.

KOPONEN, J. (1988), 'War, Famine, and Pestilence in Late Precolonial Tanzania: A Case for Heightened Mortality', *International Journal of African Historical Studies*, 21.

KOSO-THOMAS, O. (1987), *The Circumcision of Women: A Strategy for Eradication* (London: Zed).

KRAUSE, L. B. (1988), 'Hong Kong and Singapore: Twins or Kissing Cousins?', *Economic Development and Cultural Change*, 36.

KRISHNA, RAJ (1963), 'Farm Supply Response in India-Pakistan: A Case Study of the Punjab Region', *Economic Journal*, 73.

KRISHNAJI, N. (1987), 'Poverty and Sex Ratio: Some Data and Speculations', *Economic and Political Weekly*, 22.

KRISHNAMACHARI, K. A. V. R., RAO, N. P., and RAO, K. V. (1974), 'Food and

Nutritional Situation in the Drought Affected Areas of Maharashtra: A Survey and Recommendations', *Indian Journal of Nutrition and Dietetics*, 11.

KRISHNAN, T. N. (1985), 'Health Statistics in Kerala State, India', in Halstead, S. B., *et al.* (eds.) (1985), *Good Health at Low Cost*.

—— (1989), 'Kerala's Health Transition: Facts and Factors', mimeo, Center for Population Studies, Harvard University.

KULA, E. (1988), 'The Inadequacy of the Entitlement Approach to Explain and Remedy Famines', *Journal of Development Studies*, 25.

—— (1989), 'Politics, Economics, Agriculture and Famines', *Food Policy*, 14.

KULKARNI, S. N. (1974), *Survey of Famine Affected Sinnar Taluka* (Pune: Gokhale Institute of Politics and Economics).

KUMAR, B. G. (1985), 'The Ethiopian Famine and Relief Measures: An Analysis and Evaluation', mimeo, UNICEF.

—— (1986), 'Ethiopian Famines 1973–1985: A Case Study', paper presented at a Conference on Food Strategies held at WIDER, Helsinki, 21–5 July 1986; Working Paper No. 26, WIDER, 1987; to be published in Drèze, J. P., and Sen, A. K. (eds.) (forthcoming), *The Political Economy of Hunger*.

—— (1987), 'Poverty and Public Policy: Government Intervention and Levels of Living in Kerala, India', unpublished Ph.D. thesis, University of Oxford.

—— (1988), 'Consumption Disparities, Food Surpluses and Effective Demand Failures: Reflections on the Macroeconomics of Drought Vulnerability', Working Paper No. 229, Centre for Development Studies, Trivandrum.

—— and STEWART, F. (1987), 'Tackling Malnutrition: What Can Targeted Nutritional Intervention Achieve?', paper presented at a Conference on Poverty in India, Queen Elizabeth House, Oxford, Oct. 1987.

KUMAR, S. K. (1979), 'Impact of Subsidised Rice on Food Consumption and Nutrition in Kerala', Research Report No. 5, International Food Policy Research Institute, Washington, DC.

—— and LIPTON, M. (1988), 'Editors' Introduction', *World Development*, 16.

KUZNETS, P. W. (1988), 'An East Asian Model of Economic Development: Japan, Taiwan, and South Korea', *Economic Development and Cultural Change*, 36.

KUZNETS, S. (1966), *Modern Economic Growth* (New Haven: Yale University Press).

KYNCH, J. (1985), 'How Many Women are Enough? Sex Ratios and the Right to Life', in *Third World Affairs 1985* (London: Third World Foundation).

—— (1987a), 'Food Scarcity and Jail Population in British India', mimeo, Institute of Economics and Statistics, Oxford.

—— (1987b), 'Some State Responses to Male and Female Need in British India', in Afshar, H. (ed.) (1987), *Women, State and Ideology: Studies from Africa and Asia*.

—— (1988), 'Scarcities, Distress and Crime in British India', paper presented at the 7th World Congress of Rural Sociology, Bologna, July 1988.

—— and Sen, A. K. (1983), 'Indian Women: Well-Being and Survival', *Cambridge Journal of Economics*, 7.

LABONNE, M. (1984a), *Sur la question alimentaire en Afrique* (Paris: Institut National de la Recherche Agronomique).

—— (1984b), *Origines et perspectives de la crise alimentaire dans les pays du Sahel* (Paris: Institut National de la Recherche Agronomique).

LADEJINSKI, W. (1973), 'Drought in Maharashtra: Not in a Hundred Years', *Economic and Political Weekly*, 17 Feb.

LAL, D. (1983), *The Poverty of 'Development Economics'* (London: Institute of Economic Affairs).

LALLEMAND, S. (1975), 'La Sécheresse dans un village Mossi de Haute-Volta', in Copans, J., *et al.* (1975), *Sécheresses et famines du Sahel*.

LANDMAN, J., and WALKER, S. (1987), 'Towards Food and Nutrition Security in Jamaica: The Nutrition Perspective', in Leslie, K. A., and Rankine, L. B. (eds.) (1987), *Papers and Recommendations of the Workshop on Food and Nutrition Security in Jamaica in the 1980s and Beyond*.

LANGFORD, C. (1984), 'Sex Differentials in Mortality in Sri Lanka: Changes since the 1920s', *Journal of Bio-social Science*, 16.

—— (1988), 'Sex Differentials in Sri Lanka: Past Trends and the Situation Recently', mimeo, London School of Economics.

LANGSTEN, R., and CHOWDHURY, S. A. (1984), 'The Demographic Effects of Famine in Contemporary Bangladesh', mimeo, Carolina Population Center, University of North Carolina.

LAPPÉ, F. M., and COLLINS, J. (1979), *World Hunger: Ten Myths* (London: IFDP).

—— —— (1980), *Food First: The Myth of Scarcity* (London: Souvenir Press).

LARDINOIS, R. (1982), 'Une conjoncture de crise démographique en Inde du Sud au XIXe siècle: la famine de 1876–1878', *Population*, 37.

—— (1985), 'Famine, Epidemics and Mortality in South India', *Economic and Political Weekly*, 20.

—— (1987), 'Population, famines et marché dans l'historiographie indienne', *Annales économies, sociétés, civilisations*, 3.

LAWRENCE, P. (ed.) (1986), *World Recession and the Food Crisis in Africa* (London: James Currey).

League of Red Cross and Red Crescent Societies (1986), 'The Red Cross Policy on the Nutritional Aspects of Relief Operations', Resolution passed at the XXVth International Conference of the Red Cross, Geneva, Oct. 1986.

LEE, R. D., ARTHUR, W. B., KELLEY, A. C., RODGERS, G., and SRINIVASAN, T. N. (eds.) (1988), *Population, Food and Rural Development* (Oxford: Clarendon Press).

LEE, R. P. L. (1982), 'Comparative Studies of Health Care Systems', *Social Science and Medicine*, 16.

—— (1983), 'Problems of Primary Health Care in a Newly Developing Society: Reflections on the Hong Kong Experience', *Social Science and Medicine*, 17.

LEFTWICH, A., and HARVIE, D. (1986), 'The Political Economy of Famine', Discussion Paper No. 116, Institute for Research in the Social Sciences, University of York.

LEGAL, P. Y. (1984), 'Alimentation et énergie dans le développement rural en Cabo Verde', Série Énergie, Alimentation et Développement, No. 2, Centre International de Recherche sur l'Environnement et le Développement, École des Hautes Études en Sciences Sociales, Paris.

LEGRAIN, C. (1980), 'Nutrition et santé des enfants aux Îles du Cap Vert', *Environnement africain*, Nos. 14, 15, 16, ENDA, Dakar.

LEITINGER, I. A. (1985), 'Women's Legal Status and Role Choices in Six Latin American Countries: A Cross-Cultural Longitudinal Analysis (1950–70) and a Single-Case Update (1980)', Working Paper No. 91, Office of Women in International Development, Michigan State University.

LELE, U., and CANDLER, W. (1984), 'Food Security in Developing Countries: National Issues', in Eicher, C. K., and Staatz, J. M. (eds.) (1984), *Agricultural Development in the Third World*.

LEONTIEF, W., *et al.* (1977), *The Future of the World Economy* (New York: Oxford University Press).

LESLIE, J. (1987), 'Interactions of Malnutrition and Diarrhoea: A Review of Research', in Gittinger, J. P., *et al.* (eds.) (1987), *Food Policy*.

—— (1988), 'Women's Work and Child Nutrition in the Third World', *World Development*, 16.

LESLIE, K. A., and RANKINE, L. B. (eds.) (1987), *Papers and Recommendations of the Workshop on Food and Nutrition Security in Jamaica in the 1980s and Beyond* (Kingston: Caribbean Food and Nutrition Institute).

LESOURD, M. (1986), 'Sécheresse et émigration aux Îles du Cap Vert', paper presented at a conference on 'Comparaison des sécheresses dans le Nordeste brésilien et le Sahel africain', IHEAL, Paris, Jan. 1986.

LEVINE, R. A. (1988), 'Women's Schooling and Patterns of Fertility and Child Survival', mimeo, forthcoming in *Educational Research*.

LEVINSON, F. J. (1972), *Morinda: An Economic Analysis of Malnutrition Among Young Children in Rural India* (Cambridge, MA and Ithaca, NY: MIT/Cornell University Press).

LEYS, R. (1986), 'Drought and Drought Relief in Southern Zimbabwe', in Lawrence, P. (ed.) (1986), *World Recession and the Food Crisis in Africa*.

LI, L. (1982*a*), 'Food, Famine and the Chinese State', *Journal of Asian Studies*, 41.

—— (1982*b*), 'Feeding China's One Billion: Perspectives from History' in Cahill, K. (ed.) (1982), *Famine*.

—— (1987), 'Famine and Famine Relief: Viewing Africa in the 1980s from China in the 1920s', in Glantz, M. (ed.) (1987*a*), *Drought and Hunger in Africa*.

LIEBERMAN, S. S. (1984), 'An Organisational Reconnaissance of the Employment Guarantee Scheme', *Indian Journal of Public Administration*, 30.

—— (1985), 'Field-Level Perspectives on Maharashtra's Employment Guarantee Scheme', *Public Administration and Development*, 5.

LIEDHOLM, C., and KILBY, P. (1989), 'The Role of Non-Farm Activities in the Rural Economy', in Williamson, J. G., and Panchamukhi, V. R. (eds.) (1989), *Balance Between Industry and Agriculture in Economic Development*, ii: *Sector Proportions* (London: Macmillan).

LIN, T. B., LEE, R. P. L., and SIMONIS, U. (eds.) (1979), *Hong Kong: Economic, Social and Political Studies in Development* (New York: M. E. Sharpe).

LINNEMANN, H. (1981), *MOIRA: A Model of International Relations in Agriculture* (Amsterdam: North Holland).

LIPTON, M. (1977), *Why Poor People Stay Poor: Urban Bias in World Development* (London: Temple Smith).

—— (1983), 'Poverty, Undernutrition and Hunger', World Bank Staff Working Paper No. 597, World Bank, Washington, DC.

—— (1986), 'Food Production Data: Does Anyone Care?', paper presented at a Workshop on Statistics in Support of African Food Policies and Strategies, Brussels, May 1986.

—— (1987*a*), 'Limits of Price Policy for Agriculture: Which Way for the World Bank?', *Development Policy Review*, 5.

—— (1987b), 'Variable Access to Food', in Gittinger, J. P., et al. (eds.) (1987), Food Policy.

—— (1988a), 'The Poor and the Poorest: Some Interim Findings', World Bank Discussion Paper No. 25, World Bank, Washington, DC.

—— (1988b), 'A Rejoinder to Ray', Development Policy Review, 6.

—— (1988c), 'The Place of Agricultural Research in the Development of Sub-Saharan Africa', World Development, 16.

LITTLE, I. (1982), Economic Development (New York: Basic Books).

LITTLE, P. O., and HOROWITZ, M. M. (1987), 'Subsistence Crops Are Cash Crops: Some Comments with Reference to Eastern Africa', Human Organization, 46.

LLOYD, C. B., and NIEMI, B. T. (1979), The Economics of Sex Differentials (New York: Columbia University Press).

LOEWENSON, R. (1984), 'The Health Status of Labour Communities in Zimbabwe: An Argument for Equity', dissertation presented for the M.Sc. Degree in Community Health in Developing Countries, University of London.

—— (1986), 'Farm Labour in Zimbabwe: A Comparative Study in Health Status', Health Policy and Planning, 1.

—— and SANDERS, D. (1988), 'The Political Economy of Health and Nutrition', in Stoneman, C. (ed.) (1988), Zimbabwe's Prospects: Issues of Race, Class, State and Capital in Southern Africa.

LOFCHIE, M. F. (1975), 'The Political and Economic Origin of African Hunger', Journal of Modern African Studies, 13.

—— (1987), 'The Decline of African Agriculture: An Internationalist Perspective', in Glantz, M. (ed.) (1987a), Drought and Hunger in Africa.

—— and COMMINS, S. E. (1982), 'Food Deficits and Agricultural Policies in Tropical Africa', Journal of Modern African Studies, 20.

LOMBARD, J. (1985), Disponibilités alimentaires en céréales et stratégies de survie en pays Serer (Dakar: ORSTOM).

LONGHURST, R. (1986), 'Household Food Strategies in Response to Seasonality and Famine', IDS Bulletin, 17.

—— (1987), 'Famines, Food and Nutrition: Issues and Opportunities for Policy and Research', Food and Nutrition Bulletin, 9.

—— (1988), 'Cash Crops, Household Food Security and Nutrition', IDS Bulletin, 19.

LOPEZ, A. D. (1983), 'The Sex Mortality Differentials in Developed Countries', in Lopez, A. D., and Ruzicka, L. T. (eds.) (1983), Sex Differentials in Mortality: Trends, Determinants and Consequences.

—— and RUZICKA, L. T. (eds.) (1983), Sex Differentials in Mortality: Trends, Determinants and Consequences (Canberra: Australian National University).

LOUTFI, M. F. (1980), Rural Women: Unequal Partners in Development (Geneva: ILO).

LOVEDAY, A. (1914), The History and Economics of Indian Famines (London: A. G. Bell and Sons; reprinted by Usha Publications, New Delhi, 1985).

LOWGREN, M. (1985), 'A Nutritional Sejour to Africa', mimeo, League of Red Cross and Red Crescent Societies.

LUGAN, B. (1976), 'Causes et effets de la famine "Ramanura" au Rwanda, 1916–18', Canadian Journal of African Studies, 10.

LUNDAHL, M. (1983), 'Insuring Against Risk in Primitive Economies: The Role of Prestige Goods', in Söderström, L. (ed.) (1983), Social Insurance.

LUTHRA, S., and SRINIVAS, S. (1976), 'Famine in India: A Select Bibliography', mimeo, Social Science Documentation Centre, New Delhi.

McALPIN, M. (1983a), *Subject to Famine: Food Crises and Economic Change in Western India, 1860–1920* (Princeton: Princeton University Press).

—— (1983b), 'Famine, Epidemics, and Population Growth: The Case of India', in Rotberg, R. I., and Rabb, T. K. (eds.) (1983), *Hunger and History*.

—— (1987): 'Famine Relief Policy in India: Six Lessons for Africa', in Glantz, M., (ed.) (1987a), *Drought and Hunger in Africa*.

McCANN, J. (1987), 'The Social Impact of Drought in Ethiopia: Oxen, Households, and Some Implications for Rehabilitation', in Glantz, M. (ed.) (1987a), *Drought and Hunger in Africa*.

McCORKLE, C. (1987), 'Foodgrain Disposals as Early Warning Famine Signals: A Case From Burkina Faso', *Disasters*, 11.

McCRINDLE, J. W. (1877), translation of *Ancient India* by Megasthenes.

—— (1901): *Ancient India as Described in Classical Literature* (Westminster: Constable and Co. Ltd.).

McELROY, M. B., and HORNEY, M. J. (1981), 'Nash Bargained Household Decisions: Toward a Generalization of Theory of Demand', *International Economic Review*, 22.

McGINN, N. F., SNODGRASS, D. R., KIM, Y. B., KOM, S. B., and QUEE-YOUNG (1980), *Education and Development in Korea* (Cambridge, MA: Harvard University Press).

McHENRY, D. F., and BIRD, K. (1977), 'Food Bungle in Bangladesh', *Foreign Policy*, 27.

McKEOWN, T. (1976), *The Modern Rise of Population* (London: Edward Arnold).

—— and LOWE, C. R. (1966), *An Introduction to Social Medicine* (Oxford: Blackwell).

McKERROW, R. J. (1979), 'Drought in Ethiopia 1977/1979', *Disasters*, 3.

MACKINTOSH, M. (1985), 'Economic Tactics: Commercial Policy and the Socialization of African Agriculture', *World Development*, 13.

McLEAN, W. (1986), 'A Profile of Mali with Focus on Current Food Shortages', mimeo, London School of Hygiene and Tropical Medicine.

—— (1987), 'Assessment of the Food Emergency in Mali 1983–85', paper presented at the 5th IDS Food Aid Seminar on The Use of Information in Emergencies, Apr. 1987.

—— (1988), 'Intervention Systems in Food Crises: The Role of International Agencies', paper presented at the Seventh International Congress for Rural Sociology, Bologna, Italy, June 1988.

McNEILL, W. H. (1976), *Plagues and People* (Garden City, NY: Anchor Press).

MAGANDA, B. F. (forthcoming), 'Surveys and Activities of the Central Bureau of Statistics Related to Food Monitoring', to be published in Downing, T., *et al.* (eds.) (forthcoming), *Coping With Drought in Kenya: National and Local Strategies*.

MAHIEU, F. R., and NOUR, M. M. (1987), 'The Entitlement Approach to Famines and the Sahelian Case: A Survey of the Available Literature', mimeo, WIDER, Helsinki.

MAHMUD, W., and MAHMUD, S. (1985), 'Age–Sex Aspects of the Food and Nutrition Problems in Rural Bangladesh', ILO Working Paper, WEP10-6/WP74, Geneva.

MAKSUDOV, M. (1986), 'Ukraine's Demographic Losses 1927–1938', in Serbyn, R., and Krawchenko, B. (eds.) (1986), *Famine in Ukraine*.

MALENBAUM, W. (1956), 'India and China: Development Contrasts', *Journal of Political Economy*, 64.

—— (1959), 'India and China: Contrasts in Development Performance', *American Economic Review*, 49.

—— (1982), 'Modern Economic Growth in India and China: The Comparison Revisited, 1950–1980', *Economic Development and Cultural Change*, 31.

MALLET, A. (1980), 'Social Protection of the Rural Population', *International Social Security Review*, 33.

MALLORY, W. H. (1926), *China: Land of Famine* (New York: American Geographical Publishing Society).

MALTHUS, T. R. (1798), *Essay on the Principle of Population as it Affects the Future Improvement of Society* (London: J. Johnson).

—— (1800), *An Investigation of the Cause of the Present High Price of Provisions* (London).

MAMADOU, P. T. (1987*a*), 'Dans quelles mesures la place des individus détermine leur droit à la nourriture: example du pays Senoufo (nord Côte d'Ivoire)', mimeo, Université Nationale de Côte d'Ivoire, Abijan.

—— (1987*b*), 'La Notion des droits, de la privation, de la pauvreté et de la famine chez les Natara Rouges—Senoufo du nord de la Côte d'Ivoire', mimeo, Université Nationale de Côte d'Ivoire, Abijan.

MANDAZA, I. (ed.) (1986), *Zimbabwe: The Political Economy of Transition 1980–1986* (Dakar: CODESRIA).

MANN, C. K., and HUDDLESTON, B. (eds.) (1986), *Food Policy: Frameworks for Analysis and Action* (Bloomington: Indiana University Press).

MANSER, M., and BROWN, M. (1980), 'Marriage and Household Decision Making: A Bargaining Analysis', *International Economic Review*, 21.

MANSERGH, N. (ed.) (1971), *The Transfer of Power 1942–7*, iii (London: HMSO).

—— (ed.) (1973), *The Transfer of Power 1942–7*, iv (London: HMSO).

MAO ZEDONG (TSE-TUNG) (1974), *Mao Tse-tung Unrehearsed, Talks and Letters: 1956–71* (London: Penguin Books).

MARCHIONE, T. J. (1977), 'Food and Nutrition in Self-Reliant National Development: The Impact on Child Nutrition of Jamaica Government Policy', *Medical Anthropology*, 1.

—— (1984), 'Evaluating Primary Health Care and Nutrition Programmes in the Context of National Development', *Social Science and Medicine*, 19.

MARGLIN, F. (1986), 'An Anthropological View on Food, Hunger and Poverty', paper presented at a conference on Food Strategies held at WIDER, Helsinki, July 1986.

MARGLIN, S. (1976), *Value and Price in the Labour-Surplus Economy* (Oxford: Clarendon).

MARI BHAT, P. N. (forthcoming), 'Mortality and Fertility in India, 1881–1961', to be published in Dyson, T. (ed.) (forthcoming), *India's Historical Demography: Studies in Famine, Disease and Society* (London: Curzon Press).

MARRACK, J. R. (1947), 'Investigations of Human Nutrition in the United Kingdom During the War', *Proceedings of the Nutrition Society*, 5.

MARTORELL, R. (1987), 'Body Size, Adaptation, and Function', paper presented at the 86th Annual Meeting of the American Anthropological Association, Nov. 1987, Chicago.

—— and SHARMA, R. (1985), 'Trends in Nutrition, Food Supply and Mortality Rates', in Halstead, S. B., *et al.* (eds.) (1985), *Good Health at Low Cost*.

MARX, K. (1844), *The Economic and Philosophic Manuscript of 1844*, English translation (London: Lawrence and Wishart).

—— (1852), *The 18th Brumaire of Louis Bonaparte* (2nd ed. 1869).

—— (1857–8), *Grundrisse der Kritik der politischen Okonomie*; 1939 and 1941 (Moscow: Marx-Engels-Lenin Institute); English trans. by M. Nicolaus (1973): *Grundrisse: Foundations of the Critique of Political Economy* (Harmondsworth: Penguin); also part trans. with supplementary texts of Marx and Engels, and with an Introduction by Eric Hobsbawm (1964), *Pre-Capitalist Economic Formations* (London: Lawrence and Wishart).

—— (1875), *Critique of the Gotha Programme*, English trans. (New York: International Publishers).

—— (1887), *Capital: A Critical Analysis of Capitalist Production*; English trans. by S. Moore and E. Aveling; edited by F. Engels (London: Sonnenschein; republished by Allen and Unwin, 1938).

MASEFIELD, G. B. (1963), *Famine: Its Prevention and Relief* (Oxford: Oxford University Press).

MASON, J. B., HABICHT, J. P., TABATABAI, H., and VALVERDE, V. (1984), *Nutritional Surveillance* (Geneva: World Health Organization).

—— HAAGA, J. G., MARKS, G., QUINN, V., TEST, K., and MARIBE, T. (1985), 'Using Agricultural Data for Timely Warning to Prevent the Effects of Drought on Child Nutrition: An Analysis of Historical Data from Botswana', mimeo, Cornell University Agricultural Experiment Station.

MASON, L., and BROWN, R. (1983), *Rice, Rivalry and Politics* (Notre Dame: University of Notre Dame Press).

MATA, L. (1978), *The Children of Santa Maria Cauque: A Prospective Field Study of Health and Growth* (Cambridge, MA: MIT Press).

—— (1985), 'The Fight Against Diarrhoeal Diseases: The Case of Costa Rica', in Vallin, J., and Lopez, A. D. (eds.) (1985), *Health Policy, Social Policy and Mortality Prospects*.

—— and ROSERO, L. (1988), 'National Health and Social Development in Costa Rica: A Case Study of Intersectoral Action', Technical Paper No. 13, Pan American Health Organization, Washington, DC.

MATHUR, K., and BHATTACHARYA, M. (1975), *Administrative Response to Emergency: A Study of Scarcity Administration in Maharashtra* (New Delhi: Concept).

MATIZA, T., ZINYAMA, L. M., and CAMPBELL, D. J. (1988), 'Household Strategies for Coping with Food Insecurity in Low Rainfall Areas of Zimbabwe', paper presented at the Fourth Annual Conference on Food Security Research in Southern Africa, Oct.–Nov. 1988, Harare, Zimbabwe.

MATTHEWS, A. (1988), 'Growth and Employment Considerations in the Food vs. Export Crops Debate', *IDS Bulletin*, 19.

MAXWELL, S. (1978a), 'Food Aid, Food For Work and Public Works', Discussion Paper No. 127, Institute of Development Studies, University of Sussex.

—— (1978b), 'Food Aid for Supplementary Feeding Programs: An Analysis', *Food Policy*, 4.

—— (1988), 'Editorial', *IDS Bulletin*, 19.

—— and Fernando, A. (1987), 'Cash Crops in Developing Countries: The Issues, the Facts, the Policies', paper presented at a Workshop on Cash Crops held at the Institute of Development Studies, University of Sussex, 5–6 Jan. 1987.

MAYER, J. (1974), 'Coping with Famine', *Foreign Affairs*, 53.

—— (1975), 'Management of Famine Relief', in Abelson, P. H. (ed.) (1975), *Food: Politics, Economics, Nutrition and Research*.

MAYOUX, L. (1988), 'Income Generation for Women in West Bengal', mimeo, University of Cambridge.

MAZUMDAR, V. (1985), *Emergence of Women's Questions in India and the Role of Women's Studies* (New Delhi: Centre for Women's Development Studies).

MBITHI, P., and WISNER, B. (1972), *Drought and Famine in Kenya: Magnitude and Attempted Solutions* (Nairobi: Institute for Development Studies).

MEADE, J. E., *et al.* (1968), *The Economic and Social Structure of Mauritius* (London: Frank Cass).

MEADOWS, D. N., *et al.* (1972), *The Limits to Growth* (Washington, DC: Potomac).

MEDINA, E., and KAEMPFFER, A. (1982), 'La salud en Chile durante la década del setenta', *Revista Médica de Chile*, 110.

MEEGAMA, S. A. (1985), 'The Mortality Decline in the "Fast-Declining" Countries', in *International Population Conference, Florence, 1985*, ii (Liège: International Union for the Scientific Study of Population).

MEHTA, S. R. (1981), *Social Development in Mauritius* (New Delhi: Wiley).

MEIER, G., and STEEL, W. F. (eds.) (1987), *Industrial Adjustment in Sub-Saharan Africa* (Washington, DC: Economic Development Institute, World Bank).

MEILLASSOUX, C. (1974), 'Development or Exploitation: Is the Sahel Famine Good Business?', *Review of African Political Economy*, 1.

—— (1976), *Femmes, greniers et capitaux* (Paris: Maspéro).

MEINTEL, D. (1983), 'Cape Verde: Survival Without Self-Sufficiency', in Cohen, R. (ed.) (1983), *African Islands and Enclaves* (Beverley Hills: Sage).

—— (1984), *Race, Culture and Portuguese Colonialism in Cape Verde*, Foreign and Comparative Studies, African Series 41, Maxwell School of Citizenship and Public Affairs, Syracuse University.

MELLOR, J. W., and AHMED, R. (eds.) (1988), *Agricultural Price Policy for Developing Countries* (Baltimore: Johns Hopkins).

—— DELGADO, C. L., and BLACKIE, C. L. (eds.) (1987), *Accelerating Food Production in Sub-Saharan Africa* (Baltimore: Johns Hopkins).

—— and DESAI, G. (eds.) (1985), *Agricultural Change and Rural Poverty: Variations on a Theme by Dharam Narain* (Baltimore: Johns Hopkins).

—— and JOHNSTON, B. (1984), 'The World Food Equation: Interrelationships Among Development, Employment and Food Consumption', *Journal of Economic Literature*, 22.

MELVILLE, B., LAWRENCE, O., WILLIAMS, M., FRANCIS, V., COLLINS, L., and ARCHER, E. (1988), 'Childhood Malnutrition in Three Ecological Zones in Western Jamaica', *Ecology of Food and Nutrition*, 20.

—— WILLIAMS, M., FRANCIS, V., LAWRENCE, O., and COLLINS, L. (1988), 'Determinants of Childhood Malnutrition in Jamaica', *Food and Nutrition Bulletin*, 10.

MENCHER, J. (1980), 'The Lessons and Non-lessons of Kerala: Agricultural Labourers and Poverty', *Economic and Political Weekly*, 15.

—— (1988), 'Peasants and Agricultural Labourers: An Analytical Assessment of Issues Involved in Their Organizing', in Srinivasan, T. N., and Bardhan, P. K. (eds.) (1988), *Rural Poverty in South Asia*.

MENDEZ, J. C. (ed.) (1979), *Chilean Economic Policy* (Santiago: Budget Directorate, Government of Chile).

—— (1980), *Chilean Socio Economic Overview* (Santiago: Budget Directorate, Government of Chile).

MESA-LAGO, C. (1969), 'Availability and Reliability of Statistics in Socialist Cuba', *Latin American Research Review*, 4.

—— (1971), 'Cuba: teoría y práctica de los incentives', Occasional Paper No. 7, Center for Latin American Studies, University of Pittsburgh.

—— (1978), *Social Security in Latin America* (Pittsburgh: University of Pittsburgh Press).

—— (1979), 'Cuban Statistics Revisited', *Cuban Studies*, 9.

—— (1983a), 'Social Security and Extreme Poverty in Latin America', *Journal of Development Economics*, 12.

—— (1983b), *La economía en Cuba socialista: una evaluacíon de dos décadas* (New Mexico: University of New Mexico Press).

—— (1985a), 'Health Care in Costa Rica: Boom and Crisis', *Social Science and Medicine*, 21.

—— (1985b), *El desarrollo de la seguridad social en América Latina*, Estudios e Informes de la CEPAL, Naciones Unidos, Santiago, Chile.

—— (ed.) (1985c), *The Crisis of Social Security and Health Care*, Latin American Monograph and Document Series, No. 9, Center for Latin American Studies, University of Pittsburgh.

—— (1985d), 'Alternative Strategies to the Social Security Crisis: Socialist, Market and Mixed Approaches', in Mesa-Lago, C. (ed.) (1985c), *The Crisis of Social Security and Health Care*.

—— (1986), 'Comparative Study of the Development of Social Security in Latin America', *International Social Security Review*, 2.

—— (1988a), 'Social Insurance: The Experience of Three Countries in the English-Speaking Caribbean', *International Labour Review*, 127.

—— (1988b), 'Social Security in Latin America and the Caribbean', paper presented at a Workshop on Social Security in Developing Countries held at the London School of Economics, 4–5 July 1988; to be published in Ahmad, S. E., *et al.* (eds.) (forthcoming), *Social Security in Developing Countries*.

—— (1988c), 'Jamaica', unpublished report prepared for the International Labour Organization, Geneva.

—— and DIAZ-BRIQUETS (1988), 'Costa Rica y Cuba', *Annuario de estudios centro americano*, 14.

—— and PEREZ-LOPEZ, J. (1985), 'A Study of Cuba's Material Product System, Its Conversion to the System of National Accounts, and Estimation of Gross Domestic Product per Capita and Growth Rates', World Bank Staff Working Paper No. 770, World Bank, Washington, DC.

MESAROVIC, M. D., and PESTEL, E. (1974), *Mankind at Turning Point* (New York: Dutton).

MEUVRET, J. (1946), 'Les Crises de subsistance et la démographie de la France d'ancien régime', *Population*, 1.

MICHELL, T. (1988), *From a Developing to a Newly Industrialised Country: The Republic of Korea, 1961–82* (Geneva: ILO).

MIDGLEY, J. (1984a), *Social Security, Inequality and the Third World* (Chichester: Wiley).

—— (1984b), 'Social Assistance: An Alternative Form of Social Protection in Developing Countries', *International Social Security Review*, 3/84.

—— (1986), 'Industrialization and Welfare: The Case of the Four Little Tigers', *Social Policy and Administration*, 20.

MIES, M. (1982), *The Lace Makers of Narsapur: Indian Housewives Produce for the World Market* (London: Zed Press).

MILL, J. S. (1859), *On Liberty* (repr. Harmondsworth: Penguin, 1974).

MILLER, B. (1981), *The Endangered Sex: Neglect of Female Children in Rural North India* (Ithaca, NY: Cornell University Press).

MINHAS, B. (1974), *Planning and the Poor* (New Delhi: Chand & Co.).

—— JAIN, L. R., KANSAL, S. M., and SALUJA, M. R. (1987), 'On the Choice of Appropriate Consumer Price Indices and Data Sets for Estimating the Incidence of Poverty in India', *Indian Economic Review*, 22.

MINOGUE, M. (1983), 'Mauritius: Political, Economic and Social Development in a Small Island', *Manchester Papers on Development*, 8.

MITRA, ASHOK (1977), *Terms of Trade and Class Relations: An Essay in Political Economy* (London: Frank Cass).

MITRA, ASOKE (1980), *Implications of Declining Sex Ratios in India's Population* (Bombay: Allied Publishers).

MITTER, S. (1988), 'Managing the Drought Crisis: The Zimbabwe Experience, 1982–83', undergraduate essay, Harvard University.

MODY, N. (1972), 'To Some, a God-Send', *Economic and Political Weekly*, 23 Dec.

MOHS, E. (1983a), 'Infectious Diseases and Health in Costa Rica: The Development of a New Paradigm', *Pediatric Infectious Diseases*, 1.

—— (1983b), *La salud en Costa Rica* (San José: Editorial Universidad Estatal a Distancia).

MOKYR, J. (1985), *Why Ireland Starved* (London: Allen and Unwin).

MOLYNEUX, M. (1981), 'Women's Emancipation Under Socialism: A Model for the Third World?', *World Development*, 9.

MOMSEN, J. H., and TOWNSEND, J. (eds.) (1987), *Geography of Gender in the Third World* (London: Butler and Tanner).

MONCKEBERG, F. (1983), 'Socioeconomic Development and Nutritional Status: Efficiency of Intervention Programs', in Underwood, B. (ed.) (1983), *Nutrition Intervention Strategies in National Development*.

—— MARDONES, R., and VALIENTE, S. (1984), 'Evolución de la desnutrición y mortalidad infantil en Chile en los últimos años', *Creces*, 10.

MONDOT-BERNARD, J. (1982), 'Les Études en nutrition et alimentations dans les pays du Sahel: bibliographie analytique', mimeo, Club du Sahel, OECD, Paris.

MONTGOMERY, R. (1985), 'The Bangladesh Floods of 1984 in Historical Context', *Disasters*, 9.

MORALES, E., and ROJAS, S. (1986), 'Relocalización Socio-espacial de la pobreza: políticas estatal y presión popular, 1979–85', Documento de Trabajo No. 280, FLACSO, Santiago.

MORAN, C. (1989), 'Economic Stabilisation and Structural Transformation: Lessons from the Chilean Experience', *World Development*, 17.

MORAN, E. (1982), 'The Evolution of Cape Verde's Agriculture', *African Economic History*, 11.

MORAN, R., *et al.* (1988), 'Jamaica: Summary Review of the Social Well-Being Program', Report No. 7227-JM, World Bank, Washington, DC.

MOREMI, T. C. (1988), 'Transition from Emergency to Development Assistance: Botswana Experience', paper presented at a Conference on Nutrition in Times of Disasters, World Health Organization, Geneva, 27–30 Sept. 1988.

MORGAN, R. (1985), 'The Development and Applications of a Drought Early Warning System in Botswana', *Disasters*, 9.

—— (1986), 'From Drought Relief to Post-Disaster Recovery: The Case of Botswana', *Disasters*, 10.

—— (1988), 'Social Welfare Policies and Programmes and the Reduction of Household Vulnerability in the Post-Independence SADCC States of Southern Africa', paper presented at a Workshop on Social Security in Developing Countries held at the London School of Economics, 4–5 July 1988; to be published in Ahmad, S. E., *et al.* (eds.) (forthcoming), *Social Security in Developing Countries*.

MORIO, S., and TAKAHASHI, S. (1986), 'Socio-economic Correlates of Mortality in Japan', in Ng Shui Meng (ed.) (1986), *Socio-economic Correlates of Mortality in Japan and ASEAN*.

MORIS, J. (1988), 'Failing to Cope with Drought: The Plight of Africa's Ex-pastoralists', *Development Policy Review*, 6.

MORLEY, D., ROHDE, J., and WILLIAMS, G. (eds.) (1983), *Practising Health for All* (Oxford: Oxford University Press).

MORRIS, M. D. (1974), 'What is a Famine?', *Economic and Political Weekly*, 9.

—— (1975), 'Needed—A New Famine Policy', *Economic and Political Weekly*, Annual Number.

—— (1979), *Measuring the Conditions of the World's Poor: The Physical Quality of Life Index* (Oxford: Pergamon).

MORRISON, B., and WAXLER, N. (1986), 'Three Patterns of Basic Needs Distribution within Sri Lanka: 1971–73', *World Development*, 14.

MORRIS-PEEL, S. (1986), 'A Review of the Health and Nutritional Aspects of the League's Drought Relief Operations in Chad, Mali and the Sudan 1984–86', mimeo, Institute of Development Studies, University of Sussex.

MOSLEY, W. H. (1985*a*), 'Will Primary Health Care Reduce Infant and Child Mortality? A Critique of Some Current Strategies with Special Reference to Africa and Asia', in Vallin, J., and Lopez, A. (eds.) (1985), *Health Policy, Social Policy and Mortality Prospects*.

—— (1985*b*), 'Remarks', in Halstead, S. B., *et al.* (eds.) (1985), *Good Health at Low Cost*.

—— and CHEN, L. C. (eds.) (1984), *Child Survival: Strategies for Research* (New York: Population Council).

Moto (1983), 'Facing the Drought', *Moto Magazine*, Harare.

MOUTON, P. (1975), *Social Security in Africa: Trends, Problems and Prospects* (Geneva: ILO).

MUELLBAUER, J. (1987), 'Professor Sen on the Standard of Living', in Sen, A. K. (1987*a*), *The Standard of Living*.

MUJICA, R., and ROJAS, A. (1986), 'Mapa de la extrema pobreza en Chile: 1982',

Documento de Trabajo, Instituto de Economía, Pontificia Universidad Católica de Chile, Santiago.

MUKHOPADHYAY, S. (1981), 'Women Workers in India: A Case of Market Segmentation', mimeo, ILO-ARTEP.

—— (ed.) (1985a), *The Poor in Asia: Productivity-Raising Programmes and Strategies* (Kuala Lumpur: Asia and Pacific Development Centre).

—— (ed.) (1985b), *Case Studies on Poverty Programmes in Asia* (Kuala Lumpur: Asia and Pacific Development Centre).

MUNDLE, S. (1974), 'Relief Planning in Maharashtra', *Indian Journal of Public Administration*, 20.

MUNIZ, J. G., FABIAN, J. C., and MAURIQUEZ, J. C. (1984), 'The Recent Worldwide Economic Crisis and the Welfare of Children: The Case of Cuba', *World Development*, 12.

MUQTADA, M. (1981), 'Poverty and Famines in Bangladesh', *Bangladesh Development Studies*, 9.

MURAGE, F. G. (forthcoming), 'Agricultural Yields, Production and Monitoring Methods of the National Cereals and Produce Board', to be published in Downing, T., *et al.* (eds.) (forthcoming), *Coping with Drought in Kenya*.

MURDOCH, W. W. (1980), *The Poverty of Nations: The Political Economy of Hunger and Population* (Baltimore: Johns Hopkins).

MURRAY, C. J. L. (1987), 'A Critical Review of International Mortality Data', *Social Science and Medicine*, 25.

—— and CHEN, L. C. (1989), 'Patterns of the Health Transition', mimeo, Center for Population Studies, Harvard University; to be published in Chen, L. C., *et al.* (eds.) (forthcoming), *Social Change and Health*.

MURTHY, N., HIRWAY, I., PANCHAMUKHI, P. R, and SATIA, J. K. (1988), 'Social Services Design, Delivery and Impact in Relation to the Poor', mimeo, Indian Institute of Management, Ahmedabad.

MWALUKO, E. P. (1962), 'Famine Relief in the Central Province of Tanganyika, 1961', *Tropical Agriculture*, 39.

MWANGI, W. M. (1986), 'Alternatives for Improving Production, Employment and Income Distribution in Kenyan Agriculture', mimeo, Institute of Development Studies, University of Sussex.

MWENDWA, H. (forthcoming), 'Agricultural and Livestock Monitoring Using Aerial Photography', in Downing, T., *et al.* (eds.) (forthcoming), *Coping with Drought in Kenya: National and Local Strategies*.

NADARAJAH, T. (1983), 'The Transition from Higher Female Mortality to Higher Male Mortality in Sri Lanka', *Population and Development Review*, 9.

NAG, M. (1985), 'The Impact of Social and Economic Development on Mortality: Comparative Study of Kerala and West Bengal', in Halstead, S. B., *et al.* (eds.) (1985), *Good Health at Low Cost*.

—— (1988), 'The Kerala Formula', *World Health Forum*, 9.

—— (1989), 'Political Awareness as a Factor in Accessibility of Health Services: A Case Study of Rural Kerala and West Bengal', *Economic and Political Weekly*, 25 Feb.

NAGARAJ, K. (1986), 'Infant Mortality in Tamil Nadu', mimeo, Madras Institute of Development Studies.

—— (1989), 'Female Workers in Rural Tamil Nadu—A Preliminary Study', mimeo, Madras.

NAGI, M. H. (1986), 'The Welfare State in Kuwait: Policy Issues and Impact', *Sociology and Social Welfare*.

NARAIN, DHARM (1965), *The Impact of Price Movements on Areas Under Selected Crops in India, 1900–1939* (Cambridge: Cambridge University Press).

—— (1988), *Studies on Indian Agriculture*, ed. K. N. Raj *et al.* (Delhi: Oxford University Press).

NASH, J. F. (1950), 'The Bargaining Problem', *Econometrica*, 18.

NASH, T. (1986), 'Report on Activities of the Child Feeding Centre in Korem', mimeo, Save the Children Fund, London.

NATHAN, A. J. (1965), *A History of the China International Famine Relief Commission* (Cambridge, MA: East Asian Research Center).

NAYYAR, R. (1987), 'Female Participation Rates in Rural India', *Economic and Political Weekly*, 22.

NEE, V. (1986), 'The Peasant Household Economy and Decollectivization in China', *Journal of Asian and African Studies*, 21.

NEGUS, D. (1985), 'Aid with Dignity: Helping Malian Nomads to Survive Drought in 1984', *Disasters*, 9.

NELSON, H. (1983), 'Report on the Situation in Tigray: December 1983', mimeo, Manchester University.

NEUMANN, C. G., BWIBO, N. O., CARTER, E., WEINBERG, S., JANSEN, A. A., CATTLE, D., NGARE, D., BAKSH, M., PAOLISSO, M., and COULSON, A. H. (forthcoming), 'Impact of the 1984 Drought on Food Intake, Nutritional Status and Household Response in Embu District', to be published in Downing, T. E., *et al.* (eds.) (forthcoming), *Coping with Drought in Kenya: National and Local Strategies*.

NEWBERY, D. (1987a), 'Agrarian Institutions for Insurance and Stabilization', mimeo, Churchill College, Cambridge; Published in Bardhan, P. K. (ed.) (1989), *The Economic Theory of Agrarian Institutions* (Oxford: Oxford University Press).

—— (1987b), 'When Do Futures Destabilize Spot Prices?', *International Economic Review*, 28.

—— and STIGLITZ, J. (1981), *The Theory of Commodity Price Stabilization: A Study in the Economics of Risk* (Oxford: Clarendon).

NEWHOUSE, P. (1987), 'Monitoring Food Supplies', *UNDRO News*, Jan./Feb. 1987.

NEWMAN, L. F., CROSSGROVE, W., KATES, R. W., MATTHEWS, R., and MILLMAN, S. (eds.) (forthcoming), *Hunger and History: Food Shortage, Poverty and Deprivation* (Oxford: Blackwell).

NEWMAN, P. (1970), 'Malaria Control and Population Growth', *Journal of Development Studies*, 6.

—— (1977), 'Malaria and Mortality', *Journal of American Statistical Association*, 72.

NG SHUI MENG (ed.) (1986a), *Socio-economic Correlates of Mortality in Japan and ASEAN* (National Institute for Research Advancement, Japan, and Institute of Southeast Asian Studies, Singapore).

—— (1986b), 'Socio-economic Correlates of Mortality in Singapore', in Ng Shui Meng (ed.) (1986a), *Socio-economic Correlates of Mortality in Japan and ASEAN*.

NIJIM, B. K. (1985), 'Spatial Aspects of Demographic Change in the Arab World', in Hajjar, S. G. (ed.) (1985), *The Middle East: From Transition to Development*.

Nordic Conference on Environment and Development (1987), background papers, mimeographed.

NORGAN, N. G. (1988), 'Chronic Energy Deficiency and the Effects of Energy

Supplementation', in Schürch, B., and Scrimshaw, N. (eds.) (1988), *Chronic Energy Deficiency: Consequences and Related Issues* (Lausanne: IDECG Secretariat).

NUSSBAUM, M., and SEN, A. K. (eds.) (forthcoming), *Quality of Life* (Oxford: Clarendon).

Nutrition Foundation of India (1988), *Profiles of Undernutrition and Underdevelopment: Studies of Poor Communities in Seven Regions of the Country* (New Delhi: Nutrition Foundation of India).

Office of Foreign Disasters Assistance (1985), *OFDA Annual Report, FY 1985* (Washington, DC: USAID).

O'GRADA, C. (1988a), 'For Irishmen to Forget?—Recent Research on the Great Irish Famine', Working Paper No. WP88/7, Centre for Economic Research, University College, Dublin.

—— (1988b), *Ireland Before and After the Famine: Explorations in Economic History 1800–1930* (Manchester: Manchester University Press).

—— (forthcoming), *The Great Famine in Irish History* (London: Macmillan).

OHADIKE, P.O. (1983), 'Evolving Indications of Mortality Differentials by Sex in Africa', in Lopez, A., and Ruzicka, L. T. (eds.) (1983), *Sex Differentials in Mortality: Trends, Determinants and Consequences*.

O'LEARY, M. (1980), 'Response to Drought in Kitui District, Kenya', *Disasters*, 4.

OLSEN, W. (1984), 'Kenya's Dual Grain Market: The Effects of State Intervention', mimeo, Food Studies Group, Oxford.

OMAWALE and McLEOD, J. (1984), 'Food Consumption and Poverty in Rural Jamaica', *Ecology of Food and Nutrition*, 14.

OMVEDT, G. (1980), *We Will Smash This Prison! Indian Women in Struggle* (London: Zed).

O'NEILL, O. (1987), *Faces of Hunger* (London: Allen and Unwin).

OSMANI, S. R. (1982), *Economic Inequality and Group Welfare* (Oxford: Clarendon).

—— (1986), 'The Food Problems of Bangladesh', paper presented at a Conference on Food Strategies held at WIDER, Helsinki, 21–5 July 1986; Working Paper No. 29, WIDER, 1987; to be published in Drèze, J. P., and Sen, A. K. (eds.) (forthcoming), *The Political Economy of Hunger*.

—— (1987a), 'Nutrition and the Economics of Food: Implications of Some Recent Controversies', Working Paper No. 16, WIDER; to be published in Drèze, J. P., and Sen, A. K. (eds.) (forthcoming), *The Political Economy of Hunger*.

—— (1987b), 'On Some Recent Controversies in the Measurement of Undernutrition', paper presented at a Conference on Poverty, Undernutrition and Living Standards held at WIDER, Helsinki, 27–30 July 1987; to be published in Osmani, S. R. (ed.) (forthcoming), *Nutrition and Poverty*.

—— (1988a), 'Social Security in South Asia', paper presented at a Workshop on Social Security in Developing Countries held at the London School of Economics, 4–5 July 1988; to be published in Ahmad, S. E., *et al.* (eds.) (forthcoming), *Social Security in Developing Countries*.

—— (1988b), 'Food and the History of India: An "Entitlement" Approach', Working Paper No. 50, WIDER, Helsinki.

—— (ed.) (forthcoming), *Nutrition and Poverty* (Oxford: Clarendon).

—— and CHOWDHURY, O. H. (1983), 'Short Run Impacts of Food for Work Programme in Bangladesh', *Bangladesh Development Studies*, 11.

O'SULLIVAN, G., EBRAHIM, S., O'SULLIVAN, J., and TATTS, C. (1980), 'Nutritional

Status of Laotian Refugee Children in Uban Camp, Thailand', *Journal of Epidemiology and Community Health*, 34.

OTTEN, M. W. (1986), 'Nutritional and Mortality Aspects of the 1985 Famine in North Central Ethiopia', mimeo, Centre for Disease Control, Atlanta, USA.

OUGHTON, E. (1982), 'The Maharashtra Droughts of 1970–73: An Analysis of Scarcity', *Oxford Bulletin of Economics and Statistics*, 44.

OXFAM (1972, 1973), unpublished field reports.

OXFAM/UNICEF (1986), 'Nutritional Surveillance and Drought Monitoring Project, Darfur, Report of March/April Survey 1986', mimeo.

PACEY, A., and PAYNE, P. (eds.) (1985), *Agricultural Development and Nutrition* (London: Hutchinson).

PADMINI, R. (1985), 'The Local Purchase of Food Commodities: "Cash for Food" Project', mimeo, UNICEF, Addis Ababa.

PANIKAR, P. G. K. (1985), 'Health Care System in Kerala and Its Impact on Infant Mortality', in Halstead, S. B., *et al.* (eds.) (1985), *Good Health at Low Cost.*

—— (1986), 'Financing Health Care in China', *Economic and Political Weekly*, 21.

—— and SOMAN, C. R. (1984), *Health Status of Kerala* (Trivandrum: Centre for Development Studies).

—— —— (1985), 'Recent Trends in the Health Status of Indian Children: A Reappraisal', Working Paper No. 209, Centre for Development Studies, Trivandrum.

PANKHURST, A. (1985), 'Social Consequences of Drought and Famine: An Anthropological Approach to Selected African Case Studies', unpublished MA dissertation, Department of Social Anthropology, University of Manchester.

—— (1986), 'Social Dimensions of Famine in Ethiopia: Exchange, Migration and Integration', paper presented to the 9th International Conference of Ethiopian Studies, Moscow.

PANKHURST, R. (1961), *An Introduction to the Economic History of Ethiopia from Early Times to 1800* (London: Lalibela House).

PAPANEK, H. (1987), 'The World Is Not Like Us: Limits or Feminist Imagination', paper, presented at the 82nd Annual Meeting of the American Sociological Association.

—— (1989), 'Socialization for Inequality: Entitlements, the Value of Women, and Domestic Hierarchies', mimeo, Center for Asian Development Studies, Boston University.

PARIKH, K. (1986), 'Chronic Hunger in the World: Impact of International Policies', paper presented at a Conference on Food Strategies held at WIDER, Helsinki, 21–5 July 1986; to be published in Drèze, J. P., and Sen, A. K. (eds.) (forthcoming), *The Political Economy of Hunger*.

—— and RABAR, F. (eds.) (1981), *Food for All in a Sustainable World* (Laxenburg: IIASA).

PARK, C. K., and YEON, H. C. (1981), 'Recent Developments in the Health Care System of Korea', *International Social Security Review*, 2/81.

PARK, P., and JACKSON, T. (1985), 'Lands of Plenty, Lands of Scarcity: Agricultural Policy and Peasant Farmers in Zimbabwe and Tanzania', OXFAM, Oxford.

PASSMORE, R. (1951), 'Famine in India: An Historical Survey', *Lancet*, 303.

—— (1974), *Handbook on Human Nutritional Requirements* (Rome: FAO).

PATEL, M. (1980), 'Effects of the Health Service and Environmental Factors on Infant

Mortality: The Case of Sri Lanka', *Journal of Epidemiology and Community Health*, 34.

PATIL, S. (1973), 'Famine Conditions in Maharashtra: A Survey of Sakri Taluka', *Economic and Political Weekly*, 28 July.

PAYNE, P. R. (1985), 'Nutritional Adaptation in Man: Social Adjustment and their Nutritional Implications', in Blaxter, K., and Waterlow, J. C. (eds.) (1985), *Nutritional Adaptation in Man*.

—— (1987a), 'Undernutrition: Measurement and Implications', paper presented at a Conference on Poverty, Undernutrition and Living Standards held at WIDER, 27–30 July 1987; to be published in Osmani, S. R. (ed.) (forthcoming), *Nutrition and Poverty*.

—— (1987b), 'Malnutrition and Human Capital: Problems of Theory and Practice', in Clay, E., and Shaw, J. (eds.) (1987), *Poverty, Development and Food*.

—— and LIPTON, M., with LONGHURST, R., NORTH, J., and TREAGUST, S. (1988), 'How Third World Rural Households Adapt to Dietary Energy Stress', mimeo, International Food Policy Research Institute, Washington, DC.

PEARSON, R. (1986); 'Lessons from Famine in Sudan (1984–1986)', mimeo, UNICEF, Khartoum.

PEBERDY, M. (1985), *Tigray: Ethiopia's Untold Story* (London: Relief Society of Tigray UK Support Committee).

PEEK, P., and RAABE, C. (1984), 'Rural Equity in Costa Rica: Myth or Reality?', Working Paper No. 67, Rural Employment Policy Research Programme, ILO, Geneva.

PENG, X. (1987), 'Demographic Consequences of the Great Leap Forward in China's Provinces', *Population and Development Review*, 13.

PERERA, P. D. A. (1985), 'Health Care Systems of Sri Lanka', in Halstead, S. B., *et al.* (eds.) (1985), *Good Health at Low Cost*.

PERKINS, D. H. (1983), 'Research on the Economy of the People's Republic of China: A Survey of the Field', *Journal of Asian Studies*, 42.

—— (1988), 'Reforming China's Economic System', *Journal of Economic Literature*, 26.

—— and YUSUF, S. (1984), *Rural Development in China* (Baltimore: Johns Hopkins).

PHILLIPS, M. A., FEACHEM, R. G., and MILLS, A. (1987), 'Options for Diarrhoea Control', EPC Publication No. 13, Evaluation and Planning Centre for Health Care, London School of Hygiene and Tropical Medicine.

PHONGPAICHIT, P. (1982), *From Peasant Girls to Bangkok Masseuses* (Geneva: ILO).

PIAZZA, A. (1986), *Food Consumption and Nutritional Status in the People's Republic of China* (Boulder: Westview).

PINOCHET, Augusto (1976), 'We Are Truly Independent Thanks to the Efforts of All Chileans', public presidential address, reprinted in Mendez, J. C. (ed.) (1979), *Chilean Economic Policy*.

PINSTRUP-ANDERSEN, P. (1985a), 'The Impact of Export Crop Production on Human Nutrition', in Pinstrup-Andersen, P., and Biswas, M. (eds.) (1985), *Nutrition and Development*.

—— (1985b), 'Food Prices and the Poor in Developing Countries', *European Review of Agricultural Economics*, 12.

—— (1987), 'Nutrition Interventions', in Cornia, G., *et al.* (eds.) (1987), *Adjustment With a Human Face*.

—— (ed.) (1988a), *Consumer-Oriented Food Subsidies: Costs, Benefits and Policy Options for Developing Countries* (Baltimore: Johns Hopkins).

—— (1988b), 'Assuring Food Security and Adequate Nutrition for the Poor', in Bell, D. E., and Reich, M. R. (eds.) (1988), *Health, Nutrition and Economic Crisis*.

—— (ed.) (forthcoming), *The Political Economy of Food and Nutrition*.

—— and ALDERMAN, H. (1988), 'The Effectiveness of Consumer-Oriented Food Subsidies in Reaching Rationing and Income Transfer Goals', in Pinstrup-Andersen, P. (ed.) (1988a), *Consumer-Oriented Food Subsidies: Costs, Benefits and Policy Options for Developing Countries*.

—— and BISWAS, M. (eds.) (1985), *Nutrition and Development* (Oxford: Oxford University Press).

—— and JARAMILLO, M. (1986), 'The Impact of Technological Change in Rice Production on Food Consumption and Nutrition in North Arcot, India', mimeo, International Food Policy Research Institute, Washington, DC.

PLATTEAU, J. P. (1988a), 'The Food Crisis in Africa: A Comparative Structural Analysis', Working Paper No. 44, WIDER; to be published in Drèze, J. P., and Sen, A. K. (eds.) (forthcoming), *The Political Economy of Hunger*.

—— (1988b), 'Traditional Systems of Social Security and Hunger Insurance, paper presented at a Workshop on Social Security in Developing Countries held at the London School of Economics, 4–5 July 1988; to be published in Ahmad, S. E., *et al.* (eds.) (forthcoming), *Social Security in Developing Countries*.

PLEASE, S., and AMOAKO, K. (1984), 'The World Bank's Report on Accelerated Development in Sub-Saharan Africa: A Critique of Some of the Criticisms', *African Studies Review*, 27.

POLEMAN, T. T. (1981), 'Quantifying the Nutrition Situation in Developing Countries', *Food Research Institute Studies*, 18.

POLLAK, R. A. (1983), 'A Transaction Cost Approach to Families and Households', mimeo, University of Pennsylvania.

POPKIN, S. L. (1979), *The Rational Peasant: The Political Economy of Rural Society in Vietnam* (Berkeley: University of California Press).

POSNER, R. (1980), 'A Theory of Primitive Society, With Special Reference to Law', *Journal of Law and Economics*, 23.

POTTIER, J. (1988), *Migrants no More: Settlement and Survival in Mambwe Villages, Zambia* (Manchester: Manchester University Press).

PRABHAKAR, M. S. (1975), 'Death in Barpeta', *Economic and Political Weekly*, 10.

PRESCOTT, N., and JAMISON, D. (1985), 'The Distribution and Impact of Health Resource Availability in China', *International Journal of Health Planning and Management*, 1.

PRESTON, S. (1975), 'The Changing Relation Between Mortality and Level of Economic Development', *Population Studies*, 29.

—— (1980), 'Causes and Consequences of Mortality Declines in Less Developed Countries During the Twentieth Century', in Easterlin, R. A. (ed.) (1980), *Population and Economic Change in Developing Countries*.

—— KEYFITZ, N., and SCHOEN, R. (1972), *Causes of Death: Life Tables for National Populations* (New York: Seminar Press).

PRESVELAN, C., and SPIJKERS-ZWART, S. (eds.) (1980), *The Household, Women and Agricultural Development* (Wageningen: Veenman and Zonen).

PRINDLE, P. H. (1979), 'Peasant Society and Famines: A Nepalese Example', *Ethnology*, 1.

PROSTERMAN, R. L. (1984), 'The Decline of Hunger-Related Deaths', The Hunger Project Papers, No. 1, The Hunger Project, San Francisco.

Public Institution for Social Security (1985), 'Recent Developments in the Social Security System in Kuwait', *Asian News Sheet*, 15.

PUTTERMAN, L. (1986), *Peasants, Collectives and Choice* (Greenwich, Conn.: JAI Press).

—— (1988), 'Ration Subsidies and Incentives in the Pre-reform Chinese Commune', *Economica*, 55.

PYATT, G. (1987), 'A Comment on "Growth and Equity in Developing Countries: A Reinterpretation of the Sri Lankan Experience" by Bhalla and Glewwe', *World Bank Economic Review*, 1.

QI, W. (1988), 'South Korea and Taiwan: A Comparative Analysis of Economic Development', Discussion Paper No. 252, Institute of Development Studies, University of Sussex.

QUINN, V. (1986), 'Malawi: Agricultural Development and Malnutrition', paper presented at the SOEC/WFC Workshop on Statistics in Support of African Food Strategies and Policies, Brussels, 13–16 May 1986.

—— COHEN, M., MASON, J., and KGOSIDINTSI, B. N. (1987), 'Crisis-Proofing the Economy: The Response of Botswana to Economic Recession and Drought', in Cornia, G., *et al*. (eds.) (1987), *Adjustment with a Human Face*.

RACZYNSKI, D. (1987), 'Social Policy, Poverty, and Vulnerable Groups: Children in Chile', in Cornia, G., *et al*. (eds.) (1987), *Adjustment with a Human Face*.

—— and OYARZO, C. (1981), 'Por qué cae la tasa de mortalidad infantil en Chile?', Colección Estudios CIEPLAN 6, Estudio No. 55, Santiago, Chile.

—— and SERRANO, C. (1985), *Vivir en la pobreza: testimonios de mujeres* (Santiago: CIEPLAN-PISPAL).

RAHMATO, D. (1987), *Famine and Survival Strategies: A Case Study From Northeast Ethiopia* (Geneva: International Institute for Relief and Development).

—— (1988), 'Peasant Survival Strategies', mimeo, Institute of Development Research, Addis Ababa University.

RAJARAMAN, I. (1974), 'Constructing the Poverty Line: Rural Punjab, 1960–61', Discussion Paper No. 43, Research Program in Economic Development, Princeton University.

RAM, N. (1986), 'An Independent Press and Anti-hunger Strategies: The Indian Experience', paper presented at a Conference on Food Strategies held at WIDER, Helsinki, 21–5 July 1986; to be published in Drèze, J. P., and Sen, A. K. (eds.) (forthcoming), *The Political Economy of Hunger*.

RAMACHANDRAN, V. K. (1986), 'Socioeconomic Characteristics of Agricultural Labourers in a Vanguard Agrarian Region: A Case Study of Gokilapuram Village, Madurai District', unpublished Ph.D. thesis, University of Madras.

RAMALINGASWAMI, P. (1987), 'Women's Access to Health Care', *Economic and Political Weekly*, 22.

RAMALINGASWAMI, V., DEO, M. G., GULERIA, J. S., MALHOTRA, K. K., SOOD, S. K., OM PRAKASH, and SINHA, R. V. N. (1971), 'Studies of the Bihar Famine of 1966–67', in Blix, G., *et al*. (eds.) (1971), *Famine: Nutrition and Relief Operations in Times of Disaster*.

RANGASAMI, A. (1974), 'A Generation Being Wiped Out', *Economic and Political Weekly*, 30 Nov.

—— (1985), '"Failure of Exchange Entitlements" Theory of Famine: A Response', *Economic and Political Weekly*, 20.

RAO, V. K. R. V. (1982), *Food, Nutrition and Poverty in India* (Brighton: Harvester Press).

RASHID, S. (1980), 'The Policy of Laissez-Faire during Scarcities', *Economic Journal*, 90.

RATCLIFFE, J. (1983), 'Social Justice and the Demographic Transition: Lessons from India's Kerala', in Morley, D., *et al.* (eds.) (1983), *Practising Health for All*.

RATNAVALE, A. (1986), 'Famine in the Sahel: The Situation from 1979 to 1984', mémoire présenté en vue de l'obtention du Diplôme, Institut Universitaire de Hautes Études Internationales, Geneva, Switzerland.

RAVALLION, M. (1984), 'How Much is a Transfer Payment Worth to a Rural Worker?', *Oxford Economic Papers*, 36.

—— (1987a), *Markets and Famines* (Oxford: Clarendon).

—— (1987b), 'Market Responses to Anti-Hunger Policies: Effects on Wages, Prices and Employment', Working paper No. 26, WIDER; to be published in Drèze, J. P., and Sen, A. K. (eds.) (forthcoming), *The Political Economy of Hunger*.

—— (1987c), 'Growth and Equity in Sri Lanka: A Comment', mimeo, World Bank, Washington, DC.

—— (1987d), 'The Economics of Famine: An Overview of Recent Research', Working Papers in Trade and Development, No. 87/13, The Australian National University Research School of Pacific Studies; to be published in Pearce, D. W., and Rau, N. J. (eds.) (forthcoming), *Economic Perspectives: An Annual Survey of Economics* (New York: Harwood).

—— (1988), 'Income Effects on Calorie Undernutrition', mimeo, Australian National University.

RAVENHILL, J. (ed.) (1986), *Africa in Economic Crisis* (New York: Columbia University Press).

RAY, A. (1988a), 'A Response to Lipton's (June 1987) Review of "World Development Report 1986"', *Development Policy Review*, 6.

—— (1988b), 'Postscript', *Development Policy Review*, 6.

RAY, T. (1984), 'Drought Assessment: Kenya', mimeo, USAID/Kenya, Nairobi.

RAYNAUT, C. (1977), 'Lessons of a Crisis', in Dalby, D., *et al.* (eds.) (1977), *Drought in Africa 2*.

REARDON, T., MATLON, P., and DELGADO, C. L. (1989), 'Coping with Food Insecurity at the Household Level in Drought-Affected Areas of Burkina Faso', *World Development*, 17.

REDDY, C. R. (1985), 'Rural Labour Market in Varhad: A Case Study of Agricultural Labourers in Rain-Fed Agriculture', WEP Working Paper No. 75, ILO, Geneva.

REDDY, S. (1988), 'An Independent Press Working Against Famine: The Nigerian Experience', *Journal of Modern African Studies*, 26.

REICH, M. (1989), 'Another Look at Political Will and Good Government in the Health Transition', Health Transition Seminar, mimeo, Harvard University.

Relief and Development Institute (1985), 'Strengthening Disaster Preparedness in Six African Countries', report prepared for the Ford Foundation, Relief and Development Institute, London.

Relief Society of Tigray (1983), 'The Drought and its Effects', mimeo, REST, Khartoum.

REPETTO, R. C. (1981), *Economic Development, Population Policy and Demographic Transition in the Republic of Korea* (Cambridge, MA: Harvard University Press).

Republic of Korea, Bureau of Social Welfare, Ministry of Health and Social Affairs (1979), 'Changing Family Patterns and Social Security Protection: The Case of the Republic of Korea', *International Social Security Review*, 1.

REUTLINGER, S. (1977), 'Malnutrition: A Poverty or Food Problem', *World Development*, 5.

—— (1984), 'Policy Implications of Research on Energy Intake and Activity Levels with Reference to the Debate on the Energy Adequacy of Existing Diets in Developing Countries', in *Energy Intake and Activity* (New York: Alan Liss).

—— (1985), 'Food Security and Poverty in LDCs', *Finance and Development*, 22.

—— and ALDERMAN, H. (1980), 'The Prevalence of Calorie-Deficient Diets in Developing Countries', *World Development*, 8.

—— and BIGMAN, D. (1981), 'Feasibility, Effectiveness and Costs of Food Security Alternatives in Developing Countries', in Valdés, A. (ed.) (1981), *Food Security for Developing Countries*.

—— and SELOWSKY, M. (1976), *Malnutrition and Poverty: Magnitude and Policy Options* (Baltimore: Johns Hopkins).

Review of African Political Economy (1979), 'The Roots of Famine', special double issue.

—— (1985), *War and Famine*, special issue.

REYNOLDS, N. (1984), 'Citizens, the State and Employment: Public Works as the Core of a Rural Development Strategy', Carnegie Conference Paper No. 234, Southern African Foundation for Economic Research, Harare.

RICARDO, D. (1822), draft text of speech for delivery in Parliament, included in Sraffa, P. (ed.) (1971), *The Works and Correspondence of David Ricardo*, v (Cambridge: Cambridge University Press).

RICHARDS, P. (1986), *Coping with Hunger* (London: Allen and Unwin).

RICHARDSON, J. H. (1956), 'Social Security Problems, with Special Reference to the British West Indies', *Social and Economic Studies*, 5.

RICHARDSON, R., and KIM, B. W. (1986), 'Adjustments to Policy Changes: The Case of Korea, 1960–1985', Report No. DRD 239, Labor Markets Division, Development Research Department, World Bank, Washington, DC.

RIDDELL, R. C., and associates (1989), 'Manufacturing Africa: Performance and Prospects of Seven Countries in Sub-Saharan Africa', mimeo, Overseas Development Institute, London.

RINGEN, S. (1987), *The Possibility of Politics: A Study of the Economy of the Welfare State* (Oxford: Clarendon).

RISKIN, C. (1986), 'Feeding China: The Experience Since 1949', paper presented at a Conference on Food Strategies held at WIDER, Helsinki, 21–5 July 1986; Working Paper No. 27, WIDER, 1987; to be published in Drèze, J. P., and Sen, A. K. (eds.) (forthcoming), *The Political Economy of Hunger*.

—— (1987), *China's Political Economy: The Quest for Development since 1949* (Oxford: Oxford University Press).

—— (1988), 'Reform: Where is China Going?', mimeo, Columbia University.

—— (forthcoming), 'Hunger and Poverty in China since 1949', to be published in Newman, L. F., *et al.* (eds.) (forthcoming), *Hunger and History*.

RIVERS, J. P. W. (1982), 'Women and Children Last: An Essay on Sex Discrimination in Disasters', *Disasters*, 6.

—— (1988), 'Nutritional Biology of Famines', in Harrison, G. A. (ed.) (1988), *Famines*.

—— HOLT, J., SEAMAN, J., and BOWDEN, M. (1976), 'Lessons for Epidemiology from the Ethiopian Famine', *Annales de la Société Belge de Médicine Tropicale*, 56.

ROBSON, J. R. K. (ed.) (1981), *Famine: Its Causes, Effects and Management* (New York: Gordon and Breach).

ROCH, J., HUBERT, B., NGYRIE, E., and RICHARD, P. (1975), 'Selective Bibliography on the Famines and the Drought in the Sahel', *African Environment*, 1.

ROCHFORD, S. C. (1981), 'Nash-Bargained Household Decision-Making in a Peasant Economy', mimeo.

RODRIGUEZ, A. V. (1986), 'El gasto público en programas de seguridad social: estudio de su efecto redistributivo en 1982', Instituto de Investigaciones en Ciencias Económicas, Universidad de Costa Rica, San José.

ROGERS, B. (1980), *The Domestication of Women* (London: Tavistock).

ROHDE, J. (1983), 'Health for All in China: Principles and Relevance for Other Countries', in Morley, D., *et al.* (eds.) (1983), *Practising Health for All*.

ROHRBACH, D. D. (1988), 'The Growth of Smallholder Maize Production in Zimbabwe (1979–1985): Implications for Food Security', in Rukuni, M., and Bernsten, R. H. (eds.) (1988), *Southern Africa: Food Security Policy Options*.

ROJAS, A. (1986), 'Extrema pobreza: concepto cuantificación y caracterización', *Estudios públicos*, 24.

ROSE, T. (1985), *Crisis and Recovery in Sub-Saharan Africa* (Paris: OECD).

ROSEMBERG, M. B. (1979), 'Social Security Policy Making in Costa Rica: A Research Report', *Latin American Research Review*, 14.

—— (1983), *Las luchas por el seguro social en Costa Rica* (San José: Editorial Costa Rica).

ROSENZWEIG, M. R. and SCHULTZ, T. P. (1982), 'Market Opportunities, Genetic Endowments, and Intrafamily Resource Distribution', *American Economic Review*, 72.

—— BINSWANGER, H. P., and McINTIRE, J. (1988), 'From Land Abundance to Land Scarcity: The Effects of Population Growth on Production Relations in Agrarian Economies', in Lee, R. D., *et al.* (eds.) (1988), *Population, Food and Rural Development*.

ROSERO, L. (1984), 'Las políticas socio-economicas y su efecto en el descenso de la mortalidad', in Asociación Demográfica Costarricense (1984), *Mortalidad y fecundidad en Costa Rica*.

—— (1985a), 'Infant Mortality Decline in Costa Rica', in Halstead, S. B., *et al.* (eds.) (1985), *Good Health at Low Cost*.

—— (1985b), 'The Case of Costa Rica', in Vallin, J., and Lopez, A. (eds.) (1985), *Health Policy, Social Policy and Mortality Prospects*.

ROSS, C. G. (1983), 'A Program for Food Grain Self-Sufficiency in the Sahel', paper presented at the Fifth Conference of the Club du Sahel, Brussels, 26–8 Oct. 1983.

ROSS, D. (ed.) (1980), *Aristotle: The Nicomachean Ethics* (Oxford: Oxford University Press).

ROTBERG, R. I., and RABB, T. K. (eds.) (1983), *Hunger and History: The Impact of Changing Food Production and Consumption Patterns on Society* (Cambridge: Cambridge University Press).

ROTH, A. E. (1985), *Axiomatic Models of Bargaining* (Berlin: Springer Verlag).

ROTHSCHILD, E. (1976), 'Food Politics', *Foreign Affairs*, 54.

—— (1977), 'The Economics of Starvation' and 'The Rats Don't Starve', *New York Times*, 10 and 11 Jan.

RRC–UNICEF (1984), 'Local Purchase of Food Commodities Project, Ethiopia 1984: Evaluation Report', mimeo, RRC–UNICEF, Addis Ababa.

—— (1985), 'Evaluation Report on Cash for Food Project in Dodota Wereda (Chilalo, Arsi, Ethiopia)', mimeo, RRC–UNICEF, Addis Ababa.

RUBINSTEIN, A. (1987), 'Perfect Equilibrium in a Bargaining Model', in Binmore, K., and Dasgupta, P. (eds.) (1987), *The Economics of Bargaining*.

RUIZ, O. (1980), 'Economic Politics and the Nutritional State of the Urban Poor in Chile 1968–1976', in Solimano, G., and Taylor, L. (eds.) (1980), *Food Price Policies and Nutrition in Latin America* (Tokyo: United Nations University).

RUKUNI, M. (1988), 'The Evolution of Smallholder Irrigation Policy in Zimbabwe: 1982–1986', *Irrigation and Drainage Systems*, 2.

—— and BERNSTEN, R. H. (eds.) (1988), *Southern Africa: Food Security Policy Options*, Proceedings of the Third Annual Conference on Food Security Research in Southern Africa, 1–5 Nov. 1987 (University of Zimbabwe–Michigan State University Food Security Research Project, Department of Agricultural Economics and Extension, Harare).

—— and EICHER, C. K. (eds.) (1987), *Food Security for Southern Africa* (Harare, UZ–MSU Food Security Project, University of Zimbabwe).

RUZICKA, L. T. (1984), 'Mortality in India', in Dyson, T., and Crook, N. (eds.) (1984), *Indian Demography*.

—— and Lopez, A. D. (1983), 'Conclusions and Prospects', in Lopez, A. D., and Ruzicka, L. T. (eds.) (1983), *Sex Differentials in Mortality*.

SACHS, I. (1986), 'Growth and Poverty: Some Lessons from Brazil', paper presented at a Conference on Food Strategies held at WIDER, Helsinki, 21–5 July 1986; to be published in Drèze, J. P., and Sen, A. K. (eds.) (forthcoming), *The Political Economy of Hunger*.

SAENZ, L. (ed.) (1982), *Análisis de la situación alimentaria-nutricional en Costa Rica* (San José, Costa Rica: Ministerio de Salud).

—— (1985), 'Health Changes During a Decade: The Costa Rican Case', in Halstead, S. B., *et al.* (eds.) (1985), *Good Health at Low Cost*.

SAGAR, D. (1988), 'Rural Poverty in India: An Evaluation of the Integrated Rural Development Programme in Uttar Pradesh and Bihar', unpublished M.Phil. thesis, Department of Land Economy, University of Cambridge.

SAHN, D. E. (1986), *Food Consumption Patterns and Parameters in Sri Lanka: Causes and Control of Malnutrition* (Washington, DC: International Food Policy Research Institute).

—— (1987), 'Changes in Living Standards of the Poor in Sri Lanka During a Period of Macroeconomic Restructuring', *World Development*, 15.

—— and EDIRISINGHE, N. (forthcoming), 'The Politics of Food Policy in Sri Lanka: From Basic Human Needs to an Increased Market Orientation', to be published in Pinstrup-Andersen, P. (ed.) (forthcoming), *The Political Economy of Food and Nutrition*.

SAITH, A. (ed.) (1987), *The Reemergence of the Chinese Peasantry* (London: Croom Helm).

SAMARASINGHE, S. W. R. de A. (1988), 'Sri Lanka, A Case Study from the Third World', in Bell, D. E., and Reich, M. R. (eds.) (1988), *Health, Nutrition and Economic Crisis.*

SAMUELS, A. (1987), 'Health Sector Review: 1987', report prepared for the Ministry of Health, Government of Jamaica, Kingston.

SAMUELSON, P. A. (1955), 'Diagrammatic Exposition of a Theory of Public Expenditure', *Review of Economics and Statistics*, 37.

SANDERS, D. (1982), 'Nutrition and the Use of Food as a Weapon in Zimbabwe and Southern Africa', *International Journal of Health Services*, 12.

—— and DAVIES, R. (1988), 'Economic Adjustment and Current Trends in Child Survival: The Case of Zimbabwe', *Health Policy and Planning*, 3.

SANDFORD, S. (1977), 'Dealing with Drought and Livestock in Botswana', Report to the Government of Botswana, Gaborone.

SANTANA, S. M. (1987), 'The Cuban Health Care System: Responsiveness to Changing Population Needs and Demands', *World Development*, 15.

SANYAL, S. K. (1988), 'Trends in Landholding and Poverty in Rural India', in Srinivasan, T. N., and Bardhan, P. K. (eds.) (1988), *Rural Poverty in South Asia.*

SARMA, J. S. (1983), *Contingency Planning for Famines and Other Acute Food Shortages: A Brief Review* (Washington, DC: International Food Policy Research Institute).

SCARPACI, J. L. (1985), 'Restructuring Health Care Financing in Chile', *Social Science and Medicine*, 21.

SCHEETZ, T. (1987), 'Public Sector Expenditures and Financial Crisis in Chile', *World Development*, 15.

SCHELLING, T. C. (1960), *The Strategy of Conflict* (Cambridge, MA: Harvard University Press).

SCHEPER-HUGHES, N. (ed.) (1987), *Child Survival: Anthropological Perspectives on the Treatment and Maltreatment of Children* (Dordrecht: Reidel).

SCHIFF, M., and VALDÉS, A. (1988), 'Nutrition: Alternative Definitions and Policy Implications', mimeo, International Food Policy Research Institute; forthcoming in *Economic Development and Cultural Change.*

SCHMIDT-WULFFEN, W. (1985), 'Dürre- und Hungerkatastrophen in Schwarzafrika —das Fallbeispiel Mali', *Geographische Zeitschrift*, 73.

SCHWARE, R. (1982), 'Official and Folk Flood Warning Systems: An Assessment', *Environmental Management*, 6.

SCITOVSKY, T. (1985), 'Economic Development in Taiwan and South Korea, 1965–81', *Stanford Food Research Institute Studies*, 19.

SCOTT, E. (ed.) (1984), *Life Before the Drought* (Boston: Allen and Unwin).

SCOTT, J. (1976), *The Moral Economy of the Peasant* (New Haven: Yale University Press).

SCRIMSHAW, N. (1987a), 'Biological Adaptation in the Maintenance of Nutrition and Health', paper presented at the 86th Annual Meeting of the American Anthropological Association, Nov. 1987, Chicago.

—— (1987b), 'The Phenomenon of Famine', *Annual Review of Nutrition*, 7.

—— TAYLOR, C. E., and GOPALAN, J. E. (1968), *Interactions of Nutrition and Infection*, WHO Monograph No. 57, World Health Organization, Geneva.

SEAMAN, J. (1987), 'Famine Mortality in Ethiopia and Sudan', paper presented at a IUSSP seminar on Mortality and Society in Sub-Saharan Africa, Yaoundé, Cameroon, Oct. 1987.

—— HOLT, J., and RIVERS, J. (1978), 'The Effects of Drought on Human Nutrition in an Ethiopian Province', *International Journal of Epidemiology*, 7.

—— —— (1980), 'Markets and Famines in the Third World', *Disasters*, 4.

—— RIVERS, J., HOLT, J., and MURLIS, J. (1973), 'An Inquiry into the Drought Situation in Upper Volta', *Lancet*, No. 7832.

SEAVOY, R. E. (1986), *Famine in Peasant Societies* (Connecticut: Greenwood Press).

SECKLER, D. (1982), 'Small but Healthy?: A Basic Hypothesis in the Theory, Measurement and Policy of Malnutrition', in Sukhatme, P. V. (ed.) (1982a), *Newer Concepts in Nutrition and Their Implications for Policy*.

—— (1984), 'The "Small but Healthy?" Hypothesis: A Reply to Critics', *Economic and Political Weekly*, 19.

SEELEY, J. A. (1986a), *Famine in Africa: A Guide to Bibliographies and Resource Centres* (Cambridge: African Studies Centre).

—— (1986b), *Famine in Sub-Saharan Africa: A Select Bibliography* (Cambridge: African Studies Centre).

SEIDL, C. (1988), 'Poverty Measurement: A Survey', in Bos, D., Rose, M., and Seidl, C. (eds.) (1988), *Welfare and Efficiency in Public Economics* (Berlin: Springer-Verlag).

SELIGSON, M. A. (1980), *Peasants of Costa Rica and the Development of Agrarian Capitalism* (Madison: University of Wisconsin Press).

SELWYN, P. (1983), 'Mauritius: The Meade Report Twenty Years After', in Cohen, R. (ed.) (1983), *African Islands and Enclaves* (Beverley Hills: Sage).

SEN, A. K. (1960), *Choice of Techniques* (Oxford: Blackwell).

—— (1970), *Collective Choice and Social Welfare* (San Francisco: Holden-Day; republished, Amsterdam: North-Holland, 1979).

—— (1976a), 'Famines as Failures of Exchange Entitlements', *Economic and Political Weekly*, 11.

—— (1976b), 'Poverty: An Ordinal Approach to Measurement', *Econometrica*, 44.

—— (1976c), 'Real National Income', *Review of Economic Studies*, 43.

—— (1977a), 'Starvation and Exchange Entitlements: A General Approach and Its Application to the Great Bengal Famine', *Cambridge Journal of Economics*, 1.

—— (1977b), 'Rational Fools: A Critique of the Behavioural Foundations of Economic Theory', *Philosophy and Public Affairs*, 6; repr. in Sen, A. K. (1982a), *Choice, Welfare and Measurement*.

—— (1980), 'Equality of What?', in McMurrin, S. (ed.) (1980), *Tanner Lectures on Human Values* (Cambridge: Cambridge University Press); repr. in Sen, A. K. (1984a), *Resources, Values and Development* and also in Rawls, J., *et al.* (eds.) (1987), *Liberty, Equality and Law* (Cambridge: Cambridge University Press).

—— (1981a), *Poverty and Famines* (Oxford: Clarendon).

—— (1981b), 'Public Action and the Quality of Life in Developing Countries', *Oxford Bulletin of Economics and Statistics*, 43.

—— (1982a), *Choice, Welfare and Measurement* (Oxford: Basil Blackwell).

—— (1982b), 'Food Battles: Conflicts in Access to Food', Coromandel Lectures, New Delhi; repr. in *Food and Nutrition*, 10 (1984).

—— (1982c), 'How is India Doing?', *New York Review of Books*, 29.

—— (1982*d*), 'The Right Not To Be Hungry', in Floistad, G. (ed.) (1982), *Contemporary Philosophy*, vol. ii (The Hague: Martinus Nijhoff).

—— (1983*a*), 'Development: Which Way Now?', *Economic Journal*, 93.

—— (1983*b*), 'Poor, Relatively Speaking', *Oxford Economic Papers*, 35; repr. in Sen, A. K. (1984*a*) *Resources, Values and Development*.

—— (1984*a*), *Resources, Values and Development* (Oxford: Basil Blackwell).

—— (1984*b*), 'Family and Food: Sex Bias in Poverty', in Sen, A. K. (1984*a*), *Resources, Values and Development*.

—— (1985*a*), *Commodities and Capabilities* (Amsterdam: North-Holland).

—— (1985*b*), 'Well-Being, Agency and Freedom: The Dewey Lectures 1984', *Journal of Philosophy*, 82.

—— (1985*c*), 'Women, Technology and Sexual Divisions', *Trade and Development (UNCTAD)*, 6.

—— (1985*d*), 'A Sociological Approach to the Measurement of Poverty: A Reply to Professor Townsend', *Oxford Economic Papers*, 37.

—— (1986*a*), 'Food, Economics and Entitlements', *Lloyds Bank Review*, 160; to be repr. in Drèze, J. P., and Sen, A. K. (eds.) (forthcoming), *The Political Economy of Hunger*.

—— (1986*b*), 'The Causes of Famine: A Reply', *Food Policy*, 11.

—— (1987*a*), *The Standard of Living*, Tanner Lectures with discussion by J. Muellbauer and others, ed. G. Hawthorn (Cambridge: Cambridge University Press).

—— (1987*b*), *On Ethics and Economics* (Oxford: Blackwell).

—— (1987*c*), 'Gender and Cooperative Conflicts', Working Paper No. 18, WIDER, Helsinki; to be published in Tinker, I. (ed.) (forthcoming), *Persistent Inequalities*.

—— (1987*d*), 'Reply: Famines and Mr. Bowbrick', *Food Policy*, 12.

—— (1987*e*), *Hunger and Entitlements* (Helsinki: WIDER).

—— (1988*a*), 'Freedom of Choice: Concept and Content', *European Economic Review*, 32.

—— (1988*b*), 'Capability and Well-Being', paper presented at a Conference on The Quality of Life held at WIDER, Helsinki, July 1988; to be published in Nussbaum, M., and Sen, A. K. (eds.) (forthcoming), *Quality of Life*.

—— (1988*c*), 'Africa and India: What Do We Have to Learn From Each Other?', in Arrow, K. J. (ed.) (1988), *The Balance Between Industry and Agriculture in Economic Development*, i: *Basic Issues* (London: Macmillan).

—— (1988*d*), 'Food and Freedom', Sir John Crawford Memorial Lecture, to be published in *World Development*.

—— (1988*e*), 'Property and Hunger', *Economic Philosophy*, 4.

—— (1988*f*), 'Sri Lanka's Achievements: How and When', in Srinivasan, T. N., and Bardhan, P. K. (eds.) (1988), *Rural Poverty in South Asia*.

—— (1989*a*), 'Women's Survival as a Development Problem', *Bulletin of the American Academy of Arts and Sciences*, 43, 2.

—— (1989*b*). 'Indian Development: Lessons and Non-lessons', *Daedalus*, 118.

—— and SENGUPTA, S. (1983), 'Malnutrition of Rural Children and the Sex Bias', *Economic and Political Weekly*, 19 (annual number).

SENAUER, B., and GARCIA, M. (1988), 'The Determinants of Food Consumption and Nutritional Status Among Preschool Children: Evidence from the Rural Philippines', Staff Paper Series, No. P88-33, Department of Agricultural and Applied Economics, University of Minnesota.

—— and YOUNG, N. (1986), 'Impact of Food Stamps on Food Expenditures', *American Journal of Agricultural Economics*, 68.

SERBYN, R., and KRAWCHENKO, B. (eds.) (1986), *Famine in Ukraine* (Edmonton: University of Alberta Press).

SHAH, C. H. (1982), 'The Demand for Higher-Status Food and Nutrition in Rural India: The Experience of Matar Taluka', *Food and Nutrition Bulletin*, 8.

SHAMA SASTRY, R. (1967), *Kautilya's Arthasastra* (Mysore: Mysore Publishing House).

SHAO, Y. (1988), *Health Care in China* (London: Office of Health Economics).

SHAWCROSS, W. (1984), *The Quality of Mercy: Cambodia, Holocaust and Modern Conscience* (New York: Simon and Schuster).

SHEETS, H., and MORRIS, R. (1974), *Disaster in the Desert: Failure of International Relief in West African Drought* (Washington: Carnegie Endowment for International Peace).

SHERBINY, N. A. (1984), 'Expatriate Labor Flows to the Arab Oil Countries in the 1980s', *Middle East Journal*, 38.

SHETTLES, L. B. (1958), 'Biological Sex Differences with Special Reference to Disease, Resistance and Longevity', *Journal of Obstetrics and Gynaecology of the British Empire*, 65.

SHIGEMATSU, I., and YANAGAWA, H. (1985), 'The Case of Japan', in Vallin, J., and Lopez, A. (eds.) (1985), *Health Policy, Social Policy and Mortality Prospects*.

SHUKLA, R. (1979), *Public Works during Drought and Famines and Its Lessons for an Employment Policy* (Ahmedabad: Sardar Patel Institute of Economic and Social Research).

SIDER, R. J. (1980), *Cry Justice: The Bible on Hunger and Poverty* (New York: Paulist Press).

SIGMUND, P. E. (1984), 'Chile: Free-Market Authoritarianism', in Wesson, R. (ed.) (1984), *Politics, Policies and Economic Development in Latin America*.

SINGER, H., and MAXWELL, S. (1979), 'Food Aid to the Developing Countries: A Survey', *World Development*, 7.

—— WOOD, J., and JENNINGS, T. (1987), *Food Aid: The Challenge and the Opportunity* (Oxford: Clarendon).

SINGH, I. (1988), 'Land and Labor in South Asia', World Bank Discussion Paper No. 33, World Bank, Washington, DC.

SINGH, S. K. (1975), *The Indian Famine, 1967* (New Delhi: People's Publishing House).

SMALE, M. (1980), 'Women in Mauritania: The Effects of Drought and Migration on Their Economic Status and Implications for Development Programs', report prepared for the Office of Women in Development, US Agency for International Development, Washington, DC.

SMITH, A. (1776), *An Inquiry into the Nature and Causes of the Wealth of Nations*; republished in Campbell and Skinner (1976).

SMITH, R. (1987), *Unemployment and Health* (Oxford: Oxford University Press).

SMOUT, T. C. (1978), 'Famine and Famine-Relief in Scotland', in Cullen, L. M., and Smout, T. C. (eds.) (1978), *Comparative Aspects of Scottish and Irish Economic History 1600–1900*.

SNOWDON, B. (1985), 'The Political Economy of the Ethiopian Famine', *National Westminster Bank Quarterly Review*, November.

SOBHAN, R. (1979), 'Politics of Food and Famine in Bangladesh', *Economic and Political Weekly*, 14.

—— (1986), 'Politics of Hunger and Entitlements', paper presented at a Conference on Food Strategies held at WIDER, Helsinki, 21–5 July 1986; to be published in Drèze, J. P., and Sen, A. K. (eds.) (forthcoming), *The Political Economy of Hunger*.

SOBHAN, S. (1978), *Legal Status of Women in Bangladesh* (Dhaka: Bangladesh Institute of Law and International Affairs).

Society for International Development (1985), *Report of the North–South Roundtable on the Crisis in Africa* (Islamabad: NSRT).

SÖDERSTRÖM, L. (ed.) (1983), *Social Insurance* (Amsterdam: North-Holland).

SOETERS, R. (1986), 'Pitfalls with Weight for Height Measurements in Surveys of Acute Malnutrition', *Tropical Doctor*, 16.

SOLIMANO, G., and HAIGNERE, C. (1984), 'Free-Market Politics and Nutrition in Chile: A Grim Future after a Short-Lived Success', Working Paper No. 7, Center for Population and Family Health, Faculty of Medicine, Columbia University.

SOROKIN, P. A. (1942), *Man and Society in Calamity: The Effects of War, Revolution, Famine and Pestilence Upon Human Mind, Behaviour, Social Organization and Cultural Life* (New York: E. P. Dutton and Co.).

—— (1975), *Hunger as a Factor in Human Affairs* (Gainsville: University of Florida Press).

SPERLING, L. (1987a), 'Food Acquisition During the African Drought of 1983–84: A Study of Kenyan Herders', *Disasters*, 11.

—— (1987b), 'Wage Employment Among Samburu Pastoralists of Northcentral Kenya', *Research in Economic Anthropology*, 9.

SPITZ, P. (1978), 'Silent Violence: Famine and Inequality', *International Social Sciences Journal*, 30.

—— (1980), *Drought and Self-Provisioning* (Geneva: UNRISD).

SPRING, A. (1986), 'Women Farmers and Food in Africa', in Hansen, A., and McMillan, E. E. (eds.) (1986), *Food in Sub-Saharan Africa*.

SPYCKERELLE, L. (1987), 'Integrated Natural Resources Management in Cape Verde', term paper, Institute of Development Studies, University of Sussex.

SRINIVASAN, T. N. (1981), 'Malnutrition: Some Measurement and Policy Issues', *Journal of Development Economics*, 8.

—— (1983), 'Malnutrition in Developing Countries: The State of Knowledge of the Extent of Its Prevalence, Its Causes and Its Consequences', background paper prepared for FAO's Fifth World Food Survey.

—— (1987), 'Undernutrition: Concepts, Measurement and Policy Implications', paper presented at a Conference on Poverty, Undernutrition and Living Standards held at WIDER, 27–30 July 1987; to be published in Osmani, S. R. (ed.) (forthcoming), *Nutrition and Poverty*.

—— and BARDHAN, P. K. (eds.) (1974), *Poverty and Income Distribution in India* (Calcutta: Statistical Publishing Society).

—— —— (eds.) (1988), *Rural Poverty in South Asia* (New York: Columbia University Press).

SRIVASTAVA, H. S. (1968), *History of Indian Famines and Development of Famine Policy 1858–1918* (Agra: Sri Ram Mehra and Co.).

STANDING, G., and SHEEHAN, G. (eds.) (1978), *Labour Force Participation in Low Income Countries* (Geneva: ILO).

STAVIS, B. (1982), 'Ending Famines in China', in Garcia, R., and Escudero, J. (eds.) (1982), *Drought and Man*, ii.

STEELE, I. (1985), 'Mali Battles Drought', *Africa Emergency Report*, Apr.–May 1985.

STEIN, Z., SUSSER, M., SAERGER, G., and MAROLLA, F. (1975), *Famine and Human Development: The Dutch Hunger Winter of 1944/45* (New York: Oxford University Press).

STEINBERG, D. I. (1988), 'Sociopolitical Factors and Korea's Future Economic Policies', *World Development*, 16.

STEWART, F. (1985), *Planning to Meet Basic Needs* (London: Macmillan).

—— (1987), 'Supporting Productive Employment Among Vulnerable Groups', in Cornia, G., *et al.* (eds.) (1987), *Adjustment with a Human Face*.

—— (1988), 'Basic Needs Strategies, Human Rights and the Right to Development', Ld'A-QEH Development Studies Working Paper No. 2, Queen Elizabeth House, Oxford.

STEWART, P. J. (1988), 'The Ecology of Famine', in Harrison, G. A. (ed.) (1988), *Famines*.

STICHTER, S., and PARPART, J. (1988), *Patriarchy and Class: African Women in the Home and Workforce* (Boulder: Westview).

STIGLER, J. G. (1945), 'The Cost of Subsistence', *Journal of Farm Economics*, 27.

STONEMAN, C. (ed.) (1988), *Zimbabwe's Prospects: Issues of Race, Class, State and Capital in Southern Africa* (London: Macmillan).

STREETEN, P. (1984), 'Basic Needs: Some Unsettled Questions', *World Development*, 12.

—— (1987), *What Price Food?* (London: Macmillan).

—— (1989), 'The Politics of Food Prices', in Islam, N. (ed.) (1989), *Balance between Industry and Agriculture in Economic Development*, vol. v (London: Macmillan).

STREETEN, P., with BURKI, S. J., MAHBUB UL HAQ, HICKS, N. and STEWART (1981), *First Things First: Meeting Basic Needs in Developing Countries* (New York: Oxford University Press).

STYCOS, J. M. (1982), 'The Decline of Fertility in Costa Rica: Literacy, Modernization and Family Planning', *Population Studies*, 36.

SUBBARAO, K. (1989), 'Improving Nutrition in India: Policies, Programs and Impact', Discussion Paper No. 49, World Bank, Washington, DC.

SUBRAMANIAM, V. (1975), *Parched Earth: The Maharashtra Drought 1970–73* (Bombay: Orient Longmans).

SUH, S. M. (1984), 'Effects of the Current World Recession on the Welfare of Children: The Case of Korea', in Jolly, R., and Cornia, G. (eds.) (1984), *The Impact of World Recession on Children*.

—— and WILLIAMSON, D. (1987), 'The Impact of Adjustment and Stabilization Policies on Social Welfare: The South Korean Experiences During 1978–1985', in Cornia, G., *et al.* (eds.) (1987), *Adjustment with a Human Face*.

SUKHATME, P. V. (1961), 'The World's Hunger and Future Needs in Food Supplies', *Journal of Royal Statistical Society*, Ser. A, Vol. 124.

—— (1969), 'The Incidence of Protein Deficiency in India', *Indian Journal of Medical Research*, 57.

—— (1973), 'The Protein Problem', *Everyman's Science*, 8.

—— (1977), *Nutrition and Poverty* (New Delhi: Indian Agricultural Research Institute).

—— (ed.) (1982a), *Newer Concepts in Nutrition and Their Implications for Policy* (Pune: Maharashtra Association for the Cultivation of Science).

—— (1982*b*), 'Measurement of Undernutrition', *Economic and Political Weekly*, 16.

—— and MARGEN, S. (1978), 'Models of Protein Deficiency', *American Journal of Clinical Nutrition*, 31.

—— —— (1982), 'Autoregulatory Homeostatic Nature of Energy Balance', *American Journal of Clinical Nutrition*, 35; also repr. in Sukahtme, P. V. (ed.) (1982*a*), *Newer Concepts in Nutrition and Their Implications for Policy*.

SUNDARAM, K., and TENDULKAR, S. D. (1981), 'Poverty Reduction in the 6th Plan', Working Paper No. 233, Delhi School of Economics.

SUPER, J. C. and WRIGHT, T. C. (eds.) (1985), *Food, Politics and Society in Latin America* (Lincoln and London: University of Nebraska Press).

SVEDBERG, P. (1986), 'Undernutrition in Sub-Saharan Africa: A Critical Assessment of the Evidence', Working Paper No. 15, WIDER; to be published in Drèze, J. P., and Sen, A. K. (eds.) (forthcoming), *The Political Economy of Hunger*.

—— (1988), 'Undernutrition in Sub-Saharan Africa: Is There a Sex Bias?', Working Paper No. 47, WIDER, Helsinki.

SWAMINATHAN, MADHURA (1988), 'Inequality and Economic Mobility: An Analysis of Panel Data from a South India Village', D.Phil. dissertation, Oxford University.

SWAMINATHAN, M. C., RAO, K. V., and RAO, D. H. (1969), 'Food and Nutrition Situation in the Drought-Affected Areas of Bihar', *Journal of Nutrition and Dietetics*, 6.

SWAMINATHAN, M. S. (1986), *Sustainable Nutrition Security for Africa: Lessons from India* (San Francisco: The Hunger Project).

SWAMY, S. (1986*a*), 'A Comparative Perspective of the Economic Growth of China and India: 1870–1985', mimeo, Harvard University; to be published as a monograph.

—— (1986*b*), 'Efficiency, Productivity and Income Distribution in China and India: 1952–84', mimeo, Harvard University.

SWANBERG, K. G., and HOGAN, E. (1981), 'Implications of the Drought Syndrome for Agricultural Planning in East Africa: The Case of Tanzania', Discussion Paper 120: 1–49, Harvard Institute for International Development.

SWANN, N. L. (trans.) (1950), *Food and Money in Ancient China*, an annotated translation of Pan Ku's *Han Shu 24*, with related texts (Princeton: Princeton University Press).

SWIFT, J. (1977), 'Sahelian Pastoralists—Underdevelopment, Desertification, and Famine', *Annual Review of Anthropology*, 6.

—— (1982), 'The Future of African Hunter-Gatherer and Pastoral Peoples', *Development and Change*, 13.

—— (1985), 'Planning Against Drought and Famine in Turkana, Northern Kenya', mimeo, Institute of Development Studies, University of Sussex.

—— (1989), 'Why Are Rural People Vulnerable to Famine?', in Chambers, R. (ed.) (1989), *Vulnerability: How the Poor Cope*.

—— (forthcoming), 'Planning Against Drought and Famine in Turkana: A District Contingency Plan', to be published in Downing, T. E., *et al.* (eds.) (forthcoming), *Coping with Drought in Kenya: National and Local Strategies*.

SZRETER, S. (1986), 'The Importance of Social Intervention in Britain's Mortality Decline c. 1850–1914: A Re-interpretation', *Social History of Medicine*, 1.

TABOR, S. (1983), 'Drought Relief and Information Management: Coping Intelligently with Disaster', Family Health Division, Ministry of Health, Government of Botswana.

Tabutin, D. (1975), 'Origines, composantes et conséquences de l'évolution démographique à Maurice', Working Paper No. 19, Département de Démographie, Université Catholique de Louvain, Belgium.

—— and Sombo, N. (1983), 'Tendances et causes de la mortalité à Maurice depuis 1940', Working Paper No. 115, Départment de Démographie, Université Catholique de Louvain, Belgium.

Taeuber, I. B. (1958), *The Population of Japan* (Princeton: Princeton University Press).

Tagwireyi, J. (1988), 'Experiences in Increasing Food Access and Nutrition in Zimbabwe', paper presented at the Fourth Annual Conference on Food Security Research in Southern Africa, Oct.–Nov., Harare, Zimbabwe.

Talbot, R. B., Hawley, J., and Poorman, J. (1985), *Selected Bibliography on World Food Politics and Policies* (Ames: Iowa State University Press).

Taryam, A. O. (1987), *The Establishment of the United Arab Emirates 1950–85* (London: Croom Helm).

Taylor, C. E. (1983), 'Synergy Among Mass Infections, Famines, and Poverty', in Rotberg, R. I., and Rabb, T. K. (eds.) (1983), *Hunger and History*.

Taylor, L. (1975), 'The Misconstrued Crisis: Lester Brown and World Food', *World Development*, 3.

—— (1988a), *Varieties of Stabilization Experiences: Towards Sensible Macroeconomics in the Third World* (Oxford: Clarendon).

—— (1988b), 'Macro Effects of Myriad Shocks: Developing Countries in the World Economy', in Bell, D. E., and Reich, M. R. (eds.) (1988), *Health, Nutrition and Economic Crises*.

Taylor, W. (1983), 'An Evaluation of Supplementary Feeding in Somali Refugee Camps', *International Journal of Epidemiology*, 12.

Teuscher, T. (1985), 'Report on Nutritional Aspects of the Ongoing LRCS Food-Aid Program', internal report, League of Red Cross and Red Crescent Societies, Geneva.

Thomas, D., Strauss, J., and Henriques, M. H. (1988a), 'How Does Mother's Education Affect Child Height?', Discussion Paper No. 89, Development Economics Research Centre, University of Warwick.

—— —— —— (1988b), 'Child Survival, Height for Age and Household Characteristics in Brazil', Discussion Paper No. 90, Development Economics Research Centre, University of Warwick.

Thomas, J. W., Burki, S. J., Davies, D. G., and Hook, R. H. (1976), 'Public Works Programs in Developing Countries: A Comparative Analysis', World Bank Staff Working Paper No. 224, World Bank, Washington, DC.

—— (1986), 'Food for Work: An Analysis of Current Experience and Recommendations for Future Performance', Discussion Paper No. 213, Harvard Institute for International Development, Cambridge, MA.

Tilly, C. (1975), 'Food Supply and Public Order in Modern Europe', in Tilly, C. (ed.) (1975), *The Formation of National States in Europe* (Princeton: Princeton University Press).

—— (1978), *From Mobilization to Revolution* (Reading, MA: Addison-Wesley).

Tilly, L. A. (1971), 'The Food Riot as a Form of Political Conflict in France', *Journal of Interdisciplinary History*, 2.

—— (1983), 'Food Entitlement, Famine, and Conflict', in Rotberg, R. I., and Rabb, T. K. (eds.) (1983), *Hunger and History*.

—— (1986), 'Sex and Occupation in Comparative Perspective', mimeo, New School for Social Research, New York.

The Times (1985), 'Harare Health Drive Cuts Infant Mortality', *The Times*, 4 Nov. 1985.

TIMMER, C. P. (1984), *Private Decisions and Public Policy: The Food Price Dilemma in Developing Countries* (Cambridge, MA: Harvard Business School).

—— (1986), *Getting Prices Right: The Scope and Limits of Agricultural Price Policy* (Ithaca: Cornell University Press).

—— (1988), 'Food Policy and Economic Adjustment', in Bell, D. E., and Reich, M. R. (eds.) (1988), *Health, Nutrition and Economic Crises*.

—— FALCON, W., and PEARSON, S. (1983), *Food Policy Analysis* (Baltimore: Johns Hopkins).

TINKER, I. (ed.) (forthcoming), *Persistent Inequalities* (New York: Oxford University Press).

TITMUSS, R. M. (1950), *History of the Second World War: Problems of Social Policy* (London: HMSO).

—— and ABEL-SMITH, B. (1968), *Social Policies and Population Growth in Mauritius* (London: Frank Cass).

TOBERT, N. (1985), 'The Effect of Drought Among the Zaghawa in Northern Darfur', *Disasters*, 9.

TOMIC, B. (1983), 'Descentralización y participación popular: la salud rural en Costa Rica', Monografias Sobre Empleo No. 34, Institute of Social Studies, PREALC, International Labour Office.

TORCHE, A. (1985), 'Una evaluación económica del programa nacional de alimentación complementaria (PNAC)', *Cuadernos de economía*, 22.

TORDOFF, W. (1988), 'Local Administration in Botswana', *Public Administration and Development*, 8.

TORRY, W. I. (1979), 'Anthropological Studies in Hazardous Environments: Past Trends and New Horizons', *Current Anthropology*, 20.

—— (1984), 'Social Science Research on Famine: A Critical Evaluation', *Human Ecology*, 12.

—— (1986a), 'Drought and the Government–Village Emergency Food Distribution System in India', *Human Organization*, 45.

—— (1986b), 'Morality and Harm: Hindu Peasant Adjustments to Famines', *Social Science Information*, 25.

—— (1987), 'Evolution of Food Rationing Systems with Reference to African Group Farms in the Context of Drought', in Glantz, M. (ed.) (1987a), *Drought and Hunger in Africa*.

—— (1988a), 'Famine Early Warning Systems: The Need for an Anthropological Dimension', *Human Organization*, 47.

—— (1988b), 'Information for Food: Community Famine Surveillance in Sudan', mimeo, Department of Sociology/Anthropology, West Virginia University.

TOULMIN, C. (1983), 'Economic Behaviour Among Livestock-Keeping Peoples: A Review of the Literature on the Economics of Pastoral Production in Semi-arid Zones of Africa', Occasional Paper No. 25, School of Development Studies, University of East Anglia.

TOWNSEND, P. (1979a), *Poverty in the United Kingdom* (Harmondsworth: Penguin).

—— (1979b), 'The Development of Research on Poverty', in Department of Health and Social Security, *Social Science Research: The Definition and Measurement of Poverty* (London: HMSO).

—— (1985), 'A Sociological Approach to the Measurement of Poverty: A Rejoinder to Professor Amartya Sen', *Oxford Economic Papers*, 37.

—— and DAVIDSON, N. (eds.) (1982), *Inequalities in Health* (Harmondsworth: Penguin).

TOYE, J. (1987), *Dilemmas of Development* (Oxford: Basil Blackwell).

TURTON, D. (1977), 'Response to Drought: The Mursi of Southwestern Ethiopia', *Disasters*, 1.

—— (1985), 'Mursi Response to Drought: Some Lessons for Relief and Rehabilitation', *African Affairs*, 84.

—— and TURTON, P. (1984), 'Spontaneous Resettlement After Drought: An Ethiopian Example', *Disasters*, 8.

TWOSE, N. (1984), *Cultivating Hunger* (Oxford: OXFAM).

UNDERWOOD, B. (ed.) (1983), *Nutrition Intervention Strategies in National Development* (New York: Academic Press).

UNDRO (1984), 'Sécheresse en Mauritanie', internal report, Office of the United Nations Disaster Relief Coordinator, Geneva.

—— (1986), *UNDRO in Africa 1984–85* (Geneva: Office of the United Nations Disaster Relief Coordinator).

UNICEF (1987a), *The State of the World's Children 1987* (Oxford: Oxford University Press).

—— (1987b), 'Sri Lanka: The Social Impact of Economic Policies During the Last Decade', in Cornia, G., *et al.* (eds.) (1987), *Adjustment with a Human Face*.

—— (1988), *The State of the World's Children 1988* (Oxford: Oxford University Press).

—— (1989), *The State of the World's Children 1989* (Oxford: Oxford University Press).

United Nations (1987), *First Report on the World Nutrition Situation*, Administrative Committee on Coordination, Subcommittee on Nutrition, United Nations.

—— (1988), 'Mortality of Children Under Age 5: World Estimates and Projections, 1950–2025', Population Studies No. 105, Department of International Economic and Social Affairs, United Nations, New York.

United Nations Office for Emergency Operations in Africa (1985a), *Status Report on the Emergency Situation in Africa* (New York: OEOA).

—— (1985b), *Supplement to the Status Report on the Emergency Situation in Africa* (New York: OEOA).

United States Department of Agriculture (1986), 'Sub-Saharan Africa: Situation and Outlook Report', Economic Research Services, United States Department of Agriculture.

UPPAL, J. N. (1984), *Bengal Famine of 1943: A Man-Made Tragedy* (Delhi: Atma Ram).

USAID (1982), 'Cape Verde: Food for Development Program (PL480 Title II, Section 206)', mimeo, USAID, Washington, DC.

—— (1983), 'U.S. Aid to Zimbabwe: An Evaluation', AID Program Evaluation Report No. 9, US Agency for International Development, Washington, DC.

VAIDYANATHAN, A. (1985), 'Food Consumption and Size of People: Some Indian Evidence', *Economic and Political Weekly*, 20.

—— (1987), 'Poverty and Economy: The Regional Dimension', paper presented at a Workshop on Poverty in India, Queen Elizabeth House, Oxford, Oct. 1987.

VALAORAS, V. G. (1946), 'Some Effects of Famine on the Population of Greece', *Milbank Memorial Fund Quarterly Bulletin*, 24.

VALDÉS, A. (ed.) (1981), *Food Security for Developing Countries* (Boulder: Westview).

VALDES-BRITO, J. A., and HENRIQUES, J. A. (1983), 'Health Status of the Cuban Population', *International Journal of Health Services*, 13.

VALIENTE, S., MONCKEBERG, F., and GONZALEZ, N. (1985), 'The Political Economy of Nutrition in Chile', paper presented at a IFPRI/UNU workshop on the Political Economy of Nutritional Improvements, Berkeley Springs, W. Va.

VALLIN, J., and LOPEZ, A. D. (eds.) (1985), *Health Policy, Social Policy and Mortality Prospects* (Liège: International Union for the Scientific Study of Population).

VAN APPELDOORN, G. J. (1981), *Perspectives on Drought and Famine in Nigeria* (London: Allen and Unwin).

VAN BINSBERGEN, A. (1986), 'Cape Verde: Food Aid Resource Planning in Support of the National Food Strategy', paper presented at a WFP–ADB Seminar on Food Aid in sub-Saharan Africa, Abijan, Sept. 1986.

VATUK, S. (1979), 'The Sharing and Giving of Food in South Asian Society', draft paper prepared for the Social Science Research Council Committee on South Asia.

VAUGHAN, M. (1985), 'Famine Analysis and Family Relations: 1949 in Nyasaland', *Past and Present*, 108.

—— (1987), *The Story of an African Famine: Hunger, Gender and Politics in Malawi* (Cambridge: Cambridge University Press).

VIAL, I., MUCHNIK, E., and KAIN, J. (1987), 'Chile's Main Nutrition Intervention Programs: A Synthesis', mimeo, Institute of Nutrition and Food Technology, Santiago.

—— —— —— (1988), 'Evolution of Chile's Main Nutrition Intervention Programs', mimeo, University of Chile and Catholic University, Santiago.

VISARIA, L. (1985), 'Infant Mortality in India', *Economic and Political Weekly*, 20.

VISARIA, P. (1961), *The Sex Ratio of the Population of India*, Monograph 10, Census of India 1961 (New Delhi: Office of the Registrar General).

VIVEROS-LONG, A. (1986), 'Changes in Health Financing: The Chilean Experience', *Social Science and Medicine*, 22.

VOGLAIRE, A. (1988), 'La Théorie économique à l'épreuve des faits: le cas de la grande famine irlandaise de 1845–1849', unpublished M.Sc. thesis, Facultés Universitaires Notre-Dame de la Paix, Namur, Belgium.

VON BRAUN, J. (1988), 'Households' Responses to Severe Food Shortages in Two Very Different African Settings: Rwanda and The Gambia', transcript of a presentation made at a Workshop on Famine and Famine Policy held at Tufts University, 25 Mar. 1988.

—— (forthcoming), 'Social Security in Sub-Saharan Africa: Reflections on Policy Challenges', mimeo, International Food Policy Research Institute; to be published in Ahmad, S. E., *et al.* (eds.) (forthcoming), *Social Security in Developing Countries*.

—— and KENNEDY, E. (1986), 'Commercialization of Subsistence Agriculture: Income and Nutritional Effects in Developing Countries', Working Papers on Commercialization of Agriculture and Nutrition, No. 1, IFPRI, Washington, DC.

—— —— (1987), 'Cash Crops Versus Subsistence Crops: Income and Nutritional Effects in Developing Countries', in Gittinger, J. P., *et al.* (eds.) (1987), *Food Policy*.

—— —— and BOUIS, H. (1989), 'Comparative Analysis of the Effects of Increased Commercialization of Subsistence Agriculture on Production, Consumption, and

Nutrition', mimeo, International Food Policy Research Institute, Washington, DC.

VON KOHL, M. A. (1988), 'Cash for Food in Ethiopia', INTERCOM–UNICEF, No. 47.

WADDELL, E. (1974), 'Frost over Ningini: A Retrospect on Bungled Relief', *New Guinea*, 8.

WADE, R. (1983), 'South Korea's Agricultural Development: The Myth of the Passive State', *Pacific Viewpoint*, 24.

—— (1988), 'State Intervention in "Outward-Looking" Development: Neo-classical Theory and Taiwanese Practice', in White, G. (ed.) (1988), *Developmental States in East Asia*.

WALDRON, I. (1983), 'The Role of Genetic and Biological Factors in Sex Differences in Mortality', in Lopez, A. D., and Ruzicka, L. T. (eds.) (1983), *Sex Differentials in Mortality: Trends, Determinants and Consequences*.

WALFORD, C. (1978), 'On the Famines of the World: Past and Present', *Journal of Statistical Society*, 41.

WALKER, G. A., *et al*. (1986), 'Maternal Mortality in Jamaica', *Lancet*, 1.

—— ASHLEY, D. E. C., McCAW, A. M., and BERNARD, G. W. (1987), 'Maternal Deaths in Jamaica', *World Health Forum*, 8.

WALKER, P. (1987), 'Food for Recovery: Food Monitoring and Targeting in Red Sea Province, Sudan 1985–87', mimeo, OXFAM, Oxford.

—— (1988), 'Famine and Rapid Onset Disaster Warning Systems: A Report by the International Institute for Environment and Development for the Red Cross', mimeo, International Institute for Environment and Development, London.

WALKER, T. S., SINGH, R. P., and ASOKAN, M. (1986), 'Risk Benefits, Crop Insurance, and Dryland Agriculture', *Economic and Political Weekly*, 21.

WALLACE, H. M., and EBRAHIM, G. J. (eds.) (1981), *Maternal and Child Health Around the World* (London: Macmillan).

WALLICH, C. (1983), 'Savings Mobilization through Social Security: The Experience of Chile during 1916–17', World Bank Staff Working Paper No. 553, World Bank, Washington, DC.

WALLSTAM, E. (1985), 'A Nutritional Perspective on LORCS' Drought Relief Operations in Eastern and Southern Africa', internal report, League of Red Cross and Red Crescent Societies, Geneva.

WALTER, J., and WRIGHTSON, K. (1976), 'Dearth and Social Order in Early Modern England', *Past and Present*, 71.

WALTON, G. M. (ed.) (1985), *National Economic Policies of Chile* (Greenwich, Conn.: JAI Press).

WANGWE, S. (1986), 'The Contribution of Industry to Solving the Food Problem in Africa', paper presented at a Conference on Food Strategies held at WIDER, Helsinki, 21–5 July 1986; to be published in Drèze, J. P., and Sen, A. K. (eds.) (forthcoming), *The Political Economy of Hunger*.

WARE, H. (1984), 'Effects of Maternal Education, Women's Roles, and Child Care on Child Mortality', in Mosley, W. H., and Chen, L. C. (eds.) (1984), *Child Survival: Strategies for Research*.

WATERSON, T., and SANDERS, D. (1984), 'Zimbabwe: Health Care Since Independence', *Lancet*, 18 Feb.

WATKINS, S., and MENKEN, J. (1985), 'Famines in Historical Perspective', *Population and Development Review*, 11.

WATTS, M. J. (1983), *Silent Violence: Food, Famine and Peasantry in Northern Nigeria* (Berkeley: University of California Press).

—— (1984), 'The Demise of the Moral Economy: Food and Famine in a Sudano-Sahelian Region in Historical Perspective', in Scott, E. (ed.) (1984), *Life Before the Drought*.

WEBER, M. T., STAATZ, J. M., HOLTZMAN, J. S., CRAWFORD, E. W., and BERNSTEN, R. H. (1988), 'Informing Food Security Decisions in Africa: Empirical Analysis and Policy Dialogue', Staff Paper No. 88–58, Michigan State University, East Lansing.

WEDDERBURN, D. (ed.) (1974), *Poverty, Inequality and Class Structure* (Cambridge: Cambridge University Press).

WEINER, D. (1987), 'Agricultural Transformation in Zimbabwe: Lessons for a Liberated South Africa', paper presented at the Annual Meeting of the Association of American Geographers, Portland, Oregon, 23–6 Apr. 1987.

—— (1988), 'Land and Agricultural Development', in Stoneman, C. (ed.) (1988), *Zimbabwe's Prospects*.

—— and MOYO, S. (1988), 'Wage Labor, Environment and Peasant Agriculture', mimeo, Zimbabwe Institute of Development Studies, Harare; forthcoming in *Journal of African Studies*.

WEISBROD, A. (1969), 'Collective Action and the Distribution of Income: A Conceptual Approach', in Joint Economic Committee, *The Analysis and Evaluation of Public Expenditure* (Washington, DC: US Government Printing Office).

Welfare State Programme (forthcoming), *The Welfare Audit: The Extent and Effectiveness of the Welfare State since 1974* (Oxford: Oxford University Press).

WERNER, D. (1983), 'Health Care in Cuba: A Model Service or a means of Social Control—or Both?', in Morley, D., *et al.* (eds.) (1983), *Practising Health for All*.

WERTHEIM, J. (1979), 'Cuba: Economic Change and Education Reform, 1955–1974', World Bank Staff Working Paper No. 317, World Bank, Washington, DC.

WESSON, R. (1984a), 'Costa Rica, Problems of Social Democracy', in Wesson, R. (ed.) (1984), *Politics, Policies and Economic Development in Latin America*.

—— (eds.) (1984b), *Politics, Policies and Economic Development in Latin America* (Stanford: Hoover Institution Press).

WESTERGAARD, K. (1986), *People's Participation, Local Government and Rural Development: The Case of West Bengal, India* (Copenhagen: Centre for Development Research).

WHEELER, E. F. (1984), 'Intrahousehold Food Allocation: A Review of Evidence', mimeo, London School of Hygiene and Tropical Medicine.

—— and ABDULLAH, M. (1988), 'Food Allocation Within the Family: Response to Fluctuating Food Supply and Food Needs', in de Garine, I., and Harrison, G. A. (eds.) (1988), *Coping with Uncertainty in Food Supply*.

WHITE, G. (ed.) (1988), *Developmental States in East Asia* (Basingstoke: Macmillan).

WHITEHEAD, A. (1985), 'Gender and Famine in West Africa', mimeo, University of Sussex.

—— (1986), 'Rural Women and Food Production in Sub-Saharan Africa', paper presented at a Conference on Food Strategies held at WIDER, Helsinki, 21–5 July 1986; to be published in Drèze, J. P., and Sen, A. K. (eds.) (forthcoming), *The Political Economy of Hunger*.

WIDDOWSON, E. M. (1976), 'The Response of the Sexes to Nutritional Stress', *Proceedings of the Nutrition Society*, 35.

WIGLEY, T. M., INGRAM, M. G., and FARMER, G. (eds.) (1981), *Climate and History* (Cambridge: Cambridge University Press).

WILL, P. E. (1980), *Bureaucratie et famine en Chine au 18e siècle* (Paris: Mouton).

WILLIAMS, A. (1987), 'What is Health and Who Creates It?', mimeo, University of York.

WILLIAMS, B. (1987), 'The Standard of Living: Interests and Capabilities', in Sen, A. K. (1987a), *The Standard of Living*.

WILLIAMSON, J. (ed.) (1988), *Balance Between Industry and Agriculture in Economic Development* (London: Macmillan).

WILSON, F., and RAMPHELE, M. (1989), *Uprooting Poverty: The South African Challenge* (Cape Town: W. W. Norton & Co.).

WILSON, G. (1987a), *Money in the Family—Financial Organisation and Women's Responsibility* (Aldershot: Avebury Publishers).

—— (1987b), 'Patterns of Responsibility and Irresponsibility in Marriage', in Brannen, J., and Wilson, G. (eds.) (1987), *Give and Take in Families*.

WINTER, J. M. (1986), *The Great War and the British People* (London: Macmillan).

WISNER, B. G. (1977), 'The Human Ecology of Drought in Eastern Kenya', unpublished Ph.D. Dissertation, Clark University, Worcester.

WOHLT, P., ALLEN, B. J., GOIE, A., and HARVEY, P. W. (1982), 'An Investigation of Food Shortages in Papua New Guinea', mimeo, Institute of Applied Social and Economic Research, Boroko, Papua New Guinea.

WOLF, M. (1987), *Revolution Postponed: Women in Contemporary China* (Stanford: Stanford University Press).

WOOD, D. H., BARON, A., and BROWN, V. W. (1986), *An Evaluation of the Emergency Food Assistance Program: Synthesis Report* (Washington, DC: USAID).

WOODHAM-SMITH, C. (1962), *The Great Hunger* (United Kingdom: Hamish Hamilton).

World Bank (1980), *Poverty and Human Development* (Washington, DC: World Bank).

—— (1981), *Accelerated Development in Sub-Saharan Africa: An Agenda for Action* (Washington, DC: World Bank).

—— (1983a), *China: Socialist Economic Development* (3 vols.) (Washington, DC: World Bank).

—— (1983b), *Zimbabwe: Population, Health and Nutrition Sector Review* (Washington, DC: World Bank).

—— (1984a), *China, The Health Sector*, World Bank Country Study (Washington, DC: World Bank).

—— (1984b), *Towards Sustained Development in Sub-Saharan Africa: A Joint Program of Action* (Washington, DC: World Bank).

—— (1985), *China: Long-Term Development Issues and Options* (Baltimore: Johns Hopkins).

—— (1986), *Poverty and Hunger: Issues and Options for Food Security in Developing Countries* (Washington, DC: World Bank).

—— (1988a), *The World Bank's Support for the Alleviation of Poverty* (Washington, DC: World Bank).

—— (1988b), *The Challenge of Hunger: A Call to Action* (Washington, DC: World Bank).

World Food Programme (1986a), 'Lessons Learned from the African Food Crisis: Evaluation of the WFP Emergency Response (note by the Executive Director)', WFP/CFA: 22/7, World Food Programme, Rome.

—— (1986*b*), 'Lessons Learned from the African Food Crisis: Summary Evaluation Report on the WFP Emergency Response', WFP/CFA: 22/7, Add. 1, World Food Programme, Rome.

—— (1986*c*), 'Recent Developments in Regard to the Main Aspects Covered by the Evaluation', WFP/CFA: 22/7, Add. 2, World Food Programme, Rome.

—— (1986*d*), 'Interim Evaluation Summary Report on Project Ethiopia 2488', WFP/CFA: 21/14-A (WPME) Add. 1, World Food Programme, Rome.

—— (1986*e*), 'Aide alimentaire d'urgence fournie à la suite de la sécheresse 1984–85 au Niger', mimeo, World Food Programme, Niamey.

World Health Organization (1983), *Primary Health Care: The Chinese Experience* (Geneva: WHO).

—— (1984), 'Nutrition Surveillance: Morbidity and Mortality from the 1983 Famine', *Weekly Epidemiological Record*, 59.

—— (1986), 'Intersectoral Action for Health', background document prepared for the 39th World Assembly of the World Health Organization, Geneva, May 1986.

—— (1988), 'Nutrition: Sex Bias of Nutritional Status of Children 0–4 Years', *Weekly Epidemiological Record*, 20 May.

WRIGHT, K. (1983), *Famine in Tigray: Eye Witness Report* (London: Relief Society for Tigray).

WRIGHT, W. (1882), *The Chronicle of Joshua the Stylite* (Cambridge: Cambridge University Press).

WRIGLEY, C. (1976), 'Changes in East African Society', in Low, D. A., and SMITH, A. (eds.) (1976), *History of East Africa* (Oxford: Clarendon).

WRIGLEY, E. A. (1969), *Population and History* (London: Weidenfel and Nicholson).

WYNNE, E. A. (1980), *Social Security: A Reciprocity System Under Pressure* (Boulder: Westview).

WYON, J. B., and GORDON, J. E. (1971), *The Khanna Study* (Cambridge, MA: Harvard University Press).

XU SU-EN (1985), 'Health Statistics of the People's Republic of China', in Halstead, S. B., *et al.* (eds.) (1985), *Good Health at Low Cost*.

YANG, SHUZHANG, and DOWDLE, N. (1985), 'Trends and Levels of Mortality in China', paper presented at an International Symposium on China's National Sample Fertility Survey, Beijing.

YAO, F. K., and KONE, H. (1986), 'The African Drought Reported by Six West African Newspapers', Discussion Paper No. 14, African Studies Center, Boston University.

YEH, R. (1984), 'Urban Low Income Housing in South East Asia', in Richards, P. J., and Thomson, A. M. (eds.) (1984), *Basic Needs and the Urban Poor* (London: Croom Helm).

YEON, H. C. (1982), 'Medical Insurance Programme and Its Future Development in Korea', *International Social Security Review*, 30.

—— (1986), 'Social Welfare Policies in the Republic of Korea', *International Social Security Review*, 34.

YOON, S. B., and PARK, T. K. (1985*a*), 'Strategies and Programmes for Raising the Productivity of the Poor and the Eradication of Poverty in Korea', in Mukhopadhyay, S. (ed.) (1985*a*), *The Poor in Asia: Productivity-Raising Programmes and Strategies*.

—— —— (1985*b*), 'An In-Depth Follow-Up Study of a Poor Rural Village of

Jukchon', in Mukhopadhyay, S. (ed.) (1985*b*), *Case Studies on Poverty Programmes in Asia*.

YORK, S. (1985), 'Report on a Pilot Project to Set Up a Drought Information Network in Conjunction with the Red Crescent Society in Darfur', *Disasters*, 9.

YOUNG, H. (1987), 'Selective Feeding Programmes in Ethiopia and East Sudan, 1985/1986', *Disasters*, 11.

YOUNG, K., WOLKOWITZ, C., and McCULLAGH, R. (1981), *Of Marriage and the Market: Women's Subordination in International Perspective* (London: CSE Books).

ZAHLAN, R. S. (1978), *The Origins of the United Arab Emirates* (London: Macmillan).

ZENG YI (1988), 'Changing Demographic Characteristics and the Family Status of Chinese Women', *Population Studies*, 42.

ZINYAMA, L. M., CAMPBELL, D. J., and MATIZA, T. (1988), 'Traditional Household Strategies to Cope with Food Insecurity in the SADCC Region', in Rukuni, M., and Bernsten, R. H. (eds.) (1988), *Southern Africa: Food Security Policy Options*.

NAME INDEX

SUBJECT INDEX

adaptation and adjustment, nutritional 38, 39–40, 40–2, 45
administrative problems 17, 85–7, 89–93, 94–5, 100–2, 107–9, 110–13, 117–18, 125, 150, 181–2, 192–3, 195–6, 210–13, 217–20, 227, 262–6
adversarial politics, role of vii, 19, 68, 84, 126, 133, 138, 154, 197, 212–14, 225, 239, 241–2, 259, 262, 263–4, 272, 275, 276–9
African successes in famine prevention, case studies 133–8, 138–46, 146–52, 152–8, 158–61, 257, 263–6
aged people 14, 43–4, 80–1, 137, 219, 243
Angola 70, 275
Australia 184, 257

Bangladesh 52, 95, 116
famine of 1974 8, 23, 27–30, 80, 94
'bargaining problems' 49–50, 57
basic capabilities 12–13, 14–15, 16, 42–5, 177–8, 226, 258, 267–8
basic needs fulfilment and economic growth 187–8, 190–7
Bengal famine of 1943 5, 23, 46, 48–9, 55, 126, 210, 212, 265
Benin 70
Bhutan 178
Bihar (India) 8, 92, 131
bonded labour 74
'boom famines' 4–5, 48–9
Botswana 33, 69–71, 85, 91, 96, 152–8, 159, 160, 260, 263
Brazil 180, 187, 189, 192, 258
'breakdown position' 49, 56, 57, 58–9
Burkina Faso 70, 71
Burma 189
Burundi 70

Cameroon 70, 91
capabilities 12–13, 15, 42–5, 176, 177–8, 182, 225, 258, 260–2, 267, 269
Cape Verde 70, 71, 96, 133–8, 158, 159, 160, 260, 263
cash crops 76–7, 169–70, 172–6, 271–2
cash support for entitlement protection 18, 95–102, 102–3, 113–18, 124, 137, 140, 156, 160, 172–6, 264, 266
Chad 71, 91, 93, 95, 275
children and child mortality 39, 57, 58, 78, 79–81, 109–13, 137–8, 182, 193, 249, 250, 265–6

Chile 184–6, 199, 200, 226, 229–40, 246, 247, 250, 268, 278
China
achievements and experiences of 3, 8, 17, 51–3, 59, 96, 107, 180, 184, 185, 186, 199, 200, 201–2, 204–25, 246, 247, 250, 251–2, 257, 258, 268, 269, 277, 278
comparisons with India 8, 204–5, 206–9, 210–14, 221–5, 278
famine of 1958–61 8, 24, 55, 80, 205, 210–14, 277, 278
gender inequality in 17, 51–3, 56, 59, 216–20, 223–24, 266
post-reform experiences of 215–21, 258, 277
classes 9, 11, 17, 30, 48, 59, 107–8, 238, 272, 277, 278
commodities *vis-à-vis* capabilities 12–13, 43–5, 176, 261–2
contingency planning, for famine prevention 81–4, 117, 264
co-operative conflicts 11–12, 17–18, 47–50, 51–4, 56–9, 218–19
Costa Rica 33, 34, 184, 185, 186, 199, 200, 226, 229–30, 240–6, 247, 250, 251, 258, 268, 269, 278
Côte d'Ivoire 70
Cuba 174, 184–6, 199, 200, 226, 229, 240–6, 247, 249–51

Debt, international 34, 183, 273–4, 275
democracy and public action vii, 17–19, 84, 126, 133, 138, 152, 212–13, 230, 239, 241–2, 248, 259, 263–4, 275, 276–7, 278–9
dietary adjustments 37–8, 77, 80, 88
disabled people 43–4, 119–21, 137, 154, 266
diversification of production 34, 76–7, 160–1, 168–71, 171–6, 270–3
droughts 12, 26, 47, 86, 92, 126–33, 134–5, 138–9, 141–3, 148–9, 154, 263, 264

early warning and early action 81–4, 139, 154, 159, 263–4
East Europe 257, 279
East and South-east Asia 52, 58–9
ecology 31–3, 46–7, 166–8, 168–70, 201, 273–4
education, role of 13, 14, 15–16, 135, 191–3, 196–7, 224, 240, 241–2, 248, 250, 258, 259, 261–2, 267, 268, 270, 271